HANDBOOK OF
INTERNATIONAL SOCIAL WORK

HANDBOOK OF INTERNATIONAL SOCIAL WORK

Human Rights, Development, and the Global Profession

EDITED BY

LYNNE M. HEALY

ROSEMARY J. LINK

OXFORD
UNIVERSITY PRESS

OXFORD
UNIVERSITY PRESS

Oxford University Press, Inc., publishes works that further
Oxford University's objective of excellence
in research, scholarship, and education.

Oxford   New York
Auckland   Cape Town   Dares Salaam   Hong Kong   Karachi
Kuala   Lumpur   Madrid   Melbourne   Mexico City   Nairobi
New Delhi   Shanghai   Taipei   Toronto

With offices in
Argentina   Austria   Brazil   Chile   Czech Republic   France   Greece
Guatemala   Hungary   Italy   Japan   Poland   Portugal   Singapore
South Korea   Switzerland   Thailand   Turkey   Ukraine   Vietnam

Copyright © 2012 by Oxford University Press, Inc.

Published by Oxford University Press, Inc.
198 Madison Avenue, New York, New York 10016
www.oup.com

Oxford is a registered trademark of Oxford University Press

Library of Congress Cataloging-in-Publication Data

Handbook of international social work : human rights, development, and the
global profession / edited by Lynne M. Healy, Rosemary J. Link.
    p. cm.
  Includes bibliographical references and index.
  ISBN 978-0-19-533361-9 (hardcover : alk. paper) 1. Social service—International
cooperation. 2. Social service—History. 3. Human rights—International cooperation.
4. Economic development—Social aspects. I. Healy, Lynne M. II. Link, Rosemary J.
III. Title.

HV40.35.H36 2012
361.3—dc23   2011026312

Dedicated to the memory of our beloved sisters,

Deborah Evelyn Moore and Josephine Melanie MacRae,

who brought us much joy in their too short lives.

ACKNOWLEDGMENTS

Many people have inspired and assisted us as we worked to develop and complete this volume. First, we thank our authors. Their expertise and hard work made publication of a comprehensive and state-of-the-art book possible. We also acknowledge the contributions of the members of the Advisory Board, especially their wise counsel as we proposed the contents and structure of the book. The editors at Oxford University Press have been unwavering in their support and have provided valuable assistance in seeing this book through to publication. Senior editor, Maura Roessner, recognized the growing importance of international social work; she suggested that the time was right for a major reference work on the topic and has remained with the project through to conclusion.

We would both like to add a special acknowledgment of the late Dr. Katherine A. Kendall (1910–2010) who has been a source of inspiration for our careers in international social work. We each had the privilege of knowing and working with Katherine for several decades. We have benefited greatly from her brilliance, undaunting commitment to international social work, and support for more junior colleagues. We are confident that she would have greeted this book with enthusiasm.

Finally, we acknowledge and appreciate the encouragement and professional support of our educational institutions: for Lynne Healy, the University of Connecticut School of Social Work and for Rosemary Link, Simpson College, Iowa.

CONTENTS

THE EDITORS AND ADVISORY BOARD

The Editors:

Lynne M. Healy, Professor and Director, Center for International Social Work Studies, School of Social Work, University of Connecticut, West Hartford, Connecticut, USA.

Rosemary J. Link, Associate Vice President of Academic Affairs, Evening, Weekend, and Graduate Programs, Simpson College, Indianola, Iowa, USA.

Advisory Board:

Doreen Elliott, former Chair, Global Commission, Council on Social Work Education, Professor of Social Work & Distinguished Teaching Professor, School of Social Work, University of Texas, Arlington, USA.

Julia Guevara, Assistant Vice President for Academic Affairs, Assessment, Accreditation, and Planning; Professor of Social Work, Grand Valley University, Michigan, USA.

Karen Lyons, Editor in Chief, *International Social Work* (2005-2009) Emeritus Professor of International Social Work, London Metropolitan University, London, UK.

James Midgley, Harry and Riva Specht Professor of Social Work and Dean Emeritus, School of Social Welfare, University of California–Berkeley, USA.

Ngoh Tiong Tan, Professor and Dean, School of Human Development and Social Services, SIM University, Singapore.

Abye Tasse, Immediate Past-President, International Association of Schools of Social Work (2004–2008), Advisor to the President, University of Nouakchott, Nouakchott, Mauritania.

Gabi Čačinovič Vogrinčič, Professor and founding Dean of Family Social Work and Family Psychology, School of Social Work, University of Ljubljana, Slovenia.

Maureen Wilson, Professor and Associate Dean, Faculty of Social Work, University of Calgary, Canada.

CONTRIBUTORS

Tatsuru Akimoto, DSW
President, APASWE
Director and Professor
Asian Center for Welfare in Society
Social Work Research Institute
College of Social Work
Kiyose, Tokyo
Japan

Jean Ayoub, MA, MS
Secretary General
International Social Service-General Secretariat
Geneva
Switzerland

Gary Bailey, MSW, ACSW
Associate Professor, President of IFSW
School of Social Work
Associate Clinical Professor
School of Nursing and Health Sciences
Simmons College
Boston, Massachusetts
USA

Peta-Anne Baker, PhD
Lecturer in Social Work,
Coordinator, Social Work Unit
Department of Sociology, Psychology, and Social Work
University of the West Indies
Mona
Jamaica

Angeline Barretta-Herman, PhD
Associate Vice President for Academic Affairs
Office of Academic Affairs
University of St. Thomas
St. Paul, Minnesota
USA

Amy Bess, MSW
Senior Practice Associate
Human Rights and International Affairs
National Association of Social Workers
Washington, DC
USA

Lois Bosch, PhD
Associate Professor, Director
Department of Social Work
Augsburg College
Minneapolis, Minnesota
USA

Martha Bragin, PhD
Associate Professor
Hunter College School of Social Work
City University of New York
New York, New York
USA

Annamaria Campanini, PhD
Professor in Social Work, President of EASSW
Corso di Laurea in Servizio Sociale
Università Milano Bicocca
Milano
Italy

Moon Choi, PhD
Postdoctoral Fellow
Department of Epidemiology and
    Community Health
School of Medicine
Virginia Commonwealth University
Richmond, Virginia
USA

Elaine Congress, DSW
Professor and Associate Dean
Graduate School of Social Service
Fordham University
New York, New York
USA

Joanne Corbin, MSS, MPH, PhD
Chair, Research Sequence
Associate Professor
School for Social Work
Smith College
Northampton, Massachusetts
USA

Denys Correll, BA, BSocAdmin
Executive Director
International Council on Social Welfare
Entebbe
Uganda

Charles "Chuck" Cowger, PhD
Professor Emeritus
School of Social Work
University of Missouri-Columbia
Columbia, Missouri
USA

Professor Emeritus
School of Social Work
University of Illinois
Urbana-Champaign
USA

Govind Dhaske, MSW
Social Work Researcher
Doctoral Student
Indiana University School of Social Work
Indianapolis, Indiana
USA

Lena Dominelli, PhD
Professor of Applied Social Sciences
Associate Director, Institute of Hazard, Risk and
Resilience Research
Durham University
Durham
United Kingdom

Doreen Elliott, PhD
Professor of Social Work
& Distinguished Teaching Professor
University of Texas at Arlington
School of Social Work
Arlington, Texas
USA

Andy Elvin, MA
Chief Executive
Children and Families Across Borders
London
United Kingdom

Christina L. Erickson, PhD
Assistant Professor
Department of Social Work
Augsburg College
Minneapolis, Minnesota
USA

Thomas P. Felke, PhD
Assistant Professor
Social Work Division
College of Professional Studies
Florida Gulf Coast University
Fort Myers, Florida
USA

Kristin M. Ferguson, PhD
Associate Professor
School of Social Work
University of Southern California
Los Angeles, California
USA

Nigel Hall, MSc
IFSW Representative
Senior Lecturer
School of Social Work
Kingston University
London
United Kingdom

Scott Harding, PhD
Associate Professor
School of Social Work
University of Connecticut
West Hartford, Connecticut
USA

Jesse Harris, PhD
Professor
School of Social Work
University of Maryland
Baltimore, Maryland
USA

Lynne M. Healy, PhD
Professor
School of Social Work
University of Connecticut
West Hartford, Connecticut
USA

Sven Hessle, PhD
Editor in Chief, *International
Journal of Social Welfare*
Department of Social Work
Stockholm University
Stockholm
Sweden

Kimberly Hinds, MSW
Former Lecturer in Social Work
Department of Sociology, Psychology, and Social Work
University of the West Indies
Mona
Jamaica

M. C. "Terry" Hokenstad, PhD
Ralph S. and Dorothy P. Schmitt Professor
Mandel School of Applied Social Sciences
Case Western Reserve University
Cleveland, Ohio
USA

Dorothee Hölscher, MSocSc
Lecturer
School of Social Work and
Community Development
University of KwaZulu-Natal,
Howard College Campus
Durban
South Africa

Nathalie Huegler, MA
Practicing Senior Social Worker, London
Part-time Lecturer
Faculty of Applied Social Sciences
London Metropolitan University
London
United Kingdom

Gunn Strand Hutchinson, PhD
Associate Professor
Section for Social Work, Faculty of Social Sciences
University of Nordland
Bødo
Norway

Lorne Jaques, PhD
Associate Professor
Faculty of Social Work
University of Calgary
Calgary, Alberta
Canada

Therese Jennissen, PhD
Associate Professor
School of Social Work
Carleton University
Ottawa, Ontario
Canada

Jay T. Johnson, PhD
Assistant Professor
Geography Department and Global Indigenous Nations
Studies Program
University of Kansas
Lawrence, Kansas
USA

Hugo Kamya, PhD
Professor
School of Social Work
Simmons College
Boston, Massachusetts
USA

Pat Lager, MSW
Director of International Programs
College of Social Work
Florida State University
Tallahassee, Florida
USA

Christine Lambert, MS
Director
Director of Case Management
International Social Service
General Secretariat
Geneva
Switzerland

Horace Levy, MA, STL
Research Fellow
Institute of Criminal
Justice and Security
University of the West Indies
Mona
Jamaica

Kathryn Libal, PhD
Assistant Professor
School of Social Work
University of Connecticut
West Hartford, Connecticut
USA

Rosemary J. Link, PhD
Associate Vice President of Academic Affairs
Evening, Weekend, and Graduate Programs
Simpson College
Indianola, Iowa
USA

Colleen Lundy, PhD
Professor
School of Social Work
Carleton University
Ottawa, Ontario
Canada

Karen Lyons, PhD
Emeritus Professor (International Social Work)
Faculty of Applied Social Sciences
London Metropolitan University
London
United Kingdom

Robin Mama, PhD
Dean, Professor
School of Social Work
Monmouth University
West Long Branch, New Jersey
USA

Susan Mapp, PhD
Associate Professor and Chair
Department of Social Work
Elizabethtown College
Elizabethtown, Pennsylvania
USA

Golam M. Mathbor, PhD
Professor, Associate Dean
The Wayne D. McMurray School of
Humanities and Social Sciences
Monmouth University
West Long Branch, New Jersey
USA

Sally Mathiesen, PhD
Associate Professor
School of Social Work
San Diego State University
San Diego, California
USA

John Maxwell, PhD
Retired Senior Lecturer in Social Work
Former Deputy Dean
Faculty of Social Sciences
University of the West Indies
Mona
Jamaica

Goutham M. Menon, PhD
Associate Professor
Department of Social Work
College of Public Policy
University of Texas at San Antonio
San Antonio, Texas
USA

James Midgley, PhD
Harry and Riva Specht Professor
School of Social Welfare
University of California–Berkeley
Berkeley, California
USA

Lengwe-Katembula Mwansa, PhD
Associate Professor
Department of Social Work
University of Botswana
Gaborone
Botswana

Vimla Nadkarni, PhD
Professor, Founder Dean
School of Social Work
Tata Institute for Social Sciences
Mumbai
India

Mary Nash, PhD
Senior Lecturer
School of Health and Social Services
Massey University
Palmerston North
New Zealand

Carolyn Noble, PhD
Professor, Head Social Work Unit (FP)
School of Social Sciences and Psychology
Victoria University
Footscray
Australia

Felicity Northcott, PhD
Director
Arthur C. Helton Institute for the
Study of International Social Service
International Social Service, USA
Baltimore, Maryland
USA

Irene Queiro-Tajalli, PhD
Professor, Interim Director of Labor
Studies Program
School of Social Work
Indiana University
Indianapolis, Indiana
USA

Frank B. Raymond, PhD
Dean Emeritus, Distinguished Professor Emeritus
College of Social Work
University of South Carolina
Columbia, South Carolina
USA

Narda Razack, PhD
Associate Dean, External Faculty
Liberal Arts and Professional Studies
York University
Toronto, Ontario
Canada

Elisabeth Reichert, PhD
Professor
School of Social Work
Southern Illinois University
Carbondale, Illinois
USA

Dennis J. Ritchie, PhD
Elisabeth Shirley Enochs Endowed
Chair in Child Welfare
Professor
Department of Social Work
George Mason University
Fairfax, Virginia
USA

Jini L. Roby, JD, MSW
Associate Professor
School of Social Work
Brigham Young University
Provo, Utah
USA

Letnie F. Rock, PhD
Lecturer, Department Head
Department of Government, Sociology,
and Social Work
University of the West Indies
Cave Hill
Barbados

Julie Gilbert Rosicky, MS
Executive Director
International Social Service, USA
Baltimore, Maryland
USA

Karen Smith Rotabi, PhD
Assistant Professor
School of Social Work
Virginia Commonwealth University
Richmond, Virginia
USA

Allison Rowlands, PhD
Director Practice Standards
NSW Department of Human Service–Community
Services
Australia

Uma A. Segal, PhD
Professor
School of Social Work
University of Missouri–St. Louis
St. Louis, Missouri
USA

Silvia Staub-Bernasconi, PhD
Professor for Social Work und Human Rights
Centre for Postgradual Studies in Social Work
Berlin
Germany

Member of the Academic Board and Lecturer
International Doctoral Studies in Social Work
(INDOSOW)
Faculty of Social Work, University of Ljubljana
Slovenia

Ngoh Tiong Tan, PhD
Professor and Dean
School of Human Development and Social Services
SIM University
Singapore

Rebecca L. Thomas, PhD
Associate Professor
School of Social Work
University of Connecticut
West Hartford, Connecticut
USA

W. Duffie VanBalkom, PhD
Professor
Faculty of Education
University of Calgary
Calgary, Alberta
Canada

Katherine van Wormer, PhD
Professor
Department of Social Work
University of Northern Iowa
Cedar Falls, Iowa
USA

Gabi Čačinovič Vogrinčič, PhD
Professor
Faculty of Social Work
University of Ljubljana
Ljubljana
Slovenia

Julia Watkins, PhD
Executive Director
Council on Social Work Education
Alexandria, Virginia
USA

Janice Wood Wetzel, PhD
Chief Representative
International Association of Schools of Social Work
United Nations
New York, New York
USA

Lincoln O. Williams, MA
Head/Senior Lecturer
Social Welfare Training Centre (Open Campus)
University of the West Indies
Mona
Jamaica

Maureen Wilson, PhD
Professor
Faculty of Social Work
University of Calgary
Calgary, Alberta
Canada

Stuart Wilson, MA
UN Representative
HelpAge International
New York, New York
USA

Joseph Wronka, PhD
Professor
School of Social Work
Springfield College
Springfield, Massachusetts
USA

Michael Yellow Bird, PhD
Professor
Department of Social Work
Humboldt State University
Arcata, California
USA

Michael J. Zakour, PhD
Associate Professor
Division of Social Work
West Virginia University
Morgantown, West Virginia
USA

Darja Zaviršek, PhD
Professor
Faculty of Social Work
University of Ljubljana
Ljubljana
Slovenia

Jelka Zorn, PhD
Senior Lecturer
Faculty of Social Work
University of Ljubljana
Ljubljana
Slovenia

HANDBOOK OF
INTERNATIONAL SOCIAL WORK

1

Introduction

LYNNE M. HEALY AND ROSEMARY J. LINK

Interest in international social work has expanded dramatically over the past few decades. Increased interest is evident throughout the world, but it is particularly noticeable in industrialized countries, where social work has become institutionalized and sometimes inward looking. Globalization continues to affect people's well-being from individual to national levels, and it particularly disadvantages some. Everywhere, however, globalization and its effects heighten awareness of international issues. The goal of the *Handbook on International Social Work* is both to respond to and encourage the trend of growing interest in international or global social work[1]. The social work editors at Oxford University Press initiated the idea of a reference work on international social work several years ago and approached us to develop and edit the volume.

The expanding focus on international social work is evident in many ways. There has been an explosion of relevant literature, including books on international or global social work published in Asia, Europe, Australia, and North America. The number of regional and international journals in the field has grown, and the long-established journal *International Social Work* expanded from four to six issues per year in response to increased submissions of relevant articles. Many social work educational programs throughout the world now offer a focus on international or global social work, while others have increased their content on global issues and human rights or have expanded opportunities for student and faculty exchange. The major international social work organizations have also collaborated over the past decade to issue new policy statements and standards for ethics and social work education.

The context of the profession's growing interest is a world full of urgent social problems and policy challenges. Within the past decade, human migration has continued to increase and to affect a growing number of nations, bringing the human effects of conflict, poverty and disasters to new settings. Cataclysmic natural disasters have stalled or reversed development gains in countries such as Haiti, Myanmar, Indonesia and Pakistan and shaken confidence in the ability of nations with greater resources to cope with mass devastation. An upsurge in weather-related natural disasters has increased concern about climate change and the potential impact on human settlements. Just as the authors began final review of the manuscript for production, one of the strongest and most devastating earthquakes in recorded history has struck Japan. The human toll from the earthquake and resulting tsunami is exacerbated by damage to nuclear reactors. As aftershocks rumble across the affected area, the financial and nuclear aftershocks are being felt across the world, underscoring once again our interdependence in a globalized environment.

In 2009, a global food crisis coincided with an ongoing fiscal crisis to interrupt the modest progress being made toward meeting the globally agreed upon Millennium Development Goals. Poverty and high levels of unemployment continue to cause human misery, yet gains in levels of education and reduction in rates of new HIV infections are positive developments. Recent expressions of demand for democracy and good governance in countries in the Middle East offer both opportunities and risks for improved human well-being or intensified repression.

Within this context of global challenges, the concerns of the profession of social work are inevitably international. Thus, it seemed to be time to develop a reference book on international social work.

The purpose of the *Handbook on International Social Work* is to provide an introduction to a wide range of topics in international social work garnered from many countries and regions and to suggest resources for further exploration by readers. The target audience for the book includes social work educators, students, and practitioners; we also hope that professionals and colleagues in other disciplines will find the book of interest. We have aimed to produce a volume that is useful to practitioners, teachers, and students across the world. We recognize, however, the limitations of language and therefore the fact that the book is currently accessible only to those with reading knowledge of English. As translation and language conversion programs improve, the barriers of language may be eased.

We initially planned the volume with the assistance of an international advisory board. Members of the board suggested additions and deletions to our proposed list of chapters and suggested authors with expertise in needed areas. We are particularly grateful that a number of the advisers agreed to write chapters for the book. In all these areas, their assistance has enhanced the final product, and we thank them. (A list of Advisory Board members can be found at the beginning of the book.)

In this *Handbook*, we attempt to provide a comprehensive collection of current knowledge on international social work. Comprehensiveness, of course, is an impossible target, and we acknowledge that areas are missing. As the work neared completion, new and changing realities emerged, underscoring the topics already included. The British Petroleum (BP) deepwater oil spill in the Gulf of Mexico adds to the environmental concerns addressed in Section IV; continuation of the global fiscal crisis affects issues of poverty and unemployment and underscores the need to understand global financial organizations, as addressed in Section VI; the 2011 earthquake in Japan and the catastrophic flooding in Pakistan that followed a devastating earthquake in Haiti in 2010 reinforce the importance of disaster prevention and response; and so forth. We can accurately state that the book is a wide-ranging treatment of most aspects of the field of international social work. The subtitle for the Handbook, *Human Rights, Development and the Global Profession*, was selected as we realized how extensively these themes are reflected in the collection and in contemporary international social work.

A signature strength of the *Handbook* is the diversity of our authors. The chapter authors are drawn from many countries and cultures. Each is an expert in the topic of his or her chapter, and together they reflect a worldwide set of perspectives on global issues and international practice. Chapter authors are from Jamaica, Barbados, the United States, Canada, England, Italy, Norway, Slovenia, Sweden, India, Japan, Singapore, Australia, New Zealand, South Africa, Botswana, South Korea, and Switzerland. Still others, although settled in one of the previously listed countries, were originally from other countries, including Argentina, Bangladesh, India, and Uganda.

INSTRUCTIONS TO AUTHORS

The *Handbook* is intended to provide brief overviews of a wide range of topics, brief in order to keep the length of the volume manageable with more than seventy chapters. We worked with our authors to encourage chapters of similar length. However, some chapters are modestly longer than others, reflecting the scope of the particular chapters or the need to cover a wide range of material. In a similar vein, we asked authors to keep their reference lists modest and to carefully select the most important references for further study.

Specific terminology was left open to the authors; they chose and defined terms, and therefore there is some variation in usage. Countries may be referred to alternatively as developing, industrialized, Global North or Global South, or Two-Thirds World. We hope this adds to the appreciation of global diversity and does not confuse readers.

We asked our authors to write from a global perspective. This proved to be one of the most engaging challenges for the editors and for the authors. It reinforced that almost all of us see the world from our own national and cultural vantage points—even those of us who have devoted our professional careers to living and working in the international context. It is difficult to think and write globally. We applaud our authors for their efforts. By design, a modest number of chapters draw heavily on experiences in a single country, generalizing the lessons that a case example offers to other countries and to global policy development. And, again by design, the chapters in Section VIII, Social Work Around the World, are regional or subregional in scope.

DIMENSIONS OF INTERNATIONAL SOCIAL WORK AS REFLECTED IN THE *HANDBOOK*

Our definition of international social work is broad but also has many specific elements; it is both practice oriented and value based. This book presents international social work as the following:

- A way of looking at and appreciating the world (worldview)
- Practice informed by international knowledge
- Practice, concern, and action on globally experienced social issues
- Participation in international professional organizations

- Understanding of the global profession
- Development and human rights
- A future and action-oriented movement for global change.

First, we view international social work as a way of looking at and appreciating diversity and the global character of issues facing social work. This global professional worldview carries responsibilities for global action, as identified in the concluding chapter of the book and suggested throughout. Furthermore, these responsibilities apply to all members of the profession regardless of their location, although access to resources and what is often referred to as *privilege* may assign a larger share of responsibilities to some. To fulfill these responsibilities, social workers need an understanding of the profession as it exists in various parts of the world and of the functions and possibilities offered by its international organizations. We also see the interrelationship of global issues and local practice and policy. Thus, international social work is also practice informed by international knowledge, particularly practice in those areas at the interface between the domestic and the international or global. Our definition served as a conceptual road map as we developed the table of contents for the book.

Overview of the Sections of the *Handbook*
Section I of the book addresses theories and concepts underlying international social work. It begins with an introductory chapter analyzing evolving perspectives on the definition of international social work. Following this introduction, chapters explore five central concepts that inform international social work: globalization, development, human rights, social exclusion, and social justice. Readers will see reference to these concepts in later chapters in the volume.

In Section II, two chapters provide insights into the history of social work. The first focuses on the development of the profession, emphasizing beginnings and critical periods in the history of social work. It is followed by a chapter on the involvement of the profession in the global struggle for gender equality.

Sections III and IV address the methods and content of international social work practice. Chapters in Section III focus on methods of practice relevant to international social work. These include chapters on working with immigrants and refugees, international adoption, trauma counseling, intercountry casework, social and community development, disaster response, representation of social work at international bodies such as the United Nations (UN),

cross-cultural communication, and conflict resolution. Section IV, Global Social Issues, is an extensive section with twenty-three chapters, each addressing a specific issue that social workers tackle in their practice. These issues, ranging from aging to youth, also pose policy challenges at the global level and invite professional contributions to ongoing policy developments. Although not an exhaustive treatment of the arenas of social work practice, Section IV demonstrates the broad scope of the profession's globally relevant activities and contribution. Some of the chapters in Sections III and IV address similar topics, such as natural and human-made disasters. Chapter 34 in Section IV provides a global overview of the problem of disasters, while the related Chapter 15 in Section III focuses on social work interventions for response and recovery. Similarly, both sections contain chapters on migration, providing practice strategies in Section III and an overview of migration as a global issue in Section IV.

Sections V and VI introduce key global organizations. Four international social work and social welfare organizations—the International Federation of Social Workers (IFSW), the International Association of Schools of Social Work (IASSW), the International Council on Social Welfare (ICSW), and the International Consortium for Social Development (ICSD)—are presented in Section V. A concluding chapter explores social work ethics from a global perspective, underscoring the central role of ethical principles in defining the profession. Section VI begins with an overview of UN agencies and programs, emphasizing those most closely related to social work concerns. The other chapters in the section present the work of humanitarian and advocacy nongovernmental agencies (NGOs) and international economic organizations. Though not usually identified as social welfare organizations, the policies and programs of the World Bank, International Monetary Fund, and World Trade Organization affect human well-being and often shape local and global responses to social problems.

The role of social work education is key to ensuring that social workers are prepared to address global challenges, whether in their local practice or on a larger scale. Chapters in Section VII address current models for internationalizing social work curricula, for arranging international field placements that enhance students' professional development, and for running international exchange initiatives that reflect mutuality and reciprocity. Reflecting the growing availability of communication technologies, another chapter identifies ways in which these technologies can be used to enhance international education, exchange, and research. The final chapter in Section VII reprints an important international study of the extent to which social work educational programs in diverse countries reflect consistency with the global standards adopted by the IASSW and IFSW in 2004.

Understanding ways in which social work practice is similar or different in various parts of the world is essential if social workers are to consider themselves as part of a global profession. Section VIII contains seven chapters, each providing an overview of social work in a region or subregion of the world. Given the complexity and diversity within regions, some authors had a huge challenge in presenting unifying perspectives while illustrating great variation. How, for example, does one write about social work in Asia when the continent is home to half the world's population and includes many cultures, peoples, and nations? Yet, we asked an author to do just that. We recognize the ongoing struggle to capture and appreciate local uniqueness in a regional collective.

International social work is more than the sum of concerns about global issues and social work practice strategies. We have chosen to more fully explore the arenas of development and human rights in this book. These two conceptual and practice areas have been central thrusts in the work of global organizations over the past two decades. They are highly consistent with core values of social work; we therefore assert that human rights and the promotion of human well-being through development efforts offer concrete avenues for international social work practice and provide the field with a globally relevant value-based compass. These topics are discussed in numerous chapters, and explored in more depth in Sections IX and X. The chapters in Section IX on development address sustainable social development projects, microenterprise, and methods for measuring developing progress. The concluding chapter analyzes prospects for the survival and adaptation of the European welfare state as a model for addressing human well-being in the twenty-first century.

An overview of global human rights laws and implementation machinery opens Section X on human rights. This chapter is followed by four chapters that explore, respectively, the human rights of women, the rights of children, the rights of persons with disabilities, and issues of rights and sexual orientation. These chapters examine both the policy instruments available to social workers worldwide and examples of their application in practice. The chapters also signal the opportunity inherent in collaborating with the UN and the policies and conventions that are now established as international law.

In the final section, chapters on careers in international social work and on career mobility for social workers across borders bring the focus back to the profession. By sharing their journeys in social work away from their countries of origin, social workers illustrate the humility that is needed to offer professional insights in new cultural and economic contexts. Finally, the concluding chapter highlights the challenge for this still-new century. The last fifty years of the profession made an impact across borders and brought many professionals together in sharing knowledge, identifying practice opportunities, and establishing human rights protocols, conventions, and laws. During the next fifty years, the social work profession is charged with fully implementing these laws, especially in relation to tackling poverty, establishing social and economic justice, and securing an end to oppression.

We have kept the appendices to a minimum. We include two of the most important documents issued by the profession in the twenty-first century—the international statement of ethical principles and the body of the Global Standards for the Education and Training of the Social Work Profession. Because they are referred to in many chapters, we include the Millennium Development Goals agreed to by the members of the UN in 2000 and augmented since then. Finally, we have included a short summary of the guidelines for psychosocial intervention in emergencies, issued by the Inter-Agency Standing Committee (IASC) of UN agencies and NGOs. This document has the potential to inform social work practice in the international arena and should be widely disseminated and discussed.

It has been a monumental undertaking to decide on the contents of this volume and then to recruit and guide a globally diverse group of authors to its completion. We hope the *Handbook on International Social Work: Human Rights, Development and the Global Profession* will be a useful addition to the professional literature and will encourage social workers to incorporate a global perspective into their practice and professional identity.

NOTE

1. International social work and global social work are often used interchangeably in the social work literature. We use the term *international* because the term is more inclusive, as explained in Chapter 2. In our usage, international social work includes global social work.

SECTION I

Theories and Concepts Underlying
International Social Work

2

Defining International Social Work

LYNNE M. HEALY

"Two characteristics of social work—the broad economic and intellectual background which it demands, and the deep moral root from which it springs, make its international application almost indispensable" (Jebb, 1929, p. 642). Today, more than eight decades after Jebb delivered these words to the First International Conference of Social Work, international social work is truly indispensable. To be relevant and effective in the twenty-first century, social work must have an enhanced presence in international practice and policy. Global trends now affect the lives of social workers and those they serve as community members, service users, and professionals. Major problems affecting human well-being in the globalized environment demand social work attention. "Globalization influences and creates the social issues we deal with, it creates the context of our practice and education through its impact on the political and cultural landscape within which we practice, educate and learn" (Payne & Askeland, 2008, p. 154). Indeed, it is difficult to comprehend or act on the issues facing the profession without global understanding. As Khinduka (1999) put it, "many problems of the contemporary world can neither be analyzed intelligently nor combated effectively without a transnational perspective" (p. xi). Those who believe in the mission of social work and its competence as a helping profession therefore embrace a more global agenda and role. The rationale for international social work is both pragmatic and value based. It is on these premises that the *Handbook on International Social Work* has been developed.

In many ways, social work has always been an international profession; the founders were keenly interested in and involved in international exchange. During some periods and in some sections of the world, this international orientation was forgotten or pushed aside. Beginning in the last years of the twentieth century, however, international interest and activity have accelerated. This c' er reviews the reasons

for intensified interest in global issues and the scholarly treatment of the definition of international social work. It then illuminates the editors' definition; in general terms, this definition is spelled out in the table of contents of the book. As noted in the Preface, our conceptual map guided the development of the plan for the book.

EVOLUTION OF INTEREST IN INTERNATIONAL SOCIAL WORK

Recent historical research has revealed strong interest in the international exchange of ideas among the founders of social work (Kendall, 2000). The rapid spread of both the Charity Organization Society and the settlement movement from Europe to the United States demonstrates that international technology transfer was essential to the development of social work in the late nineteenth century. In 1928, the First International Conference of Social Work drew approximately 2500 participants from forty-two countries representing six continents. Out of these meetings emerged three international professional bodies that continue their work today, the International Association of Schools of Social Work, the International Council on Social Welfare, and the International Federation of Social Workers. Educators at the 1928 meeting discussed plans for an international school of social work to further the goal of cross-national exchange of ideas and practices. Although never realized, this indicates the strength of the international commitment and vision among these early leaders of the profession.

The profession of social work is now in its second century. Social work has been established on every inhabited continent, and on every continent, organized educational programs in social work have existed for more than half a century. Thus, it can be said that social work is a global profession in terms of its reach. The profession is continuing to mature and develop in a highly globalized context; global trends in every sphere of life—economy, security, health, environment, and culture—affect social work practice, practitioners, and clients of social work interventions. As Link and Ramanathan (2011) point out, "local and national borders are no longer sufficient limits for our information sources and ethical practice" (p. 1). Standards in human rights are increasingly negotiated at the global level, and social provisions and programs are modeled and emulated across borders (Healy, 2008). Communication technologies facilitate rapid and frequent exchange of ideas across the globe and access to information about local and global developments. Globalization has led to new social problems and increased awareness of others that have long existed; increasingly, these problems are experienced in most or even all countries. These shared social problems and the movement of people across borders challenge the very notion of a domestic social work practice. Thus, Lorenz was accurate when he said, "All social work is enmeshed in global processes of change" (1997, p. 2).

The social work profession has moved since the beginning of the twenty-first century to further its global presence through a new global definition of social work, a revised set of ethical principles that recognize both the imperative of universal values and the complexities of many local expressions, and the first ever adopted Global Standards for Education and Training of the Social Work Profession (IASSW/IFSW, 2004; see appendix for text). There is growing interest, therefore, in the international aspects of social work and in specifying and promoting a dimension of the profession called *international social work*.

DEFINITIONS OF INTERNATIONAL SOCIAL WORK: A REVIEW OF THE LITERATURE

What is international social work? Many scholars have addressed this question. Use of the term dates back to at least the 1920s, but scholarship on the topic has intensified in the early twenty-first century. The first specific mention of the term *international social work* may have been in a 1928 speech written for the First International Conference of Social Work by Eglantyne Jebb of England (Jebb, 1929). Referring to the work of Save the Children, International Migration Service, and other organizations, she said that there had been "a rapid and surprising increase in actual international social work since the Great War" (p. 650) and called on delegates to increase the scope of international

social work. Decrying the lack of international research, she concluded that "international social work demands constant contact between social workers on an international intellectual basis" (p. 651).

Proposed definitions of international social work can be categorized as general or specific, broad or narrow, and functional or value based. At the most general level, international social work can be defined as any aspect of the profession that involves more than one country. This draws on the dictionary definition of *international* as meaning "of, relating to or affecting two or more nations" and "active, known or reaching beyond national boundaries"(Merriam-Webster, 2011). In 1984, Sanders and Pederson defined international social work broadly and generally as "those social work activities and concerns that transcend national and cultural boundaries" (p. xiv); they advised scholars to keep the definition broad and open to encourage further work. An example of a narrow and specific definition is the one developed by a study committee of the US Council on Social Work Education (CSWE) in the 1950s. After considering more expansive definitions, the committee recommended that the term *international social work* be limited to the international work done by social workers through the United Nations (UN) and international nongovernmental organizations (NGOs) (Stein, 1957).

Writings on international social work published during the 1970s and 1980s emphasized more general ideas of the importance of an international perspective and the value of comparative study. Boehm (1976) loosely defined international social work as including the obvious work of international agencies but also comparative analysis and its contribution to transnational exchange of ideas and innovations. Little was written about practice roles during this period. In 1999, Lyons wrote that international social work "is a nebulous concept, with elements of cross-national comparison and applications of international perspectives to local practice, as well as participation in policy and practice activities which are more overtly cross-national or supra-national in character" (p. 12).

More recently, a number of functional or practice-focused definitions have emerged. These definitions have earlier precedents, however. Particularly notable is the definition published by George Warren in the *Social Work Yearbook* in 1939. He identified four specific functions or activities as international social work: intercountry casework (work across borders to resolve case situations); international relief and assistance to victims of wars and disasters; international cooperation on issues of social concern through global organizations, such as the International Labour Organization or League of Nations; and international exchange of social work knowledge through international conferences on social work.

Scholars in the twenty-first century have developed functional definitions similar to the ideas expressed by Warren. Healy (2008) linked the impact of globalization with a call for professional action on global practice and policy issues. Her definition identified four major professional functions as elements of international social work: domestically based practice and policy advocacy in situations with international dimensions, international professional exchange of personnel and ideas, practice in international relief and development organizations, and participation in global policy formulation and advocacy. Cox and Pawar (2006) added an emphasis on the "global and local promotion of social work education and practice" (p. 20) to ensure that the profession is established throughout the world. Thus, their definition begins, "International social work is the promotion of social work education and practice globally and locally, with the purpose of building a truly integrated international profession that reflects social work's capacity to respond appropriately and effectively, in education and practice terms, to the various global challenges that are having a significant impact on the well-being of large sections of the world's population" (p. 20). With its action and practice emphasis, the definition fits within the category of a functional definition, but it also includes (as do most) value dimensions. It introduces an integrated perspectives approach incorporating global, human rights, and ecological and social development perspectives.

An idea floated early in the 1960s was to define international social work as the fourth major practice method to complement casework, group work, and community organization. Goldman (1962) proposed this as a logical step in expanding social work attention beyond the community level to seek "international solutions to international problems" (pp. 1–2), much as a caseworker seeks individual solutions to problems of individuals. It does not appear that this idea generated significant interest.

Several authors have critiqued the existing definitions of international social work, instead espousing a value-driven focus. Ahmadi (2003) called for focusing or refocusing international social work on promotion of human rights, democracy, social justice, conflict prevention, and peace. Haug (2005) critiqued the Western domination of the field. Her definition is clearly value focused: "International social work includes any social work activity anywhere in the world, directed toward global social justice and human rights, in which local practice is dialectically linked to the global context" (p. 133). Payne and Askeland (2008) argue for postmodern analysis to combat the growing inequality and injustice that result from globalization. Increasingly, definitions of international social work link functions with value-focused ends.

Some scholars reject the validity of an international or global social work. Webb (2003) argues that social work is inherently local and requires deep understanding of local culture. He therefore states that social work "has no clearly identified or legitimate mandate in relation to globalization" and concludes that "'global social work' is a practical impossibility" (p. 193) and no more than a vanity for the profession. Though space precludes extensive discussion here, Webb's arguments appear to be based on a narrow definition of social work that excludes its policy and advocacy functions.

Definitional Debates: How Broad Is International Social Work?

International Versus Global

Some scholars and educational programs use the term *global social work* interchangeably with *international social work*, while others argue that *global* connotes a more worldwide vision and concern. Indeed, dictionary definitions cast *global* as meaning "of, relating to or involving the entire world" (Merriam-Webster, 2011). We have maintained the term *international social work* in the book since it can encompass both the truly global dimensions of concern and those practice or policy situations that involve only a few countries or regions. *Global social work* would be a more limiting term in spite of the fact that it suggests a broad view. It should be noted, however, that *international* includes the word *nation* and therefore may reinforce the dominance of the nation-state ideal and national sovereignty in global relations. For a profession striving for less division in the world, this aspect of terminology should be considered further.

Breadth of Definitions

There are debates over the scope of international social work. Nagy and Falk (2000), among others, question whether work with immigrants and refugees should be considered part of the field. They argue that this work is intercultural or multicultural but not international. Most contemporary scholars disagree and include work with international populations as an important dimension of international social work (Healy, 2008, 2004; Lyons, Manion, & Carlsen, 2006).

In this book, the authors propose that multicultural and international social work overlap and are not mutually exclusive but can be distinct. Multicultural social work focuses on understanding the importance of culture in people's lives, access to resources, and ways of communicating with one another. Carter and Qureshi (1995) define *culture* as "a learned system of meaning and behaviors that is passed from one generation to the next" (p. 241). Culture always relates to socialization and sometimes to national borders, politics, and geography. Whereas multicultural practice relates to awareness of roots, identity, language, customs, nonverbal communication, and rituals, the practice of international social work is broader in scope and includes political dimensions and the work of international organizations such as the UN and OXFAM. These transnational institutions generate international policy instruments that are crucial social policy and practice resources for social workers, as indicated in several chapters in this book. International social work practice seeks to engage with cultural, social, economic, and political forces that affect individuals, families, and communities. Summing up her study of social agencies in California, Xu (2006) concluded, "Theories, practices and strategies of international social work, as well as understanding international and global phenomena that impact local communities, can be of substantial benefit to social workers and their daily interactions with clients, particularly in ethnically and culturally diverse areas" (p. 490).

Other scholars have questioned the relationship between the national origin of the practitioner and the content of the practice, arguing that simply traveling to another country to practice social work does not make this practice part of international social work (Akimoto, 1995). In his recent book, Hugman (2010) ties together his discussion of definitions by endorsing the notion of crossing borders as core to international social work: "In summary, we may say the 'international social work' refers to practice and policy concerning situations in which professionals, those who benefit from their services or the causes of the problems that bring these two actors together have traveled in some way across the borders between nations. That is, social work is international when the social worker, the service user or the social issue moves between or connects two or more countries" (p. 20). This issue is far from settled; however, international

social work is a more robust concept when the substance of the practice issues, rather than the origins of the practitioner, involves more than one country.

The Editors' Definition of International Social Work

As discussed in the Introduction, the intent of this book is to present a wide-ranging collection of current knowledge on international social work. The editors' definition of international social work is therefore broad and encompasses theory, practice, and values. Based on our working definition, this book presents international social work as

- a way of looking at and appreciating the world (worldview) and acknowledging the impact of globalization on human well-being;
- practice, including locally based practice, informed by international knowledge;
- practice, concern, and action on globally experienced social issues;
- participation in international professional organizations and dialogue;
- understanding the global profession;
- promotion of development and human rights; and
- a future and action-oriented movement for global change.

We define international social work as a multidimensional concept. The purposes of international social work are to promote global social justice and human well-being and to ensure the ongoing relevance of locally based practice by calling attention to global realities that affect local conditions. Although the *Handbook* calls for increased attention to global issues, we also recognize the continuing relevance of the nation-state to practice and policy along with the growing impact of global forces.

LEGACY OF COLONIALISM AND THE EXPORT MODEL: ENDURING TENSIONS

Discussions of international social work continue to elicit concerns that the concept embodies imperialistic notions and is Western in orientation (Gray, 2005; Webb, 2003). Professional social work originated in Europe and North America at the end of the nineteenth century, a century of imperialistic expansion and domination of Africa, much of Asia, and the Caribbean by the United States and European powers. Domination was far reaching, disrupting patterns of family, culture, and religion; expropriating natural and human resources; and drawing boundaries for the convenience of the colonizers without regard for local rationalities. The effects have been long lasting and are replicated in newer forms of domination by the international economic order. These issues are explored in later chapters of the book, especially in the chapters on globalization, development, and regulation of the global economy. Social work was introduced to some countries in Asia and Africa by Western missionaries and by officials of colonial governments. In other cases, social work arrived in newly independent nations under UN auspices or through bilateral aid projects. Almost always it involved heavy use of Western consultants and educators. Thus, the association of the social work profession with imperialism and colonialism has challenged the premises of an international profession.

Within this context, international exchange has at times been characterized by unselective imposition and borrowing of foreign models of education and practice. Uncritical export of social work concepts and relationships based on superior–inferior status has created distrust of internationalism, much as the negative effects of globalization on poorer peoples and countries have created resistance. The legacy of the export model remains a barrier to support for internationalizing the profession.

Gray and Fook (2004) identified four sets of related tensions affecting social work: globalization-localization, Westernization–indigenization, multiculturalism–universalization, and universal–local standards. The drive to include international perspectives in the profession is indeed stronger in colonizing countries; the profession in colonized countries has been subject to a steady influx of international influences, often uninvited and unwelcome. Link and Ramanathan (2011) note the importance of addressing the "tension between establishing universal principles of social work through international collaboration in research and practice, while respecting indigenous uniqueness, distinct local traditions and cultural strength" (p. 10). Dominelli (2005) recommends looking at international social work "as a form of practice that localizes the global and globalizes the local" (p. 505), ensuring that internationalization and indigenization are seen as compatible and equally essential in the maturation of the profession. As addressed later in the book, exchange relationships based on reciprocity and mutuality must replace the export model. Internationalism in the twenty-first century demands "equality, mutuality, reciprocal

benefits, and a true exchange of ideas around the globe" in a form of international networking (Elliott & Segal, 2008, p. 355). This is consistent with Ahmadi's idea of international social work as "a project of partnership between diverse social actors" (2003, p. 14).

The editors firmly endorse antiracist and anticolonial perspectives as critical to social work; however, we believe that social work must embrace a vision of active internationalism in which professionals work together on important global issues with true reciprocity and mutuality. Although the profession must acknowledge the negative aspects of its history, it can also celebrate the "transnational dimension of social work" and "movement of individuals and exchange of ideas about practice" that contributed to its founding (Penna, Paylor, & Washington, 2000, p. 119). Further, the profession can create a new history of active engagement with the critical issues of our times. The development of the Global Standards for the Education and Training of the Social Work Profession in the early twenty-first century can be cited as an example. Responding to both internal and external pressures, international professional organizations worked for several years to develop globally agreed-upon guidelines for social work education. This was a project fraught with the dangers of reproducing Western hegemonic control and definitions of social work education. However one judges the final product, it is widely agreed that the process was conducted as a global collaborative effort to advance professional education.

A final consideration in the ongoing debates about the definition of international social work is whether it is useful to further develop it as a separate dimension of social work. An alternative view is that all social work is embedded in a global reality and should be taught and practiced with an international perspective. Though conceptually attractive, this approach is likely to dilute attention to international issues.

IS THERE A THEORY OF INTERNATIONAL SOCIAL WORK?

The review of the definitions of international social work and the expansion of scholarly writing on the topic suggest a maturation of ideas. In the first section of the *Handbook*, chapters exploring globalization, development, human rights, social inclusion and exclusion, and social justice represent a critical mass of theories that support international social work. In later chapters, diverse authors demonstrate how these underlying ideas fit with social work theories of human behavior and the social environment, cultural diversity, and social change and are enriched by the overarching principles of social work ethics and values. International social work, then, is based on the marriage of critical, globally relevant interdisciplinary theories and concepts with social work knowledge and values. By continuing to refine our understanding and expanding the global presence of social work, its development as a profession will also mature.

More than a decade ago, Ramanathan and Link (1999) summarized the importance of moving forward with internationalizing social work. They wrote that becoming more global will allow social work to "1. Confirm our collective vision and mission for the next millennium. 2. Strengthen the goals of the profession. 3. Be heard and understood more clearly by other professions, politicians and community groups. 4. Move forward in joint work across borders, to gather our experience in achieving social and economic justice. 5. Role-model ways to simultaneously respect indigenous approaches, which address unique needs, and embrace global cooperation, which improves the universals of the human condition" (p. 230). Recognizing that on one level, social work is a practice linked to specific nations, "at another level it is also an international social movement, concerned to work for social justice worldwide" (Banks, Hugman, Healy, Bozalek, & Orme, 2008, p. 336). In addressing the drive for justice and serious social challenges, a scholar from Zimbabwe encourages us to be bold: "The profession just must become more aggressive, and more adventurous, if it is to be taken seriously and indeed if it is to become more relevant" (Mupedziswa, 1992, p. 29). Through this volume, we encourage social workers to be more adventurous and assertive in including a global perspective in their learning and work.

REFERENCES

Ahmadi, N. (2003). Globalization of consciousness and new challenges for international social work. *International Journal of Social Welfare, 12*, 14–23.

Akimoto, T. (1995). Towards the establishment of an international social work/welfare concept. (Unpublished paper). Japan Women's University, Kanagawa, Japan.

Banks, S., Hugman, R., Healy, L., Bozalek, V., & Orme, J. (2008). Global ethics for social work: Problems and possibilities. *Ethics and Social Welfare, 2*(3), 324–338.

Boehm, W. (1976). Editorial. *International Social Work, 19*(3), 1.

Carter, R. T., & Qureshi, A. (1995). A typology of philosophical assumptions in multicultural counseling and training. In J. G. Pontevotta, L. A. Suzuki, &

C. M. Alexander (Eds.), *Handbook of multicultural counseling* (pp. 239–262). Thousand Oaks, CA: Sage.

Cox, D., & Pawar, M. (2006). *International social work: Issues, strategies, and programs.* Thousand Oaks, CA: Sage.

Dominelli, L. (2005). International social work: Themes and issues for the twenty-first century. *International Social Work, 48*(4), 504–507.

Elliott, D., & Segal, U. A. (2008). International social work. In B. W. White, K. M. Sowers, & C. N. Dulmus (Eds.), *Comprehensive handbook of social work and social welfare* (Vol. 1, pp. 343–376). Hoboken, NJ: Wiley.

Goldman, B. W. (1962). International social work as a professional function. *International Social Work, 5*(3), 1–8.

Gray, M. (2005). Dilemmas of international social work: Paradoxical processes in indigenization, universalism and imperialism. *International Journal of Social Welfare, 14*(3), 231–238.

Gray, M., & Fook, J. (2004). The quest for a universal social work: Some issues and implications. *Social Work Education, 23*(5), 625–644.

Haug, E. (2005). Critical reflections on the emerging discourse on international social work. *International Social Work, 48*(2), 126–135.

Healy, L. M. (2008). *International social work: Professional action in an interdependent world.* New York: Oxford University Press.

Healy, L. M. (2004). Strengthening the link: Social work with immigrants and refugees and international social work. *Journal of Immigrant and Refugee Services, 2*(1/2), 49–67.

Hugman, R. (2010). *Understanding international social work: A critical analysis.* Basingstoke, Hampshire: Palgrave Macmillan.

IASSW/IFSW. (2004). *Global standards for social work education and training.* Accessed August 25, 2009, from www.iassw-aiets.org.

Jebb, E. (1929). International social service. In *International Conference of Social Work: Proceedings, Volume 1.* First Conference, Paris, July 8–13, 1928.

Kendall, K. A. (2000) *Social work education: Its origins in Europe.* Alexandria, VA: Council on Social Work Education.

Khinduka, S. (1999). Foreword. In C. S. Ramanathan & R. J. Link (Eds.), *All our futures: Principles and resources for social work practice in a global era* (pp. xi–xii). Belmont, CA: Brooks/Cole (Wadsworth).

Link, R. J., & Ramanathan, C. S. (2011). *Human behavior in a just world: Reaching for common ground.* Lanhan, MD: Rowman & Littlefield.

Lorenz, W. (1997, August). *Social work in a changing Europe.* Paper presented at the Joint European Regional Seminar of IFSW and EASSW on Culture and Identity. Dublin, Ireland, August 24, 1997.

Lyons, K. (1999). *International social work: Themes and perspectives.* Aldershot: Ashgate.

Lyons, K., Manion, K., & Carlsen, M. (2006). *International perspectives on social work: Global conditions and local practice*. Basingstoke, Hampshire: Palgrave/Macmillan.

Merriam-Webster, (2011). On line dictionary. Accessed March 29, 2011 from www.merriam-webster.com/dictionary.

Mupedziswa, R. (1992). Africa at the crossroads: Major challenges for social work education and practice towards the year 2000. *Journal of Social Development in Africa*, 7(2), 19–38.

Nagy, G., & Falk, D. (2000). Dilemmas in international and cross-cultural social work education. *International Social Work*, 43(1), 49–60.

Payne, M., & Askeland, G. A. (2008). *Globalization and international social work: Postmodern change and challenge*. Aldershot, Hampshire: Ashgate.

Penna, S., Paylor, I., & Washington, J. (2000). Globalization, social exclusion and the possibilities for global social work and welfare. *European Journal of Social Work*, 3(2), 109–122.

Ramanathan, C. S., & Link, R. J. (1999). *All our futures: Principles and resources for social work practice in a global era*. Belmont, CA: Brooks/Cole (Wadsworth).

Sanders, D.S. & Pedersen, P. (Eds.) (1984) *Education for international social welfare*. Manoa: University of Hawaii and Council on Social Work Education.

Stein, H. (1957, January). *An international perspective in the social work curriculum*. Paper presented at the Annual Program Meeting of the Council on Social Work Education, Los Angeles, January 1957.

Warren, G. (1939). International social work. In R. Kurtz (Ed.), *Social work yearbook 1939* (pp. 192–196). New York: Russell Sage Foundation.

Webb, S. A. (2003). Local orders and global chaos in social work. *European Journal of Social Work*, 6(2), 191–204.

Xu, Q. (2006). Defining international social work: A social service agency perspective. *International Social Work*, 49(6), 679–692.

3

Globalization

MAUREEN WILSON

Globalization is a term describing a growing interconnectedness and integration of economies across national borders, through the movement of capital, goods, services and technology, and also involving the diffusion of social, cultural and political ideas. While globalization is not new, in its modern form the process of global economic integration has been dramatically accelerated, becoming more widespread, more complex and more institutionalized. Because of its broad implications for human and environmental well-being, globalization is of vital importance to social work. In this chapter we examine the contested meanings of globalization, its impacts, prescriptions for addressing those impacts, and some ways in which social work is uniquely positioned to contribute responses to these challenges.

THE GLOBALIZATION DEBATES

Global economic integration has its champions and its critics. Its champions have argued that free markets and deregulation, allowing each country to specialize in its areas of competitive advantage, will result in greater efficiencies and outputs, and benefits for all. Its critics tend to object not to globalization per se (the growth of international trade or the spread of access to technologies or new ideas) but to the predominantly neoliberal rules under which this phenomenon has operated in its contemporary form. These debates echo nineteenth century liberal–conservative controversies over free trade, with open markets advocated by (liberal) industrial capitalists and protectionism preferred by (conservative) traditional oligarchies. They also reflect nineteenth century concerns regarding the potential for social turmoil created by the globalization of capital.

The modern era of globalization is characterized by the global hegemony of the neoliberal ideas by which it is governed. Neoliberalism is an ideology that assumes the inherent wisdom of the market and makes the market central in governing economic, social, and political life. It thus assumes that the rules of the market should govern societies, rather than the other way around. A pivotal concept in neoliberalism is that of *competition*, which is valued for its ability to get things done in the most efficient ways possible. According to this doctrine, allowing the talents of the most able to find expression will eventually benefit everyone: The rising tide of capitalism will lift all boats. Those advancing a neoliberal perspective thus tend to see globalization as both inevitable and beneficial (Friedman, 2005).

The neoliberal global agenda is advanced through *structural adjustment programs*. These generally involve cuts in government spending, strong promotion of exports, privatization of public enterprises, removal of controls on trade and exchange, deregulation of wages and prices, weakening of environmental protection, and in general the removal of any laws or regulations interfering with commercial interests. The neoliberal view, advanced by transnational corporations and their allies, and sectors hegemonized by these, is that labor markets need to be more "flexible," and social programs cut, to deal with international competition. Thus neoliberals advocate cuts in unemployment insurance, repeal of labor-protective laws ("labor market deregulation"), weakening of union power, and cuts to social programs.

At the international level, this is expressed through advocacy of "free trade" in goods and services, free circulation of capital, and freedom of investment, with rules codified in trade agreements and enforced by multilateral institutions such as the World Bank, the International Monetary Fund, and the World Trade Organization (Chossudovsky, 2003; Klein, 2007). The ideological orientation underlying these policies is referred to as *globalism*. This neoliberal perspective on global economic integration is an extension of the modernization model of development described in James Midgley's chapter 4 in this volume.

Voices opposing this perspective point out that a natural consequence of the application of this doctrine—promoting competition among individuals, businesses, and nations—is that there will be winners and losers. Globalization, thus, is producing a small number of fortunate winners and an overwhelming world majority who are excluded from the benefits of globalization. Musings on these developments in relation to the widespread belief in a free-enterprise doctrine—involving what Galbraith (1993) called a "theological" belief in the inherent wisdom of the market[1]—led one economist to declare an apparent epidemic of "mad economists disease" (Cameron, 1996). In a resonance of Polanyi's historical research demonstrating that national markets are not "natural" but depend on the creation and maintenance of a complicated infrastructure of laws and institutions, Kozul-Wright and Rayment declare, "It is a dangerous delusion to think of the global economy as some sort of 'natural' system with a logic of its own: It is, and always has been, the outcome of a complex interplay of economic and political relations" (2004, pp. 3–4). In addition, there is unease related to a perception that the diffusion of ideas tends to be one way—from the center outward—with views on democracy and human rights and, perhaps more importantly, the promotion of an "intellectual blueprint . . . based on a belief about the virtues of markets and private ownership" (Przeworski et al., 1995, p. viii).

Further concern is expressed that "free" trade agreements, constraining governments to act in accordance with commercial considerations at the expense of the interests of their own citizens or the environment, represent threats to democracy and to national sovereignty. Trade agreements giving corporations the power to sue governments should laws or regulations interfere with commerce, it is argued, result in the concentration of economic and political power in the hands of corporate elites. This expansion of "rights" and "freedoms" for corporations, with the dismantling of trade and investment barriers, is seen as having disempowered people and governments, transferring power into the hands of global corporations (Korten, 1996, 2009).[2] In other words, the free trade agreements that allow the interests of corporations to trump those of governments and the structural adjustment policies associated with globalism have reduced the capacity and right of governments to protect their citizens from these impacts (Klein, 2007).

Challenges to neoliberal globalism have come also from within corporate and political elites as cracks in the Washington consensus. By the turn of the twenty-first century, as economic, social, environmental, and political crises proliferated throughout the world, increasing numbers of people at the "center" had been questioning the wisdom of the neoliberal "miracle" (Soros, 1998). Important corporate and political figures were calling for reform, or at least for some kind of "supervision" of capital. In a May 1999 speech, World Bank chief economist Dr. Joseph Stiglitz criticized the single-minded preoccupation with inflation that resulted in macroeconomic policies stifling growth; he noted that there were "signs . . . of a growing fissure between the IMF's thinking and that of its sister organization, the World Bank" (Elliot, 1999, p. 14). The same year, Canadian Finance Minister Paul Martin plainly stated that "simply put, in an institutional and legal vacuum, private markets cannot serve social interests, nor can they serve economic interests" ("In praise of regulation," 1999). The Tobin Tax, Nobel Prize–winning economist James Tobin's proposal for a punitive tax on short-run speculative financial transactions, was just one of a number of initiatives being proposed to rein in out-of-control capital. The 2008 global market collapse brought home the crucial importance of these issues, seeming to create overnight neo-Keynesians in corporate circles, with a recognition of the need for reregulation in the interest of capital accumulation (Martinez, 2009).

NEOLIBERAL GLOBALIZATION AND HUMAN WELFARE: THE DEVELOPMENT GAP

Is globalization good or bad for human welfare? From one perspective, the answer is that it is unquestionably good. From another, the answer is-well, it depends upon who you are.

Globalization is not new,[3] nor is concern about its human impacts. In the mid-nineteenth century, Marx and Engels (2005) anticipated both the triumphant globalization of capital and the accompanying social turmoil. While waxing eloquent on the achievements of capitalism, they argued that in its insatiable appetite for growing production and profits, it inevitably creates both social turmoil and instability: "The bourgeoisie cannot exist without constantly revolutionizing the instruments of production, and thereby the relations of production, and with them the whole relations of society . . . constant revolutionizing of production, uninterrupted disturbance of all social conditions, everlasting uncertainty and agitation" (p. 44). As Panich (1998) observed, "the social and ecological effects of today's global capitalism confirm . . . the *Manifesto's* warning that the failure to construct a democratic, egalitarian, communal social order out of the class struggles that capitalism generates can only result in humanity's 'common ruin'" (p. 5).

Notwithstanding the claims of free trade advocates that everyone would benefit from global economic integration, the promised broad improvements to human welfare resulting from deregulation and global competition have been little in evidence. Rather, the disparities that have grown over past decades between rich and poor, both within and between countries, persist. In 1999, the United Nations Development Programme (UNDP) called the "inequitable effects of globalization driven by markets and profit . . . a grotesque and dangerous polarization between people and countries benefiting from the system and those that are merely passive recipients of its effects" (UNDP, 1999, p. 1). A decade later, the *World of Work Report* by the International Labour Organization (ILO) concluded that the worldwide gap between richer and poorer households had widened since that time, and that "financial globalization—caused by deregulation of international capital flows—has been a major driver of income inequality" (ILO, 2008, p. 2). 43% of the global workforce earns less than $2 per day (Ransom, 2009), and the number of people going hungry is increasing. In September 2008, CARE International reported that "[in the past two years] another 100 million people have been pushed into hunger and can no longer afford food" (p. 1).

Globalization may have helped to reduce poverty in some of the largest and strongest economies, such as those of China and India (United Nations [UN], 2009), but levels of global inequality continue to be very high (Anand, Segal & Stigliz, 2010). Recent decades have been described as a "development disaster for many of the world's poorest countries where key indicators of human development not only failed to progress but began to register reversals based on both income and capability indicators" (Fukuda-Parr & Stewart, 2010, p. 247). While the 1.3 billion people living in the world's poorest countries lived on an average annual income of $573, following the 2008 financial crisis $15 trillion in public funds were used to bail out private banks. $15 trillion is approximately one-fourth of the world's total income (Ransom, 2009).

Further, the growing economic and political power of businesses and investors in recent decades, strengthened immensely by globalization (Stanford, 2008),

has produced a mounting concern that inequalities in wealth and power are fueling the global climate crisis (Nikiforuk, 2008; Worth 2009b). Climate change, in turn, disproportionately affects the poorest of the poor through flooding, malaria, malnutrition, diarrhea, rising world food prices, and increasing numbers of so-called natural disasters. Thus there is an additional sense in which "the rich world owes the poor world an ecological debt" (Worth, 2009a, p. 8).

Addressing the Human Impacts of Globalization

Neither champions nor opponents of globalization speak with single voices. However, it is clear that prescriptions for ameliorating negative human impacts of globalization vary with one's perspective on the nature and sources of the problem.

From a neoliberal perspective, global economic integration is both inevitable and beneficial. Development and the distribution of resources are best left to the invisible hand of the market; through an evolutionary process, the fittest (the best able to compete in a global market economy) will rise to the top, and the benefits will trickle down to everyone. Thus, in terms of addressing human problems associated with the processes of globalization, proponents of this position are likely to either

- argue that there is really no problem because benefits from the success of those at the top will trickle down to benefit all, or
- acknowledge that some people are temporarily dislocated or disadvantaged in the process of globalization and that some individuals or groups may need to be provided with temporary assistance as they adjust to the new global economy.

Hence, although there may be acknowledgment of some "painful" aspects of the application of these policies, as some people are "temporarily" dislocated or disadvantaged, any ameliorative actions involve temporary assistance for these persons in adjusting to the new global economy. In this way, even studies documenting dismal human consequences of globalization may avoid identifying any fault in the dominant neoliberal paradigm in operation in producing these results, instead suggesting that what is needed is better *management* of globalization. One UNDP report (1997), for example, put forward a series of strategies its member countries could adopt for a "managed globalization," including fairer trade policies, better terms for poor countries to enter markets, and investment in education of the poor, which would "make markets work for people, not people for markets" (p. 91). Taking as a given the rush to globalization, it elides the question of what would produce the political will to implement these policies.

Opponents of neoliberal globalization are inclined to point to the degradation of social, economic, and environmental conditions that accompanies the processes of neoliberal globalization for the vast majority of the world's population. "Just as the market has proved incapable of controlling the dangerous excesses of international finance, it is failing to reduce greenhouse gas emissions, or to kick-start the dramatic shift towards zero-carbon economies we so desperately need" (Worth, 2009b, p. 11). These results are seen as being at odds with social justice, as ordinary people worldwide are dislocated and thrown out of work and needed social programs are dismantled while a small number of people become very rich. Thus, regarding the human problems associated with globalization, opponents have argued for one or more of the following:

- With the overwhelming world majority excluded from the benefits of globalization, social safety nets should be strengthened, not weakened, to address the needs of the victims of this process, or that
- Nothing should be done, because the global capitalist system, containing the seeds of its own destruction, will eventually be replaced by a more equitable system through the leadership of self-emancipated working classes, and/or that
- Support should be given to new forms of social, economic, and political organization emerging through the efforts of those rooted in the everyday struggles of ordinary people.

With respect to the latter, it is contended that the evolution of new open, self-organizing systems, drawing on insights from the field and reinforced by developments in scientific understanding of living systems over the past four decades,[4] can help develop socially, economically, and ecologically sustainable communities. This does not necessarily entail the rejection of a belief in "survival of the fittest" but rather an identification with biological evidence that the "fittest" who survive are likely to be those best able to operate cooperatively (Barlow, 1992).

CIVIL SOCIETY RESPONSES: GLOBALIZATION FROM BELOW

In the context of the shrinking ability of governments to protect their citizens from negative effects of globalization, and in the absence of significant effective leadership from mainstream political parties, academia, or other traditional forces of opposition, civil society organizations worldwide have been moving into the breach. Working at social and political levels, as well as on the terrain of economic survival, a wide range of groups and organizations is now engaged in confronting perceived threats of corporate globalization to democracy, economic justice, the environment, and protection of the commons. The growing convergence of circumstances between underclasses of North and South has produced a set of conditions ripe for cross-national alliances around these issues. Thus consequences of the economic globalization process have been the globalization of poverty and the emergence of a Global South transcending traditional North–South borders and giving impetus to alliance building among like-minded groups.

Popular movements—citizen's groups including labor organizations; community groups; faith-related and ecumenical coalitions; women's, environmental, indigenous peoples', civil rights, seniors', and student organizations; antipoverty alliances; and nongovernmental organizations (NGOs) addressing any number of social and political issues—have been forming international networks, solidarity linkages, and coalitions. Citizens' movements, for example, have organized worldwide boycotts against landmines and have developed shareholder campaigns and lawsuits against businesses and banks that provide loans or investments to repressive regimes, cause environmental damage, or are complicit in human rights abuses.

La Via Campesina, an international movement of peasants, small- and medium-sized producers, landless people, rural women, indigenous people, rural youth, and agricultural workers was formed to "develop solidarity and unity among small farmer organizations in order to promote gender parity and social justice in fair economic relations; the preservation of land, water, seeds and other natural resources; food sovereignty and sustainable agricultural production based on small and medium-sized producers" (www.viacampesina.org/en/). Fair trade networks have promoted trade and business relationships among grassroots groups, and specific bilateral trade relationships have been developed, such as those that have developed between Central American producer cooperatives and Japanese consumer cooperatives and between Nicaraguan Miskitu Indians and Canadian aboriginal groups around management of forest and fishing industries. In more industrialized countries, a movement toward community-supported agriculture supports small local farmers as ordinary consumers seek more ethical ways to purchase goods and services. These and other linkages make up a kind of parallel globalization, or "globalization from below."

Opposition to the hegemony of the neoliberal approach to globalization is perhaps best summed up in the "one no, many yeses" theme of the World Social Forum. Meeting in various places around the world as a counterpoint to the annual World Economic Forum in Davos, Switzerland, the WSF represents a broad-based civil society rejection of the neoliberal global agenda (the "no") and an affirmation of the multiplicity of alternatives that are generated through the creative genius of ordinary people (the "yeses").

Social Work Responses: Becoming an Ally

In preparation for a workshop with a group of social workers, I asked an undergraduate class to brainstorm a comparison between neoliberal and social work perspectives. The class came up with the list in Table 3.1.

This brief snapshot captures some of the tension between the neoliberal global project and social work values. As the late Professor Gayle Gilchrist James (2003) observed,

> "Principles of human rights and social justice are fundamental to social work. . . . Every social worker has the *opportunity* to matter and, hopefully, the *capacity* to do so."

How can social workers best respond to this global challenge? Clearly social work values have much in common with the goals and aspirations of the above-described civil society organizations, and it appears that some of the most promising countervailing forces to neoliberal hegemony, both in practice and in the development of accompanying theory, tend to come from those rooted in popular struggles. Thus it is not surprising that social workers all over the world are already allied with the popular movements they hope will help to build a more equitable and sustainable globalization process. However, the answers as to how we work in relation to these processes are more complex than simply deciding whose "side" we are on.

Social workers have the ability to bring a range of roles and skills to this work. What are needed are both

TABLE 3.1. CONTRASTING NEOLIBERALISM AND SOCIAL WORK

Neoliberal	Social work
Free market economy	People-centred
Survival of the fittest	Inclusiveness
Globalism	Self-determination
Privatization	Cooperation
Competition	Compassion
Corporatization	Antioppressive
Modernization	Participation
Economics of supply and demand	Empowerment
Targeted social programs	Universal social programs
Power over	Power with
Capitalistic base	Empathy
English as language of business	Reciprocity
Private	Public
Globalism	Environmental sustainability
Economics driven	Social justice
Promotes elite power	Grassroots organizing
Individualism ("*I*")	Collectivism ("*we*")
"Development"	Education
Blaming the victim	Awareness
Oppressive	Cross-border organizing
	Socially driven
	Human rights
	Egalitarian
	Recognition of culture/ language
	Minority rights
	Gender awareness

skills of conceptualizing this reality, and more effective means of acting to change it- though not necessarily in that order. Most of these needed skills are in fact already present in social work, which owes a debt to both Gramsci and Freire for their explication (Whitmore & Wilson, 2005). Susan George (1997) presented an important challenge in observing that the Gramscian recognition of the importance of the struggle for ideological hegemony, the "war of ideas," in recent decades seems to have been taken more to heart by the champions of neoliberal economic doctrine than it has by more progressive forces. This work needs to be reclaimed by those united in the search for social justice and a more equitable distribution of resources.

It is perhaps also time to revisit another Gramscian notion: the leadership potential in *organic intellectuals* who contribute not by virtue of holding the social role of an intellectual but by virtue of their intimate connection to, and reflections on, the struggles of daily life (Gramsci, 1976). This lesson, developed by Paulo Freire (1970) to dramatic effect in popular education (education for critical consciousness) with Latin American and African underclasses, has come to significantly influence how social work is conceived (Wilson & Prado, 2007).

Social workers can bring important conceptual and practical skills to work both on the terrain of the "war of ideas" and on the terrains of political and economic action. The *conceptual skills* include attention to analysis of the historical contexts in which we work as well as an ability to distinguish, carry out, and share the skills of both structural and conjunctural analysis. This must include knowledge of what globalization is (under the current rules), including the nature of neoliberalism (the rules of engagement), its current manifestations, the human consequences of neoliberal globalization, and current government and civil society responses to these consequences. It implies the ability to analyze broad social forces (structural analysis), to analyze the particular moment and its possibilities (conjunctural analysis), and to use and share these insights in relation to the intersection of personal troubles and public issues and in practice directly addressing structural issues.

Central among the many *practical skills* social workers can bring are the skills for working with people to identify and clarify issues to be addressed, to design short- and long-term strategies and tactics for addressing the issues, to clarify the desired results (outcomes, impacts) for each, to identify indicators for the desired results, to plan for action, to implement and evaluate change (using reflection on experience, successes, and setbacks to inform subsequent actions), and to build community capacity for these activities.

With these skills, as Professor Gilchrist James (2003) has reminded us, social workers are uniquely equipped both to engage in social policy process (formulation, critique, change) and to be effective allies of groups, organizations, and movements addressing issues of human rights and social justice. This work may include a variety of approaches, from work in a given moment toward fine-tuning the neoliberal model to ameliorate its consequences for the most vulnerable, to work toward the creation of a range of alternatives. Since there is no road map or blueprint for this work, skills of structural and conjunctural analysis become critical as we "make the road by walking" (Horton & Freire, 1990).

There is a sense in which all social work is international social work. Because national social policies are circumscribed by the rules of international trade agreements, these form part of the context for all of our work. However, it would be a mistake to assume that because of this, we should focus exclusively on the international level in our attempts to influence policy. Signatories of international agreements do not operate in a vacuum; they answer to constituencies at home. Thus, the effectiveness of international action related to social policies depends on the effectiveness of work at the local, regional, and national levels.

Globalization is not new, and it is inherently neither good nor evil. However, in its modern form it has produced results putting it at odds with social work values related to human rights and social justice. Social workers, well placed to assist in the transformation of this phenomenon, are already engaged in the process of bringing modern-day globalization back into democratic accountability, in order to address the social development goal of enhancing human welfare in ways that are determined by people themselves.

NOTES

1. Galbraith (1993) notes, "In accepted free-enterprise attitudes and doctrine, the market is a neutral and accurate reflection of external influences; it is not supposed to be subject to an inherent and internal dynamic of error. This is the classic faith" (p. 23). "Economists . . . sought to exculpate the market [for the crash of 1929], holding deeper factors . . . responsible for the business decline. This was evasion bordering on nonsense" (p. 89). "Markets . . . are theologically sacrosanct. . . . Accepted in reputable market orthodoxy is . . . the inherent perfection of the market. . . . Yet clearly the speculative episode, with increases provoking increases, is within the market itself. And so is the culminating crash. Such a thought being theologically unacceptable, it is necessary to search for external influences" (pp. 106–107).

2. Yet, as Korten has commented, "even CEOs are extremely limited by the imperatives of global competition from acting socially responsibly. When they do, they are quickly replaced. When they do not, they are rewarded greatly" (IFG, 1996, p. 12).

3. Held, McGrew, Goldblatt, and Perraton (1999) identify four historical eras during which this has occurred. Early forms of globalization were present during the Roman Empire, the Parthian empire (247 BCE-224 CE), and the Han Dynasty (202 BCE-220 CE). During the Islamic Golden Age (700 CE-1200 CE or later), Muslim traders and explorers established an early globalization of crops, trade, knowledge, and technology across the Old World; during the Mongol Empire (1206–1368) there was greater economic integration along the Silk Road. A wider form of globalization began around the turn of the sixteenth century, with Portugal and Spain entering into exploration,

colonization, and trade in Africa, South America, and Southern and Eastern Asia. The Iberian powers were followed shortly by France and England, with the British establishing a huge and powerful global empire. The nineteenth century was a period of rapid growth in international trade and investment between the European imperial powers and their colonies and, later, the United States. However, this began to break down with World War I and then collapsed with the gold standard crisis and Great Depression in the late 1920s and early 1930s.

4. As explicated by Capra (1996), these developments transcend the historic division between the study of pattern (form, quality, order) and substance (structure, quantity, matter), the Cartesian split between mind and matter, through the integration of the linking element of process. Based on insights from a variety of sources, including nonlinear mathematics made possible by the powerful new computers that became available in the 1970s, new research in microbiology (challenging the view of evolution as resulting only from random mutations and natural selection), and new developments in psychology (the Santiago theory of cognition), this emerging "unified theory" also resonates with ancient knowledge from various corners of the world. According to Capra, the growing interest in nonlinearity has produced a number of theories sharing the following characteristics: They deal with open systems operating far from equilibrium, they describe the spontaneous emergence of new structures and new forms of behavior (a phenomenon known as *self-organization*), they include internal feedback loops, and they are formulated in terms of nonlinear equations.

REFERENCES

Anand, S., Segal, P. & Stiglitz, J. E. (2010). Introduction. pp. 1–23. In S. Anand, P. Segal, & Stiglitz, J. E. (Eds.), *Debates in the measurement of global poverty.* New York: Oxford University Press.

Barlow, C. (Ed.). (1992). *From Gaia to selfish genes: Selected writings in the life sciences.* Cambridge, MA: MIT Press.

Cameron, D. (1996, August). Mad economists's disease. *Canadian Forum, 76*(7), 8.

Capra, F. (1996). The Web of Life. *Resurgence, 178,* 24–29.

CARE International. (2008, September). Living on the edge of emergency: Paying the price of inaction. Available: http://reliefweb.int/rw/lib.nsf/db900SID/SHIG-7JLCMK?OpenDocument.

Chossudovsky, M. (2003). *The globalization of poverty and the new world order.* Ottawa: Global Research.

Desmarais A. A. (2007). *La Vía Campesina: Globalization and the Power of Peasants.* Black Point, Nova Scotia: Fernwood Publishing.

Elliot, C. (1999). *Locating the Energy for Change: An Introduction to Appreciative Inquiry.* Winnipeg: International Institute for Sustainable Development.

Freire, P. (1970). *Pedagogy of the oppressed.* New York: Seabury Press.

Friedman, T. L. (2005). *The world is flat.* New York: Farrar, Strauss & Giroux.

Fukuda-Parr, S., & Stewart, D. (2010). Unequal development in the 1990s: Growing gaps in human capabilities. In A. Sudhir, P. Segal, & J. E. Stiglitz (Eds.), *Debates in the measurement of global poverty* (pp. 246–261). New York: Oxford University Press.

Galbraith, J. K. (1993). *A short history of financial euphoria.* New York: Penguin.

George, S. (1997). How to win the war of ideas: Lessons from the Gramscian right. *Dissent, 44*(3), 47–53.

Gramsci, A. (1976). *Selections from the prison notebooks* (Q. Hoare & G. Nowell Smith, Trans., Eds.). New York: International Publishers.

Held, D., McGrew, A., Goldblatt, D., & Perraton, J. (1999). *Global transformations: Politics, economics and culture.* Palo Alto, CA: Stanford University Press.

Horton, M., & Freire, P. (1990). *We make the road by walking: Conversations on education and social change.* Philadelphia: Temple University Press.

In praise of regulation for the market's sake. (1999, June 9). *Globe and Mail*, p. A4.

International Forum on Globalization (IFG). (1996, Fall). *IFG News* 1.

International Labour Organization (ILO). (2008). *World of work report 2008.* Available: www.ilo.org/global/About_the_ILO/Media_and_public_information/Press_releases/lang–en/WCMS_099377/index.htm.

James, G. G. (2003, February). Address to Student Social Action Day, Faculty of Social Work. University of Calgary, Alberta, Canada.

Klein, N. (2007). *The shock doctrine: The rise of disaster capitalism.* New York: Metropolitan Books.

Korten, D. (2009). Beyond bailouts: Let's put life ahead of money. *Yes! 48*(Winter), 12–15.

Korten, D. (1996). *When corporations rule the world.* West Hartford, CT: Kumarian Press.

Kozul-Wright, R., & Rayment, P. (2004). *Globalization reloaded: An UNCTAD perspective.* Discussion Paper 167. New York: United Nations.

Martinez, M. A. (2009). *The myth of the free market: The role of the state in a capitalist economy.* Sterling, VA: Kumarian Press.

Marx, K., & Engels, F. (2005). Manifesto of the Communist Party. In P. Gasper (Ed.), *Manifesto of the Communist Party: A road map to history's most important political document.* Chicago: Haymarket Books.

Nikiforuk, A. (2008). *Tar Sands: Dirty Oil and the Future of a Continent.* Vancouver: Greystone Books.

Panich, L. (1998, May 2). Where the Left began. *Globe and Mail*, p. A5.

Polanyi, K. (2001). *The Great Transformation.* Boston: Beacon Press.

Przeworski, A., Bardhan, P., Bresser Pereira, L. C., Bruszt, L., Choi, J. J., Comisso, E. T., et al. (1995). *Sustainable democracy*. Cambridge: Cambridge University Press.

Ransom, D. (2009). The age of possibility. *New Internationalist, 421*, 13–19.

Soros, G. (1998). *The crisis of global capitalism: Open society endangered*. New York: Public Affairs.

Stanford, J. (2008). *Economics for everyone: A short guide to the economics of capitalism*. Halifax and Winnipeg: Fernwood.

United Nations Development Programme (UNDP). (1999). *Human development report*. Cary, NC: Oxford University Press.

United Nations Development Programme (UNDP). (1997). *Human development report 1997*. Available: www.undp.org.

United Nations (UN). (2009). *Millennium Development Goals report 2009*. Available: www.un.org/millenniumgoals/.

Whitmore, E., & Wilson, M. G. (2005). Popular resistance to global corporate rule: The role of social work. In I. Ferguson, M. Lavalette, & E. Whitmore (Eds.), *Globalisation, global justice and social work* (189–206). London & New York: Routledge.

Wilson, M. G., & Prado Hernández, I. (2007). The liberatory tradition in Nicaraguan social work. In I. Ferguson & M. Lavalette (Eds.), *Radical social work in an era of globalisation* (pp. 73–90). Birmingham, UK: Venture Press.

Worth, J. (2009a, January/February). Four principles for climate justice. *New Internationalist, 419*, 8.

Worth, J. (2009b, April). Can climate catastrophe be averted? *CCPA Monitor*, 10–13.

4

Development

JAMES MIDGLEY

Development has been an intellectual and policy preoccupation of global importance since the mid-twentieth century. Although the concept of development is rooted in philosophical speculation about the nature of social change and progress, it assumed a distinctly economic connotation when it was popularized after World War II (Arndt, 1987). It also had a political connotation, reflecting the intention of the nationalist independence movements of the Global South to transform their predominantly agrarian societies into modern nation-states. Development, it was believed, would be achieved by adopting economic policies that promoted industrialization, significantly expanded wage employment, and raised standards of living. Although the former imperial powers promised to assist, the geopolitical power struggles of the postwar era fostered competition for their loyalty. As the leaders of the United States and the Soviet Union vied for global influence and supported the development efforts of governments that aligned with them, development became a key geopolitical project.

The following provides an overview of development over the last half century. It begins with the formative focus of development on economic issues and the way it was linked to national and global politics. Criticisms of the narrow economic approach to development are briefly reviewed and the reformulation of the concept to embrace a multifaceted process involving social, gender, and ecological dimensions is discussed. The effects of neoliberal ideas on development since the 1980s and the challenge of persistent poverty and deprivation are examined. Finally, the achievements of development effort and challenges for the twenty-first century are considered.

DEVELOPMENT AS AN ECONOMIC PROJECT

In its early formulation, development was economistic in that it was almost entirely concerned with issues of capital mobilization, industrial investments, and wage-employment expansion. In addition to drawing on the social sciences, development policy was inspired by the massive social and economic changes brought about by industrialization in the West, the Soviet Union, and Japan in the late nineteen and early twentieth centuries. Like the newly independent nations, these countries had an agrarian past in which the vast majority of their populations lived in poverty and eked out a living in subsistence or near-subsistence agriculture. Since the eighteenth century, industrialization had drawn the rural poor of Western Europe and North America into wage employment, and living standards improved dramatically. Through deliberate policy intervention, industrialization in Japan and the Soviet Union also fostered the expansion of wage employment, reducing the number of people in poverty. In addition, both countries demonstrated that the process of industrialization could be accelerated through government planning. Provided that the right policies were adopted, industrialization could bring about equally substantive economic and social changes in the Global South.

A standard economic development model that drew on these experiences was widely adopted in the 1950s. Formulated by leading development economists, the model was based on the contention that most colonized societies had dual economic sectors composed of a small but modern urban and plantation economy and a large coexisting agrarian economy in which the vast majority of the population lived and worked (Booke, 1953). While the urban sector was dynamic and productive, the agrarian sector was characterized by subsistence poverty. Dual-sector theorists proposed that the modern sector be expanded through capital investments that would stimulate manufacturing and commercial activities and draw surplus labor out of subsistence agriculture into modern wage employment. International aid, foreign direct investment, commercial borrowing, and even domestic capital mobilization would provide the capital needed to expand the modern sector. The theoretical insights of Keynesian economics as well as empirical and historical research on industrialization in Europe provided the basis for this policy.

At the time, policy makers focused on initiating an endogenous, import-substituting process that promoted economic development within individual countries (Lewis, 1955), but they also recognized that international aid and foreign investment were needed if capital for industrial development were to be mobilized. However, the use of aid to exert geopolitical influence sullied the process. Aid was often linked to military technologies that did little to foster sustained development. Mismanagement and poor economic planning also limited the effectiveness of aid. Despite the efforts of the Non-Aligned Movement, which emerged out of the Bandung Conference in Indonesia in 1955, development was inextricably linked to neoimperialist struggles for global domination. President Truman's Four Points and President Kennedy's Alliance for Progress reflected Cold War competitiveness, as did Soviet development initiatives.

The world powers also sought to exert influence through multilateral agencies, such as the World Bank and the United Nations, but had limited success. Both of these organizations were founded at the end of the Second World War and soon began to shape international development efforts. In addition to its peacekeeping and diplomatic activities, development emerged as a major preoccupation for the United Nations and its affiliate agencies. The United Nations Development Decades provided the impetus for concerted action on economic and social development, and various United Nations human rights initiatives augmented these efforts. The United Nations also played a leading role in promoting social development through convening the World Summit for Social Development in 1995 and sponsoring the Millennium Development Goals. The World Bank was primarily concerned in its early years with funding large-scale development projects, but, under the presidency of Robert McNamara and subsequently of James Wolfensohn, it focused attention on poverty and supported a variety of projects that sought to improve social conditions for the world's poor. However, as will be shown, the World Bank's subsequent role in diffusing market liberal economic development policies through structural adjustment programs undermined these efforts (see Chapter 47 and Chapter 49 for more on the United Nations and World Bank).

TRANSCENDING ECONOMIC DEVELOPMENT

Although the economistic conception of development was widely implemented in the 1950s and 1960s, it was frequently criticized and numerous attempts to reformulate it were made. An early contribution came from sociologists and political scientists, known as the *modernization theorists*, who sought to augment the economic premises of development by stressing the need for cultural, demographic, political, and attitudinal changes that would facilitate economic growth. Traditional institutions, they argued, needed to change so that people would embrace modern economic activities. Long-established cultural obligations, extended families, political institutions, and cultural beliefs needed to be replaced by individualism, acquisitiveness, and entrepreneurship (Hozelitz, 1960; Inkeles & Smith, 1974; McClelland, 1964).

As may be expected, these ideas were vigorously challenged by traditionalists and agrarian populists who rejected the need for urbanization and rapid industrialization and resisted the pressures of modernity. Instead, they extolled the virtues of prevailing social and cultural institutions, especially in the rural communities of the Global South (Kitching, 1982). Other critics, known as *dependency theorists*, challenged the idea that the problem of mass poverty could be solved through endogenous development. They argued that it was highly unlikely that developing countries would experience authentic economic progress while they were part of a global, exploitative capitalist system. Although their neo-Marxist analysis was weak on policy, the dependency theorists offered a powerful critique of the modernization approach (Cardoso, 1972; Frank, 1974, 1967; Rodney, 1972). Some advocated the delinking of development efforts from the global economy, and others proposed that the governments of the Global South assert their autonomy and negotiate improved terms of trade. In time, these ideas found expression in a number of North–South initiatives, such as the Brandt Commission (1980), and greater emphasis was placed on creating new global trade relationships that were beneficial to the developing world.

In contrast to the dependency school's critique of global capitalism, some scholars and policy makers were more pragmatically concerned with the problems of mass poverty and deprivation in the nations of the South. Known as *developmentalists*, they challenged the argument that rapid growth through industrialization would automatically raise standards of living for all (Griffin, 1978; Myrdal, 1970; Seers, 1969).

Instead, they emphasized the need for social policy interventions targeted at the rural poor and the large numbers of migrants who had come to the cities in search of work. They were particularly concerned with the plight of migrants engaged in informal-sector activities. The rapid growth of the informal sector, they argued, demonstrated that the economic development model, which had promised to create large-scale wage employment through industrialization, was unworkable. The persistence of poverty in both rural and urban areas suggested that it would take many decades before wage employment would expand sufficiently to absorb surplus labor from the agrarian sector. They insisted that social policies that directly tackled the problems of poverty, ill health, illiteracy, and malnutrition be implemented.

These ideas were echoed by the international agencies. As noted earlier, the World Bank under the presidency of Robert McNamara paid more attention to the problem of poverty and increased its lending for antipoverty projects. In the 1970s, the International Labour Organization (ILO) urged developing countries to make a determined effort to meet the basic social needs of their people rather than focus on industrial development (ILO, 1976; Streeten & Burki, 1978). The World Health Organization encouraged its member states to replace conventional hospital-based curative medical care with more appropriate community-based interventions (Newell, 1975). Similarly, the United Nations Children's Fund (UNICEF) assisted its member states in focusing on the needs of young children and their mothers and adopting policies that would ensure that their basic health, nutritional, and educational needs were addressed.

The developmentalist approach was augmented by the advocacy of policies that focused on gender and ecological issues. Proponents of the conventional economic development model, as well as neo-Marxist dependency writers, had paid scant attention to these issues. Gender analysts were understandably critical of the way that women's roles in and contributions to development had been ignored, and they insisted that women participate fully when development policies were being formulated (Beneria, 2003; Boserup, 1970; Moser, 1989; Porter & Judd, 1999; Shiva, 1989). Environmentalists criticized the emphasis on industrialization and economic modernization, which they believed not only harmed the natural environment but fostered a consumer culture that promoted acquisitive values and undermined cooperative systems of support (Brundtland Commission, 1983;

Daly, 1996; Mishan, 1967). These ideas were compatible with a concern about growing inequality and the problem of distorted development in many developing countries (Midgley, 1995). Though economic growth had indeed raised standards of living for the urban elite and emerging middle class, poverty remained endemic. Development would only be meaningful, critics claimed, if the benefits of economic growth were equally distributed and fostered inclusivity and solidarity. This, they argued, could be achieved without harming economic growth (Ahluwalia, 1976).

STAGNATION, GROWTH, AND GLOBALIZATION

In seeking to mobilize capital for industrialization, many governments in the Global South borrowed extensively on international commercial markets. They also became indebted to the Western donor nations. When global interest rates were low, these governments managed their debts, but with the oil shocks of the 1970s and rampant inflation in the West, political leaders such as President Reagan in the United States and Prime Minister Thatcher in Britain adopted anti-inflationary policies that significantly raised interest rates. This caused widespread indebtedness among countries that had borrowed liberally when interest rates were low. As balance of payments worsened and currencies collapsed, many governments sought emergency credit from donor nations and multilateral organizations such as the International Monetary Fund and World Bank.

By this time, the formative Keynesian influence in development thinking had been eroded and replaced by a radical commitment to free market liberalism. In academic circles, Western aid agencies, the World Bank, and the International Monetary Fund, neoliberalism became the new orthodoxy. However, with a few notable exceptions, such as the military regime in Chile, its tenets were not enthusiastically adopted by the governments of the South. Nevertheless, the neoliberal approach diffused widely and exerted a powerful influence. By the 1980s, liberalized markets, entrepreneurship, deregulation, and denationalization were widely regarded as essential for economic progress. Integration into the global economy through trade liberalization was also believed to be a precondition for economic development.

The adoption of market liberalism was also facilitated by the imposition of structural adjustment programs. These programs were imposed as a condition for the payment of emergency credit from the International Monetary Fund and the World Bank.

As noted earlier, many developing countries had borrowed freely on international commercial markets, but as interest rates soared in the 1980s, many were unable to meet their debt repayments and sought help from the International Monetary Fund and the World Bank. Structural adjustment programs were designed to ensure that these debts were repaid, and they usually required massive cuts in public expenditures, civil service layoffs, retrenchments in health and education programs, and the introduction of user fees at schools, clinics, and hospitals. Structural adjustment had a serious impact on human capital development. In many countries where health, education, and other social service programs were retrenched, school attendance and health and nutritional standards declined.

Despite the promise that marketization would promote rapid economic recovery, many developing economies stagnated. In addition, the incidence of poverty in many parts of the South increased. This was particularly evident in Africa, South Asia, and parts of South and Central America. With the adoption of market liberalism, government public services were decimated, many civil servants were laid off, and education and health budgets were retrenched. Many governments introduced user fees for medical care and schooling, which had an adverse effect on millions of poor people. These problems were exacerbated by an increase in ill health, the HIV pandemic, higher rates of malnutrition, and a rise in violence, military intervention, and dictatorship.

Proponents of neoliberal development policy downplayed these harsh realities. Some claimed that patience was needed since it would take time for market-based development policies to work. Others drew attention to the success of a few, mostly East Asian nations, which had based their development policies on exports rather than the conventional endogenous import-substitution approach. These tiger economies, as they became known, had been able to secure access to Western markets and had undoubtedly prospered. However, while neoliberals touted their achievements, few mentioned that the East Asian governments had actively planned and managed the development process. Ignoring the role of the state, they claimed that market capitalism offered a viable solution to the poverty problem in the South. With the collapse of the Soviet Union and the adoption of market policies by the Yeltsin government, neoliberalism appeared to be triumphant.

As noted earlier, few governments in the Global South were avid supporters of market liberalism. Nevertheless, many embraced export-led development policies even though relatively few were able to emulate the achievements of the tiger economies. The major exception was China, where the government cautiously adopted a market-based but state-directed development strategy in the late 1980s. By the turn of the century, wage employment in China had increased exponentially, the country had become a major exporter of manufactured goods, and standards of living had risen dramatically even though inequality and mass poverty in the rural areas remained serious problems. Similarly, government-directed economic liberalization in other large developing countries such as Brazil and India fueled economic growth. In both countries, a sizable middle class has slowly emerged even though poverty and deprivation remain widespread.

DEVELOPMENT ACHIEVEMENTS AND CHALLENGES FOR THE TWENTY-FIRST CENTURY

Although hundreds of millions of people in the Global South have experienced significant improvements in living conditions over the last half century, the promise of prosperity for all through economic growth has not been realized. The number of people in the Global South with an income below the one-dollar-a-day poverty line declined during the 1990s from about 1.27 billion to 1.19 billion—a fall of about 80 million (Hall & Midgley, 2004); however, many hundreds of millions of people continue to live in poverty and deprivation. In reality, the incidence of global poverty declined largely because of the fall in poverty in East Asia, particularly in China (World Bank, 2001). Smaller declines were recorded in Latin America, the Caribbean, and the Middle East, but the incidence of poverty in South Asia is still high. Unfortunately, in sub-Saharan Africa, the number of people living below the one-dollar-a-day line increased by about 15 million during the 1990s. The increase in poverty in the sub-Saharan region was also accompanied by a decrease in life expectancy associated with the HIV and AIDS pandemic as well as frequent political and social conflict that cost the lives of millions.

On the other hand, compared with conditions at the end of World War II, when most of the world lived under European colonialism, incomes and standards of living have improved significantly. A smaller proportion of the Global South was living in poverty at the beginning of the twenty-first century than at the end of the Second World War, and in many developing countries, life expectancy has increased and infant mortality has declined. Access to education and health care has also improved, and many more people are now in regular wage employment. However, this does not mean that the problems of poverty and deprivation have been solved. On the contrary, hundreds of millions continue to live in abject misery. Clearly, the persistence of absolute poverty will pose a huge challenge to development efforts in the twenty-first century. This challenge will undoubtedly be exacerbated by the global recession experienced at the end of the first decade of the century.

The mixed record of development has resulted in different interpretations and policy prescriptions. Whereas some development scholars and policy makers believe that the development project has been a colossal failure (Escobar, 1995; Munck, 1999; Rahnema, 1997), others are more optimistic. Although recognizing the enormity of the task, they believe that redoubled efforts to promote sustainable economic growth and raise incomes and standards of living can succeed. Some believe that increased international cooperation can enhance development effort and that multilateral agencies such as the United Nations, with its advocacy of social development and the Millennium Development Goals, can provide effective leadership (United Nations, 1996, 2005). Others take the view that developing countries need to more vigorously challenge the continued geopolitical hegemony of the West if they are to attain development goals, and there are signs that this is already happening. As the governments of developing countries have become increasingly frustrated by the Western nations that have used international trade institutions such as the World Trade Organization to further their own interests, their leaders have successfully stymied the Doha Round of trade negotiations and insisted on improved terms. Although the trade impasse is unresolved, many governments in the Global South have become resolute in their efforts to resist superpower domination (see Chapter 49).

Development thinking has also become more multifaceted. Instead of the narrow focus on economic growth and industrialization that characterized the formative years of development effort, more emphasis is now placed on social, ecological, gender, and other noneconomic dimensions of development. Also, although development was initially seen as a state-directed project, the contributions of voluntary organizations, local communities, women's groups, and faith-based organizations have been recognized. It has also been recognized that human rights, peace, and international cooperation are critical to future success. Of course, the reformulation of the concept of development and the application of development ideas in many contexts, institutions, and organizations has complicated matters. But it has also fostered lively academic and policy debates that are indicative of a greater willingness among development scholars and policy makers to pragmatically consider different approaches. This attitude augurs well for future policy innovations and responses to the rapidly changing realities of the time. As the global recession negatively affects the lives of hundreds of millions around the world, flexibility and innovation in development thinking will be urgently needed.

REFERENCES

Ahluwalia, M. (1976). Inequality, poverty and development. *Journal of Development Economics, 3*(4), 309–342.

Arndt, H. W. (1987). *Economic development: The history of an idea.* Chicago: University of Chicago Press.

Beneria, L. (2003). *Gender, development and globalization.* New York: Routledge.

Booke, J. (1953). *Economics and economic policy in dual societies.* Haarlem: Willink.

Boserup, E. (1970). *Women's role in economic development.* London: Allen and Unwin.

Brandt, W. (1980). *North-South: A programme for survival.* London: Pan Books.

Brundtland Commission. (1983). *Our common future: From one earth to one world.* Geneva: World Commission on Environment and Development.

Cardoso, F. H. (1972). Dependency and development in Latin America. *New Left Review, 74,* 83–89.

Daley, H. (1996). *Beyond growth.* Boston: Beacon Press.

Escobar, A. (1995). *The making and unmaking of the Third World.* Princeton, NJ: Princeton University Press.

Frank, A. G. (1974). *On capitalist underdevelopment.* New York: Oxford University Press.

Frank, A. G. (1967). *Capitalism and underdevelopment in Latin America.* New York: Monthly Review Press.

Griffin, K. (1978). *International inequality and national poverty.* London: MacMillan.

Hall, A., & Midgley, J. (2004). *Social policy for development.* Thousand Oaks, CA: Sage.

Hozelitz, B. F. (1960). *Sociological factors in economic development.* New York: Free Press.

Inkeles, A., & Smith, D. H. (1974). *Becoming modern.* London: Heinemann.

International Labour Office (ILO). (1976). *Employment, growth and basic needs: A one world problem.* Geneva: Author.

Kitching, G. (1982). *Development and underdevelopment in historical perspective.* London: Methuen.

Lewis, W. A. (1955). *The theory of economic growth.* London: Allen & Unwin.

McClelland, D. (1964). A psychological approach to economic development. *Economic Development and Cultural Change, 12*(2): 320–324.

Midgley, J. (1995). *Social development: The developmental perspective in social welfare.* Thousand Oaks, CA: Sage.

Mishan, E. J. (1967). *The costs of economic growth.* Harmondsworth, England: Penguin.

Moser, C. O. N. (1989). *Gender planning and development: Theory, practice and training.* London: Routledge.

Munck, R. (1999). Deconstructing development discourses: Of impasses, alternatives and politics. In R. Munck & D. O'Hearn (Eds.), *Critical development theory: Contributions to a new paradigm* (pp. 196–210). New York: Zed Books.

Myrdal, G. (1970). *The challenge of world poverty.* Harmondsworth, England: Penguin.

Newell, K. (Ed) (1975). *Health by the people.* Geneva: World Health Organization.

Porter, M., & Judd, E. (Eds.). (1999). *Feminists doing development: A practical critique.* New York: Routledge.

Rahnema, M. (1997). Towards post-development: Searching for signposts, a new language and new paradigms. In M. Rahnema & V. Bawtree (Eds.), *The post-development reader* (pp. 377–403). New York: Zed Books.

Rodney, W. (1972). *How Europe underdeveloped Africa.* Dar-es-Salaam: Tanzania Publishing House.

Seers, D. (1969). The meaning of development. *International Development Review, 3*(1), 2–6.

Shiva, V. (1989). *Staying alive: Women, ecology and development.* London: Zed Books.

Streeten, P., & Burki, S. J. (1978). Basic needs: Some issues. *World Development, 6*(3), 411–421.

United Nations. (2005). *Investing in development: A practical plan to achieve the Millennium Development Goals.* New York: Author.

United Nations. (1996). *Report of the World Summit for Social Development: Copenhagen, 6–12 March 1995.* New York: Author.

World Bank. (2001). *World Development Report, 2000/2001: Attacking poverty.* Washington, DC: Author.

Human Rights and Their Relevance for Social Work as Theory and Practice

SILVIA STAUB-BERNASCONI

Human rights have a long tradition in social work theory and practice, first more implicitly and, from about 1970, more explicitly. I would like to remember just a few stations of the human rights discourse in social work, beginning with *A New Consciousness and an Ancient Evil* by Jane Addams (1912), where she writes about the problem of prostitution as organized slavery and economic enterprise. Then we have to remember the struggle of many social workers for the women's vote, the demonstrations for decent working conditions and wages in front of the Washington Capitol, and the organization of the sweatshop workers and the toilet-cleaning women in Chicago. Furthermore, there is the well-documented organized protest against World War I at the International Congress of Women at The Hague in 1915.

In England, Eglantyne Jebb was the first person to make a draft for the Declaration on the Rights of the Child, which was adopted by the League of Nations in 1924 but then was forgotten until the new convention, ratified in 1989. In the foreword of *Social Welfare and Human Rights*, the proceedings of the International Conference on Social Welfare in 1968 in Helsinki, Eugen Pusić writes: "If there is one basic value premise for all the professions in the field of welfare it is the affirmation of human rights. And if there is one major complex of technical problems common to all the sectors of the field—from case-work to social security and from delinquency to rehabilitation—it is the question of how to implement, protect, and make real their human rights in the everyday life of people under stress" (p. vi). And in 1992, parallel to the UN World Conference on Human Rights in Vienna, a manual appeared titled *Human Rights and Social Work* by the UN Centre for Human Rights in Geneva as joint cooperation between representatives of the International Federation of Social Workers (IFSW) and of the International Association of Schools of Social Work (IASSW).

The more recent documents of the scientific and professional community (IASSW/IFSW) relating explicitly to human rights include the International Definition of the Social Work Profession, the Ethics in Social Work: Statement of Principles, and the Global Standards for the Education and Training of the Social Work Profession (IFSW, 2004) (see Appendices A & B). The international definition, for example, reads:

> The social work profession promotes social change, problem solving in human relationships and the empowerment and liberation of people to enhance well-being. Utilising theories of human behavior and social systems, social work intervenes at the points where people interact with their environments. Principles of human rights and social justice are fundamental to social work. (pp. 5–7)

Then, in 2001, the Committee of Ministers of the Council of Europe made the recommendation (Rec [2001]1) not only to integrate obligatory seminars about human rights into the curriculum of social work but also to make sure that they are implemented into the daily practice. The newest document is now Standards in Social Work Practice meeting Human Rights issued by IFSW European Region (2010).

The relevance of these documents for the future of social work education and practice is due to increasing globalization, which means that almost all local social problems—be they poverty, hunger, unemployment, displaced persons and economically forced migration, political refugees, postconflict reconstruction, drug dependency, or diseases such as AIDS—are largely determined by the structure and dynamics of world society and its institutions, including the World Trade Organization (WTO), the World Bank, the

International Monetary Fund (IMF), and the legislation of the European Union, especially those dealing with trade (e.g., GATS, TRIPS) (Lyons, Manion, & Carlsen 2006; Healy 2001).

Taking seriously the documents of the international associations means not only integrating human rights into the curriculum but something more challenging: bringing human rights as a central, regulative idea into the whole discipline and practice of social work, which means bringing it into the debates about social work's object and explanatory base as well as its value base and practice. Thus, my further considerations in this chapter address this challenge, answering the following questions of social work as action science (*Handlungswissenschaft*): *(1)* What are human rights violations in the problem or action field of social work? *(2)* How can one explain human rights violations? *(3)* What does human dignity mean as the philosophical and ethical base of human rights, and is it possible to avoid colonialism in the name of human rights? *(4)* What roles do human rights play in the professional mandate of social work? *(5)* How can human rights be discussed, claimed, and implemented on the social micro, mezzo, and macro levels? (Staub-Bernasconi 2008, 2010)

HUMAN RIGHTS VIOLATIONS AS AN ADDITIONAL DIAGNOSTIC CATEGORY

Historically and culturally, human rights, their invocation, and the further development of their philosophical, religious, ethical, and political movements are answers to experiences of injustice, the extreme powerlessness of individuals, groups, or members of social categories (minorities) to change their situation. Experiences of injustice—as both objective and interpreted facts—point to problems of dependency of powerful social actors or problems of a power structure. They make us conscious of what human beings are capable of doing to each other: causing fear, pain, humiliation, social exclusion, torture, destruction, and extermination. They show us that human beings have to be protected from other human beings, that the dignity of human beings has to be protected from the stranglehold of (*Wuergegriff*), the destructive actions and consequences of other human beings. By *stranglehold*, I mean the social rules and norms of power structures, which make discrimination and privileges, the tyranny of exploitation, cultural colonization, classism, sexism, racism, and unfair procedures, possible. It is the problem of structural violence

(Galtung, 1975) for which nobody has to take direct responsibility (Staub-Bernasconi, 2007).

Vulnerable Individuals and Groups as Clients of Social Work

If we look at the clients of social work, most belong to vulnerable groups. Their vulnerability is due to the fact that all human beings are dependent on others and social systems for the satisfaction of their needs and wishes and thus for their well-being. Vulnerable groups have the following characteristics: They are specially suited as scapegoats for experienced or feared structural threats (downward social mobility) and as a consequence for a politics of symbolic upgrading and disrespect for others by the threatened. Yet "prejudice must already exist against particular groups or individuals before scapegoating starts. . . . the individuals in question must appear to be too weak to fight back successfully when attacked. And finally, the society must sanction the scapegoating through its own institutional structure" (Saenger, 1953, cited in Blumenfeld & Raymond, 2000, p. 24).

The Complex Relationship Between Victims and Victimizers (Offenders)

The difference between victims and active agents of human rights violations is sometimes not as clear as one would like. Social workers have almost no difficulties identifying the state, the economy, or the health, legal, or education systems as active agents of violations. They also have no difficulties diagnosing inhuman, patriarchal, capitalistic political structures as discriminating and repressive. More difficult is the diagnosis of inhuman organizational structures in social, youth, health care, or community work—in short, social welfare. Social workers further hesitate to identify human rights violations by their clients, such as when clients try to solve their problems with violence. In these cases we sometimes confuse the explanation of a fact with the ethical and moral judgment of the fact. Especially difficult is the identification of actors of human rights violations when an agency belongs to a religious denomination or promotes advocacy for clients but is in fact an instrument of political or economic power or has an ethic that violates human rights. A human rights orientation requires a pitiless diagnosis that doesn't respect loyalties.

Multiple studies show that in many cases there is a complex relationship of passive and active victimization in the same person, interaction field, family, youth gang, organization, or even social movement. This type of relationship calls for differential, professional diagnosis. A human rights orientation doesn't replace but complements the diagnostic process (Arnegger, 2005; see also Karls & Wandrei's 1994 PIE instrument about discrimination). To prevent the idea of human rights from becoming inflated—a moral guillotine—it is necessary to develop scales defining minor, middle, and serious human rights violations and their consequences.

HUMAN RIGHTS AND THE BASIC SCIENTIFIC DISCIPLINES OF SOCIAL WORK

On the actor level, one has to ask how individuals become exploiters; rapists; oppressors; dictators; traffickers of refugees, women, or children; torturers; or blindly obeying functionaries, employees, or soldiers. What is their biography and what kind of experiences might change their thinking and behavior in a decisive way? And what are the psychological, social, and cultural explanations for becoming a victim?

On the level of the social power structures, one has to ask what the processes are of building and institutionalizing a power structure with rules of discrimination, privilege, and exclusion (e.g., the wage differences between men and women, the exclusion of certain students from school, the greed wages of managers, the trade rules between rich and poor countries and regions). How can one explain the genesis of rules of dominance and oppression in families, educational institutions, churches, social welfare, health care, and so on? And what determines the development of cultural/religious beliefs (religious beliefs are a part of culture) and constitutional rules that, according to traditions of interpretation, allow or even prescribe structural as well as direct violence, such as discrimination against minorities, women, children, and the elderly; female genital mutilation; or the death penalty, as well as the very restrictive rules for (illegal) migrants following racial and ethnic divides, apartheid, the Nuremberg laws, and so on?

The Problematic Construction of a Western Cultural and Genetic Continuity of the Idea of Human Dignity and Human Rights

Many accounts of the development of human rights show the construction of a linear history of ideas that follows a determinate "development scheme" (Bielefeldt, 2007, p. 43). According to this scheme, first notions of human dignity are found in the Bible or Koran (men as God's image or representatives of God on earth), then in the writings of antique philosophers Seneca and Epictetus, the Magna Carta in 1215, the English Bill of Rights in 1689, the Reformation, the French Revolution, and finally the UN Charter and the Universal Declaration of Human Rights from 1945 to 1948.

This description is a teleological one, which means that historical texts and events are interpreted from a result—the actual state of recognized human rights—and are brought into a systematic line (Bielefeldt, 2007, p. 45). This procedure implies historically and empirically wrong interpretations. For example, slavery, condemned and outlawed today, is no problem in the Bible (e.g., Moses; the letter to Philemon). In several texts, the notion of being God's image was reserved only for men and not for women (1. Kor. 12; 13). Seneca didn't mean the egality of all men; he only desired to alleviate the inhuman consequences of the attribution of a higher and lower value (status) to individuals. The Magna Carta was mainly a document to secure the feudal privilege structure of its conceivers. And Jefferson didn't include slaves in the Declaration of Independence. The Declaration of the Rights of Man and of the Citizen in 1789 didn't include the women; even worse, Olympe de Gouges, who wrote two years later a Declaration of the Rights of Woman and the Female Citizen, died on the scaffold.

The claiming of such heritages leads directly to an imperialistic understanding of human rights. In addition, all the resistance, the inquisition policies of the religious and secular power holders, and the fights, revolts, and revolutions for their implementation with their huge trace of blood in the "western history of the development of human rights" (Bielefeldt, 2007, p. 49) are rarely mentioned in this development scheme.

HUMAN DIGNITY AS METAVALUE AND HUMAN RIGHTS—PRAGMATIC UTOPIAS AND THE SEARCH FOR AN OVERLAPPING CONSENSUS

The value base of human rights refers to human dignity. However, there are many competing definitions of dignity. One can distinguish two lines of tradition. The first relies on a heteronomous conception of a transcendental dowry as an objective value that is due to the prefactual existence given by God or nature. Whereas for the believer the law of God is revealed in the act of believing, the law of the nonbeliever is part of his reason and thus an act of rational cognition. The utopian Marxism replaced the revelation of the divine laws with the deterministic economic laws of history—history seen as a totality, created by a total, unified act of revolution. In practice we have a shift from priests to philosophers and then to political interpreters of the relevant laws (Tiedemann, 2006, p. 58).

In contrast to these definitions of human dignity, we have autonomous conceptions, which, according to Tiedemann can't be reconciled with heteronomous ones. Kant, the most prominent representative of the autonomous conceptions, postulates the moral autonomy of human beings, a postulate that leads to the "claim to institutionalize this autonomy as general freedom rights and equality-based participation in defining legislation" (*gleichberechtigte republikanische Mitgesetzgebung*) (Bielefeldt, 1998, p. 15). In fact, it is difficult to reconcile absolute divine law with laws made by human beings. The only bridge between the two concepts of dignity might be the fundamental idea of being accepted by God regardless of compliance with good behavior or duties and the central idea of human rights that their implementation may not be dependent on good behavior by the rights holder. Further foundations of human dignity recur to the notion of reciprocity in interpersonal, repression-free communication (Habermas) or of respect in contrast to humiliation, as within an asymmetric helping process (Margalit, 1999, p. 23).

THE SEARCH OF AN OVERLAPPING CONSENSUS

The question is now whether there is a necessity to find a common definition for this cacaphony of definitions of human dignity. This might be difficult in a multicultural, multireligious society. To raise a special cultural heritage claim upon the definition would mean to declare human rights as the property of Western (occidental) or Islamic or Asian values, which would be a perversion of the idea of human dignity. The alternative is to find political-legal rules for the respect of human dignity (Bielefeldt, 2007) and to clearly define the limits of tolerance. The same holds for social work. Thus, human rights can be in open conflict with discriminatory, repressive elements of religious and secular belief systems and ethics.

Therefore, the notion of human dignity isn't an empty concept. It means equality without assimilation and justifies the inalienability of fundamental rights. According to this postulate, human rights differ from other rights, which people can determine according to

their own preferences and the existing power relationships; according to these interests, they even can decide to renounce them (see Nazi Germany). Following Rawls, one can define this search for a common denominator as the search for an overlapping consensus that asks for political-legal structures by which the state or another actor doesn't impose one of the competing definitions of human dignity to others. This overlapping consensus is much more than a modus vivendi (i.e., an informal agreement to live with differences since the alternative would be worse). This consensus can be, for example, that the freedom of expression is to protect, that torture has to be condemned absolutely, that education is a right for all, and so on. It can also be an agreement about the claim that all human beings want to be free of corporal pain, violence, fear, humiliation, poverty, discrimination, repression, and exclusion, and to guarantee this, a society needs laws. A larger definition of this overlapping consensus could be that these freedom claims point to universal human needs that are interpreted by very different religious, cultural, and political beliefs, some of which can be inhuman, which is the reason rights must be protected universally (Obrecht, 2007).

Human Rights Are Pragmatic Utopias: Article 28

Those who read Article 28 of the UN Declaration of Human Rights (issued on December 10th, 1948) and confront it with the actual situation of our world might be caught by despair, hopelessness, or cynicism: "Everyone is entitled to a social and international order in which the rights and freedoms set forth in this Declaration can be fully realized."

There is a big difference between plain utopias, ideals with exorbitant claims for which one isn't able to say who is in charge to change things, and, on the other side, Article 28 as a reality-based, pragmatic utopia. With pragmatic utopias, one can indicate precisely what policies and measures have to be conceptualized, what resources are necessary, and what political and professional decisions have to be envisaged. Since the World Conference on Human Rights in Vienna in 1993, human rights conventions are part of the binding international law and one knows who are their promoters and enemies. In addition, one knows the conventions, protocols, comments, recommendations, actors, and procedures as basic knowledge about how to complain to the UN or the European Court on Human Rights about a human rights violation.

We also need pragmatic utopias to operationalize social work goals, but they often can't be implemented without compromises. This is almost always the case when one should respect both freedom and social rights, the latter requiring the mostly compulsory redistribution of wealth. Furthermore, the rights of children might question and constrain the rights of parents and vice versa (Prior, 2003). This calls for professional mediation processes guided by criteria of social justice and procedural fairness (Montada & Kals, 2001).

FROM THE DOUBLE VOCATIONAL TO THE PROFESSIONAL TRIPLE MANDATE OF SOCIAL WORK

The commonly shared notion is that social work has a double mandate of help and control—help as the mandate of the client, control as the mandate of society represented by the social agency. A double mandate characterizes a vocational activity, which relies mainly on simple or complex techniques to reach a defined goal. A profession has a triple mandate, which consists of both previously mentioned mandates as well as a mandate from the profession itself as third party. This third mandate has the following components:

- A scientific descriptive and explanatory base for its policies, interventions, and methods, which are reliable for solving or preventing social problems
- An ethical base, that is, a professional code of ethics that is in the case of social work explicitly oriented toward human rights and social justice.

Both elements constitute the relative autonomy of the profession and, if necessary, the legitimacy to partially modify or even refuse mandates from the agency as well as from clients. The code of ethics with its reliance on human dignity and rights is also a base for the critical questioning of local, national, and international laws and juridical procedures. Are they just legal in a positivistic sense, or are they also legitimate, implementing human dignity and well-being (e.g., immigration laws, welfare laws)? Relying on this triple mandate, one shouldn't have to debate endlessly about whether social work has a political mandate for social change or whether professional and critical or structural social work are incompatible approaches to social problems. With the third mandate, social work has the legitimate theoretical and ethical mandate for the criticism of society and social

agencies as well as for science-based advocacy and social change. This doesn't question direct citizen participation but complements it.

SOCIAL RIGHTS AS A MAIN FOCUS OF SOCIAL WORK AS PROFESSION

The international definition of social work mentions not only human rights but also emphasizes social justice as main ethical guidelines for social work. Although social justice is part of the human rights discourse, it makes sense to mention it separately, because social work is confronted with extensive violations of social rights (Reichert 2007, Staub-Bernasconi 2007, Wronka 2007). At the Vienna World Conference on Human Rights, 173 states declared solemnly that human rights are "universal, indivisible, interdependent and inalienable" (UN doc. A/CONF. 157/23, Part I, para. 5); however, one can't overlook the fact that liberal and democratic human rights are much more discussed parts of UN recommendations, and monitored than are social human rights. The violation of freedom rights provokes a huge protest from all kinds of groups, movements, and media demanding immediate intervention. Yet, since the end of the Cold War over 300 million people have died from poverty-caused conditions, and each year there are at least 18 million more deaths. This number is increasing with the financial and economic crisis as of 2011. A much larger number lives under the conditions of life-threatening poverty, within which it is almost impossible to stand up for one's interests and rights.

This gigantic range of denial of human rights as a form of structural violence occurs within an international framework of social rules (mainly of the Bretton Woods Institutions) that "work for the profit of governments, economic organizations, and (rich) citizens of the rich countries and also for the elites of the poor countries" (Pogge, 2008, p. 170). The denial of social rights occurs in a social vacuum without echo. A survey in Germany showed that almost all people interviewed either didn't know about social rights or denied them the status of human rights (Sommer, Stellmacher, & Bähler, 2003). According to these results, not even the minimal conditions are present to make social rights violations a public issue.

Yet, the asymmetry between civil and social rights has been considerably reduced as of December 2008, when the UN plenary session (Vollversammlung) accepted the right for individual complaints for social rights by adopting the Optional Protocol to the International Covenant on Economic, Social, and

Cultural Rights. When and if it enters into force by the states, it will be an important avenue for social work action.

ACTORS, RESOURCES, PROCEDURES, AND METHODS

According to a narrow notion of human rights protection, it is the responsibility and task of the states. It is true that the state has to respect the freedom of individuals, to protect them from inhuman intervention by third parties, and to fulfill legitimate demands by actively providing the resources for the realization of freedom, democratic, and social rights. A broader conception of human rights has the goal of establishing a human rights culture in everyday life as well as in social communities and organizations (Ife, 2001; Wronka, 2007). This calls for a much broader range of actors in charge, including economic organizations with their enormous power, nongovernmental organizations (NGOs), religious organizations and, since the Vienna conference of 1993, also professions, which are confronted daily with human rights violations and are also in danger of being violators themselves. These professions include police officers, nurses, physicians, teachers, lawyers, educators, international development and cooperation personnel, and social workers. Another already established group of promoters is human rights activists, who often are exposed to many risks, including the danger of injuries, imprisonment, torture, and loss of life.

The students of the Berlin Master of Social Work in "Social Work as a Human Rights Profession" (founded 2002) are active in the following fields of human rights practice:

- Human rights education in various contexts (primary school, universities of applied sciences, universities)
- Human rights projects encompassing the individual, local, and national levels (e.g., contribution to shadow reports to the UN Committee on Economic, Social and Cultural Rights – in short Social Rights)
- Human rights–based international social work
- Human rights innovation in the agency where one works (introduction of human rights in social diagnosis, assessment of human rights violations of the organization itself, formulation of social policies for vulnerable groups) etc.
- Research projects.

For the narrower conception of human rights protection, one needs close cooperation with lawyers; for the broad conception, one can use various social work methods such as resource mobilization, consciousness raising, mediation, and empowerment. More specific methods include using the official instruments of the UN for complaints, monitoring, lobbying, and, more and more, also whistle blowing. But in many cases, one needs civil courage to stand up against actors in a power sructure. It could be the end of a career, or one's life and the lives of family members and collaborators may be threatened.

Gore (1969), former director of the Tata School of Social Sciences in Mumbai, India, summarized what is meant by the introduction of human rights into social work:

> It is a role that differs from that of a rebel and also from the one of a repairman (or repairwoman). . . . Yet, it compels the profession to see beyond the fashions and prejudices of the present so as to identify and promote instrumental values and practices necessary for the realization of the goals of human dignity and equality. . . . It will disturb the complacence of the individual social worker who may be tempted to acquiesce in the values of the local community even when they conflict with the broader values of the profession. It will require and compel the organized profession to take clear positions on social issues. . . . We shall be even more aware of the fact that as the world is peopled by many cultures and values there will be need for the affirmation on an acceptable common denominator. The Universal Declaration of Human Rights provides this necessary standard and direction to all constructive action. (pp. 67–68)

REFERENCES

Addams, J. (1912). A New Consciousness and an Ancient Evil. New York: Macmillan.

Arnegger, M. (2005). Soziale Arbeit als Menschenrechtsprofession in der diagnostischen Praxis. *Neue Praxis*, H. 5, 682–694.

Bielefeldt, H. (2007). Menschenrechte in der Einwanderungsgesellschaft—Plaedoyer für einen aufgeklaerten Multikulturalismus. Transcript, Bielefeld.

Bielefeldt, H. (1998). *Philosophie der Menschenrechte*. Darmstadt: Primus.

Blumenfeld, W. J., & Raymond, D. (2000). Prejudice and discrimination. In M. Adams et al. (Eds.), *Readings for diversity and social justice: An anthology on racism,* antisemitism, sexism, heterosexism, ableism, and classism (Fn 9, pp. 21–30). London: Routledge.

Galtung, J. (1975). Strukturelle Gewalt. In *Beitraege zur Friedens- und Konfliktforschung*. Hamburg: Reinbeck.

Gore, M. S. (1969). Social work and its human rights aspects. In International Council on Social Welfare, *Social welfare and human rights*. Proceedings of the XIVth Intern. Conference on Social Welfare, Helsinki/Finland, August 1968. New York: Columbia University Press for ICSW (pp. 56–68).

Healy, L. M. (2001). *International social work: Professional action in an interdependent world*. New York: Oxford.

Ife, J. (2001). *Human rights and social work: Towards rights-based practice*. Cambridge, UK: Cambridge University Press.

IFSW. (2004). Supplement of International Social Work(ISSN 0020-8728), London: Sage. Accessible at www.ifsw.org.

International Federation of Social Workers European Region e.V. (2010): Standards in Social Work Practice meeting Human Rights. Berlin.

Karls, J., & Wandrei, K. E. (1994). *PIE manual—Person-in-Environment system*. Washington: NASW.

Lyons, K., Manion, K., & Carlsen, M. (2006). *International Perspectives on Social Work. Global Conditions and Local Practice*. Hampshire, Palgrave Macmillan.

Margalit, A. (1999). *Politik der Wuerde. Ueber Achtung und Verachtung*. Frankfurt: Fischer.

Montada, L. & Kals, E. (2001). Mediation, Beltz, Weinheim/Basel.

Obrecht, W. (2007). *Umrisse einer biopsychosozialen Theorie menschlicher Bedürfnisse*. (Unpublished manuscript), Vienna University of Economics and Business, Vienna.

Pogge, T. (2008). Das Recht auf ein Existenzminimum. In I. Richter (Ed.), *Transnationale Menschenrechte.*

Schritte zu einer weltweiten Verwirklichung der Menschenrechte (pp. 121–138). Opladen: Barbara Budrich.

Prior, P. M. (2003). Removing children from the care of adults with diagnosed mental illnesses—a clash of human rights? *European Journal of Social Work*, 6(2), 179–191.

Pusić, E. (1969). Foreword. In International Council on Social Welfare, *Social Welfare and Human Rights*, Proceedings of the XIVth International. Conference on Social Welfare, Helsinki/Finland, August 1968. New York: Columbia University Press for ICSW (pp. v–vii).

Sommer, G., Stellmacher, J., & Bähler, E. (2003). *Einstellung der Deutschen zu Menschenrechten*. Pressekonferenzunterlage zum Tag der Menschenrechte, December 10, 2003.

Reichert, E. (2007) (Ed.), *Challenges in human rights: A social work perspective*. New York: Columbia University Press.

Staub-Bernasconi, S. (2008). Soziale Arbeit und Menschenrechte—Oder: Was haben Menschenrechte in der Sozialen Arbeit zu suchen? *Widersprueche, 107*, 9–32.

Staub-Bernasconi, S. (2010). *Soziale Arbeit als Handlungswissenschaft*. Bern/Stuttgart/Wien: UTB/Haupt, 2nd ed.

Staub-Bernasconi, S. (2007). Economic and social rights: The neglected human rights. In E. Reichert (Ed.), *Challenges in human rights: A social work perspective* (pp. 128–161). New York: Columbia University Press.

Tiedemann, P. (2006). *Was ist Menschenwuerde?* Darmstadt: Wissenschaftliche Buchgesellschaft.

Wronka, J. (2007). *Human rights and social justice*. London: Sage.

Social Exclusion and Inclusion

KAREN LYONS AND NATHALIE HUEGLER

The notion of social exclusion and the need to implement policies and programs that combat marginalization and facilitate social inclusion has gained currency in many parts of the world over the past few decades. Social exclusion is often associated with poverty: In a World Bank survey of what poverty means to people who are poor, the respondents identified that poverty is not just a lack of material goods but extends to lack of power; feelings of dependence and inferiority; injustice, exclusion and lack of opportunities; and receipt of poor quality social services (Narayan, Chambers, & Shah, 2000). However, just as poverty might prevent people from fully participating in civil society, so some populations may feel marginalized or excluded by the attitudes and behaviors of neighbors, institutions, and whole political systems. This may be particularly the case if individuals or groups are perceived as different from their local community or host society, for instance because of disability, ethnicity, or immigration status.

It has been rumored that the term *social exclusion* became popular as a basis for policy developments in Europe in the early nineties when two leading politicians, Prime Minister Thatcher and Chancellor Kohl, declared that poverty no longer existed in their respective countries (UK and Germany) (personal communication, confidential comment by an EC official, IFSW European Experts meeting, Brussels, April, 1990). Whatever its policy origins, in the European Union a paradigm shift occurred (Schulte, 2002) from a series of antipoverty programs prevalent in the 1980s to new programs aimed at the inclusion of people who were marginalized or excluded from mainstream society and its services. However, the notion of social exclusion extends beyond Europe, and the terms *marginalization* and *social exclusion and inclusion* have entered the vocabulary of social and community development workers around the world involved in projects aimed at particular population groups, including those who constitute an ethnic minority.

In this chapter we examine the theoretical origins of the concept of social exclusion, give some examples of particular policies and programs aimed at addressing social exclusion, and consider how the concept might have global relevance in the context of social workers' concerns with human rights and global citizenship.

DEFINING TERMS

Background

Social exclusion has been described as a contested term (Burchardt, Le Grand, & Piachaud, 2002; Munck, 2005). Its roots can be traced to Weber's concept of social closure, a process of subordination through which some groups of people achieve a privileged position at the expense of other groups. In late twentieth-century France, social exclusion evolved as a normative concept describing the perceived breakdown of the social fabric of values and solidarity, which threatened society as a whole (Silver, 1994). In this context, various groups of people who had fallen through the net of solidaristic social security systems or deviated from the social norm came to be considered as *the excluded*, including people with disabilities, single parents, people with drug or alcohol dependencies, unemployed people, and immigrants in the poor neighborhoods of major cities (Burchardt et al., 2002; Silver, 1994). The concept was soon embraced in European policy, and at the Lisbon Summit in 2000, European Union member states agreed on promoting social cohesion and inclusion as a strategic goal. In countries of Anglo-Saxon liberal tradition, *poverty* had been a key concept for social analysis "in terms of competitive interactions under scarcity, and the problems of collective action arising from these" (Jordan, 1996, p. 4). However, social exclusion terminology began to gain political popularity in 1980s Britain under a Conservative government that denied the existence of poverty. It was fully embraced by the incoming New Labour government in 1997 with the establishment of a dedicated government body, the Social Exclusion Unit.

United Nations Efforts

Attention to social inclusion has been enhanced by United Nations (UN) efforts. One of the ten commitments made at the World Summit for Social Development in Copenhagen in 1995 is to promote *social integration*, a term sometimes used interchangeably with *social inclusion*. Social integration was defined in the 1995 Copenhagen Declaration and Programme of Action as "the capacity of people to live together with full respect for the dignity of each individual, the common good, pluralism and diversity, non-violence and solidarity, as well as their ability to participate in social, cultural, economic and political life" (UN, 1995, p. 39). Indeed, the promotion of social integration along with the eradication of poverty and promotion of full employment are the three major action pillars of the outcome documents from Copenhagen. The emphasis on inclusion is clear in the stated goals: "The aim of social integration is to create 'a society for all,' in which every individual, each with rights and responsibilities, has an active role to play" (UN, 1995, p. 95).

The UN Commission for Social Development has followed up with periodic review of the Copenhagen commitments. In 2009 and 2010, the commission's major theme for its work was social integration and inclusion. Nongovernmental organizations (NGOs) have also joined the global discussions through policy statements submitted to the commission. The International Council on Social Welfare (ICSW) urged attention to involvement and participation of excluded groups and to the roles of diverse sectors. "Such involvement and participation in decision-making and identification of their own needs will be a key determinant and outcome of social mobilisation and integration efforts. Governments, private sector and civil society need to work jointly to identify the causes of vulnerability and address social exclusion at the community level. Organisations of civil society are particularly well placed to accomplish this task" (ICSW, 2009, p. 9).

Conceptual Issues

Social exclusion is generally seen as a broader concept than poverty in that it refers to "the dynamic process of being shut out, fully or partially, from any of the social, economic, political and cultural systems which determine the social integration of a person in society" (Walker & Walker, 1997, p. 8, as cited in Levitas, 2005). In this view, inclusion and exclusion go beyond the question of access to resources, touching on issues such as identity, location, health, self-determination, and discrimination. Notwithstanding its European conceptual roots, social exclusion has been linked to terms that have been more common in other regions, such as *ghettoization, marginalization,* or the *underclass* in the American context (Burchardt et al., 2002). The concept has also been criticized as "intrinsically problematic" (Levitas, 2005, p. 7) because the division of societies into included majorities and excluded minorities can lead to poverty and disadvantage being treated as peripheral, pathological, and residual problems while overall social inequalities are ignored.

Perhaps even more than any other social sciences concept, social exclusion has been used to fit a variety of political agendas. Levitas (2005) distinguishes three main discourses that frame the causes and remedies of exclusion. Representatives of a redistributionist discourse on social exclusion (RED) are concerned with reducing inequalities by changing the distribution of power and wealth in societies through the full realization of citizenship rights. In contrast, the moral underclass discourse (MUD) focuses explicitly, and in more subtle ways, on the morally or culturally rooted deficits and behavior of the excluded themselves, criticizing welfare systems as encouraging dependency. As a value-laden discourse emphasizing individual responsibility, family stability, and community cohesion, it has gendered implications (e.g., a problem-focused view on single mothers) and can also take highly racialized forms. A third strand, the social integrationist discourse (SID), is particularly dominant in European social policy approaches and emphasizes (re)insertion into the labor market as a remedy for exclusion. Its narrow focus on paid employment has been criticized for neglecting the value of unpaid work (e.g., the caretaking roles often taken on by women) and for further marginalizing some groups of people with disabilities.

The focus on social integration through employment in many European social exclusion debates and programs has contributed to a view of the concept itself as Eurocentric. As a result, questions have been raised about the applicability of the concept internationally, both in countries of the Global South where the majority of the population might lack formal employment opportunities, and in the North, where many migrants are systematically excluded through restrictive government policies or where, for indigenous people, much more is at stake than simply access to decent work (Munck, 2005, 2009).

In order to have relevance globally, social exclusion therefore needs to be conceptualized in a broad sense. For example, a UK Department for International Development policy paper refers to social exclusion as a process of systematic disadvantage of certain groups "because they are discriminated against on the basis of their ethnicity, race, religion, sexual orientation, caste, descent, gender, age, disability, HIV status, migrant status of where they live" (2005, p. 3). The concept also needs to focus not only on the excluded but also on the excluders and the dynamics of power that allow the unequal distribution of resources and opportunities. This gives rise to further debate about the powers of definition inherent in creating boundaries between the excluded and the included. A focus on the contextual nature of social exclusion defines it as a multidimensional concept that highlights relational, structural, and dynamic aspects of inequality. From this perspective, links can also be drawn between social exclusion and a denial of the full realization of human rights (Healy, 2001), and it is a theme to which we shall return at the end of the chapter after considering some policy examples.

SOCIAL EXCLUSION IN POLICY PROGRAMS AND RESEARCH

In this section we report on the application of the concept of social exclusion. We include attempts by national governments or regional bodies to address social exclusion through specific social policies and programs as well as the use of the concept to analyze social developments in a particular country.

A European Example: The Roma

One minority group that has been the focus of policies aimed at combating social exclusion in Europe is the Roma; 2005 to 2015 has been deemed by twelve European countries as the Decade for Roma Inclusion. The Roma are a traditionally mobile population concentrated in central Europe but extending to Ireland and the Mediterranean countries. They are sometimes referred to as *Gypsies* (a corruption of their supposed origins in Egypt) or *Travelers* (but not everyone so labeled is necessarily of Roma stock) and also include other ethnic minority groups such as the Sinti, Ashkali, and Kale. There are no precise figures for the size of this population, but it includes millions of people; the European Commission has described the Roma as "Europe's biggest ethnic minority . . . characterised

by discrimination and far-reaching exclusion from Mainstream society" with "disproportional rates of poverty and unemployment, poor health status and lower life expectancy" (EU Press Release, 2009, p. 1).

While member states of the European Union remain responsible for national policies and programs concerning the Roma population residing within their borders, the European Commission has aimed at facilitating social inclusion of the Roma in four ways. First, in relation to rights, the Roma are covered by EU legislation prohibiting discrimination on grounds of ethnic origin; second, there are policies and events aimed at providing a framework for exchange and mutual learning about positive initiatives between countries; third, financial support (for example, for vocational training schemes) has been provided through the European Social Fund; and fourth, the commission has sought to increase the human capital of the Roma population by offering direct work experience and training to young Roma (ten placements for five months each, twice a year, since 2000) in the European Commission itself (EU Press Release, 2009).

In 2009 a new initiative was launched under which member states can apply for European Union funding from a new fund totaling 5 million euros to develop programs that enable "access to mainstream education, mainstream jobs and mainstream housing" (EU Press Release, 2009). Housing is particularly important since considerable efforts have been made in many countries in recent years to settle the Roma people, but this often means their location is on the margins of urban areas in poor housing with limited local facilities, including schools and health services. There may also be little work available in the locality, and the negative reputation of the Roma and prejudices of local communities may prevent their employment. (For a critique based on an Irish example, see Dunphy, 2009).

Additionally, just as the gender dimension in poverty was identified as the feminization of poverty (for example, see Van Wormer, 1997), information pertaining to the Roma inclusion initiative includes a reference to the need for attention to the gender dimension of Roma-related policies. Similarly, in line with developments in other areas of professional policy and practice, there is recognition of the need to include Roma people themselves as actors in the development and implementation of new programs. It therefore seems appropriate for social professionals to be involved in local policy development and implementation of such programs, and it is important that their training includes anti-oppressive practices as well as cultural competence and skills in collaborative working practices with both service users and colleagues in other occupations and agencies.

Examples From Other Parts of the World

The recognition of the social exclusion of some groups and efforts to counter it are not an exclusively European concern, although the connection with discrimination against ethnic minorities may not be as apparent elsewhere. For instance, a paper on the UNESCO Management of Social Transformations (MOST) website described the overall goal of an antipoverty program in Chile as "achiev[ing] the social integration of indigent families by bringing them into the public network of social services, by making them, in other words, real rather than purely formal citizens" (Palma & Urzua, 2005, p. 5). The national Chile Solidario system developed since 2000 provides a social protection network for the poorest families together with immediate assistance and longer-term skills development. Participating families are required to sign a contract committing them to meet stated conditions in exchange for receiving certain benefits (e.g., psychosocial support, cash subsidies, preferential access to opportunities for work and skills development). The authors note that in three years of operation, the scheme could be regarded as successful in terms of coverage and low dropout rates. However, they are critical of the extent to which the program is led by people with professional and technical skills; there is little opportunity for citizen participation in either defining the problem or possible solutions. (See also a more recent paper by Saracostti [2008], which summarizes the program and identifies the role of social workers).

The theme of social exclusion is also evident in a recent book about China (Logan, 2008). Two factors have apparently combined to produce marginalized young men in many Chinese cities. The first is the rapid increase in urbanization with the migration of primarily younger family members from rural areas in search of work. Authors of one chapter point out how such migrants engage in a form of circular migration in which they do not invest in their new homes or communities because of the need to send money home and their intention to return home for specific occasions if not in the longer term (Wu & Rosenbaum, 2008). The second factor is the result of the long established one-child policy in a cultural context where males have preferential status. This has resulted in an excess of young men for whom marriage and

a family life consistent with cultural expectations are unlikely, if not ruled out completely. Messner, Liu, and Karstedt (2008) suggest that such men participate in migration to urban areas but are likely to feel alienated and become part of a deviant subculture excluded from the opportunities afforded by modernization to members of mainstream society. Elsewhere, another Chinese author has used the concept of social exclusion to examine the plight of urban street children and to suggest policy directions that should be pursued to address their plight (Xu, 2009).

Finally, although rarely identified as social exclusion, the theme of marginalization in relation to ill health or disability is evident in many of the papers in a special issue of the journal *International Social Work* focusing on social work and health. In one paper in particular, an example drawn from the author's experience illustrates how the Aboriginal population in Australia may be discouraged if not excluded from use of mainstream health services (Giles, 2009). However, Giles also identifies the many interrelated factors that have an impact on health and challenges social workers to develop services that ensure inclusion of marginalized groups.

IMPLICATIONS FOR INTERNATIONAL SOCIAL WORK

Earlier, we looked at different discourses on social exclusion, including the criticism of a Eurocentric bias in some policy applications. We now consider the implications of a social exclusion perspective for international social work. Assuming basic common ground between the various forms of social work in localities worldwide, the definition of social work agreed upon by the International Federation of Social Workers (IFSW) and International Association of Schools of Social Work (IASSW) (2004) refers to concepts such as *social change, liberation of people to enhance well-being, human rights*, and *social justice*. With social work's focus on "the points where people interact with their environments" (IFSW and IASSW, 2004), it seems evident that a key concern is whether people are shut out or able to participate. From previous discussions in this chapter, it is also clear that constructing people as being either in or out is problematic, obscuring the dynamic and multidimensional nature of social exclusion.

As a set of processes that emphasize both wider (global) and more localized levels of human interaction, globalization draws particular attention to inequalities and social exclusion (Payne & Askeland, 2008). This happens both through dynamics that create new scenarios of exclusion (such as the exploitation of labor in poor countries by transnational corporations or the international migration of people uprooted by political, social, and economic change) and through greater knowledge of disparities as a result of worldwide communication networks. From a position that challenges postcolonial hegemony and oppression, social exclusion can be constructed as something experienced particularly by people from the poor Global South and perpetuated by those from the wealthier Global North. However, a simplistic North–South divide neglects the fact that various forms of deprivation affect people around the world, just as some elites in the South have profited from exploitation. Social workers therefore have to engage in differentiated analyses of how exclusion affects people in communities, countries, and regions worldwide.

Given the commitment of the profession to social justice and human rights, social workers are particularly concerned with the plight of excluded groups and can, as such, be agents of inclusion. However, through their actions and being part of political and social structures, they can also reinforce marginalization and exclusion (Payne & Askeland, 2008). For example, in relation to working with refugees and asylum seekers, social workers' roles have involved challenging oppressive immigration systems, performing rights-based advocacy, and providing access to essential material and psychosocial resources, but they have also involved the enactment of restrictive welfare policies that form part of secondary immigration control measures (Briskman & Cemlyn, 2005).

There are also examples of the devastating consequences of social workers assuming knowledge of the best interests of excluded groups, particularly where the behaviors and cultural practices of those groups are considered deviant or deficient, such as policies and practices relating to the stolen generation of Aboriginal children removed and placed with white Australian families or in institutions. In the context of the various discourses on social exclusion presented earlier, many social workers might consider that their work is committed to redistribution and social integration, but practice that is moralistic, exclusionary, and oppressive is both inherent in the profession's history and an ongoing risk.

Globalization and cultural diversity provide additional challenges for social workers, especially where they deal with issues of protection alongside dilemmas of inclusion. An example of the complex interactions of these factors is the role of social workers in relation to the practice of female genital cutting (FGC).[1] Social workers' ethical codes and human rights principles invoke, first and foremost, a clear duty to protect children at risk of suffering this harmful practice. At the same time, social workers are also faced with the possibility that children will be excluded in communities where FGC continues to have cultural meaning or that the communities themselves will become marginalized through global condemnation, increasing the risk of the practice being driven underground and future interventions prevented (Dustin & Davies, 2007; Khaja, Barkdull, Augustine, & Cunningham, 2009). An inclusion perspective places the necessary intervention of protecting children and upholding their right to safety from harm in a wider context of dialogue and participatory negotiation within communities and across societies with the aim of stopping this and other harmful practices without relinquishing communities' rights to maintain traditional values (Ife, 2008). Such a perspective also overcomes the assumption that only Western approaches challenge the discrimination against women; many women have challenged FGC from within their communities, thus providing scope for inclusive social movements that struggle for social justice.

The full realization of citizenship rights for all people has been put forward as the true opposite of social exclusion. However, from an international perspective, traditional notions of citizenship based on membership of a particular nation-state only offer limited inclusion, excluding migrants and refugees. Debates about forms of global citizenship have gained popularity in recent years, but the concepts have yet to be further defined and developed. The universal application and contextual realization of human rights (Ife, 2008) provide a starting point for such debates and for social work aimed at promoting social inclusion on local, national, regional, and global levels.

CONCLUDING COMMENTS

The origins and understandings of social exclusion are contested and particularly associated with Europe. However, there are worldwide examples of the adoption of the concept in policy and research contexts.

Most people who are socially excluded lack financial resources, and they also experience other forms of disadvantage and actual discrimination and oppression. The effects of marginalization and exclusion have a differential impact on different sectors of the population (e.g., according to age, sex, race, or disability) in different places. For example, in many societies, people with disabilities or who are immigrants are particularly vulnerable to marginalization and social exclusion. We have seen various policy efforts to counter social exclusion and promote inclusionary practices over the last decade or so, and social workers clearly have a part to play in such efforts. However, such initiatives often focus on the problems of those who are marginalized (for example, through financial assistance and training and employment schemes). It is equally important to address public attitudes and the practices of professionals in their dealings with people who are socially excluded so that the human and civic rights of minority populations are promoted and the goal of social inclusion is achieved.

NOTE

1. Female genital cutting is a traditional cultural practice of removing female genitalia without any medical indication, often resulting in extreme physical and emotional harm. It is estimated to affect around two million women, particularly children between the ages of four and thirteen. The majority of communities practicing FGC are located in Africa, but it is also practiced in some immigrant communities in Northern countries (Dustin & Davies, 2007; Khaja et al., 2009).

REFERENCES

Briskman, L., & Cemlyn, S. (2005). Reclaiming humanity for asylum-seekers: A social work response. *International Social Work, 48*(6), 714–724.

Burchardt, T., Le Grand, J., & Piachaud, D. (2002). Introduction. In J. Hills, J. Le Grand, & D. Piachaud (Eds.), *Understanding social exclusion* (pp. 1–12). Oxford: Oxford University Press.

Department for International Development (DFID). (2005). *Reducing poverty by tackling social exclusion.* London: Author.

Dunphy, S. (2009, May 9). I'm a social worker but even I am angry with the Travellers. *Irish Independent* (Weekend Review), p. 8.

Dustin, D., & Davies, L. (2007). Female genital cutting and children's rights: Implications for social work practice. *Child Care in Practice, 13*(1), 3–16.

EU Press Release. (2009, April 24). www.stop-discrimination.info (accessed May 16, 2009).

Giles, R. (2009). Developing a health equality imagination: Hospital practice challenges for social work priorities. *International Social Work, 52*(4), 517–530.

Healy, L. (2001). *International social work: Professional action in an interdependent world.* New York: Oxford University Press.

Ife, J. (2008). *Human rights and social work: Towards rights-based practice* (2nd ed.). Melbourne: Cambridge University Press.

International Council on Social Welfare (ICSW). (2009). *Statement on the priority theme: Social integration.* Statement of the International Council on Social Welfare to the United Nations Commission for Social Development, 47th Session, February 2009. Utrecht: Author.

International Federation of Social Workers (IFSW) and International Association of Schools of Social Work (IASSW). (2004). *Ethics in social work, statement of principles.* Berne: IFSW.

Jordan, B. (1996). *A theory of poverty and social exclusion.* Cambridge: Polity Press.

Khaja, K., Barkdull, C., Augustine, M., & Cunningham, D. (2009). Female genital cutting: African women speak out. *International Social Work, 52*(6), 727–741.

Levitas, R. (2005). *The inclusive society? Social exclusion and New Labour* (2nd ed.). Basingstoke: Palgrave Macmillan.

Logan, J. R. (Ed.). (2008). *Urban China in transition.* Oxford: Blackwell.

Messner, S., Liu, J., & Karstedt, S. (2008). Economic reform and crime in contemporary urban China: Paradoxes of a planned transition. In J. R. Logan (Ed.), *Urban China in transition* (pp. 271–293). Oxford: Blackwell.

Munck, R. (2009). Social integration. *Global Social Policy, 9*(1), 16–18.

Munck, R. (2005). Social exclusion: New inequality paradigm for the era of globalization? In M. Romero & E. Margolis (Eds.), *The Blackwell companion to social inequalities* (pp. 31–49). Oxford: Blackwell.

Narayan, D., Chambers, R., & Shah, M. (2000). *The voice of the poor: Crying out for change* (Vol. 2). Washington, DC: World Bank.

Palma, J., & Urzua, R. (2005). *Anti-poverty policies and citizenry: The 'Chile Solidario' experience.* MOST Policy Papers, 12, UNESCO. Available at http://www.unesco.org/new/en/social-and-human-sciences/themes/social-transformations/most-programme/

Payne, M., & Askeland, G. A. (2008). *Globalisation and international social work: Postmodern change and challenge.* Aldershot: Ashgate.

Saracostti, M. (2008). The Chile Solidario system: The role of social work. *International Social Work, 51*(4), 566–572.

Schulte, B. (2002). A European definition of poverty: The fight against poverty and social exclusion in the member states of the European Union. In P. Townsend and D. Gordon (Eds.), *World poverty: New policies to defeat an old enemy* (pp. 119–145). Bristol: Policy Press.

Silver, H. (1994). Social exclusion and social solidarity: Three paradigms. *International Labour Review, 133*(5–6), 531–578.

United Nations (UN). (1995). *The Copenhagen Declaration and Programme of Action: World Summit for Social Development.* New York: Author.

Van Wormer, K. (1997). *Social welfare: A world view.* Chicago: Nelson Hall.

Walker, A., & Walker, C. (Eds.). (1997). *Britain divided: The growth of social exclusion in the 1980s and 1990s.* London: CPAG.

Wu, W., & E. Rosenbaum. (2008). Migration and housing: Comparing China and the United States. In J. R. Logan (Ed.), *Urban China in transition* (pp. 250–267). Oxford: Blackwell.

Xu, Z. (2009). Urban street children in China: A social exclusion perspective. *International Social Work, 52*(3), 401–408.

Social Justice

DOROTHEE HÖLSCHER

In 2000, the International Federation of Social Work (IFSW) and the International Association of Schools of Social Work (IASSW) adopted the current definition of social work, the beginning section of which reads, "The social work profession promotes social change, problem solving in human relations and the empowerment and liberation of people to enhance well-being. . . . *Principles of human rights and social justice are fundamental to social work* [emphasis added]" (IFSW, 2000, p. 1). Thus, social justice constitutes one of the defining principles of social work and is often used as a point of reference when social workers wish to anchor their work ethically, be it practice or scholarly work. Haug's (2005) conceptualization of international social work illustrates this point: "International social work includes any social work activity anywhere in the world, directed toward *global social justice* [emphasis added] and human rights, in which local practice is dialectically linked to the global context" (p. 133).

Frequently, however, social work theorists and practitioners assume a level of clarity and consensus within the profession regarding the concept of social justice that does not necessarily exist (compare, for example, Dominelli, 2008, and Ferguson, 2008). McGrath Morris (2002) and Mullaly (2002) claim that the notion of social justice remains undertheorized in social work ethical discourse, and Humphries (2008) notes that to date, "the concept . . . remains ambiguous and not clearly articulated" (p. 24).

In other words, there is a need to interrogate the concept of social justice regarding its evolving meaning, scope, and inherent tensions in relation to the diverse theory and practice contexts of social work. This chapter begins with a brief review of social justice discourses in social work to date. The section that follows considers suggestions regarding the lines along which our understanding of social justice might be broadened. This is before the background of globalization, which appears to be undermining the previously taken-for-granted centrality and ability of states as agencies to promote (or hinder) the furtherance of social justice within and beyond their territories. Concepts of state sovereignty and membership are key to understanding the aspects of globalization that require international social work to revisit previous assumptions concerning the scope of social justice.

The implications of these arguments for international social work are then explored in a twofold manner. Looking inward, there is the role of social work with cross-border migrants vis-à-vis the question of whether, and if so how far, the latter are entitled to provisions of social justice in their host societies. This problematic illustrates the mutually reinforcing nature of human rights and social justice, justifying the close proximity in which human rights and social justice tend to appear in much social work literature. Looking outward, the final section engages some of the issues emerging from the increasing role of social workers as global citizens in addressing injustices of global scale. Practical difficulties flowing from the notion of global citizenship aside, the social connection model reviewed here holds some useful pointers with regard to possible roles of international social work at a macro level.

Overall, the presence of social injustice anywhere exacerbates processes and cements structures of social exclusion, thus hampering the furtherance of human rights both within and across societies. In other words, thorough reconceptualization of social justice is a prerequisite for the ability of international social work to advance the cause of social justice, which in turn is a corequisite for the promotion of social inclusion and human rights worldwide (for further exploration of these concepts, see Chapters 5 and 6).

THE CONCEPTUAL DEVELOPMENT OF SOCIAL JUSTICE AS A GUIDING PRINCIPLE OF SOCIAL WORK

Current literature on social work ethics draws on a number of theoretical sources to inform its engagement with social justice. The conceptual roots of social justice can be found in nineteenth-century socialist, social democratic, and labor movements. However, the mainstreaming of class analysis of societies gained momentum with the institutionalization of welfare states in Western democracies after World War II. Rawls's (1971) seminal work, *A Theory of Justice*, stands in this tradition. Social workers have praised Rawls for providing "a rigorous philosophical argument for long standing social work values" (Swenson, cited in McGrath Morris, 2002, p. 365). Of particular attraction to social work has been Rawls's *original position*. Starting from the premise that "individuals . . . would . . . minimise disparities in resource allocation in the event that they might [themselves] become a member of a disadvantaged group" (p. 367), Rawls uses an imagined situation—the *"original position"*—to develop his *"basic principles of justice"*, thereby providing a rationale for redistribution of resources within society. In this context, Rawls draws out attention to the distribution of financial and material resources: *distributive justice*.

Drawing on Rawls's (1971) notion of a "basic structure of society" (p. 7), Barry (2005) suggests that "if we want to ask how far a society's institutions work together to produce social justice . . . we have to work back . . . from their . . . contribution to a just distribution of rights, opportunities and resources" (p. 17). The conceptualization of social justice as distributive justice draws attention almost inadvertently to the class divisions of societies. This is a conceptual limitation that has been critiqued by theorists of recognition, one of whom is Young (1990), prominently introduced to social work discourse by Mullaly (2002):

> Equating the scope of social justice with distribution only is misleading in two ways: (1) the social structures, processes, and practices that cause the mal-distribution in the first place are ignored; and (2) the limits of the logic of extending the notion of distribution to such non-material goods and resources as rights and opportunities are not recognised. (p. 33)

This argument shifts the focus of the debate to the institutional context of exclusionary practices, such as the "rules and norms that guide [the said social structures, processes and practices], and the language and symbols that mediate social interaction within them" (Mullaly 2002, p. 33). Thus, the meaning of Rawls's (1971) rights and opportunities is shifted:

> Rights refer to doing more than having, to social relationships that enable or constrain action. . . . Similarly, opportunity . . . is a condition of enablement, rather than possession which usually involves a system of social rules and social relations, as well as an individual's skills and abilities.
> —(Young as cited in Mullaly, *2002*, p. 34)

Centering on societies' "internal status hierarchies" (Fraser, 2008, p. 12), then, theorists of recognition are concerned with the question of how status inequalities along the lines of race and gender, among other things, marginalize entire social groups, rendering them partially if not completely voiceless, thereby hindering their ability to successfully voice claims toward just access to rights, opportunities, and resources for their members. Theories of *recognition* have been mainstreamed by feminism, black consciousness, and other civil rights movements, especially from the 1960s onward.

Drawing on the arguments of both distributional theories and theories of recognition, Ife and Tesoriero (2006) thus propose a social justice perspective that understands social injustice as social, political, and economic exclusion, primarily along lines of race, class, and gender. Thus, social injustice is structural in as far as it emanates from institutionalized processes that advantage the members of specific race, class, and gender groups in terms of accessing rights, opportunities, and resources by means of systematically disadvantaging *Others*.

In so far as social justice refers to the distribution of rights, opportunities, and resources, it raises questions not only around the (re)distribution of benefits but also around "the morally proper distribution . . . of . . . burdens among all of *society's members* [emphasis added]" (Mullaly, 2002, p. 32). Such questions imply the existence of a finite amount of (re)distributable resources in any society. In order to conceptualize social justice, international social work must therefore reconsider the scope of justice: Who is to receive and who is to give what?

Flowing from the assumption of finite resources to which people ought to have rights and opportunities is the understanding that there ought to be some form of membership in a collective held together by some notion of solidarity as the legitimate base for such claims, even if this means imposing certain burdens on those members who are comparatively better off. Questions of membership belong within a complex that Fraser (2008) calls "the proper *frame* [emphasis added] within which to consider first order questions of just distribution or reciprocal recognition in the given case" (p. 15).

In other words, the way social justice is framed is a function of admission criteria for membership in a certain collective, which may—justly or unjustly—exclude *Others* from being considered subjects of social justice. This form of exclusion potentially gives rise to a specific set of injustices beyond maldistribution and misrecognition. Fraser (2008) calls this type of injustice *misframing* and describes it as a metalevel injustice as opposed to the substantive justice concerns of distribution and recognition: There can be no distributive justice for, and no just recognition of, persons who are not considered to be legitimate members by the reference group to whom they are addressing their claims.

The conceptual roots of framing questions, or membership questions, might best be located in the arguments developed first in the nineteenth century by internationalist labor movements. Such debates regained momentum in the 1970s with the proliferation of solidarity movements accompanying the liberation movements in various former colonies and again in the context of accelerated globalization from the 1990s onward, when parts of the former solidarity movements began focusing on the presence of forced and economic migrants in their midst while other parts evolved into global justice and antiglobalization movements.

Rawls (1999) regards social justice as a system of distribution within but not across societies, which he conceptualizes as relatively closed nation-state systems with clearly demarcated territorial boundaries and members being their respective citizens. Though this view has been strongly criticized by a number of theorists (as will be shown), it remains uncommon among social work scholars to interrogate the taken-for-granted convergence of societal boundaries with state borders and the assumption that these are indeed the most the appropriate demarcation lines for the scope of social justice. For example, Barker (cited in Lundy & van Wormer, 2007) describes social justice as "an ideal condition in which *all members of a society* [emphasis added] have the same basic rights,

protection, opportunities, obligations and social benefits" (p. 727), while Chu, Tsui, and Yan (2009) translate this understanding into practice and assert that "social justice is pursued by challenging *societal* [emphasis added] barriers, inequalities and injustices" (p. 287).

Inasmuch as this is not explicitly stated, it may well be assumed that many writers in social work—following Rawls—mean *states* when referring to *societies* as their frame for social justice and mean *citizens* when talking about society's *members*. These imply that the *bounds of social justice* are (or ought to be) equivalent to the existing set of *international borders*. If that is so, then the urgent question that follows for international social work is whether the boundaries of nation-states and citizenship remain the appropriate ones for delineating the scope of social justice in the context of globalization and large-scale cross-border migration.

GLOBALIZATION AND SOCIAL INJUSTICE: IMPLICATION FOR THE ROLE OF STATES AS AGENCIES OF REDRESS

The inherited international order is based on the premise that the world map is divided into distinct states, each of which covers a specific territory, separated from its neighboring states by international borders. As much as the mapping of the world along interlocking borders was completed at the end of the nineteenth century, no-man's-lands all but ceased to exist, and civil and international conflicts continue to unfold around the exact territorial demarcations of specific states.[1] The model on which this international order is based, and which continues to dominate global sociopolitical and economic discourses, is the Westphalian model of state sovereignty. This model presupposes that each state and the citizens who inhabit its territory are governed by a "dominant and unified political authority whose jurisdiction over a clearly marked piece of territory is supreme" (Benhabib, 2004, p. 4; also compare Lister, 1997).

It is mainly because of the previously uncontested role of the Westphalian state that mainstream conceptualizations of social justice in social work have tended to regard the state as the main agent to whom most if not all contests regarding social justice would be addressed. If territorial states were structures, and if citizenship were a form of membership inconsequential for people's chances to lead a good life, this point would not be worth considering. But although this assumption may have previously gone without saying, the current context of globalization lays bare its ideological nature far more glaringly than was the case in the preceding decades.

This context is characterized by an interconnected and frequently reinforcing set of global cultural, economic, social, political, and environmental developments, which are described in more detail in the chapter on globalization in this volume (Chapter 3). Relevant for the argument here is that globalization in its current form has led to a world in which poverty and inequalities not only within but also between states are increasing; in which the degree to which countries are affected by global warming and environmental degradation differs vastly; in which power over the financial resources, the extraction and processing of raw materials, and the production of industrial goods is distributed unevenly to the extreme between states and corporations; in which the majority of states do not live up to ideals of liberal democracy and constitutionality and are instead marred by internal and international conflict; and in which, as a result, well over 200 million cross-border migrants are estimated to be residing in countries other than their home countries (GCIM, 2005).

The fact therefore that citizenship of a particular state is by and large not a matter of choice but one of attribution for all save for a small cultural, political, and economic elite matters greatly. Citizenship remains an important determining factor for the allocation of rights, opportunities, and resources, as well as for recognition and for admission as a subject of justice in a context where globalization has rendered international boundaries extremely porous for some yet rigidly enforced for others. Fraser (2008) contends thus:

> Territorialising [social] justice, the Westphalian frame . . . drastically limit[s], if not wholly . . . exclude[s], binding *obligations of justice that cut across borders*. Constructing a set of territorially bounded domestic 'who', discrete and arrayed side-by-side, *this frame obscure[s] trans-border injustices*
> —[emphasis added]. (p. 55)

Unsurprisingly, assumptions affirming the role of the state as the main redistributive agency to which claims for recognition would also be addressed have been increasingly challenged. Voices have been heard at a global scale from sources as varied as

> communalists . . . who seek to locate the scope of concern in sub-national units . . . Regionalists

and trans-nationalists . . . who propose to identify the 'who' of justice with larger, though not fully universal units, such as 'Europe' or 'Islam' [as well as] globalists and cosmopolitanists . . . who propose to accord equal consideration to all human beings.

> —(Fraser, *2008*, p. 56)

However, with consensus waning as to the correct frame for social justice, disputes around who should be considered to be the relevant subjects and to which agency of redress they ought to direct their claims are bound to increase. These disputes have the potential to greatly undermine the practicability of the concept of social justice in guiding international social work.

LOOKING INWARD: SOCIAL JUSTICE AND CROSS-BORDER MIGRATION

It has been noted that at the current conjuncture, cross-border migrations of all sorts have increased dramatically worldwide at the same time as globalization has eroded the ability of states to exercise their autonomy over economic and social policy, that is, over matters of social justice. Having lost ground on state autonomy, however, is not the same as having lost ground on sovereignty. Lister (1997) claims that, "as regulators of access to territory, jobs and welfare, the power of nation states . . . could be said to be enhanced" (p. 55). In other words, because of their loss of autonomy on so many other levels, states have become preoccupied with policing access to rights, opportunities, and resources within their spheres of sovereignty, seeking to "maintain at least the illusion of control" (Morrison, 2001, p. 71). Accordingly, Bauman (2004) asserts that "in order to salvage whatever is left . . . present-day nation states . . . still claim the foundational, constitutional prerogative of sovereignty: Their right of exemption" (p. 52).

Benhabib (2004) illustrates this point by showing how the right of exemption has found its way as major "internal contradictions built into the logic of the most comprehensive international law documents of our world" (p. 11). While the 1948 Universal Declaration of Human Rights recognizes the right to emigrate (but not to immigrate), the right to enjoy asylum under defined circumstances, and the right to a nationality, it does not stipulate states' obligations that emanate from these rights.

> These rights have no specific addressees, and they do not appear to anchor specific obligations on the

part of second and third parties to comply with them. Despite the cross-border characteristics of these rights, the declaration upholds the sovereignty of individual states.

—(Benhabib, 2004, p. 11)

Still, cross-border, forced, and economic migration continues unabated across the world. In response, states have developed layered levels of social, political, and economic inclusion and exclusion of noncitizens, awarding differential residence statuses with varying restrictions and privileges based on the migrant's economic or otherwise usefulness to the country concerned. Irrespective, migrants continue to hold equal (because universal and inalienable) social and economic rights that are thus denied, albeit to varying degrees.

Unfortunately, active participation in the denial of socioeconomic rights to noncitizens by virtue of drawing and implementing lines of inclusion and exclusion between prospective service users with varying degrees of eligibility to provisions of social justice has become a defining feature of much social work with asylum seekers and other cross-border migrants across the world (compare, for example, Briskman & Cemlyn, 2005; Hayes, 2005; Humphries, 2004; Zorn, 2007). A number of scholars who have begun engaging with the ethics of social work with cross-border migrants argue therefore that practices of social justice ought to be inclusive of any person who is present within the boundaries of a particular state. Such calls are based on an implicit rather than explicit transference of the notion of universality from concepts of human rights to those of social justice. However, such a conceptual transfer is far from uncontested (compare Pogge, 2002). Thus, the presence of cross-border migrants in states where they do not hold citizenship-based rights to opportunities and resources requires international social work to reground its normative commitments to both social justice and human rights. In the words of Benhabib (2004),

We can render the distinction between 'citizens' and 'aliens', 'us' and 'them' fluid and negotiable. . . . Only then do we move towards a . . . post-national conception of cosmopolitan solidarity which increasingly brings all human beings, by virtue of their humanity alone, under the net of universal human rights, while chipping away at the exclusionary privileges of membership. (p. 21)

LOOKING OUTWARD: GLOBAL SOCIAL JUSTICE

Apart from issues surrounding the treatment of refugees and other migrants, global social justice is concerned with challenges such as the following:

Global poverty [and] economic inequality . . . the fair distribution of risks and responsibilities in addressing global environmental issues . . . the differential effects of multinational investment decisions on fragile societies, and the shape of the transnational division of labour.

—(Young, 2007, p. 9)

Considerations of global social justice are therefore related to a growing recognition of the increasing interconnectedness of the world, such as, for example, the fact that day-to-day consumption patterns of the affluent few are linked, through often complex causation chains, to the exploitation and suffering of people in distant places (Boltanski, 1999). Calls for redistribution of "material resources to address the causes and consequences of . . . absolute poverty [suffered by] hundreds of millions of people" (Young, 2007, p. 9) are, at least in general terms, shared in mainstream political discourse. Yet, Pogge (1994/2008) reminds us that the way we conceptualize the causes of world poverty matters greatly. Noting the geographical, historical, social, political, and economic interdependencies of the world, including the mutually reinforcing injustices and inequalities between nation states, he contends,

First-worlders often downplay these interdependencies and think of real societies as 'self-sufficient', 'closed', 'isolated' and 'self-contained'. Like the closely related notion that the causes of third-world poverty are indigenous, this fiction is a severe distortion of the truth—most clearly in the . . . case of today's unfortunate societies which are still reeling from the effects of slavery and colonial oppression and exploitation and are also highly vulnerable to global market forces and destabilization from abroad. (p. 253)

It is for reasons such as this that Young (2007) asserts a need for deepening levels of global democracy. She contends that "wider public discussion of policy issues within and between states, and an increased effective voice for less powerful states and peoples in making decisions about them will . . .

increase the chances that these decisions will promote global justice" (pp. 9–10), a view strongly supported and elaborated in great detail by Fraser (2008).

International social workers at this level would hence be concerned with their collective responsibilities as global citizens toward changing those institutions and social, economic, and political processes that create, perpetuate, and deepen the injustices and hardships that are often at the root of Third World poverty, conflict, and cross-border migrations in the first place.

Young's (2007) arguments are derived not so much from abstract principles and concepts as from the notion of humans' interconnectedness and interdependence, and they therefore sit well with Benhabib's (2004) notion of cosmopolitan solidarity cited previously:

> Obligations of justice arise between persons by virtue of the social processes that connect them. . . . Some of such processes [are] structural, and . . . some harms come to people as a result of structural social injustice. Claims that obligations of justice extend globally for some issues, then, are grounded in the fact that some structural social processes connect people across the world without regard to [state] boundaries.
>
> —(Young, *2007*, p. 159)

Simply by following the "rules and conventions of the communities and institutions in which we act" (Young, 2007, p. 177), social workers contribute to the production and maintenance of structural injustices across the world. Indeed, our global interconnectedness is so intricate that, for example, the mere fact that social workers use petrol to drive themselves to their offices or to visit their service users connects them to refugee-producing conflicts as diverse as the war in Iraq and the use of child soldiers in Uganda. These types of harm (over and above resulting from individual acts perpetrated by identifiable culprits) are the cumulative effects of the activities of thousands, even millions, of people across the globe, many of which are likely to be neither conscious, intentional, nor avoidable. Consequently, the moral responsibilities that derive from participation in these institutionalized processes of structural injustice are shared, forward looking, and dischargeable only through collective action (Young, 2007).

The victims of structural injustice, similar to the guilty parties, often cannot be unambiguously isolated.

In addition, those who benefit most from structural injustices (such as economic and political elites and globalization profiteers) are likely to have the least interest in making relevant changes. Conversely, those with the greatest insights into the injustices concerned and the greatest understanding of the likely effects of proposed changes on their lives are more often than not those with the least power. As Jordan and Düvell (2003) suggest, "The relevant needy populations (the 'worst off' . . .) are surely those who scratching a subsistence in Africa, Asia or remote parts of Latin America, and who make no direct claims from their needs" (p. 96). They therefore depend on the voice of those who "benefit relatively from structural injustices [and] are able to adapt to changed circumstances without suffering deprivation" (Young, 2007, p. 184).

Difficulties are bound to flow from such an appreciation of the evolving and increasingly complex interconnectedness of social work's global context, together with an appreciation of its own implication in global injustices. For one, there is the sheer impossibility of acting on every aspect of every injustice that each one of us is connected to in the absence of being able to tell the difference between those injustices that are relevant for international social work and those that are not. However, the social connection model considered here remains useful in pointing to a role of international social work at the current conjuncture: to liaise, engage, analyze, represent, advocate, and participate in collective action to democratize those institutions, policies, and processes within their spheres of influence that affect distant victims of globalization and global structural injustices most severely.

CONCLUSION

This chapter explored possible directions for a conceptualization of social justice for international social work. The review of some of the key discourses and debates to date revealed that social justice for social workers includes questions of just distribution and recognition, requiring our critical engagement with exclusionary and unjust structures and processes in contemporary societies. Where critical engagement may have been lacking so far is the question of the scope and boundaries of social justice. However, the increasingly felt impact of globalization in general and cross-border migration in particular have made the need to close this conceptual gap more apparent. International social work with its simultaneous commitment to human rights and social justice is inextricably caught between inclusion and exclusion, which are in turn embedded in the conceptualization of the sovereign state. Notions of universal human rights, citizenship, and social justice are linked to one another such that they at once constitute and pull in different directions the modern state, and with it, social work.

A further aspect of international social work that has been explored in this chapter is that of global social justice. Using social work's concern with relationships and its process orientation as a starting point allows us to draw on literature that conceptualizes moral obligations emanating from global social injustice from the vantage point of social connection. This approach has much to offer international social work at a macro level in that it gives such notions as global citizenship and cosmopolitan solidarity a practicability that might enable us to better negotiate the previously mentioned tensions between inclusion and exclusion, human rights and social justice.

The suggestions and directions for debate and exploration emanating from this chapter are just that. Further empirical research and theoretical deliberation are needed for the continuous grounding of international social work in social justice for a dynamic and rapidly changing world.

NOTES

1. The falling apart of the former Yugoslavia, the breakaway of the Eritrean nation from the Ethiopian state, and ongoing conflicts between Israel and Palestine and in the eastern provinces of the Democratic Republic of Congo (while each follows its unique logic and dynamics) are just four out of many examples that illustrate this point.

REFERENCES

Barry, B. (2005). *Why social justice matters*. Cambridge: Polity Press.

Bauman, Z. (2004). *Human waste: Modernity and its outcasts*. Cambridge, Oxford, and Malden: Polity Press.

Benhabib, S. (2004). *The rights of others: Aliens, residents and citizens*. Cambridge: Cambridge University Press.

Boltanski, L. (1999). *Distant suffering: Morality, media and politics*. Cambridge, New York, & Melbourne: Cambridge University Press.

Briskman, L., & Cemlyn, S. (2005). Reclaiming humanity for asylum-seekers: A social work response. *International Social Work, 48*(6), 714–724.

Chu, W. C. K., Tsui, M., & Yan, M. (2009). Social work as moral and political practice. *International Social Work, 52*(3), 287–298.

Dominelli, L. (2008). *Anti-racist social work* (3rd ed.). Houndmills, Basingstoke, Hampshire: Palgrave Macmillan.

Ferguson, I. (2008). *Reclaiming social work: Challenging neo-liberalism and promoting social justice*. Thousand Oaks, CA: Sage.

Fraser, N. (2008). *Scales of justice: Reimagining political space in a globalising world*. Cambridge: Polity Press.

Global Commission on International Migration (GCIM). (2005). *Migration in an interconnected world: New directions for action*. www.gcim.org/en/finalreport.html (accessed March 13, 2006).

Haug, E. (2005). Critical reflections on the emerging discourse of international social work. *International Social Work, 48*(2), 126–135.

Hayes, D. (2005). Social work with asylum seekers and others subject to immigration control. In R. Adams, L. Dominelli, & M. Payne (Eds.), *Social work futures: Crossing boundaries, transforming practice* (pp.182–194). Houndmills, Basingstoke, Hampshire: Palgrave Macmillan.

Humphries, B. (2008). *Social work research for social justice*. Houndmills, Basingstoke, Hampshire: Palgrave Macmillan.

Humphries, B. (2004). An unacceptable role for social work: Implementing immigration policy. *British Journal of Social Work, 34*(1), 93–107.

Ife, J., & Tesoriero, F. (2006). *Community development: Community-based alternatives in an age of globalization* (3rd ed.). French Forest: Pearson Education.

International Federation of Social Workers (IFSW). (2000). *Definition of social work*. www.ifsw.org/Publications/4.6e.pub.htlm (accessed August 7, 2004).

Jordan, B., & Düvell, F. (2003). *Migration: The boundaries of equality & justice*. Cambridge, Oxford, & Malden, MA: Polity Press.

Lister, R. (1997). *Citizenship: Feminist perspectives*. Houndmills, Basingstoke, Hampshire, & New York: Palgrave.

Lundy, C., & van Wormer, K. (2007). Social and economic justice, human rights and peace: The challenges for social work in Canada and the USA. *International Social Work, 50*(6), 727–739.

McGrath Morris, P. (2002). The capabilities perspective: A framework for social justice. *Families in Society, 83*(July-August), 365–374.

Morrison, J. (2001). The dark side of globalization. *Race and Class, 43*(1), 71–74.

Mullaly, B. (2002). *Challenging oppression: A critical social work approach*. New York: Oxford University Press.

Pogge, T. W. (1994/2008). An egalitarian law of peoples. In T. Brooks (Ed.), *The global justice reader* (pp. 237–257). Malden, Oxford, Carlton: Blackwell.

Pogge, T. W. (2002). *World poverty & human rights*. Cambridge: Polity.

Rawls, J. (1999). *The law of peoples*. Cambridge, MA: Harvard University Press.

Rawls, J. (1971). *A theory of justice.* Oxford: Claredon Press.

Young, I. M. (2007). *Global challenges: War, self-determination and responsibility for justice.* Cambridge & Malden, MA: Polity Press.

Young, I. M. (1990). *Justice and the politics of difference.* Princeton, NJ: Princeton University Press.

Zorn, J. (2007). Borders, exclusions and resistance: The case of Slovenia. In M. Lavalette & I. Ferguson (Eds.), *International social work and the radical tradition* (pp. 117–143). Birmingham: Venture Press.

SECTION II

History

8

The History of the Development of Social Work

LYNNE M. HEALY

Capturing the history of social work around the world in a single chapter is a difficult task[1]. This chapter summarizes the beginnings of social work in diverse parts of the world. Ways in which professionals have addressed common challenges and tensions are then discussed, including professionalization, survival in times of oppression, and expansion in times of special opportunity. Other themes of note are the role of national founders or pioneers and cross-national borrowing and adaptation of models and applications of social work, including the influence of external organizations such as the United Nations. The beginnings of the profession are highlighted to demonstrate the breadth of the spread of the profession and to suggest issues for further research to explain patterns of institutionalization, stability and instability, and indigenization.

It is difficult to identify the specific beginning of the profession of social work. Most religious traditions incorporate ideas of helping, and there have been numerous initiatives for improving the human condition throughout history. In countries where social work has developed, helping activities began under a variety of auspices. When can these activities be labeled *social work*? Is one hallmark that they became secular rather than exclusively under the control of religious personnel? Or was it when they were undertaken by people who devoted themselves to helping as a regular activity rather than an occasional one? Or did social work become a professional activity when those providing such helping services began to systematize their efforts and train others to provide services in a similar way?

Accounts of the history of social work often emphasize the founding of schools of social work. The easiest beginning date to identify is the beginning of formalized training for social work, because the founding of educational programs tends to be well documented. Earlier markers include the establishment of agencies such as settlement houses and the YWCA.

Founding of these agencies represented organized efforts to provide social services, often by paid staff who devoted themselves to this work as their main enterprise.

THE EMERGENCE OF SOCIAL WORK AS A PROFESSION

Several distinct patterns in the evolution of social work are evident. Social work schools emerged almost simultaneously in London, Amsterdam, New York, and Berlin around 1900 (de Jongh, 1972). Social services were being developed to address the human needs that grew out of the industrial revolution in Northern Europe and America. Family services, settlement houses, and assistance to orphans, widows, immigrants, and young working women sprang up in response to harsh employment conditions. Schools and courses were organized to train staff and systematize these services. It has long been thought that this was a spontaneous development; however, new research involving correspondence and papers of the day shows considerable correspondence and exchange among the founders, who traveled to learn of newly emerging models of services (Kendall, 2000).

Regarding a second pattern, de Jongh says, "I do not know of any developing country in which social work education was an original product of national development; the origins can always be traced back to strong foreign influences" (1972, p. 23). Thus, we have two patterns: social work evolving in the United States and much of Europe as an indigenous response to the conditions of late nineteenth-century life and social work being introduced into Asian and African countries by American and European experts to address the problems of underdevelopment. A third pattern, which emerged after de Jongh's work, is the introduction or reintroduction of modern social work in the countries of the former Soviet Union and Eastern Bloc, including Russia, Eastern European nations, China, and Vietnam; this process has also involved substantial foreign influence. Although much of de Jongh's argument holds true, it can also be said that exchange, borrowing, and adaptation have influenced the development of social work in Europe and North America as well as elsewhere.

Social Work Services Emerge in Europe and the United States

As summarized by Van Wormer, "Two social movements in social welfare that began at the end of the nineteenth century shaped the development of the profession of social work: the Charity Organization Societies (COS) and the settlement house establishments" (1997, p. 162). Although both developed as responses to the social ills of the times, they differed in philosophy and approach. Both institutions began in London, the COS in 1869 and the first settlement house, Toynbee Hall, in 1884. Within less than a decade, each was transplanted to the United States—remarkable examples of early technology transfer in the human services. The first COS in the United States began in 1877 in Buffalo and was followed by rapid development of societies in other cities. Hull House was founded in Chicago in 1889 following Jane Addams's visit to Toynbee Hall. The reform orientation of social work was strongly influenced by the settlement movement in the United States and Europe. The COS workers, with their emphasis on the needy individual and combination of scientific record keeping with friendly visiting, were the forerunners of social caseworkers.

These models spread to other countries, often as a result of colonial activities and missionary work. Ilona Foeldy founded a settlement in Budapest in the 1930's (Zaviršek, 2008). In India, a settlement house, the Nagpada Neighborhood house, was begun in 1926 by Dr. Clifford Manshardt, a missionary from the United States (Manshardt, 1967). The adoption of the COS in Jamaica is documented by John Maxwell (1993): "The extent to which services established in the then British West Indies colonies were conceived as export models from the mother country is reflected in the names of the programmes established in the Region. None demonstrates this more completely than the Kingston Charity Organization Society founded in 1900 which was promoted with a view to rationalizing the delivery of private charity in the community. It did not however assume the central prominence in the development of social services and the systematizing and ultimate professionalizing of social work service delivery that was achieved by

the original London Charity Organization Society" (p. 9).

The Spread of Social Work and Social Work Education

As noted, professional education may well be the cornerstone of the establishment of a profession. This section identifies the beginnings of social work education around the world. It shows early diffusion to every continent, with later periods of expansion, consolidation, and sometimes retreat. In 1899, the first full program of social work education began in Amsterdam at the Institute for Social Work Training. According to its prospectus, this was a two-year course aimed "at the methodical, theoretical and practical training of those who wish to dedicate themselves to certain important tasks in the field of social work" (United Nations, 1958, p. 109). Five fields of study were offered: welfare of the poor, housing management, Toynbee work (settlement work), child care for orphans and deserted children, and social work in factories and workshops.

There were earlier efforts of more limited scope. Octavia Hill was conducting training in England as early as 1873. In 1895, a summer institute was sponsored in Chicago by Hull House, followed by the 1898 summer school organized by the New York COS; the New York offering became a one-year course in 1904 and later became the Columbia University School of Social Work (UN, 1958). Alice Salomon began training in Germany in 1899 and opened a school of social work in Berlin in 1908 (Wieler, 1988).

In Eastern Europe, the Training School for Social Work was founded by Helena Radlinska at the Free University of Poland in Warsaw in 1925. Radlinska commented to educators at the First International Conference of Social Work that she found it difficult to balance theory and practice: "In fact, there are very few professors who combine practical experiences with academic qualifications; therefore it is difficult to correlate the practice and theory of social work" (International Conference of Social Work, 1929, p. 92). This continued to be a challenge in the early years of developing professional social work education. Early social work was most often a female profession. As late as 1937, 83 of the 179 schools of social work in the world were for women only; just 9 were reserved for men. In some European countries, including Austria, France, Hungary, Italy, Norway, Portugal, Romania, and Switzerland, the only social work training institutions were reserved for women.

In the 1920s and 1930s, schools of social work were initiated in Latin America, including Santiago,

Chile, in 1925 and the University of Buenos Aires in Argentina in the early 1930s. Collaborations between South American medical personnel and social work educators in Belgium, France, and Germany were key in beginning these schools. They were also influenced by local traditions of charity work. In Argentina, for example, a women's organization called the *Charity Society* was established in 1823 and given authority to administer institutions for children, women, and the aged. In existence until 1948, this organization has been described as "by far the most powerful charity organization in the 19th century" (Queiro-Tajalli, 1995, p. 92).

The first schools in Africa began at opposite ends of the continent, in South Africa in 1924 and in Egypt in 1936. In South Africa, training initially focused on the problems of poor whites; theory was borrowed from North America and Europe with little attention to adaptation (Mazibuko, McKendrick, & Patel, 1992). University based from the outset, the 1924 course was founded at the University of Cape Town, and within a decade, it was joined by programs in Pretoria and Stellenbosch. Though there was an opposing tradition of liberalism that advocated diversity and openness, early social work was linked to Broederbond, an Afrikaner advancement movement that opposed cultural assimilation. Two traditions of liberalism, one focusing on poverty in general and the Afrikaner focus on services to whites, continued unchanged in South African social work for decades.

The Jan H. Hofmeyr School of Social Work, founded in 1941 with assistance from the YMCA, was the first to focus on education for nonwhites (Kendall, 2000). It grew from the work of Hofmeyr, a South African philanthropist who believed in equal opportunity, and Ray Phillips, a Congregationalist missionary with a PhD from Yale. Phillips was committed to the "absolute equality of men and women of every race and condition" (Kendall, 2000, pp. 7–11), and his work in founding the school was one way to put his beliefs into action.

Social work education in the Middle East and North Africa began in Cairo in 1936, the year Egypt gained recognition as an independent nation. According to Ragab (1995), in the early stage of development, "the American model was successfully transplanted into Egypt" (p. 281). The founders were confident that the many social problems facing the new nation could be handled with an approach to social reform based on sound theory and research. "The school was an instant success. . . as the country was

teeming with idealistic, enthusiastic youth searching for a role in national reconstruction and development" (p. 284). Social services became more formalized and job opportunities grew as the government established the Ministry of Social Affairs and Labour in 1939 to provide public social services. Prior to 1939, social services in Egypt were entirely voluntary, organized by mosques and nongovernmental organizations (NGOs) (Walton & El Nasr, 1988).

From his work in the Nagpada settlement house, Manshardt became convinced "that the standard of social work in India could not be raised appreciably until a permanent School of Social Work was set up to engage in a continuous study of Indian Social Problems and to offer training for social work on a graduate basis" (Manshardt, 1941, p. 15). With financing from the trust of an Indian industrialist, Manshardt began India's first professional school in Bombay in 1936, the Sir Dorabji Tata Graduate School of Social Work (Desai, 1987). The school focused on urban problems and pioneered in training labor welfare officers to cope with the new factory labor force as families moved to Bombay from rural villages. Labor welfare has continued to be important in Indian social work. According to Kudchodkar (1963), India is another case in which the "birth and early growth of social work and its professionalization (in India) was not the product of indigenous inspiration" (p. 96). Indian social work education was heavily influenced by U.S. models for many years.

In China, social work training began in the Sociology Department at Yanjing University (now Beijing) in 1922, and it soon became the Department of Sociology and Social Services. The program was heavily influenced by American missionaries and by the YMCA and YWCA (Leung, 1995). Australian social work education began at Melbourne University in 1933 as a two-year diploma course.

Therefore, by the mid-1930s, within thirty-five years of the first appearance of social work, students were being educated as professional social workers on every inhabited continent. The spread of professional training for social service work is an impressive story of the global diffusion of innovation. It is also a story that continues to the present day.

Social Work Founders and Pioneers

Many people contributed to the development of social work. In several countries, however, the work of a few people stands out. Alice Salomon in Germany, Jane Addams and Mary Richmond in the United States, Sattareh Farman-Farmaian in Iran, Manon Lüttichau in Denmark, René Sand in Belgium, Helena Radlinska in Poland—these pioneers, among others, are noted for their multifaceted contributions in launching the profession. In many cases they initiated social services, founded educational programs to train better service providers, and even expanded their work to found national and international professional organizations. Their progressive attention to service, education, and organization expresses the core of what it means to be a profession. It is also noteworthy that each of those named here believed fervently in the value of international exchange of ideas as essential to profession building. Other individuals, such as Katherine Kendall and Eileen Younghusband, carried on the work of the founders in their efforts to spread social work around the world.

EFFORTS TO GAIN RECOGNITION AS A PROFESSION

In spite of the founders' efforts, it was not easy for social work to achieve recognition as a profession. In 1915, Abraham Flexner dismayed his audience at the U.S. National Conference of Charities and Correction by stating that social work was not a profession because it did not have a body of educationally transmissible technique and because the boundaries of social work were too broad (Popple, 1995).

Around the same time, Alice Salomon, seeing the increased demand for social workers in Germany toward the latter years of World War I, promoted uniform standards for social work schools. In Germany, state approval was needed to promulgate uniform standards because such an action required recognition of the profession. Salomon therefore called together representatives of the schools and government representatives from the Ministries of the Interior and of Education for a discussion about the need for professional recognition and standards, but the results were not positive.

As Salomon wrote in her autobiography, "the head of the public health section of the Ministry. . . finally broke out: 'You talk about a number of different things, about training for health work-for educational activities-for relief-for protection of labor-and all this you call a profession of social workers. What you talk about does not exist' (Lees, 2004, p. 152). A similar process and outcome occurred in France when social workers petitioned the minister of health for regulation as a profession. The reply was that social work 'cannot be defined. . . which makes regulations impossible'" (Lees, 2004, p. 152).

Recent Efforts

The quest for professional standing has continued. Efforts to secure accreditation and licensing or registration of social workers are seen as ways to increase professional legitimacy, although others see these as diminishing the commitment to social justice. These efforts have most often been initiated by the profession, not the public or governments. To ensure the continuing status of the profession in a new era, social workers in Hong Kong secured passage of the Social Workers Registration Ordinance in 1996, just in advance of the territory's return to China as a special administrative region; licensure began in 1998 (Chui, Tsang, & Mok, 2010). And, a 2010 article in the International Federation of Social Workers (IFSW) newsletter quotes the deputy community development minister in Zambia, who commented on the lack of licensing or certification for social workers in that country, "There is no discipline that can claim to be a profession without having the relevant requisites such as a body of knowledge, code of ethics and a professional body. How then can we social workers in Zambia claim to be professionals when we do not have standards of certification as well as practice licences?" (IFSW, 2010). In her video presentation to the 2008 IASSW Congress in Durban, Katherine Kendall reminded the audience that the United Nations has stated that social work is a profession. "What higher authority could there be?" she asked (Kendall, 2008).

SOCIAL WORK UNDER OPPRESSIVE CONDITIONS

Social work has often suffered unduly in politically oppressive contexts. Its human rights and social justice mission and focus on needs of unpopular groups have made it a target of dictators and oppressive regimes on both the political right and left. In some periods of history, the oppression of the profession led to abolishing schools and denouncing the profession as unnecessary or subversive. At times, professionals and their organizations have valiantly resisted oppression; at others, there have been instances of collaboration with evil and still other instances of modest accommodation while continuing to serve those in need to the extent feasible.

Lorenz (1994) has documented the active collaboration of some social workers with the Nazi regime in Germany and elsewhere in identifying and classifying groups of undesirables; such labeling led to sterilization and later to extermination of groups. According to Lorenz (1994), "The actual legitimation of the procedure (sterilization) depended essentially on experts such as doctors and social workers making the 'right diagnosis'" (p. 65). Social work skills and methods of assessment, diagnosis, and report writing were used to identify "unworthy life" (p. 66). "It is a fact that the welfare machinery of Nazi Germany, by 'doing its duty' willingly or reluctantly, delivered thousands of people into the hands of the henchmen of the regime, caused untold anguish and suffering, deepened divisions at all levels of society and discredited its own humanitarian ideals" (p. 63).

Lorenz believes that the strong scientific emphasis in social work at the time and promotion of the belief in value neutrality were at least partially to blame. The focus on technical methodologies for dealing with human problems and the absence of a human rights orientation allowed the methodologies of the profession to be used for evil purposes.

Under other dictatorial governments, the profession itself has been abolished. Communist ideology branded social work a "bourgeois pseudo-science" (Xia & Guo, 2002, p. 258) and an unnecessary profession, formed only to deal with the problems arising from the capitalist system. Therefore, in the 1940s following the Soviet takeover of many Eastern European countries, social work was officially abolished as a profession in Hungary, Czechoslovakia, and Romania (although work continued in Poland and Yugoslavia). China followed suit in 1952, abolishing the discipline of sociology and along with it the teaching of social work, and Vietnam did so in 1975 (Oanh, 2002). The regimes reinforced the notion of social work as unnecessary by ceasing the collection of data on social problems; therefore, the claim was made that personal and social ills no longer existed. Social work in Hong Kong, however, grew following the Communist takeover of China in 1949 as social work agencies, particularly those that had their roots in missionary work, relocated to Hong Kong. That year also saw the establishment of the Hong Kong Social Workers Association (Chui et al., 2010).

Social work in Ethiopia was similarly shut down in the 1970s when a military junta called the *Dergue* deposed the emperor and established a socialist state. Ethiopia had been a leader in social work education in Africa and was active in the International Association of Schools of Social Work (IASSW). Though the teaching of social work content continued under various disguises, the profession suffered severe setbacks for several decades until the official revival of social work education in the twenty-first century.

In other places, too, the profession and its members have come under attack for their identification with human rights. Social workers and social work students were targets of violence, including disappearance and murder, by the Pinochet regime in Chile in the 1970s and 1980s. In South Africa, antiapartheid social workers were harassed, banned, and jailed for their activities. In these settings, the courage and value-driven commitments of members of the profession can be hailed and celebrated in contrast to the activities reported by Lorenz (1994).

OPPORTUNITIES AND EXPANSION

Just as there have been periods of oppression and contraction of the profession, there have been times of opportunity and expansion. Often, these times follow periods of oppression and conflict. One important period of expansion immediately followed World War II. "For social work and social welfare, the restoration period following World War II can be described as a rich cornucopia filled with international programs, projects and opportunities" (Kendall, 1978, p. 178). The devastation in Europe and East Asia brought opportunities for social workers to become involved in the enormous international relief and rehabilitation efforts, especially through the United Nations Relief and Rehabilitation Agency (UNRRA) (Friedlander, 1949). In various capacities, social workers addressed the needs of refugees and displaced persons, orphans, and other children in need. UNRRA was the first systematic program to send social welfare experts abroad to assist other countries in developing social legislation and social service programs.

Other opportunities for postwar expansion of social work arose from nationalist and independence movements emerging throughout the developing countries of Asia, Africa, and the Caribbean. These developments led to the birth of many new social work service and educational programs accompanying the birth of new nations.

Role of the United Nations

The United Nations (UN) soon became the largest contributor to the spread of professional social work throughout the world, taking responsibility for starting schools of social work in a number of developing countries (Younghusband, 1963). When the UN was in its infancy, the Social Commission of ECOSOC (the Economic and Social Council) encouraged attention to the training of social workers and provision of technical assistance in social welfare. A series of studies and publications was initiated under the title, Technical Assistance for Social Progress. One of these, the First United Nations Survey on Social Work Education, was issued in 1950, the first of five comprehensive studies in the field. Then, in 1959, ECOSOC asked the secretary-general to do "everything possible to obtain the participation of social workers in the preparation and application of programs for underdeveloped countries" (Garigue, 1961, p. 21).

Many countries in the developing world received consultation assistance in establishing social work training. Others secured fellowships to send faculty abroad for advanced training. In addition, grants through the UN and other sources assisted directly in establishing social welfare programs and social work training. Uganda, for example, established its social work program at Makerere University in Kampala with a UNICEF (United Nations Children's Fund) grant that carried the school through its first four years (Rao, 1984). Efforts by the UN also reshaped social work in some locations. According to Asamoah (1995), "perhaps the most significant event in the 1960's for both social work practice and social work education in Africa was the first UN Conference of Ministers Responsible for Social Welfare, held in 1968. The Ministers recommended that priority in developing countries be given to social welfare and that social welfare training prepare workers for carrying out developmental roles" (p. 225). This landmark event in global social welfare helped push social work in Asia and Africa toward a social development approach.

A third period of opportunity and expansion followed the dissolution of the Soviet Union. The gradual thaw and then dramatic end of Soviet domination in Eastern Europe set in motion an avalanche of opportunities to establish social work services and educational programs in Eastern Europe and the former Soviet republics. A more gradual yet substantial opening up in China has led to much the same scenario. Following the reestablishment of social sciences in Chinese universities in the early 1980s, exploration of social work began. By 1988, four universities had been given approval by the state to develop social work courses, and books and journals began using the term *social work* (Leung, 1995). In 1988, China hosted the Conference on Social Work Education in the Asia and Pacific Region (Leung, 1995). Further developments have been rapid. In 2002, Xia and Guo reported that there were 70 schools of social work in China; as of 2008, there were 200 or more such schools and China was becoming a major constituent of IASSW membership.

What do these periods of repression followed by expansion indicate? They seem to suggest that regardless of the political and economic system in place, human needs and problems arise. Especially in conditions of rapid change and modernization, professional services are needed to replace assistance that was once provided by informal systems. Professional services also address social and individual problems that many traditional mechanisms ignore or repress, such as mental illness and domestic violence. The mission and skills of social work appear universally relevant, although with different local expressions.

CONCLUSION

Many additional themes and events could be discussed in presenting the global history of social work. Some of these are ongoing, such as the move to indigenize social work and to accommodate the pressures arising from globalization with the need for locally specific methods and priorities. Although Herman Stein declared in 1972 that social work had entered the "era of indigenization" (p. 161), the quest for appropriate accommodation between the universal and locally specific elements of the profession continues and has been reflected in recent debates over international ethical principles and educational standards.

Regionalization has had a considerable impact on social work, especially in Europe, where mobility of personnel and comparability of standards have progressed. Though not as pronounced elsewhere, pressures to encourage cross-national recognition of credentials are influencing social work in other regions. Concern that regional bodies or global trade agreements could dictate professional standards was one factor propelling the development of the 2004 Global Standards for Education and Training of the Social Work Profession (IASSW and IFSW). The standards also represent a signature advancement of the idea of global professional definition and legitimacy.

Xia and Guo's (2002) summary of the history of social work in China identifies many of the continuing themes for the development of the profession worldwide. They indicate that social work struggles to balance "the two poles of globalization and localization" and currently reflects the "trends of normalisation, professionalism and globalisation" (p. 262). They conclude that the profession must continue to develop "increased professionalisation and a more profound institutionalisation" (p. 262). Although professionalization continues to be debated, it is essential that social work services and education become institutionalized within nations and within global bodies in order for its potential to be realized. Perhaps such institutionalization will also make social work more resistant to periods of oppression.

Examination of the beginnings of social work and its continued expansion to almost every nation underscores the broad and enduring relevance of professional social work. Now well into its second century, the profession continues to evolve to address new challenges and to enhance its contributions both globally and locally. There is much to learn from this history. Social work scholars conducting historical research are enhancing understanding of the shaping of the profession. As noted earlier, Kendall's (2000) exploration of the European origins of social work in the United States revealed a surprising degree of communication and exchange among the founders on both sides of the Atlantic, Wieler's (1995) study of the contributions of refugees from Nazi Germany and Austria to theory development in American social work reorients understanding of American theory, and Zaviršek's (2008) research into the history of social work in Yugoslavia during the Communist era challenges the stereotype of social casework as the more conservative branch of social work. Zaviršek discovered that the teaching of casework was suppressed by the Tito regime because its emphasis on the individual was viewed as radical and dangerous to the socialist state, while community organization was consistent with the imposition of the state on its people. As new research is conducted, it is sure to reveal new knowledge about the global history of the profession.

Additional material on the history of social work can be found in other chapters of this *Handbook*, especially in the sections on the international professional organizations and on social work in diverse regions.

NOTE

1. Parts of this chapter appeared in L. M. Healy, (2008), *International social work: Professional action in an interdependent world*, Oxford University Press. The material published here has been considerably revised and abridged.

REFERENCES

Asamoah, Y. (1995). Africa. In T. D. Watts, D. Elliott, & N. S. Mayadas (Eds.), *International handbook on social work education* (pp. 223–239). Westport, CT: Greenwood Press.

Chui, E., Tsang, S., & Mok, J. (2010). After the handover in 1997: Development and challenges for social welfare and social work in Hong Kong. *Asia-Pacific Journal of Social Work and Development, 20*(1), 52–64.

de Jongh, J. F. (1972). A retrospective view of social work education. In IASSW (Ed.), *New themes in social work education* (pp. 22–36). Proceedings of the XVIth International Congress of Schools of Social Work, The Hague, Netherlands, August 8–11, 1972. New York: IASSW.

Desai, A. (1987). Development of social work education. In *Encyclopedia of social work in India* (pp. 208–219). New Delhi: Government of India, Ministry of Welfare.

Friedlander, W. (1949). Some international aspects of social work education. *Social Service Review, XXIII*(2), 204–210.

Garigue, P. (1961). Challenge of cultural variations to social work. *Proceedings: Council on Social Work Education APM, 1961* (pp. 9–22). New York: Council on Social Work Education.

International Conference of Social Work. (1929). *Proceedings of the First International Conference of Social Work*, Paris, July 8–13, 1928.

International Federation of Social Workers (IFSW). (2010). Zambia promises new social work law and regulation in 2010. *IFSW Newsletter* (January). Accessed January 27, 2010, from www.ifsw.org.

Kendall, K. A. (2008, July). *Looking back, looking forward: The influence of history on social work education and practice*. Panel presentation to the International Congress of Schools of Social Work, Durban, South Africa, July 21, 2008.

Kendall, K. A. (2000). *Social work education: Its origins in Europe*. Alexandria, VA: CSWE.

Kendall, K. A. (1978). The IASSW from 1928–1978: A journey of remembrance. In K. Kendall (Ed.), *Reflections on social work education 1950–1978* (pp. 170–191). New York: International Association of Schools of Social Work.

Kudchodkar, L. S. (1963). Observations. *Indian Journal of Social Work, 24*(2), 96.

Lees, A. (Ed.). (2004). *Character is destiny: The autobiography of Alice Salomon*. Ann Arbor, MI: University of Michigan Press.

Leung, J. (1995). China. In T. D. Watts, D. Elliott, & N. S. Mayadas (Eds.), *International handbook on social work education* (pp. 403–419). Westport, Connecticut: Greenwood Press.

Lorenz, W. (1994) *Social work in a changing Europe*. London: Routledge.

Manshardt, C. (1967). *Pioneering on social frontiers in India*. Bombay: Lalvani Publishing House for the Tata Institute of Social Sciences.

Manshardt, C. (1941). Education for social work. *Indian Journal of Social Work, II*(1), 12–22.

Maxwell, J. A. (1993, June). *Caribbean social work: Its historical development and current challenges*. Paper presented at the Caribbean Regional Social Work Conference, St. Michaels, Barbados, June 6–10, 1993.

Mazibuko, F., McKendrick, B., & Patel, L. (1992). Social work in South Africa: Coping with apartheid and change. In M. C. Hokenstad, S. K. Khinduka, & J. Midgley (Eds.), *Profiles in international social work* (pp. 115–127). Washington, DC: NASW Press.

Oanh, N. T. (2002). Historical development and characteristics of social work in today's Vietnam. *International Journal of Social Welfare, 11*, 84–91.

Popple, P. R. (1995). Social work profession: History. In R. Edwards (Ed.), *Encyclopedia of social work* (19th ed., pp. 2282–2292). Washington, DC: NASW Press.

Queiro-Tajalli, I. (1995). Argentina. In T. D. Watts, E. Elliott, & N. S. Mayadas (Eds.), *International handbook on social work education* (pp. 87–102). Westport, CT: Greenwood Press.

Ragab, I. A. (1995). Middle East and Egypt. In T. D. Watts, D. Elliott, & N. S. Mayadas (Eds.), *International handbook on social work education* (pp. 281–304). Westport, CT: Greenwood Press.

Rao, V. (compiler). (1984). *World guide to social work education* (2nd ed.). New York: Council on Social Work Education for the International Association of Schools of Social Work.

Stein, H. D. (1972). Cross-national themes in social work education: A commentary on the Sixteenth IASSW Congress. In IASSW (Ed.), *New themes in social work education* (pp. 155–164). New York: IASSW.

Walton, R. G., & El Nasr, M. (1988). The indigenization and authentization of social work in Egypt. *Community Development Journal, 23*(3), 148–155.

Wieler, J. (1988). Alice Salomon. *Journal of Teaching in Social Work, 2*(2), 165–171.

United Nations (UN). (1958). *Training for social work: Third international survey.* New York: Author.

United Nations (UN). (1950). *Training for social work: An international survey.* Lake Success, NY: Department of Social Affairs.

Van Wormer, K. (1997). *Social welfare: A world view.* Chicago: Nelson Hall.

Wieler, J. (1995). Destination social work: Emigres in a women's profession. In S. Quack (Ed.), *Between sorrow and strength: Women refugees of the Nazi period* (pp. 265–282). Cambridge: Cambridge University Press.

Xia, X., & Guo, J. (2002). Historical development and characteristics of social work in today's China. *International Journal of Social Welfare, 11*, 254–262.

Younghusband, E. (1963). Tasks and trends in education for social work: An international appraisal. *Social Work, 20*(3), 4–11.

Zaviršek, D. (2008, July). *Looking back, looking forward: The influence of history on social work education and practice.* Panel presentation to the International Congress of Schools of Social Work, Durban, South Africa, July 21, 2008.

Claiming Women's Places in the World: Social Workers' Roles in Eradicating Gender Inequalities Globally

LENA DOMINELLI

Social workers are committed to enhancing human well-being by providing individuals, groups, and communities with services that meet their needs. Working at the local, national, and international levels as individual professionals, through civil society organizations, and through official channels such as the United Nations (UN), they have contributed to identifying the specificity of gender inequalities that discriminate against women throughout the life span, place them at the lower echelons of the waged labor hierarchy, and ignore unpaid work in the home. They have sought a gender equality that values women's activities and opens public spaces to them. Although there are commonalities, women's experiences of gender oppression vary according to race, ethnicity, age, disability, sexual orientation, and other factors. Women's struggles became labeled *feminist*, but many women do not associate with the feminist movement (e.g., black women call themselves *womanists*). Women continue to be discriminated against despite having organized against gender inequalities for centuries. Even in progressive Sweden, women earn 80 percent of men's earnings.

Globalization has exacerbated gendered inequalities by producing winners and losers. This concerns social workers because the majority of losers are women and children. Of the 946 billionaires worldwide in 2006, 63 were women, and the richest man held $62 billion compared with the richest woman's $20 billion (Kroll & Fass, 2007). Male children are favored in many countries. Illiteracy remains higher among girls. Women bear the burden of ill health if they are of childbearing age and are sexually active. Around 600,000 women die needlessly in childbirth each year. Many women do not have the rights to control their bodies or have reproductive rights.

Women in industrializing countries are adversely affected by lack of clean water and sanitation facilities, do most of the agricultural work, and are the least likely to own land; in Cameroon, for example, women do 75 percent of the agricultural work but own 25 percent of the land. In most countries—the Nordic states, Rwanda, and Mozambique being notable exceptions—women form a majority of the population but are underrepresented among elected politicians.

This chapter explores how women, including social work educators and practitioners, have used civil society organizations, international institutions, and networking skills to promote gender equality; change economic, political, and social realities locally, nationally, and internationally; embed gains in everyday routines; and develop relevant social work curricula. Social workers have advocated for gender equality and participated in struggles for social change as individuals active in the women's movement, development workers tackling structural inequalities, therapists addressing individual women's woes, and participants in the UN, its related agencies, and international organizations such as the International Association of Schools of Social Work (IASSW), International Federation of Social Workers (IFSW), and International Council on Social Welfare (ICSW). (The IASSW, IFSW, and ICSW endorse the UN Charter and human rights conventions and contribute to shaping policy and practice.)

Some gender-blind interventions have had positive impacts on women's personal well-being. Others are overtly feminist and seek structural changes in the social distribution of power and resources (Dominelli, 2002). Social workers' activities often lack professional visibility; in fact, social workers were successful in getting the UN to recognize the professional basis of social work, but as Kendall (2010) recalls, the report she authored for the UN in 1950 was credited to the secretary-general.

NAMING WOMEN'S OPPRESSION: ORGANIZING AGAINST GENDER INEQUALITIES GLOBALLY

Women activists named their inequalities *gender oppression*. The movement for gender equality spread globally during the 1960s. United by the common aim of ending patriarchal social relations that privileged men by devaluing women's contributions to societies, including their unpaid domestic labor that facilitated family survival, a diverse women's movement ranging from radical feminists (Banks, 1981) to postmodernists (Nicholson, 1990) emerged. Thousands of women participated in a global women's movement (Ferree & Tripp, 2006), united by the desire to eradicate the oppression of women.

The movement fractured as smaller groups organized around specific demands. In the West, working-class women wanted pay equality and access to positions restricted to men; middle-class women desired control of their time, reproductive capacities, and sexual expression; and black women wanted to eliminate racial oppression (Friedan, 1963; Lorde, 1984). In industrializing countries (variously called *developing countries*, the *Global South*, *Third World*, or *Two-Thirds World*), women sought the means for raising families, including water, sanitation, food, education, and decent housing, as well as an end to exploitative Western aid (Mohanty, 1991). Differences between women constantly emerged and reemerged, reflecting unique country positions as each group prioritized local and national matters. This fluidity suggests not a global movement but a loosely organized endeavor in which various groups united to progress women's equality by leveraging support.

Group membership overlapped as women interacted around their own priorities and approaches to change (Dominelli, 1997). The Wages for Housework Campaign, for example, highlighted the importance of women's domestic work to economic and family success. Americans argued for women's role in the public sphere, while Mexican women sought decent housing for people with low incomes and exposed the complexities of women's individual and collective actions. Social workers' professional participation included organizing women's groups to raise consciousness of the links among women's personal troubles, lack of recognition, and social location. They worked to reduce women's social isolation within family relationships and challenged doctors, psychiatrists, psychologists, and police officers for ignoring social restrictions on women's well-being, especially domestic violence and mental ill health. Additionally, they developed alternative framings of social problems and created services designed and run by women.

Tensions arose between segments of the movement because some proclaimed a singular view of women's oppression while others demanded recognition of the specificity of local struggles and cultural uniqueness. Groups celebrating women's achievements in the home felt excluded. Working across borders became problematic when women in the Global South identified the contributions of women in the North as oppressive for not listening to locality-specific concerns, devaluing local cultural knowledge and traditions in problem resolution, and not acknowledging the implications of women's diverse life experiences for collective action (Mohanty, 2003). Women's unique trajectories and the legacy of divisive assumptions whereby white Western women configured other women as similar to themselves hindered the formation of transnational alliances and allowed non-governmental organizations (NGOs) distributing development funds to undermine initiatives undertaken by local women and the state (Stubbs, 2007).

These strains persist, although women in the South organized powerful collectives to advance their views locally, nationally, and internationally, particularly in the UN (Sen & Grown, 1987). Southern women also worked with women from the North in civil society organizations, which included social workers, to resolve these differences and ensure acceptance as equal partners with their own agendas and contributions to the overall effort of enhancing women's status and life circumstances. Despite differences in priorities and approaches, feminist organizers of women's rights began to listen to diverse voices within the movement, learn from one another, and use lessons gained in one country to enlighten activities elsewhere. Thus, consciousness-raising initiatives for empowering American women interacting with health professionals drew heavily on the "speak bitterness" meetings that Chinese community organizers formed to highlight domestic violence in Mao's China (Frankfort, 1972). In these meetings, women brought community members together to monitor men's behavior and shame men into behaving appropriately toward their wives.

Not all demands of the women's movement focused on single issues. Some sought to change everyday routines through which individuals related to each other in families and communities and the relationships between citizens and their nation-states. Though local domestic issues became starting points for changing social relations, they turned transnational as women sought commonalities for forging strong alliances without losing their rootedness in local concerns and traditions. This gave regional women's organizations roles in linking national concerns to international ones with the help of social workers (Mies, 1986); examples are FEMNET (African Women's Development and Communications Network) in Africa and *Encuentros* (regional meetings addressing domestic violence) in Latin America.

SOCIAL WORKERS ENGAGE WITH WOMEN'S MULTIPLE OPPRESSIONS

The contributions of social work educators and practitioners highlighted the multiple oppressions women faced locally, nationally, and internationally in the private and public domains and alongside social divisions, including race, age, and disability. Despite being labeled oppressive, social work educators and practitioners continued to press for women's equality (Dominelli, 2002). From the origins of social work as a profession in late nineteenth-century Europe, women created a profession that recognized women's contributions to the social good. However, lack of resources among women meant that it became a profession dependent on men and the state for resources. At the same time, the main concerns of the profession were poor people in general, not women's specific interests. These were picked up by individual social work practitioners and educators but did not become wider topics of concern until the second wave of feminists started challenging mainstream practices in the profession (Dominelli, 1997).

Social workers were part of and drew upon the wider social movements of the 1960s to develop practice, undertake research that highlighted multiple and persistent oppressions and actions that respected local cultures and traditions, and empower women to organize. Fraser (2003) has suggested that tackling multiple oppressions requires human rights to be supplemented with social justice. Both have been incorporated into social work interventions internationally (Healy, 2001). Parker (2006) applied these insights to disability to expose weaknesses in the International Covenant on Economic, Social and Cultural Rights (ICESCR) and Standard Rules on the Equalization of Opportunities for Persons with Disabilities for not meeting the diverse and marginalized needs of women with disabilities (Frohmader, 2002).

Increased recognition of women's multiple and fluid identities did not prevent the UN, International Monetary Fund (IMF), World Bank, and international NGOs from endorsing development policies that depicted women's identities as monolithic, fixed, and essentialized and that ignored the differential impact of place and social divisions upon women's experiences of oppression. For example, the Millennium Development Goals (MDGs) configure women's health, education, and income needs as if they were all the same. Translated into social policies at local, national, and international levels, these goals are incorporated into professional practice.

Some social workers searched for commonalities that did not submerge differences. They developed mechanisms that celebrated diversity when improving women's circumstances and creating policies to meet women's diverse needs. By recognizing difference, women can forge points of commonality that underpin collective action. Hence, struggles for women's reproductive rights in the West have differed from those in Africa, where local traditions play more prominent roles, or in China, where the Communist Party initiated the one-child policy and made contraceptive devices freely available. Respecting these differences turned women's right to abortion to their right to choose.

Women have been key actors in realizing gender equality in their localities, often inspiring women globally. A notable example is SEWA (Self Employed Women's Association), formed in 1972 in Ahmadabad, India. It includes social workers doing community development and supporting microcredit schemes to finance women's activities in holistic approaches to empowerment. SEWA has empowered 600,000 poor women as self-employed entrepreneurs, lobbied for women's rights, and followed Gandhian principles of nonviolence to secure social change.

Women's activism has led to their rights being encompassed by the Universal Declaration of Human Rights (UDHR), especially Articles 22 to 27, which refer to social services, health, and education. Redefining women's rights as human rights at the Nairobi

World Conference on Women in 1985 gave credence to a rights-based approach to women's well-being. Social workers supported this shift and the Beijing Platform for Action (issued at the 1995 World Conference on Women) that enabled a rights-based approach to link sustainable development with human rights and set equality for women as a universal goal. This approach created a grassroots universalism to accompany the specificities of women's experiences. Human rights–based universalism has been rejected by traditionalists, including religious fundamentalists who defend cultural practices that presume the subordination of women (Ferree & Tripp, 2006). Women Against Fundamentalism, a global network that includes social work educators and policy analysts, challenges this fundamentalist position (Yuval-Davis, 1997).

SOCIAL WORKERS SUPPORT GENDER EQUALITY THROUGH THE UNITED NATIONS

International social action to promote gender equality has been embedded in UN activities since its inception in San Francisco in 1945, when four female delegates from Brazil, China, Dominican Republic, and the United States urged equality of rights among men and women in its charter. They stimulated action by nineteen female delegates who demanded a commission for women at the UN's first General Assembly in London. This was granted in 1947 as the Commission on the Status of Women to promote women's equality and rights under the auspices of the Economic and Social Council (ECOSOC).

The IASSW obtained consultative status in ECOSOC in 1947 and benefited from the boundless energies of Katherine Kendall as social affairs officer at the UN (Kendall, 2010). The organization retains that status, contributing to UN deliberations as a civil society organization. Its activities include attending summits; changing policies, especially those affecting social development, old age, women, and racial equality; organizing seminars and educational exchanges for staff and students (Dominelli, 2010); developing curricula (Healy, 2001); and providing training in social work. The reconstruction of Europe under the United Nations Relief and Rehabilitation Administration (UNRRA) and UNHCR (United Nations High Commissioner for Refugees) established social work practices that continue. Some have been gender blind—initiatives highlighting social development—while others have focused

specifically on women, such as actions by the IASSW Women's Caucus, including its significant contributions to the 1995 Beijing conference (Dominelli, 1998).

Ongoing United Nations Efforts on Gender Equality

Progress on gender equality remains uneven. Women activists, including social workers, were delighted when the UN declared 1975 the International Women's Year and held the First World Conference on Women in Mexico City. This was followed by the Decade for Women, building institutions that promoted women's equality within a framework of social and human development for men and women in industrializing countries. March 8 was proclaimed International Women's Day to celebrate women's achievements. In 1979, the UN adopted the Convention on the Elimination of All Forms of Discrimination Against Women (CEDAW). Ratified by 177 countries (but not the United States), CEDAW was the first human rights treaty to focus specifically on women, and it signaled the UN's role as advocate for and guardian of women's human rights and involvement in development (Ferree & Tripp, 2006). For a more in-depth examination of CEDAW, see Chapter 67 on human rights of women later in this volume. The Second World Conference on Women in Copenhagen in 1980 and the third conference in Nairobi in 1985 highlighted the importance of monitoring progress. Disagreements about purposes, roles, and positions in social development led to acrimonious exchanges in Mexico City and Copenhagen. Delegates from industrializing countries felt that those from the West dominated proceedings and programs of work.

Subsequent dialogues enhanced understanding of diversity, reduced the privileging of Western women, strengthened women's resolve to support each other by recognizing different standpoints, and redefined women's concerns away from simply critiquing patriarchal relations to embracing struggles for social justice and human rights. This brought economic, social, and political domination under feminists' gaze and encouraged women to seek commonalities while acknowledging differences in struggles against all inequalities. These dialogues reinforced views of women as agents of change and highlighted their interdependencies. Dialogue eased relationships between women and enabled those at the Nairobi conference to engage with each other, promote specific issues, and build solidarity that affirmed each group's contributions to the overall objective of improving women's lives in accordance with local goals and perceptions. This dialogue created new networks, such as Development Alternatives with Women for a New Era (DAWN) and Grassroots Organizations Operating Together in Sisterhood (GROOTS). These networks highlight the significant roles enacted by women from industrializing countries, the women's confidence in setting agendas that met their needs, and organization in achieving them. *Women's empowerment* became buzzwords in these networks (Sen & Grown, 1987).

Mohanty (2003) recently articulated the feminist solidarity model that seeks commonalities between women and assists them in addressing diversities and needs. Social workers supported these goals and networks and brought them into play at the Fourth World Conference on Women in Beijing in 1995. Fearing that the Nairobi conference reflected lower international priorities for women, they used the World Conference on Human Rights in Vienna in 1993 to mobilize against violence against women and insist on the relevance of human rights to women. Women's equality was also discussed at the UN's 1994 International Conference on Population and Development in Cairo, where social workers were present. Controversies regarding women's reproductive rights led to these rights being reformulated as important to economic development and slowing population growth rather than the right of women to control their bodies. Social workers argued for women's right to information about and access to contraceptive devices to enhance women's health in caring for families.

Women in Development

Parallel processes between these events resulted in women being acknowledged as central to development, a view articulated by Women in Development (WID). Feminists in industrializing countries initially challenged WID for emphasizing Western women's definitions of development and stereotyping other women. This view was consistent with earlier demands that the UN prioritize poverty, non-Western models of modernization and development, and the centrality of women to a country's economy. Their efforts were supported by a (re)emerging women's movement in the West that pressed for the inclusion of women in initiatives affecting the Global South, an issue initially raised by Boserup (1970). Women redefined their roles in economic development as integral to a social and human development that promotes social justice

(Yuval-Davis, 1997). Increasing pressures from women, chiefly from countries reacquiring independence after colonization; strong civil society organizations that advanced women's interests (Sylvester, 1994); and feminist research and scholarship led to demands for funding for women's initiatives. These produced the United Nations Development Fund for Women (UNIFEM), International Research and Training Institute for the Advancement of Women, Women's World Banking (loan guarantees), and International Women's Tribune Centre (communications). Social workers participated in these organizations, raising similar debates in their ranks as did women more generally.

During the 1990s, women's attention moved toward environmental and anti-globalization movements to resist corporate entrepreneurs who were undermining their interests. Women's research and experiences exposed corporations as impoverishing women, appropriating intellectual property rooted in local knowledge and land, and degrading environments where women raised their families (Mies, 1986). Feminist activists like Vandana Shiva and Arundhati Roy, renowned for opposing environmental degradation and exploitation of women's labor and knowledge by global capital, demanded development that enhanced human life. This included safe physical environments, respect and dignity in meeting needs, and economic growth for all.

Slow progress in improving human well-being, including women's conditions globally, and the persistence of gender inequalities led the UN to include targets for gender equity in the MDGs in 2000. These targeted poverty, the well-being of women and children, education, and health. Targets set by the MDGs seem unreachable and have reduced gender equality to a few measurable indicators in education and maternal mortality. In 2006, the UN Educational, Scientific, and Cultural Organization (UNESCO) estimated that of $11 billion needed annually to provide primary schooling for children in industrializing countries, only $7 billion became available. Most analysts blame reduced resources, reduced commodity prices, and expensive food and fuel. Correll (2008) critiqued the conceptual weaknesses of the MDGs for moving away from the commitments reached at the Copenhagen World Summit for Social Development in 1995, where the ICSW, IFSW, and IASSW played prominent roles. Copenhagen's more holistic, integrated intervention programs would have better served the needs of women and children. Social workers have supported the fulfillment of the MDGs in the

Global South but critiqued their failures to address structural inequalities (Dominelli, 2010).

The new millennium ushered in a backlash that reasserted patriarchal relations privileging men in family relationships and public life. This backlash diminished the role of women in the UN and reduced upfront support for their activities. Significant in this regard was the UN Security Council's rejection of Mary Robinson for a second term as commissioner for human rights for being too outspoken (Crossette, 2002).

SOCIAL WORKERS SUPPORTING WOMEN'S EQUALITY TRANSFORM THE IASSW

The IASSW became a target of women's transformative action. It can be proud of its beginnings, when Alice Salomon, a German academic and researcher with a specific interest in women, became the first chair of the International Committee of Schools of Social Work in Paris in 1928. Women did not head the organization after she left office until 1964, when Eileen Younghusband became president. She was succeeded by men until Lena Dominelli's election in 1996. This emphasizes that even in a profession where the front lines and academy are dominated by women, men disproportionately occupy the top posts. Before 1990, IASSW involvement in UN initiatives on women occurred primarily through individual female members of IASSW. A group of women considered the exclusion of women in IASSW so serious that they organized a Women's Caucus at the 1984 Montreal Congress to press for their inclusion in its decision-making structures and conference proceedings (Dominelli, 1998).

The Women's Caucus, later renamed the Women's Interest Group (WIG) and given a specific voting position on the IASSW Board, involved a substantial number of member schools. Its followers, active in the women's liberation movement in their own countries, played major roles in developing gender-sensitive and feminist materials for use in social work curricula and fieldwork placements and opened up new areas for research and practice in domestic violence, child sexual abuse, and female offenders (Campbell, 1992).

In the early 1990s, WIG members prepared papers for the Copenhagen World Summit for Social Development as the IASSW reaffirmed its role internationally and promoted women's issues in the IASSW and UN. Janice Wood Wetzel as chair of WIG and Lena Dominelli as vice president worked with others to plan presentations on mental ill health and domestic violence for the Beijing conference. Working with other women in NGO deliberations in Huairou, China, they mobilized around women's concerns and conveyed these to government delegates for inclusion in the Beijing Platform for Action that the UN adopted. This platform embodied women's rights as human rights, strengthening coalitions that supported women's equality and scrutinizing policies for their gender-specific impact. Women's activities suffered a blow in 2004 when the United States withdrew support for the Beijing platform. In contrast, the European Union has been active in Beijing Plus Five (2000) and Beijing Plus Ten (2005) and has gender mainstreamed its own institutions.

The IASSW adopted the Beijing platform at its 1998 Congress and contributed seminars in the follow-up to the World Summit on Social Development, Beijing Plus Five Conference in New York, and related activities in Geneva and Vienna. Women's issues were included in IASSW submissions on social development, resisting racism and xenophobia, active old age, and social services for all. Limited resources have subsequently reduced some of the organization's innovative thrust on gender equality.

CONCLUSIONS

Women continue to fight to claim their places despite gains in gender equality. Although their endeavors have influenced theory and practice in social work, the bulk of women's aspirations remain unrealized across the world. Each country has its own women's movement, feminist or otherwise. These are committed to promoting the well-being of women, men, and children, albeit each in its own terms, giving a global movement of women a rich diversity and commitment to working together under the right conditions, valuing each others' contributions from their own perspectives while working toward common aims. Social workers back these goals through various roles and means. Their responses to eradicating gender oppression over forty years have linked the local with the global and have included support for the following:

* Political, social, and economic rights of citizenship in particular nation-states
* Cultural rights to protect social traditions
* Local language rights and exposure of power relations embedded in their formulation

* End of unequal power relations in interpersonal relationships and social structures that disadvantage women
* Reproductive rights and bodily integrity for women in managing pregnancy and bodily health
* Rights to the following:
  o Sexual expression
  o Education
  o Housing
  o Food and other basic needs like shelter, clothing, heating, and lighting
  o Security, both economic and physical
  o Peace
* Environmental rights, including clean water, reliable sanitation facilities, and unpolluted land, air, and skies

The struggle to realize these demands continues; no group of women has achieved all their rights except as short-term promises at the most legalistic level.

The IASSW has had an uneven involvement in women's issues. Its first leader was deeply involved in the women's equality movement of the early twentieth century. It was at the UN in 1947 when it acquired consultative status as one of the few NGOs present at an exciting point in human history. Its concerns soon became more generalized and lost a gender-specific focus. As an organization, it did not engage fully with the specificity of women's issues in the UN again until the mid-1990s, although a Women's Caucus (now the Women's Interest Group) was formed at the Montreal Congress in 1984 to promote women's specific interests and eventually secure a voting position on the IASSW Board at the Congress in Washington in 1992 (Dominelli, 1998). The challenge for the organization remains how to best support women's struggles for gender equality—by supporting women's issues as women's issues or by improving the position of all people in the hopes that women's specific concerns will be addressed as a by-product? It is a question that troubles the UN and its member governments.

REFERENCES

Banks, O. (1981). *Faces of feminism.* London: Martin Robinson.

Boserup, E. (1970). *Women's role in economic development.* New York: St. Martin's Press.

Campbell, K. (Ed.). (1992). *Critical feminism: Argument in the disciplines.* Buckingham: Open University Press.

Correll, D. (2008). News and views from ICSW. *International Social Work, 52*(2), 285–288.

Crossette, B. (2002). An era of women leaders ends at the UN. *WeNews,* September 12, Accessed at HYPERLINK "http://www.womensenews.org"

Dominelli, L. (2010). *Social work in a globalizing world.* Cambridge: Polity Press.

Dominelli, L. (2002). *Feminist social work theory and practice.* Cambridge: Polity Press.

Dominelli, L. (1998). Women organising: The Women's Caucus of the International Association of Schools of Social Work. In E. Fernandez, K. Heycox, L. Hughes, & M. Wilkinson (Eds.), *Women's participation in change* (pp. 1–10). Sydney: IASSW.

Dominelli, L. (1997). *Sociology for social work.* London: Macmillan.

Ferree, M. M., & Tripp, A. M. (Eds.). (2006). *Global feminism: Transnational women's activism, organizing, and human rights.* New York: New York University Press.

Frankfort, E. (1972). *Vaginal politics.* New York: Quadrangle Books.

Fraser, N. (2003). Social justice in the age of identity politics: Redistribution, recognition and participation. In N. Fraser & A. Honneth (Eds.), *Redistribution or recognition? A political-philosophical exchange* (pp. 7–95). London: Verson.

Friedan, B. (1963). *The feminine mystique.* New York: Bell.

Frohmader, C. (2002). *There is no justice just us! The status of women with disabilities in Australia.* Tasmania: Women with Disabilities.

Healy, L. (2001). *International social work: Professional action in an interdependent world.* Oxford: Oxford University Press.

Kendall, K. (2010). *Essays on a long life: Jottings and random thoughts.* Alexandria, VA: CSWE.

Kroll, L., & Fass, A. (2007). The world's billionaires. *Forbes, Special Report,* 8 March.

Lorde, A. (1984). *Sister outsider.* New York: Falling Wall Press.

Mies, M. (1986). *Patriarchy and accumulation on a world scale: Women in the international division of labour.* London: Zed Press.

Mohanty, C. T. (2003). *Feminism without borders: Decolonizing theory, practicing solidarity.* Durham and London: Duke University Press.

Mohanty, C. T. (1991). Cartographies of struggle: Third World women and the politics of feminism. In C. T. Mohanty, A. Russo, & L. Torres (Eds.), *Third World women and the politics of feminism* (pp. 1–50). Bloomington, IN: Indiana University Press.

Nicholson, L. (Ed.). (1990). *Feminism/postmodernism.* London: Routledge.

Parker, S. (2006). International justice: The United Nations, human rights and disability. *Journal of Comparative Social Welfare, 22*(1), 63–78.

Sen, A., & C. Grown. (1987). *Development crises and alternative visions: Third World women's perspectives.* New York: Monthly Review Press.

Stubbs, P. (2007). Community development in contemporary Croatia: Globalisation, neoliberalism and NGO-isation. In L. Dominelli (Ed.), *Revitalising communities in a globalising world* (pp. 161–174). Aldershot: Ashgate.

Sylvester, C. (1994). *Feminist theory and international relations in a postmodern era.* Cambridge: Cambridge University Press.

Yuval-Davis, N. (1997). *Gender and nation.* London: Sage.

SECTION III

International Social Work Practice

10

Work With Immigrants and Refugees

UMA A. SEGAL

Migration worldwide continues to increase as people move in, through, and out of countries and regions. Increasing openings of borders, as in the European Union; greater physical border controls, as in the southern United States; and ongoing perceptions of border fluidity, as in the African Union, present unprecedented opportunities and challenges to policy makers, service providers, businesses, and migrants themselves. Less mentioned in discussions on migration is movement within and through South and Central America, South Asia and the Pacific Rim, and the Middle East and Central Asia.

As borders become more porous, eyes turn to nations with relatively large migration flows, looking for answers to questions about policy, impact on the labor force, integration, and implications for governmental programs. However, receiving countries may or may not have the most effective answers. With a multitude of areas under discussion, at least one of three is voiced by most nations: the presence of an unauthorized immigrant population, the loss of a workforce through emigration, and the social and economic integration of migrants. Implications are complex, and social work is ideally suited to address issues of entry, adaptation, and exit.

Practice is generally associated with direct services; nevertheless, those working with immigrant groups should practice across modalities, recognizing their intervention potential through policy practice, community practice, and administration in addition to direct practice with immigrants. Trained to address behavior in environmental contexts, social workers must assess appropriate points of intervention at the macro, mezzo, and micro levels. This chapter discusses general issues facing newcomers and host nations, suggests implications for social work practice, and provides resources for further information.

THE PROCESS OF MIGRATION

The phenomenon of immigration is neither novel nor recent, and though migration may be a response to crises, it is often a search for better opportunities. This is evident in Lyons and Huegler's Chapter 72, which presents a strong overview of migration patterns worldwide and indicates that the cross-national movement begins not when immigrants arrive at a host country's borders but long before, while they are still in their home countries. The process of emigration from the home country through adjustment to the receiving nation is lengthy and complex, with the success of the immigrant dependent on the interplay of personal resources and environmental factors.

Figure 10.1 identifies the salient factors in the immigration process, suggesting that practitioners must focus on reasons immigrants left their homelands, their experience of migration, the resources they bring for functioning in unfamiliar environments, and the receptiveness of host countries (both politically and socially) to their presence. Regardless of the time since entry, immigrants constantly face a duality of cultures and must function within frequently conflicting expectations.

Moving to another country is arduous, even under optimal circumstances. It usually requires elaborate preparation, great financial costs, loss of social and family ties, acquisition of a new language, and learning an alien culture. International patterns of immigration around the world have altered dramatically through the twentieth century and into the twenty-first; however, regardless of changes in immigration laws, most immigrants and refugees encounter discrimination and oppression at one time or another. They are denied opportunities or even are victimized because

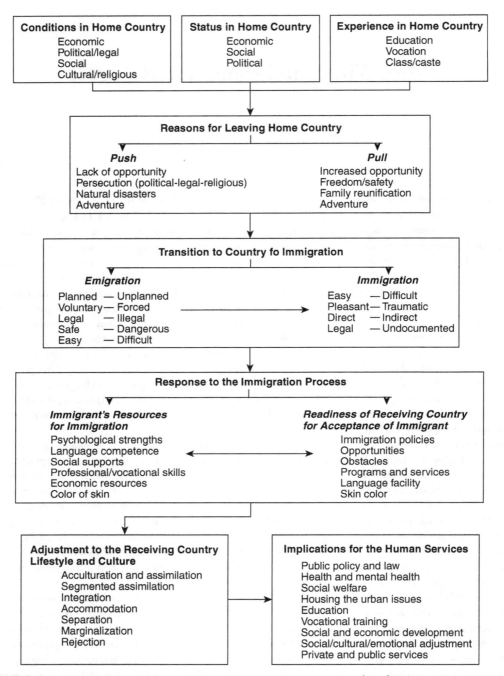

FIGURE 10.1: Model or framework for the immigrant experience. From Segal, U. A. (2002). *A framework for immigration: Asians in the United States.* New York: Columbia University Press, p. 4.

of the color of their skin, the accent with which they speak, or the clothing they wear.

Despite difficulties, overt and institutionalized discrimination, and sometimes few apparent resources,

most migrants stay in their chosen countries, establishing themselves and raising children. Although host countries may cause cultural conflicts, erect language barriers, or marginalize newcomers, they still offer migrants more opportunities and freedom than the homelands do, and immigrants draw on all their tangible and intangible resources for survival. Sometimes these are insufficient for successful adaptation, and social workers may need to intervene across the spectrum of modalities, from policy development and implementation to the direct delivery of services.

WORKING WITH IMMIGRANT AND REFUGEE COMMUNITIES

Despite a person-in-environment orientation, social work has a tendency to address immigrant and refugee issues from a micro perspective. It behooves service providers to also assess whether mezzo-level changes are needed in existing organizations to provide adequate services in ethnic communities or at the macro level of policy implementation. Policies on social and family welfare, housing, education, physical and mental health, and criminal justice substantially color the daily lives of immigrants, as they do for all citizens of a nation.

Immigration and Immigrant Policy

Immigration policies determine who is let into a country and under what circumstances, while immigrant policies identify the programs and opportunities to which immigrants have access in the host nation. Social workers may be involved in policy formulation, advocacy, and implementation that is equitable and maximizes benefits to the host country as well as the immigrant. They will likely influence immigrant policies as advocates for access to services available to all citizens as well as for programs that facilitate social and economic integration.

Community Practice

As one follows migration patterns, it becomes clear that there are trajectories of movement from one nation to another, and as networks develop, minority immigrant communities are established in the host country. Local residents are often unprepared for the entry groups of newcomers, particularly those who appear different from themselves. Community social workers can minimize xenophobia and enhance integration efforts by educating both the new and long-term residents about each other and by facilitating dialogue. Schools are often effective vehicles for accessing and uniting groups because they draw all communities through common interests in children's education. Outreach efforts mobilizing communities through neighborhood associations and services can enhance integration at the grassroots level.

Administration and Program Development

Administrators and program developers in social service agencies may implement policy with sensitivity to immigrants and develop programs of immigrant integration at the local level. Collaborations across organizations and services within communities are effective in identifying immigrant needs and developing or tailoring programs to address those that are most pressing. Increased consciousness of the immigrant experience and economic, sociocultural, and psychological issues associated with translocation can help create a milieu appropriate for immigrants. Periodic in-service training that focuses on understanding the changing demographic landscape of organizations and related issues will make workers aware of immigrants, their effects on other groups in the environment, and the latter's level of acceptance of this new population.

Direct Services

Cultural competency is essential in working with immigrant populations and requires understanding both the culture of the country of origin and the immigration experience (Chan, 2003), including the circumstances leading to departure. All people who migrate, willingly or not, leave behind much that is familiar—culture, language, environment, climate, family, friends, social system, norms of behavior, and so on. Women in particular often follow husbands, having to work harder than their spouses to reestablish social and professional networks (Salaff & Greve, 2004). Furthermore, regardless of a nation's willingness to accept these new arrivals (immigration debates indicate substantial divisions), much in the host country is strange and bewildering and traditional support systems are inaccessible.

When immigrants are able to cope psychologically with the stresses of relocating, they are more likely to be successful in adaptation. Without sufficient economic access, social and emotional support, and perhaps therapy, they may fail to find the immigration experience satisfactory, resenting their lives in the new land, pining for the familiarity of their homeland, and even exhibiting socially inappropriate or dysfunctional behaviors (Segal, 2002). Lum (2003) proposes a four-component framework for cultural competence: *cultural awareness*, or cognizance of one's own life experiences and contact with other cultures, with a conscious assessment of these in forming personal biases; *knowledge acquisition*, or learning about other diverse groups' demographic characteristics, culture, experience of oppression, and unique strengths and critically evaluating that knowledge; *skill development*, or tempering social work intervention patterns with acquired knowledge of cultural diversity and self-assessment, perhaps developing nontraditional skills appropriate to client culture; and finally, *inductive learning*, or learning based on the knowledge and experience emerging from the preceding components. Practitioners should educate others in cultural competency.

Developing Professional Relationships

In client systems not of the dominant society, several issues confound effective service provision and intervention.

Part of providing interventions for immigrant and refugee families is removing barriers between the family and the social workers. A number of barriers (Figure 10.2) prevent the use of mainstream services as well as the services of anyone outside the immediate or extended family. The more significant barriers include the following:

1. It may be culturally unacceptable to accept strangers' assistance. Help from someone outside the family unit can be a source of shame and guilt, resulting in significant resistance to help provided by social workers.

2. A number of communication differences may exist between the social worker and the client. Language itself may be a major barrier, and more subtle differences may exist in the use of nonverbal cues and an understanding of topics of taboo. These can work in concert to erect significant barriers to communication and interpretation.

3. A tremendous value is placed on the privacy of the family, and regardless of the pressures the family experiences, it colludes in silence to prevent outsiders from inspecting and intervening in its matters.

4. There may be a general mistrust of authority by many immigrants and refugees who enter the United States and other Western countries from nations where freedom is limited and oppression is prevalent. Because of fears of exposure and the ramifications of expressing needs or weaknesses, including a fear of deportation, many immigrants and refugees do not disclose the depth or range of adjustment problems they experience.

Resistance, communication barriers, personal and family background, and ethnic community identity (Lum, 1992) are exacerbated by the experiences of many immigrants and refugees, who closely guard

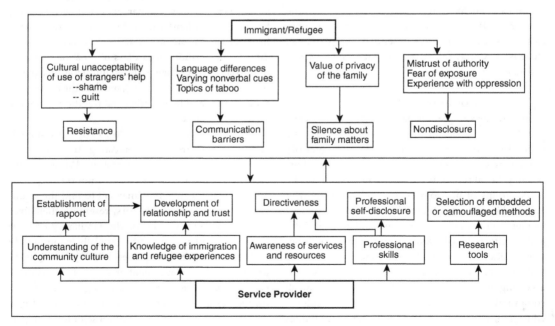

FIGURE 10.2: Working with immigrants and refugees. Adapted from Segal, U. A. (2002). *A framework for immigration: Asians in the United States.* New York: Columbia University Press, p. 377.

information because of fear (perhaps unfounded) of exposure, past experience with oppression, and mistrust of authority. Many immigrants and most refugees arrive from nations in which they do not have the freedom of speech or of choice. The mistrust of authority, including the possibility of deportation, can erect formidable barriers to open communication. Along with ameliorating these issues through good rapport, service providers can establish credibility and expert authority, effectively use directiveness, and engage in appropriate self-disclosure.

All practitioners must be alert to conditions that can hinder working relationships with immigrants and refugees. Interventions, services, and resources offered with awareness of their implications for other cultures will enable practitioners to explain the process with relevance to these clients. When service-provider credibility, rapport, and sensitivity are established, most immigrants and refugees will benefit from assistance. Prudent self-disclosure must be used to increase credibility and authority, while understanding must be used to develop the relationship.

Mainstream practitioners who use translators may find more resistance in establishing trust because the immigrant must contend with two unfamiliar people. In addition, it is essential that the translator be *(1)* bicultural and able to understand the nuances of both the immigrant culture and host-country culture; *(2)* knowledgeable about social work, its values, and approaches; and *(3)* able to translate both language and context. Though a bilingual, bicultural person from the immigrant's community can be an effective translator, client concerns about privacy can sabotage such an individual's usefulness. Clients often bring their children (frequently rather young ones) to serve as translators because they can be trusted. This results in parent–child role reversals, making the child the cultural broker in negotiating the system and placing undue responsibility on the child, perhaps adding to the stresses in the family.

Issues facing immigrants and refugees are substantially greater for newer arrivals; however, difficulties may persist through the lives of the first generation of immigrants. Cultural and social conflicts often emerge between first- and second-generation immigrants, bringing these populations to the attention of service providers at another point of the immigrant experience. With increasing focus on the integration of new arrivals, there is a tendency to overlook people who have been in a country for several years yet have problems that are different from the problems of native populations. Nevertheless, as practitioners begin to work with particular immigrant and refugee groups, they will develop an appreciation of the immigrant and refugee experience, hone their skills of assessment to recognize the unique experiences of these populations, and identify appropriate intervention techniques in delivering services.

Assessment and Intervention

In working with immigrants and refugees, assessment and intervention processes must occur both within the context of the host country as well as in the context of the immigration and cross-cultural experience. Hence, although behaviors that are exhibited should be assessed for appropriateness, it is also necessary that the service provider determine whether appropriateness is culturally bound. Level of involvement of the family and the community may also differ based on cultural background, and high levels of involvement could represent either healthy interdependence or dysfunction.

In assessments, some behaviors are universally unacceptable (e.g., stealing another person's property); however, others are idiosyncratic to particular societies. A common point of divergence in behavior between, for example, people born in the United States and many immigrants is the use of eye contact. In several nations, those who are younger, subordinate, or female are not permitted to make or sustain eye contact with those who are older, superior, or male. In the United States, such behavior is associated with being shifty or engaging in avoidance. It is then the responsibility of the worker to *(1)* observe the behavior, *(2)* understand it in light of the client's cultural norms, *(3)* determine if it is necessary that the client change the behavior because it is essential for survival in this society, *(4)* work with the client in understanding why it is essential that this pattern of behavior be changed, and *(5)* help the client deal with the dissonance associated with changing patterns of behavior, including the meaning these changes may have for others in the client's community. Thus, not only must social workers help individuals change their behavior, understand the host-country culture, and negotiate the system, they must also help them cope with the greater ramifications of these interventions in their community group.

Service Utilization

Extant literature suggests that immigrants underutilize social services (Chen, Jo, & Donnell, 2004), and once refugees have become self-sufficient and can support themselves, most move away from public assistance. After initial struggles in adjustment, many immigrants and refugees establish an acceptable pattern and quality of life. Areas of sociocultural change (particularly gender-role relationships) start emerging early in the immigrant experience, but families attempt to address these by themselves. Additional crises emerge when family expectations and intercultural and intergenerational differences threaten long-established traditions. Social service providers have interpreted lack of service use as indicative of personal strengths and high levels of adjustment, but this may only be evidence of familial privacy (Segal, 2002).

Academia

Several disciplines point to a gap between academics and practitioners, and though service providers have been slow to address immigrant and refugee concerns, social work academics and researchers may have been even slower. With the ease of transportation and communication coupled with the declining labor force in many developed nations and the rising population in developing countries, migration is not only inevitable, it is essential. It is time that social work academics recognize the growing impact of immigration movements and educate practitioners and the profession through training and research.

SERVICES FOR IMMIGRANT AND REFUGEE COMMUNITIES

There is a tendency among several immigrant and refugee groups to rely only on themselves and to minimize the use of the supportive services that are available in mainstream society. When they do have the resources to cope with their difficulties, minimization of professional support services is a strength. On the other hand, because of the tendency toward privacy, family loyalty, group sense, and issues of shame, there is an aversion to accessing even the immigrant and refugee communities themselves for assistance. Because problems are not visible to mainstream social services, service providers fail to reach out and educate these populations regarding available support options.

Thus, needs are not met by mainstream social services because many immigrants and refugees believe that the mainstream culture does not understand them, and they do not trust the natives because of common patterns of discrimination or paternalism. Hence, individuals within the family and the family itself may be extremely needy, unhealthy, or dysfunctional yet seek little external support, and social

services in turn may feel that there is no need because these groups do not express it.

Outreach and educational efforts must encourage the utilization of services that serve as surrogates for the extended family in providing support and guidance to individuals and families when their physical, financial, social, and emotional resources are insufficient. Ongoing debates continue about who should be the service providers for ethnic minorities. There is disagreement about whether ethnic services best meet the needs of their own community or whether services provided by more inclusive mainstream organizations are more effective. Furthermore, there is discussion about whether programs and services should be culture specific, whether similarities or differences should establish the foundation of service delivery, and whether the theory that drives intervention, the intervention itself, methods of evaluating effectiveness, and research methods should be adapted based on the culture of the target population.

In the absence of perceived cultural awareness on the part of service providers, especially in sensitive areas such as money management, family discord, and limited language proficiency, immigrants and refugees are more likely to forego existing services. Thus, whether or not there is a qualitative difference between immigrant and refugee service organizations and organizations that provide services to immigrants and refugees as part of a larger mission, perceptions of them differ in the community. Though immigrants and refugees may even agree that both types of organizations may be equally competent, the level of comfort they report is higher for organizations that target their groups.

CONCLUDING COMMENTS

Mainstream social service providers should recognize that the absence of immigrants and refugees among their caseloads does not necessarily mean a lack of need in these populations. In the long run, it behooves host-country social services and society in general to extend assistance to these new immigrants, whose numbers continue to grow. As micro- and mezzo-level social work services begin addressing immigrant and refugee concerns, it becomes important to focus also on macro-level social policies that may affect immigrants and refugees. Clearly immigrant and refugee policies have significant implications for who enters the nation and under what conditions, but all social policies can affect these groups as much as they affect the native population. Service providers must ensure that immigrants and refugees are aware of the rights and opportunities provided by the range of public policies and that they avail themselves of the resources they may need to function adequately. Furthermore, service providers at the micro and macro levels may need to include an awareness of immigrant and refugee needs in their advocacy and lobbying efforts as they seek to influence legislators and policy makers.

Immigrants and refugees worldwide constitute extremely diverse populations, and underlying the challenges of working with immigrants and refugees is a far-reaching xenophobia both of the immigrants and by them. It is difficult to assess who should be responsible for ameliorating difficulties—is it the host or the self-invited newcomer? For any immigrant community, it is a long road from the country of origin. The physical distance may be great, but the social, psychological, and emotional distance is always greater. Nevertheless, the human condition and its similarities bind people together to a greater extent than most of us tend to accept. Regardless of social norms, culture, religion, or language, all people have the same desires for health and the ability to provide for their families. All people experience joy, fear, pain, hope, despair, and the entire range of emotions. All are vulnerable, need other human beings, and are influenced by environmental factors.

For immigrants, as for all people, much depends on the personal resources they possess, but even more important is the readiness of the receiving country to accept immigrants and their descendents. Immigration policies may reflect the interests of the nation in allowing entry to certain groups of people; however, it is the opportunities and obstacles that immigrants and their offspring encounter daily that affect adjustment and mutual acceptance. In today's global village, migration is expected to continue to increase. Immigrants and host nations must make a conscious effort to adapt to each other—it is neither the exclusive responsibility of the host nation nor of the immigrant, and social workers, with their focus on the intersection of the person and the environment, are ideally suited to be brokers across this divide.

REFERENCES

Chan, S. (2003). Psychological issues of Asian Americans. In P. Bronstein & K. Quina (Eds.), *Teaching gender and multicultural awareness: Resources for the psychology classroom* (pp. 179–193). Washington, DC: American Psychological Association.

Chen, R. K., Jo, S-J., & Donnell, C. M. (2004). Enhancing the rehabilitation counseling process: Understanding the obstacles to Asian Americans' utilization of services.

Journal of Applied Rehabilitation Counseling, 35(1), 29–35.

Lum, D. (2003). *Culturally competent practice: A framework for understanding diverse groups and justice issues*. Pacific Grove, CA: Brooks/Cole.

Lum, D. (1992). *Social work practice with people of color*. Pacific Grove, CA: Brooks Cole.

Segal, U. A. (2002). *A framework for immigration: Asians in the United States*. New York: Columbia University Press.

ADDITIONAL RESOURCES

Balgopal, P. R. (Ed.). (2000). *Social work practice with immigrants and refugees*. New York: Columbia University Press.

Chang-Muy, F., & Congress, P. E. (Eds.). (2008). *Social work with immigrants and refugees: Legal issues, clinical skills, and advocacy*. New York: Springer.

Fong, R. (Ed.). (2004). *Culturally competent practice with immigrant and refugee children and families*. New York: Guilford Press.

Forced Migration Online (FMO). University of Oxford, Department of International Development. www.forcedmigration.org.

Lacroix, M. (2006). Social work with asylum seekers in Canada: The case for social justice. *International Social Work*, 49(1): 19–28.

Hajdukowski-Ahmed, M., Khanlou, N., & Moussa, H. (2008). *Not born a refugee woman: Contesting identities, rethinking practices*. Oxford: Berghahn Books.

Hayes, D., & Humphries, B. (2004). *Social work, immigration and asylum: Debates, dilemmas and ethical issues for social work and social care practice*. London: Jessica Kingsley.

Humphries, B. (2004). An unacceptable role for social work: Implementing immigration policy. *British Journal of Social Work*, 34, 93–107.

International Migration Review. www.wiley.com/bw/journal.asp?ref=0197-9183.

International Organization for Migration (IOM). www.iom.int.

Jansen, S., & Lofving, S. (2009). *Struggles for home: Violence, hope and the movement of people*. Oxford: Berghahn Books.

Journal of Immigrant and Refugee Studies. www.tandf.co.uk/journals/journal.asp?issn=1556-2948&linktype=5.

Migration Policy Institute (MPI). www.migrationinformation.org.

Nash, M., Wong, J., & Trlin, A. (2006). Civic and social integration: A new field of social work practice with immigrants, refugees and asylum seekers. *International Social Work*, 49(3), 345–363.

National Association of Social Workers (NASW). www.socialworkers.org/resources/abstracts/abstracts/immigrants.asp.

New York Times topics: Immigration and emigration. http://
topics.nytimes.com/topics/reference/timestopics/
subjects/i/immigration_and_refugees/index.html.

Potocki-Tripodi, M. (2002). *Best practices for social work
with refugees and immigrants*. New York: Columbia
University Press.

Sakamoto, I. (2007). A critical examination of immigrant
acculturation: Toward an anti-oppressive social work
model with immigrant adults in a pluralistic society.
British Journal of Social Work, 37(3), 515–535.

Salaff, J. W., & Greve, A. (2004). Can women's social networks migrate? *Women's Studies International Forum,
27*(2), 149–162.

US Citizen and Immigration Services. www.uscis.gov/
portal/site/uscis.

US Committee for Refugees and Immigrants.
www.refugees.org.

William, C., Soydan, H., & Johnson, M. (1998). *Social work
and minorities: European perspectives*. London:
Routledge.

11

International Adoption

KAREN SMITH ROTABI

Intercountry adoption (ICA) as it is known today dates back to late 1940s, when children orphaned during World War II were adopted by families in other nations. What began as a relatively uncommon practice grew in frequency in the 1980s and 1990s and surged at the millennium, resulting in a quiet migration (Selman, 2002). It is estimated that nearly one million children departed from their home countries to adoptive placements worldwide between the 1940s and 2010 (Selman, 2009). Families in the United States have adopted at least half of these children, and this country has become known as the Adoption Nation (Pertman, 2001).

As a phenomenon, ICA is linked to later marriages and lower fertility rates in industrialized nations and poverty, inadequate social care systems, and the shame of illegitimacy in less developed nations. It underscores a number of ethical concerns ranging from social justice and human rights considerations to sound child welfare interventions (Hollingsworth, 2003). ICA often involves unique trans-racial and cross-cultural family development considerations that take place in a globalized context in which issues of poverty and wealth can create complicated experiences for the families affected by ICA, with the actors ranging from the birth family to the child, the adoptive family, and social workers.

Many internationally adopted children have experienced highly positive outcomes, especially compared with children who languish in institutions and suffer from malnutrition, psychological problems, and other health conditions that inhibit sound growth and development. However, one must be cautious about viewing ICA as a viable large-scale child welfare intervention, because the number of children affected is relatively small compared with the millions of orphaned and vulnerable children worldwide. Also, younger and more desirable children are most frequently adopted rather than older children or children with disabilities. Most children sent for adoption throughout the world in recent history were quite young, and the pursuit of such adoptees has created in some instances a black market for babies and young children (Kapstein, 2003; Smolin, 2004, 2006).

A BRIEF HISTORY: BEGINNING WITH WAR

The modern history of ICA dates back to World War II, and conflict is a common thread across many ICA-sending nations—that is, nations that provide children for ICA. From 1948 to 1953, 5800 European children were adopted by American citizens. European children were also adopted within the continent; for example, 70,000 Finnish children were adopted by Swedes during this period, and Sweden remains a significant receiving nation (Selman, 2009). Also, Spain is a very active receiving nation today.

Also at this time, a few Americans were adopting Asian children from Japan and China, but it was the Korean conflict in the early 1950s that prompted the first significant ICA surge from that region. In response, the US government passed legislation allowing war orphans and children fathered by American soldiers to enter the nation under new immigration rights (Bergquist, Vonk, Kim, & Feit, 2007). To date, well over 100,000 Korean children have been sent for adoption, mainly to the United States and Canada. Until 1995, South Korea was the single largest source of children worldwide despite its low birth rate and growing economy (Selman, 2009). This trend is credited largely to the stigma of illegitimacy in Korea, which dates back to Confucius and deeply engrained beliefs about bloodlines and paternal acknowledgment (Bergquist et al., 2007). ICA is controversial in South Korea, and there are signs that the nation is moving toward eventual cessation of the practice, but the long-term plan is currently uncertain.

The Vietnam War also resulted in several thousand children being adopted from Southeast Asia, culminating in the dramatic Operation Babylift in April 1975 during which several thousand children were evacuated during the fall of Saigon and subsequently sent for adoption (Bergquist, 2009). After the war, adoptions largely ceased for a time but resumed in the early 1990s. Then, under international scrutiny for adoption irregularities, Vietnam closed ICA from 2003 to 2004 to implement reform, and corrupt government officials were imprisoned. The system reopened only to close again in 2008 due to child abandonment fraud and a great deal of pressure from the US Department of State.

Cambodia and Guatemala, which also have experienced prolonged conflict in recent years, had surges in ICA where thousands of healthy young children were sent for adoption. Both countries were later effectively closed following findings of serious adoption fraud (Rotabi, 2008). Illegal payments to birth mothers, coercion, and falsified documents have been at the root of problems in both countries (Bunkers, Groza, & Lauer, 2009; Rotabi & Bunkers, 2008; Rotabi, Morris, & Weil, 2008). In 2008, evidence of child theft began to emerge in Guatemala, and law enforcement has been engaged in investigations of such allegations, specifically focusing on several children now residing with adoptive families in the United States (Rotabi, 2009).

At the end of the Cold War, adoption activity increased dramatically in former Soviet nations, including Romania, Russia, and Ukraine, as poverty and postconflict reconstruction resulted in an opportunity for adoption. Though political and economic instability sets the stage for a surge in adoption, this surge does not always occur. For example, the recent conflict in the Middle East is not expected to result in the sending of large numbers of Muslim children, mainly for cultural and religious reasons. These include issues of traditional societies, such as tribal ties, as well as Islamic Sharia law. What the West calls *adoption* is more limited and ultimately is viewed as a guardianship (called *kefala*) instead.

Romania has played a particularly important role in ICA history. Under the oppressive reproductive policies of Romanian dictator Ceausescu, which forbade birth control and required women to have at least five children (Albrecht, 2006), thousands of children were abandoned in institutions, often in abhorrent conditions. When the Iron Curtain fell, the world learned of these children and the result was a rapid surge in adoptions of Romanian children, numbering

10,000 in 1990 and 1991 alone (Selman, 2009). Problems soon followed, however. Many of the children had severe attachment disorders, and some were diagnosed with reactive attachment disorder, which didn't improve significantly despite adoptive parents' efforts. There were several well-publicized stories of poor placements of children with serious attachment disorders resulting in adoption disruption and dissolution, and in rare but notorious cases, extreme child abuse and even homicide. Romania declared a self-imposed adoption moratorium in 2001. This was in reaction to the aforementioned problems as well as outside political pressure during the nation's bid to enter into the European Union, which does not come as a surprise given the more cautious attitude of some Europeans toward ICA (Albrect, 2006).

Although there was a brief slowdown in ICA during the late 1990s, it surged again at the millennium and peaked in 2004. There has been a radical decline since that time (Selman, 2009). In the final years of the surge and up to 2008, the three most frequent sending nations were China, Russia, and Guatemala. The decline in these particular nations is due to a variety of reasons. The slowdown in Guatemala is due mainly to international concerns about child sales and theft (Rotabi, 2008; Rotabi & Bunkers, 2008; Rotabi, Morris, & Weil, 2008). China, on the other hand, began to place more stringent standards on prospective families in 2007 in addition to giving domestic adoptions precedence over international adoptions. As a result, their process slowed considerably and now special needs children are those most available for ICA.

Russia's slowdown, which began in 2005, has been attributed to agency reaccreditation and also to the negative beliefs and attitudes of Russian citizens toward ICA, which have resulted from sensationalistic press accounts of inappropriate or even illegal adoption placements, mainly in the United States. Such stories include a case in 2008, when a young Russian adoptee died from heat exposure because he was left in a parked car in the summer heat, and then a case in 2010 where a young adoptee was sent back from the United States to Moscow unaccompanied with nothing more than a note of explanation claiming that the boy was deeply disturbed (Rotabi & Heine, 2010). In addition, there was a highly publicized case that involved a pedophile adopting and abusing a five-year-old girl named Masha. Details of her abuse and the sale of her image in an Internet pornography scheme are documented in US congressional testimony.

THE HAGUE CONVENTION FOR INTERCOUNTRY ADOPTION

The Hague Convention for Intercountry Adoption (HCIA) has also contributed to the ICA slowdown. This international agreement dating back to 1993 was signed by approximately eighty nations and prohibits the sale, theft, and trafficking of children under the guise of ICA. The HCIA requires sending nations to ensure that ICA serves the best interests of the child. Specifically, the sending nation must *(1)* make an active effort to keep the child within the family and kinship group, or, if this is not possible, *(2)* attempt to place the child domestically. Once these options have been explored, the child may be *(3)* freed for ICA. When there is evidence of child sales or theft, the sending nation is expected to intervene with legal and human services (Rotabi, 2008). For more about the HCIA, see www.hcch.net and www.hagueevaluation.com.

The HCIA is consistent with the United Nations Convention on the Rights of the Child (1989), which includes a number of articles related to adoption. Pertinent articles are summarized in Table 11.1.

Though not without criticism related to practical implementation (Bartholet, 2007), the HCIA has generally been welcomed by the United Nations Children's Fund (UNICEF) and other international organizations working to strengthen the capacity of child welfare systems and ultimately protect vulnerable children and families.

WHY IS THE CONVENTION NECESSARY? A CASE STUDY

Although there has been good social work practice in ICA, there have also been instances of irregularities, inconsistent law enforcement, and even scandal.

Because families typically pay on average at least US$25,000 during the adoption process, the opportunity for corruption is real, especially in nations where bribery is customary (Rotabi et al., 2008; US Government Accountability Office [GAO], 2005). In impoverished sending nations, birth families are particularly vulnerable to child theft and sales.

Operation Broken Heart was a US federal investigation of Lauryn Galindo and Lynn Devin's adoption business (Seattle Adoptions International), which involved unethical and illegal activities, including bribery, visa fraud, and money laundering (a classic organized-crime activity). The investigation also uncovered sales of children, the disturbing use of unsanitary stash houses for waiting children, and other unsavory activities required to carry out illegal sales and trafficking of children under the guise of ICA.

Galindo traveled to Cambodia, where she claimed to engage in humanitarian work, including ICA. She claimed to be an adoption facilitator but was not actually a trained child welfare professional. Devin operated the adoption agency from her personal residence. Together, the sisters successfully developed an international child trafficking scheme that placed approximately 700 children with adoptive families.

The investigating officer described the activities of the sisters as follows. Devin operated the US side of the adoption business while Galindo would facilitate the Cambodian side of the process using her contacts in the Cambodian government, to whom she admitted paying what she called *tips* (i.e., bribes). In this process, a false paper trail was created, the children's true identities were erased, and the children were laundered, so to speak (Smolin, 2004, 2006). With new names and histories, the information was placed

---

TABLE 11.1. SUMMARY OF RELATED ARTICLES OF THE UN CONVENTION ON THE RIGHTS OF THE CHILD

Article 7	Every child has the right to a name and nationality and to know and be cared for by her or his parents.
Article 8	Every child has a right to preserve her or his identity, including nationality, name, and family relations.
Article 9	Children cannot be separated from their parents against their will, except when competent authorities determine it to be in the child's best interests.
Article 11	Governments have a responsibility to protect children against illegal separation or adoption.
Article 20	Children who are deprived of their family must receive alternative care with due regard to the child's ethnic, religious, cultural, and linguistic background.
Article 21	Governments have a responsibility to ensure that all rules and processes involving adoption are respected and to ensure that there are protections against selling or kidnapping children.

on falsified birth certificates to obtain Cambodian passports, and visa fraud occurred when the unsuspecting adoptive parents immigrated the children as orphans.

The investigation revealed that Galindo collaborated with a number of Cambodians who recruited poor birth families for child sales. Recruiters told prospective birth mothers of the wonderful life awaiting their children in the United States and showed pictures of previously adopted children living happily with their new families. Some birth families were led to believe that they could regularly visit their children and even reclaim them at any time. Families were paid US$20 to US$200 and a bag of rice. Recruiters received US$50 commission for each child secured and worked on contingency—a practice associated with irregular adoptions.

Adoptive families were instructed to carry US$3,500 in crisp hundred-dollar bills when they traveled to Cambodia to pick up their children; they were told that the money would be used as donations for humanitarian purposes in Cambodia. Large groups of parents would travel to Cambodia to pick up the children, handing the cash directly to Galindo. The money did not go to children's services but rather funded a lavish lifestyle—over a million dollars' worth of assets were seized by the US government due to tax fraud. Galindo and Devin both served brief prison sentences because their activities were not covered under US human trafficking laws and sentencing was based on lesser crimes, including tax evasion.

IN BALANCE: A CASE STUDY OF GOOD INTERCOUNTRY ADOPTION PRACTICES

A sibling group of five entered the child protection system in the United Kingdom as foster children removed from serious physical abuse. The children, ranging in ages from late adolescence to five years old, were British citizens, as were their parents, who had originally emigrated from Kenya. When it became clear that the UK child protection authority was going to terminate parental rights for the youngest two children to be freed for adoption, the case was complicated by concerns about the rights of the children to a kinship placement because all of the extended family lived in other nations. The children had relatives in Kenya as well as the United States, including paternal grandparents and an interested aunt. All three nations involved, the United Kingdom, the United States, and Kenya, honor the HCIA, which prioritizes kinship care. When the US-based aunt applied for

a kinship adoption, the UK government responded to this possibility with caution because of the complexities of such a case requiring thoughtful international social work collaboration. Upon negotiation, a US social worker carried out the home study, and the entire family, including the birth mother, actively collaborated with the UK child welfare services in making kinship adoption a reality.

In time, the two youngest children were adopted by their aunt in the United States and all processes met the criteria of the HCIA, including work through Central Authority networks, approved providers, financial transparency, and adoption best practices (e.g., appropriate prospective parent training, home study assessments, and so on). On the US side of the process, an HCIA-accredited agency was involved in the placement activities, and appropriate follow-up care was provided to the family as the children transitioned from the United Kingdom to the United States. This follow-up care included postplacement reports detailing the children's adjustment to their new family life.

PERSISTENT ISSUES FOR SOCIAL WORKERS TO CONSIDER

The previous case is an example of good practice between the United Kingdom and United States, specifically for relative adoption placement between two nations with relatively consistent child welfare systems. However, just because a nation has signed and ratified the HCIA does not mean its processes are transparent and just. For example, Smolin (2004, 2006) has documented serious problems with India's adoption system, including child trafficking. In the absence of government response to the problem, a few individuals and groups have created websites and blogs about adoption fraud. Parents for Ethical Adoption Reform (http://www.pear-now.org/) and Ethica (www.ethicanet.org/) are two of many grassroots resources designed to inform prospective families about the risks of ICA.

A significant number of ICA nations have not signed or ratified the HCIA and thus are not bound by it. For example, Russia has signed the HCIA but has not been enforcing it and is known to have serious graft and corruption problems, including allegations that organized crime has been involved in ICA (Riben, 2007). Also, most African nations also have not signed the HCIA, and a recent surge in Ethiopian adoptions places that nation at risk (Rotabi, 2010), especially given the large number of children available and the history of human sales and trafficking in Africa. Some receiving agencies have begun to focus exclusively on non-HCIA nations because the adoption process is less regulated, and inevitably adoption fraud problems will persist.

INTERCOUNTRY ADOPTION AND SOCIAL WORK PRACTICE

When carried out to the fullest extent, direct practice with children and families involved in ICA includes a variety of activities in both the sending and receiving nations, as outlined in Table 11.2.

Social workers carry out assessments for both sides of the adoption process. Birth-parent summaries documenting the child's social and medical history are completed for full disclosure to the prospective family. Also, home studies determine whether a prospective family meets the social and legal criteria for child placement, including motivation to adopt and ability to parent. This requires the involvement of two different human service systems and social work practices in two different countries. The bridges in this process are the ICA organizations, the child welfare and adoption authorities of each nation, and immigration services. Often social workers are brokers in this process, which

TABLE 11.2. IDEAL INTERCOUNTRY ADOPTION ACTIVITIES

Sending Nation: Core Social Work Practices	Receiving Nation: Core Social Work Practices
Note: All activities that lead to a decision to release child to ICA are supposed to either support biological families in caring for their child OR attempt to place a child in a domestic care situation including adoption (in country) prior to the ICA decision.	
Unbiased birth-parent counseling when the parents are known and ethical relinquishment services	Prospective parent counseling about and for adoption; may be in the form of basic information
OR	
Appropriate child abandonment procedures to ensure the child is not stolen or sold and is a bona fide abandonment case	
Placement assessments to determine a child's placement potential for in-country care or ICA	Placement assessments to determine a prospective family's capacity to adopt as part of the family's home study, which then results in report writing
Birth-parent social and medical history investigation and report writing (based on birth-parent interviews in ideal cases)	
Child institutional care practices, including early childhood and youth interventions to enhance growth and development so that children may be ready for placement transition	Training of prospective families and agency social workers in relevant ICA content, including child development and medical issues as well as country-specific topics and issues of institutionalized children
Training of institution staff in appropriate child care strategies	Provision of support programs for families during the placement process, including training, in order to assist with the transition and follow-up care—including post-placement assessments and reports and referrals as needed
Social service administration of adoption practices (including judicial and immigration requirements) with oversight of ethical relinquishment practices	Social service administration of adoption practices (including judicial and immigration requirements) with oversight of ethical placing activities in a transparent system
Documentation of the process and long-term storage of adoption records	Documentation of the process and long-term storage of adoption records

Note: This table indicates what services *should* look like. It is a relatively accurate reflection of services in HCIA sending nations such as China and in HCIA receiving nations such as the US, Canada, and European nations. Some sending nations have not developed adequate services for planning and delivery of ethical adoption protocol. This also applies to some receiving nations.

is typically characterized by bureaucratic paperwork for immigration, long wait times, and in some cases, contingency planning when waiting children become ill or other problems arise. These case management functions intersect with the highly sensitive issues of ethical termination of parental rights or relinquishment (in sending nations) and determination of a family's ability and readiness for child placement (in receiving nations).

Placement activities are complicated by the fact that many children who have languished in institutions have developmental delays and medical problems, some of which are quite profound (Rotabi & Heine, 2010). As a result, adoption social workers may need to provide enhanced services beyond the time of placement. Instead of simply helping receiving families deal with the transition of a new child, they may be asked to provide follow-up social services or referrals tailored to a child's special needs, including both emotional and medical care. All of this work must be done with a clear service plan that has allowances for adoption disruptions and dissolutions.

Though there are models of good practice, at this time clear and consistent strategies of ICA placement support over sustained periods and across the child's developmental trajectory have not been modeled consistently throughout the United States or any other nation. Also of concern, birth families in sending countries typically receive little or no support following relinquishment even though they, too, face difficult transitions of loss and grief. It is important for social workers to create and carry out ethical practices to protect these vulnerable families.

CONCLUSION

Social work as a professional discipline has been anchored in child welfare and human rights since its inception. Child adoption is an important area of social work practice that has been expanded to include ICA in a globalized world in which people are communicating and moving from place to place with greater ease. Undoubtedly there are many families and children who have benefited from ICA, and regardless of the bad news about adoption fraud and human rights abuses, we must embrace the fact that ICA is a legitimate manner in which to build a family. However, there are inherent problems when a wealthy and industrialized nation receives children from a less developed nation with multiple vulnerabilities related to poverty and corruption. Combine these issues with pressures of family displacement due to conflict and natural disasters, and a number of practice issues

emerge, ranging from policy practice, such as developing appropriate administrative polices to enhance human services and limit fraud, to direct practice and placement activities that support birth and placement families for a smooth and ethical transition.

The HCIA and the UN Convention on the Rights of the Child are important international policies from which country-specific legal codes have been developed (Roby & Ife, 2009; Link, chapter 68 this volume). Social workers are well suited to respond to these standards given the profession's commitment to ethics and professional capacity in social service administration, case management, counseling, family support, and psychosocial education. It is particularly important to begin with a greater focus on birth families and family preservation first, as required by the HCIA, to ensure ethical adoptions.

REFERENCES

Albrecht, S. (2006). *Intercountry adoption: A Swiss perspective.* (Unpublished master's thesis). University of Cape Town, South Africa.

Bartholet, E. (2007, November 4). Slamming the door on adoption. *Washington Post.* Retrieved November 5, 2007, from www.washingtonpost.com/wp-dyn/content/article/2007/11/02/AR2007110201782.html.

Bergquist, K. J. S. (2009). Operation Babylift or Babyabduction? Implications of the HagueConvention on the humanitarian evacuation and "rescue" of children. *International Social Work, 52*(5), 621–633.

Bergquist, K. J. S., Vonk, M. E., Kim, D. S., & Feit, M. D. (2007). *International Korean adoption: A fifty-year history of policy and practice.* Binghamton, NY: Haworth Press.

Bunkers, K. M., Groza, V., & Lauer, D. (2009). International adoption and child protection in Guatemala: A case of the tail wagging the dog. *International Social Work, 52*(5), 649–660.

Hollingsworth, L. D. (2003). International adoption among families in the United States: Considerations of social justice. *Social Work, 48*(2), 209–217.

Kapstein, E. B. (2003). The baby trade. *Foreign Affairs, 82*(6), 115–125.

Pertman, A. (2001). *Adoption nation: How the adoption revolution is transforming America.* New York: Basic Books.

Riben, M. (2007). *The stork market: America's multi-billion dollar unregulated adoption industry.* Dayton, NJ: Advocate.

Roby, J. L., & Ife, J. (2009). Human rights, politics, and intercountry adoption: An examination of two sending countries. *International Social Work, 52*(5), 661–671.

Rotabi, K. S. (2010, June). From Guatemala to Ethiopia: Shifts in intercountry adoption leaves Ethiopia vulnerable for child sales and other unethical practices. *Social*

Work and Society News Magazine. Available from www. socmag.net/?p=615.

Rotabi, K. S. (2009, August). Guatemala City: Hunger protests amid allegations of child kidnapping and adoption fraud. *Social Work and Society News Magazine*. Retrievable from www.socmag.net/?p=540.

Rotabi, K. S. (2008, Jan/Feb). New intercountry adoption requirements. *Immigration Law Today*, 12–15.

Rotabi, K. S., & Bunkers, K. M. (2008, November). Intercountry adoption reform based on the Hague Convention on Intercountry Adoption: An update on Guatemala in 2008. *Social Work and Society News Magazine*. Retrievable from www.socmag. net/?tag=adoption.

Rotabi, K. S., & Heine, T. M. (2010). Commentary on Russian child adoption incidents: Implications for global policy and practice. *Journal of Global Social Work Practice*. Available from www.globalsocialwork. org/vol3no2/Rotabi.html.

Rotabi, K. S., Morris, A. W., & Weil, M. O. (2008). International child adoption in a post-conflict society: A multi-systemic assessment of Guatemala. *Journal of Intergroup Relations*, *XXXIV*(2), 9–41.

Selman, P. (2009). The rise and fall of intercountry adoption in the 21st century. *International Social Work*, 52(5), 575–594.

Selman, P. (2002). Intercountry adoption in the new millennium: The "quiet migration" revisited. *Population Research and Policy Review*, 21(3), 205–225.

Smolin, D. M. (2006). Child laundering: How the intercountry adoption system legitimizes and incentivizes the practices of buying, trafficking, kidnapping, and stealing children. *Wayne Law Review*, 52(113), 113–200.

Smolin, D. M. (2004). Intercountry adoption as child trafficking. *Valparaiso University Law Review*, 39(2), 281–325.

US Government Accountability Office (GAO). (2005). *Foreign affairs: Agencies have improved the intercountry adoption process, but further enhancements are needed*. Publication No. GAO-06-133. Retrieved January 8, 2007, from www.gao.gov/new.items/d06133.pdf.

12

Trauma Counseling

ALLISON ROWLANDS

This chapter explores the concept of trauma and ways in which social workers can intervene. Definitions of traumatic events and some approaches to assisting people who have experienced a traumatic event are discussed. While many professions intervene after traumatic events and provide support for survivors, the contribution of social work is the focus. The impact of traumatic events on children and their development is particularly highlighted. The chapter considers social work intervention along a continuum from individual to community and from a single traumatic event to a large-scale disaster.

WHAT IS TRAUMA AND ITS IMPACT?

A traumatic event is an out-of-the-ordinary experience that involves life-threatening elements, an overwhelming sense of powerlessness, and a change in worldview (Herman, 1992; Raphael, 1986). Traumatic events overwhelm the ordinary systems of care that give people a sense of control, connection, and meaning (Herman, 1992). Experiencing such an event evokes a normal physical and psychological reaction to the strength of the experience. This reaction is to be expected; it is a natural reaction to an abnormal situation (Kanel, 2003; Raphael & Meldrum, 1994). The normalization or educational aspect of therapy is critical in dealing with this reaction.

Potential traumatic events include war, terrorism, natural disaster, suicide, murder, sexual assault, domestic violence, severe childhood abuse and neglect, motor vehicle and workplace accidents, and sudden unexpected deaths. How people respond is influenced, among other things, by their personal vulnerability or resilience (Herman, 1992), the levels of support available, and the nature of their relationship with any victims. Traumatic loss is the loss of a close attachment figure occurring in association with sudden, unexpected, untimely, or otherwise traumatic circumstances of death (Raphael, 1983).

Post-Traumatic Stress Disorder (PTSD) was first included in the diagnostic manual of the American Psychiatric Association (APA) in 1980. It is the most common mental health disorder following exposure to a traumatic event (Norman, 2000). At the time, traumatic events were described as outside the range of usual human experience (APA, 1980). Herman (1992) argues, however, that traumatic events are a common part of human experience, including war, sexual and domestic violence, and child abuse. Certainly for social work in hospitals, family services, child and youth services, and general welfare services, people who have experienced violent and traumatic events frequently receive assistance, whether on a voluntary or involuntary basis.

Reactions to trauma include hyperarousal (startle responses, nightmares, vigilance), intrusion (reliving, reenacting), and constriction (numbing, avoidance, dissociation, inability to plan, loss of feelings of affection or the ability to express them). We now know that neurotransmitters, hormones, cortical areas of the brain, and the nervous system play a much greater role in trauma responses and the development of PTSD than previously understood (James & Gilliland, 2005). Once the danger has passed and the person is safe, the body no longer needs to function on an emergency basis. However, if the stress is prolonged, the nervous system may continue to function as if the emergency were still continuing. Intense and continuous stress can cause permanent physical changes in the brain, which will be referred to later in the chapter with regard to children's traumatic experiences.

A corollary of these reactions is the tendency to disconnect from people, including relationships, groups, and community. Because of the potential for damage to these relationships, researchers and clinicians advocate the importance of social support. Assuring safety and rebuilding trust and a sense of control are critical (Herman, 1992; Raphael, 1986; Silove, 2005). The community therefore has an important role, which can be enacted through such rituals as welcoming returning soldiers or holding memorial services for communities affected by natural disaster. (The community can also be extremely unhelpful, for example in attitudes and legal processes following sexual assault.) This heralds the potential for many effective interventions at the community level that social workers can initiate.

Raphael (2005) cautions that it is a normal reaction to be hyperaroused, to be focused on images, to be fearful of something returning, and to try to be numb and shut out some of the issues. Studies have suggested that in the first month, the acute severe reaction that disables people might be called *acute stress disorder*, and PTSD is frequently diagnosed.

The diagnostic criteria for PTSD are explicit (APA, 2000):

- The occurrence of a severe traumatic event (as defined by society)
- Reexperiencing and intrusive symptoms (flashbacks, nightmares)
- Numbing symptoms
- Arousal symptoms (irritability, sleep disturbances, hyperalertness)

It is generally accepted that natural catastrophes cause less PTSD than human-made acts of trauma, especially when the trauma directly affects the social support system of the family. Examples include the Holocaust, hostage taking, and sexual assault of both children and adults (James & Gilliland, 2005; Raphael, 1986, 2005; Tan, 2009).

The affected person's cognitive processing of the event is how the mind attempts to come to terms with the experience (Raphael & Meldrum, 1994), and the phases of remembering and avoiding continue until the experience is integrated (Marmar & Horowitz, 1988). The recovery environment and social support are vital in assisting recovery.

INTERVENTION PRINCIPLES AND MODELS: FROM INDIVIDUAL TO COMMUNITY

Interventions by social workers in trauma situations span a continuum from direct individual assistance based on crisis intervention principles to in-depth and long-term counseling therapies, intervention with small groups and families, and community development and social action–oriented intervention. Research, particularly participatory action and empowerment research, is also a form of intervention that contributes to the knowledge base while affording an opportunity to include affected people and facilitate the recovery process (Rowlands, 2004). Some of these approaches will be discussed in this section.

Crisis Intervention

Fundamental to an immediate response to people who have experienced a traumatic event is crisis intervention.[1] Crisis intervention has a distinguished history originating in Lindeman's work in the United States in the 1940s (Kanel, 2003). Theoretical models such as psychoanalytic, existential, humanistic, cognitive-behavioral, family system, and strengths approaches have contributed to crisis intervention over time. Kanel's model of crisis intervention builds on this rich history and entails three key components: developing and maintaining rapport, identifying the problem, and coping. Provision of crisis intervention at an appropriate point after a traumatic event could ameliorate more severe post-traumatic stress responses at a later time.

Core interpersonal helping skills[2] are employed in developing rapport. Identifying the problem is the heart of assessment, although assessment is also a continuous process occurring throughout intervention. Identifying the precipitating event entails exploring its meaning for the individual and the subjective distress and impact on functioning. Techniques include statements that are supportive, educational, empowering, or reframing. The third component, coping, addresses coping behavior, including the person's own attempts at coping, the person's own ideas regarding new coping behaviors, and alternative ideas, including group approaches such as support and self-help groups or other appropriate referrals.

Trauma Intervention

Crisis intervention is appropriate immediately following an event and is a time-limited intervention over approximately six weeks. The key considerations in trauma interventions are consistent with crisis intervention, but trauma interventions are not time limited and may often be provided at a considerable time after the event. Key principles are restoring a sense of safety, remembering and mourning, reconnecting, and acknowledging commonality (Herman, 1992). Therapeutic processes include establishing trust, providing education, ensuring social support, and dealing with the trauma itself (Raphael, 2005; Raphael & Meldrum, 1994). Catharsis through the individual helping relationship or a group situation must be paced according to the person's need. The person must have sufficient trust in the helping relationship and must know that the listener can bear it (Herman, 1992; Raphael & Meldrum, 1994). Adequate social support and building on the person's strengths are recognized by key authors, although a more explicit person-in-environment and strengths perspective is seldom articulated—a real contribution that social work can make in this sphere (Rowlands, 2004).

Psychological trauma and bereavement can occur together, such as in the particular circumstances of horrific deaths. Closely allied with a trauma response is grief, whether it involves a traumatic loss or the loss of a sense of safety in the world or relationships. Normal or complicated grief reactions are to be expected and not confused with depression. One expects angry protest, searching and yearning for the lost one, scanning, looking for the lost person, sadness, and mourning (Raphael, 2005). If normal grief does not continue, depression and other behavioral changes can follow, particularly in situations of traumatic loss. Interventions involve working through the circumstances of the death, the cause of the trauma, and the loss (i.e., reviewing the history of the lost relationship and the grief processes).

Therefore, in addition to skilled counseling for those who have experienced a traumatic event or loss, capacity building in the health and social services systems, including adequate training and supervision of workers, is required.

Social Support Interventions

Scaffolding family and social support systems is increasingly recognized as critical in mitigating the impact of trauma experiences (Raphael & Stevens, 2007; Rowlands, 2004; Silove, 2005). For example, after a disaster there should be a focus on reuniting separated families, finding shelter, and ultimately finding a permanent home that is socially and culturally appropriate (Raphael, 2005). In the disaster context, both formal and informal social structures are affected in major ways; therefore, interventions to support social systems are more critical than generally has been understood (Tan, 2009). Common ties, such as neighborhood connections and personal networks that have been destroyed in a disaster, need assistance to be rebuilt, because a person's sense of home, community, and belonging is instrumental in psychological recovery as well as the social recovery of the community.

Social rituals, for example memorials and testimonies, are important to support the process of grieving and make meaning of the traumatic event (Emergency Management Australia, 2004; Raphael, 1986, 2005; Raphael & Stevens, 2007; Silove, 2005). Cultural issues are also paramount, as is the inclusion of local community members in recovery planning, which should be managed by local services as much as possible. Intervening at the community level after a disaster therefore calls for community development strategies as well as social planning and action research, all models of intervention within social work (Rowlands, 2004; Tan & Rowlands, 2008).

Silove (2005) adds further support to the holistic model of trauma intervention when he argues that there is insufficient distinction within the medical framework between common, self-limiting psychological responses to trauma and persisting reactions that become complicated and disabling. Silove (2005) indicated "that the best therapy for acute stress reactions is social: providing safety, reuniting families, creating effective systems of justice, offering opportunities for work, study and other productive roles, and re-establishing systems of meaning and cohesion—religious, political, social and cultural" (p. 75). Mental health interventions are clearly needed for those complicated and disabling reactions that affect small minorities of people exposed to a traumatic event, such as the 2004 Indian Ocean tsunami. At the same time, understanding the objectives and processes of social interventions is essential. Decades of research have shown that survivors do well in relation to their capacity to reestablish social networks and a viable way of life. Therefore Western mental health models should attend more to the role of social agency, including work, in promoting stable well-being and mental health (Summerfield, 2005).

As Silove (2005) and Summerfield (2005) have suggested, a medical model has been privileged in providing greatly needed therapeutic interventions to survivors of trauma, and the value of the psychiatric and psychological knowledge base is assured. However, there is a tension in the integration of these ideas with those of an approach based more on strengths and solutions and even more so in adopting community development interventions, that is, broadening the focus of interest beyond the individual, couple, or family unit (Rowlands, 2004).

A Strengths Approach

A strengths perspective focuses on strengths and present abilities, maximizing the person's opportunities to make decisions and enhance quality of life, as opposed to focusing on deficits and problems in adjustment

(Saleebey, 2006). A strengths approach enables people who have experienced traumatic events to have more control over their lives and to have a greater voice in institutions, service, and situations that affect them (Shardlow, 1998). Some traumatized clients have recognized personal strengths, such as compassion, optimism, or heightened ability to deal with future stress, when positive language is used and survival acknowledged. Hence, listening for something positive that came from the event and fostering client descriptions of strengths and competence is used in the strengths perspective (Norman, 2000; Rowlands, 2004). Further, the strengths perspective assumes that the individual and community are the experts of their own situation and can best decide what they want and need (Saleebey, 2006; Tan, 2009).

Strength and resilience are highly correlated (Herman, 1992; Priestley & Hemingway, 2006). Resilience is the resourcefulness of people, families, and communities and their ability to bounce back, including the contribution of culture and history in recovering from traumatic events. Because one can never know the limit of a person's capacity for growth and change, the worker must take seriously the client's hopes and dreams and recognize the resource-rich environment surrounding them. Thus, the worker's assessment needs to look for successes, hopes, and dreams; look for the person's strengths and resources; and recognize the person's expertise.

Principles of liberation and empowerment underpin the strengths approach and link to heroism and hope. The converse is alienation and oppression, anxiety and evil, the experience of trauma and violence. Therefore, the tenets of the strengths approach are entirely consistent with those of trauma counseling: empowerment, membership and inclusion, resilience, healing and wholeness, dialogue and collaboration (Herman, 1992; Raphael, 1986, 2005; Saleebey, 2006).

A strengths focus can also be applied to intervention at the community level, adopting the assets-based model of community development (Kretzmann & McKnight, 2005). This approach harnesses individual and community skills and assets and is based on development driven by the community itself rather than external agencies, a principle of recovery planning (Emergency Management Australia, 2004). Community development itself as a social work mode of intervention aims to reestablish the community as the location of significant human experience and the meeting of human need. This development can focus on any of six dimensions: social, economic, cultural, personal or spiritual, environmental, and political (Ife, 2002). Building upon the resources that the community already controls and harnessing those that are not yet available facilitates community recovery from trauma or disaster. Community members' capacities and locally based services and groups can all be tapped to provide resources and expertise in recovery.

THE IMPACT OF TRAUMATIC EXPERIENCES ON CHILD DEVELOPMENT: DIRECTIONS FOR THERAPEUTIC INTERVENTION

The traumatic impacts of child maltreatment and appropriate interventions to ameliorate them are becoming increasingly recognized (Taylor & Siegfried, 2005). Severe trauma during childhood can have a devastating effect on the development of the brain and all its functions—emotional, cognitive, behavioral, and physiological (Child Safety Commissioner, 2007; Ko et al., 2008; Perry, 2006). The body's physiological reaction to a traumatic event creates an altered neurological state, the severity of which depends on previous experiences of trauma, the extent of social support available, and existing resilience factors. Children are more vulnerable to trauma than adults because of the developing nature of their brains and neurological systems (Child Safety Commissioner, 2007). "Traumatic and neglectful experiences during childhood cause abnormal organization and function of important neural systems in the brain, compromising the functional capacities mediated by these systems" (Perry, 2006, p. 29).

Chronic childhood trauma interferes with the capacity to integrate sensory, emotional, and cognitive information into a cohesive whole (Child Safety Commissioner, 2007). Developmental delays that ensue include cognitive, language, motor, and socialization skills. The capacity to regulate emotions and reactions (affect regulation) is also built during early childhood. This capacity is impaired by attachment difficulties and trauma, leading traumatized children to have difficulties in controlling their anger and impulses and regulating strong feelings. These children are described as hyperaroused, where they are reactive, hypervigilant, and alarmed, or dissociated, where they are disengaged, numb, and compliant.

Children in the child welfare system, especially those in foster care, have experienced abuse and neglect, domestic violence, removal from their families, and often multiple placements, schools, and peer groups. Assessment must address the child's complete trauma history. Social workers, foster and adoptive parents, and teachers play important roles in facilitating post-trauma recovery (Taylor & Siegfried, 2005).

It is also necessary to assess a child's true age, which is separate from chronological, emotional, social, cognitive, physical, or moral age (Perry, 2006, p. 48), using psychometric measures and semistructured interviews. History is the most critical component, especially primary caregiving during early childhood. Key to this history is the caregiver's own history of primary caregiving, because we parent the way we were parented.

Intervention as early as possible affords the best outcomes for traumatized children. A safe environment is a prerequisite to recovery and healing (Herman, 1992; Perry, 2006). Children need to feel safe and secure in their living environment. They need caring adults to acknowledge their hurt, provide nurturance, and contain their difficult behaviors. This places considerable demands on the child's carers (whether they be family, kinship, or foster carers). Providing training and support to carers is an indirect yet powerful intervention. Children also need help reducing overwhelming emotion, making new meaning of their trauma history and current experiences, and addressing the impact of trauma and subsequent changes in their behavior, development, and relationships. Additionally, it is important to support positive, stable relationships in the child's life and to support family and caregivers (Ko et al., 2008).

"Children with fundamental attachment problems due to early childhood neglect need many, many positive nurturing interactions with trustworthy peers, teachers, and caregivers" (Perry, 2006, p. 37). Interventions need to be developmentally appropriate while also approximating age-appropriate activities. Pets are therapeutic because of the unconditional acceptance they provide. For children with hypervigilance, impulsivity, and anxiety, repetitive activities are indicated, such as dance, drumming, music, and massage, rather than talking therapies. Such patterned, repetitive, and rhythmic activities are central elements of healing and grief rituals in aboriginal cultures (Perry, 2006).

For a child who has experienced severe neglect, one therapy session a week will not provide sufficient healthy relational interactions to permit the child to catch up from years of relational poverty. More effective is intervening to create a therapeutic web using any healthy and invested people in the child's life, such as teachers, coaches, foster parents, siblings, extended family, neighbors, and youth ministers (Ducker & Trenoweth, 2009; Perry, 2006).

WORKER SELF-CARE

Social workers are not immune to the powerful impacts of working with individuals and communities affected by trauma. Good self-care strategies and access to supervision are essential. The work may at times become overwhelming for personal reasons, such as identifying someone like oneself or identifying with children who are deceased. Social workers also need to make meaning of what has happened and process their experiences.

Workers' emotional reactions can include anger at the oppressor, anger at the client, anger at society over its failure to help, fear of personal vulnerability, anxiety over ability to assist, guilt over being exempted from suffering, numbed responsiveness after hearing traumatic stories over and over, helplessness, disillusionment, and the assumption of too much responsibility. These impacts can occur whether the worker is providing counseling or community-level interventions (Emergency Management Australia, 2004).

Self-care strategies include the following:

- Time management and maintaining work–life balance (taking breaks, holidays, private time)
- Maintaining a healthy lifestyle (exercise; relaxation; hobbies; nutrition; sleep; reduced consumption of alcohol, nicotine, and caffeine; careful driving)
- Personal awareness (developing more self-awareness and reflective skills, expressing feelings, being assertive, talking slowly, listening more)

Professional supervision is necessary for work with individual clients and can be advantageous for teams in disaster situations, for example. The opportunity to debrief after particularly stressful interactions and to explore personal and professional boundaries is warranted. There are many opportunities for social support and team building in crisis and trauma work.

Research on vicarious trauma, burnout, and compassion fatigue is rapidly expanding and is beyond the scope of this chapter. Recognition of burnout symptoms is the first step to addressing it successfully. Employers carry a responsibility to provide adequate supervision and provide training to staff to raise awareness. Organizational strategies to burnout-proof an agency, so to speak, include limiting working hours per week, ensuring lunch breaks are taken, providing ongoing staff development, providing regular skilled supervision, providing adequate administrative and technical support, debriefing after critical events such as a child's death, assigning reasonable caseloads, and ensuring staff and client safety is paramount (James & Gilliland, 2005).

CONCLUSION

A common response from workers invested in this field is that they see the best of human nature. Contributing in this way provides its own rewards despite the very real concerns raised previously. And despite the evidence of the impact of trauma on children and adults, for some survivors, there is evidence of growth through the experience. Survivors talk of increased maturity and strength, more self-assurance, greater appreciation of loved ones, increased empathy and care for others, and a greater appreciation of life itself (Dyregrov, 1997).

Any intervention anywhere needs to be culturally sensitive and respectful of a society's ways of healing after traumatic exposures. Recognition of the cultures of meaning and understanding of what has happened, reaction, and recovery are critical in working in a collaborative and consultative way with communities that have been affected by trauma. This is a very human issue, and it takes great sensitivity (Raphael, 2005).

NOTES

1. A *crisis* is defined as a stressful precipitating event, the perception of which leads to subjective distress where usual coping methods fail, leading to a lower level of functioning in an individual (Kanel, 2003).

2. Attending behavior, questioning, paraphrasing, reflecting, summarizing.

REFERENCES

American Psychiatric Association (APA). (2000). *Diagnostic and statistical manual of mental disorders (DSM IV)*. Washington, DC: American Psychiatric Association.

American Psychiatric Association (APA). (1980). *Diagnostic and statistical manual of psychiatric disorders (DSM III)*. Washington, DC: American Psychiatric Association.

Child Safety Commissioner. (2007). *Calmer classrooms: A guide to working with traumatized children*. Melbourne: Child Safety Commissioner. www.ocsc.vic.gov.au (accessed 1 July 2009).

Ducker, H., & Trenoweth, S. (2009). *A room at the top*. North Sydney: William Heinemann.

Dyregrov, A. (1997). Traumatic grief—growing at different life stages. In *Trauma, Grief & Growth—finding a pathway to healings*. Keynote address, proceedings of Joint National Conference 1997, pp 1–13. University of Sydney, Sydney.

Emergency Management Australia. (2004). *Recovery: Australian Emergency Manual Series*. Canberra: Emergency Management Australia. www.ema.gov.au (accessed 25 June 2009).

Herman, J. (1992). *Trauma and recovery*. New York: Basic Books.

Ife, J. (2002). *Community development: Community-based alternatives in an age of globalization* (2nd ed.). Frenchs Forest, Australia: Pearson.

James, R. K., & Gilliland, B. E. (2005). *Crisis intervention strategies*. Belmont, CA: Brooks Cole.

Kanel, K. (2003). *A guide to crisis intervention* (2nd ed.). Pacific Grove, CA: Wadsworth.

Ko, S. J., Ford, J. D., Kassam-Adams, N., Berkowitz, S. J., Wilson, C., Wong, M., Brymer, M. J., & Layne, C. M. (2008). Creating trauma-informed systems: Child welfare, education, first responders, health care, juvenile justice. *Professional Psychology: Research and Practice*, 39(4), 396–404.

Kretzmann, J. P., & McKnight, J. L. (2005). *Discovering community power: A guide to mobilizing local assets and your organization's capacity*. ABCD Institute. http://www.abcdinstitute.org/docs/kelloggabcd.pdf (accessed 26 March 2011).

Marmar, C. R., & Horowitz, M. J. (1988). Diagnosis and phase-oriented treatment of post-traumatic stress disorder. In J. P. Wilson, Z. Harel, & B. Kahana (Eds.), *Human adaptation to extreme stress: From the Holocaust to Vietnam* (pp. 81–103). Cleveland: Cleveland State University.

Norman, J. (2000). Constructive narrative in arresting the impact of post-traumatic stress disorder. *Clinical Social Work Journal*, 28(3), 303–319.

Perry, B. D. (2006). Applying principles of neurodevelopment to clinical work with maltreated and traumatized children. In N. B. Webb (Ed.), *Working with traumatized youth in child welfare* (pp. 27–52). New York: Guilford Press.

Priestley, M., & Hemingway, L. (2006). Disability and disaster recovery: A tale of two cities? In N. T. Tan, A. Rowlands, & F. K. O. Yuen (Eds.), *Asian tsunami and social work practice* (pp. 23–42). New York: Haworth Press.

Raphael, B. (2005, March). *The human face of disaster*. Paper presented to Academy of Science, Canberra, 31 March 2005. www.naf.org.au/tsunami/robertson-raphael.htm (accessed 6 October 2005).

Raphael, B. (1986). *When disaster strikes*. New York: Basic Books.

Raphael, B. (1983). *The anatomy of bereavement*. New York: Basic Books.

Raphael, B., & Meldrum, L. (1994). Helping people cope with trauma. In R. Watts & D. de la Horne (Eds.), *Coping with trauma: The victim and the helper* (pp. 1–20). Brisbane: Australian Academic Press.

Raphael, B., & Stevens, G. (2007). Disaster and response: Science, systems and realities. *Journal of Social Work in Disability and Rehabilitation*, 5(3/4), 1–22.

Rowlands, A. (2004). Reappraising social work's contribution to recovery from disaster and trauma: Applying a strengths perspective. *Asia Pacific Journal of Social Work*, 14(2), 67–85.

Saleebey, D. (Ed.). (2006). *The strengths perspective in social work practice*. Boston: Pearson.

Shardlow, S. (1998). Values, ethics and social work. In R. Adams, L. Dominelli, & M. Payne (Eds.), *Social work: Themes, issues and critical debates* (pp. 23–33). Basingstoke: Macmillan.

Silove, D. (2005). The best immediate therapy for acute stress is social. *Bulletin of World Health Organization*, 83, 75–76.

Summerfield, D. (2005). What exactly is emergency or disaster 'mental health'? *Bulletin of World Health Organization*, 83, 76.

Tan, N. T. (2009). Disaster management: Strengths and community perspectives. *Journal of Global Social Work Practice*, 2(1). Accessed March 26, 2011, at http://www.globalsocialwork.org/vol2no1_Tan.html.

Tan, N. T., & Rowlands, A. (2008). Social re-development following the Indian Ocean tsunami. *Social Development Issues*, 30(1), 47–58.

Taylor, N., & Siegfried, C. B. (2005). *Helping children in the child welfare system heal from trauma: A systems integration approach*. National Child Traumatic Stress Network Systems Integration Working Group. www.nctsnet.org (accessed 28 June 2009).

13

International Social Service: Addressing the Need for Intercountry Casework

FELICITY NORTHCOTT, JULIE GILBERT ROSICKY, ANDY ELVIN, JEAN AYOUB, AND CHRISTINE LAMBERT

This chapter defines the meaning of international social service and intercountry casework, reviews the kinds of intercountry cases most commonly encountered, and identifies how to prepare the next generation of social workers to address transnational casework. The experiences of International Social Service (ISS), a major provider of intercountry services, is used to illustrate the discussion; therefore, the chapter provides an overview of the organization and two of its Branches, the International Social Service of the United Kingdom (ISS UK) and International Social Service, USA (ISS-USA).

Broadly conceptualized, the definition of *international social service* is a three-pronged one: social work in a particular country with individuals from outside of that country (immigrants and refugees, for example), social work that requires working across international borders (international adoption, abduction, document and relative tracings, home studies, child welfare checks), and, finally, social work undertaken by social workers of one country in another country (ISS-USA, 2010).

Today, 3% of the world's population, or nearly 200 million people, live in a country other than the one in which they were born. These people often find themselves in need of legal and social services as a result of being in an unfamiliar place. Their needs may vary widely, and it is imperative that social workers understand the cultural, social, and emotional differences between themselves and their clients. Culturally relevant social work is the cornerstone of transnational or intercountry social work and therefore of the case agency, ISS. It is optimal when social agencies engaged in this work use social workers who are native to the country in which they are working. By doing so, the potential for misinterpreting situations is lessened.

Within the United States, for example, the National Association of Social Workers (NASW) has clear guidelines on cultural competence and working with diverse client populations (NASW, 2001). NASW Standard 3, Cross-Cultural Knowledge, states that "social workers shall have and continue to *develop specialized knowledge and understanding about the history, traditions, values, family systems, and artistic expressions* of major client groups that they serve" (emphasis added). Furthermore, NASW Standard 5, Service Delivery, says that "social workers *shall be knowledgeable about and skillful in the use of services available in the community and broader society and be able to make appropriate referrals for their diverse clients*" (emphasis added).

Social workers who encounter cases with an international component must learn to trust the skills of their counterparts in other countries. These professionals have the specialized cultural knowledge to interpret and analyze situations within their own country with greater expertise than an outsider. Systems and styles of reports will be different from country to country. Regardless, it is important that fellow social workers from other countries are accorded professional respect.

HISTORY AND BACKGROUND OF INTERCOUNTRY CASEWORK

Intercountry casework was developed and refined by ISS, an organization committed to protect, defend, and support persons, especially children, who are separated from their family as a result of international displacement or migration. As Warren wrote in an article originally published in 1930, "Case work becomes international when the peculiar problems of local clients have their roots and some elements in another country" (1939b, p. 644). The 1939 *Social Work Yearbook* defined international social casework and referred to the early work of ISS, then known as the International Migration Service. Warren identified international social casework as one of four components of international social work and defined it as "the application of case work methods to the problems of families and individuals whose social adjustments require cooperative action in two or more countries" (Warren, 1939a, p. 192).

Such cases usually arise in the context of migration and are exacerbated by complex laws that apply differentially in different countries. As Warren indicates, migration and the various laws "tend to separate families for temporary or prolonged periods of time, and thus to weaken family unity" (p. 192–193). International social case work therefore has to do with assistance in migration, assistance to refugees, service to families separated by restrictive immigration laws or by involuntary or premeditated desertion, the search for lost relatives, organizing the help of relatives in one country for dependents in another, obtaining documents to assist qualification for different categories of public relief, deportations, the repatriation of families to countries of origin, the placing of children with relatives in other countries, and in fact with many of the types of family situations familiar to local social services" (p. 193).

International Social Service: A Case Study

For more than eight decades, ISS has been the lead agency practicing and refining intercountry or international casework. It was founded in 1924 under its original name, the International Migration Service, by representatives from the United States, the United Kingdom, Czechoslovakia, France, Greece, Poland, and Switzerland in response to increased migration from Europe in the nineteenth and twentieth centuries (Cox, 1984). The ISS network gradually expanded to reestablish family links and to protect and defend children separated from their family across borders. The organization changed its name to International Social Service in 1946 (Social Welfare History Archives, 2010). The role of ISS is providing psychosocial and legal expertise in child and family matters in an international context. Today, ISS is a worldwide network of staff and volunteers that has strengthened its expertise in order to enable the protection, defense, and support of internationally separated children and families. Migrants in need, such as refugees, internally displaced persons, and unaccompanied minors, remain a primary concern to ISS.

Structure

The ISS network includes 600 staff and more than 3000 volunteers. The organization operates in more than 100 countries. The General Secretariat, led by the secretary-general and based in Geneva, is the heart of the network. It defines ways to implement the ISS mission, policies, and objectives. Beside coordinating and monitoring the actions of the network, it provides active support to its members, such as capacity building. The fourteen national Branches[1] are legally autonomous nonprofit organizations. The five Affiliated Bureaus[2] are either governmental or nongovernmental bodies that, in addition to their main activities, undertake assignments as ISS members. Correspondents are either governmental or nongovernmental organizations (NGOs) or individuals that primarily handle casework.

The governing bodies of ISS include the International Council, the Governing Board, and the Professional Advisory Committee. The International Council is made up of the representatives of the Branches, Affiliated Bureaus, and Correspondents, and it elects the Governing Board. The Governing Board, composed of the international president, the treasurer, three elected board members from the Branches and Affiliated Bureaus, and the chair of the Professional Advisory Committee, defines the framework of the ISS network; defines its mission, policies, and objectives; and supervises the secretary-general. The Professional Advisory Committee (PAC) is made up of the directors of the all the Branches and Affiliated Bureaus. It advises the General Secretariat about programmatic issues and is represented on the Governing Board by the elected chair of the PAC.

Partnership

Close and sustainable partnerships with international intergovernmental organizations and relevant NGOs are essential for effective intercountry work. For example, ISS maintains such partnerships with the United Nations Children's Fund (UNICEF), UN High Commissioner for Refugees (UNHCR), Committee on the Rights of the Child (CRC), International Committee of the Red Cross (ICRC), International Federation of Red Cross and Red Crescent Societies (IFRC), Hague Conference on Private International Law, and Inter-American Children's Institute (IIN). Many NGOs involved in international work maintain consultative status with the UN in order to participate in relevant policy discussions and remain abreast of developments. The ISS has consultative status with the UN Economic and

Social Council (ECOSOC), UNICEF, the European Council (EC), and the Organization of American States (OAS). The ISS also participates in diverse working groups, such as the NGO group for the Convention on the Rights of the Child, the International Council on Social Welfare (ICSW), and the NGO Committee on UNICEF.

International Social Service Activities Across the Globe

Activities of ISS include implementation of both prevention and support activities related to children and families in accordance with the International Bill of Human Rights and the Convention on the Rights of the Child.

Intercountry Casework

Today, ISS assists in individual cases of social and legal need by *(1)* establishing a link between social services in different countries and *(2)* providing accurate and complete information that enables service providers to make decisions in the best interest of the child. In cases of family conflict, ISS can act as a mediator between the parties. This includes conflicts regarding custody and visitation rights. The agency makes a social report of the children's family environments and provides psychological support prior to reestablishing family links. In 2008, ISS handled 25,000 cases worldwide.

Development Projects

The organization raises awareness about the difficulties of migration, the realities of the trip, and opportunities that are available at home. The ISS network, in close collaboration with national partners, also provides assistance to immigrants upon arrival in the country of destination, temporary shelter, food and medical assistance, language training, and psychological support.

Capacity Building and Technical Advice

Training and technical support on specific subjects related to child protection and international social work methodology are provided by ISS. It also supports legislative and administrative reform processes at all levels, organizes training seminars at the university level for social workers, and develops practical tools for professionals working on child protection issues.

Research and Advocacy

The organization is the hub of policies and legislative practices on research, knowledge sharing, best practices, and expertise on child protection. Special attention is given to children deprived of their family and unaccompanied and separated children. The organization produces position papers, thematic fact sheets, and other publications. It also advocates for the ratification and implementation of national and international standards on child protection and related issues. The General Secretariat houses the International Reference Centre for the Rights of Children Deprived of their Family (ISS/IRC), a program dedicated to questions linked to adoption and children without parental care. It is a service provider for twenty intercountry adoption (ICA) central authorities worldwide.

Two ISS Branches are presented next to give readers more detail about practical operations and cases.

How ISS-USA Works

The ISS Branch in the United States, ISS-USA, is a nonprofit, nongovernmental social work agency that manages cases across international borders. It is the national contractor for the Department of Health and Human Services (HHS), Administration for Children and Families, Office of Refugee Resettlement, and US Repatriation Program. The US Repatriation Program provides travel and relocation assistance to eligible American citizens in foreign countries who are destitute, are mentally ill, or are unaccompanied minors who need to be returned to the United States. Assistance is provided in the form of a loan, and repatriates are expected to pay HHS back for services received if they are able.

Specifically, ISS-USA caseworkers receive referrals from Department of State workers in embassies or consulates in other countries via e-mail, and then they coordinate travel and care to be received with states and local providers at the location of final US destination via e-mail and phone. Ultimately, the repatriating US citizens travel to the United States, are met by a social worker and maybe a psychologist or appropriate professional upon arrival at the airport, and are transported to a hospital or shelter to receive care. All coordination of services is done via e-mail and phone. Caseworkers must be extremely knowledgeable about what information needs to be provided to ensure appropriate treatment when the person arrives. They must also be staunch advocates for the repatriate and follow up with the consulates and social workers in the United States to confirm that all the details have been attended to and services are ultimately delivered.

Intercountry case management services are also provided by ISS-USA, including document and relative tracings, home studies for kinship or adoptive placement, child protection alerts, and postplacement follow-up on children placed in the United States from another country or on American children placed overseas by ISS partners in other countries. In cases where children are separated from family across borders, the ISS believes, and the Convention on the Rights of the Child establishes (Link, chapter 68 this volume) that all children have the right to have their family searched for and evaluated for suitability so that they may be placed with family when it is in their best interest. No child should be denied access to family simply because of the reluctance of the child welfare system to place US children with kin in other countries. In some cases, reluctance to place stems from perceptions based on the quality or timeliness of the home study or from perceptions about the quality of services available in another country (Gomez, Berger Cardoso, & Thompson, 2009). In addition, logistical barriers, conflicting child welfare mandates, and lack of familiarity with intercountry placement procedures, all factors shown to influence the placement of children with kin across borders (Cardoso, Gomez & Padilla, 2009), should be overcome so that borders do not become barriers to placement.

An example of such a case would be a US citizen in foster care whose parents were recently deported to Guatemala The court would have to decide whether to allow the child to remain in foster care, to terminate parental rights so that the child could be adopted, to place the child with other relatives in the United States, or to return the child to Guatemala to either live with the parents or other relatives. In this case, the department of social services or department of children and family services (the titles of child welfare agencies differ from state to state) in the United States would request a home study in Guatemala from ISS-USA, who would contact its colleagues in Guatemala to conduct the home study and refer the case. The completed home study would be reviewed by ISS, translated from Spanish to English, and sent to the party requesting the home study.

Services do not end with the home study. It is critical to help all parties take a global perspective when weighing the benefits and risks of returning the child to another country (e.g., Guatemala) versus keeping the child in the United States. Specifically, parties must avoid using their own experiences of life in the United States, and perhaps their impressions of life in other countries, to make a decision about what a child needs. Furthermore, if the decision is to place a child with family outside the United States, then culturally appropriate transition services must be implemented

to ensure that the child makes a positive adjustment during transition and afterward. Finally, postplacement reports are necessary to ensure that the child receives all needed services and appropriate care after placement.

Each year, ISS-USA works with more than seventy-five countries. The majority of the organization's intercountry social work involves Germany, Mexico, the United Kingdom, the Dominican Republic, Greece, Canada, Guatemala, and Honduras.

The casework of ISS-USA has developed in response to the following factors:

o Numbers of children who will enter the US child welfare system as a result of being part of a family with mixed immigration status
o Cost to local, state, and national agencies charged with the care of these children as the population of children awaiting permanency determinations grows
o Pressure on individual social service providers and agencies to provide comprehensive care, make reasonable efforts on behalf of the children, and work toward family reunification regardless of where the family lives

As ISS-USA casework has grown and evolved, so has the need to ensure appropriate access to research, training, and technical assistance on matters involving the placement of children with family members across international borders. In response to this need, ISS-USA launched the Arthur C. Helton Institute for the Study of International Social Service. The mandate of the institute is to provide training, technical assistance, and research on issues related to children separated from their families across international borders. The institute is also the advocacy arm of the agency and works to ensure that all children are provided with the same due diligence in being reunited with their families in a safe and timely manner regardless of where that family may live.

How ISS UK Works
The ISS Branch in the United Kingdom, ISS UK, is a nonprofit, nongovernmental social work agency called Children and Families Across Borders (CFAB) that handles international social work cases in the United Kingdom. Similar to ISS-USA, ISS UK assists children in public care by organizing assessments of family members overseas for children and young people in foster care in the United Kingdom. The organization also works with its partners overseas

to arrange assessments of extended family in the United Kingdom for children in care in other countries. For example, a local authority contacted ISS UK about a two-year-old child whose mother had been arrested at a UK airport on suspicion of importing illegal substances. The child was placed in a foster home where his native language was not spoken. His mother suggested a family in the Netherlands (friends of hers in her country of origin) who might care for him. ISS UK was able to work with ISS Netherlands to ensure that the relevant authority in the Netherlands obtained a temporary custody order for the child and that the family was able to accept the child into their care. The family in the Netherlands traveled to the United Kingdom to collect the child. Then ISS UK and the UK social workers supervised a departure visit between the child and his mother in prison. Social services in the United Kingdom had arranged for an ISS assessment of the family as a potential long-term care option. ISS Netherlands reported that the child has settled into his Dutch foster home with the friends of his mother. The child only stayed four nights in the UK foster home before being placed with the mother's friends in the Netherlands.

The organization also handles a large number of referrals related to families where there are child protection concerns crossing borders. Additionally, ISS UK provides unique services to address the following:

- **Advice Line** – CFAB has an advice line is free to all, social workers, Court officers, private individuals, solicitors, charity workers and central government officers. Advice is free and in 2010 we received over 1700 calls to our advice line.
- **Children in Care** – We arrange assessments overseas of extended family members who put themselves forward as carers for children looked after. Not only does all research show that children's outcomes are more positive when placed in extended family as opposed to the care system, there is also the issue of the significant cost of the looked after population. All assessments are carried out by social work staff, qualified and registered in the country concerned. We also arrange assessments of extended family in the UK for our partner agencies overseas where children are in state care.
- **Child protection alerts** – We ensure that vital child protection information is passed promptly to the appropriate agency in the

country that the child has travelled to. In this way we ensure that children at risk who are taken across international borders do not get lost in the system or fall between services. We also receive a significant number of alerts from overseas which we pass on to UK authorities.

- **Welfare Checks** – We can arrange welfare checks overseas on children who are visiting a country for a significant length of time and about whom there are concerns. This can cover children who do not meet child protection thresholds but about whom UK social workers have cause for concern. This service is also available for children subject to plans of protection who are visiting family or holidaying abroad provided sufficient notice is given (generally 3–4 weeks).
- **Unaccompanied Minors** – We can assist in re-establishing contact with family at home or helping to establish how young people came to the UK. In this area of work we ensure that the young person wants contact to be re-established and is aware of the issues. We do not work to return young people to their country of origin unless they wish to do so.
- **Child abduction** – We offer a mediation service to work with both parents to try to agree to a care arrangement that allows the child to grow up knowing both parents and having a positive relationship with both parents. Abduction cases often involve adults putting their own needs before those of the children, and we work to focus attention on the best interests of the child. We generally work in countries who are not signatories to the 1980 Hague Convention
- **Child Trafficking** – We work closely with a number of UK statutory and voluntary agencies to support young people who have been trafficked. Our role is to arrange assessments in the young person's country of origin to ascertain if it is safe for them to return and that they have family who will protect and care for them if they choose to return. Often families are unaware that the child has been trafficked believing they have gone abroad for a better life. We are also involved in setting up projects overseas for returning trafficked children.
- **Private Fostering** – We can help establish what the knowledge, wishes and feelings of

the parents are in cases where children are privately fostered. We can also help establish the process by which the child became privately fostered. This can include making sure parents are aware of, and consent to who is caring for their children, that they have agreed to this and that they are fully aware of any concerns there may be about their child

- **Leave to remove cases** – In leave to remove cases we are able to procure assessments of the situation the child is potentially moving to. These assessments can include: comment on the education/health and related services available in the proposed domicile, interviews with extended family members in proposed domicile covering commitment to supporting child and parent and their attitude to ongoing contact with other parent, and comment on the proposed residence of the child in the new domicile. We can also arrange a follow up assessment if and when the child relocates.
- **Police and Social Services checks** – We can offer access to these checks in most countries where they are available.
- **Travel Assistance** – We run the travel assistance scheme for the UK Government. This scheme allows immigrants with permanent status in the UK to choose to return to their country of origin if their life in the UK has become difficult and they have better prospects in their country of birth. Each case is assessed by a social worker and only those in whose best interests it is to return are eligible for support. The individuals have to apply and volunteer for this scheme, there is no coercive element
- **Libya Project** – Each year we promote contact between mothers, grandparents and extended family with children whose fathers have abducted them to Libya. Libyan law does not allow for the return of such children but via our scheme and ongoing mediation work, we are able to promote an ongoing and positive relationship between the children and their mothers. This scheme is currently suspended pending developments in Libya.

Similar to ISS-USA, ISS UK has responded to the growing and diverse situations that cause children to be separated from family members across borders by training social workers, court staff, police, and other child welfare professionals. In addition, ISS UK has led advocacy efforts to highlight the rise in child trafficking and child abductions in the United Kingdom and to actively promote the UN Convention on the Rights of the Child.

Each year, ISS UK works with over 100 countries, most often with Spain, Australia, Poland, New Zealand, South Africa, Pakistan, the United States, India, Bangladesh, and Nigeria. It also increasingly works with states of the former Soviet Bloc Especially Poland, Lithuania and Romania.

LOOKING TO THE FUTURE OF INTERCOUNTRY SOCIAL WORK

In its eighty-five-year history, ISS has witnessed many causes for migration. In recent years, there is a growing need for coordinated intercountry social services in far more countries than ever before, particularly in developing parts of the world. While migration continues to occur for all the same reasons as in the past (war, economic and educational opportunities, natural disasters, religious freedom), more people are migrating for other reasons, such as human trafficking, climate change, HIV and AIDS, and poverty. Furthermore, there has been a growing trend of migration among elderly and aging populations seeking to return to their homelands to live out their remaining months or years.

Regardless of the reason or the population, it is understood throughout the ISS federation that no one better understands the social work needs of a population than those living in that culture. Relying on the coordination of homegrown expertise from one country to another is the best way to coordinate information with all concerned parties. However, it is not enough to merely share this information. A great deal of training is still needed to be able to interpret and understand this information to put it to the best possible use between social work experts in two countries. What is needed to make this information usable is a respect for and understanding of

- international and national laws that guide social work practice in one's own country and internationally,
- social work systems in one's own country and in other countries,
- one's own values and biases and how they might affect one's judgment, and
- resources available in one's own country and around the globe and how to maximize use of existing resources.

Because we live in a global society, exemplified by the diversity of the people within our own borders and more frequent work across borders, the need to expand current social work training to include the previous list is more pressing than ever. In addition, it is necessary to consider the challenge of how to train more social workers, particularly in countries that have limited social work capacity. We need to train more globally minded social workers who have expertise in domestic and international laws and systems, understand their own biases and values and how they affect their worldview, and knowledge about the wide variety of resources that exist both within and outside their country. By developing global social work capacity in both content and scope, ISS and others can enhance the ability to provide coordinated expert social work across borders.

NOTES

1. Australia, Germany, Belgium, Canada, Greece, Hong Kong, Italy, Japan, the Netherlands, the Philippines, Switzerland, United Kingdom, United States, and Venezuela

2. France, Israel, New Zealand, Portugal, and South Africa

REFERENCES

Berger Cardoso, J., Gomez, R., & Padilla, Y. (2009). What happens when family resources are across international borders? An exploratory study on kinship placement in Mexican immigrant families. *Child Welfare, 88*(6), 67–84.

Cox, D. R. (1984). *Intercountry casework: Some reflections on sixty years experience of International Social Service, 1924–1984.* Geneva: ISS.

Gomez, R., Berger Cardoso, J., & Thompson, S. (2009) Kinship care with Hispanic children: Barriers and obstacles to policy and practice implementation. In S. Quintero (Ed.), *Child welfare issues and perspectives* (pp. 1–16). Happague, NY: Nova Science.

International Social Service, USA (ISS-USA). (2010). www.iss-usa.org.

National Association of Social Workers (NASW). (2001), *NASW standards for cultural competence in social work practice.* Washington, DC: Author.

Social Welfare History Archives. (2010). Website. Minneapolis: Social Welfare History Archives at University of Minnesota. Available at: http://special. lib.umn.edu/swha/

Warren, G. (1939a). International social work. In R. H. Kurtz (Ed.), *Social work yearbook, 1939* (pp. 192–196). New York: Russell Sage Foundation.

Warren, G. L. (1939b). Some aspects of international case work. In F. Lowry (Ed.), *Readings in social case work 1920–1938: Selected reprints for the case work practitioner* (pp. 644–650). New York: Columbia University Press.

14

Social Development and Social Work

DOREEN ELLIOTT

This chapter addresses social development in the context of international social work and social welfare, reviews its relationship with the profession of social work, and analyzes its impact on global social work practice. It addresses the following questions: What is social development? How is it applicable to social work practice? What are some applications of social work practice in countries around the world?

WHAT IS SOCIAL DEVELOPMENT?

In the context of social work in the United States, social development is often seen as synonymous with community development or with childhood socialization, or it is seen is as an approach to social welfare applicable only to emerging economies. The work of the United Nations Development Programme (UNDP) on the Human Development Index and the annual Human Development Reports for the last twenty years is based on the human development framework of Amartya Sen and Mahbub ul Haq, and it looks remarkably consistent with social development goals, values, and approaches (Sen, 2000). This overlapping terminology has created confusion within the profession in the Global North around what exactly is the domain of social development.

Some clarification therefore is necessary to place the present discussion in context, and given the limited space available and the fact that the focus of this paper is social development and social work practice, only the briefest review of social development ideas is presented here. This review is just sufficient to help readers understand the place of social development in social work practice worldwide and its potential for practice in developed economies. Readers are encouraged to further explore the references cited for more detailed discussions.

The approach to social development discussed in this chapter derives from the idea of social development as a social welfare approach first started by the British in colonial Africa between the First and Second World Wars. Midgley (1994, 1995) has documented the history of social development and further explicated it from many perspectives in the context of social welfare. Discussions on the topic are also to be found in Chapters 4 and 62 through 65 of this volume.

In defining social development, Midgley (1995) emphasizes the connection between social and economic development and the idea of planned change for universal optimal life conditions. In this respect social development brings a much-needed economic perspective to social work and social welfare. Despite the profession's history of advocating on behalf of the world's poor, to date social work has had little involvement with economics in most countries. Accreditation standards for social work education in the United States, for example, do not require courses or other content in economics for Master of Social Work training. Problem assessment is most often clinical and related to individual pathology, and while the profession has long claimed a person-in-environment perspective, the environment is linked mainly to social and cultural environmental factors rather than economic factors. This is less true of social work in the developing world, which is much closer to social development. So social development is a potential bridge between social work in developing and developed economies, and as such it has potential as a model for global social work practice.

Generally agreed-upon values of social development are that it is

- optimizing of human conditions and experience worldwide;
- focused on an investment approach to building human and social capital and assets;
- strongly grounded in concepts of social and economic justice;

- emphatic of inclusion, growth, and empowerment from cultural, political, and economic perspectives;
- interdisciplinary with a strong social science base, drawing from economics, sociology, and political science;
- based on human rights and the importance of participation and democracy; and interventionist or statist in that structural, institutional, and social change are regarded as essential and government intervention may be required to make the necessary changes (Falk, 1984; Meinert & Kohn, 1987; Midgley, 1995; Paiva, 1997; Sanders, 1982).

These values have been clearly expressed and operationalized by the United Nations (UN) in the landmark statement issued from the World Summit for Social Development in Copenhagen in 1995. The statement vowed, in the interests of world peace, to put people at the center of development, eradicate poverty, achieve equality between men and women worldwide, and promote equal access for all to education and health care (World Summit for Social Development, 1995). The UN Millennium Development Goals (MDGs) represent a global agreement arising out of a summit of world leaders in 2000 to achieve the following lofty goals by 2015: Eradicate extreme poverty and its concomitant hunger; provide universal education; achieve gender equality; reduce child mortality and HIV, AIDS, malaria, and other diseases; improve reproductive health; ensure a sustainable environment; and create a global partnership for development (UNDP, 2000). The UNDP continues to monitor progress and communicate best practices toward achieving the MDGs.

HOW IS SOCIAL DEVELOPMENT APPLICABLE TO SOCIAL WORK PRACTICE?

Given the previously described characteristics, social development offers a paradigm for social work that is both national and international, and it offers a progressive model of social work practice linking both micro and macro approaches. It therefore is vital for international social work, and this is generally recognized in the literature. For instance, Billups, Meinert, and Midgley (1994) analyze issues associated with the relationship between social work and social development. Midgley and Livermore

(1997) discuss implications of social development for social work education. Asamoah, Healy, and Mayadas (1997) suggest that social development along with human rights and cultural competence are important considerations in international social work practice. Healy (2008) includes social development as well as human rights, multiculturalism, and social exclusion as relevant theoretical approaches to international social work. Cox and Pawar (2006) offered an integrative perspectives theoretical framework for international social work with social development, human rights, and ecological perspectives. In discussing social development and social work in the context of feminist practice, Dominelli (1997) argues that power relations must also be considered as part of social development in international social work practice.

There are numerous other discussions of social work and social development in relation to themes. Table 14.1 shows examples only of the literature; it is not by any means a comprehensive list for reasons of space.

Social development offers a progressive model of social work practice with goals of social justice and empowerment of oppressed, marginalized, or excluded populations. It is an asset-based approach consistent with a strengths and empowerment perspective.

The progressive nature of social work practice based on social development arises out of the fact that such an approach is developed in response to injustice, discrimination, exclusion, or marginalization, and to that extent it is reactive. However, its predominant characteristic is proactive, with emphasis on human rights, prevention, planning, sustainability, advocacy, structural and institutional change, growth, and investment. It therefore addresses discrimination and oppression through structural change. These characteristics are in strong contrast to traditional approaches, which center on maintenance or reactive responses to a crisis with little preventative intervention (Stein, 1976).

A social development perspective introduces new terminology into social work practice, such as *building assets*, *social capital*, and *human capital*, and it addresses distorted development, sustainability, microlending, and microenterprise as new interventive techniques in the fight against poverty. Table 14.2 summarizes some of the differences between a traditional Western model of social policy with a residual emphasis and the type of social work practice arising from these policies compared with a model based on social development.

TABLE 14.1. THEMES ADDRESSING SOCIAL WORK AND SOCIAL DEVELOPMENT IN A GLOBAL CONTEXT

Theme Linking Social Work and Social Development	Author and Date
Community development	Estes, 1997
Women	Dominelli, 1997
Microenterprise	Livermore, 1996
	Raheim, 1996
Multicultural practice	Midgley, 1991
Ethnic minorities in China	Smith, 2003
Social work education	Estes, 1994
Technology transfer	Billups & Juliá, 1996
Australian social work	Gray & Crofts, 2008
Social work and social development in Asia	Kwok, 2008
Social justice	Banerjee, 2005
Sub-Saharan Africa	Noyoo, 2000
Group work	Mayadas & Elliott, 1995

There has been considerable discussion regarding the compatibility of social work with social development; nevertheless, at the level of goals, values, and themes, as Table 14.2 indicates, there is evidence of global application. However, there have been few attempts to operationalize social development as a practice model. Discussion has remained at the conceptual model, and there is little mention of interventive techniques and skills. Hollister (1977) identified core skills and proposed that social development might be a specialty within social work. Billups (1994) proposed social development as an organizing framework for social work practice, and Elliott (1993)

proposed an integrative approach linking micro and macro practice in social work based on a systems approach.

Elliott and Mayadas (1996) and Mayadas and Elliott (2001) suggest that a major barrier to the acceptance of social development–based social work in the Global North is its applicability to clinical practice. They attempt to demonstrate that not only is it possible to link the two but that the linking brings about important new dimensions for clinical and direct practice. Moreover, the authors have presented and operationalized a model of social work practice based on social development and applied

TABLE 14.2. COMPARISON OF SOCIAL DEVELOPMENT AND TRADITIONAL SOCIAL WORK AND POLICY APPROACHES

Traditional Policy and Practice Approaches	Social Development Policy and Practice Approaches
Clinical/labeling approaches (e.g., *DSM IV*) Individual pathology, deficit model	Strengths, asset-based approaches
Services that sometimes create stigma and focus on the need for the client to change (i.e., victim blaming)	Human rights, advocacy, and empowerment
Help limited to subsistence and focused on income maintenance (e.g., TANF)	Building sustainable family and microeconomies
Temporary and short-term interventions (i.e., band-aid approaches)	Creating change in societal structures and institutions
Help offered as a last resort after a crisis has occurred	Planned prevention and development
Distorted development (i.e., rich getting richer and poor getting poorer)	People-centered sustainable development
Consumption	Building human and social capital

Table 14.2 is developed from figures in Elliott (1993, 2010).

it to practice with immigrants and disaster (Elliott, 2010; Elliott & Mayadas, 1999, 2000; Mayadas & Elliott, 2002). Midgley and Conley (2010) have drawn together readings on social work and the social development and social investment approach in a book titled *Developmental Social Work* that includes a strong international perspective and that promises to provide a more comprehensive theoretical and applied approach to social work from a social development perspective.

A SOCIAL DEVELOPMENT–BASED SOCIAL WORK PRACTICE MODEL

The practice model proposed by Mayadas and Elliott is an integrative model combining both micro and macro social work interventions. It is based on four interventive systems: social investment, economic participation, political empowerment, and human investment.

The social investment system of interventions recognizes that poverty and exclusion worldwide have significant social costs for humanity. This system focuses on building infrastructure such as housing, environmental sustainability, child care, health care, and education. Social investment also includes ecosystem problems, such as food and water shortages and erosion of living areas through economic globalization and global climate change. Interventions to build environmental sustainability are included here.

In the economic investment system, the linking of social and economic development characteristic of social development is essential. In an advanced economy, poor people are excluded from work, property, assets, and credit, and in a rural economy, they are excluded from land ownership. Microenterprise, microlending, and asset-building approaches are geared toward the acquisition of assets, land and property ownership, access to education, and participation in the local economy.

The political empowerment system addresses the interests of marginalized and excluded populations. It focuses on service recipients in terms of advocacy and empowerment and on the conscientization and imperative of service providers to change institutions and structure of services responsible for exclusion, discrimination, and oppression. This system focuses on participatory planning and decision making, advocacy, social justice and human rights, and equal access to resources such as food, water, health care, and education, as indicated in the MDGs.

The human investment interventive system works with microsystems such as individuals and families. However, it shifts from the traditional deficit model to empowerment, strengths-based, and solution-focused approaches. It includes creating a sustainable family microeconomy and capacity building in terms of building resources available to families in need. The model is more fully explicated with diagrams and applications in Elliott and Mayadas (2000) and Elliott (2010).

This model is just one contribution. More models need to be developed in order to further the potential of social development in the global practice of social work. In particular, testable models identifying skills as well as interventive techniques would address the criticisms that social development remains at a conceptual level and has not been sufficiently operationalized.

WHAT ARE SOME SOCIAL DEVELOPMENT APPLICATIONS TO SOCIAL WORK PRACTICE GLOBALLY?

Social development may have few theoretical models of social work practice, but there is ample evidence of the operationalization of its goals and principles in practice worldwide. The following text notes just a few of these as mainly successful practice applications at various levels of operation.

Aside from the work of the UNDP on human development mentioned earlier, other UN agencies are focusing efforts on social development goals and principles. Two examples are from the World Bank and the International Labour Organization (ILO). In 2005, the World Bank launched its initiative of addressing poverty through social development, which is defined as transforming institutions to empower people. This initiative is also designed to change the much criticized approaches of the World Bank by creating organization-wide strategies for social development (World Bank, 2005). In 2004, the ILO reported on its social development–based initiative focused on creating fair globalization and adequate work for all (ILO, 2004).

Several countries have based social policies and service delivery, including social work, along social development lines; notable among them are South Africa and New Zealand. Midgley (2001) and Gray (2006) report on the progress of the 1997 implementation of a social development framework for South African social welfare services, including social work, as part of the Reconstruction and Development Programme (RDP) initiated by the African National Congress (ANC). The implementation of the policies outlined in the *White Paper for Social Welfare* (RSA, 1994) involved far-reaching changes for the organization of social work practice. Given subsequent changes in political power and a return to macro-based economic policy, Gray argues that social development could not succeed in this context. She further posits that social development as applied to social work was not well understood and that more conceptual clarity is needed. Midgley proposes that the South African experience of implementing a social development–based social policy and services system offers valuable experience for other countries. Noyoo (2000) argues that social workers need to understand a broader economic perspective to understand, for example, the impact of economic structural adjustment programs in sub Saharan Africa, as well as dicusses the impact of social development and implications for social work in South Africa.

Lunt (2009) documents the change in New Zealand social welfare policies and services from a neoliberal approach to a social development model. Intended to address welfare dependency, poverty, and violence, welfare services were reformed under the Ministry of Social Development. A social investment model building social and human capital in families and communities is key to the new welfare approach. Though the system is based on classic social development theory, Lunt raises questions about people being considered investments instead of acknowledging their intrinsic value as human beings.

These examples have referred to large UN programs and countries adopting a wholesale philosophy of social policy and services based on social development. In addition, there are many programs around the world that partially implement social development ideas; three are indicated here as examples.

- In Bangladesh, Integrated Social Development Effort (ISDE) is a nongovernmental organization (NGO) set up by social workers to address rural poverty through the creation of self-sustaining rural communities. It is a partnership of NGOs and deals with challenging social conditions, including empowering rural women such as those in the foothills of the Hindu Kush-Himalayas. It was first established to respond to dire social conditions after the 1991 cyclone. Later the organization focused on adult literacy and formed 525 centers to bring literacy and numeric education to 34,260 learners (of whom 15,750 were adults). Through a primary health-care program, it also focused on reproductive and child health for 5000 households in Chakaria thana, focusing particularly on postnatal care, immunization, and growth monitoring of malnourished children. The program also includes the prevention of sexually transmitted diseases, including AIDS (ISDE, 2009).

- In the United States, the Administration for Children and Families operates the Assets for Independence (AFI) program. This program funds community-based nonprofits and government agencies to implement individual development matched-savings accounts as an approach to addressing poverty. These funds may then be used for setting up a small business, making a deposit on a home mortgage, or paying for education (AFI, 2009).

- In the United Kingdom, the Child Trust Fund (CTF) is an example of a state following social investment and asset-based policies. At birth, each child born in the United Kingdom is given a government grant atbirth of 250 pounds sterling. This is doubled for low-income families. A further grant is given at the age of seven. Parents may make additional contributions. The account may not be drawn until the child reaches the age of eighteen (CTF, 2009).

This chapter has discussed some basic concepts of social development and looked at the links between social development and social work over approximately twenty-five years. Examples have been given from the literature where social development concepts are applied to aspects of social work practice. The fact that there is some conceptual uncertainty around the implementation of social development and social work practice at the theoretical level is evident in the example from South Africa. The lack of theoretical practice models possibly contributes to this. An example of one theoretical model is presented and a call is made for more models to improve the application of social development within the social work profession. Lacking also is a systematic research effort to evaluate programs based on social development outside the UN. This is an essential requirement for further development of the model. However, these examples selected from international social work practice suggest that social development provides an appropriate but underused model for social work practice globally.

REFERENCES

Assets for Independence (AFI). (2009). Assets for Independence program. www.acf.hhs.gov/programs/ocs/afi/ (accessed July 13, 2009).

Asamoah, Y., Healy, L. M., & Mayadas, N. S. (1997). Ending the international domestic dichotomy: New approaches to a global curriculum for the millennium. *Journal of Social Work Education, 33*(2), 389–401.

Bannerjee, M. M. (2005). Social work, Rawlsian social justice and social development. *Social Development Issues, 27*(1), 6–24.

Billups, J. O. (1994). The social development model as an organizing framework for social work practice. In R. G. Meinert, J. T. Pardeck, & W. P. Sullivan (Eds.), *Issues in social work: A critical analysis.* Westport, CT: Auburn House.

Billups, J., Meinert, R. G., & Midgley, J. (1994). Redefining social development: Diverse conceptualizations and new approaches. *Social Development Issues, 16*(3), 1–19.

Billups, J., & Juliá M. C. (1996) Technology transfer and integrated social development: International issues and possibilities for social work. *Journal of Sociology and Social Welfare, 23*(2), 175–188.

Child Trust Fund (CTF). 2009. Key facts about the Child Trust Fund. www.childtrustfund.gov.uk/templates/Page_____1177.aspx (accessed July 13, 2009).

Cox, D., & Pawar, M. (2006). *International social work: Issues, strategies, and programs.* Thousand Oaks, CA. Sage.

Dominelli, L. (1997). International social development and social work: A feminist perspective. In M. C. Hockenstad & J. Midgley (Eds.), *Issues in international social work* (pp. 74–91). Washington, DC: NASW Press.

Elliott, D. (1993). Social work and social development: Towards an integrative model for social work practice. *International Social Work, 36,* 21–36.

Elliott, D. (2010). A social development model for incorporating disaster planning, management and relief in the social work curriculum. In D. Gillespie & K. Danso (Eds.), *Disaster Concepts and Issues: A Guide for Social Work Education and Practice* (Chapter 5, pp 89–110). Alexandria, VA: Council on Social Work Education.

Elliott, D. & Mayadas, N. S. (1999) Infusing Global Perspectives into Social Work Practice. In R. Link & C. S. Ramanathan (Eds.), *Innovations in Global Social Work: All our Futures* (Chapter 4, pp. 52–68). San Francisco, CA: Brooks/Cole.

Elliott, D., & Mayadas N. S. (2000). International perspectives on social work practice. In P. Allen-Meares & C. Garvin (Eds.), *The handbook of social work direct practice* (Chapter 30, pp. 633–650). Thousand Oaks, CA: Sage.

Elliott, D., & Mayadas, N. S. (1996). Social development and clinical practice in social work. *Journal of Applied Social Sciences, 21*(1), 61–68.

Estes, R. (1997). Social work, social development and community welfare centers in international perspective. *International Social Work, 40*(1), 43–55.

Estes, R. (1994). Education for social development: Curricular issues and models. *Social Development Issues, 16,* 69–89.

Falk, D. (1984). The social development paradigm. *Social Development Issues, 8*(4), 4–14.

Gray, M. (2006). The progress of social development in South Africa. *International journal of social welfare, 15*(Suppl. 1), S53–S64.

Gray, M., & Crofts, P. (2008). Social development and its relevance to Australian social work. *Australian Social Work, 61*(1), 88–103.

Healy, L. M. (2008). *International social work* (2nd ed.). New York: Oxford University Press.

Hollister, D. (1977). Social work skills and social development. *Social Development Issues, 1*(1), 9–20.

Integrated Social Development Effort (ISDE). (2009). Integrated Social Development Effort (ISDE) Bangladesh.http://www.isdebangladesh.org/ (accessed April 14, 2011).

International Labour Organization (ILO). (2004). *A fair globalization: Creating opportunities for all.* Report of the World Commission on the Social Dimension of Globalization. www.ilo.org/public/english/wcsdg/docs/report.pdf (accessed July 13, 2009).

Kwok, J. (2008). Social work and social development in Asia. *International Social Work, 51*(5), 699–704.

Livermore, M. (1996). Social work, social development and micro-enterprises: Techniques and issues for implementation. *Journal of Applied Social Sciences, 21*(1), 37–44.

Lunt, N. (2009). The rise of a social development agenda in New Zealand. *International journal of social welfare, 18,* 3–12.

Mayadas, N. S., & Elliott, D. (2001). Psychosocial approaches, social work and social development. *Social Development Issues, 23*(1), 5–13.

Mayadas, N. S. & Elliott, D. (2002). Social Work's Response to Refugee Issues: A Global Response. In P. K. Visvesvaran (Ed.) *SOCIAL WORK TODAY — Present Realities & Future Prospects (The Madras School of Social Work Golden Jubilee Commemorative Volume)* (Chapter 2, pp. 107–119). Chennai, India: Madras School of Social Work & Society for Education & Research.

Mayadas, N. S., & Elliott, D. (1995). Developing professional identity through social groupwork: A social development model for social work education. In M. D. Feit, J. H. Ramey, J. S. Woodarski, & A. R. Mann (Eds.), *Capturing the power of diversity* (Chapter 7, pp. 89–107). New York: Haworth Press.

Meinert, R., & Kohn, E. (1987). Towards operationalization of social development concepts. *Social Development Issues, 10*, 4–18.

Midgley, J. (1995). *Social development: The developmental perspective in social welfare.* Thousand Oaks, CA: Sage.

Midgley, J. (1994). Defining social development: Historical trends and conceptual formulations. *Social Development Issues, 16*(3), 3–19.

Midgley, J. (1991). Social development and multi-cultural social work. *Journal of Multi-Cultural Social Work, 1*(1), 85–10.

Midgley, J., & Livermore, M. (1997). The development perspective in social work: Educational implications for a new century. *Journal of Social Work Education, 33*(3), 573–586.

Midgley, J. (2001). South Africa: The challenge of social development. *International Journal of Social Welfare, 10*, 267–275.

Midgley, J., & Conley, A. (Eds.). (2010). *Developmental social work.* New York: Oxford University Press.

Noyoo, N. (2000). Social development in sub-Saharan Africa: Lessons for social work practice in South Africa. *International Social Work, 43*(4), 453–465.

Paiva, J. F. X. (1977). A conception of social development. *Social Service Review, 51*(2), 326–336.

Raheim, S. (1996). Micro-enterprise as an approach for promoting economic development in social work: Lessons from the self-employment investment demonstration. *International Social Work, 39*(1), 69–82.

R.S.A. (Parliament of the Republic of South Africa) (1994). *White Paper on Reconstruction and Development.* Government Gazette Vol. 353, No. 16085. Pretoria, South Africa, Government Printer.

Sanders, D. (1982). *The developmental perspective in social work.* Manoa, HI: University of Hawaii Press.

Sen, A. (2000). A decade of human development. *Journal of Human Development, 1*(1), 17–23.

Smith, A. E. (2003). Social work and ethnic minorities' social development in the People's Republic of China. *International Social Work, 46*(3), 403–419.

Stein, H. D. (1976). Social work's developmental and change functions: Their roots in practice. *Social Service Review, 50*(1), 1–10.

United Nations' Development Programme (UNDP). (2000). Millenium Development Goals. www.undp.org/mdg/ (accessed July 13, 2009).

World Bank. (2005). Empowering people by transforming institutions: Social development in World Bank operations. http://siteresources.worldbank.org/EXTSOCIALDEVELOPMENT/Resources/244362-1164181732580/SDStrategy-Full.pdf (accessed July 13, 2009).

World Summit for Social Development. (1995). Copenhagen declaration on social development. www.un.org/esa/socdev/wssd/decl_intro.html (accessed July 13, 2009).

Disaster Relief and Management: Readiness, Response, and Recovery

GOLAM M. MATHBOR

Disasters seem to be increasing, whether caused by nature or by human activities, especially those activities that disregard the environment. Disaster can strike anywhere, including in rich industrialized countries, where their occurrence can highlight long-standing structural failures in addressing social problems (Dominelli, 2007). Regardless of the type of disaster or location, vulnerable populations routinely experience vast inequities in terms of emergency response (Zakour, 2007). The strong link between poverty and heightened vulnerability to natural disasters calls for social justice. Vulnerability is the physical, social, economic, political, or other susceptibility to a destabilizing phenomenon of natural or human cause (Zakour, 2007). Buckland and Rahman (1999) note that communities that are well trained, culturally, socially, and psychologically, in disaster preparedness are better prepared and more effective responders to the aftermath of disasters.

The movement toward preparedness at the local level was a real weakness during Hurricane Katrina (Light, 2005). Smith (2007) noted that existing warning systems in some communities are not specifically understandable by local cultures. Many people in the area affected by the 1991 Bangladesh cyclone heard warning signals three to six hours before the storm surge hit but did not take refuge in shelters, and a similar situation occurred in the devastation of Hurricane Katrina. People were not evacuated in time due to a lack of well-coordinated plans among the organizations involved.

In contrast, no deaths occurred among indigenous people of the Andaman Islands during the 2004 tsunami devastation because of their understanding of early warning systems. As another example, Tropical Cyclone Sidr, which hit low-lying coastal regions in November 2007, was the deadliest storm to strike Bangladesh in the last decade, killing more than 3100 people. Credit goes to the Bangladesh Red Crescent Society for an effective early warning system and its volunteers, who evacuated 3.5 million people to shelter houses before the storm struck.

Mortality from disaster is generally greatest in areas with the poorest socioeconomic conditions (Guha-Sapiro, 1991). Related deaths were largely attributable to a lack of decent housing capable of providing shelter during the Bangladesh cyclone of 1991. The poor are hardest hit because by definition they only have access to the lowest-cost assets (land and housing), making them vulnerable (Smith, 2007). Pyles (2007) analyzed the association between community characteristics before a disaster and the survival or failure after disaster of eight communities that experienced the Midwest floods of 1993 in the United States. They found that high poverty rates in communities were associated with failure to survive (Pyles, 2007, p. 321). Communities characterized by higher levels of physical, human, and social capital were better prepared and more effective in responding to disaster, such as in the case of the 1997 Red River flood in Canada. Therefore, in assessing the vulnerability of communities, one must assess not only risks but also the resistance of physical infrastructure to disaster and the resilience of the community after being destabilized by a natural or human-made disaster.

There are significant differences between developing and developed countries regarding disaster relief and management, as summarized in the following table. Disaster managers must take these differences into consideration while devising strategies and techniques for effective management of disasters.

Social workers need to be prepared in anticipation of disaster rather than waiting until disaster strikes.

TABLE 15.1. DIFFERENCES BETWEEN DEVELOPING
AND DEVELOPED COUNTRIES

Developing Countries	Developed Countries
• Less dependency on government	• Dependent on government
• Heavy reliance on military	• Military as backup
• Reliance on NGOs and civil society	• NGOs supplement
• Fewer rules	• More rules
• Remote areas	• Easier accessibility
• Lack of technology	• High technology
• Difficult communication	• Better communication
• Interpersonal communication	• Impersonal communication
• Fewer possessions	• Material possessions
• Extended families	• Families far apart
• Village life	• Anonymity
• Lack of formal services	• Community services
• Use of tents	• No tents
• Difficult or no infrastructure	• Existing infrastructure
• Use of shelter houses	• Use of public facilities
• Built-in social capital	• Not built-in social capital

Social work curricula need to incorporate disaster management so that a new generation of social workers will be trained and prepared for disasters. Ongoing training must also be developed for practicing social workers. The preamble of the US National Association of Social Workers (NASW) Code of Ethics for example explicitly states that "the primary mission of the social work profession is to enhance human well-being and help meet the basic human needs of all people, with particular attention to the needs and empowerment of people who are vulnerable, oppressed and living in poverty" (www.naswdc.org/pubs/code/default.asp). However, social work has not yet developed or prioritized disaster management as an integral part of curriculum and practice. The social work profession is highly grounded in the principles of social justice and human rights. Its active involvement in disaster management is pivotal to create a plan that links vulnerable populations to required resources before, during, and after a disaster (Mathbor, 2007). Social work professionals use invisible community assets such as solidarity, social cohesion, social interaction, and social networks to enhance the capacity of individuals, groups, communities, and organizations, thereby ensuring social development. Evidently, the enhancement of social development facilitated by social workers and community allows

for a stronger, more cohesive response to disasters (Mathbor, 2008).

DEFINITION OF DISASTER

Disaster can be defined as a hazard that causes significant damage to a vulnerable community or locality, resulting in deaths, property loss, and so on. It is defined by the World Health Organization (WHO) as any occurrence that causes damage, ecological disruption, loss of human life, and deterioration of health and health services on a scale sufficient to warrant an extraordinary response from outside the affected community or area.

Classification of Disaster

Generally, disaster is classified into two types— natural and human made. Considering the nature, causes, and sources of disaster, it can then be classified into two distinct but overlapping categories:

1. Natural disaster: Disaster caused by nature, such as earthquakes, cyclones, volcanoes, erosion, and hurricanes
2. Human-made disaster: Disaster caused by human beings, either deliberately or accidental, such as fire, terrorism, riot, pollution, accidents, and war

Causes of Disaster

To understand the causes of disaster, the following formula can be used:

Disaster = Hazard × Vulnerability / Capacity.

A hazard can be a disaster if it affects certain portions of society to such an extent that people need an extraordinary response from outside the community. Absence of capacity can be termed *vulnerability*, and similarly, capacity lacks vulnerability. Vulnerability is a political-ecological concept in that it refers to the relationship of people with their environment and the political economy of a society and culture that shapes and conditions this relationship (Zakour, 2007).

The Action Impact Matrix (AIM) is an analytical tool that helps to study the interlinkages that exist among seemingly independent policies, activities, and issues. Professor Mohan Munasinghe of Sri Lanka has developed this innovative tool in order to assess the vulnerability and adaptation of communities to natural disasters. He argues that the mechanism of identifying and analyzing economic, environmental, and social interactions plays a key role in the implementation of sustainable development goals and identification of major impacts on development goals under disaster conditions, including future climate-change hazards. Unique features of the AIM methodology are as follows (MIND, 2006):

1. Determine the most important national goals and policies.
2. Determine critical vulnerability and adaptation (VA) areas relevant to climate change.
3. Determine status of VA areas subject to only natural climate variability.
4. Determine impacts of climate change on VA areas.
5. Identify how goals and policies might affect VA areas.
6. Identify how VA areas might affect goals and policies.
7. Prioritize most important interactions and determine appropriate remedial policies and measures.
8. Perform more detailed studies and analysis of key interactions and policy options previously identified.

Figure 15.1 depicts how to calculate the effects of vulnerabilities on development, and Figure 15.2 helps to enumerate development effects on vulnerabilities.

		Economic				Environmental				Social		
		(1) Agriculture & Livestock	(2) Hydro Energy	(3) Infrastructure, incl. transport	(4) Industry & Tourism	(5) Water resources (excl. hydro use)	(6) Forest Resources	(7) Bio-diversity (flora & fauna)	(8) Coastal resources, Wetlands	(9) Human Settlements & Livelihoods	(10) Human health
(R1)	RISK 1: Storms and Floods	+1	+2	–1	–1	+2	–	–	–1	–2	–2
(R2)	RISK 2: Droughts	–2	–2	–	–	–2	–1	–	–	–1	–1
	Development Goals/Policies										
(A)	Economic Growth	–1	–2	–1	–1				–1		–1
(B)	Poverty alleviation - Equity	–1	0	–1		–1			–1*	–2	–1
(C)	Food Security	0	–1	–1	0				–1		
(D)	Employment	0	–1	0	–1				–1		0
(E)	Trade & Globalisation	–1	0		–1				–1		
(F)	Macroeconomic stabilization	–1	–1	–1	–1				–1	–1	–1
(G)	Public Sector Reform										
(H)	Environment	–0	–1		–1	–1	–1	–1	–1	–1	

Sectors most affected by droughts
Sectors most affected by floods (and droughts)
Sectors which affect all policy goals
Goals most affected by hazards
Goals moderately affected by hazards

FIGURE 15.1. Vulnerabilities Effects on Development (VED).

		Areas of Vulnerability									
		Economic				Environmental				Social	
		(1)	(2)	(3)	(4)	(5)	(6)	(7)	(8)	(9)	(10)
		Agriculture & Livestock	Hydro Energy	Infrastructure, incl. transport	Industry & Tourism	Water resources (excl. hydro use)	Forest Resources	Bio-diversity (flora & fauna)	Coastal resources, Wetlands	Human Settlements & Livelihoods	Human health
	Development Goals/Policies										
(A)	Economic Growth	+1	+1	+2/3	+2	−1	−1	−1	−1	+2	+1
(B)	Poverty alleviation - Equity	+1		+1						+2	+2
(C)	Food Security	+2		+1		−1	−1	−1		+1	+2
(D)	Employment	−1		+1	+2					+2	+1
(E)	Trade & Globalisation	+1		+2	+2			−1		+1	+2
(F)	Macroeconomic stabilization	−1		+1	+1					+1	+1
(G)	Public Sector Reform	+1		+2	+2	+1				+1	+1
(H)	Environment	−1		0	−1	+2	+2	+2	+2		+2
(R1)	RISK 1: Storms and Floods	+1	+2	−1	−1	+2	−	−	−1	−2	−2
(R2)	RISK 2: Droughts	−2	−2	−	−	−2	−1	−	−	−1	−1

FIGURE 15.2. Development Effects on Vulnerabilities (DEV).

Items in these figures can be expanded to include other issues and goals based on unique circumstances in disaster-prone communities.

DISASTER CYCLE

There are three stages in the disaster cycle:

1. Readiness (preparedness): Planning how to respond to a disaster
2. Response: Minimizing the hazards created by an emergency
3. Recovery: Returning the community or environment to normalcy

Disaster Readiness: Before the Disaster

In this phase, disaster managers develop plans of action for the time when disaster strikes. *Disaster readiness* refers to the effective readiness measures to expedite emergency action, rehabilitation, and recovery. It includes emergency warnings, emergency shelter, emergency evacuation plans, and maintenance of resources and training of personnel. An effective model of readiness from Bangladesh is described next.

The idea of a Cyclone Preparedness Programme (CPP) started in 1965, when the Bangladesh Red Crescent Society (BDRCS; formerly the national Red Cross) requested that the International Federation of Red Cross and Red Crescent Societies (IFRC; formerly the League of Red Cross and Red Crescent

Societies) support the establishment of a warning system for the population living in the coastal belt. In 1966, the IFRC and the Swedish Red Cross began to implement a pilot scheme for cyclone preparedness that consisted of both impersonal and personal warning equipment.

During the international seminar, Disaster Planning, Management, and Relief: New Responsibilities for Social Work Education, held in St. Michael, Barbados, in January 2007, Geoff Loane, head of ICRC regional delegation for the United States and Canada, noted that

> Bangladesh has the most exposed and vulnerable coastline to flooding with the largest population presence of anywhere in the world. On an annual basis, thousands of persons are displaced and lives destroyed through flooding. Anticipation of floods in Bangladesh is thus somewhat straightforward and because of this a greater emphasis can be placed on preparation and response. Again it is not surprising that the country has one of the best prepared local capacities for disaster response and for anyone trying to draw lessons in relation to coping mechanisms, this case study provides fascinating insight into how societies manage their disaster response mechanism.
>
> —(Loane, 2007, p. 14)

The CPP experience shows that proper guidance; transparency; access to information at all stages, such as project proposal, planning, implementation, and evaluation stages of development initiatives; and recognition of people's worth are needed in the disaster management project (Mathbor, 2007, p. 365). Volunteers' sincerity and firm commitment to the fundamental principles of the Red Cross movement, such as humanity, impartiality, neutrality, independence, voluntary service, unity, and universality, which were cultivated through a sustained training program, not only enhanced the effectiveness of CPP but also saved many lives in recent disasters that hit the coastal areas of Bangladesh. Many of the 2004 tsunami victims in South and Southeast Asia could have been saved if there had been similar preparedness programs in the areas.

Volunteers with CPP are well-trained cadres in disaster management. They are also familiar with the local community and its resources, such as shelter locations, relief programs, and rehabilitation programs, as well as the evacuation plan to follow at the time of disaster. Ongoing interaction among the members as well as with the project people (Functionaries/Officials of CPP) helps avoid mistrust and misunderstanding in the development process. Local people come forward to join CPP on a voluntary basis. Year-round training generates leadership qualities, management skills, the tendency to serve humanity, and solidarity among the volunteers. Volunteers feel satisfied by the social recognition of their relentless efforts to help distressed people of the community.

The program operates through an effective chain of command using a communication networking system that is quick to respond to the immediate needs of the coastal communities. This communication system consists of both personal and impersonal methods of communication. Volunteers are seen as

Matrix AED
Effects of key VA areas on development goals and policies

	Vulnerability & Adaptation (VA) Areas		
	Economic	Environmental	Social
	....	....	....
Dev. Goals/Policies			
(A)			
(B)			
(C)			
(D)			

Matrix DEA
Effects of development goals and policies on key VA areas

	Vulnerability & Adaptation (VA) Areas		
	Economic	Environmental	Social
	....	....	....
Dev. Goals/Policies			
(A)			
(B)			
(C)			
(D)			

FIGURE 15.3. Telecommunication Network of CPP.

the magnetic catalyst to convey program messages to the people; thus, CPP conducts year-round training for volunteers. It also uses local media in disseminating program messages to people, such as by staging dramas, showing films and video shows, and so on.

Figure 15.3 depicts impersonal communication (i.e., telecommunication network) of CPP from headquarters to cyclone-prone localities. Figure 15.4 presents various stages of impersonal communication, such as use of high-frequency (HF) equipment at Zonal to Thana levels (A) and very high-frequency (VHF) equipment at Union levels (B), and it illustrates personal communications, such as megaphone, mike, and direct contact at the Unit (C) and Village (D) levels. Figure 15.5 is the organizational chart of a Unit Committee and the specific tasks assigned in various committees that serve 2000 to 3000 people.

Before any disaster, governments should undertake disaster mitigation and preparedness programs. The following suggestions can be considered at the preparedness stage of disaster management.

1. Create more awareness and provide information about what to do at the time of disaster via posters, billboards, mass-media advertising, and so on.
2. Regularly update existing forecasting systems.
3. Preserve foods at regional stocks to serve the affected people effectively.
4. Provide an ongoing training program for community-based organizations (CBOs), nongovernmental organizations (NGOs), and government officials about search and rescue, evacuation, first aid, and other logistics.

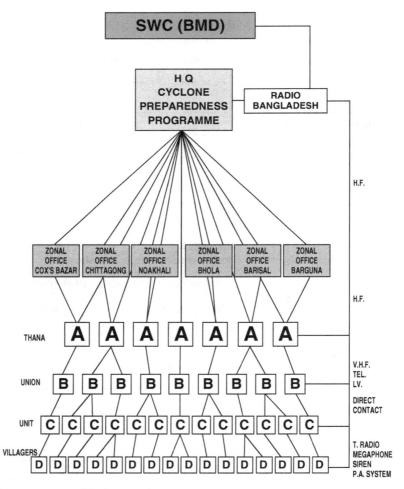

FIGURE 15.4. Dissemination of Cyclone Signals.

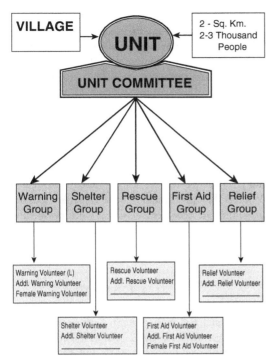

FIGURE 15.5. CPP Unit Committee.

Disaster Response: During the Disaster

The response phase includes the mobilization of the necessary emergency services and first responders in the disaster-affected area. Here, necessary emergency services include search and rescue, evacuation, demand analysis, resource analysis, emergency relief (e.g., food, water, sanitation, first aid), and logistic supply (e.g., tents). First responders include firefighters, police, social workers, volunteers, CBOs, and NGOs.

This author has developed a model that emphasizes three steps to building social capital based on the World Bank classification of social capital from the perspective of poverty reduction and community capacity building: bonds, bridges, and links.

1. *Bonding within communities:* Utilization of social capital starts with bonding within the community. Social integration, social cohesion, solidarity, networking, two-way communication, sustained interaction among members, effective coordination of community activities, collaboration and support of member activities, fostering leadership qualities, and giving a hand to other community members are all useful attributes for bonding within communities. these attributes can be cultivated through

recreational activities, religious and spiritual gatherings, political and institutional affiliations, economic and business activities, physical infrastructure building, and psychological and social supports.

2. *Bridging among communities:* The next level is reaching out to other communities within the society. At this point groups and interested citizenry can form a coalition to identify needs and make joint collaborative efforts to meet the needs.

3. *Linking communities through ties with financial and public institutions:* The historic relationship developed between communities and the government, including financial institutions, has generally assisted in mitigating the consequences of natural disasters. This Effectiveness in working together has proved crucial in mobilizing community resources, expertise, professionals, and volunteers both before disaster strikes and in the recovery work that takes place during and afterward (Mathbor, 2007, pp. 362–363).

All efforts of relief should be administered under the exclusive umbrella of the government. In this phase, the government should mobilize the first responders to expedite the following operations:

1. Search and rescue operations
2. Evacuation to shelter houses
3. Needs analysis (e.g., food, safe water, first aid, medical services, mobile hospitals)

Disaster Recovery: After the Disaster

The aim of disaster recovery is to restore the affected area to its previous state. It includes the following:

1. Rehabilitation: Cleaning up the debris, rebuilding destroyed houses and property, reemployment, and so on
2. Reconstruction: Rebuilding or repairing essential infrastructure (e.g., roads, hospitals, schools)

In this phase, the attention of the government should be on rehabilitation and reconstruction:

1. Providing assistance in rebuilding affected houses by giving aid and interest-free loans

2. Supplying fertilizer and hybrid seeds as well as agricultural loans to affected farmers
3. Reemploying people who have lost their jobs, providing (free of cost or with interest-free loans) the means of production (e.g., fishing nets, fishing boats, cows, goats) as necessary
4. Rationing on temporary basis
5. Selling rice and essential goods in open market during this period
6. Learning the lessons from present disasters

ROLE OF SOCIAL WORK IN DISASTER RELIEF AND MANAGEMENT

Adger and colleagues (2005) note that social and ecological vulnerability to disasters and outcomes of any particular extreme event are influenced by buildup or erosion of resilience both before and after disasters occur. The authors further state that resilient social-ecological systems incorporate diverse mechanisms for living with, and learning from, change and unexpected shocks. Social work is a discipline that originated from a grassroots movement that continuously dealt with unexpected shocks by utilizing people's strengths. Mukhier (2006) reports that psychosocial support—previously considered soft and not tangible in terms of assistance to those affected by disasters—was shown to be important after the devastating 2003 earthquake that struck Bam, Iran, and it is now a key component for any effective emergency response.

Dr. Ariyaratne, the founder and president of Sarvodaya (the largest NGO in Sri Lanka), made these remarks on the value of social work after the 2004 tsunami:

> Most of our full-time workers and thousands of volunteers from unaffected areas worked around the clock taking a lot of risks and undergoing hardship. However, none of them demanded additional salaries or extra payment for overtime work. Neither did they seek any cheap publicity or recognition. They only shared the sufferings of those who lost their loved ones and possessions to the Tsunami and tried to make the lives of the survivors at least a little bit easier. They helped satisfy the survivors' immediate, basic physical, psychological, and social needs and were rewarded with the dispassionate joy of loving and serving true Sarvodaya (sacrifice) spirit.
>
> —(Sarvodaya, 2006, p. 5)

Social workers are well connected to the people they serve, know about their unique locations, are familiar with community resources and leadership potentials, and are equipped with the necessary knowledge base to address issues at micro, meso, and macro levels. In March of 2006, NASW convened a meeting on disasters and disparities as they relate to social work and NASW, examining issues in the wake of the unprecedented disasters of the last several years. "It is very important for social workers to focus on the issues of disparities when addressing disasters," said Dr. Elizabeth Clark, NASW Executive Director. "While other professionals have valuable skills for responding to disasters, the social work perspective takes into account the many factors that affect access—or lack of access—to services and resources" (Stoesen, 2006, p. 5).

CONCLUSION

Although plans, resources, and logistics are vital in disaster relief and management, consideration must also be given to the social capital of the community. it is evident that the CPP, AIM, and social capital theory are three key strategies that should be considered by the organizations working in this field as they strengthen disaster policies and management.

As stated in the beginning of this chapter, communities that are well trained culturally, socially, and psychologically are better prepared and more effective responders to the aftermath of disasters. This applies to the social work profession, where proper training is critical to all stages of disaster planning and mitigation; however, the current social work curriculum teaches little about the role of the social worker in disaster management. Trained social workers need to understand their role as one of being realistic, being able to advocate for the client and community, being supportive and assisting with available resources, teaching empowerment, and being culturally competent by taking into account community values. Training also needs to focus on types of disasters and understanding disaster relief and management.

REFERENCES

Adger, W. N., et al. (2005). Social-ecological resilience to coastal disasters. *Science, 309*, 1036–1039. Washington, DC: American Association of the Advancement of Science.

Bangladesh Red Crescent Society (BDRCS). (1996). *CPP at a glance*. Dhaka: Author.

Buckland, J., & Rahman, M. (1999). Community development and disaster management: A case study of three rural communities in the 1997 Red River flood in Canada. Menno Simons College, Retrieved from http://www.unwinnipeg.ca/~msc/FLDRPTV2.htm. Winnipeg, Manitoba.

Dominelli, L. (2007). Editorial. *International Social Work, 50*(3), 291–294.

Guha-Sapiro, D. (1991). Rapid assessment of health needs in mass emergencies: Review of current concepts and methods. *World Health Statistics Quarterly, 44,* 171–181.

Light, P. (2005, September 4). Lessons Learned: Hurricane Katrina and Wilma Hit U.S. Gulf Coastal States, *Boston Globe.*

Loane, G. (2007). Multidimensional domains of disaster response for social work practice: preparedness, response, recovery, and mitigation. In *Proceedings of the International Seminar on Disaster Planning, Management, and Relief: New responsibilities for social work education* (pp. 12–18). St. Michael, Barbados: Council on Social Work Education.

Mathbor, G. M. (2008). *Effective community participation in coastal development.* Chicago: Lyceum Books.

Mathbor, G. M. (2007). Enhancement of community preparedness for natural disasters: The role of social work in building social capital for sustainable disaster relief and management. *International Social Work, 50*(3), 357–369.

MIND (Munasinghe Institute for Development). (2006). *Second International Conference on Sustainable Hazard Reduction, Rehabilitation, Reconstruction, and Long-Term Development report.* Colombo, Sri Lanka: Author.

Mukhier, M. (2006). Surviving the Bam earthquake: Psychosocial support helps people to heal. *Optimist: Looking Beyond the Horizon.* Retrieved April 27, 2006, from www.optimistmag.org/gb/0014/one.php.

Pyles, L. (2007). Community organizing for post-disaster social development: Locating social work. *International Social Work, 50*(3), 321–333.

Sarvodaya. (2006). *Waves of compassion: Sarvodaya's Tsunami to Deshodaya Plan after six months of action.* Colombo, Sri lanka: Author.

Smith, M. (2007). A social justice framework for teaching disaster-related knowledge and skills. In *Proceedings of the International Seminar on Disaster Planning, Management, and Relief: New Responsibilities for social work education* (pp. 110–114). St. Michael, Barbados: Council on Social Work Education.

Stoesen, L. (2006). Experts examine disasters, disparities. *NASW News,* April 2006, p. 5. Washington, DC: NASW.

Zakour, M. J. (2007). Vulnerability: A central concept encompassing the multidimensionality of disaster. In *Proceedings of the International Seminar on Disaster Planning, Management, and Relief: New responsibilities for social work education* (pp. 71–76). St. Michael, Barbados: Council on Social Work Education.

16

Representing Social Work at the United Nations and Other International Bodies

ROBIN MAMA

The social work profession has a rich history of participating in and influencing the work of the United Nations (UN) and its affiliate agencies. The work of nongovernmental organizations (NGOs) at the founding conference of the UN in San Francisco in 1945 played a key role in establishing what has come to be a formal relationship between civil society and the UN. Article 71 of the UN Charter cemented this relationship by allowing the Economic and Social Council (ECOSOC) to make consultative arrangements with NGOs (UN, 2003). The number of NGOs at the founding conference numbered 1200; at present 3172 NGOs have consultative status with ECOSOC (UN, 2009a). Three of the leading social work organizations that have consultative status with the UN are as follows:

- International Association of Schools of Social Work (IASSW)—received consultative status in 1947
- International Federation of Social Workers (IFSW)—received consultative status in 1959
- International Council on Social Welfare (ICSW)—received consultative status in 1972.

This chapter focuses primarily on representing social work at the UN through the IFSW, of which the author is an appointed representative.

OVERVIEW

Since its inception, the UN has served as the primary institution for nations to work toward peace and development based on the principles of justice, human dignity, and well-being for all (UN, 2009b). It is where governments to meet to discuss concerns and make decisions on a collective scale (Cronin, Mama, Mbugua, & Mouravieff-Apostol, 2006). Once decisions are made, the work that is involved in making these decisions a reality falls to civil society. The relationship of the UN with civil society is a detailed and sometimes complex one. The eligibility requirements for civil society to engage in consultative relationship with the UN, the rights and obligations of civil society in consultative status, procedures for withdrawal or suspension of consultative status, and how the UN Secretariat supports this consultative relationship is outlined in ECOSOC resolution 1996/31 (UN, 1996).

The UN sees itself as being in partnership with civil society to achieve the mandates of the decisions of the UN and its affiliate agencies. Without the work of civil society to implement and put into action its conventions, resolutions, treaties, and declarations, the work of the UN would come to a halt. Governments cannot do this work alone—they need civil society. However, the decision-making power of the UN rests with the 192 governments that have joined the UN. "The term *consultative status* was chosen deliberately to indicate a secondary role—being available to give advice but not part of the decision-making process" (Cronin et al., 2006, p. 211).

Most NGOs publically acknowledge their consultative status, but when they describe their work, the term *advocacy* is often used instead of *consultation*. "Consultation has more of a passive status—you wait to be called upon for your advice or expertise. Advocacy is active, purposeful, and directed at specific issues. It reflects the actual work that NGOs undertake at the United Nations" (Cronin et al., 2006, pp. 211–212).

Social work has been present within the UN since its inception. Healy (2001) provides a detailed description of the history of social work in the international arena in her book, *International Social Work* (2001).

This history has included social activism, pacifism, policy advocacy, and research and program development. International policy advocacy forms the major part of the work undertaken by NGO social workers affiliated with the UN. In examining the issues in global policy that are currently on the world stage, they are the same issues that are important to social work: poverty, human rights, health, migration, and the status of women and children. Social work skills in policy analysis are very valuable. They help to determine when and what action to take when advocating for policy change. International policy advocacy includes supporting policies that the UN is proposing, being involved in writing or commenting on proposed policy, and working within the NGO committee system to influence UN delegates to introduce new policy or change existing policy.

When advocating for policy change within the UN system, NGO representatives need to advocate on behalf of individuals, groups, and communities worldwide. Efforts must be culturally appropriate, and as representatives of an international organization that has members from all parts of the globe, there must be an understanding of the cultural elements that are present in each issue. No one approach can dominate a representative's thinking or actions, and most work undertaken will be interdisciplinary, as will be seen from the following discussion.

CURRENT ROLES AND CONTRIBUTION OF SOCIAL WORK

Representing the social work profession at the UN is an important task that cannot be learned overnight. It takes determined study and experience to fully understand the role of a representative and how to begin to influence the UN system. The UN has its own culture, language, protocols, and ways of doing work that must first be understood to fully appreciate where and when one can advocate. Each person who represents an NGO at the UN is a liaison between the organization and the UN. Work done by that representative must therefore relate directly to the work of these two organizations. Though representatives are guided by the purpose and goals of the organizations they are representing, they are present at the UN by invitation, so all their work must be professional, credible, and legitimate. Representatives should not be trying to further their own agenda through their work at the UN.

The General Assembly (GA) regularly meets at UN Headquarters in New York between September and December each year. Work by the delegates during this time is often completed as a group; however, when the GA is not in session, its work is carried out by six committees, other subsidiary bodies, and the UN Secretariat. The six committees include the following:

- First Committee—Disarmament and International Security
- Second Committee—Economic and Financial
- Third Committee—Social, Humanitarian, and Cultural
- Fourth Committee—Special Political and Decolonization
- Fifth Committee—Administrative and Budgetary
- Sixth Committee—Legal.

The work of the Third Committee is of the greatest importance to social work, and so IFSW representatives in New York follow this committee closely (Cronin et al., 2006). Representatives attend open meetings of the Third Committee and also attend briefings that highlight the work of the UN in general. Although ECOSOC-accredited NGO representatives have a fair amount of access to the UN, a number of meetings and discussions are closed to the NGO community. For example, the Security Council is generally closed to NGO representatives, except on occasion when the council chooses to extend an open invitation to the NGO community.

There are five IFSW representatives on the New York team, and each person covers a substantive area of concern to IFSW. It is important to represent IFSW at the Commission for Social Development, the Commission on the Status of Women, and the Permanent Forum on Indigenous Issues. It is also important to work in coalition with other NGO representatives on important issues that relate to the UN's work, so IFSW representatives are members of the NGO Committee on the Status of Women, the NGO Committee on Ageing, the NGO Committee on the Family, and the NGO Committee on Mental Health, to name a few.

The IFSW also has teams at the UN in Geneva and Nairobi. Social work representation in Geneva differs from that in New York because of the presence of the Office of the High Commissioner for Human Rights. Much of the work that is done in Geneva focuses on human rights and child rights. There is also social work representation at the International Labour

Organization (ILO). A major contribution of the Geneva team was the drafting of the training manual on human rights and social work that was published by the former Centre for Human Rights in 1992. The Geneva team was also heavily involved in the Secretary-General's Study on Violence against Children (Cronin et al., 2006). In Nairobi, the work of the IFSW team focuses on the work of the Human Settlements Programme, UN-HABITAT, which promotes socially and environmentally sustainable human settlements, working to achieve adequate shelter for all. The Nairobi team is a member of a subcommittee of the Cities Alliance Consultative Group, which works on city slums and other urban management initiatives. The Nairobi team also participates in the African Great Lakes Initiative, which is aimed at supporting peace and stability in Africa (Cronin et al., 2006).

The IASSW also has a team of representatives at the New York UN Headquarters. These representatives are responsible for relating to specific NGO committees, such as the NGO Committee on Mental Health or the NGO Committee on Social Development. In an article on the contribution of social work to human rights, Healy (2008) describes four ways that social work contributes to human rights: through expressions in official documents, contributions of social work leaders, representation and action, and involvement in critical incidents. These are exactly the ways that social work is represented at the UN.

As an example of expressions in official documents, NGO representatives often write statements for the annual Commission for Social Development or the Commission on the Status of Women, expressing their organization's concerns or views on the stated theme or agenda of the commission. The IFSW statement for the 47th Session of the Commission for Social Development in 2009 spoke to the theme of social integration on the issues of poverty eradication and full employment (ECOSOC, 2009). The IFSW made specific recommendations on social integration as it applied to employment and poverty. As part of the record of the Commission for Social Development, it is hoped that these types of recommendations provide useful discussion for governments as they debate the theme of the commission and work toward a plan of action at the end of the commission. It is further hoped that delegates include these recommendations in their own plans for their country. If so, an NGO might be then called upon for assistance or guidance in interpreting or implementing the recommendations.

During these commissions, NGOs also hold side events, or workshops that are held during the times when the commission has no active sessions. These side events usually last for one to two hours and are on topics related to the theme of the commission. Representatives of NGOs, UN staff, delegate staff, and others are drawn to the side events to learn of new approaches, best practices, and issues of concern that might also help influence the work of the commission and the development of the plan of action. These events also give UN and delegate staff additional resources to call upon from civil society. They often highlight the contributions of social work and its leaders to the UN (a number of social work experts have been chosen to work with the UN on various issues).

Social work also has been represented at the UN in the development of new conventions. The most recent convention that entered into force on May 3, 2008, was the Convention on the Rights of Persons with Disabilities. A number of NGO representatives (several of them representing social work) made substantive recommendations for the text of the convention and its implementation. Their contributions helped to make the newest convention inclusive and applicable to the rights of all persons with disabilities—in fact, the definition of disability itself was changed because of social work's contribution to the language of this convention.

Every NGO representative at the UN wants to be able to influence governments and thus decision making at the highest level. The NGO Committee on the Family had that influence on the ambassador of Benin, who believed that the UN was not addressing family issues adequately. The ambassador proposed that the International Year of the Family be organized in 1994. This UN observance of the family drew considerable attention to the policies, programs, and strategies for supporting families. Since 1994, several publications and research studies have provided valuable information on issues affecting families around the world (Cronin et al., 2006).

These examples illustrate some of the impact that social work has had on the UN though NGO representatives. The work of the UN also has an impact on NGOs and their work. For example, an IFSW team member works with the NGO Committee on Indigenous Issues. Her work and the knowledge she gained from working with the NGO committee led her to draft a policy statement for IFSW on indigenous people. "An important part of IFSW's work has been to represent social work's views on major world issues through development of policy position papers and through its consultative status with the UN" (Healy, 2001, p. 57). The IFSW International Policy on Indigenous Peoples was approved in 2005 after going through a process of deliberation by IFSW member organizations around the world. "An international approach to a major social problem is formulated and an international policy is defined through a democratic process, where all member social work associations are invited to make comments and proposals. Finally, the IFSW General Meeting decides on approval through voting. In this way, social workers from around the world have been able to agree on international platforms for major social work issues" (Johannesen, 1997, p. 156).

SUMMARY

Social work representation at the UN is carried out through several international social work organizations. Representatives of these organizations focus a good deal of their work on international policy advocacy, where representatives work to understand the circumstances and forces that affect various groups and populations and then bring these conditions to light at the UN, advocating for change where possible. Social work representatives also work toward enhancing human rights and bringing human rights issues to the attention of the UN community. This work is accomplished by working with UN staff, NGO committees, and other social work leaders within the UN system. Representatives are engaged in writing statements for UN commissions, holding side events on key issues during the commissions, and commenting on new policies and initiatives that are proposed by the GA.

Social workers who are not affiliated with the UN but who have a vested interest in global social policy can also have an impact on the UN and its global agenda. One vehicle for this has been the Annual Social Work Day at the UN that is held every spring and is sponsored jointly by the IFSW and IASSW. Thousands of social workers, social work faculty, and social work students have come to these half-day conferences over the last twenty-eight years and have been inspired by the program and also by meeting other social workers who have similar international interests. Many of the attendees have gone on to graduate social work programs that specialize in global social work. Some have gone to work with the Peace Corps or AmeriCorps programs, and others have volunteered for international organizations overseas.

Another way to influence global policy and the work of the UN is by working with the national office of the National Association of Social Workers (NASW) and the state chapters of the organization. A number of state chapters have formed international committees that work to highlight international and global issues in their state, which can then affect the work of the national office. Many NASW delegates have brought forth new policy statements, such as a recent policy statement on human trafficking and modern-day slavery (Salet, 2006). Statements like these help to support the work of the UN on human trafficking and can then be used by NGO representatives in their work at the UN. Representatives rely on the expertise and research of social workers in writing statements or holding side events, as mentioned previously.

The social work profession has had a great deal of influence on the UN for many years, and it will continue to have an influence on global policy and advocacy as long as there are social workers who look beyond their immediate, everyday work to see the links of their work to the global stage. They have the opportunity to influence global advocacy at the state and national levels. Social work education that focuses on human rights and global issues will continue to broaden the experience of students who will be the next vanguard representing the profession at the UN and its affiliate agencies.

REFERENCES

Cronin, M., Mama, R. S., Mbugua, C., & Mouravieff-Apostol, E. (2006). Social work and the United Nations. In N. Hall (Ed.), *Social work: Making a difference* (pp. 209–224). Switzerland: IFSW.

Economic and Social Council (ECOSOC). (2009). E/CN.5/2009/NGO/5. Retrieved February 1, 2009, from www.un.org/esa/socdev/csd/2009_ngostats.html.

Healy, L. M. (2008). Exploring the history of social work as a human rights profession. *International Social Work, 51*(6), 735–748.

Healy, L. M. (2001). *International social work: Professional action in an interdependent world.* New York: Oxford University Press.

Johannesen, T. (1997). Social work as an international profession. In M. C. Hokenstad & J. Midgley (Eds.), *Issues in international social work: Global challenges for a new century* (pp. 146–158). Washington, DC: NASW Press.

Salet, E. P. (2006). Human trafficking and modern-day slavery. NASW Practice Update, November.

United Nations (UN). (2009a). Consultative status with ECOSOC. Retrieved February 8, 2009, from www.un.org/esa/coordination/ngo.

United Nations (UN). (2009b). The United Nations: An introduction for students. Retrieved February 1, 2009, from www.un.org/cyberschoolbus/unintro/unintro.asp.

United Nations (UN). (2003). Charter of the United Nations (revised ed.). New York: UN Department of Public Information.

United Nations (UN). (1996). Resolution 1996/31: Consultative relationship between the United Nations and non-governmental organizations. Retrieved January 30, 2009, from www.un.org/documents/ecosoc/res/1996/eres1996-31.htm.

17

Cultural Efficacy in Communication and Practice in Global Context

LOIS BOSCH

The world in which you were born is just one model of reality. Other cultures are not failed attempts at being you: they are unique manifestations of the human spirit.

WADE DAVIS, *National Geographic Magazine*

For many, the world seems increasingly smaller and more tightly bound together. We are told that the world is flat (Friedman, 2006), that citizens are born in one world, living in another (Spindler & Stockard, 2006), with the realization that globalization has resulted in a gap in which the rich get richer and the poor get left further behind (Isaak, 2005). Styles (1993) describes the twenty-first century as the "international century" (p. 507) owing to the confluence of technology, cyberspace, and ethnic diversity and the concomitant impact on society. Indeed, countries with declining populations augment their workforce with migrants from countries with increasing population rates (Mor Barak, 2005), resulting in increased globalization in the workplace and, consequently, in the community. Adjusting to diversity and cultural differences has become the norm rather than the exception.

What is the effect of this increasing globalization on the role of social work? Much of social work practice takes place with marginalized people, including new citizens, recent immigrants, and refugees. As a result of the changing world dynamic, social work education increasingly emphasizes preparation for professional practice with a diverse group of clients. Social workers understand how important cultural sensitivity is; indeed, one of the hallmarks of good social work practice is cultural competence. The challenge for all helping professionals, including social workers, is delivering services that respect the dignity of the individual while providing for the greater common good. This chapter presents the global and cross-cultural context of social work practice; the concepts of cultural competence, cultural encapsulation,

and cultural efficacy; the case for the importance of culturally effective practice; and suggested practice principles.

THE ROLE OF CULTURE IN SOCIAL WORK PRACTICE

Cultural competence, as defined by the National Association of Social Workers (NASW) Code of Ethics, "requires workers to take reasonable steps to understand and be sensitive to clients' cultures and social diversity" (Reamer, 2006, p. 16). To work effectively in cross-cultural settings, social workers must become aware of their own worldview and value systems (Lum, 1999). Sue (2006) outlines four components of cultural competence, including awareness of one's own biases, understanding the worldviews of others, developing appropriate practice approaches, and understanding the forces of oppression that inhibit cultural competence.

Whether in social work practice or when traveling abroad, one may find *cultural encapsulation* (Wrenn, 1985, as cited in Marsella & Pedersen, 2004), which inhibits cultural competence. Included in cultural encapsulation are five identifying features: *(1)* Reality is defined by particular cultural assumptions (all people think like I do), *(2)* people assume their view is the right one (therefore, the British drive on the wrong side rather than the left side of the road), *(3)* assumptions are not dependent upon proof but are truth (all people want to be free, or all parents want to participate in their child's educational program), *(4)* solutions to problems are quick fixes (the best way to raise children is . . .), and *(5)* people are judged from one's own cultural frame of reference (the way we do things here). Western social workers may understand a client's need to establish trust through conversation but hold to the view that the real work of the relationship comes with the clinical intervention. The underlying assumption may be that at this stage social workers assert their expert knowledge and experience to help the client.

Cultural efficacy extends the concept of cultural competence and implies two conditions: that the professional can effectively communicate with people of different cultural backgrounds and that, in contrast to cultural encapsulation, "neither the caregiver's nor the patient's culture is the preferred or more accurate view" (Nuñez, 2000, p. 1072). Cultural efficacy is another evolution of the term *cultural competence*. According to Nuñez (2000), cultural competence "implies a discrete knowledge set that focuses on the culture of the patient only as something 'other' and therefore aberrant from the norm" (p. 1072). In other words, a dominant model of cultural competence sets the social worker at the center of the cultural arena and reaches out to those who are not within the same cultural sphere. This perception can lead the social worker to a particular cultural reference point, where the worker can understand the Other (client) only within the context of the worker's own culture. Cohen (2001) suggests that such views are privileged, reflecting a "self-centered, ethnocentric view of the world" (p. 159).

For example, recently a judge related to an audience her perspective in child protective services: Above all, the child's physical and emotional safety must be preserved, which might include removal of the child from the home. Suddenly, one member of the audience stood up and vehemently disagreed with the judge. This person maintained that within her culture, the most important thing was to preserve the sense of community, regardless of the needs of the individual. At this point, both the judge and the speaker were in conflict with no easy resolution. Social workers are likely to encounter similar circumstances throughout their practice. These different perspectives are an important part of diversity and represent tensions in understanding and working with cultural differences. Such tensions are likely to be evident in social work practice frequently.

In spite of these tensions, some practitioners and social work students may fail to understand how cultures vary. Cohen (2001) suggests that many college students have difficulty understanding that other cultures are different from their own. They may be unable to see that one must assume a neutral stance when understanding other cultures. According to Cohen, "Different societies are programmed by different cultural software. Not better, not worse, just different" (p. 159). How to act appropriately can be negotiated from a point of neutrality. Adopting a neutral attitude, although challenging, can be considered a work in progress to be developed in conversation and dialogue with others.

In the helping services, Nuñez (2001) proposes that cultural efficacy requires attention to three systems—the client system, the worker system, and the helping environment system. Nuñez suggests that not enough attention is paid to the influence of the helping environment culture, such as in the medical community. The impact of hospital bureaucracy makes most people act differently regardless of cultural background. Therefore, the oppression and opportunities available in the helping environment are both important cultural considerations. This extends to the use of medically prescribed treatment (e.g., surgery or medications). What might be considered medically necessary to professionals might be considered offensive to those from other cultures.

Moving to cultural efficacy requires moving away from cultural encapsulation. Culturally competent social workers may feel themselves temporarily slowed down by cultural differences and that sooner or later, the real work of the relationship can begin. Within a model of cultural efficacy, the social worker must understand that the beginning of the relationship may be the real work.

Furthermore, the paradigm of cultural efficacy holds the perception that other cultures have something to offer, regardless of economic status. This is true not only in the one-to-one client–worker relationship but also within the research and policy arena. A particular challenge in Western social work is persuading some social work students and practitioners to experience other developing cultures as having something to teach them about social work. Travel to developing countries involves more than what Western practitioners can bring to developing countries (e.g., economic aid, technical knowledge) but also what developing countries can contribute to the global practice of social work. Cohen (2001) poses the term *alternity*, defined as "the existence of others possessing different and equally valid world views and ways of life" (p. 151). This is particularly evident when traveling to developing countries on study tours, where students and practitioners meet with social workers from other countries. The tour participants' first instinct may be to learn *about* rather than to learn *from* those professionals. Students may feel more comfortable volunteering to help others, ignoring the possibility that they may be the ones who need to learn.

Within the efficacy paradigm of cultural communication, determining what is normal becomes culturally defined. Even the "word 'normal' becomes a trap for judging others" (Link & Ramanathan, 2011, p. 105). What is best or right for a person or group must be considered from the unique view of the cultural context in which it occurs. Social workers must consider the differences for clients from high- versus low-context societies. Members from high-context societies, such as Taiwan, El Salvador, or India, interpret much of communication from the context, or setting, rather than the actual words. Such cultures "accept, even encourage, conclusions that tolerate greater ambiguity" (Kalyanpur & Harry, 1999, p. 7). This is in contrast to low-context societies, such as the United States, Germany, or Great Britain, where emphasis is placed on the transmitted message (Mor Barak, 2005).

Other contrasts to consider are individual versus collectivist societies, where the rights of the individual are weighed with the good of the community. When a US judge presumes that the safety of the individual supersedes the rights of the community, how does this affect immigrants from other countries or cultures? What is the social worker's response to these cultural definitions? This poses significant ethical dilemmas for the social worker and challenges the ethical, culturally sensitive practice. Who is right? Well, it depends. According to the International Federation of Social Workers (IFSW) Ethics in Social Work: Statement of Principles, social workers are often caught in the delicate balance between individual and societal demands. Further, the IFSW principles advocate for understanding the whole person and recognizing "all aspects of a person's life" (www.ifsw.org/en/p38000324.html).

HOW TO PROMOTE CULTURAL EFFICACY

How do we learn to practice with cultural efficacy? Here are some suggestions.

1. Go beyond knowing yourself. In developing cultural efficacy, one should understand one's own culture and the relevant aspects of the client's culture. In addition, the culture of the helping environment will have an impact on the client and the worker. Schools, hospitals, and other institutions have expectations of client systems. For example, disability can be considered socially constructed. What is seen as a problem to be solved in one culture may not be perceived as a problem in other cultures. The Individuals with Disabilities Education Act (IDEA) legislates how special education services are delivered in the United States. Within the legislation is the expectation that parents will be empowered to act as advocates for their children in special education. However, not all parents want to be an advocate or see that as their role; they may perceive this as an intrusion into the realm of the professional. What is the role of the social worker in accommodating the cultural expectation of parents in these situations while maintaining the child's right to an appropriate public education? Social workers should ask and be willing to listen carefully to parents.

2. Recognize the "fluid nature of culture" (Ruddock & Turner, 2007, p. 367), which includes an awareness of ecological fallacy. Not all people from a culture act the same, and not all problems affect everyone the same. The practitioner can develop skills to discern when clients are acting in congruence with their culture or are experiencing difficulty and how to authentically intervene as needed. Social workers can become familiar with the use of interpreters, learn another language, learn the history of the culture, and consult with community cultural guides.

3. Educate social work students and practitioners for the global, cross-cultural context of social work. One way to do this is to internationalize the social work curriculum. Other helping professions are attempting this as well. For example, Marsella and Pedersen (2004) suggest that internationalizing the curriculum should be a goal to prepare practitioners of counseling psychology to meet the new demands of our times. They go on to suggest that ethnocentric attitudes of Western psychology are a major obstacle to achieving this goal and that Western ideology has little "resonance in many of the more than 5000 cultures found in today's world" (2004, p. 414). Internationalizing the social work curriculum should mean not just providing study tourism but also facilitating global research to merge ideas from a variety of theoretical and cultural sources.

4. Encourage international travel in culturally sensitive ways. Focus on questions of how various cultures approach social work problems. International travel can be a useful strategy to facilitate deeper cultural learning and sensitivity among social work students and practitioners (Danzig & Jing, 2007; Ruddock & Turner, 2007). Study tours should emphasize the contributions made to the global understanding of social work practice and the human condition from as many cultural perspectives as possible.

5. Use international examples in the classroom and staff development opportunities. Where possible, consider international examples to promote understanding and sensitivity to non-Western thinking. Challenge social work staff and students to consider how other cultures inform us about effective social work practice. This includes the Slovenian approach to services for older adults, Mexican models emphasizing neighborhood and community services, Indian use of microcredit lending to women in poverty (Bagati, 2003), the Norwegian paradigm of environment around person rather than person in environment, and the US models of intrapersonal, individual counseling and casework, to mention a few.

6. Facilitate the use of intergroup dialogue among students and professionals. Intergroup dialogue encourages deep listening without judgment and helps us understand the differences and similarities between groups (Rodenborg & Bosch, 2008). The goal of dialogue is to facilitate mutual understanding between disparate groups. Use of dialogue emphasizes the safety of group members through confidentiality and experienced facilitation. Through hearing the experiences of other group members, the individual is able to develop empathy and awareness.

7. Examine so-called universally held truths within the context of different cultures. What do they mean for social work practice within another culture? For instance, Western culture places high value on democratic, egalitarian status. The IFSW Ethics in Social Work: Statement of Principles and the NASW Code of Ethics promote the value of self-determination, which may be antithetical for people from other cultures.

What happens when the social worker from a high-egalitarian culture supervises workers from two groups with unequal status in their home country? How does the supervisor engage workers who may refuse to work with each other? What are the cultural implications as well as economic implications? In this situation, one alternative is that the social work supervisor can use the skill of listening in negotiating a solution. The supervisor can respond to the observation that the workers are refusing to work together and request their reactions as well as their solutions to overcome the barriers. All the while, the supervisor should acknowledge that people have a right to their emotional response and that they can move ahead more easily if they feel heard.

8. Consider the reflective practitioner (Schön, 1983) as a model for practice. Use of the reflective model of practice highlights a move away from technical rationalism, which emphasizes the dominance of expert opinion and its bias that professionals know best. Though empiricism may have answers, empirical research is not the only thing to consider in viewing solutions to problems. The use of reflective practice recognizes the importance of informal helping systems (Schön, 1983). Using reflective practice will help the social worker focus with the client in determining appropriate evidence-based interventions.

Because of its dual focus on the person and the environment, social work is uniquely poised to practice within the global and cross-cultural context. Moreover, the IFSW, with its principles of client self-determination and treatment of the whole person, demonstrates the shared and common fundamental professional values and principles of social work. Historically, social work has emphasized starting where the client is and responding to the uniqueness of the individual. The challenge for social work is to understand how the institutional environment complicates and shapes the cultural reality of the worker and the client. As members of an agency-based profession, we know how to influence organizational improvement. As the practitioner and client work together to understand their own cultural realities, they can begin to understand how to further the helping process. Cultural efficacy serves as a vehicle for this work. As the context for social work practice become more and more global, social workers will need new skills and tools to practice effectively in that context.

REFERENCES

Bagati, D. (2003). Microcredit and empowerment of women. *Journal of Social Work Research and Evaluation,* 4(1), 19–34.

Cohen, R. (2001). Living and teaching across cultures. *International Studies Perspectives, 2,* 151–160.

Danzig, A., & Jing, W. (2007). From tourist to learner: International travel and cultural encounters as a lens for teaching and administration. *ISEA, 35*(1), 78–91.

Friedman, T. (2006). *The world is flat.* New York: Farrar, Straus & Giroux.

Isaak, R. (2005). *The globalization gap: How the rich get richer and the poor get left further behind.* Upper Saddle River, NJ: Prentice Hall/Financial Times. (6), 577–587.

Kalyanpur, M., & Harry, B. (1999). *Culture in special education.* Baltimore: Paul H. Brookes.

Link, R., & Ramanathan, C. (2011). *Human Behavior in a Just World: Reaching for common ground.* New York: Rowman & Littlefield.

Lum, D. (1999). *Culturally competent practice: A framework for growth and action.* Pacific Grove, CA: Brooks-Cole.

Marsella, A., & Pedersen, P. (2004). Internationalizing the counseling psychology curriculum: Toward new values, competencies, and directions. *Counseling Psychology Quarterly, 17*(4), 413–423.

Mor Barak, M. (2005). *Managing diversity: Toward a globally inclusive workplace.* Thousand Oaks, CA: Sage.

Nuñez, A. (2000). Transforming cultural competence into cross-cultural efficacy in women's health education. *Academic Medicine, 75*(11), 1071–1080.

Reamer, F. (2006). *Ethical standards in social work: A review of the NASW Code of Ethics* (2nd ed.). Washington, DC: NASW Press.

Rodenborg, N., & Bosch, L. (2009). Intergroup dialogue: Introduction. In A. Gitterman & R. Salmon (Eds.), *Encyclopedia of social work with groups* (pp. 78–80). New York: Routledge.

Ruddock, H., & Turner, D. S. (2007). Developing cultural sensitivity: Nursing students' experiences of a study abroad programme. *Journal of Advanced Nursing, 59*(4), 361–369.

Schön, D. (1983). *The reflective practitioner: How professionals think in action.* New York: Basic Books.

Spindler, G., & Stockard, J. (2006). *Globalization and change in 15 cultures: Born in one world, living in another.* Belmont, CA: Wadsworth.

Styles, M. (1993). The world as a classroom. *Nursing and Health Care, 14,* 507.

Sue, D. (2006). *Multicultural social work practice.* Hoboken, NJ: Wiley.

18

Cultural Conflict and Conflict Resolution

NGOH TIONG TAN

This chapter focuses on culture, conflict, and conflict resolution. Social work actively engages culture in micro, meso, and macro settings. Social workers, especially those in the international front, should be competent in cross-cultural intervention and conflict resolution. The chapter is divided into two sections. The first addresses culture, culture in context, and cultural competence. The second focuses on conflict resolution, alternative dispute resolution, and management of cultural conflict.

There are many types of culture conflicts, such as interpersonal and community conflict, conflicts between subcultures, class conflict, and ethnic conflict. Social workers in multicultural societies and a globalized world need to be well versed in both principles and skills of mediation and conflict management. Conflict and culture are tools for social change: Conflict provides the impetus for change and culture adjusts to a more functional way of relating and adapting to the social environment (Tan, 1987).

WHAT IS CULTURE?

Culture implies the integrated pattern of human behavior that includes "thoughts, communications, actions, customs, beliefs, values and institutions of racial, ethnic, religious, or social groups" (Cross, Bazron, Dennis, & Issacs, 1989, as cited in http://www.ncccurricula.info/culturalcompetence.html). It uses a particular set of knowledge and values to make sense of what is going on, helping us interpret or find meaning in our experiences. Culture is thus shared by people, and it is created and maintained through relationships. It is also useful for differentiating one group from another.

Cultures are different ways of life and thus each culture is unique. When cultures interact, they are bound to create friction and thus adjustments are needed for people to relate effectively with one another.

Cultures can interact in ways that are destructive or constructive. Constructive conflict management and engagement minimize the negative and yield positive outcomes.

Conflict is part of life and social workers routinely deal with it, be it within a family, between people or groups, in organizations, or in the community. Differences are often the reason for conflict, though not necessarily. Diversity can also enrich relationships and communities. Cultural conflict and conflict resolution can present opportunities for change and interpersonal growth as well as enhance intergroup understanding.

Edward Hall's metaphors of culture include the ideas of cultures as models, like the air we breathe and the living, interlocking ecosystems. According to Hall (1976), cultures are used to differentiate one group from another. Every metaphor of culture has its uses and limits (www.culture-at-work.com/concept2.html).

Culture must be flexible enough to accommodate many circumstances. It may be described as optional behavior in that whatever "proves satisfactory will continue to be selected and reinforced by a variety of people in many contexts over time." Thus there are unique cultural patterns that are both dynamic and complex. This avoids a simplistic notion of culture while still being able to provide "guidance about typical or workable options" (http://www.culture-at-work.com/concept3.html and Hall, 1976).

Ethnicity is more than genetic traits and blood ties. According to Culture at Work, it contains a set of cultural practices "determined by the formal or informal decisions of the ethnic group" that one belongs to. It is "the boundary between one group and another, the dichotomy, the comparison that produces cultural patterns" (http:// www.culture-at-work.com/concept2.html). This boundary-marker metaphor is helpful in deciding which issues are readily negotiable and which will be difficult to resolve.

CULTURE AND CONTEXT

Social work practice is found in many multicultural settings. Each person lives within a culture and culture is also within a person. This provides the cultural identity for the person as well as cultural context with its meaning and resources. If culture is the way of life, then technically every conflict has cultural significance in that the conflict is due to different perspectives and ways of life.

There are many meanings of the word *culture*, such as national culture and ethnic culture. Subgroup culture could include various cultural groups that people are socialized into. The culture concept has also been applied to organizational culture, religious culture, peer culture, professional culture, culture of poverty, youth culture, and the like. Culture is found in every human niche and context.

On a global level, the world can be divided into key cultural blocks; for example, the East and the West are cultural blocks. Asian cultures have been termed *high context* and American cultures *low context* (Hall, 1976). These concepts describe cultural differences between societal groups. High context refers to societies where people live in communities or have close connections over a length of time. Cultural behaviors are not made explicit because most members know what to do and what to think, which are developed through years of interacting one with another. Low-context cultures are "societies where people tend to have many connections but of shorter duration or for some specific reason" (http://www.culture-at-work.com/highlow.html). Cultural behaviors have to be spelled out explicitly so that people will know how to behave.

It is difficult for an outsider to enter a high-context culture because close relationships take time to develop. Conversely, it is relatively easy to enter low-context cultures (Hall, 1976) "because the environment contains much of the information you need to participate" in the community. When one enters a high-context situation, "it doesn't immediately become a low context culture," and even in low-context cultures learning the language or religious practices can be difficult (http://www.culture-at-work.com/highlow.html and Hall, 1976).

In the East, interpersonal harmony, respect, and responsibility hold complex human relations together. Confucian countries, for example, exhort these virtues and value a long-term perspective of relationships. Social relations are governed by *li*, which are social rules governing behavior or observable patterns of behavior (Chang, 2000). Asian and Confucian values are slowly giving way to Western values; for example, there is increasing acceptance of no-fault divorce in China (Barnes, 2006). All these social contexts have implications for culture conflict and conflict resolution.

Males and females have different upbringings and subcultures. Studies show significant effects of gender differences on the outcome of conflict and the selection of strategies for conflict management (Kleinke, 1977). Men, for example, are more likely than women to blame their spouses and avoid emotional involvement in conflict situations. Confrontation as a male strategy tends to be more aggressive, competitive, and coercive, while females prefer more compromising (Berryman-Fink & Brunner, 1987), less aggressive and more prosocial strategies (Margolin, 1987).

Social workers seek to understand cultural traditions and practices, as well as gender dynamics, when working within different social contexts. Subcultural issues are actively addressed in the social intervention.

CULTURAL COMPETENCE IN INTERNATIONAL SOCIAL WORK

Cultural competence is a critical factor for effective social work practice and relates directly to intervention in situations of conflict. It refers to the competence to work across cultures and for constructive engagement for positive change. There are varying contexts of service and social work arenas, including ethnic-based services, self-help community organizations, culture groups, and religious-based services that provide spiritual support and resources. Each of these needs specialized knowledge for effective assessment and intervention.

Cross et al. (1989) state that "cultural competence is a set of congruent behaviors, attitudes, and policies that come together in a system, agency, or among professionals and enable that system, agency, or professionals to work effectively in cross-cultural situations" (http://www.ncccurricula.info/culturalcompetence.html). Cultural competency on the social worker's part includes knowledge of the history, values, and beliefs of the client's culture and the understanding that the "person of an ethnic background is not a duplicate of all people of that culture"(http://www.ncccurricula.info/culturalcompetence.html).

Each person and community is unique, and cultural competency starts with respecting the similarities as well as the differences.

Knowledge and skills are both required for cultural competence. The knowledge component, including knowledge of cultural theories, people and community groups, and organizational dynamics of different societies, provides an essential base for practice. The skills component is being able to work effectively with individuals, community groups, organizations, and societies.

It is vital to begin by being aware of and learning more about various groups and then being able to communicate more effectively with specific clients. *Cultural awareness* can be defined as the process of "self-examination of one's own biases towards other cultures and the in-depth exploration of one's cultural and professional background" (http://www. transculturalcare.net/Cultural_Competence_Model. htm; see: Campinha-Bacote, 2002). Awareness is a good start but not sufficient to bring about change. The skills to effect social change are vital for social work practice.

Papadopoulos, Tilki, and Taylor's model for developing cultural competence (Papadopoulos, 2003) is a four-stage model that starts with cultural awareness, followed by the acquisition of cultural knowledge and the development of cultural sensitivity. It requires recognition of one's biases, prejudices, and constraints. Developing cultural awareness requires humility, self-understanding, and acceptance of one's own cultural identity. Self-awareness must not only be an intellectual exercise but also must involve one's emotion to be effective.

Cultural sensitivity is "knowing that cultural differences as well as similarities exist, without assigning values, that is, better or worse, right or wrong, to those cultural differences" (http://cecp.air.org/cultural/Q_howdifferent.htm and National Maternal and Child Health Center, 1997). The principles for cultural competence and ethnic-sensitive practice are summarized as follows:

1. Incorporating the importance of culture into the entire social work process of assessment, planning, intervention, evaluation, and termination.
2. Considering the dynamics that result from cultural difference and actively seeking relevant cultural knowledge and service adaptation to meet culture-specific needs of the client system.

3. Seeking to actively collaborate with indigenous social workers and helpers in delivering appropriate social work intervention.

CONFLICT MANAGEMENT AND CONFLICT RESOLUTION

Competence in the resolution of conflict is an important aspect of cultural competence. Effective conflict management is based on understanding the meaning of the conflict, the conflict process, and skills in negotiation, facilitation, and mediation.

Fisher and Ury (1991) describe approaches to resolving disputes based on interest, rights, and power. The focus on interest means that the underlying needs, desires, and concerns, or "things one cares about," are of primary importance to the conflict resolution. A rights-based approach relies on the "independent standards with perceived legitimacy or fairness to determine who is right." Power is the "ability to coerce someone to do something he would not otherwise do," and this approach does not address underlying issues and concerns that create distress (Ury, Brett, & Goldberg, 1988, p. 7).

Tan (1987) proposed a seven-step process model of conflict resolution as the model for keeping peace:

1. Commitment to resolution
2. Definition of conflict
3. Negotiation
4. Agreement
5. Contracting
6. Implementation of change
7. Evaluation.

In the first step, commitment to resolution, the collaborative mode is introduced and the emphasis is on reciprocity. It is important to create a mutual expectation that it is beneficial to resolve the conflict. Framing the issue is vital to conflict resolution because it helps narrow the scope of the workable problem area. It defines the conflict that needs to be resolved and specifies the needs of both parties (Tan, 1987).

During negotiation, the social worker helps the parties bargain from their own interests within established ground rules and structures, such as following the norms of equality, staying with objective facts, sharing information, and adopting a nonblaming posture. To reach an agreement, the parties have to find common goals, clarify common grounds, and create positive actions. It is good to summarize any agreement that is achieved so that both parties are clear as to what they are agreeing to. Contracting makes explicit the specific responsibilities of the parties concerned, emphasizing, again, mutual responsibilities and ownership of the solution.

After reaching an agreement, it is necessary to follow up with the implementation of change. It is crucial to develop conditions that are conducive for task performance and to acknowledge and reward the positive actions of both parties. Finally, in evaluation, the worker checks on the implementation schedule to see whether the needs that gave rise to the conflicts are met and if alternative structures are needed to reduce future conflicts (Tan, 1987).

Modern societies rely more on formal channels of conflict resolution than in the past. The police keep law and order and the courts administer justice. Adjudication becomes a primary avenue to get grievances resolved. In the past twenty years there has been a movement to "give conflict back to the people" (Christie, 1977, p. 8), and alternative dispute resolutions forums such as mediation, arbitration, and med-arb, a combination of the two, have been developed. Community Boards and Neighborhood Justice Centers deal with mediation of community conflicts. Peer mediation has been introduced in schools and grievance processes instituted in industries as transformative mediation (Tan & Lee-Partridge, 2000). Mediation must emphasize participation of members of the community and suit social, cultural, and political contexts (Tan, 2002).

Mediation

Mediation is a goal-directed, time-limited, task-oriented process of conflict management in which the parties in conflict attempt to reach a consensual settlement facilitated by a mediator (Tan, 1988). It facilitates clarification of issues, identifies alternatives, reduces acrimony between the parties, assists the parties in resolving any controversy, and helps the parties reach mutual agreement (Tan, 1988). Mediation provides an effective forum for dealing constructively with conflict.

Social workers need to actively engage indigenous ways of resolving conflict. As much as possible, local conflict resolution principles and models, such as the Native mediation model or the Indian panchayat system of conflict resolution, should be used (Kruk, 1997; Gutierrez, Alvarez, Nemon, & Lewis, 1996). Native Americans have developed a model for conflict

resolution using the four compass directions (Kruck, 1997):

East: Set the climate for conflict resolution.

South: Tell the story.

West: Discover what is important.

North: Create solutions.

There are four stages of mediation similar to the Native American mediation circle:

1. In the introduction, the worker explains the rules and process of mediation.
2. Storytelling is the time to allow the parties to tell their own stories and then state their wishes. The mediator listens, clarifies, and ensures that all parties have fair time to express themselves.
3. The problem-solving stage, like the conflict resolution process, involves framing the issue, emphasizing common ground, focusing on positive behaviors, and keeping communication channels open. The mediator's role is help disputants generate solutions, weigh the consequences, and make decisions they can live with.
4. Agreement is the final stage of mediation. The mediator summarizes the agreement, identifies the various responsibilities, works on an implementation time frame, and evaluates the process.

Indians have developed the panchayat model, which involves local mediators in dispute settlements. This system is practiced even in faraway communities of Indian emigrants. The panchayats make concessions and facilitate agreements more frequently than do village elders in India. Mediations are thus strongly influenced by the panchayat system. Cultural efficacy is achieved using local mechanisms of conflict resolution.

The mediator's skills for successful conflict management and agreement include gaining the trust and confidence of the parties concerned. This involves achieving good rapport with the parties and being able to discover the real issues and interests. A skilled mediator understands the dynamics of the situation and promotes good interparty communication and relations as well as a favorable climate for negotiation.

Since time is limited, the mediator must establish priorities, educate parties on the negotiation process and how they can use it efficiently to reach agreement, and make wise decisions. Sometimes the mediator demands reality testing so that the settlement is realistic and workable.

Concept of Functional Culture for Social Work Practice

There are several types of culture conflict, including ethnic conflict, gender conflict, class conflict, and cross-national or international conflict. Conflict serves different functions, and within each culture there are different rules for conflict resolution. How does social work respond to cultural patterns that are dysfunctional in adapting within the larger social context?

Each family and subgroup functions in a specific way in its culture. In working toward change in the family and community, whatever does not hinder the functionality of the culture group should be retained and preserved as its identity. Each family or group looks at behaviors in relation to its own values and beliefs. As a principle, whatever value, attitude, or behavior stands in the way of healthy functioning of the group should be changed. The social worker working across cultures may challenge dysfunctional values and behaviors such as the use of violence in socialization and control.

Working with a family, group, or community is a collaborative effort. The concept of functional culture is adapted to the context. What does the group define as functional or useful and appropriate? The functionalist approach starts with what the family or group wants in relation to the presenting issue. What will happen if the symptom or problem is taken away? What difference would the family or group like to see?

The cross-cultural social worker observes the dynamics of the family and community and helps the family redefine and respond to what is good for them. Norms are reexamined and healthy functioning and wellness are defined collaboratively with the clients in this process. Violence, for example, depends on culture, and the type of violence is correlated with class and ethnicity. A culture that oppresses women and children needs to be challenged and changed. Roles of men, women, and children could be redefined so that they do not oppress each other. How can the father use his authority and position in the family to protect members of the family instead of abusing them? The way to resolve potential culture conflict between practitioners and clients is to help the clients define operational norms so that they can function more effectively within their life situations.

Macro Conflicts, Prevention, and Ethics

Singapore has developed confidence and harmony circles as a way to foster interethnic ties and promote better interethnic relations in its multicultural society. Harmony circles comprise members from grassroots organizations, self-help groups, schools, and other social institutions. They work closely with schools, community organizations, and other grassroots organizations to promote interracial harmony and bonding.

It is vital that policies that enhance social integration, such as integrated housing, schools, and other service delivery systems, be thoughtfully developed and implemented. Principles of social justice counteract discriminatory policies and practices so as to ensure social equality and peace. These are preventive strategies to ensure racial harmony.

Social work can help foster mutual appreciation and peaceful living among different peoples and communities. The social work approach to ethnic relations is to develop positive human and community relationships. It is the profession's agenda to support social networks that contribute to peaceful interethnic relations that promote social integration and self-determination rather than segregation. Prevention strategies enhance positive interaction and reduce fear, ignorance, and discrimination.

It is important that social workers adhere to the international professional code of ethics. Ethical principles that culturally competent social workers subscribe to include impartiality, neutrality, and confidentiality. Social workers should be prompt in attending to clients' needs and the conflict managed without unnecessary delays. Any conflict of interest on the part of the social worker should be declared. Finally, it is vital to obtain informed consent for both research and practice of mediation and conflict management.

CONCLUSIONS

Everyone is inevitably part of two or more cultures, and each culture has values, beliefs, and behaviors that could conflict with another. Interpersonal conflict resolution takes into consideration the culture and the context of the person. Cross-cultural competence is important for effective social work practice.

On a macro level, societies all over the world are in transition. With greater interconnectedness through globalization, societies have become more diverse (MacRaild, 1998; Tan & Rowlands, 2004). There is increasing multiculturalism in every country, and when these cultures interact, the differences sometimes result in conflict. Historically, ethnic relations have been fraught with tensions and conflicts. The development of tensions could be used constructively for effecting social change, addressing discrimination, and reducing prejudice. Preventive measures, social policy, and legislation are needed to strengthen positive and enriching experience of cross-cultural relations.

Are there fault lines and clashes between civilizations (Huntington, 1996)? Yes, conflicts are inevitable, but the social worker's agenda is to work toward greater social justice and social integration, conditions that will engender peace.

REFERENCES

Barnes, B. E. (2006). *Culture conflict and mediation in the Asian Pacific*. Lanham, MD: University Press of America.

Berryman-Fink, C., & Brunner, C. (1987). The effects of sex of source and target on interpersonal conflict management styles. *Southern Speech Communication Journal, 53*, 38–48.

Campinha-Bacote, J. (2002). The process of cultural competence in the delivery of healthcare services: A model of care. *Journal of Transcultural Nursing, 13*(3), 181–184.

Chang, W. C. (2000). Qing, Li, Fa: An exploration of the fairness heuristic of the Chinese. In N. T. Tan & J. E. Lee-Patridge (Eds.), *Alternative dispute resolution*, (pp. 123–132). Singapore: Centre for Advanced Studies, National University of Singapore.

Christie, N. (1977). Crime as property. *British Journal of Criminology, 17*, 1–15.

Cross, T., Bazron, B., Dennis, K. W., & Issacs, M. R. (1989). *Towards culturally competent systems of care*. Washington, DC: Georgetown University Child Development Center.

Fisher, R., & Ury, W. (1991). *Getting to yes*. Boston: Penguin.

Gutierrez, L., Alvarez, A. R., Nemon, H., & Lewis, E. A. (1996). Multicultural community organizing: A strategy for change. *Social Work, 41*(5), 501–508.

Hall, E. (1976). *Beyond culture*. New York: Doubleday.

Huntington, S. (1996). *The clash of civilizations*. New York: Simon and Schuster.

Kleinke, C. L. (1977). Compliance to requests made by gazing and touching experimenters in field settings. *Journal of Experimental Social Psychology, 13*, 218–223.

Kruk, E. (1997). *Mediation and conflict resolution in social work and human services*. Chicago: Nelson Hall.

Margolin, G. (1987). The multiple forms of aggressiveness between marital partners: How do we identify them? *Journal of Marital and Family Therapy, 13*, 77–84.

MacRaild, D. M. (1998). *Culture, conflict and migration*. Liverpool: Liverpool University Press.

National Maternal and Child Health Center on Cultural Competency. (1997). As cited in: http://www.ncccurricula.info/culturalcompetence.html.

Papadopoulos, R. (2003). Papadopoulos, Tilki and Taylor's model for the development of cultural competence in nursing. *Journal of Health, Social and Environmental Issues, 4*(1), 5–7.

Tan, N. T. (2002). Community mediation in Singapore: Principles for community conflict resolution. *Conflict Resolution Quarterly, 19*(3), 289–301.

Tan, N. T. (1988). *Development of an assessment instrument for family mediation*. (Unpublished PhD thesis). University of Minnesota, Minneapolis.

Tan, N. T. (1987). A conceptual model for peace through constructive conflict resolution. *Social Development Issues, 10*(3), 46–53.

Tan, N. T., & Lee-Partridge, J. E. (Eds.). (2000). *Alternative dispute resolution*. Singapore: Centre for Advanced Studies, National University of Singapore.

Tan, N. T., & Rowlands, A. (2004). Globalisation, international welfare and social work practice. In N. T. Tan & A. Rowlands (Eds.), *Social work around the world III* (pp. 5–12). Berne, Switzerland: IFSW Press.

Ury, W. L., Brett, J. M. & Goldberg, S. B., (1988). *Getting Disputes Resolved Designing Systems to Cut the Costs of Conflict*. San Francisco: Jossey Bass Publishers.

SECTION IV

Global Social Issues

19

Global Aging

M. C. "TERRY" HOKENSTAD AND MOON CHOI

The globe is graying! Unprecedented population aging is taking place around the world. Both the number and proportion of older persons (sixty years of age and older) have been steadily increasing over the past half century. In 2006, this number surpassed 700 million as compared with 200 million in 1950. According to United Nations projections, this number will reach 2 billion by 2050. Today, the global population of older persons is growing by 2.6% a year, whereas the overall yearly population growth is 1.1%. Lower fertility rates in almost all countries are resulting in an increasing percentage of seniors (United Nations, 2007b).

In the past, the population aging process has been most evident in developed countries. The postindustrial nations of Europe and North America, along with Japan, Australia, and New Zealand, currently have the largest proportions of older people. However, now the developing world is also experiencing population aging. Currently, 64% of all people sixty years of age and older live in developing countries. By 2050, this number will increase to 80%. The speed of change is greatest in Asia, Latin America, and the Caribbean, where the sixty-to-seventy-nine age group is growing by 3.3% and the eighty-plus age group by almost 5% each year. Africa is aging at a slower rate, but the proportion of the African population over sixty years of age will increase by 310% between now and 2050. Thus, the aging population is a worldwide phenomenon (HelpAge International, 2008).

The fastest growing segment of older people is those who are eighty years of age and older. This oldest-old population is increasing by 3.9% per year. Today, one in eight of the sixty-plus population is over eighty years of age. By 2050, this ratio will be approximately two persons aged eighty or older for every ten older persons. Also, women compose the majority of the older population. Today, they outnumber older men by about seventy million. Among the eighty-plus population, women are almost twice as numerous as men. Because of their additional longevity and less time spent in the labor market, older women are particularly at risk for social isolation and economic deprivation (United Nations, 2007b).

This demographic revolution has major implications for social welfare policy and social work practice. Policy challenges include the coverage and cost of pension programs for an increasing number of older people who have retired from the labor market. Challenges also encompass the adequacy and efficiency of health care for citizens who are living longer with chronic illness. Social workers must focus on a growing amount of isolation, abuse, and neglect among their older client group. Social workers also must develop and adapt social development strategies, particularly for elderly clients without pensions or outside of the formal labor market. The United Nations has addressed these and other challenges stemming from population aging in its Madrid International Plan of Action on Ageing.

MADRID INTERNATIONAL PLAN OF ACTION ON AGEING: RECOMMENDATIONS FOR ACTION

Population aging provides new opportunities associated with the active participation of older generations in both the economy and society at large. It also poses important challenges, especially those related to the financial viability of pension systems, the costs of health-care systems, and the full integration of older people as active agents of societal development (United Nations, 2007a). Facing these challenges and opportunities associated with an aging population, the Madrid International Plan of Action on Ageing (MIPAA), a product of the Second World Assembly on Ageing in Madrid (2002), outlines three priority directions for action that have implications for international social work: (1) older persons and development, (2) advancing health and well-being into old age, and

(3) ensuring enabling and supportive environments (United Nations, 2003).

Priority Direction I: Older Persons and Development

Although older persons can be essential resources to their communities, they face great risk of marginalization. They often experience both social devaluation and poverty upon leaving the labor market, and financial market fluctuations also contribute to income and social insecurity. Overall, 80% of the world's population is not sufficiently protected in old age against income risks (United Nations, 2007a). Certain groups are particularly vulnerable to poverty and social devaluation in old age due to cultural and institutional biases for examples, women, persons with disabilities, and older migrants. For this reason, the MIPAA recommends social security programs for older persons around the world, particularly for socially and economically disadvantaged groups (United Nations, 2003).

Another recommendation is that older persons be enabled to continue income-generating work for as long as they want and are able to do so. An aging-friendly labor market requires increased recruitment of older persons and elimination of exclusion or discrimination against them. Lifelong education and training is a prerequisite for older persons' participation in employment. Besides economic participation, older persons also should be given equal opportunity to participate in social, cultural, and political activities. Promoting and strengthening solidarity among generations and mutual support are key elements for social development (United Nations, 2003).

In many developing and transitioning countries, urbanization and industrialization cause the exodus of young adults from rural areas, leaving older adults behind with few resources. The MIPAA recommends social policies and programs that are designed and implemented to improve living conditions and infrastructure in rural areas. Additionally, in emergency situations such as natural disasters, war, and terrorism, older persons are especially vulnerable due to isolation, disability or lack of physical stamina, and loss of family caregivers. Thus, government and humanitarian relief agencies should provide services to facilitate coping with crises such as displacement, land dispossession, and loss of property (United Nations, 2003).

Priority Direction II: Advancing Health and Well-Being Into Old Age

The World Health Organization (WHO) defines *health* as a state of complete physical, mental, and social well-being, not merely the absence of disease and infirmity. The MIPAA uses this definition and also incorporates the WHO life-course perspective on aging: *(a)* Health promotion and disease, disability, and injury prevention contribute to health in old age, and *(b)* the health of older persons must be considered in the context of events throughout the life span. Given the life-course perspective on aging, disadvantaged groups such as women and ethnic minorities tend to experience accumulated health problems in old age, and special attention to those groups is needed (United Nations, 2003).

Health-promotion activities and equal access of all social groups to health care and services throughout life are cornerstones of healthy aging. Expansion of educational and training opportunities in geriatrics and gerontology for health and social service professionals, paraprofessionals, and informal caregivers is also critical to advance the health and well-being of older persons. In addition, individual efforts to maintain a healthy lifestyle throughout the life span are important for healthy aging.

Adequate policies are required to meet the growing need for care and treatment of an aging population. For people living with disabilities, preservation of maximum functional capacity and full societal integration are crucial. Adequate mental health care, which is frequently overlooked, is also essential for quality of life in old age. Various losses and life changes can often lead to an array of mental health disorders in old age. Thus, the United Nations calls for the development and implementation of national and local strategies to prevent and treat mental illness in older persons. Finally, the MIPAA calls for special attention to be given to the increasing prevalence of HIV and AIDS among the older population (United Nations, 2003).

Priority Direction III: Ensuring Enabling and Supportive Environments

The MIPAA section that focuses on enabling and supportive environments gives major attention to policies and programs that *(1)* promote "aging in place" in the community, *(2)* provide a continuum of care for older persons and their caregivers, and *(3)* focus on the prevention and reduction of elder abuse (United Nations, 2003).

Aging in one's home is considered an ideal among most people. Providing affordable housing options with transportation and support systems for older persons is critical to promote aging in place. Despite changing family structures such as increasing divorce rates and decreasing marriage and birth rates, families throughout the world still perform major caregiving roles. In this context, older persons serve as caregivers as well as receivers of informal care. Thus, the MIPAA emphasizes the need for programs and services that support family caregivers of frail older people.

Action to prevent and reduce all forms of elder neglect and abuse is another major MIPAA objective. Educational programs to raise awareness of the growing problem of elder mistreatment and to reduce stereotyping of older people are essential to prevent abuse, neglect, and exploitation of older persons. In addition, the MIPAA calls for the creation of social services to identify and act on cases of neglect and abuse. Social service professionals are encouraged to play a major role in the prevention and handling of elder abuse (United Nations, 2003).

SOCIAL WORK AND GLOBAL AGING

The International Federation of Social Workers (IFSW) International Policy on Ageing and Older Adults (2008) points out that social workers are well qualified to create and implement programs and services that benefit older people around the world. Social workers have a grounding in cultural competence and are qualified to advocate for age-related policies and programs that are responsive to the wide diversity of older persons in many countries. Social work also articulates values of social justice and human rights at all levels of intervention, from policy implementation to clinical practice. Finally, social workers have knowledge and skills that enable them to assist older people living in the community as well as in institutional settings. Thus, IFSW states that social workers should play a crucial role in implementing the MIPAA priority directions.

Social Work Roles With Older Persons and Development

In developing countries, about 342 million older persons lack adequate income security, and poverty is a growing social problem. Some countries are making gradual progress in addressing the problem of stable income for elders. Recently, India introduced limited pensions for some segments of the informal labor force (United Nations, 2007a). An important role for social workers in the field of social development is organizing older people to advocate for accessible, affordable, and sustainable old-age pension programs designed to meet country-specific conditions. A good

example of this advocacy for social development is the Resource Integration Centre (RIC) in Bangladesh, which brought a delegation of older people together to meet national and district-level politicians and administrators to discuss income needs and pension programs (HelpAge International, 2006a).

Increasing industrialization and urbanization have led to growing isolation of the older generation in developing countries. Young adults are moving to the cities to seek employment, and aging members of the family are left in rural areas to manage for themselves. Older persons in rural areas are often excluded from both economic and social resources. Social workers employed by social development agencies help the rural elderly establish microenterprises to support themselves. Samridhi day-care centre, set up in rural India, is an example of this type of program. This center helps elderly women learn traditional crafts. It also provides the women with raw materials and the infrastructure needed to earn an income through craft making (United Nations, 2007a).

Social isolation is also a problem for older people in poor and geographically isolated areas of more developed countries. Creative strategies are needed to provide social services in such environments. For example, Australian social workers use teleconferencing group counseling to address personal problems and reduce loneliness (Findlay, 2003). Social workers are involved in several levels of intervention in their work with poor and isolated older people around the world.

Social Work Roles in Advancing Health and Well-Being Into Old Age

As part of its active aging program, launched at the Second World Assembly on Ageing, WHO is promoting positive images of aging. Active aging has come to mean the process of optimizing opportunities for health and participation to improve quality of life as people age. Additionally, WHO is emphasizing the concept of enablement—restoring the functioning of and expanding the participation of older people in all aspects of society—instead of disablement (WHO, 2006). This concept of active aging fits well with the strengths approach of social work, which accentuates participation and prevention in working with older people.

Social workers in many countries have professional responsibilities in both health-care services and disease prevention programs that focus on older people. Their roles include direct services, such as counseling and case management, as well as coordinating and managing programs in home health-care agencies, hospitals, and nursing homes.

Social workers in Singapore, for example, coordinate mobile medical clinics for senior citizens (Ow, 1999). As another example, Danish social workers participate in home visits to all citizens aged seventy-five years and older for the purpose of health promotion and disease prevention in accordance with social policy in Denmark (Vass, Avland, Hendricksen, Philipson, & Rils, 2007).

In many countries, social workers in the field of community mental health are placing more emphasis on the mental health needs of older persons. At the same time, social work expertise is applied to programs addressing the cognitive disabilities facing many older persons, such as Alzheimer's disease and other dementias. In Sweden, social work expertise is used in adult day-care programs for dementia patients. Such programs provide respite for family caregivers while enabling cognitively frail elders to remain in the community and out of institutions (Jarrott, Zarit, Berg, & Johansson, 1998).

Finally, social workers provide information about the prevention and risks of HIV and AIDS to older persons as well as social support to those with the disease and their caregivers. Caregiver support is particularly important in developing countries because 90% of AIDS care is provided at home, most often by older women (HelpAge International, 2005). In this context, social work education in African countries, such as Uganda and South Africa, gives special attention to preparing students for HIV and AIDS work.

Social Work Roles in Aging and Supportive Environments

The immediate living environment has a major impact on the well-being of older persons in all parts of the world. Changes in family structures due to declining fertility rates, modernization, and patterns of migration have created challenges for elder care in all countries. In developing countries, traditional informal approaches to care have been under increasing stress, and in developed countries, where elders most often live alone or with a spouse, care outside of the family is often needed.

Social workers play an important role in assessing the needs of older people who need formal support to remain in their own homes. They determine the types and amounts of services needed for both frail elders and family members who provide informal care. Case management and counseling are two key components of this role. Social workers in many developed countries carry out these functions of elder care in diverse settings (Hokenstad, 2006).

Formal care is less available in many developing countries, wherein family members play a key role in providing care to older adults. Thus, the role of social workers involves facilitating support programs for family caregivers, who are often older women. A number of program initiatives for female caregivers are underway in Africa. For example, support groups for older women in Mozambique help to reduce their costs of care and to increase their income. HelpAge International, with the support of UNAIDS (Joint UN Programme on HIV/AIDS), has implemented a program in several African countries to increase the visibility of older female caregivers and document the need for policies and programs for caregiver support (HelpAge International, 2006b).

Caregiver stress and the erosion of family support structures are major risk factors for elder abuse in the home. Institutional abuse occurs most often when staff are poorly trained or overworked, or when care standards are low or inadequately monitored. Countries around the world vary in their responses to elder abuse and neglect. Social services for abused, neglected, or exploited older people are generally provided through existing health and social service networks. Roles of social workers include identifying and investigating suspected abuse, linking victims with medical and social services and providing appropriate counseling to those in need. Social workers have also been at the forefront of advocacy efforts to initiate or improve protective legal statutes and to expand services (Hokenstad, 2006).

A Challenge for International Social Work

As the demographic revolution continues, increasing numbers of helping professionals will be needed to provide health care and social services for older people around the world. This increase in skilled professional helpers will require more attention to education in the field of aging; thus, IFSW (2009) has called for the expansion of gerontological education for all social workers as well as the recruitment and training of more specialists in work with older people. This challenge must be met if international social work is to effectively serve the growing older population.

REFERENCES

Findlay, R. A. (2003). Interventions to reduce social isolation amongst older people: Where is the evidence? *Ageing & Society, 23,* 647–658.

HelpAge International. (2008). Global ageing statistics. Retrieved March 28, 2009, from http://www.helpage.org/resources/ageing-data/global-ageing-statistics.

HelpAge International. (2006a). *Ageways, 67*. London: Author.

HelpAge International. (2006b). Older women: The invisible carers. *Ageing in Africa, 27*, 1–2.

HelpAge International. (2005). *Annual review 2004/2005*. London: Author.

Hokenstad, M. C. (2006). *Older persons in a changing society: Report to the United Nations*. Cleveland, OH: Case Western Reserve University.

International Federation of Social Workers (IFSW). (2009). International Policy on Ageing and Older Adults. Retrieved May 21, 2009, from www.ifsw.org/p38000214.html.

Jarrott, S. E., Zarit, S. H., Berg, S., & Johansson, L. (1998). Adult day care for dementia: A comparison of programs in Sweden and the United States. *Journal of Cross-Cultural Gerontology, 13*, 99–108.

Ow, R. (1999). Social work in a multicultural context. *International Social Work, 42*(1), 7–14.

United Nations (UN). (2007a). *World economic and social survey 2007: Development in an ageing world—60th anniversary edition, 1948–2007*. New York: Author.

United Nations (UN). (2007b). *World population ageing 2007*. New York: Author.

United Nations (UN). (2003). *Second World Assembly on Ageing 2002: Political Declaration and Madrid International Plan of Action on Ageing*. New York: Author.

Vass, M., Avland, K., Hendricksen, C., Philipson, L., & Rils, P. (2007). Preventive home visits to older people in Denmark. *Zeitschrift für Gerontologie und Geriatrie, 40*(4), 209–216.

World Health Organization. (2006). Active ageing. Retrieved January 1, 2009, from http://www.who.int/ageing/active_ageing/en/index.html.

20

Child Abuse and Neglect

LETNIE F. ROCK

The abuse of children has been chronicled throughout history and across continents. Crosson-Tower (2008) notes, "Since ancient times, children have been viewed as property to be sold, given, or exploited by adults. Throughout history, children have been overworked, prostituted, and physically maltreated for a variety of reasons" (p. 20). However, despite the indignities they have suffered, their safety and protection only became a matter of professional and public interest after the publication of an article on the battered child syndrome in 1962 (Kempe & Kempe, 1994). This publication was instrumental in rousing international concern about the violence meted out to children by their caretakers. The physical abuse and neglect of children was the early focus of attention until it was acknowledged that children are mistreated in other ways as well. This chapter presents a global overview of familial child abuse and neglect, and gives insights on the problem in the English-speaking Caribbean (referred to as *the Caribbean* in this chapter).

OVERVIEW OF CHILD ABUSE AND NEGLECT

Definitions

Child abuse is generally classified as physical, sexual, and emotional or psychological abuse, and neglect is classified as medical, physical, psychological, educational, lack of supervised care, and abandonment. These concepts have been "defined and redefined throughout history" (Crosson-Tower, 2008, p. 1), and yet no universal definitions exist. Definitions tend to reflect various professional orientations, including medical, legal, psychological, sociological, and social work (Besharov, 1990), and they may also reflect a cultural orientation. Nevertheless, the definitions have some elements in common. For example, definitions of physical abuse tend to focus on whether the behavior that is perpetrated is deliberate, or with intent to harm the child. Definitions of sexual abuse generally take into consideration the statutory age of consent and the fact that the behavior is perpetrated for the gratification of the adult. In the case of emotional or psychological abuse, definitions tend to focus on deliberate and unintentional behaviors that may or may not be observable. Whereas the abuse of children generally entails acts of commission, neglect results from acts of omission.

Child abuse and neglect have been destroying the lives of children around the world for centuries, and the problem continues to cause international worry. The present-day child protection movement is therefore universal in scope and is supported by the United Nations (UN) and its various international bodies, such as the United Nations Children's Fund (UNICEF) and United Nations Development Fund for Women (UNIFEM) (now part of UN Women), and by the World Health Organization (WHO). Other international organizations including regional organizations specific to each area of the globe, local governmental and nongovernmental organizations (NGOs) (such as Save the Children), and civil society groups also champion the right of children to protection from abuse and neglect.

Through its 1989 Convention on the Rights of the Child (CRC), the UN has drawn tremendous international attention to the plight of children and to the realization that, due to their vulnerability, children are entitled to special care and protection in their homes, in institutions, educational settings, the workplace and in their communities. The CRC emphasizes the responsibility of parents as well as the extended family in the care and protection of children, the obligation of governments to support legal and other administrative measures necessary for the protection of children and the vital role of local communities and the international community in helping to ensure that children are accorded their rights (UNICEF, 1989). In the CRC, *child abuse* is defined as all forms of maltreatment and exploitation of children by parents and others responsible for their care. This encompasses all conditions detrimental to the well-being of children and includes physical, emotional, and sexual abuse and neglect or negligent treatment (Articles 19, 34, 36, and 39); child labor (Article 32); the illicit use of and trafficking in narcotic drugs by children (Article 33); torture and deprivation of liberty (Article 37); the sale, trafficking, and abduction of children (Articles 11 and 35); and children's involvement in armed conflict (Article 38).

Global Scope of Abuse and Neglect

It has been customary to focus on familial child abuse and neglect—that is, the abuse of children by their parents, caretakers, other family members, and relatives—because this type of violence is pervasive and accounts for much of the violence experienced by children (UN, 2006). However, with the horrific stories of children suffering through institutional and societal abuse and the knowledge that these sources are integrally involved with familial abuse, these types of abuse have also been receiving much attention. Societal abuse may be conceived as the sum of a society's "actions, beliefs, and values that impede the healthy development of its children" (Giovannoni, 1985, p. 194), while institutional abuse refers to maltreatment "perpetrated on children through society's institutions" (pp. 195–196), such as the educational, legal, health-care, and social welfare systems.

Many theoretical approaches have been proposed to explain the causes of child abuse and neglect. These have generally focused on individual, family, or societal risk factors. However, it is increasingly being acknowledged that the social, economic, legal, and political systems in some countries also contribute to the abuse of children, whether intentionally or unintentionally. For example, in societies where socioeconomic policies lead to large-scale poverty and degradation that affect families, where socially sanctioned practices such as corporal punishment known to be harmful to children are condoned and institutionalized, where children are exploited for profit through their labor, where children are involved in armed conflict, and where the existing legislation fails to protect them, children's well-being and survival are seriously jeopardized. The UN reports that "growing income inequality, globalization, migration, urbanization, health threats, in particular the HIV/AIDS pandemic, technological advances and armed conflict" (UN, 2006, p. 13) have all affected how children are treated.

Research studies have consistently identified a large number of child, perpetrator, parental and family, cultural, community, and environmental risk factors, which may vary from family to family and from society to society (Crosson-Tower, 2008; Gil, 1971; Rock, 2002; UN, 2006; UNICEF, 2007a). Some of these include the age and gender of the child, whether the child has a disability, poor parenting, disciplinary tactics that involve violent behavior, cultural practices, social isolation of families, and so on.

The emerging research indicates that child maltreatment exists in every country of the world, cutting across "culture, class, education, income and ethnic origin" (UN, 2006, p. 5). All children are potentially at risk; this includes special groups of children such as children with disabilities, children of illegal immigrants, children of minority and marginalized groups, street children, children in conflict with the law, refugee children, and children who are displaced because of natural disasters and emergencies (UN, 2006).

Several reports highlight the global problem, painting a grim picture. The most recent international, in-depth research that details the nature, extent, and causes of violence against children is the Secretary-General's Study on Violence against Children (UN, 2006). This study, which involved over 133 UN member states, "confirms that violence exists in every country of the world . . . is socially approved, and is frequently legal and State-authorized" (p. 5). The study indicates that according to International Labour Organization (ILO) estimates for 2004, 218 million children were involved in child labor, which included forced or bonded labor, prostitution, pornography, and trafficking. The study report also cites WHO statistics estimating that during 2002, 150 million girls and 73 million boys under age eighteen were sexually abused in various ways, and it notes that "trafficking in human beings, including children, within countries and across international borders is a major international concern" (p. 21).

Save the Children UK (2008) reports that millions of children around the globe are exposed to abuse, violence, exploitation, and neglect; that 1.8 million children are abused for profit; that over 300,000 children around the world are soldiers; that an increasing number of children unaccompanied by caregivers are crossing international borders in Africa (Save the Children UK, 2007b); and that child trafficking is a problem in many countries, including the United Kingdom (Save the Children UK, 2007a). The National Society for the Prevention of Cruelty to Children (NSPCC) (2010) reports that in the United

Kingdom, 27, 900 children and young people were the subjects of child protection interventions during 2007 and 29, 200 during 2008, 34,100, during 2009 and 39, 100 during 2010.

National child abuse statistics for the United States indicate that "nearly 3.6 million children received a CPS [child protective services] investigation or assessment" during 2006; that of this number, approximately 25.2% "were determined to have been abused or neglected"; and that "an estimated 905, 000 children were found to be victims" (US Department of Health and Human Services [USDHHS], 2006, p. 1). In 2009 "more than 3.6 million (duplicate) children were subjects of at least one report and received one or more dispositions. One-fifth of these children were found to be victims" (USDHHS, 2009, p. 20) of maltreatment.

Reports of abuse and neglect have generally increased in many societies (UN, 2006). This increase in reporting may be due to increased public education and awareness of the problem and the fact that more people are prepared to report the problem to the authorities. However, it cannot be ruled out that in some societies, more children are being victimized. Research also indicates that there is still underreporting of cases (UNICEF, 2006). Accurate reporting may be a problem in some societies because the criteria used by professionals and the general public for reporting incidents of child abuse differ in many respects, and these criteria determine which cases get reported and which do not. Some well-intentioned citizens do not know where to report a suspected case of abuse or neglect, and some feel that they have no right to intervene in the lives of others (Crosson-Tower, 2008). Additionally, cases that involve familial sexual abuse that occurs in the privacy of the home and the sexual abuse of children perpetrated by adults via the Internet are rarely reported.

Variation in the legal ages for sexual consent, marriage, employment, and criminal responsibility in several countries also affects how children are treated and has implications for reports of child maltreatment. Giovannoni (1985) suggests that anomalies in the legislation of countries can present difficulties in defining who is and is not a child in some contexts, and the ambiguities can promote unequal treatment of children as well as variations in the rights and protection accorded them under the law.

CHILD ABUSE IN THE CARIBBEAN

The English-speaking Caribbean, which will be used as an example in this chapter, includes the countries of Jamaica, Trinidad and Tobago, Barbados, St. Vincent and the Grenadines, St. Kitts and Nevis, Antigua and Barbuda, St. Lucia, Grenada, Montserrat, Dominica, Anguilla, the British Virgin Islands, the Turks and Caicos Islands, Belize in Central America and Guyana in South America. The Caribbean is affected by many of the social and economic problems that plague the world, including the scourge of child abuse and neglect; "violence is a regular feature of the lives of many Caribbean children" (UNICEF, 2007a, p. 15).

The rate of violence against children in some countries of the Caribbean is among the highest in the world (UNICEF, 2007a). UNICEF (2006) reports that "available data on the extent of child abuse and neglect indicates that the problem is endemic in the Caribbean region and large numbers of children are believed to be affected" (p. 16). The violence takes many forms and includes familial child abuse and neglect; violence against children in the community and on the streets; violence against children in school, in institutions, and at work; and children's exposure to domestic and societal violence (Crawford-Brown, 1999; UNICEF, 2006). The poor socioeconomic conditions in some Caribbean countries, prevalence of domestic violence, cultural sanctioning of the physical punishment of children, increased drug trafficking, and escalating societal violence in countries such as Jamaica, Trinidad, and Guyana have all contributed in one way or another to rising child abuse rates (UNICEF, 2007a).

In the Caribbean, familial child abuse includes physical, sexual, and emotional abuse; abandonment; and the witnessing of domestic violence, while familial neglect is generally categorized as physical, psychological, educational, and medical neglect and the inadequate supervision of children. Familial child abuse is not always reported because it generally occurs in the privacy of the home, and some abusive and negligent practices are viewed as normal within the culture (UNICEF, 2006).

One such practice is the corporal punishment of children, which has been implicated in cases of physical child abuse in the Caribbean (Rock, 2002; Le Franc 2002; UN, 2007a; UNICEF, 2006). This cultural practice is institutionalized in both the school and home and is used pervasively and legitimately as a common disciplinary tactic (Payne, 1989; UN, 2005). It has been the subject of much debate in Caribbean countries (Barrow, 2003), and any suggestion to reform the laws to prohibit its use is generally opposed. It is not uncommon for people to state, "When I was a child, I was beaten by my parents and the beatings have made me into a better adult today," or for parents to tell children, "I brought you into the world and I can take you out." Furthermore, there is the "religious reinforcement which admonishes parents not to 'spare the rod'" (Barrow, 2003, p. 46). Garbarino (1977) and Gil (1970) suggest that there is a link between child maltreatment and the cultural sanctioning of physical punishment. Garbarino (1977) notes that the presence of prevailing cultural norms that support the use of physical force can make the difference between abuse and nonabuse for at-risk families; that for child abuse to occur within families, there must be a cultural justification for the use of force against children; and that "there must be a generally held belief that children are the property of their parents to be cared for as they see fit" (p. 32).

Inconsistencies in legislation with regard to the age at which children can perform certain adult behaviors also constitute a problem for Caribbean countries. The age at which children can legally give consent, marry, be employed, and be held responsible for criminal activity varies and is generally disadvantageous for children.

Documenting the true extent of child abuse and neglect in the Caribbean is nearly impossible. Apart from the cultural sanctioning of abusive behavior, the lack of reporting, and the gray areas in the legislation, there is a lack of proper reporting protocols, lack of mandatory reporting laws and formalized systems for responding to reports, and relatively few agencies specializing in child protection (NCH/UNICEF CAO, 2002). These deficiencies in the child protection systems of the various countries hamper the reporting of cases, and therefore "official data on abuse are limited and may vary widely between countries and between years within a country" (UNICEF, 2007a, p. 66).

Despite this problem, the number of reported cases is still "a cause for concern" (Barrow, 2003). Reports range from 224 cases of abuse in Dominica in 2002 (UNICEF, 2006) to 761 cases in Barbados from 2005 to 2006 (UNICEF, 2007b). Although mandatory reporting is widespread in North America and Europe, only a few countries in the Caribbean, including Belize (1999) and Jamaica (2004), have adopted mandatory reporting. Unfortunately, these laws are not fully enforced due to inadequate support systems. There is a critical need for adequate legislation, child abuse reporting, and management protocols in several countries, and UNICEF is providing support in this regard (UNICEF, 2009).

The corporal punishment of children that is so commonplace in the Caribbean is also prevalent in other countries around the globe. Some countries are debating legislation to end the practice, while several others have legislation in place. The Global Initiative to End All Corporal Punishment of Children (2009) reports that "at the start of 2009, children in 23 countries have equal protection from assault, with corporal punishment prohibited in all settings, including the family home: Austria, Bulgaria, Costa Rica, Croatia, Cyprus, Denmark, Finland, Germany, Greece, Hungary, Iceland, Israel, Latvia, Netherlands, New Zealand, Norway, Portugal, Romania, Spain, Sweden, Ukraine, Uruguay, and Venezuela" (p. 2).

ROLES OF SOCIAL WORK AND IMPLICATIONS FOR RESEARCH, POLICY, AND PRACTICE

By virtue of its mandate, the social work profession must be concerned about child abuse and neglect, including risk factors, and the effects of abuse on children, families, and communities. Child abuse and neglect can destroy the lives of children and their families. No form of child abuse takes place in isolation of other types. "Physical violence is often accompanied by psychological violence" (UN, 2006, p. 16) and may occur in combination with sexual abuse and neglect. Some children may suffer the effects for a lifetime despite therapeutic intervention. Such effects include socioemotional disorders, physical injury, intellectual and cognitive disorders, personality disorders, neurological disorders, and inappropriate behaviors.

The causes of child abuse are multifaceted (United Nations, 2006). This means that for social workers to be effective in helping children and families, they must develop certain competencies and be trained to perform various micro-, meso-, and macro-level roles as they work with those affected and build preventive strategies for child protection. These strategies include intensive work with affected children, families, and offending family members; advocacy on behalf of children; and research that can inform evidence-based practice and policy development. The development of relevant policies and intervention strategies for the prevention of child abuse and neglect together with appropriate therapeutic interventions with abused children and their families can be instrumental in combating the problem. Current challenges to the profession in relation to the maltreatment of children include training for child protection workers in techniques of assessment, planning, and intervention in their disposition of cases; advocacy for at-risk and abused children and their families; and advocacy for adequate protective legislation.

A great deal of research exists on the topic of child maltreatment. However, in some countries such as those in the Caribbean, there is a dearth of research, particularly social work research (Rock & Valtonen, 2002). In the Caribbean, the available data on child abuse and neglect are still largely derived from social service agencies, family courts, crisis centers, and one-off, small-scale (usually qualitative) studies. "This prevents trend analyses, as well as the kinds of comparisons between victims, non-victims, abusers and non-abusers necessary for the identification of risk factors and determinants" (Le Franc, 2001, p. 288).

CONCLUSION

Child abuse is a global phenomenon with a long history, but solutions to reduce and eradicate the problem are still emerging. Countries around the world must realize that many of their cultural practices and socioeconomic policies are harmful to children, and they must take measures to protect children from the scourge of abuse and to ensure their survival and well-being.

The social work profession has a role to play in the prevention of abuse and neglect and the rehabilitation of affected children and families. Social work practitioners, educators, and researchers must continue to examine the problem of child abuse and neglect from a variety of perspectives. Such inquiries will provide empirical evidence and refine theoretical perspectives that can provide alternative approaches to explaining the problem.

The need for research, education, and training and for cultural sensitivity and competence among social workers in accordance with the Global Standards for the Education and Training of the Social Work Profession is critical (See Appendix B). Training is sorely needed, because inadequately trained workers in the field will continue to affect how case decisions are made and how well children are protected.

The situation in the Caribbean in regard to child abuse and neglect and the care and protection of children may be similar to what is occurring in other parts of the world, especially in countries where physical punishment is accepted as the norm, where abusive cultural practices are condoned, and where social work is emerging as a profession. According to the UN (2006), "harmful traditional practices affect children disproportionately" (p. 17), for example WHO reports indicate that female genital mutilation "is prevalent in Africa, and also occurs in some parts of Asia and within immigrant communities in Europe, Australia, Canada, and the United States of America" (p. 17).

Prevention of child abuse in countries around the world will require greater understanding of and respect for the rights of children, greater emphasis on the responsibilities of parents toward their children, fundamental changes in societal values and cultural norms that condone abusive behaviors toward children, and the development of programs and socioeconomic policies aimed at ameliorating the situations that are generally found in abusive families and that produce social stress and frustration. In addition to the global initiative for prevention, the role of individual governments and social agencies in the prevention of child maltreatment and its attendant ills is underscored.

REFERENCES

Barrow, C. (2003). Children and social policy in Barbados: The unfinished agenda of child abuse. *Caribbean Journal of Social Work, 2*, 36–53.

Besharov, D. J. (1990). Improved research on child abuse and neglect through better definitions. In D. J. Besharov (Ed.) *Family violence research and public policy issues* (pp. 42–52). Washington, DC: The AEI Press.

Crawford-Brown, C. (1999). *Who will save our children? The plight of the Jamaican child in the 1990's.* Kingston, Jamaica: Canoe Press University of the West Indies.

Crosson-Tower, C. (2008). *Understanding child abuse and neglect* (7th ed.). New York: Pearson.

Giovannoni, J. M. (1985). Child abuse and neglect: An overview. In J. Laird & A. Hartman (Eds.), *A handbook of child welfare: Context, knowledge, and practice* (pp. 193–212). New York: The Free Press.

Garbarino, J. (1977). The human ecology of child maltreatment: A conceptual model for research. *Journal for Marriage and the Family, 30*, 721–735.

Gil, D. J. (1971). A socio-cultural perspective on physical child abuse. *Child Welfare, 50*(5), 389–395.

Global Initiative to End All Corporal Punishment of Children. (2009). Newsletter 6.

Le Franc, E. (2002). Child abuse in the Caribbean: Addressing the rights of the child. In C. Barrow (Ed.), *Children's rights, Caribbean realities* (pp. 285–304). Kingston, Jamaica: Ian Randle.

Kempe, R. S., & Kempe, C. H. (1994). Child abuse. In J. Bruner; M. Cole, & B. Lloyd (Eds.), *The developing child series* (pp. 1–136). Cambridge, MA: Harvard University Press.

National Children's Home (NCH), & United Nations Children's Education Fund (UNICEF) Caribbean Area Office (CAO). (2002). *Social services delivery in the Organization of Eastern Caribbean States and Turks and Caicos Islands (OECS). A research component of the project: Family law and domestic violence legal and judicial reform in the OECS and Turks and Caicos Islands.* Barbados: Author.

National Society for the Prevention of Cruelty to Children (NSPCC). (2010). Children subject to child protection plans – England 2006-2010. Retrieved from http://www.nspcc.org.uk/Inform/research/statistics/ england_wdf49858.pdf (accessed April 3, 2011).

Rock, L. F. (2002). Child abuse in Barbados. In C. Barrow (Ed.), *Children's rights, Caribbean realities* (pp. 305–329). Kingston, Jamaica: Ian Randle.

Rock, L. F., & Valtonen, K. (2002). Identifying a programme of social work research in the Eastern Caribbean. *Journal of Eastern Caribbean Studies*, 27(3), 49–68.

Payne, M. (1989). The use and abuse of corporal punishment: A Caribbean view. *Child Abuse and Neglect*, 13, 389–401.

Save the Children. (2008). Protecting children. Retrieved from www.savethechildren.org.uk/en/31_58.htm (accessed December 29, 2008).

Save the Children. (2007a). Child trafficking in England: Three reports on the evidence and agency responses to child trafficking. Retrieved from www.savethechildren.org.uk/en/54_3039.htm (accessed December 29, 2008).

Save the Children. (2007b). Children crossing borders: Report on unaccompanied minors who have travelled to South Africa. Retrieved from www.savethechildren.org.uk/en/54_3163.htm (accessed December 29, 2008).

United Nations (UN). (2006). *United Nations Secretary-General's Study on Violence against Children: General Assembly report of the independent expert for the United Nations Study on Violence against Children*. New York: Author.

United Nations (UN). (2005). *Ending legalized violence against children: Report for Caribbean regional consultation—the UN Secretary-General's Study on Violence against Children*. London: Global Initiative to End All Corporal Punishment of Children.

United Nations Children's Education Fund (UNICEF). (2009). Child abuse: The number one threat to Caribbean childhood. Retrieved from www.unicef.org/lac/media_10551.htm (accessed March 31, 2009).

United Nations Children's Education Fund (UNICEF). (2007a). *Situation analysis of women and children in the Eastern Caribbean*. Barbados: UNICEF Office for Barbados and the Eastern Caribbean.

United Nations Children's Education Fund (UNICEF). (2007b). *Child protection in Barbados: The need for a national reporting protocol*. Barbados: UNICEF Office for Barbados and the Eastern Caribbean.

United Nations Children's Education Fund (UNICEF). (2006). *Violence against children in the Caribbean Region: Regional assessment. The United Nations Secretary-General's Study on Violence against Children*. Panama: Child Protection Section, UNICEF Regional Office for Latin America and the Caribbean.

United Nations Children's Education Fund (UNICEF). (1989). *Convention on the Rights of the Child. Adopted by the General Assembly of the United Nations on 20 November, 1989*. New York: Author.

U.S. Department of Health and Human Services. (2006). Chapter 3, Children: Child maltreatment. Retrieved from www.acf.hhs.gov/programs/cb/pubs/cm06/chapter3.htm (accessed 29 December, 2008).

United States Children's Bureau (2010). Child maltreatment 2009. US. Department of Health and Human Services, Administration on Children Youth and Families. Washington DC: US Government Printing Office. Retrieved from www.acf.hhs.gov/programs/cb/pubs/cm09/cm09.pdf (accessed April 3, 2011).

21

Child Labor and Work

DENNIS J. RITCHIE

The phenomenon of children working is neither new nor limited to a certain group of nations. Throughout the world children have always worked and continue to do so today. However, controversies concerning working children abound. Children engage in a wide variety of work across a span of ages in an array of settings. Some of this work is viewed positively and other forms negatively. Not all work that children engage in is viewed as something bad or as something that should be eliminated. In order to understand this topic and associated issues, it is necessary to clarify definitions, types of work, and the distinction between child labor and child work.

The terms *economically active children, working children*, and *children's work* have been used interchangeably and refer to a broader concept than *child labor*. They refer to children engaged in some type of work within the household, family farm, or outside the family. This type of work is not necessarily detrimental to the child's development and well-being; indeed, much of children's work is viewed as something positive for children and families. In some circumstances the child's and family's survival may depend on the child contributing to family income, either directly by her or his own production or indirectly by giving the adult(s) increased time to produce income, such as in cases where a child provides childcare for siblings. Some cultures and families view children's work as expected and valued, as contributing to the child's development or socialization, or as a type of vocational education. The International Labour Organization (ILO) defines *economic activity* as inclusive of "most productive activities undertaken by children" regardless of pay, hours, or legality; it does not include household chores or time spent in school (ILO, 2006, p. 5).

The concept of child labor is narrower in scope. Some forms of children's work clearly have a negative impact on children's development and health (both physical and mental) and negatively affect their biopsychosocial functioning and overall well-being.

These situations occur when work interferes with ability to obtain a formal education or exposes children to potentially harmful hazards and risks. Children often are more vulnerable than adults to certain hazards and risks presented in particular forms of work, such as using machinery, carrying heavy loads, or being exposed to chemicals.

Economically active children and child laborers are found in every region of the world: in developed and developing nations, in both the Global North and Global South (ILO, 2004; McKechnie, 1999). It is estimated that 317 million children between the ages of five and seventeen are economically active worldwide, with 218 million of them classifiable as child laborers and 126 million of these involved in hazardous work (ILO, 2006). The Asia and Pacific region has the largest number of working children, but sub-Saharan Africa has the largest proportion (greater than one in every four). The vast majority of these children, 69%, work in the agricultural sector; 22% work in services and only 9% in industry. Other major sectors of child labor include mining, child soldiers, human trafficking of children, commercial sexual exploitation of children, and domestic labor (ILO, 2009a).

Child labor and hazardous work, as distinguished from innocuous children's work, are concepts that are somewhat open to interpretation, and individual nations decide what constitutes each. Determination of whether particular forms of work are categorized as child labor depends on the context; considerations include the child's age, the type of work and number of hours, and the conditions surrounding the work. International child labor standards have been established to help distinguish between acceptable child work and unacceptable child labor. It has been easier to reach a consensus concerning the most extreme forms of child labor, such as those involving human trafficking and other forms of slavery, where children are separated from family and exploited while being exposed to serious harm.

INTERNATIONAL STANDARDS ON CHILD LABOR

The international legal system that guides individual nations and serves as the foundation for the global movement against child labor rests upon two primary ILO conventions working in concert with the UN Convention on the Rights of the Child (CRC) (1989). These are the ILO Minimum Age Convention, 1973 (No. 138) and the ILO Worst Forms of Child Labour Convention, 1999 (No. 182). *Child* is defined as a person under the age of eighteen.

Convention No. 182 establishes the worst forms of child labor as a top priority to be targeted and eliminated, without losing sight of the long-range goal to eliminate all forms. Each ratifying member state commits itself to immediate actions to prohibit and eliminate the worst forms, which Article 3 defines as

(a) all forms of slavery or practices similar to slavery, such as the sale and trafficking of children, debt bondage and serfdom and forced or compulsory labour, including forced or compulsory recruitment into armed conflict;

(b) the use, procuring or offering of a child for prostitution, for the production of pornography or for pornographic performances;

(c) the use, procuring or offering of a child for illicit activities, in particular for the production and trafficking of drugs as defined in the relevant international treaties;

(d) work, which by its nature or the circumstances in which it is carried out, is likely to harm the health, safety, or morals of children. (ILO, 1999).

ILO Recommendation No. 190, which accompanies Convention No. 182, provides guidelines for determining what qualifies as the hazardous work referred to in Article 3(d). It calls for consideration of the following in determining what forms are likely to harm children's health, safety, or morals:

(a) work which exposes children to physical, psychological or sexual abuse;

(b) work underground, under water, at dangerous heights or in confined spaces;

(c) work with dangerous machinery, equipment and tools, or which involves the manual handling or transport of heavy loads;

(d) work in an unhealthy environment which may, for example, expose children to hazardous substances, agents or processes, or to temperatures, noise levels, or vibrations damaging to their health;

(e) work under particularly difficult conditions such as work for long hours or during the night or work where the child is unreasonably confined to the premises of the employer. (ILO, 1999, R190, II 3).

Convention No. 138 provides a framework for establishing minimum ages for various categories of work, and violations result in categorization as child labor. The basic minimum age for employment is normally set at fifteen, but developing countries may set it at fourteen. It further specifies that children should not enter full-time employment below the age required for completion of compulsory schooling. The minimum age for light work is thirteen, or twelve for developing countries; light work is that which does not interfere with schooling or vocational education nor harm children's health and development. The minimum age for engaging in hazardous work is eighteen but may be allowed at sixteen under strict conditions.

Article 32 of the United Nations Convention on the Rights of the Child (CRC) (1989) specifically addresses child labor:

State Parties recognize the right of the child to be protected from economic exploitation and from performing any work that is likely to be hazardous or to interfere with the child's education, or to be harmful to the child's health or physical, mental, spiritual, moral or social development.

It is noteworthy that this convention is the most widely and rapidly ratified in the history of the UN. Many articles indirectly relate to child labor, such as those covering the right to education and social security.

Great progress has been made toward the universal ratification of both ILO conventions. Convention No. 182 (now at 169 of the 183 member states) has been the most rapidly ratified convention in the ninety-year history of the ILO and has mobilized strong international support for No. 138 (now at 151 ratifications, a fourfold increase since adoption of No. 182).

OVERVIEW OF PROGRESS, CHALLENGES, AND ISSUES

Progress to Date

There is reason to be optimistic concerning child labor. The ratification success rate of the three conventions has resulted from a concerted international movement against child labor and for children's rights, which has been linked to the Education for All, Child Rights, Anti-Poverty, and Pro Human Development movements exemplified by the UN Millennium Development Goals. Fyfe (2007) presents an excellent historical and analytical description of this worldwide movement to end child labor, which started in the early nineteenth century, began to accelerate its impact on child labor in the 1980s, and continues to the present. Within this movement, the ILO assumes a "convening role and provides policy leadership through its standards" and the "largest . . . programme of technical cooperation" (Fyfe, 2007, p. 3).

The ILO is a tripartite United Nations agency comprising representatives from governments, workers, and employers. Founded in 1919 based on a vision that lasting peace is built upon decent treatment of working people, it is committed to promoting social and economic justice and human and labor rights. It is the global body responsible for developing and overseeing international labor standards. After the UN adopted the CRC in 1989, the ILO dedicated itself to assisting nations in dealing with child labor. In 1992 it established its International Programme on the Elimination of Child Labour (IPEC), which became the principal global program exclusively focused on child labor. It has turned into the largest technical cooperation program of the ILO and has spearheaded the international movement against child labor. It provides a wealth of invaluable resources to advocates working to eliminate child labor internationally, nationally, and locally, including more than 1800 publications and advocacy materials. One can learn more about IPEC and access its many resources via its website (www.ilo.org/ipec). The IPEC Statistical Information and Monitoring Programme on Child Labour (SIMPOC) offers resources and assistance in data collection, analysis, and documentation related to child labor.

Significant progress in the struggle against child labor has been documented. The UN has taken the lead via multiple agencies, most notably the ILO and IPEC, but other partners are also instrumental in the movement. For example, the ILO and IPEC have forged partnerships with governments, other international agencies, employers and their organizations, workers organizations (including unions), private businesses, universities, the media, faith-based groups, children and their families, and a variety of nongovernmental organizations (NGOs) throughout the world representing women's and children's human

rights, education, health, food security, and poverty reduction.

Understanding Children's Work (UCW) is an interagency cooperative research project that has contributed to the success of the movement and helped shape the course of future action. It was created in 2000 by three main international agencies concerned with children, labor, and development—the United Nations Children's Fund (UNICEF), the ILO, and the World Bank—with goals to improve child labor data collection, analysis, research, and assessment of interventions at national and local levels (Fyfe, Roselaers, Tsannatos, & Rosati, 2003). One can learn more about UCW and its many resources via its website (www.ucw-project.org).

The ILO's 2006 global report is often cited for documenting the success experienced in reducing child labor from 2000 to 2004, delineating accomplishments and challenges, and establishing a goal of eliminating the worst forms of child labor by 2016. This goal is viewed as within reach based on the positive changes that have occurred and the ongoing strength of the movement. There was an 11% decline in the number of child laborers worldwide and an even more striking drop in children doing hazardous work—a 26% decline overall and a 33% decline among five- to fourteen-year-olds. "The more harmful the work and the more vulnerable the children involved, the faster the drop" (ILO, 2006, p. vii). This evidences the success attributable to targeting the worst forms of child labor as the top priority.

Remaining Challenges

Salient challenges still need to be addressed. The ILO 2006 global report cites the mainstreaming of child labor elimination into principal human rights and development frameworks as a major challenge, particularly linking to the UN Millennium Development Goals aimed at poverty reduction. Reduction of child labor will play a key role in those targets related to education, which in turn are linked to poverty reduction.

Poverty and lack of access to quality education are two of the primary determinants of child labor cited throughout the literature. They are intertwined and linked to child labor as both determinants and consequences. Guarcello, Lyon, and Rosati (2008) explicate the interplay between education and child labor and the connection between the movements toward education for all and the elimination of child labor. Child labor is an obstacle to children attending school, and lack of access to quality education encourages children to not attend school and to engage in labor. Children and families weigh the costs and benefits of child labor and education and make decisions based on their view of the likely consequences of investment in each. Children living in poverty are more likely to engage in child labor. Those who invest in child labor rather than education are more likely to end up with limited earning power and remain in poverty. Those who combine child labor and schooling are likely to perform poorly in school and thereby limit future opportunities.

Additional threats to human development and human rights, including serious health threats like the HIV/AIDS pandemic and the marginalization and exclusion of vulnerable populations, are also key factors in understanding and intervening in child labor. Though poverty is most often considered the primary reason why children work, IPEC asserts that other reasons, such as the AIDS pandemic in sub-Saharan Africa, can force children into working when their parents are sick or when they eventually become orphaned (ILO, 2009b). Dorman (2008) conducted an extensive literature review on the relationships among child labor, education, and health, concluding that although child labor is now considered a "human capital problem, measurable by its impacts on education and health" (p. 47), there is a need for investigation into links between types and intensity of work and precise outcomes for children based on age, gender, and socioeconomic status.

A gender perspective paying special attention to the girl child is certainly needed. A recent report (ILO, 2009c) notes that the global economic crisis may push more children into child labor and have an even greater impact on girls. According to IPEC, children's gender can "determine at what age they are sent to work and in which particular occupation . . . [and] may affect a child's access to education and assistance" (ILO, 2009b). When families with limited resources are facing tough decisions, those from cultures that place a higher value on the education of boys may keep girls out of school and in the workplace. Girls are also disproportionately involved in many of the worst forms of child labor, such as being trafficked into sexual exploitation or domestic labor. Much of their work is hidden from public view, making them particularly vulnerable and potentially undercounted. Girls are more likely to be responsible for household chores and, coupled with work outside the home, they face a double burden that increases their exclusion from education and limits future opportunities. As a result almost two-thirds of the world's illiterate population is female.

Other vulnerable and marginalized populations require special attention as well. These include children with disabilities, racial and ethnic minorities, children affected by natural disasters, and immigrant and migrant children.

INTERVENTIONS IN CHILD LABOR

The movement recognizes that child labor is a complex problem that requires a holistic view to fully understand and effectively intervene to reduce and eliminate it across global, national, and local levels. The professional literature comprises various disciplines and perspectives and reflects the complex, interdisciplinary nature of the phenomenon. Predominant interventions to eliminate child labor aim to provide access to quality education and social and economic development programs to address poverty and other forms of violence that threaten human rights and development. Interventions also address the specific physical and psychosocial health effects of child labor.

Woodhead (2004) critically focuses on the psychosocial impact of child work. He emphasizes that work can be both a hazard and an asset in children's lives, and he stresses the importance of viewing the situation in context of children's lives. It is essential to understand various perspectives, including those of the children themselves. Woodhead calls for more personalized, localized child-centered interventions that take into consideration risks, benefits, and the best interest of the child. He suggests that hazard assessments be accompanied by assessment of the child's and parents' perceptions of the economic and psychosocial rewards provided by the work, which may be viewed as essential to their welfare.

It is widely recognized that building quality education programs that children can access is a key strategy for reducing child labor. Since child labor is largely an economic decision for families facing poverty—a weighing of the costs and benefits of work versus school—critical interventions include those that address income security, credit availability, access to basic services, provision of a social safety net, and views on education.

Conditional Cash Transfer Programs

Conditional cash transfer (CCT) programs are a promising intervention to address poverty and reduce child labor. These programs are a form of social security that provides cash to families. The cash transfer is conditional, however, on certain behaviors and commitments of the families that are designed to develop human capital in their children. Common examples include conditions related to health and education; the cash payment is continued if parents ensure that children receive immunizations and checkups and/or that the children attend school.

With roots in Latin America, CCTs are now sprouting up throughout the world. Mexico and Brazil have been leaders in the field, having developed the earliest, largest, and most extensive programs. Mexico's CCT program named *PROGRESA* started in 1997 and was renamed *Oportunidades* in 2001; it began by serving about 300,000 households and now serves five million. Brazil's Bolsa Familia currently benefits approximately eleven million families and is the largest CCT program in the world; it merged the federal conditional and unconditional cash transfer programs that provided minimum income grants to encourage primary education, food security, and subsidies for cooking gas.

Most CCT programs do not specifically include reduced child labor as a condition, and they do not always result in a reduction. Certainly, targeting increased school attendance and poverty reduction can lead to a decrease in child labor. Further research is needed focusing on the impact of CCTs on child labor, including determining whether successes in specific countries can be replicated in others and whether school attendance as a condition leads to a decrease in child labor or whether children then merely combine school and work.

Brazil's Program for the Eradication of Child Labor (PETI) has been incorporated into *Bolsa Familia* and has proven to be effective by lengthening the school day and establishing the reduction of child labor as a condition. The World Bank has published a report examining CCT rationale, conceptualization, and effectiveness (Fiszbein & Schady, 2009). The report concludes that CCTs have improved the lives of people living in poverty. It further states that "although CCT's generally have not resulted in reductions in the labor market participation of adults, they have led to substantial decreases in child labor. . . . Reduced child work by CCT beneficiaries has been found in Brazil, Cambodia, Ecuador, Mexico, and Nicaragua" (p. 16).

Rosati and Lyon (2006) identify three broad categories of policy and program options needed to sustainably reduce child labor. They call for targeting children at risk of involvement in child labor, children already engaged in and harmed by child labor, and children requiring immediate direct action due to their involvement in the worst forms of child labor.

Preventive interventions are needed that identify and target the causal factors. Preventive efforts need to be complemented by interventions of removal, rehabilitation, and social integration of children who have been involved in child labor.

SOCIAL WORK AND CHILD LABOR

The holistic, ecosystemic perspective of social work is well suited for analyzing and synthesizing the multifaceted, complex, interrelated aspects (i.e., determinants and consequences) of child labor. Addressing the phenomenon of child labor fits well with social work's definition, purpose, and values. The reader is referred to the International Definition of Social Work (IASSW/IFSW, 2001) and its statements on the profession's mission and values. Social work practice focuses on "meeting human needs and developing human potential. Human rights and social justice serve as the motivation and justification for social work action." Social workers strive to "alleviate poverty and to liberate vulnerable and oppressed people in order to promote social inclusion," and they work together with those who are disadvantaged to achieve these goals (IASSW/IFSW International Definition of Social Work, 2001, Values section).

Social work needs to increase research and action into the determinants and consequences of child labor throughout the world, because it is indeed a global problem. We need research that critically examines the phenomenon and that is linked to social action, addressing all forms of child labor in all geographic areas in both the Global South and North. Action research on child labor with special attention to vulnerable subpopulations (for example, girls, immigrants and migrants, and children with disabilities) is particularly lacking. Social workers can identify and involve all key stakeholders in any given situation of child labor and can especially help "give voice" to the children, helping to empower them to critically reflect on their situation and effect planned social change to realize and protect their full human rights and development.

The specialized knowledge concerning child labor that social workers might need to acquire to effectively address the problem is readily available. Potential resources to help social workers join and contribute to the worldwide movement against child labor and its negative consequences have been cited throughout this chapter. The IPEC and UCW websites are especially good starting points.

Even though social work is well positioned to tackle child labor as a global and local problem, the profession has paid limited attention to it. A paucity of professional social work literature exists on the topic. There has been some literature on a few specific forms of child labor, such as "street children" (e.g., Ferguson, 2006) and human trafficking (e.g., Estes & Weiner, 2002; Roby, 2005). Otis, Pasztor, and McFadden (2001) discussed child labor being outside the professional child welfare radar screen in the twenty-first century, despite the contrary being true in the early twentieth century, when social work reformers led a call for the elimination of hazardous child labor. These authors called for a renewed commitment by child welfare professionals and advocates, but child labor has not become a major focus of social work to date. It is time for social work to again commit itself to tackling this problem, to help lead the way and assume a major role in the movement to eliminate child labor and respond to those children and families who are already affected.

REFERENCES

Dorman, P. (2008). *Child labour, education and health: A review of the literature.* Geneva: International Labour Office.

Estes, R. J., & Weiner, N. A. (2002). *The commercial sexual exploitation of children in the U.S., Canada and Mexico.* Philadelphia: University of Pennsylvania School of Social Work Center for the Study of Youth Policy. Retrieved June 20, 2009, from www.sp2.upenn.edu/restes/CSEC_Files/Complete_CSEC_020220.pdf.

Ferguson, K. M. (2006). Responding to children's street work with alternative income-generation strategies. *International Social Work, 49*(6), 705–717.

Fiszbein A. & Schady N. (2009). *Conditional cash transfers: Reducing present and future poverty.* Washington, DC; The World Bank Group. Retrieved March 31, 2011 from http://siteresources.worldbank.org/INTCCT/Resources/5757608-1234228266004/PRR-CCT_web_noembargo.pdf

Fyfe, A. (2007). *The worldwide movement against child labour: Progress and future directions.* Geneva: International Labour Office.

Fyfe, A; Roselaers, F; Tsannatos, Z & Rosati, F. (2003). Understanding children's work, *The World Bank Economic Review.* 17(2), 311–314.

Guarcello, L., Lyon, S., & Rosati, F. C. (2008). Child labour and education for all: An issue paper. *The Journal of the History of Childhood and Youth.* 1(2), 254–266.

International Association of Schools of Social Work/International Federation of Social Workers (IASSW/IFSW). (2001). *Definition of social work.* Retrieved July 7, 2009, from www.iassw-aiets.org.

International Labour Organization (ILO). (2009a). *Child labour by sector.* Retrieved June 10, 2009, from www.ilo.org/ipec/areas/lang–en/index.htm.

International Labour Organization (ILO). (2009b). *Related issues: AIDS, gender . . .* Retrieved June 10, 2009, from www.ilo.org/ipec/facts/related/lang–en/index.htm.

International Labour Organization (ILO). (2009c). *Give girls a chance: Tackling child labour, a key to the future.* Geneva: International Labour Office.

International Labour Organization (ILO). (2006). *The end of child labour: Within reach.* Geneva: International Labour Office.

International Labour Organization (ILO). (2004). *Child labour: A textbook for university students.* Geneva: International Labour Office.

International Labour Organization (ILO). (1999). Worst Forms of Child Labor Convention No. 182.

International Labour Organization (ILO). (1973). Minimum Age Convention No. 138.

McKechnie, J. (1999). Child labor: The view from the North. *Childhood, 6*(11), 89–100.

Otis, J., Pasztor, E. M., & McFadden, E. J. (2001). Child labor: A forgotten focus for child welfare. *Child Welfare, 80*(5), 611–622.

Roby, J. L. (2005). Women and children in the global sex trade: Toward more effective policy. *International Social Work,* 48, 136–137.

Rosati, F. C., & Lyon. S. (2006). *Tackling child labour: Policy options for achieving sustainable reductions in children at work.* Rome: Understanding Children's Work Project. Retrieved March 26, 2011, from http://info.worldbank.org/etools/docs/library/251035/day8-TacklingchildlabourApril8Se1.pdf.

United Nations Convention on the Right of the Child (CRC). (1989). www.unicef.org/crc/.

Woodhead, M. (2004). *Psychosocial impacts of child work: A framework for research, monitoring and intervention.* Rome: Understanding Children's Work Project. Retrieved March 23, 2011, from http://www-wds.worldbank.org/external/default/WDSContentServer/WDSP/IB/2008/05/20/000333037_20080520023027/Rendered/PDF/437620WP0UCW0s1Box0327368B01PUBLIC1.pdf.

22

Child Soldiers

JOANNE CORBIN

Media images of young children dressed in military fatigues carrying rifles, accounts of US soldiers in the Middle East encountering children pointing weapons at them, and published accounts of children caught in the middle of ethnic and political instability have brought the experiences of child soldiers into the public's awareness. The public is presented with stark contrasts of young children behaving in ways that are expected of adults under the most difficult circumstances.

Social workers working with former child soldiers are confronted with understanding and reconciling many such contrasts. One example is a conversation I had with a lawyer who wanted to know about the experiences a former child soldier may have had in his country of origin, a country in the midst of a long-standing armed conflict. The lawyer was determining whether this former child soldier was a victim or perpetrator of violence in order to proceed with his application for amnesty in the United States. The reality is that this child and others like him experienced many violent acts as receivers of violence, actors in violence, and witnesses to violence. Every aspect of the topic of child soldiers is just as difficult to categorize.

This chapter provides an overview of child soldiers, including definitions, ways that children become involved in armed conflict, their experiences during armed conflict, and interventions to support their reintegration into society. Social workers encounter families from countries that are experiencing or have experienced armed conflict. Family members, including children, may have been involved in the violence. Social workers must deepen their awareness and knowledge of these children's experiences, because such understanding is critical for practice, research, and policy that is informed by and responsive to these children's specific needs.

OVERVIEW: SCOPE OF THE ISSUE

Number of Child Soldiers

Children under eighteen are involved in 75% of the world's armed conflicts (University of British Columbia, 2005). There are an estimated 100,000 to 200,000 child soldiers in government, paragovernment, and nongovernment armed forces and groups (Achvarina & Reich, 2006) in eighty-six countries and territories (Coalition to Stop the Use of Child Soldiers, 2008). Of the conflicts that involve children, 80% involve children under fifteen (University of British Columbia, 2005). The average age of a child soldier is nine to ten (Acharvarina & Reich, 2006). Approximately one-third of child soldiers are girls.

Definitions

The sentiment that children are entitled to protection appears in the Geneva Declaration of the Rights of the Child, which states, "The child must be given the means requisite for its normal development, both materially and spiritually" (League of Nations, 1924). This is echoed in subsequent international human rights policies, such as the UN's Universal Declaration of Human Rights (1948), the Declaration of the Rights of the Child (U.N.,1959), and the Convention on the Rights of the Child (CRC) (OHCHR, 1989). It was not until 1989 that an age criterion provided in the CRC defined a child as "every human being below the age of eighteen years unless under the law applicable to the child, majority is attained earlier" (OHCHR, 1989).

In accordance with this definition, the CRC (OHCHR, 1989) established eighteen as the minimum age for recruitment of an individual into an armed force or group and participation in hostilities. The Optional Protocol to the Convention on the

Rights of the Child on the Involvement of Children in Armed Conflict (OHCHR, 2000) stipulates that government and nongovernment armed groups should ensure that individuals under eighteen do not involuntarily participate in such groups. There is international debate about whether children between the ages of fifteen and eighteen can voluntarily join an armed force or armed group. The Coalition to Stop the Use of Child Soldiers (2008) defines a child soldier as "any person below the age of 18 who is a member of or attached to government armed forces or any other regular or irregular force or armed political group whether or not an armed conflict exists" (p. 9). International humanitarian law as reflected in the Rome Statute of the International Criminal Court (United Nations, 2002) considers the conscription or enlistment of children under the age of fifteen into national armed forces or using them to participate in hostilities to be a war crime.

Opposing perspectives of age-based criteria in international human rights policies and humanitarian laws center on the historical, cultural, and contextual factors that influence concepts of childhood (Rosen, 2005). Children have historically been involved in armed conflicts; for example, boys fought in the American Revolution, the Civil War, and World War I, and they fought in Britain's military beginning in the Middle Ages (Rosen, 2005). There are cultural variations in the understanding of when children take on adult roles; youths in Angola, for example, undergo cultural rites of adulthood around the age of fourteen (Lamberg, 2004). Age-based definitions also may be considered paternalistic; for example, young people under eighteen in Sri Lanka and El Salvador have made autonomous decisions to participate in a military or an armed group. Some young people may join militaries for the training and education that is provided. The age-based criteria for participation in militaries or armed groups attempt to find the balance between the benefits of youths' right to participate in an armed group and the risks of abuse, injury, and death (Breen, 2007).

Despite efforts to develop universally accepted age-based criteria, the involvement of children under eighteen in government and nongovernment armed groups appears to be a growing phenomenon (University of British Columbia, 2005). The percentage of intrastate conflicts involving ethnic, religious, and political differences has increased. Intrastate conflicts account for 95% of current armed conflicts, often in developing countries. The vast majority of child soldiers are associated with nongovernment

armed groups involved in intrastate conflicts. Africa has become the region where the percentage of armed conflicts is the highest (40%), closely followed by Asia (37%) (Ploughshares, 2008).

Pathways for Conscripting Children

Children become soldiers through four broad pathways: voluntary enlistment, legal recruitment, lack of viable alternatives, and forced recruitment. First, some children voluntarily join nongovernment groups fighting oppressive governments, as in the case of Israel and occupied Palestinian territory (Rosen, 2005). Second, many children are legally recruited into government armed forces and government-sponsored armed groups; Myanmar has provided an example of this type of recruitment (Coalition to Stop the Use of Child Soldiers, 2008). Third, children may join government forces and nongovernment armed groups as a result of poverty, lack of basic needs, lack of viable livelihoods, or lack of protection if they do not join, such as in the case of the Liberation Tigers of Tamil Eelam (Tamil Tigers) in Sri Lanka (Raman, 2006). Lastly, some children are forced to join under threats of death to themselves or relatives or are abducted into government or nongovernment armed groups, as in the case of the Lord's Resistance Army (LRA) in Uganda.

Poverty, lack of educational resources, increasing numbers of children without parents, and availability of weapons that are easier for children to use have been offered as explanations for children's recruitment into armed conflicts. These may be common factors where children are involved in armed groups; however, Achvarina and Reich (2006) found that the lack of protection and safety of children in internally displaced person (IDP) and refugee camps was the strongest variable associated with children's involvement in armed groups. Due to increasing intrastate conflicts, the population in conflict-affected areas is often relocated to IDP or refugee camps for safety. A tragic consequence is that children in these camps are extremely vulnerable to being coerced or forced to join armed groups.

EXPERIENCES OF CHILDREN IN ARMED CONFLICT

Roles

Child soldiers perform many roles, including fighting in direct combat, setting explosives, acting as spies, carrying food and other equipment, cooking, performing domestic labor, and being used for sexual exploitation (Coalition to Stop the Use of Child Soldiers, 2008). Not all children perform the same roles or have the same experiences; for example, 48% to 87% of children were involved in direct combat (Bayer, Klasen, & Adam, 2007). Girls may not have to fight on the front lines, although they often do, as in the armed conflicts in Liberia and Uganda. McKay and Mazurana (2004) found that females forced into armed groups perform the same roles as males in addition to traditional female gender-role activities, such as food preparation, cleaning, and producing and raising children (McKay & Mazurana, 2004). And although girl soldiers nearly always experience rape or are expected to provide sexual services, girls in Sri Lanka may not have been subjected to these expectations due to cultural prohibitions (Lamberg, 2004). It is important to remember that boys are also sexually abused during armed conflict—recent studies have found that 6% to 22% of boy soldiers have been forced to engage in sex (Bayer , Klasen, & Adam, 2007; Betancourt, Borisova, et al., 2008).

Experiences

As a result of their involvement in these various roles, children in armed conflict are exposed to and experience unimaginable violence. Reported experiences of former child soldiers include witnessing torture, beatings, and violent killings; having to torture or kill others; being forced to engage in sexual acts; having to burn homes and steal from civilians; being seriously beaten or injured; and losing relatives or close friends (Bayer et al., 2007; Derluyn, Broekaert, Schuten, & De Temmerman, 2004; Kanagaratnam, Raundalen, & Asbjørnsen, 2005; Kohrt et al., 2008). The sexual victimization of girls results in children being born in armed conflict; 18% of girl soldiers abducted in Uganda gave birth during their captivity (Derluyn et al., 2004). On average, former child soldiers were exposed to six to eleven traumatic events (Bayer et al., 2007; Derluyn, Broekaert, Schuten, & DeTemmerman, 2004).

The subjective experiences of child soldiers depend on the circumstances of their involvement in the armed conflict. Many children are forced into armed conflict, while others join with varying degrees of volition. Children's experiences will be affected by their perception of self-agency. In Sri Lanka, former child soldiers reported that ideological commitment was a factor in their decision to fight with one of the Tamil groups. Girls in Sri Lanka and the Philippines experienced gender equality since they were trained and placed in positions of power similar to boys (Kanagaratnam et al., 2005; Lamberg, 2004).

Physical, Psychological, and Social Effects

Child soldiers experience a multitude of physical effects, including injuries and disabilities from gunshot wounds, landmine accidents, and other physical hardships. Other health-related issues include malnutrition, respiratory illnesses, skin infections, auditory and visual impairments, and untreated sexually transmitted diseases. Substance abuse is also a concern because drugs are used by some armed groups to desensitize children to the violence.

The psychological effects of armed conflict for child soldiers include depression, anxiety, post-traumatic stress, and bereavement. Former child soldiers in Sierra Leone had persistent psychological distress such as nightmares, recurring and intrusive thoughts, and sadness related to their exposure to violence (Betancourt, Simmons, et al., 2008). Percentages of child soldiers reporting clinically significant post-traumatic stress disorder (PTSD) symptoms range from 35% to 97% (Bayer et al., 2007; Derluyn et al., 2004). In Nepal, 39% to 62% had significant mental health symptoms, including poorer outcomes for depression, PTSD, and functional impairment (Kohrt et al., 2008). Psychological effects can be long lasting, as indicated by 85% of former child soldiers from Sri Lanka reporting clinically significant PTSD symptom scores six years after exposure to conflict (Kanagaratnam et al., 2005).

The type of exposure to violence can make a difference on a child's psychological symptoms and later reintegration into society. Exposure to intimate victimization (such as rape or forced drug use) and perpetration (such as injuring, killing, or taking part in such) were stronger predictors of depression, anxiety, hostility, and PTSD than were witnessing violence or being a victim (Betancourt, Borisova, et al., 2008). Further, higher levels of PTSD symptoms in former child soldiers were associated with less openness to reconciliation and more feelings of revenge; openness to reconciliation increased for those who had been out of the armed group more than two months (Bayer et al., 2007). In addition, the longer child soldiers were with their armed groups, the more they continued to use violence to control others upon return to their communities (Boothby & Knudsen, 2000).

The identities of child soldiers are also affected by their experiences. The decisions they may have had to make about inflicting violence or observing violence often contrast with their understanding of who they were prior to living through armed conflict. Additionally, the social roles that many former child soldiers had as a child or sibling before involvement in conflict have changed as they have lost parents and other family members. These children may be the sole survivors of a family that was killed, or they may return home to take on the role of caring for younger siblings.

The social worlds of child soldiers change drastically with the loss of family members and friends, broken social networks, and disrupted social identities. Many children had to attack family members or steal food and other provisions from their former villages. They may fear harassment and isolation from community members due to the actions they committed or negative perceptions about child soldiers. Many child soldiers have missed years of education and have difficulty finding ways to support themselves and engage in meaningful activities. Programs to increase the sensitivity of community members to the experiences of former child soldiers in Mozambique were key factors in their successful reintegration (Schollmeyer, 2006). Gender is always an important factor to consider in understanding the social effects for girls in armed conflict. Upon return to their communities, girls' experiences are qualitatively different than boys'. Girls have to deal with the consequences and stigma of sexual violation, including returning with children born during their involvement with the armed group. The experiences of girl soldiers during and after involvement in armed conflict tend to be underreported due to shame, stigma, and cultural norms.

RETURNING HOME

Child soldiers leave armed groups through escape, rescue, or cessation of conflict. The communities to which these children return have the challenge of reintegrating them while attending to the pressing needs of the community. All aspects of these communities, villages, and refugee or IDP camps have been severely affected by the armed conflict, including diminished availability of basic needs such as food, shelter, health care, and livelihood or educational opportunities. It is important to remember that everyone living in these contexts has lived with the same violence (or the threat of this violence) as the child soldiers have.

Rehabilitation and Reintegration

Psychological and social rehabilitation programs for former child soldiers have been shaped by humanitarian policies such as the UN's Convention on the Rights of the Child (OHCHR, 1989). The UN works with nongovernmental agencies to develop the disarmament, demobilization, and rehabilitation (DDR) programs that support the reintegration of former child soldiers (Breen, 2007). Disarmament involves collecting the weapons of former combatants, demobilization is the process of ending the former child soldier's connection with the armed force by removing the child from the armed group and identifying the child's family, and rehabilitation involves preparing former child soldiers to return to their families and providing support in the form of psychosocial counseling, social skills, and income-generating activities. These rehabilitation programs provide former child soldiers with needed resources during the reintegration process; however, the provision of these resources to child soldiers in a community where everyone has been tremendously affected by violence and has similar needs often causes tension between the returning children and others in the community. In addition, the receiver of these services is identified as a former child soldier, which may be an identification that does not aid the child as he or she is reconnecting to the social network.

Positive reintegration is supported by the ability of former child soldiers to engage in socially accepted livelihood activities, return to school, reestablish good relationships, and help rebuild homes and schools destroyed during the conflict (Schollmeyer, 2006). These socially and culturally valued activities provide normative experiences and reestablish former child soldiers' roles within the community, thereby supporting psychosocial healing (Farwell & Cole, 2002).

Psychosocial Interventions

Interventions to address child soldiers' psychological and social needs have focused on strategies to support constructive coping skills to manage the trauma and distress that some children experience and to support prosocial behaviors that enable children to rejoin families and communities. Such interventions include art, dance, sports, and social skills groups. Psychosocial interventions must incorporate ethnically and culturally appropriate understandings of physical health, mental health, and well-being. Practitioners should understand how physical and mental health, including the dimensions of wellness, disease, and healing, are conceptualized within a specific culture.

Traditional cultural healing ceremonies and involvement of the church were key elements in postwar reconstruction in Mozambique. The ceremonies helped resolve distress and suffering of the heart and repair the social relationships that were destroyed in the war (Gibbs, 1994; Honwana, 2006). Traditional cleansing ceremonies were also important for child soldiers in northern Uganda. A former girl soldier who was abducted at fifteen was able to escape with three children after eight years with the LRA. Her family believed she died in the fighting and publically mourned her. Upon her return to the IDP camp, a traditional cleansing ceremony, called *stepping on the egg*, was conducted by a traditional leader to cleanse the spiritual impurities that she was exposed to during her abduction. An additional ceremony, called *returning the tears*, was conducted to undo the mourning process. Such traditional ceremonies are used to aid psychological and social reconnection between the returning person and the family and larger community (Corbin, 2008).

Implications for Social Work

Social workers must deepen their knowledge about the specific armed conflicts that former child soldiers have experienced; this applies to all areas of social work, including practice, policy, education, and research. Children's experiences in armed conflict are complex, and factors such as the history of conflict in a specific country, the degree of volition that an individual had in becoming a child soldier, and the type of exposure to violence affect a child soldier's experience. Though practitioners should expand their knowledge about specific armed conflicts, they should not assume that the experiences of armed conflict are the most pressing concern for the individual. The most salient issues may be difficulties in the individual's current living situation concerning housing, employment, education, disconnection from one's culture or communal network, and adaptation to another culture.

Areas of inquiry for research include exploring the strengths of former child soldiers and of their communities during reintegration. Both contribute to the process of healing and recovery. Implications for policy include an increased presence of social workers in organizations that shape human rights and humanitarian policies related to child soldiers (e.g., age-based definitions of childhood). Increasing the voice of social workers in these forums can enrich such discussions by bringing a focus on the complex biopsychosocial needs of child soldiers.

CONCLUSION

Hundreds of thousands of children under the age of eighteen are involved in armed groups in 37% of the world's countries and territories. This chapter reviewed the key issues affecting these children, including the historical involvement of children in war, the challenge of universal age-based criteria, children's experiences in armed conflicts, and the process of reintegration. Children are vulnerable to becoming child soldiers as a result of political, religious, ethnic, cultural, economic, and social instability in their countries. Social workers must gain as full an understanding as they can of the specific context of armed conflict and the subjective experiences of child soldiers in order to work effectively with such children, their families, and their communities.

REFERENCES

Achvarina, V., & Reich, S. (2006). No place to hide: Refugees, displaced persons and the recruitment of child soldiers [Electronic version]. *International Security, 31*(1), 127–164.

Bayer, C. P., Klasen, F., & Adam, H. (2007). Association of trauma and PTSD symptoms with openness to reconciliation and feelings of revenge among former Ugandan and Congolese child soldiers. *Journal of the American Medical Association, 298* (5), 555–559.

Betancourt, T., Borisova, I., Rubin-Smith, J., Gingerich, T., Williams, T., & Agnew Blais, J. (2008). *Psychosocial adjustment and social reintegration of children associated with armed forces and armed groups: The state of the field and future directions: A report prepared for Psychology Beyond Borders*. Austin, TX: Psychology Beyond Borders.

Betancourt, T., Simmons, S., Borisova, I., Brewer, S. E., Iweala, U., & De La Soudiere, M. (2008). High hopes, grim reality: Reintegration and the education of former child soldiers in Sierra Leone [Electronic version]. *Comparative Education Review, 52*(4), 565–587.

Boothby, N. G., & Knudsen, C. M. (2000). Children of the gun. *Scientific American, 282*(6), 60–65.

Breen, C. (2007). When is a child not a child? Child soldiers in international law [Electronic version]. *Human Rights Review, 8*(2), 71–103.

Coalition to Stop the Use of Child Soldiers. (2008). *Child soldiers global report 2008: Summary*. Retrieved February 27, 2008, from www.childsoldiersglobalreport.org.

Corbin, J. N. (2008). Returning home: Resettlement experiences of formerly abducted children in northern Uganda. *Disasters, 32*(2), 316–335.

Derluyn, I., Broekaert, E., Schuten, G., & De Temmerman, E. (2004). Post-traumatic stress in former Ugandan child soldiers. *Lancet, 363*(9412), 861–863.

Farwell, N., & Cole, J. B. (2002). Community as a context of healing: Psychosocial recovery of children affected by war and political violence [Electronic version]. *International Journal of Mental Health, 30*(4), 19–41.

Gibbs, S. (1994). Post-war social reconstruction in Mozambique: Re-framing children's experience of trauma and healing. *Disasters, 18*(3), 268–276.

Honwana, A. (2006). *Child soldiers in Africa*. Philadelphia: University of Pennsylvania Press.

Kanagaratnam, P., Raundalen, M., & Asbjørnsen, A. E. (2005). Ideological commitment and posttraumatic stress in former Tamil child soldiers. *Scandinavian Journal of Psychology, 46*, 511–520.

Kohrt, B. A., Jordans, M. J. D., Tol, W. A., Speckman, R. A., Maharjan, S. M., Worthman, C. M., & Komproe, I. H. (2008). Comparison of mental health between former child soldiers and children never conscripted by army groups in Nepal. *Journal of the American Medical Association, 300*(6), 691–702.

Lamberg, L. (2004). Reclaiming child soldiers' lost lives. *Journal of the American Medical Association, 292*(5), 553–554.

League of Nations. (1924). *Geneva Declaration of the Rights of the Child*. Geneva: UN Documents Cooperation Circles. Retrieved January 5, 2009, from www.un-documents.net/gdrc1924.htm.

McKay, S., & Mazurana, D. (2004) *Where are the girls? Girls in the fighting forces of northern Uganda, Sierra Leone and Mozambique: Their lives during and after war*. Montreal: Center for Rights and Democracy.

Ploughshares. (2008). 30 wars greet the 2008 "Day of Global Cease-Fire." Waterloo, Ontario: Project Ploughshares. Retrieved February 17, 2009, from www.ploughshares.ca/libraries/ACRText/ACRPressrelease08.pdf.

Raman, N. (2006). Outrage over child soldiers in Sri Lanka. *Christian Science Monitor, 99*(3), 7.

Rosen, D. M. (2005). *Armies of the young: Child soldiers in war and terrorism*. New Brunswick, NJ: Rutgers University Press.

Schollmeyer, J. (2006). Re child soldiers: Lost boys found. *Bulletin of the Atomic Scientists, 62*(3), 11.

United Nations. (2002). Rome Statute of the International Criminal Court. The Hague: Author. Retrieved February 27, 2009, from www.icc-cpi.int/NR/rdonlyres/EA9AEFF7-5752-4F84-BE94-0A655EB30E16/0/Rome_Statute_English.pdf.

United Nations. (1948). The Universal Declaration of Human Rights. New York: Author. Retrieved January 7, 2009, from www.un.org/Overview/rights.html.

United Nations Office of the High Commissioner for Human Rights (OHCHR). (2000). Optional Protocol to the Convention on the Rights of the Child on the Involvement of Children in Armed Conflict. General Assembly Resolution 54/263. Geneva: Author. Retrieved on March 18, 2011 from http://www2.ohchr.org/english/law/crc-conflict.htm.

United Nations Office of the High Commissioner for Human Rights (OHCHR). (1989). Convention on the Rights of the Child. General Assembly Resolution 44/25. Geneva: Author. Retrieved on March 18, 2011 from http://www2.ohchr.org/english/law/crc.htm.

United Nations (U.N.). (1959). *Declaration of the Rights of the Child*. General Assembly, 14th session, Resolution 1386. UN Documents: Gathering a Body of Global Agreements. Retrieved on March 18, 2011 from http://www.un-documents.net/a14r1386.htm.

University of British Columbia. (2005). Human security report: War and peace in the 21st century. New York: Oxford University Press. Retrieved February 27, 2009, from www.humansecurityreport.info/HSR2005_PDF/Part1.pdf.

WEBSITES FOR FURTHER INFORMATION

Coalition to Stop the Use of Child Soldiers. www.child-soldiers.org/home.

Human Rights Watch: Child Soldiers. www.hrw.org/en/topic/children039s-rights/child-soldiers.

UNICEF in Emergencies. www.unicef.org/emerg/index_childsoldiers.html.

23

Children in and of the Street

KRISTIN M. FERGUSON

The world population of street children encompasses multiple groups of street-working children, street-living children, and children at risk of migrating to the streets. Extant definitions of these groups include the classification proposed by Lusk (1989) and promoted by UNICEF (United Nations Children's Fund) (Rizzini, Rizzini, Munoz-Vargas, & Galeano, 1995). This typology categorizes street children along a continuum according to their stage in the process of street migration and acculturation. At one end of the continuum, *children at high risk* are those who live in poverty in surrounding slums or squatter communities. Although they maintain ties with their families and often attend school, they tend to be minimally supervised by parents and other adults, spend time working or socializing in the streets, and manifest signs of academic desertion. *Children on the streets* are those who earn their living working in the streets but maintain some family ties. They may either return home daily to sleep or sleep in the streets due to long distances to the worksite. *Children of the streets* are those who are completely on their own, frequently live with other street children, and largely do not attend school. They embrace the street lifestyle and often perform illegal activities to supplement their income, finance a drug addiction, fulfill their basic needs, or simply survive (Ennew, 1994).

Other country-specific and regional conceptualizations of street children and other vulnerable children also exist in the literature. Kenyan service providers proposed nine overlapping categories of at-risk children, including AIDS orphans, children who are heads of households, and children living with HIV or AIDS (Ferguson & Heidemann, 2009). The HIV and AIDS pandemic in many African countries has created new categories of vulnerable children who migrate to the streets to meet their needs in the absence of parental and community support systems (Lombe & Ochumbo, 2008).

In the United States and other industrialized countries, street children may include *runaway* or *homeless youths*, who have left home for one or more nights without notifying their parents or guardians; *throwaway youths*, who have left home because their parents asked them to leave or locked them out; and *independent youths*, who do not have a home to which they can return (Halcon & Lifson, 2004). Youths who live on the streets may also be part of biological *homeless families* or fictive *street families* (Denfeld, 2007).

Most street children never uniformly fit into static groups but tend to oscillate between groups, progressing from one category to another throughout their lives. Factors such as culture, geographical context, age, and the evolutionary nature of street migration all contribute to the complexity of establishing a consistent definition as well as to the difficulty of obtaining precise data of their exact numbers (De la Barra, 1998). Although somewhat imprecise, for the purposes of this chapter the author adopts the United Nations definition of *street children* as "any boy or girl. . . . [under the age of eighteen] for whom the street (in the widest sense of the word, including unoccupied dwellings, wasteland, etc.) has become his or her habitual abode and/or source of livelihood, and who is inadequately protected, supervised, or directed by responsible adults" (Lusk, 1992, p. 294).

GLOBAL OVERVIEW OF CHILDREN IN AND OF THE STREET

One of the most pressing global challenges is the increasing number of children living and working on the streets of urban centers. According to UNICEF (2006), over 100 million children across the world live and work on the streets in order to survive. Most street children are male, although worldwide estimates of females range from one-fourth to one-third of the total street-child population (UNICEF, 2006).

Street children who live and work in urban centers participate in the informal street economy by selling commercial items, washing car windshields at intersections, shining shoes, collecting recyclables and other items from garbage sites, and begging. Some child street workers may also earn a living through theft, prostitution, drug trafficking, or other illicit activities. Often having little or no protection, these children are frequently exposed to exploitative employment, illegal substances, urban crime, and abuse by authorities. They perform unskilled and labor-intensive tasks in the streets for long hours while receiving minimal pay, all of which can affect their health, safety, and psychosocial and moral development. Given these negative effects, child street work constitutes one of the worst forms of child labor (International Labour Organization [ILO], 1999).

Factors Leading Children to the Streets

Myriad individual, familial, and structural factors precipitate the movement of children into the streets to live or work. Individual risk factors include school difficulties and dropping out, unwanted pregnancies, gang involvement, and alcohol and substance abuse (Halcon & Lifson, 2004). Other children seek street employment to complement their families' struggling incomes; many poor families depend on the earnings of their children to meet their basic needs. The incomes derived from these children's labor oftentimes maintain their families above the poverty line (Grootaert & Patrinos, 1999). Likewise, many disadvantaged children depend on income from work to finance their education and that of their siblings (Mickelson, 2000).

Problems in children's families of origin also influence child street migration. Street children are highly likely to come from multiproblem families, characterized by familial conflict, physical and sexual abuse, neglect, and economic hardship (Cauce et al., 2000). Parental mental illness and substance abuse are also frequently cited among the reasons youths leave home. Additional family factors such as poverty, residential instability, and homelessness are also implicated in the reasons children leave home (Halcon & Lifson, 2004).

Structural influences on child street migration include economic crises, unemployment, and labor exclusion of marginal groups. For example, in Brazil, children's informal economic street activity—selling food or artisan products, performing tricks, washing cars, begging, and even stealing—became a primary means of economic subsistence and survival for many poor families, who were most affected by the 1999 financial crisis (Mickelson, 2000). Families living in poverty who face unemployment often seek job opportunities in the informal economy. In this unregulated and often invisible labor realm, the children of these and other poor families find fertile ground for precarious employment (Rizzini et al., 1995).

Additionally, uncontrolled urban growth and the prolific sprawl of marginal shantytowns are two demographic shifts that have occurred in many industrializing countries over the past several decades. Street children are likely to come from these informal shantytowns, often erected on invaded land located in the low flood lands or precarious hillsides surrounding urban centers (Aptekar, 1994). Political strife in many countries throughout Latin America and Africa has also contributed to forced and voluntary in-migration of residents, largely from rural regions to precarious urban areas (Ayuku, Kaplan, Baars, & de Vries, 2004; Pinzón-Rondón, Hofferth, & Briceño, 2008).

Health and Mental Health Status

Once on the streets, children are commonly involved in high-risk survival behaviors to meet their basic needs (Halcon & Lifson, 2004). Street behaviors may include prostitution or survival sex (participating in sexual acts in exchange for money, food, lodging, clothing, or drugs), pimping, pornography, panhandling, theft, selling stolen goods, mugging, dealing drugs, and conning others for goods. Compounding these high-risk behaviors, many street children also have histories of depression, low self-esteem, trauma, self-harm, substance abuse, and physical and sexual abuse (Cauce et al., 2000).

Street children's high-risk behaviors make them particularly susceptible to various health problems. Common physical illnesses among this population include respiratory and skin infections, gastrointestinal problems, and malnutrition. Street children are also disproportionately affected by sexually transmitted diseases and HIV and AIDS (Halcon & Lifson, 2004).

Socially, street children often have limited formal job skills as well as low literacy and educational levels (Epstein, 1996). Patterns of intermittent and persistent residence on the streets are precipitated by the children's limited educational and employment skills, which can ultimately lead to their social exclusion. In countries that lack national systems to locate truant children and the accompanying social services to incorporate them back into the formal educational system, street children often do not attend school (Ayuku et al., 2004; Trussell, 1999).

Service Utilization

Despite the myriad issues that street children confront, considerable evidence indicates their limited use of services. Often treatment for their physical and mental health issues is inadequate or absent altogether; street children tend to have limited service engagement outside of frequenting local drop-in centers for food, clothing, and showers (Raleigh-DuRoff, 2004). Limited service engagement among this population can be explained by their distrust of adults and institutions, transient nature, low self-esteem, and concern for daily survival (De Rosa et al., 1999).

To meet their basic needs in the absence of frequent formal service use, street children are commonly embedded in social support networks on which they rely, particularly those who do not regularly use agency services (Unger, Kipke, Simon, & Johnson, 1998). Social support among street children is useful in helping them survive on the streets and endure daily stressors. Street peers, often referred to as *street families*, provide each other with companionship and material aid as well as with emotional support for mental health issues, such as depression (Trussell, 1999).

POLICY FRAMEWORKS AND SOCIAL WORK CONTRIBUTIONS WITH STREET AND WORKING CHILDREN

There are multiple frameworks to guide policymakers and social work professionals in working with street children. One framework presented in Ferguson (2006) consists of four dimensions of social policy initiatives and practice responses for street children, which build on conceptual maps presented in Lusk (1989), Rizzini and Lusk (1995), Karabanow (2003), Karabanow and Clement (2004), and Dybicz (2005). These are social-control, paradoxical, residual social welfare, and social development policies.

According to this framework, social-control policies are supported by the underlying assumption that children who live and work in the streets are deviants to be controlled, or children who knowingly break the law. Social interventions and programs designed under this ideology follow a correctional, institutional approach and include juvenile detention and reform schools as well as physical threats and abuse by authorities (Karabanow & Clement, 2004). Review of various correctional interventions suggests that not only has this approach achieved low success rates in reintegrating children into their families and communities, but it is also labor and cost intensive (Dybicz, 2005).

Further, correctional interventions are controversial in light of stipulations for child protection outlined in the Convention on the Rights of the Child (UNICEF, 1989). As such, governmental and nongovernmental organizations (NGOs) are increasingly moving away from this approach.

Paradoxical social policies, on the other hand, reflect the underlying assumption that street children are miniature adults with financial responsibilities to the family. One social intervention created under this ideology provides government subsidies, or conditional cash transfers (CCTs), to families to remove their children from the streets and incorporate them in the formal education system. Some well-known examples of CCT programs in Latin America include Oportunidades (formerly PROGRESA) in Mexico, Social Protection Network (SPN) in Nicaragua, Bolsa Familia in Brazil, Family Assignment Program (PRAF) in Honduras, and Chile Solidario in Chile. Adaptations of the Mexican Oportunidades program also exist in African countries, such as Zambia and Malawi, as well as in the United States in New York (Nigenda & González-Robledo, 2005; Rockefeller Foundation, 2007). Although CCT programs have undoubtedly reduced poverty among the poorest families, the overall results regarding children's academic achievement as a result of increased school enrollment have been mixed (de Janvry & Sadoulet, 2006; Skoufias, Parker, Behrman, & Pessino, 2001). In many countries experimenting with CCTs, the monetary assistance is often both less than what the child makes in the street economy and insufficient to cover basic school costs (Nigenda & González-Robledo, 2005).

Another intervention designed under paradoxical social policies consists of creating attractive social service programs within the street milieu (e.g., drop-in centers) that attend to the children's needs yet fail to address the risk factors in their families and communities that precipitate their movement into the streets to live or work (Fernandes, 2007). A criticism of this approach is that street-based programs may even attract at-risk children into the streets in search of the services and benefits offered. Similarly, given the street-based services available, many children are able to meet their basic needs while continuing to live in the streets and engage in high-risk survival behaviors, such as prostitution, theft, and substance use (Gaetz & O'Grady, 2002). Although street-based services aim to mitigate the health, emotional, and social problems of street children, this approach can in effect sustain the livelihoods and behaviors of these young people on the streets.

Third, residual social welfare policies, or means-tested measures to rehabilitate or reeducate street children, stem from the assumption that street children are underdeveloped victims of their surrounding circumstances who need to be assisted. Efforts to help children under this approach include shelters, rehabilitative programs, and charitable works (Karabanow & Clement, 2004). Although programs designed under residual policies may address the children's immediate needs, they are often ineffective in promoting long-term change due to their dependence on external funding as well as on the will of the children to exit the streets. Although efficacy data are lacking, this approach has been criticized as promoting Western, middle-class, and Christian values, thus rendering it questionable for street children from diverse socioeconomic groups, cultures, and religions (Dybicz, 2005).

Finally, social development policies emanate from the belief that street children are autonomous agents of social change and protagonists of their own futures. Social development strategies include using resource development and income-generation initiatives, incorporating children and adults in the formal educational system or providing them with informal education, and enhancing local political involvement and decision-making capacities. Interventions designed under this approach use psychoeducation, societal consciousness raising, and empowerment to incorporate street children in the formal economy and educational system and to prevent their social and labor exclusion (Dybicz, 2005; Karabanow, 2003).

In the extant literature, various examples exist of using a developmental approach, including microenterprises and other social enterprise interventions, with street youths. The International Labour Organization (2003) has documented several successful examples of using vocational cooperatives and microenterprises to help child street workers and their parents replace family income following the withdrawal of child laborers from the informal economy. For instance, in Pakistan, the Directorate of Manpower and Training offers vocational training courses in car repair, tailoring, and electricity to boys and girls who were previously child workers in the informal sector. Similarly, in El Salvador, former child workers participate in apprenticeships and microenterprises as a means to acquire technical skills and generate income. A related community benefit of such initiatives is stimulation of local economic development by creating jobs for youths and goods and services for purchase by the surrounding community.

Mexico currently uses a model of *triangular solidarity* to bring together various sectors, including NGOs, public institutions, and corporations, to address the street-youth phenomenon. In this model, nonprofit organizations, such as Covenant House, assist street children in exiting the street milieu and receiving the necessary physical health, mental health, and social services to lead self-sufficient lives. The public sector (through the Ministry of Education) then provides these young people with vocational training and certification programs to teach them skills and increase their employability. Finally, local and national corporations agree to hire youths who have completed the training program (Ferguson, 2004).

Children's Development Banks (CDB), or Bal Vikas Banks, which are owned, managed, and operated by street children themselves, currently serve hundreds of street children in India, Bangladesh, Pakistan, Afghanistan, and Nepal (Meyer, Masa, & Zimmerman, 2010). Operating as cooperative banking systems, CDBs enable street children who are members to save and withdraw money as well as to receive loans for economic development activities. Across South Asia, CDBs have been successful in teaching street children valuable business skills, assisting them in saving for their futures and securing loans for new businesses, and providing them with a path out of poverty and social exclusion.

Similarly, Kenyan NGOs commonly have income-generating cooperatives through which street children learn vocational skills, create products for consumption or sale, and earn income for themselves and their families. Kenyan NGOs that operate within international networks in the United States and Europe are able to export artisan products made by the children for sale abroad. For example, an Eldoret NGO sponsors a cooperative of street girls and orphans that makes beaded home decorations and jewelry, which are sold in Germany and Netherlands by program supporters (Ferguson & Heidemann, 2009).

In the United States, the Reciprocity Foundation in New York is a social enterprise that facilitates the permanent exit of homeless and high-risk youths from the streets and social services by assisting them in starting sustainable careers in fashion, graphic design, and marketing within the formal economy. Industry professionals teach the young people marketable job skills and mentor them in becoming leaders of their own socially responsible enterprises. Staff employ a sustainable approach by offering services in both professional development and personal well-being (Reciprocity Foundation, 2007).

Implications for the Social Work Profession

The implications of this review of street children include the need to develop policy and practice responses that are holistic, collaborative, and asset based. Evaluation research of interventions suggests that organizations offering integrated services in one location are most successful in addressing street children's various needs (Dybicz, 2005). Programs that can provide multiple services (e.g., shelter, food, education, employment, counseling, and health care) will ultimately have greater success helping children exit the streets and preparing them for adulthood compared with programs offering one-dimensional services. When holistic services are not feasible due to funding limitations, it is important for organizations to develop collaborative networks among service providers and to use interagency referrals to ensure that the children receive the comprehensive services they need. Given the increasing numbers of street children, the opportunity is ripe for governmental and nongovernmental organizations to work cooperatively and to maximize resources in serving this vulnerable population.

Recognizing the inherent resiliency of street children, it is also vital to adopt an asset-based approach that builds upon the children's strengths and skills. In working with this population, social work professionals can increase the human capital of street youths by equipping them with technical skills, such as computer literacy, carpentry, electricity, farming, and sewing. Vocational cooperatives and small businesses that provide structured work hours can serve as a gateway to access additional schooling or to complete compulsory education. Participation in economic ventures can also assist young people financially, both with personal savings and in making contributions to their family incomes. Lastly, because social development responses are embedded in social relationships in the community, they both embody and produce social capital for those involved (Putnam, 2000). As such, social work professionals can help street youths use their preexisting social networks to form cooperatives and small businesses. In turn, this organization of peers around common goals strengthens the social and labor networks among members for future collaboration.

CONCLUSION

The millions of children under the age of eighteen who live and work on the streets around the world require attention from social workers and other policy makers. As noted earlier in the chapter, descriptive categories of street children are not discrete, fixed, or homogeneous but rather encompass multiple subgroups. A complex interplay of individual, familial, and structural factors contribute to child street migration. Among multiple policy and practice responses, the social development approach offers promise in incorporating street children in the formal economy and educational system. Overall, successful policy and practice responses need to be holistic, collaborative, and asset based.

REFERENCES

Aptekar, L. (1994). Street children in the developing world: A review of their condition. *Cross-Cultural Research*, 28(3), 195–224.

Ayuku, D. O., Kaplan, C., Baars, H., & de Vries, M. (2004). Characteristics and personal social networks of the on-the-street, of-the-street, shelter and school children in Eldoret, Kenya. *International Social Work*, 47(3), 293–311.

Cauce, A. M., Paradise, M., Ginzler, J. A., Embry, L., Morgan, C. J., Lohr, Y., & Theofelis, J. (2000). The characteristics and mental health of homeless adolescents: Age and gender differences. *Journal of Emotional and Behavioral Disorders*, 8, 230–239.

Denfeld, R. (2007). *All God's children: Inside the dark and violent world of street families*. New York: Public Affairs.

De Janvry, A., & Sadoulet, E. (2006). Making conditional cash transfer programs more efficient: Designing for maximum effect of the conditionality. *World Bank Economic Review*, 20(1), 1–29.

De la Barra, X. (1998). Poverty: The main cause of ill health in urban children. *Health Education and Behavior*, 25(1), 46–59.

De Rosa, C. J., Montgomery, S. B., Kipke, M. D., Iverson, E., Ma J. L., & Unger, J. B. (1999). Service utilization among homeless and runaway youth in Los Angeles, California: Rates and reasons. *Journal of Adolescent Health*, 24(6), 449–458.

Dybicz, P. (2005). Interventions for street children: An analysis of current best practices. *International Social Work*, 48(6), 763–771.

Ennew, J. (1994). *Street and working children: A guide to planning*. London: Save the Children.

Epstein, I. (1996). Educating street children: Some cross-cultural perspectives. *Comparative Education*, 32(3), 289–303.

Ferguson, K. (2006). Responding to children's street work with alternative income generation strategies. *International Social Work*, 49(6), 705–717.

Ferguson, K. (2004). Shaping street-children organizations across the Americas: The influence of political, social and cultural contexts on Covenant House and Casa Alianza. *Social Thought*, 23(4), 85–102.

Ferguson, K., & Heidemann, G. (2009). Organizational strengths and challenges of Kenyan NGOs serving orphans and vulnerable children: A template analysis. *International Journal of Social Welfare, 18,* 354–364.

Fernandes, A. L. (2007). *Runaway and homeless youth: Demographics, programs, and emerging issues.* CRS Report for Congress. Washington, DC: Congressional Research Service.

Gaetz, S., & O'Grady, B. (2002). Making money: Exploring the economy of young homeless workers. *Work, Employment & Society, 16*(3), 433–456.

Grootaert, C., & Patrinos, H. A. (Eds.). (1999). *The policy analysis of child labor: A comparative study.* Washington, DC: World Bank.

Halcon, L. L., & Lifson, A. R. (2004). Prevalence and predictors of sexual risks among homeless youth. *Journal of Youth and Adolescence, 33,* 71–80.

International Labour Organization (ILO). (2003). *Investing in every child: An economic study of the costs and benefits of eliminating child labour.* ILO International Programme on the Elimination of Child Labour. Geneva: Author.

International Labour Organization (ILO). (1999). C182 Worst Form of Child Labour Convention, 1999 (Article 3). Retrieved on March 18, 2011, from www.ilo.org.

Karabanow, J. (2003). Creating a culture of hope: Lessons from street children agencies in Canada and Guatemala. *International Social Work, 46*(3), 369–386.

Karabanow, J., & Clement, P. (2004). Interventions with street youth: A commentary on the practice-based research literature. *Brief Treatment and Crisis Intervention, 4*(1), 93–108.

Lombe, M., & Ochumbo, A. (2008). Sub-Saharan Africa's orphan crisis. *International Social Work, 51*(5), 682–698.

Lusk, M. W. (1992). Street children of Rio de Janeiro. *International Social Work, 35*(3), 293–305.

Lusk, M. W. (1989). Street children programs in Latin America. *Journal of Sociology and Social Welfare, 16*(1), 55–77.

Meyer, J., Masa, R. D., & Zimmerman, J. M. (2010). Overview of child development accounts in developing countries. *Children and Youth Services Review, 32*(11), 1561–1569.

Mickelson, R. A. (2000). Globalization, childhood poverty, and education in the Americas. In R. A. Mickelson (Ed.), *Children on the streets of the Americas: Globalization, homelessness and education in the United States, Brazil and Cuba* (pp. 11–39). New York: Routledge.

Nigenda, G., & González-Robledo, L. M. (2005, June). *Lessons offered by Latin American cash transfer programmes, Mexico's Oportunidades and Nicaragua's SPN: Implications for African countries.* London: DFID Health Systems Resource Centre.

Pinzón-Rondón, A. M., Hofferth, S., & Briceño, L. (2008). Children working in the streets of Colombian cities: Different pathways to the street lead to different populations. *Children and Youth Services Review, 30,* 1417–1424.

Putnam, R. D. (2000). *Bowling alone: The collapse and revival of American community.* New York: Simon & Schuster.

Raleigh-DuRoff, C. (2004). Factors that influence homeless adolescents to leave or stay living on the street. *Child and Adolescent Social Work Journal, 21*(6), 561–571.

Reciprocity Foundation. (2007). Reciprocity Foundation: Designing a better future. Retrieved on March 18, 2011, from www.reciprocityfoundation.org/aboutus.php.

Rizzini, I., & Lusk, M. W. (1995). Children in the streets: Latin America's lost generation. *Children and Youth Services Review, 17*(3), 391–400.

Rizzini, I., Rizzini, I., Munoz-Vargas, M., & Galeano, L. (1995). Brazil: A new concept of childhood. In C. Szanton Blanc (Ed.), *Urban children in distress: Global predicaments and innovative strategies* (pp. 55–99). Florence, Italy: Gordon and Breach.

Rockefeller Foundation. (2007, March). Opportunity NYC: Recognizing the day-to-day challenges faced by the poor. Retrieved on March 18, 2011, from www.rockefellerfoundation.org/what-we-do/where-we-work/new-york-city/opportunity-nyc.

Skoufias, E., Parker, S. W., Behrman, J. R., & Pessino, C. (2001). Conditional cash transfers and their impact on child work and schooling: Evidence from the PROGRESA program in Mexico. *Economía, 2*(1), 45–96.

Trussell, R. P. (1999). The children's streets: An ethnographic study of street children in Ciudad Juárez, Mexico. *International Social Work, 42*(2), 189–199.

Unger, J. B., Kipke, M. D., Simon, T. R., & Johnson, C. J. (1998). Stress, coping, and social support among homeless youth. *Journal of Adolescent Research, 13*(2), 134–157.

United Nations Children's Fund (UNICEF). (2006). *The state of the world's children 2006: Excluded and invisible.* New York: Author.

United Nations Children's Fund (UNICEF). (1989). Convention on the Rights of the Child. Retrieved on March 18, 2011, from www2.ohchr.org/english/law/crc.htm.

ADDITIONAL WEBSITES FOR MORE INFORMATION ON STREET CHILDREN

Consortium for Street Children: www.streetchildren.org.uk.

Covenant House (worldwide locations): www.covenant-house.org.

PANGAEA Worldwide Resource Library: http://pangaea.org/street_children/kids.htm.

Street Kids International: www.streetkids.org.

24

Community Violence

HORACE LEVY

Violence, both criminal and community, is a rising problem around the planet. Multiple killings of innocent people in schools or other crowded places by a lone gunman seeking to redress a received scorn are now a regular occurrence in some developed countries. Yet these pale beside the thousands slain in the war in Iraq and the hundreds in collateral damage in Palestine and Pakistan. The World Health Organization (WHO) reports that violence kills more than 1.6 million people every year. It is the leading cause of death for those between the ages of fifteen and forty-four, accounting for 14 percent of deaths among males and 7 percent among females. A homicide is committed almost every minute—1424 every day—and youth homicide rates in particular have increased in many parts of the world. Yet, according to the experts, most violent acts take place behind closed doors and are never included in the statistics (WHO, 2002). At a country level, South Africa and Colombia for several years had the record annual rate of homicides—over 60 per 100,000 people.

The Caribbean, especially Jamaica, is no exception to these numbers. A leading Jamaican criminologist reports that "over the last two decades, there have been significant increases in the rate of violent crime in the ten Caribbean countries for which data are available" (Harriott, Brathwaite, & Wortley, 2004). These other Commonwealth countries are beginning to show a pattern similar to that of Jamaica, though not as yet to the same extreme.

COMMUNITY VIOLENCE IN JAMAICA: A CASE STUDY

This chapter focuses on Jamaica, a country where street violence now exceeds levels in South Africa and Colombia. It emphasizes community violence in particular and the community gangs that are its source. A case study is put forward, an offering of experiences and lessons that others elsewhere may find helpful in confronting similar scenes. The first stop is a brief

account of the gravity of the problem nationally, the next an analysis probing causes and effects, and the third a description of an unusual countering approach carried out by social workers and an indication of its impact. The chapter concludes with lessons learned in the hopes that they can be applied in other contexts around the world.

Incidence and Causal Factors

After declining over several decades, property crimes are now on the rise thanks to harsh economic circumstances, but the relentless climb of homicidal violence is the more threatening reality. With 1674 murders in 2005 in a population of only 2.6 million (64 per 100,000), reduced in 2008 only marginally (60 per 100,000) to nearly 7 per day, Jamaica has the grim distinction of world leader in the killing profession. A social epidemic has built up over the years and is now almost out of control, spurred along by sensationalist reporting in both print and electronic media. Though most homicides are the work of organized criminals, a significant number are the doing of young men in community gangs, as discussed later in the chapter.

Harriott (2008) sees the violence as growing into a subculture, a truly troubling thought. Fresh thresholds are regularly crossed—bodies with slashed throats in a barrel, killings in a crowded plaza at midday, indiscriminate drive-by shootings, targeting of women and children, beheadings, massacres of groups of three and five. And though homicide, especially in its brutal executions, is more than just a useful measuring stick, other indicators also accentuate the depth of the climate of violence. These include, for example, the popularity of capital punishment for murder, Christian clergymen offering themselves as hangmen, the crowd clamoring for a police station to turn over to them the man detained for the cruel rape and slaying of a nine-year-old boy, and frequent Old Testament eye-for-eye voicings.

History

How did Jamaicans get to this point? This is the recurring question. Wherever they go overseas, they are known as assertive, hard-working people; only in recent years have they become known as homicidal. Back in 1962, the year of national independence, the records tell of sixty-three homicides, an acceptable level internationally. It was in that decade, though, that the numbers began to increase, with politicians distributing guns as they climbed into seats of power.

Along with the guns went the creation over that decade and the next of *garrisons*, communities in which apartments in housing estates were reserved for followers of the sitting members of parliament. Garrisons consolidated partisan hold on broader areas, and the constituencies established zones of intolerance—no supporter of a rival party (if person and property were to remain unassailed) was allowed to even voice a rival view—as well as armed camps of defense and attack that also provided refuge for criminals wanted by police. What this resulted in was conflict between neighboring communities on opposing sides of the political fence. Elections were the periodic flash points for explosions of violence involving firearms, but in reality these were the peaks of ongoing low-level wars, and at the center of this conflict were and are the community gangs.

The prime effect of the garrison gangs and their gun culture has been the destruction of community and the sanctioning of violence. Community is about people with all their differences living together, creating meaning, and helping individuals find their identity. Garrisons are about domination, violence, exclusion, and the foisting of a party identity on young people. They destroy community spirit and social capital regardless of whether organized top–down directives enforce order and calm. If political views mean that people must be pushed out of their birthplace, no true community is there. The twelve to fifteen garrisons that formed over several decades across the capital city Kingston and other urban centers have spread a miasma of violence across the country.

Although politics through the garrisons has been historically the source of the violence, several other factors are involved. Principally, these are an absence of economic opportunity, extrajudicial police conduct coupled with courts that work against the poor, and serious deficits in parenting, family life, and schooling —all told, a thorough social exclusion.

Economic Factors

In a national context of a flat 1 percent GDP annual growth over the past two decades, people in the inner city have seen nothing but prolonged hardship. Youth unemployment averaged 32 percent (Planning Institute of Jamaica [PIOJ], 2007a) over the past decade (with rates even higher in specific communities and for females), and inequality between top and bottom quintiles stands at 6.5 to 1 (PIOJ, 2007b). No one-on-one correlation between joblessness or poverty and violence is being argued. However, the combination of inequality (Gilligan, 2001)—very visible in a small country where SUVs and large houses are popular—pressure on males (still seen as providers for the household), idleness, and the accessibility of guns to youth for whom masculinity means having and using them, results in an explosive mix, a cycle of violence that feeds on itself.

Police Violence

The example of the police, the Jamaica Constabulary Force (JCF), does not help. Although in recent years the JCF has turned to community policing and information intelligence, the paramilitary North Ireland model on which it was originally fashioned still grips a large section and accounted for 252 killed in 2007, reduced by about a quarter in 2008. The police usually allege shootouts, but in many cases they engage in cold-blooded extrajudicial killings for which indictments or convictions have been relatively rare. According to a recent report by the respected human rights organization, Jamaicans for Justice (2008), of the nearly 3400 police shootings involving almost 1500 fatalities between 1999 and 2007, a mere 134 were brought to trial and only a single police officer was convicted of murder. This situation reflects the profound weaknesses in the constabulary force and in the office of the director of public prosecutions, which blessedly are now showing signs of being corrected.

Family Issues

Another dimension of the violence problem is found in parenting—identified by inner-city inhabitants themselves as critical—and the family. Many young parents haven't a clue what parenting means or that there is such a thing as respect for children (Brown, 2002). Beatings are the chief and only method of discipline and are often savage (Gayle, 2004), driving many boys to escape onto the streets. In any case, this is where inner-city schoolboys pass after-school or (under a misguided shift system) pre-school hours, supervision while the parent is at work being an arrangement that is often unknown. More fundamental to the problem is a "tie the heifer, loose the bull" mentality that guides thinking at the lower-income level on the ways of rearing female and male children (Chevannes, 2001). In Chevannes' (2006) view, the family has declined as a functioning unit.

If youths have found corner crews and community gangs so attractive, it is in part because of weaknesses in the Jamaican family. The most frequent family structure lasting for many years—the visiting relationship preliminary to common-law or marital union—does not provide children with the constant presence and example of a father. This is especially problematic for boys. The extended family was a working substitute for earlier generations, but in the current urban work world, 46.7 percent of single-parent household heads are out on jobs, and migration has become a regular survival route, leaving "barrel children" (i.e., children of families heavily dependent on barrels of food and clothes sent by relatives abroad) to the care of an aunt, older sister, or even themselves in the case of some teenagers (Gayle, 2004).

All of this is further compounded by a school system that, because of old-fashioned methods, has been failing to attract and keep a large percentage of male students. Until 2007, the system terminated education for those below a certain academic level after grade nine (age fifteen). The state declared itself simply unable financially to find school space for them. One-third of these teenagers, 4500 annually (JASPEV, 2004), are functionally illiterate (PIOJ, 2006) and without a trade skill. The 50,000 unemployed in the fourteen-to-twenty-four age group (PIOJ, 2007a) undoubtedly include many of their number accumulated over the years.

APPROACHES TO VIOLENCE REDUCTION

To cope with the rampant violence, three broad approaches have been tried. The first is the security approach, which began by launching a succession of a dozen special police squads. When these were ineffectual, the security approach turned to intelligence and community policing, with slow but hopeful outcomes. The second approach is electoral legislation; the Electoral Commission was established with wide powers to deal with fraud and connected violence and even to void election results. It has proved very effective in its limited area of electoral violence. The third approach is the Peace Management Initiative (PMI), a state and civil society alliance formed in 2002 by the minister of national security with the blessing of the two main political parties.

The Peace Initiative

This last approach, on which we want to focus (Levy, 2009), was a thoroughly new departure. For the first time, community violence was specifically targeted, and civil society and conversation rather than physical force and armed agents of the state were assigned to the task. Also for the first time, the state was employing social workers and applying social measures to address community violence, doing so under civil society direction. The state's input is its presence on the PMI activist board (which meets fortnightly and takes a hands-on approach); representatives of the two main political parties, several of them holding office in the government, are on the board. In addition, there is financial support and some oversight on the part of the Ministry of National Security. Civil society is present in the board membership, which includes ministers of religion, university lecturers, the Dispute Resolution Foundation director, and others. Civil society is also well represented in the actual work carried out on the ground by board members and by the field staff.

In the PMI approach, board members and staff simply walk into a community rocked by war (violence) and engage the young *shottas* (shooters) in conversation, listening carefully to each side and persuading them to meet each other in some neutral spot, generally outside the community. This encounter, when accusations and responses are leveled and accumulated rage is vented while the PMI only intervenes to cool the anger and keep the dialogue constructive, is the mediation process. It can go on for weeks or even months, the PMI appealing to the combatants to hold it (the violence) down until some settlement can be agreed on and developmental measures begun. This last topic, especially income-earning projects, surfaces early, the PMI pointing out that this possibility rests on a cease-fire assuming permanence.

The PMI meets with all who come forward, this coming forward signaling a desire to end the war, a degree of good will. The PMI feels compelled to work with such respondents and assumes no responsibility to investigate or take action on their possible past crimes or delinquencies—police matters outside the PMI's area of responsibility and competence. In fact, as the PMI recognized early on, respondents usually do not include hardened criminals, who prefer a climate of gunshots and violence. Throughout this process, the PMI keeps its distance from the police. This is essential to win and keep the trust of the shottas, even as they speak freely with one another about episodes of violence.

While this process is going forward, an auxiliary team of pastors and psychologists organized by a PMI staff person counsels those traumatized by the violent deaths of family members or close friends. This effort is directed at children especially, whose mental health and maturing can be deeply compromised, but also at adults, including men who try usually to hide the tears. The more severely hurt children are brought to a counseling center at the University of the West Indies, and many are taken along with a parent on excursions to places such as Serenity Park. Not only psychological health is at stake but also heading off revenge reprisals by those who want to even the score.

What takes place through PMI mediation and counseling efforts is a process of reconciliation and restorative justice on a microscale similar to the work on a national scale of South Africa's Truth and Reconciliation Commission (TRC). The PMI has been Jamaica's TRC, community members showing the way to the wider society, mediations sometimes starting or ending with prayer (Tutu, 1999). Homicidal violence had originally sprung, as with apartheid, out of political antagonisms, and it continues to do so in some areas. But whether from politics or over turf the deep hurt and grief flowing from so many cruel deaths and confrontations cannot at one stroke be covered up and forgotten. A current of mutual understanding, forgiveness, and exculpation has to flow, and to the credit of many, given the national eye-for-eye mentality, it has flowed, though not easily. Only over time as distrust dissipates, hurt is salved, and developmental measures come into play can a sense of community be fully restored.

Social Development

The development enabled by the PMI is not the housing, schools, and infrastructure that people tend to think of when the word *development* is used; that can come later. It is rather what some refer to as *social development*, the essential action needed for turning a cease-fire into a stable peace. The PMI's limited resources, both financial and human (four field staff and four or five occasionally helping board members), have not made it possible to give the sustained attention required to carry forward development efforts to more than a third of the community clusters, or individual communities, that compose the city and adjoining parish section (population close to one million).

The following are examples of the kind of development referred to:

- Training in conflict resolution by, for example, the Dispute Resolution Foundation
- Training in skills and trades by, for example, HEART Trust/NTA (National Training Agency)
- Small grants for group income-earning projects as well as job locating outside the community by a professional person employed for this purpose
- Intercommunity sport competitions (football, netball, corner leagues)
- Cultural activities (led by the Area Youth Foundation, for example)
- Residential retreats out of the city for fifty to seventy youths focusing on such topics as violence, revenge, sex, health, discipline, careers, and community life
- Health and opportunity fairs to put communities in touch with agencies and institutions that offer the resources they need
- Community fix-up projects (e.g., repainting a basic school)
- Cross-city and cross-country leadership conferences
- A peace council of leaders of rival adjoining communities or community sections following a formal and public peace agreement.

This last initiative, the peace council, is particularly important. It grows naturally out of weekly or fortnightly mediation meetings. The council is essential not only initially for maintaining communication between sections and thus quelling the rumors that tend to abound and lead to fresh outbreaks of violence but also for building trust and as an ongoing forum for sharing ideas and taking steps to address developmental and welfare needs. By linking with resource-rich agencies such as the Jamaica Social Investment Fund or Citizen Security and Justice Programme, the council can move toward the goal of rebuilding the community damaged by the violence.

An important aspect of the peace council is its inclusion of community police. The PMI effort and the police effort come together at this point, and it is essential that they do so. One message that the PMI

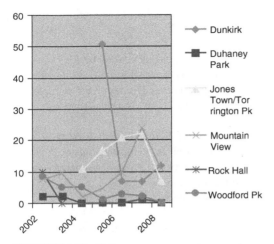

FIGURE 24.1: PMI outcomes.

constantly carries but is hard for a community corner crew to accept is to abandon reprisal, leaving it to the police to catch up with those who commit crimes against them.

Figure 24.1 shows the impact of the PMI approach in the reduction in homicides in five communities. In the sixth community, Mountain View, partisan politics in 2007, year of national elections, led to the frightening escalation depicted. Yet even there, the Community Development Council established in 2003 continues to do excellent work. It should be noted that what the chart does not show is the ending of feuding between corners or sections even where, as in Dunkirk, the homicides were too high in 2008. It should also be noted that two murders in Duhaney Park is extremely high given a population of only 2100—100 per 100,000.

CONCLUSION: LESSONS LEARNED

This chapter has sketched the seriousness of community violence in Jamaica; its original source, proximate causes, and effects; and the countering effort represented by the PMI. A small number of social workers in other agencies in the country have been using the same approach over the past few years in Southside (Kingston), Flanker (Montego Bay), and the parishes of St. Catherine and Clarendon. Data on their results are yet to be put together, but reports suggest they are positive.

From the experience of the PMI and other agencies, a number of simple lessons emerge with clarity.

The first is the requirement of *going to gangs where they are*, without police protection, of course. This is not optional if gang violence is to be ended nonviolently by social workers or civilian volunteers. There is no need to be afraid of getting hurt. Inner-city youth feel respected that "big" people from uptown are coming to see them, and more than anything else, respect is what they long for. And they are grateful for the avenue to peace.

The second lesson is the power of *engaging gang members in conversation*, not to lecture but to listen, steering to an agreement that it is more important to look to the future than to keep rehashing the past. Of course, listening sympathetically without agreeing with the first version you hear is not easy. It is difficult to persuade gang members that a face-to-face meeting with a rival will help, and it is necessary to encourage them with a promise of real after-peace assistance. Inner-city youth need help.

The third lesson is to accept that most gang members are *not criminals* (even though they may have shot and killed) *but delinquents* who can be turned off their current course without going to jail. To win and keep the trust of gangs, it is crucial to keep a distance from the police, leaving entirely to them the responsibility of finding and confining those who commit crimes.

Of course, there are many other lessons, among them the need to spot the tough criminals among the delinquents and to recognize that violence, like so much else in life, is a moving dynamic. Yesterday's two gangs may become today's citywide network with overseas connections, requiring management of large areas of the city as well as mediation. What tomorrow will bring is something that every agency that works with community violence has to unravel from scrutiny of its own situation.

REFERENCES

Brown, J. (2002). Parental resistance to child rights in Jamaica. In C. Barrow (Ed.), *Children's rights: Caribbean realities* (pp. 113–131). Kingston: Ian Randle.

Chevannes, B. (2001). Learning to be a man: Culture, socialization and gender identity in five Caribbean communities. Kingston: University of the West Indies Press.

Chevannes, B. (2006). *Betwixt and Between: Explorations in an African-Caribbean mindscape.* Kingston: Ian Randle.

Gayle, H. (2004). *Adolescents of urban St Catherine: A study of their reproductive health and survivability.* Spanish Town, St. Catherine: Children First Agency.

Gilligan, J. (2001). *Preventing violence.* London: Thames and Hudson.

Harriott, A. (2008). *Bending the trend line: The challenge of controlling violence in Jamaica and high violence societies of the Caribbean*. Kingston: Arawak.

Harriott, A., Brathwaite, F., & Wortley, S. (2004). *Crime and criminal justice in the Caribbean*. Kingston: Arawak.

Jamaicans for Justice. (2008). *Killing impunity: Fatal police shootings and extrajudicial executions in Jamaica 2005–2007*. Washington, DC: George Washington University Law School.

JASPEV. (2004). *Annual progress report on national social policy goals 2003*. Office of Cabinet.

Levy, H. (2009). *Killing streets and community revival*. Kingston: Arawak.

Planning Institute of Jamaica (PIOJ). (2006). *The transition of Jamaican youth to the world of work*. Kingston: Author.

Planning Institute of Jamaica (PIOJ). (2007a). *Economic and social survey 2006*. Kingston: Author.

Planning Institute of Jamaica (PIOJ). (2007b). *Jamaica survey of living conditions 2006*. Kingston: Author.

Tutu, D. (1999). *No future without forgiveness*. London: Rider.

World Health Organization (WHO). (2002). *World report on violence and health*. Accessible at www.who.org.

Drugs: Addictions and Trafficking

KATHERINE VAN WORMER

The subject of this chapter is drug use and the drug trafficking that sustains it. Because alcohol is also a drug and is closely associated with addiction worldwide, attention is paid to its use and abuse as well. The marketing of these substances plays a key role in the process of addiction: Traders get addicted to the huge profits from the sale of the product, and addiction among the masses creates the demand. The process of supply and demand is interactive and cyclical. It is a process that is paved in the refuse of human lives and suffering.

Following an introductory discussion of the nature of addiction, this chapter describes drug trafficking as a global enterprise with an effect on every continent. Two approaches to the problem of the drug trade are examined. The first, which is favored by the US government, involves a declaration of war on the suppliers and users of drugs. The second approach is geared toward reducing the demand for drugs through harm reduction; this approach is favored in Europe and is rapidly gaining proponents elsewhere. The chapter concludes with a discussion of the principles of harm reduction and implications for the social work profession.

THE NATURE OF ADDICTION

The ability to feel pleasure is a key motivating factor in humans (as in other animals) that preserves the species. It motivates us to seek out food, to communicate and enjoy the company of others, and to reproduce. These innate drives can get out of control, however, to the point that pleasure seeking develops into a dependency. Inevitably, there are those who would prey on the vulnerable, producing products to meet a demand that can never be satiated and enticing people into trying new and ever more addictive products. Not only do individuals become addicted to these products but whole groups of people and even nations also develop a dependency on the profits associated with commerce in mood-altering substances.

Some of this commerce, such as that in tobacco and alcohol, is legal and tightly regulated by national and international law. These legal substances cause family disruption, illness, and death. The World Health Organization (WHO) estimates that tobacco kills more than 5 million people per year, and the majority of smokers now live in lower-income countries (WHO, 2010a). Another 2.5 million deaths result from alcohol abuse (WHO, 2010b). Our concern in this paper, however, is mainly with the use, trade, and dealing of illegal substances, although alcohol addiction will be discussed later in the chapter.

According to the United Nations (2008b), nearly 200 million people use illicit drugs worldwide. Cannabis (also known as marijuana, hashish, and THC) is the most widely used drug by far with 162 million users. Methamphetamine and ecstasy follow with 35 million users. Globally, an estimated 16 million people use opiates—opium, morphine, heroin, and synthetic opiates—and some 13 million people use cocaine. Cocaine use is reaching alarming levels in Western Europe and North America.

Opium is the leading cash crop in Afghanistan, the world's top opium producer. Heroin use is common throughout Asia, with around half of heroin users injecting the drug. Transmission of HIV is closely associated with intravenous drug use in Asia because equipment is often shared among many people (Association of Southeast Asian Nations, 2007).

Globally, alcohol consumption has increased in recent decades, with all or most of the increase occurring in developing countries. This increase in consumption is often occurring in countries with little tradition of alcohol use and few methods of prevention, control, or treatment (WHO, 2009a). The problems caused by this legal drug are far more serious than those caused by illicit drugs. According to WHO, 76.3 million persons have alcohol-use disorders worldwide versus at least 15.3 million persons who have drug-use disorders.

Whereas the flow of the legally marketed products (alcohol and tobacco) is largely from the rich nations to the poor, the flow of the illicit products with which we are concerned is generally from the poor nations to the rich, from the Global South to the Global North. As the product makes its journey north, it multiplies in value at every exchange along the way. This exchange in goods and services can be viewed as a microcosm of global free trade, a complex interplay between residents from Latin America and Africa and traders and consumers of the industrialized world. As a highly prized and easily concealed product, illegal drugs are a source of revenue that is responsible for the rise and fall of governments in Latin America, a force for political corruption everywhere, and the fuel for antigovernment warfare in Afghanistan, Colombia, and Myanmar.

DRUG TRAFFICKING WORLDWIDE

The story of drug trafficking is the story of the cultivation of an organic but toxic product and of the cultivation of a global taste for a profitable market. The plot is played out in the form of killings, greed, and corruption, and looming over it all is the tragedy that is addiction. Drug trafficking tends to be accompanied by arms and human trafficking, corruption, and the subversion of legitimate state institutions, according to a United Nations Security Council (2009) report. To gain a sense of the magnitude of the destruction wrought by drug trade, consider the following headlines, all from news stories in February 2009:

- Shrinking Drug Market to Blame in Metro Vancouver Shootings, Professor Says (The Canadian Press, 2009)
- UN: Latin America Needs Help vs. Drug Traffickers (Lederer, 2009)
- Napolitano Cites Mexican Drug Cartels as Major Threat (Hsu, 2009)

The major illicit drug–supplying regions in the world include the Andean regions of Latin America, which produce cocaine from the coca plant, and Myanmar and Afghanistan in Asia, which grow the opium poppy for the production of heroin. Cannabis is the only drug produced in West Africa, but this region is a major transit center for cocaine from Latin America and heroin from the East to countries in Europe. The majority of drug couriers who are caught transporting the drugs on commercial airplanes to Europe come from Nigeria. Mexico is the major distribution center for points in the United States.

The relationship between West Africa and Europe with regard to trafficking may prove to be similar to that between Mexico and the United States (UNODC, 2008a). Similar to West African traffickers, the Mexican cartels started out as service providers to Colombian trafficking groups and were paid in drugs rather than cash. They then distributed these drugs for profits. In addition to Nigeria, Sierra Leone increasingly serves as a transshipment point for the trafficking of illegal narcotics from South America to Europe (United Nations Security Council, 2009).

Nearly all coca leaf is produced in just three countries: Colombia, Peru, and Bolivia. Colombian groups produce the most coca leaf, manage cocaine production in the other two countries, and have been chief among international traffickers in the past (United Nations, 2008b). Insurgents and warlords are making hefty profits on narcotics, estimated at $50 million to $70 million in protection payments from farmers and another $200 million to $400 million from "taxes" on drug processing and trafficking in 2008 (Lee, 2009).

The Mexican illegal drug business is a multibillion-dollar industry dominated by cartels, often family run, that operate in collusion with corrupt law officials on either side of the border. Competition among the cartels is violent. According to Mexican president Felipe Calderón, who has tried to crack down on drug trafficking, the drug wars that are sweeping the country are on a level never before seen. More than 6000 deaths were attributed to the crackdown in 2008, twice as many as in 2007, and the situation has continued to worsen (Hsu, 2009).

Men are more actively involved than women in the cultivation and sale of drug plants across the world; at the lowest and riskiest level, women often are paid to act as couriers or mules (Campbell, 2008). Poverty and the increased income that drugs provide push thousands of women into this trade each year. Some women die and others become deathly ill from carrying the drugs in their stomachs. When caught, the women are sentenced to prison in the United States and Europe and then are deported to their home countries. They thus become victims of the international war on drugs.

ATTEMPTS TO CONTROL THE SUPPLY OF DRUGS

The European Union (EU) takes a harm-reduction approach to drugs, where the focus is on reducing demand (Fukumi, 2008). In Europe, the AIDS epidemic of the 1980s catapulted harm-reduction policies into prominence. Drug use was medicalized rather than criminalized, and methadone and heroin maintenance clinics were established to monitor drug use and to provide a safe dosage under medical supervision. Clean needles can be purchased in vending machines in some countries, such as Germany. The existence of nationalized health care has enhanced the adoption of policies geared toward rehabilitation and prevention.

As Fukumi (2008) suggests, where Europeans have seen the drug trade as a threat to social security, the United States has seen it as a threat to national security. Since the 1980s, US policy has defined the situation in militaristic terms as a war that needs to be fought and won. The strategy as followed today involves attacking the flow of drugs at its source. Latin Americans are increasingly skeptical of this approach, which has led to so much bloodshed in the endless drug wars plaguing their countries. A recent report by a commission headed by three of Latin America's former presidents (representing Brazil, Mexico, and Colombia) calls for treating drug use as a health issue, as with cigarettes and alcohol, instead of a criminal issue. Writing in the *Wall Street Journal*, the three former presidents argue that the US-led war on drug crime in Latin America has failed, and the alarming power of the drug cartels is leading to drug wars, the criminalization of politics, and the politicization of crime. The corruption of the judicial and political systems, according to these leaders, is undermining the foundation of democracy in several Latin American countries. The former presidents call for the decriminalization of marijuana, which has few health risks, and an end to the war-on-drugs strategy in favor of a public-health approach:

> The war on drugs has failed. And it's high time to replace an ineffective strategy with more humane and efficient drug policies. . . . Prohibitionist policies based on eradication, interdiction, and criminalization of consumption simply haven't worked. Violence and the organized crime associated with the narcotics trade remain critical problems in our countries . . .
>
> In order to drastically reduce the harm caused by narcotics, the long-term solution is to reduce demand for drugs in the main consumer countries. To move in this direction, it is essential to differentiate among illicit substances according to the harm they inflict on people's health, and the harm drugs cause to the social fabric.

In this spirit, we propose a paradigm shift in drug policies based on three guiding principles: Reduce the harm caused by drugs, decrease drug consumption through education, and aggressively combat organized crime. To translate this new paradigm into action we must start by changing the status of addicts from drug buyers in the illegal market to patients cared for by the public-health system.

—(Cardoso, *Gaviria*, & Zedillo, 2009, p. A15)

THE TOLL OF ALCOHOL ABUSE WORLDWIDE

Recently the British medical journal, *The Lancet*, published a series on alcohol abuse worldwide. Research was based on an analysis of WHO survey statistics. The first paper in the series, by Rehm et al. (2009), presents quantitative findings concerning consumption and mortality rates across the globe. These findings, which have been widely reported in the media, are a wake-up call. Alcohol is linked to one in every twenty-five deaths (3.8%) worldwide. The European death rate was the highest at 10%. Risks are increasing in developing economies, particularly Asian countries like China and Thailand, the report notes. There and elsewhere, violent injuries, accidents, and medical conditions were the major causes of death. The death rate for men related to alcohol was approximately five times that of women. Drinking patterns vary widely from country to country, with most of the adult world population—45% of men and 66% of women—abstaining from drinking altogether.

Within Europe, Russia tallied the highest proportion of deaths—15% of deaths were linked to alcohol ("Alcohol and harm reduction in Russia," 2009). Since the Russian Treasury relies heavily on alcohol taxation, there has been little incentive to take the necessary measures to reduce drinking. About half of Russian consumption involves illicit spirits sold through organized crime and nonbeverage alcohol, which is toxic.

In their analysis of consumption rates, Rehm et al. (2009) found that across the Americas, the average drinking rate was 17 units per week, while the rate in the Middle East was a low of 1.3 units per week (each unit is about the equivalent of one drink—a medium-sized glass of wine, for example). Europeans drank at the rate of 22 units a week and North Americans at a rate of 18 units. The populations of India and the Arab nations drank the least.

Keep in mind that consumption rates alone do not tell the entire story (van Wormer & Davis, 2008). Some countries and regions with high consumption rates, such as southern Italy and Greece, have relatively low rates of problematic drinking. Drinking in those wine-growing regions is associated with meals and conviviality, and children learn to drink in the home. In contrast to the moderate Mediterranean pattern, the binge-drinking pattern of young people in Anglo-American countries is implicated in violent acts, unsafe sex, car crashes, drownings, and use of illicit drugs.

The *Lancet* report (Anderson, Chisholm, & Fuhr, 2009) called for significant harm-reduction policies. Among those that are recommended because of their proven effectiveness include a halt to alcohol marketing throughout the world, especially marketing to poor populations; high taxation of alcoholic beverages; strict drinking-and-driving legislation; limited availability coupled with action against illegal production; and the provision of help for persons with drinking problems.

ADDRESSING THE PROBLEM: A PUBLIC-HEALTH, HARM-REDUCTION APPROACH

The harm-reduction or public-health model views addiction as an adaptive response to a wide range of variables that influence behavior (Sowers & Rowe, 2009). A major variable influencing addictive behavior is biological. Today, with the help of new technologies that reveal immediate and long-term changes in the brain on drugs, we can grasp how addiction affects the brain circuits, circuits that are involved in motivation, inhibitory control, memory, and feeling rewards (NIDA, 2009). Addiction, as described on the National Institute on Drug Addiction (NIDA) website, is a brain disease; following long-term use of an addictive substance, the neurotransmitters or natural opiates of the brain are depleted to the extent that the addicted person's capacity to resist using drugs is diminished. Because the drug user no longer can feel high naturally, he or she will seek chemical relief just to feel normal. The impact on memory is key to cravings that can be overwhelming in the desire to return to those original first highs experienced under the influence of the drug (van Wormer & Davis, 2008). With regard to cocaine and methamphetamine, the cravings are especially pronounced; drug addicts commonly report the phenomenon of "chasing the first high."

Equipped with an understanding of the addiction process, we can appreciate why the traditional punitive approach to substance abuse with its heavy reliance on law enforcement does not work and why

prevention and early treatment are of the essence in reducing the supply of and demand for the drug. The global marketing of legal drugs such as alcohol and tobacco, which are carefully disguised attempts to get people hooked on the products, must be discouraged. Increasingly, in the poorest regions of the world such as sub-Saharan Africa, alcohol abuse is a major threat in terms of economic survival, the HIV epidemic, and domestic violence. The key emerging alcohol markets, according to *The Lancet* (Casswell & Thamarangsi, 2009), are in the Asian Pacific region, Africa, and Latin America. Global corporations relentlessly lobby to maintain control of their marketing activities and to challenge research findings concerning the impact of alcoholic substances on marginalized populations. The report calls on WHO and grassroots organizations to be more proactive in their efforts to monitor the sales practices of the multinational corporations. On the demand side—reducing demand for the drug—the challenge is to help people break the addiction cycle and to avoid the negative consequences of their behavior.

The harm-reduction position is stated unequivocally by WHO (2009b):

> WHO strongly supports harm reduction as an evidence-based approach to HIV prevention, treatment and care for drug users. WHO advocates for universal access of a comprehensive harm reduction package of interventions for drug injectors which include needle and syringe programmes, drug dependence treatment—in particular opioid substitution therapy—as well as risk reduction counseling, HIV counseling and testing, and HIV care and treatment.

Although social work and the harm-reduction approach are more highly integrated in Canada and Europe than in the United States, there have been promising developments in recent years. The US National Association of Social Workers (NASW) (2006), for instance, endorses a comprehensive public-health approach for the prevention of alcohol, tobacco, and other drug problems. It has also endorsed harm-reduction interventions for persons affected by such problems. And for the first time, the NASW *Encyclopedia of Social Work*, now in its twentieth edition, includes an entry on harm reduction (Davis, 2008). This entry describes policies that are considered controversial but that are pragmatic and geared toward removing inequities in the availability of treatment resources.

THE TREATMENT NEED

With its heavy emphasis on attacking supply, the United States spends around two-thirds of its drug-control budget on law enforcement, crop spraying, and interdiction and around one-third on treatment. Because of this, the number of people incarcerated for drug offenses has increased an incredible tenfold from 50,000 in 1980 to 500,000 in 2007 (Schumacher-Matos, 2009).

What is the need for treatment? According to a recent National Survey on Drug Use and Health, around 3% of the US population is in trouble with drug use and in need of treatment (US Department of Health and Human Services [DHHS], 2008).

Of these, only 17.8% of the persons who stated they needed treatment in the past year received help. Other respondents who did not receive treatment when they needed it pointed to a lack of health coverage as a key reason. The rate of persons in need of treatment for problems with alcohol was three times that of those who needed treatment for other drug use.

Illicit drug use remains common in the United States. Among persons aged twelve or older, the rate of substance dependence or abuse was highest among American Indians and Alaska Natives (19.0%) and lowest among Asians (4.3%). Other racial and ethnic groups—whites (9.4%), Hispanics (9.3%), and blacks (8.5%)—reported generally similar rates (DHHS, 2008). Of these drugs, the most commonly used is marijuana, the second most common is prescription medication, and the third most common is cocaine.

Implications for Social Work

Social workers who work in child welfare and corrections will note that the war on drugs is taking a toll on children in families affected by drug use, first in the chaos in their homes and second in their own reactive, acting-out behavior when their parents go to prison or the children are removed from the home. Social workers are further aware of the disproportionate impact that harsh antidrug laws have on minorities and other marginalized groups. Accordingly, social workers tend to be strong advocates for treatment in the community and for community corrections as a positive step in promoting the healing of families coping with addiction (NASW, 2006).

At the practice level, social workers use harm-reduction strategies based on motivational interviewing and other strengths-based approaches to help prepare people to move beyond their addictions. Consistent with principles of harm reduction, they strive to remove barriers to treatment, such as by providing child care and offering treatment for persons who are not yet ready to abstain but who are willing to consider treatment options.

Promising Developments

At the national level in the United States, recent developments indicate the emergence of a substantial movement in favor of public-health approaches—of prevention over treatment and of treatment over incarceration, especially for nonviolent drug-related offenders. These developments include drug courts, housing-first programs to provide immediate housing to persons with serious substance abuse problems, local policies that favor treatment, and statewide ballot initiatives that divert nonviolent drug offenders to treatment instead of incarceration. A recent national survey conducted by Hazelden (2009) shows that public opinion generally sees the war on drugs as a failure and favors prevention and treatment over incarceration. At the time of this writing, the new drug czar has stated that the term *war on drugs* will no longer be used.

Although policies that are so ingrained in the long-standing war on drugs are difficult to change, even some law enforcement officers are calling for reform ("Officers join group backing legalization," 2009). In New Hampshire, for example, a small but growing number of law enforcement officers have joined a group that supports legalizing drugs. The group, called *Law Enforcement Against Prohibition*, claims to have 11,000 members in ninety countries.

The UN Office on Drugs and Crime (UNODC) and WHO have a joint program on drug dependence, treatment, and care. Among the goals are to increase coverage and quality of treatment and care services for drug users in poorer countries; to "promote the development of comprehensive and integrated systems that are able to deliver a continuum of care for drug users"; to encourage policy changes that support "humane and effective prevention, treatment and care"; and to support alternatives to incarceration for drug users (UNODC & WHO, 2009, p. 3). The program also aims to support training for professionals who provide services and treatment for drug users.

CONCLUSION

As we have seen, drug trafficking is threatening to national and even global security. Lucrative profits are such a strong incentive at every level of the illicit drug trade that countries such as the United States that focus on trafficking have neglected funding for the demand-side programs of drug-use prevention and treatment. Lucrative profits are a key factor as well in the marketing of the legal drugs, alcohol and tobacco. Whereas much international attention has been paid to the need for regulation of tobacco corporations, multinational alcohol corporations have been able to freely market their products in the regions of the world that are the most impoverished. Global regulation of these industries is essential in the interests of public health. The war on drugs has been relatively counterproductive; the demand for the addictive substances continues unabated and many lives thereby destroyed.

On a daily basis, social workers deal with the personal tragedies of drug addiction, incarceration of drug users, and removal of children from homes. Whether working in a specialized treatment center, in child welfare, or in a mental health center, social workers learn firsthand of the pain caused to clients and their families through the criminalization of drug addiction. They are experiencing the end result of the trafficking in toxic drugs such as methamphetamine, a drug that may have been transported thousands of miles into their communities. Clearly, the military approach to trafficking and the punitive approach to buying, selling, and using drugs have not brought the desired result of eradication. The incarceration of large numbers of people has brought much harm to individuals and their families. Fortunately, the tide seems to be turning and a new consensus building for treatment of addiction as a public-health problem rather than a criminal justice problem. The endorsement of harm reduction by the social work profession is a welcome, pragmatic approach to substance abuse and dependency.

REFERENCES

Alcohol and harm reduction in Russia (editorial). (2009). *The Lancet, 373*(9662), 2171.

Anderson, P., Chisholm, D., & Fuhr, D. (2009). Effectiveness and cost-effectiveness of policies and programmes to reduce the harm caused by alcohol. *The Lancet, 373*(9682), 2234–2246.

Association of Southeast Asian Nations. (2007). Drug use and HIV in Asia. Jakarta. Retrieved February 2009 from http://203.90.70.117/PDS_DOCS/B1485.pdf.

Campbell, H. (2008). Female drug smugglers on the US–Mexico border: Gender, crime, and empowerment. *Anthropological Quarterly, 81*(1), 233–268.

The Canadian Press (2009, February 18). Shrinking drug market to blame in Metro Vancouver shootings, professor says. Retrieved March 2009 from www.google.com/hostednews/canadianpress/article/ALeqM5hQ7_zExO7WbUVgZwOcvaJ0NPsYiQ.

Cardoso, F., Gaviria, C., & Zedillo, E. (2009, February 23). The war on drugs is a failure. *Wall Street Journal*, p. A15.

Casswell, S., & Thamarangsi, T. (2009). Alcohol: A global priority for action. *The Lancet, 373*(9682), 2247–2257.

Davis, D. R. (2008). Harm reduction. In T. Mizrahi & L.E. Davis (Eds.) *Encyclopedia of social work* (20th ed., pp. 312–314). New York: Oxford University Press and NASW Press.

Fukumi, S. (2008). *Cocaine trafficking in Latin America*. Hampshire, UK: Ashgate.

Hazelden. (2009, February 3). Americans want insurance to cover addiction, unsure if it does. Retrieved March 2009 from www.hazelden.org/web/public/pr090209healthinsurance.page.

Hsu, S. (2009, February 26). Napolitano cites Mexican drug cartels as major threat. *Washington Post*, p. A04.

Lederer, E. (2009, February 24). UN: Latin America needs help vs. Washington Post. Retrieved February 2009 from www.washingtonpost.com/wp-dyn/content/article/2009/02/24/AR2009022402882.html.

Lee, M. (2009, February 27). U.S. sees serious threat in Mexico drug violence. *Washington Post*. Retrieved February 2009 from www.washingtonpost.com/wp-dyn/content/article/2009/02/27/AR2009022701805.html.

National Association of Social Workers (NASW). (2006). Alcohol, tobacco, and other drugs. In *Social work speaks* (7th ed., pp. 23–31). Washington, DC: NASW.

National Institute on Drug Abuse (NIDA). (2008, June). Addiction science: From molecules to managed care. Retrieved June 2009 from www.drugabuse.gov/pubs/teaching/Teaching6/Teaching2.html.

Officers join group backing legalization. (2009, February 23). *Washington Times*. Retrieved March 2009 from www.washingtontimes.com/news/2009/feb/23/nation-briefs-66251585/?page=3.

Rehm, J., Mathers, C., Popova, S., Thavorncharoensap, M., Teerawattananon, Y., & Patra, J. (2009). Global burden of disease and injury and economic cost attributable to alcohol use and alcohol-use disorders. *The Lancet, 373*(9682), 2223–2233. Original Text

Schumacher-Matos, E. (2009, February 21). Mexico, faltering, not failed. *Washington Post*, p. A13.

Sowers, K., & Rowe, W. (2009). International perspectives on social work practice. In A. R. Roberts (Ed.), *Social workers' desk reference* (2nd ed., pp. 863–868). New York: Oxford University Press.

United Nations Office on Drugs and Crime (UNODC). (2008a). Drug trafficking as a security threat in West Africa. Retrieved February 2009 from www.unodc.org/documents/data-and-analysis/Studies/Drug-Trafficking-WestAfrica-English.pdf.

United Nations Office on Drugs and Crime (UNODC). (2008b, June 26). International day against drug abuse and illicit trafficking. Retrieved March 2009 from www.unodc.org/unodc/en/about-unodc/26-June.html.

United Nations Office on Drugs, Crime (UNODC) & World Health Organization (WHO). (2009). UNODC-WHO Joint Programme on drug dependence, treatment and care. Retrieved October 2010 fromwww.unodc.org/docs/treatment/09-82847_Ebook_ENGLISH.pdf.

United Nations Security Council. (2009, January 30). *First report of the Secretary-General on the United Nations Integrated Peacebuilding Office in Sierra Leone.* Retrieved March 2009 from www.unhcr.org/refworld/docid/498aa2272.html.

US Department of Health and Human Services (DHHS). (2008). *Results from the 2007 national household survey on drug abuse.* Washington, DC: US Government Printing Office. Retrieved February 2009 from http://oas.samhsa.gov/nsduh/2k7nsduh/2k7Results.pdf.

van Wormer, K., & Davis, D. R. (2008). *Addiction treatment: A strengths perspective* (2nd ed.). Belmont, CA: Cengage.

World Health Organization (WHO). (2010a). Tobacco. Retrieved May 2010 from www.who.int/mediacentre/factsheets/fs339/en/index.html.

World Health Organization (WHO). (2010b). Alcohol. Retrieved May 2010 from www.who.int/substance_abuse/facts/alcohol/en/index.html.

World Health Organization (WHO). (2009a). Alcohol. Retrieved June 2009 from www.who.int/substance_abuse/facts/alcohol/en/index.html.

World Health Organization (WHO) (2009b). Injecting drug use and prisons. Retrieved March 2009 from www.who.int/hiv/topics/idu/en/index.html.

26

Employment, Unemployment, and Decent Work

TATSURU AKIMOTO

The global employment situation is summarized in this chapter, which begins with an international comparison of employment composition by status, industry, and occupation. Reference to informal sectors is then made, and a description of unemployment, underemployment, and decent work follows. The link between these factors and the international migration of workers is also briefly explored. Even if the same word, *employment*, is used, what it means—the reality and concept—may differ considerably, making international comparisons and analyses difficult. As far as intervention is concerned, the ILO (International Labour Organization) is the core international agency that is active in this field through setting standards and implementing technical cooperation projects whose processes provide opportunities for the field of social work to intervene.

EMPLOYMENT IN THE WORLD BY STATUS, INDUSTRY, AND OCCUPATION

Employment is typically characterized by status in employment, industry, and occupation. The employment environment varies around the world. In one country, most people may be engaged in farming, forestry, and fishery with their families, while in another country, they may work in manufacturing and service sectors as blue- and white-collar employees.

In Bangladesh, for example, two-thirds (63.5%) of working people are employers (including own-account workers) and contributing family workers, and 21.6% are employees. More than half (51.7%) work for the primary industries (i.e., agriculture, hunting, forestry, and fishing), 13.7% for the secondary industries (i.e. mining and quarrying; manufacturing; electricity, gas, and water supply; and construction), and the remaining for the tertiary industries (i.e., wholesale and retail trade, restaurants and hotels, transport, storage, communication, financing, insurance, real estate, business, community, social and personal services, and so on). More than half (51.4%) are skilled agricultural and fishery workers,[1] and the remaining (48.1%) are production and related workers, transport equipment operators and laborers, and service workers and shop and market sales workers (ILO, 2007).

In the United States, on the other hand, 7.4% of all employed are employers and contributing family workers and 92.6 % are employees; very few people (1.5%) work in the primary industries, 20.8% work in the secondary industries, and the overwhelming majority (77.7%) work in the tertiary industries. Only 0.7% are skilled agricultural and fishery workers, whereas 23.8% are production and related workers, transport equipment operators, and laborers; 48.4% are legislators, senior officials and managers, professionals, technicians and associate professionals, and clerks; and 28.0% are service workers and shop and market sales workers (ILO, 2007).

Most other countries in the world fall between these two countries. Many Two-Thirds World countries (also called *developing countries* or *countries of the Global South*) are closer to the former, and most member countries of the Organization for Economic Cooperation and Development (OECD) are closer to the latter. In Egypt, for an example, employees make up 60.0% of workers, workers in the primary industries make up 30.9%, and skilled agricultural and fishery workers make up 30.1%. In Malaysia, the percentages are 76.2%, 14.6%, and some 10%, respectively (ILO, 2007).

Although there is much criticism of modernization theory, or convergence theory (see Chapter 4), most societies seem to be shifting from an employer and family worker focus to an employee focus, from agrarian to blue-collar and white-collar workers, and from primary industry to secondary and tertiary (service) industry, albeit with some exceptions.

The Informal Sector in the Two-Thirds World

The description just given does not necessarily portray the scope of employment worldwide, particularly that in the Two-Thirds World. Consider the following examples. Yesterday, a worker was an employer asking someone to work for him, but today he is an employee being asked to work for someone. He was engaged in digging a well a few days ago, is engaged in guiding tourists today, and may be engaged in farming a neighbor's fields for a week or two starting the day after tomorrow. Another person worked for a factory as a production worker last month but is building a house as a construction worker this month. Between jobs or even at the same time every evening, they work in their stalls on the streets as food venders or as noodle cooks in the family food stand as family workers. Holding one steady, major job may often be exceptional, and holding multiple jobs at one time might be normal. Or, more extremely, they may still live in a self-sufficient economy, either partially or totally.

An ILO report on Kenya in 1972 described the informal sector for the first time. In this sector, there are many people who sell goods on streets, provide various services, run numerous microplants (very small plants sometimes known as cottage industries), and are engaged in other economic activities. These individuals and enterprises have no registration, permission, or license, and they are outside taxation, statistics, labor laws, and regulations on occupational safety and health and other labor standards, including social security and insurance schemes. Their level of technology and skills, productivity, and income tend to be very low (ILO, 1991). Before this report, the ILO, as well as governments and other entities, had been endeavoring to improve worker conditions and status, but they now recognized that the workers who were in the most need with the most difficult problems had been overlooked and unprotected. What's more, these workers exist in considerable numbers.

The concept and definition of the informal sector vary (e.g., the ILO Director-General report at the 1991 Annual General Meeting and the statistical definition adopted at the Fifteenth International Conference of Labour Statisticians in 1993). Some economic activities in developed countries are sometimes discussed under the same concept. A report presented at the 2002 ILO General Meeting, for example, differentiated the informal economy, informal employment, informal sectors, and unprotected jobs in attempting to define the concept (ILO, 2003).

Informal economic activities have expanded all over the world. The informal economy share in Africa includes nearly 80% of workers in nonagricultural employment, some 60% of workers in urban employment, and more than 90% of new jobs (Charmes, 2000). Employment in countries with developing and transition economies has been mostly created within the framework of informal economic activities (ILO, 2003).

UNEMPLOYMENT

The unemployment rate may be the most critical indicator for describing the difficulties of working people. The unemployed are generally defined as "persons above a specified age" who are "not in paid employment or self-employment," are "currently available for work," and are "seeking work . . . during the reference period" (ILO, 2007, p. 481). The unemployment rate varies considerably by country. In 2006, the unemployment rate in various countries was as follows: Thailand, 1.2%; Cuba, 1.9%; Iceland, 2.9%; and Norway, Korea, and New Zealand, around 3.5%. In contrast, the rate for Macedonia was 36.0%; Bosnia and Herzegovina, 31.1%; French Guiana, 29.1%; South Africa, 25.5%; and the West Bank and Gaza Strip, 23.2%. Most of these countries have experienced wars or other conflicts. The unemployment rate of the United States during the same period was 4.6%; Canada, 6.3%; Germany, 10.4%; and most other countries between 4% and 10% (ILO, 2007).

Convergence is not necessarily applicable to the unemployment rate. Variance is observed even among OECD countries. Also, the rate fluctuates greatly even within a country, depending on the area and time. Just a few years later in May 2009, for example, the unemployment rate of the United States had doubled to 9.4% due to the financial crisis of 2009 (USBLS, 2009). Adding the discouraged unemployed would increase the rate even further; in fact, differences in the definition of unemployment and the methodology by country have been questioned. These differences were adjusted and standardized, only to result in little change.

A more basic question once raised was, "Which workers are happier, those whose unemployment rate is 20% (e.g., in some parts of Spain and southern Italy) or those at 4% plus (e.g., in the United States)?" (Bluestone, 1999). Family and neighborhood support and stigma, social norms, and social benefits and services make a difference. Also, dividing a full-time job into two part-time jobs for two workers would lower the unemployment rate by 50%. At the other economic pole of the world, urban slum dwellers in the least developed countries would not be unemployed. They have to work taking whatever job comes, including collecting cans and papers on the streets, to eat and live for today, with no savings, stocks, or social security programs or benefits.

WORKING CONDITIONS AND DECENT WORK

The dichotomous analysis of employment versus unemployment may be of little use. Employment comprising very long working hours with very low wages or the reverse of very short working hours against one's will has been discussed under the name of *underemployment* for many years. Employment requiring very little of one's full capacity may also be named similarly termed.

Some employment involves inhumane working conditions regarding wages, hours, fringe benefits, safety and health, and participation. Benefits and social protection that often accompany formal work— housing benefits, health and medical benefits, workers' compensation insurance, severance pay and unemployment insurance, and retirement benefits— are totally lacking. There must be jobs, but the jobs must be decent ones. In the 1990s, the ILO introduced *decent work* as a key campaign term. It refers to a rather all-inclusive humane sort of work "in which rights, social protection and social dialogue must be secured, and freedom and equality, the (economic and social) safe security of life of working people exist," that is, "productive employment with which dignity as a human being is kept" (ILO in Japan [ILO-Tokyo], n.d.). Recently, decent work has been promoted as a goal of all ILO activities; it has been itemized as employment creation, the security of fundamental human rights in jobs, the expansion of social protection, and the promotion of social dialogue (e.g., Ghai, 2006).

To achieve these goals, the ILO has adopted some 200 conventions from its commencement. Because many countries, including the United States, have not ratified a number of those conventions and therefore are not bound by them, the ILO adopted the Declaration on Fundamental Principles and Rights at Work in 1998, demanding that all countries, regardless of their ratification, abide by eight core labor standards in four fields: *(1)* freedom of association and recognition of the right to collective bargaining (Conventions 87 and 98), *(2)* elimination of all forms of forced or compulsory labor (Conventions 29 and 105), *(3)* effective abolition of child labor

(Conventions 138 and 182), and *(4)* elimination of discrimination in regard to employment and occupation (Conventions 100 and 111).

The UN World Summit for Social Development in 1995[2] and World Trade Organization (WTO) Ministerial Conference in 1996 had earlier confirmed that each country was to respect these core labor standards. These standards have also been cited in various documents, such as the OECD Guideline for Multinational Enterprises, UN Global Compact, Global Reporting Initiative (GRI), and International Organization for Standardization (ISO), as well as in discussions on corporate social responsibility (CSR) (JTUC, 2009).

LABOR MARKETS AND MIGRATION

Lack of employment and disparity in working conditions—most typically wages—trigger the migration of workers. Taking wages in manufacturing industries as an example, Denmark paid hourly wages of US$33.25 (2003); Germany, $19.12 (2004); the United States, $16.56 (2005); and Spain, $14.90 (2004). Monthly wages in Korea were at $2421.25 (2005); Thailand, $197.48 (2006); China, $125.32 (2003); and India, $23.80 (2002) (JPC-SED, 2009, p. 186).[3] When adding the fringe benefits or labor costs in addition to cash payment, the gap widens even further. An accurate international comparison of wages is difficult because of differences in the content and form of labor provided, wage systems, statistical methodologies, consumer prices, significance of cash income in life, and international currency exchange rates, and the rewards for labor certainly differ greatly depending on where they are supplied, even if quality and quantity are similar.

Most people stay in the area of their birth all their lives. Some, however, move to other areas, sometimes beyond their national boundaries, seeking a better life. Besides labor market conditions, necessary factors include a spirit of challenge and competency, information on employment opportunities, and the funds to emigrate. Poverty may or may not be a cause of migration.

In 2005, 191 million migrants were living outside their countries of birth or nationality. This figure includes those who moved abroad for work, their dependents, and asylum seekers. About half of them[4] were economically active: 28.5 million in Europe and Russia, 25 million in Asia and the Middle East, 20.5 million in North America, 7.1 million in Africa, 2.9 million in Oceania, and 2.5 million in Latin

America and the Caribbean. The gender ratio was roughly 50–50 as of 2000 (ILO-Tokyo, n.d.). Movements generally are from Mexico, the Caribbean Islands, and Asia to the United States and Canada; from North Africa, Turkey, Greece, and Eastern Europe to Western Europe; from Asia to the Middle East; and from Asia and South America to Japan and Eastern Asia, although these fluctuate depending on the economic conditions in each country and region.

These migrants can be permanent or temporary, dispatched workers abroad or employees transferred abroad within corporations, and legal or illegal (undocumented) workers. The jobs in which they are engaged range from highly skilled professional work such as information technology (IT) positions to low-paid, unskilled jobs such as farming, cleaning, maintenance, manufacturing, construction, and domestic and health work. The latter often are not decent work and exist under insecure, unprotected labor conditions in an informal economy (ILO-Tokyo, n.d.). Undocumented workers are always under threat of being fired, reported, arrested, or deported and are in danger of being exploited.

Undocumented workers are people who (1) entered a country illegally; (2) entered legally with a nonworking visa (e.g., tourist visa) but are engaged in work or entered with a working visa but are engaged in work that would require another category of visa; or (3) entered legally but stay to work beyond the permitted period. There are about three million such workers in the United States and Europe, respectively.

INTERVENTION IN THE INTERNATIONAL ARENA AND SOCIAL WORK

Problems and needs arising in the social phenomena of employment and decent work must be placed in the broader perspective of the society (e.g., North and South relations, multinational corporations and globalization, and how social work interventions must be questioned). Nothing is essentially different from other fields of social work. The level of practice and research ranges from policy, program, and project design, implementation, and evaluation to direct services, and interest in topics range from poverty to human rights.

The one difference is the need for two conceptual frameworks in tandem: that of *international social work* and a tentatively named *social work of work*. The former is discussed in other sections of this volume. The latter has been labeled social work in the world of work in

the United States in the 1970s (e.g., Hyman Weiner) or workers' welfare in Japan in the 1980s (e.g., Tatsuru Akimoto), where all aspects of the lives of working people, including problems in the labor market, workplace, family, community life, and labor unions, are encompassed. US social work has been involved historically in addressing unemployment, low wages, and occupational safety and health since at least the time of Jane Addams from the beginning of the twentieth century to the 1920s and 1930s. More recently, occupational social work practice in the United States and parts of Europe may be skewed toward employee assistance programs (EAP).

The major arenas for social work activities are international agencies (UN-related agencies such as the ILO, UNDP, UNICEF, and UNHCR), international cooperation agencies of each nation-state (e.g., USAID, CEDA, JICA), and NGOs (nongovernmental organizations, including religious organizations). The ILO is the most influential international agency specializing in this domain, and it has two significant fields: (1) setting standards as described earlier and (2) sponsoring technical corporation projects. Both fields provide opportunity for social work to work, but particularly the latter is on the same turf as social work. More than a third of the budgets of these projects has been used for employment. Projects range from framing employment policies and plans and capacity building of governments at the national level to vocational training and entrepreneurship programs for women and people with disabilities at the local level. One recent emphasis in projects for employment promotion is projects for infrastructure construction through the ILO Employment-Intensive Investment Programme, which uses only technologies available in the locality and takes a local rather than national approach. Many other agencies have been implementing similar projects.

The actual involvement of professional social workers has been limited, but one example is a research project, *The shrinkage of urban slums in [five Asian cities] and their employment aspects*, carried out amid the explosion of urban slums in the twenty-first century (Akimoto, 1998). The diminishing process was reviewed historically and empirically, and a comprehensive list of employment interventions by governments and NGOs was obtained.

The companionship between the ILO and social work has been long lasting. Even the preliminary committee meeting for the founding of the International Committee of Schools for Social Work (the predecessor of International Association of Schools of

Social Work) in Berlin in 1929 was attended by an ILO representative (Kniephoff-Knebel & Seibel, 2008).

In summary, in some parts of the world, most people are self-employed or family workers in farming, fishery, and forestry, while in other parts, most people are blue-or white-collar employees in manufacturing and service industries. In some parts of the world, a majority of people are working in informal sectors or economies. Some countries have an unemployment rate of only a few percent, while other countries have rates higher than 30%. Not only the existence of employment itself but also the quality of employment are concerns under the terms of underemployment—or recently, decent work. Disparity in working conditions and the absence of employment trigger the international migration of workers. The ILO and other UN-related agencies, national aid-providing agencies, and NGOs, particularly via technical corporation projects, provide social work with arenas in which to address employment-related issues.

NOTES

1. The occupation classification in this section is ISCO-88 (International Standard Classification of Occupation of 1988).

2. One of the main themes of 1995 UN World Summit for Social Development was the realization of productive employment, the raising of poverty eradication and full employment as a goal, and the promise to build up a secure, safe, and fair society (ILO-Tokyo, n.d.).

3. Definitions of real wages of production workers may differ by country. Original data sources were various governmental statistics of each country and the ILO *Yearbook of Labour Statistics*, cited from Japanese Ministry of Health, Labour, and Welfare International Affairs Division, *International Situation Report [Kaigai Josei Hokoku]* 2005–6. The data were converted into yen in the report with the exchange rates in Japanese Cabinet Office foreign economic data [*kaigai keizai deta*] and IMF international financial statistics and then converted into US dollars by the present writer with annual average rates calculated from weighted averages of rates weekly announced by Japanese Customs Chiefs (JPC-SED, 2009, p. 186).

4. "86 million out of 175 million migrants in 2000," "Of the 200 million international migrants, 50 percent are . . . migrant workers" (www.ilo.org/migrant).

REFERENCES

Akimoto, T. (1998). Shrinkage of urban slums in Asia and their employment aspects. Bangkok: ILO Regional Office for Asia and the Pacific.

Bluestone, B. (1999). Constructing a new cross-national architecture for labor market statistics: A grant proposal to Ford Foundation (funded in 2000). Cited in Tatsuru, A. (2004). Labor market statistics and well-being: A new architecture but under construction. *Social Welfare, 44.*

Charmes, J. (2000). *Informal sector, poverty, and gender: A review of empirical evidence.* Paper commissioned for World Development Report 2000/2001. Washington, DC: World Bank.

Ghai, D. (Ed.). (2006). *Decent work: Objectives and strategies.* Geneva: International Institute for Labour Studies, ILO.

International Labour Organization (ILO). (2007). *Yearbook of labour statistics, 2007.* Geneva: Author.

International Labour Organization (ILO). (2003). *Decent work and the informal economy.* Report VI, Ninetieth Annual General Meeting, Geneva.

International Labour Organization (ILO). (1991). Director-general report: The dilemma of the informal sector. Seventy-Eighth ILO General Meeting, Geneva.

International Labour Organization (ILO). (1972). *Employment, incomes and equality: A Strategy for increasing productive employment in Kenya.* Geneva: Author.

International Labour Organization Office in Japan (ILO-Tokyo). (n.d.). Labour force migration [Rodoryoku ido] (leaflet). Tokyo: Author.

JPC-SED (Japan Productivity Center for Socio-Economic Development). (2009). *Labour statistics of use [Katsuyo rodo tokei].* Tokyo: Author.

JTUC (Japan Trade Union Congress; Rengo). (2009). Core labor standards and ILO [*Chukaku-teki rodo-kijun* to ILO]. http://www.jtuc-rengo.org (retrieved on March 20, 2009).

Kniephoff-Knebel, A., & Seibel, F. (2008). Establishing international cooperation in social work education: The first decade of the International Committee of Schools for Social Work (ICSW). *International Social Work, 51*(6), 790–812.

USBLS (United States Bureau of Labor Statistics). (2007, June 5). Employment situation: May 2009 (news release). www.bls.gov/bls/newsrels.htm (retrieved on June 18, 2009).

Environmental Degradation and Preservation

CHRISTINA L. ERICKSON

Healthy environmental systems are integral to human well-being, even to human existence itself. The concern over environmental degradation and preservation has dramatically accelerated in the past three decades as the recognition of environmental losses has grown. These environmental issues have also become increasingly important to the field of social work. Documentation of environmental injustices has become clearer in recent years, and our ethical mandate to address social injustice compels social workers to act. Environmental practice is particularly suited for international social work because of the complex connections of global natural systems.

Humans have a deep dependence on the natural living world; it is through the earth that we receive nutritional sustenance and access to air, water, land, and energy to provide for our needs and comforts. Obviously, the health of the planet is intrinsically related to each of us. However, the human connection to the natural world extends beyond our physical sustenance. We have a deep emotional need to affiliate with the natural world for our own happiness (Besthorn & Saleeby, 2003). Unfortunately, it is human activity, including the desire to improve our quality of life, that lies at the core of environmental degradation. In this chapter we examine environmental issues from the standpoint of environmental justice, some effects of environmental issues around the world, and the unique contribution that social work is positioned to offer to this very human dilemma.

ENVIRONMENTAL PROBLEMS AS SOCIAL WORK PROBLEMS

Despite our long-held principle of ecosystemic practice, social work has been slow to consider the natural environment as part of our practice. Traditional social work discourse includes a focus on the person-in-environment. This focus on the environment or ecosystem refers to the sociocultural environment (McKinnon, 2008) and has ignored the physical environment upon which human life is dependent. In fact, social work has almost completely disregarded the integration of issues of the natural environment into our existing models that include the human environment.

One explanation for this disregard is that we consider it to be the purview of other disciplines (Besthorn & Saleeby, 2003); however, the expansion of social work is critical for rectifying environmental degradation and its effect on human communities. Some social work scholars have pushed for the expansion of our understanding of environmental issues beyond that of the social environment for the people we serve (Besthorn & Saleeby, 2003; Coates, 2003; Rogge, 2003). Several authors have capably argued for the appropriateness of social work to address environmental issues for reasons of environmental justice (McKinnon, 2008; Rogge, 2003), a need and desire for natural spaces (Besthorn & Saleeby, 2003), and improvement of quality of life for vulnerable populations (Coates, 2003).

Evidence is clear that environmental problems disproportionately affect communities of people living in poverty, people of color, and women and children as well as countries or areas with less power in the global arena. In the United States, Bullard (2005) has captured and elevated the understanding of environmental issues for people of color and turned that knowledge into activism. The Principles of Environmental Justice, adopted in 1971 by the attendees of the First National People of Color Environmental Leadership Summit, state that environmental justice includes the "right to be free from ecological destruction" (Bullard, 2005, p. 299). One of the founding values of the social work profession is to respect the dignity and worth of every human being, and "when we do not respect the worth of the natural environment, we do not respect the worth and dignity of the people who reside in and depend on it" (Besthorn & Saleeby, 2003, p. 10).

A main component of social work education and practice is the amelioration of social injustice; it is social work's organizing value (Marsh, 2005). The study of environmental degradation and preservation also incorporates social justice. Environmental justice focuses on the inequitable share of environmental burdens placed on communities of color, indigenous communities, poor communities, and economies outside the current dominant economic order (Schlossberg, 2007). Simultaneously, communities of affluence have access to a disproportionate share of environmental benefits. Environmental justice includes a balance of multiple elements, such as distribution of resources, recognition of rights, participation in decisions, and change capability for individuals and communities. Environmental injustice is a process that takes away a community's capacity for health, economic well-being, and full functionality as a community (Schlossberg, 2007). This perspective of environmental justice situates the problem squarely in the realm of social work.

ENVIRONMENTAL INJUSTICES AND THEIR EFFECTS

In many poor and rural communities around the world, it is the ecosystem that provides communities their security. Water, fuel, protein sources, shelter, and vitamin and mineral sources all arise from the natural world—not a government-sponsored entitlement program (Sanjayan, 2006). When ecosystems are degraded, these communities face a loss of food systems and economic opportunities, and severe poverty often ensues. Indeed, although industrialized countries may feel more removed from their natural environment, people in these countries are also dependent on natural systems.

Decades of data have shown the strong intersections between environmental burdens and the lives of people who are marginalized. The following topics represent some of the most pressing issues in relation to the environment. Though they do not represent all of the issues faced in international environmental social work, they are some of the most compelling concerns of today.

Water

According to the World Health Organization (WHO) and United Nations Children's Fund (UNICEF) (2010), access to sources of safe drinking water has improved dramatically over the last eighteen years. Currently, 87% of the world's population has access to improved sources of drinking water, with much of this improvement occurring in India and China. However, 884 million people, many of whom live in sub-Saharan Africa, still do not have access to safe drinking water. More than 25% of residents in sub-Saharan African must walk more than thirty minutes to obtain water. Three million people die each year from waterborne diseases, most of them children under five. Water contaminated by microbial pathogens is the greatest source of death and illness on a global scale (Arthurton et al., 2007). Unfortunately, human activities are one of the greatest sources of water quality degradation.

A community's access to local water is too often affected by international conflict or agreement. There is a paucity of freshwater agreements that cross international boundaries, creating potential for future conflict (Arthurton et al., 2007). Use of water by developing countries is expected to increase by 50% by 2025 while increasing on a smaller scale in developed countries. In addition to being important for human health, water is important for the market and industry sectors, and a lack of access to water affects socioeconomic development (Arthurton et al., 2007). A compounding economic issue is the sale of water as a commodity. Lack of water on a global scale is not the concern; rather, the affordability and quality of water is. Through commoditization of water, the most vulnerable of world citizens could lose their access to it, and warfare over water rights could result (United National Development Programme [UNDP], 2007).

Climate Change

Climate change may be of the utmost importance in our efforts for environmental preservation. Simultaneously, it is one of the strongest predictors of environmental degradation. The earth has already warmed over the past century, and the Intergovernmental Panel on Climate Change predicts that this warming will continue to increase by somewhere between 1.4 and 4 degrees Celsius (Kuylenstierna & Panwar, 2007). Climate change is also accelerated by human activities, including development and other activities that increase the generation of greenhouse gases. In addition, air pollution is a factor—it is estimated that two million people die every year from the effects of air pollution, and although some cities around the globe have improved their air quality, many are still struggling (Kuylenstierna & Panwar, 2007).

The most detrimental effects of climate change will be felt first by the world's poorest citizens. Changes in rainfall will decrease available food supplies, and economic industries in some regions that rely on certain climate conditions will become vulnerable as those conditions change. As ecosystems change and environmental degradation becomes severe due to rising sea levels or changes in food systems (Friends of the Earth, n.d.), some communities will no longer be able to live on their land. Environmental or climate refugees—people displaced from their homeland due to environmental changes—are anticipated to range from 50 to 200 million people by the year 2100 (Friends of the Earth, n.d.). In low-lying, multiple-island countries such as Kiribati and Tuvalu in the South Pacific, climate change is already shifting migration patterns from outward islands to those in the center (Locke, 2009). National response plans for climate change include refugee resettlement agreements as well as efforts to maintain the quality of environmental resources for future generations (Locke, 2009).

Sanitation

Sanitation facilities—safe and sustainable methods to remove human waste—are not accessible to nearly two-thirds of the world's population (WHO & UNICEF, 2010). At the current rate of progress toward sanitation efforts, the world will not meet the UN's Millennium Development Goals (MDG). By 2015, the UN had hoped to halve the proportion of the population without access to sanitation (www.un.org/millenniumgoals/environ.shtml). Use of sanitation facilities is directly linked to income (WHO & UNICEF, 2010), and it is not surprising that the areas that have made advances are urban. Rural areas, especially those that are poor, will continue to lack access to safe sanitation beyond the 2015 MDG date. Even if the world were to meet the targets of the MDG, nearly two billion people would still be without access to basic sanitation (WHO & UNICEF, 2010), affecting the health of families and communities.

Chemical Poisons

Health disparities, such as the incidence of cancer or other diseases, have been the focus of environmental injustice research in the United States (Bullard, 2005). Since the mid-1990s, social workers in the United States have been writing about environmental toxins, especially in relation to children (Rogge, 2003). Research over the last decade has confirmed that people of color, threatened by dumping grounds and toxic waste of polluting industries, are

disproportionately affected by environmental hazards in those places most close to them, such as where they live, work, and attend school (Bullard & Wright, 1993). In the United States, localizing burdens has become common practice in policies that determine garbage sites and toxic waste disposal, often mirroring the priorities of the dominant society (Bullard, 2005).

These burdens extend across national borders as well. Exportation of toxic waste by wealthier nations to developing nations, mainly to avoid regulations and fees, is a serious issue. Toxic waste such as chemicals, computers, and other sources of technology that may leach toxins has been dumped in various parts of the developing world. Businesses in wealthy nations have profited from poor countries charging smaller fees to accept toxic trash. In the Ivory Coast, for example, 15 people were killed and another 100,000 were sickened when a Swiss trading company dumped 500 tons of toxic waste (Jolly, 2009). Other developing nations such as Somalia and Ethiopia have also been used for toxic dumping by wealthier nations.

Land Use

Natural systems form the core of subsistence in many poor communities. Natural capital accounts for approximately 26% of the wealth in developing countries (Martino & Zommers, 2007). When these natural systems become depleted or people are forcibly removed from viable land, poverty often ensues. Civilian populations can be displaced due to international conflict, forcing people into marginal ecological areas that do not sustain economic livelihoods, decreasing the capacity of their societies and communities. For these communities, poverty becomes inextricably linked with the environmental degradation surrounding them, leading to higher rates of vulnerability and lower rates of human well-being (Jager & Kok, 2007).

While some lands are depleted, other natural systems contain rich resources of environmental health that are in need of preservation. Growing evidence that some of the areas of greatest biodiversity, areas we need to protect for the importance they hold for the planet's well-being, are inhabited by people struggling to survive—often people with very little material wealth (Lloyd, 2006). The growing demand among conservationists is to save the land while simultaneously including the community and helping its citizens to escape poverty. This is an example of a clear nexus of person-in-environment in which social work can lend its knowledge. Conservation scientists need social workers. The natural environment must be integrated more fully into social work theoretical development and practice, including the benefits of the natural environment (Rogge, 2000).

CONTRIBUTIONS OF SOCIAL WORK

The call from the profession is clearly building. In 2001 the Australian Association of Social Workers found that 11% of members listed environmental issues as a top-ten priority. In recent years, The Association of Baccalaureate Social Work Program Directors, Inc. in the United States formed an environmental working group. Even more longstanding are social workers from non-Western countries who have long viewed environmental factors to be closely linked to social work practice, as reflected in the social work ethics of countries such as India and Chile (McKinnon, 2008).

The difficulty in wrestling with issues of environmental degradation and human well-being is that much of human quality of life is measured by a process that extracts resources from the natural world and provides them for human consumption. It is this system in itself that is wreaking havoc on the natural environment. "Sustainable development advocates embrace the symbiotic relationships among environmental, social and economic concerns and seeks to institutionalize a vision of development that weights them equally; to do otherwise is conceptually tantamount to building a stool with two legs" (Rogge, 2000, p. 34). Marrying the concepts of environmental preservation and human well-being is a growing movement of sustainable development. A key component to sustainability in all of these issues is balancing the development needed for quality of life for humans with the environmental degradation that development inevitably causes. Within this sustainable development movement, we must not forget the voices of the communities we serve. Based on research conducted in Cameroon, Paraguay, the Philippines, and Sri Lanka on access to decision making on environmental issues, a World Resources Institute Study concluded:

> Decisions that have significant environmental and social consequences are often made without the involvement of those whose interests are directly at stake. For poor people whose lives and livelihoods often depend on natural resources, and who are therefore most vulnerable to environmental risks, the consequences of exclusion can be especially severe. Weak access to decision-making may expose poor communities to high levels of pollution, remove them from productive land, and deprive them of the everyday benefits provided by natural resources.
>
> —(Foti & de Silva, *2010*, p. 6)

Social work is uniquely positioned to lift up the voices of those who have not traditionally been heard. One professional example is the International Federation of Social Workers (IFSW), which has already embraced environmental challenges. Through the International Policy Statement on Globalisation and the Environment (IFSW, 2005) IFSW clearly identifies the connection between a healthy planet and the advancement of human quality of life.

People share a common need for and right to a fair share of the earth's resources, including a clean, safe, and healthy environment. These basic requirements are under threat from climate change and environmental degradation. These challenges are widely recognized as the greatest priority for global cooperation. The degradation of the global environment has observable social and economic consequences and therefore has an impact on the ability of people to achieve their potential as human beings and to give expression to their human rights (IFSW, 2005).

The person-in-environment perspective and social work skills of inclusion become vital as we work toward ending environmental degradation while simultaneously expanding access to resources to improve the quality of life for people around the world. As with all justice movements, environmental preservation will come only when we listen to the voices of those who have been marginalized—those who have already experienced severe burdens because of environmental issues. Human consumption and environmental degradation go hand in hand. We cannot save the environment while ignoring the plight of those who are struggling to survive and who depend on the environment to survive. Working together to save environmental biodiversity along with cultures is an important part of conservation work. Research is still working to determine what most benefits the environment, the economy, and the cultures that inhabit an area. What is known is that "local people are often the best people in developing countries to manage these conservation areas, because they want them to survive in the long term as well" (Lloyd, 2006 p. 24).

Social Work as an Environmental Ally

It is difficult to consider the potential problems that may occur if environmental degradation is not addressed. Social workers' roles may become even more stressful and complex if we choose not to address environmental problems. For example, heat waves have produced loss of life for the most vulnerable in many corners of the globe. Extended storm seasons will increase the need for disaster response from social workers as well as the global movement of climate refugees. Loss of livelihood for many groups, including fisheries in coastal areas and land suitable for farming and crop development, will lead to changes in food systems as well as employment and skills for communities. In addition, there is the very real fear that environmental conditions may become so severe that social workers will be called to respond in traumatic circumstances, forcing us to recognize the interdependence we have with the natural world (Jones, 2010). It is the perceived separation of humans from the environment that is the greatest barrier to solving issues of environmental degradation.

The place of social work in the multidisciplinary effort to combat environmental problems has yet to be fully discerned. Joining the global and multidisciplinary actions already being taken is our first step. Social workers engage in political, health, educational, legal, and economic systems not as specialists in these areas but as committed professionals who work with these disciplines to solve problems for the clients we serve. The environment is another of these systems. We do not expect to re-create ourselves as environmental scientists but to engage in the dialogue on how these problems can be solved, advocating for social justice and inclusion of all, as we have done throughout the history of the profession. Social work contributions are key to the amelioration of environmental degradation and the preservation of natural systems. It is within social work's unique person-in-environment perspective that we will create interventions for this very human issue.

REFERENCES

Arthurton, R., Barker, S., Rast, W., Huber, M., et al. (2007). Water. In United Nations Environment Programme (UNEP) *Global environment outlook: Environment for development (GEO-4)*. Accessed at www.unep.org/geo/geo4/media/.

Besthorn, F.H., & Saleeby, D. (2003). Nature, genetics and the biophilia connection: Exploring linkages with social work values and practice. *Advances in Social Work*, 4(1), 1–18.

Bullard, R. D. (2005). *The quest for environmental justice: Human rights and the politics of pollution*. San Francisco: Sierra Club.

Bullard, R. D., & Wright, B. H. (1993). Environmental justice for all: Community perspectives on health and research needs. *Toxicology and Industrial Health*, 9(5), 821–842.

Coates, J. (2003). *Ecology and social work: Toward a new paradigm*. Nova Scotia: Fernwood.

Foti J., & de Silva, L. (2010). *A seat at the table: Including the poor in decisions for development and environment*. Washington, DC: World Resources Institute. Accessible at http://pdf.wri.org/a_seat_at_the_table.pdf.

Friends of the Earth. (n.d.) A citizen's guide to climate refugees. www.foe.org.au/resources/publications/climate-justice/CitizensGuide.pdf/view.

International Federation of Social Workers (IFSW). (2005). *International Policy Statement on Globalisation and the Environment*. Retrieved April 30, 2010, from www.ifsw.org/p38000222.html.

Jager, J., & Kok, M. T. J. (2007). Vulnerability of people and the environment: Challenges and opportunities. In United Nations Environment Programme (UNEP) 2007, *Global environment outlook: Environment for development (GEO-4)*. Retrieved from www.unep.org/geo/geo4/media/.

Jolly, D. (2009, September 17). Settlement near in Ivory Coast toxic dumping case. *New York Times*. Retrieved from www.nytimes.com/2009/09/18/business/global/18trafigura.html.

Jones, P. (2010). Responding to the ecological crisis. *Journal of Social Work Education*, 46(1), 67–81.

Kuylenstierna, J. C. I., & Panwar, T. S. (2007). Atmosphere. In United Nations Environment Programme (UNEP) 2007, *Global environment outlook: Environment for development (GEO-4)*. Retrieved from www.unep.org/geo/geo4/media/.

Lloyd, M. (2006). The poverty/conservation equation. *Nature Conservancy*, 56(2), 20–31.

Locke, J. T. (2009). Climate change-induced migration in the Pacific region: Sudden crisis and long-term developments. *Geographic Journal*, 175(3), 171–180.

Marsh, J. C. (2005). Social justice: Social work's organizing value. *Social Work*, 50(4), 293–294.

Martino, D., & Zommers, Z. (2007). Environment for development. In United Nations Environment Programme (UNEP) 2007, *Global environment outlook: Environment for development (GEO-4)*. Retrieved from www.unep.org/geo/geo4/media/.

McKinnon, J. G. (2008). Exploring the nexus between social work and the environment. *Australian Social Work, 61*(3), 256–268.

Rogge, M. E. (2003). Social development and the ecological tradition. *Social Development Issues, 22*(1), 32–41.

Rogge, M. E. (2000). Children, poverty and environmental degradation: Protecting current and future generations. *Social Development Issues, 22*(2/3), 46–53.

Sanjayan, M. A. (2006). Is poverty related to conservation? *Nature Conservancy, 56*(2), 29.

Schlossberg, D. (2007). *Defining environmental justice: Theories, movements and nature.* New York: Oxford.

United Nations Development Programme (UNDP). (2007). *Water rights and wrongs.* Glamorgan, UK: Celectron Printing.

World Health Organization (WHO) & United Nations Children's Fund (UNICEF). (2010). *Progress on sanitation and drinking water: 2010 update.* Geneva: WHO.

28

Ethnic Conflicts

DARJA ZAVIRŠEK AND JELKA ZORN

*When we discuss social work with western people, they always ask us about ethnicity and racism
in our country. We don't want to talk about diversity all the time, we want to forget what we went
through and focusing at sameness among us, not predominantly at differences.*

SOCIAL WORK TEACHER FROM BOSNIA (*Personal Communication, 2007*)

Among numerous, often incompatible definitions, *ethnic conflict* is broadly defined as political or social conflict involving one or more groups that
are identified by some markers of ethnic identity
(Gilley, 2004; Toft, 2003). Its appearance varies according to time and place. Ethnic conflict can take the form
of discriminatory policies that affect housing opportunities, material resources, and reproductive rights and
that exclude individuals and communities from participation in decision-making processes. All ethnic conflicts have a common structure of social inequality.

Historically, social workers contributed toward
the development of the biopower techniques of surveillance when they treated ethnic communities
as natural laboratories for watching people's natural
deviancy[1] (Foucault, 1990). At the same time they
supported those who survived several losses on the
material and emotional level and helped individuals
and communities to restore a sense of normalcy by
focusing on daily routine as well as on the survived
past. The chapter presents social work interventions
in the situation of ethnic conflict and its aftermath.

THEORETICAL FRAMEWORK
The difficulty of defining ethnic conflict lies within
a complex and changeable notion of ethnic identity
itself. The classic understanding of ethnicity sees it as
a person's identity marked by race, religion, shared history, territory, language, and social symbols, without
taking into consideration its constructed nature, which
can be either mobilized or delegitimized. Generally,
ethnicity is defined by two main approaches: the pri-
mordialist or organic approach, which conceives ethnic
groups as substantial, objectively defined entities, and

the constructivist approach, which defines ethnicity
in terms of participants' beliefs, perceptions, understandings, and identifications—"a perspective *on* the
world" instead of "the thing *in* the world" (Brubaker,
2004, p. 65). Therefore, the boundaries of ethnicities
and ethnic differences are not simultaneously boundaries of ethnic conflicts, and ethnic characteristics and
differences cannot be the explanatory model for ethnic
conflicts. However, they can be developed as such
in particular contexts when ethnicity becomes a device
to mobilize hatred and constructed otherness. As will
be demonstrated later, ethnic conflicts colonize the
bodily and environmental spaces (Feldman, 1991).

The concept of ethnic conflict is connected
with interrelated and often overlapping concepts
and practices, such as racist and cultural conflict,
while ethnicity is interchanging with race and culture.
Some theorists claim that the concept of ethnic conflict has only replaced the more powerful concepts
of racism and power inequality (Rommelspacher,
1995). Others have emphasized that the idea of ethnic
conflict needs to be decoupled from culture since
ethnic groups might be multicultural and cultures
might be transethnic (Fenton, 2004). And a third
group has stressed that what is often defined as ethnic
conflict would be more correctly seen as a conflict
for the control over the exploitation of natural
resources, a conflict for economic rights and goods,
and the consequences of a lack of education, democratic culture, illiteracy, and so on (Gilley, 2004;
Hintjens, 2008; see also the documentary *Dar Fur:
War for Water* by Križnar & Weiss, 2008). Brubaker
(2004) also noted that ethnicity as such is usually not
the ultimate, irreducible source of violence but that

"conflicts driven by struggles for power between challengers and incumbents are newly ethnicized, newly framed in ethnic terms" (p. 90).

If ethnic identity is flexible and constructed in order to serve particular needs of individuals and groups, it can become mobilized in some circumstances and delegitimized as a means of political expression in others. In postgenocide Rwanda, the ethnic terms *Hutu, Tutsi,* and *Twa* have been not only removed from identity cards but banned from public discourse (Hintjens, 2008). Ethnic identification has become illegal, viewed as backward and potentially dangerous. As another example, after Kosovo proclaimed the independent state in 2008, social work students disputed whether they were ethnically Albanians, Muslims, or Kosovars, and they remained divided into three ethnic identities (personal observation, University of Pristine, 2008). Those who call themselves Kosovars see this ethnic self-definition as the one which brings them closer to the "European identity" and consequently into the European Union political formation of some of the Europeans, whereas "being Albanias" distance them from the desirable "European identity" and push them outside of the socially constructed borders of Europe (Personal observation, from field work in the year 2010).

After 1991, particularly in Eastern Europe and Southeast Asia, ethnicity became almost a new political and social identity, not formally recognized and not even individually known for almost half of the twentieth century. The imagined ethnic identities that had not presented a source of serious conflict for decades were mobilized by the political elites for a new political project of shifting national and state borders. The words by a Bosnian social worker from Sarajevo quoted at the beginning of the chapter show that ethnicity does not exist per se but is a mobilization focal point in the power struggles of political elites and structural deprivation. Therefore, instead of bounding ethnic difference with ethnic conflict and hostility, the task for social workers is to understand how and under what conditions some ethnic differences become sources of serious conflict and how to prevent the de-humanization of the constructed Other.

Ethnic identity and the esentialized cultural difference might become factors in the mobilization of ethnic conflict under two conditions. One is the destabilization of state systems (Yugoslavia) and the breakup of imperial orders (Sri Lanka, Chad, Cyprus, the Western Sahara, the Soviet Union); the second is the dominance over the existing natural wealth and the competition for other resources and the cultural as well as material indignities of economic disadvantage and deprivation (Georgia, Darfur, Palestine, Congo) (cf. Fenton, 2004). In former Yugoslavia, for example, economic crisis resulted in destabilization of the federative state systems, which proved to be a fertile ground for ethnic conflicts. When the state dissolved and former republics became sovereign states, the competition of the new states for resources relied on the production of ethnic boundaries. None of the new states was spared from the ethnic conflict, either in the form of war (Croatia, Bosnia and Herzegovina, Kosovo) or the oppression of those who become ethnic minorities (as in the cases of Slovenia where some people were legally erased from the register of the citizens or in Macedonia, where ethnic Albanians, Roma and Shinti people were seen as the destabilizers of the homogenous nation state).

The constructed ethnic identity thus can be based on ethnicized and racialized elements and relations such as the social distancing, humiliation and de-humanization of people who are less valued and to whom several negative characteristics are ascribed using biological and cultural determinism and essentialism. The ethnic group that is in the position of ascribing the negative characteristics is seen as being culturally and historically the holder of the positive values and social identities that also confirm the seemingly universal ideals of beauty, virtue, and intelligence. When the dominant ethnic group ascribes to itself more positive values and virtues and assigns the negative to another ethnic group, the members of the other ethnic group are turned into internal and external Others. The belief that the minority group is intrinsically different is linked with fear and suspicions that the group possesses extra privileges and might overcome the dominant ethnic group (e.g., birth rate, wealth, knowledge). Hatred becomes a mobilizing feeling for interacting communities.

Ethnic conflicts are historically based and supported by everyday repetitional practices that have the characteristics of everyday racism (Essed, 1991). The concept of *everyday practice* presupposes that the structure of everyday life is heterogeneous, repetitive, expected, and ordinary and that everyday life is based on numerous repetitional social relations that make everyday practices and everyday situations unquestionable and taken for granted. The everyday racism upon which ethnic conflicts are founded is therefore the integration of racism in everyday life through various commonly understood practices and the activation of power relations that remain unquestioned in the perception of the dominant group. The members of the ethnic group with more structural power have more resources to make their interpretation of the world into a "common truth" and a "common knowledge" which will on the personal level create greater feelings of self-confidence, safety, and self-control. These feelings are seen as normality instead of seeing them as part of structural power inequality. Seeing structural privileges as the universal norm also means that every person who is part of the dominant ethnic group profits from them, regardless of whether they accept or reject the power relations. When racist beliefs and actions become common, repetitive, and part of everyday life, the system starts to reproduce everyday racism in the form of racist and ethnic conflict in a particular social context.

MANIFESTATIONS OF ETHNIC CONFLICTS AND SOCIAL WORK RESPONSES

War, Genocide, and mass Rape

Violent ethnic conflict often ends in war, including genocide. Fein (2002) defines genocide as "sustained purposeful action by a perpetrator to physically destroy a collectivity directly or indirectly, through interdiction of the biological and social reproduction of group members, sustained regardless of the surrender or lack of threat offered by the victim" (p. 82). Another term that was widely used to describe genocide in former Yugoslavia was *ethnic cleansing*, where multiethnic villages were targeted to be cleansed of the "ethnic enemy" (Žarkov, 2007). One of the widely used weapons of ethnic violence is rape, which has been systematically practiced in many countries facing ethnic violence. Beginning in 1992, an estimated 60,000 to 100,000 Bosnian women were victims of mass rape in detention camps, villages, and towns (Žarkov, 2007). In Congo, which has been called the country of mass rapes, in the first half of 2010 more than 7.000 women and children were raped according to the official statistics (AI Report 2010). In the context of ethnic war, the woman's body is symbolically transformed into the ethnicized enemy's territory, which has to be destroyed, humiliated, violated and conquered. The aim of war rape is not only is the ultimate humiliation of the woman's body but also the systematic enforcement of the birth of children of mixed ethnic descent and the de-humanization of the community as a whole.

Social workers need to respond to the suffering of people in a culturally appropriate way. In a situation where women have survived mass rape, talking about the traumatic experiences might only be an appropriate way of dealing with the trauma in particular contexts. Silence is a socially accepted behavior in societies where speaking about pain and suffering can only be a collective encounter, not an individual one (Zaviršek, 2008). Additionally, silence might be a way to keep a positive, uncontaminated identity in communities where surviving particular traumatic events becomes a personal stigma. Instead of seeing silence as a sign of weakness, it might sometimes mean self-protection, resistance, or even a protest. Many testimonies of Muslim women surviving war rape in Bosnia revealed that women had to choose between telling the story of the trauma and being expelled from the extended family or remaining silent. In many communities, the process of healing through talking is not culturally appropriate social behavior, and public acknowledgment of the victim of war rape might endanger the person's status within the community. In environments where hierarchization of victimhood is replicating the normative order, the victim of war rape is as stigmatized as the perpetrator. (Gender inequality, for instance, is reproduced in hierarchization of victimhood where the male victims become more honored than the female or the mother who lost the son the more honored victim than the woman who experienced mass rape.)

Ethnic wars cause forced migration as people flee violence and seek safety and shelter. Social workers need to understand and address both the consequences of traumatic life events before emigration as well as postimmigration stress in the host country. For this purpose they need to listen to the everyday stories of refugees, immigrants, and other displaced people who need to be heard, taken seriously, and empowered, while taking into consideration their strengths and resilience (Dominelli, 2002; Ramon, 2008; Seifert, 2004).

Population Policy, Forced Sterilization, and the Pathologization of Ethnic Groups

The discourse about the need for the reproduction of the dominant ethnic group and preventing the reproduction of other ethnic groups is part of mobilizing ethnic conflict. Based on the eugenic strategies formalized long ago in the first sterilization law in 1907 in Indiana, this type of population policy has had a wide impact. In Germany, "race hygiene" (*Rassenhygiene*) followed that knowledge, and at the beginning of the 1930s, the eugenic rhetoric was incorporated into state politics (Proctor, 1992).

Invented by medical professionals, race hygiene was supported by social workers keen to give proof that the Jews, Roma, and Slavs were of inferior ethnicity, and the sterilization law of Nazi Germany in 1933 prevented the reproduction of some members of undesired ethnic minorities.

Coerced sterilization is not only a past practice of ethnic violence. Several ERRC (European Roma Rights Centre) reports pay attention to the coerced sterilization of Romani women in Hungary, Slovakia, and Czech Republic after 2001, which is interpreted as a form of ethnic discrimination and violence (ERRC, 2008). Between 1996 and 2000, the Peruvian government ordered the forced sterilization of more than 250,000 women and also some men (Reynolds, 1998; *Secret sterilisation*, 1999). The governmental family planning campaign, called *Plan Verde*, wanted to prevent reproduction of the poorest Indian communities living in towns and villages (Quechua villages, for instance). These examples show that ethnic hatred, conflict, and violence cannot be separated from the economic circumstances of people being defined through their ethnic identity.

Pathologization of ethnic groups is another form of ethnic conflict. Pathologization is when the ethnic and cultural characteristics of a person or group are seen as natural, inborn marks that are described in medical terms in order to construct ethnic minorities as being prone to specific bodily and mental illnesses, pathological violence, and lesser intelligence (Zaviršek, 2007). While the dominant group is viewed in terms of good health, ethnic minorities are seen as having preconditions for poor health, being prone to mental health problems, and being contagious. In such a framework, a particular ethnicity is already seen as pathological, such as Roma across Eastern Europe, who were pathologized under Communist rule as backward, lazy, untrustworthy, and less intelligent. The notion of culture was reserved for the privileged members of society, who worked in permanent employment, whereas Roma and Shinti people (often defined as the *lumpenproletariat* of the proletarian society) were highly ethnicized while being viewed as having no culture.

Instead of pathologizing ethnic minorities, social workers need to understand their everyday life experiences from their perspective. Using the demedicalized approach, social workers can focus on strengthening social movements and grassroots initiatives of ethnic groups that are discriminated against. They can ensure that members of ethnic groups within a conflict situation gain equal access to social and medical treatment

and that professional social welfare and health support is not given only to a particular ethnic group (Ramon, 2008; Urh, 2008).

Erasure of Personal Legal Statuses, Social Rights, and the Denial of Political Subjecthood

Ethnic conflict often appears in a form of constructed invisibility of certain ethnic groups. In 1992 the new Slovenian government deprived more than 25,000 people (official holders of Yugoslav passports who came to Slovenia as economic immigrants) of their citizenship rights and erased them from the register of permanent residents of the Republic of Slovenia. They lost all social and political rights and were treated as illegal migrants vulnerable to detention and deportation (Zorn, 2005, 2009). This exclusion of internal others helped to construct a seemingly homogeneous state. In 2002, the excluded started an ongoing political campaign in order to fight collectively for their rights. The erasure of legal statuses and social rights can be seen as a manifestation of ethnic conflict in the new state, which revoked political subjecthood and constructed invisibility of certain ethnic groups. Individual stories of those erased from the register of permanent residents, embedded with injustice and deprivations (including of welfare services), are still not accepted in the master narrative of the Slovenian story of independence. The invisibility of their experiences has caused a gap between the public image of a new democratic state and the everyday experiences of excluded members of society.

In such situations social workers should become advocates for the devalued ethnic groups and offer advocacy services in order to help people get back to the system and access social rights. They may also join grassroots campaigns that contribute to a more diverse concept of citizenship and empower them as social workers.

In the aftermath of ethnic violence, some social workers become involved in peace-building processes, which Moshe (2001) defines as "a struggle to ensure that groups that have been traditionally marginalised and excluded from decision-making processes become recognized partners in defining the future development for their communities and societies. . . . Unlike the conflict that seeks to wipe out whole communities to ensure justice for one's own, peace building must lead to relationships and coexistence between communities. Peace building can thus be defined as a process that entails the creation of autonomous and interdependent communities that work for the realization of justice and equality for all people through active civil participation and community building" (p. 15).

Memory Restrictions

Ethnic conflict often causes a conflicting relationship between history and memory as political regimes gain and keep their power through the construction of memory. The official history (in the Rwandan context, Hintjens [2008] calls it an "instrument of postgenocide reconstruction") erases personal and collective memories, and the new written history often produces a collective forgetting. This is especially true in the times of (post)ethnic conflicts, when the canonized construction of dominant history as part of a nation-building project selects memories as more and less legitimate and valuable. In their daily practice, social workers are confronted with the fact that the memory of one group or individual has become memorized and commemorated while the victimhood of the others remains unrecognized, causing a hierarchization of pain and discrimination.

The master narrative that becomes part of public memory is therefore based on the exclusion of those personal memories that do not fit into the dominant public discourse. Some individuals and groups are seen as official victims of the ethnic conflict and therefore have the right to official recognition of their trauma, while others are seen as less deserving to be traumatized and are deprived of professional support and public recognition of suffering. While suffering and loss are seen as the heroic acts of some people, others experience the minimizing and silencing of trauma and personal and collective experiences. In other words, the personal memories of many people are not allowed to become part of public remembrance and narrative.

Social workers try to ensure that people have the opportunity for memory work after a violent conflict in cases when this can be seen as empowerment (Zaviršek, 2008). As explained previously, memory work over a traumatic event such as rape might not be helpful outside safe, women-centered environments, and local specificities therefore need to be taken into consideration. At the same time, social workers might get involved in political work to change the oppressive environment.

It is important for social workers to know that the denial of memory divides people long after the end of armed political conflicts and encourages ethnic and religious hatred. The transgenerational trauma continuously influences people's everyday lives, including their interpersonal relationships, interactions, and life decisions. Not having the right to the personal memory is a form of civic disability that transmits an invisible form of discrimination and causes a hierarchy of pain. Memory work facilitated by social workers is important since it provides a place for voices to be heard. The right to remember and the right to testify are constitutive processes of the democratization of everyday life. These processes need someone who listens and testifies to what has been remembered. There are some positive examples of how social workers can be initiators and take part in memory projects, such as in Chile, Israel, and former Yugoslavia (Zaviršek, 2008).

CONCLUSIONS

Social workers have to be careful not to ascribe the term *ethnic conflict* to heterogeneous situations of exclusion, inequality, and violence, but at the same time they must recognize that ethnic conflict might be the consequence of economic and political deprivation of groups and communities. They have to recognize that ethnic conflict, either violent or nonviolent, is often a consequence of ethnic mobilization produced by powerful elites to achieve certain aims.

The active involvement of social workers in times of ethnic conflict includes the following:

- Understanding under what conditions ethnic differences become sources of serious conflicts
- Recognizing the manifestations of everyday hatred, including everyday racism
- Understanding that ethnic conflicts have a common structure of social inequality, which is manifested in variety of ways (e.g., using ethnic conflict in order to gain the access to the economic goods and natural resources of the country; as war, genocide, mass rape, pathologization and forced sterilization, denial of social and political rights, memory restrictions)
- Understanding the everyday life experiences of people from their own perspective
- Becoming advocates for the devalued and discriminated-against ethnic groups and offering advocacy services to help people access social and political rights
- Ensuring the opportunity for memory work after a violent conflict in cases when this can be seen as empowerment
- Responding to suffering in culturally appropriate ways

- Getting involved in political work to change oppressive environments, including joining grassroots campaigns
- Getting involved in peace building in the aftermath of violent conflicts.

Since the experiences of ethnic conflict differ according to gender, class, age, and so on, social workers have to understand and internalize many perspectives to work with communities and individuals, including antioppressive practice (Dominelli, 2002), memory work (Feldman, 1991; Kabeera & Sewpaul, 2008; Zaviršek, 2008), advocacy work (Ramon, 2008), and practice of peace building and shared citizenship (Rommelspacher, 1995; Seifert, 2004; Moshe, 2001).

NOTE

1. Michel Foucault 's (1990 [orig. 1976]) notion of *biopower* is based on his analysis of the European period of modernity, when, in comparison with the classical period, the politics of governance started to use new strategies in the realms of medicine, hygiene, and population policy in order to control people. The strategies to control a person's body became more invisible due to the ideology of health, hygiene, and modern life and have covered their homogenizing and controlling effects.

REFERENCES

Amnesty International (2010). Mass Rapes in Walikale. Still a Need for Protection and Justice in Eastern Congo. Amnesty International Publications. www.amnesty.org.

Brubaker, R. (2004). *Ethnicity without groups*. Cambridge, MA: Harvard University Press.

Dominelli, L. (2002). *Anti-oppressive social work theory and practice*. Basingstoke and New York: Palgrave Macmillan.

Essed, P. (1991). *Understanding everyday racism: An interdisciplinary theory*. Newbury Park: Sage.

European Roma Rights Center (ERRC). (2008). Support the Campaign of Romani Survivors of Coerced Sterilisation for Apologies and Compensation. http://www.errc.org/cikk.php?cikk=2963 (accessed March 5, 2011).

Fein, H. (2002). Genocide: A sociological perspective. In A. L. Hinton (Ed.), *Genocide: An anthropological reader* (pp. 74–90). Malden, MA: Blackwell.

Feldman, A. (1991). *Formations of violence: The narrative of the body and political terror in Northern Ireland*. Chicago and London: University of Chicago Press.

Fenton, S. (2004). Beyond ethnicity: The global comparative analysis of ethnic conflict. *International Journal of Comparative Sociology, 45*(3-4), 179–194.

Foucault, M. (1990 [orig. 1976]). *History of sexuality* (Vol. 1). London: Penguin.

Gilley, B. (2004). Against the concept of ethnic conflict. *Third World Quarterly, 25*(6), 1155–1166.

Hintjens, H. (2008). Post-genocide identity politics in Rwanda. *Ethnicities, 8*(1), 5–41.

Kabeera, B., & Sewpaul, V. (2008). Genocide and its aftermath: The case of Rwanda. *International Social Work, 51*(3), 324–336.

Križnar, T., & Weiss, M. (2008). *Dar fur: War for Water* [Documentary film]. www.darfurwarforwater.com/darfur-war-for-water/ang/synopsis.html (accessed April 28, 2009).

Moshe, M. (2001). Peace building: A conceptual framework. *International Social Welfare, 10*, 14–26.

Proctor, R. N. (1992). Nazi doctors, racial medicine, and human experimentation. In G. J. Annas & M. Grodin (Eds.), *The Nazi doctors and the Nuremberg Code* (pp. 17–32). Oxford/New York: Oxford University Press.

Ramon, S. (Ed.). (2008). *Social work in the context of political conflict*. Birmingham: Venture Press.

Reynolds, J. (1998). Peru forced sterilisation allegations. BBC News. http://news.bbc.co.uk/2/hi/americas/239406.stm (accessed April 23, 2009).

Rommelspacher, B. (1995). *Dominanzkultur. Texte zu Fremdheit und Macht*. Berlin: Orlanda.

Secret sterilisation—Peru [Motion picture]. (1999). www.youtube.com/watch?v=iv9GtGl4Odk (accessed April 23, 2009).

Seifert, R. (Ed.). (2004). *Soziale Arbeit und Kriegerische Konflikte*. Münster: Lit Verlag.

Toft, M. D. (2003). *The geography of ethnic violence*. Princeton and Oxford: Princeton University Press.

Urh, Š. (2008). The development of an ethnically sensitive approach in social work in Slovenia. *European Journal of Social Work, 11*(2), 117–129.

Zaviršek, D. (2008). Social work as memory work in times of political conflict. In S. Ramon (Ed.), *Social work in the context of political conflict* (pp. 147–167). Birmingham: Venture Press.

Zaviršek, D. (2007). Pathologised ethnicities and meaningful internationalism: About the book and the network. In D. Zaviršek, J. Zorn, L. Rihter, & D. S. Žnidarec (Eds.), (2007), *Ethnicity in Eastern Europe: A challenge for social work education* (pp. 7–17). Ljubljana: Faculty of Social Work.

Zorn, J. (2009). A case for Slovene nationalism: Initial citizenship rules and the erasure. *Nations and Nationalism, 15*(29), 280–298.

Zorn, J. (2005). Ethnic citizenship in the Slovenian state. *Citizenship Studies, 9*(2), 135–152.

Žarkov, D. (2007). *The Body of War*. Duke Univ. Press, Durham and London.

HIV/AIDS: The Global Pandemic

HUGO KAMYA

The nature and extent of the HIV/AIDS global pandemic has changed considerably over the past thirty years. This chapter examines the problem of HIV/AIDS worldwide, paying special attention to sub-Saharan Africa. The chapter begins with an overview to help contextualize this problem with populations that have been seriously affected. Key controversies as well as their implications for practitioners, researchers, educators, activists, and policy makers are discussed.

Although the prevalence rate of infection has leveled, over 33 million people are still living with HIV worldwide (UNAIDS, 2009). An estimated 430,000 children under the age of fifteen became infected with HIV in 2008. Though the number of new infections among children has been declining since 2000 due to the spread of programs to prevent mother-to-child transmission, the number of children younger than fifteen years living with HIV increased from 1.6 million in 2001 to 2.1 million in 2008. Over 90% of these children live in sub-Saharan Africa (UNAIDS, 2009).

The Centers for Disease Control and Prevention (CDC) reported that at the end of 2003, an estimated 1.2 million people in the United States were living with HIV/AIDS. The CDC also estimates that over 56,000 new infections occurred in the United States in 2006. In that year, almost three-quarters of HIV/AIDS diagnoses among adolescents and adults were males; the highest proportion was among men who have sex with men (MSM), followed by persons infected through high-risk heterosexual contact. African Americans continue to be disproportionately affected. Almost half of those diagnosed with HIV/AIDS in the United States have been African Americans, with Whites making up about 30% and Hispanics about 18% (CDC, 2009).

EPIDEMIOLOGICAL OVERVIEW

There are great differences in the global distribution of HIV. Sub-Saharan Africa carries the greatest numbers, although there are greater population concentrations in South and Southeast Asia. The methods of transmission vary from region to region. They include male-to-male transmission, intravenous drug use, male-to-female transmission, perinatal transmission, transmission from female sexual worker to male client, and in some cases infection from blood products. These modes of transmission are now examined in the context of low, concentrated, and generalized epidemics.

Piot (1994) offers several probable variables that influence the spread of HIV. They include virological parameters such as infectivity and immunodeficiency; genital factors such as the presence of sexually transmitted infections (STIs), lack of male circumcision, and use of vaginal products; sexual behavior such as rate of partner change, type of sexual intercourse, size of contact with core groups, and condom use; demographic variables such as migration patterns; and economic and political factors such as poverty, war, social conflicts, health-care systems, and response to epidemics.

These factors operate differently for different groups. They can be categorized as individual, societal, infrastructural, and structural factors. Individual factors are those that directly affect the patient and that the patient has some control in changing. Societal factors are related to norms that encourage high-risk behavior. Infrastructural factors directly or indirectly facilitate the spread of HIV, and the individual has little or no control over them. Structural factors relate to developmental factors over which both the individual and the health system have little control (Cohen & Tussell, 1996). All these factors contribute to the prevalence rates in the various regions of the world. Economic disparities among the regions also contribute greatly to the differences.

A recent Ugandan study found that the following risk factors were associated with recent HIV infection: female gender; current marital status of widowed or divorced as compared with never married; living in north central Uganda; having at least two sex partners in last year; herpes type 2, report of STI in last year; being an uncircumcised man; and, among married participants, having partners outside marriage and never using condoms (Mermin et al., 2008). These factors strongly relate to differences found in high-prevalence versus low-prevalence areas for HIV.

There have been several responses to the HIV/AIDS epidemic. These responses have varied from region to region. Africa's response to the problem presents an important lens to consider. Because sub-Saharan Africa has one of the highest rates of HIV/AIDS cases, the next section will examine the case of Africa.

HIV/AIDS IN SUB-SAHARAN AFRICA: EPIDEMIC AND RESPONSE

Over the last few decades HIV/AIDS has ravaged Africa. Recent reports indicate that there are over 30 million people living with HIV/AIDS in sub-Saharan Africa, 3.5 million newly infected people, and 2.5 million dead from the disease. Of these 30 million, more than 4 million are suffering from an advanced stage of AIDS and are in need of antiretroviral treatment, yet less than 10% are receiving the needed medication. In addition, the epidemic has produced an overwhelming number of orphans. Though major successes are being reported, the statistics are overwhelming.

Women are disproportionately affected by HIV/AIDS. For example, 58% percent of HIV-positive people in sub-Saharan Africa are women and girls, and 10% of females aged fifteen to twenty-four in Kampala (Uganda's capital) are HIV positive versus 2.3% of males in the same age group. The statistics are daunting, yet it is likely that there is still a lot of underreporting, which is important for social workers to consider.

African nations have responded in disparate ways to the HIV/AIDS epidemic. Of these responses, Uganda's efforts have had the most dramatic results. Uganda was one of the first countries to face its epidemic and develop programs; social workers also became involved fairly early in the efforts (Ankrah, 1992). Uganda's multipronged program, which advocates abstinence, marital fidelity, and condoms, is credited with this success. Since the initiation of the ABC (Abstinence, Be faithful, and Condoms) approach, the percentage of infected people in Uganda declined from approximately 30% in the early 1990s to 6% in 2004 (Weisberg, 2005).

Writing about the ABC approach to HIV/AIDS, Weisberg (2005) points out that although the program has decreased overall HIV infection in Uganda, it has several limitations and targets male behaviors while failing to protect women, especially married women. One limitation of the ABC program is that it does not offer enough support to young girls who are forced into prostitution for survival. The ABC program also focuses on prevention and does not provide treatment options or resources for those who are already infected with HIV. Weisberg has argued that the decline in the HIV population is more related to the deaths that have occurred than to the effectiveness of the ABC approach. Due to the focus on abstinence, many young girls are getting married earlier and are increasing their chances of HIV infection because they are marrying older males who are already infected. In some cases, these older males have more than one partner.

Cultural practices further push women into desperate situations. Due to the large age differences between wives and husbands, Ugandan women are outliving their husbands. In Uganda, when a man dies, his extended family usually collects all of his assets, taking away the woman's property and sometimes her children. These young widows are often left with no shelter and their children are left to take care of themselves (Weisberg, 2005). Risk factors for women are discussed further in the next section.

Gender-Related Risk Factors

Biological Vulnerability

Women are more susceptible to infection because "women have larger mucosal surface area exposed to abrasions during sex, and semen has a higher concentration of HIV/AIDS than vaginal fluid" (World Health Organization [WHO], 2004, p. 3). The link between violence and HIV/AIDS can also be described through biological factors. Women are biologically at a greater risk for contracting HIV during a violent encounter of force because of the exposure to blood through vaginal lacerations or abrasions. This puts girls and young women at a higher risk of transmission because their genital tracts are more likely to tear during sex (WHO, 2004). In some cases, especially where the practice of female genital cutting is performed, women are exposed to greater incidences of trauma and tearing during sex and childbirth.

Mother-to-Child Transmission

Among infected women, nearly 80% of women are of childbearing age (Craft, Delaney, Bautista, & Serovich, 2007). Mother-to-child transmission refers to an HIV-positive woman passing the HIV virus to her baby, the main mode of HIV infection among children in developing countries. Researchers have confirmed three modes of vertical transmission: in utero (during pregnancy), intrapartum (during delivery), and postpartum (after birth through breast-feeding). Vertical transmission accounts for 90% of new infections worldwide in infants and children, a group that represents over four million deaths worldwide since the beginning of the epidemic (Vignarajah, 2004).

Sociocultural Vulnerability

There is a series of sociocultural issues that affects many groups all over the world. Biological vulnerabilities are exacerbated by sociocultural challenges, and these challenges complicate the lives of those who are at risk for contracting HIV/AIDS. For women, they include economic dependency, rape, domestic violence, and lack of power on several levels. Social work at the international level needs to pay attention to these concerns and make a commitment to international human rights.

Economic Dependency

Many women are caught in a cycle of economic dependency on men who are not equal partners in the relationship. In many societies, women lack property rights and often lose property when their husbands die. The practice of polygamy, in which men marry more than one woman, often leaves women destitute because there are fewer resources to be divided among more family members. The same practice also exposes women to greater risk of infection. Since women lack parental rights, many children are driven into poverty and destitution.

Negotiation of Sexual Relations

Most women in sub-Saharan Africa and many other societies do not have any rights to negotiate safe sexual relationships with men, particularly in marriage. Refusal to engage in sex or urging safer sex practices often results in acts of violence against women perpetrated by men who hold suspicions about women and their behavior. The assumption in the culture is that men are naturally promiscuous and it is culturally appropriate for them to have extramarital partners while the women remain monogamous. It is expected that women remain faithful to their husbands and accept or tolerate their infidelities. Women, on the other hand, can be accused of infidelity and cast out of their families. They live with shame and social stigma that further alienate them. Even more deplorable is the lack of access to social services either

because they are not available or because women lack information about their choices. Indeed, "violence against women is one of the most visible consequences of social, political, legal and cultural inequalities" (Gysels, Pool, & Nnalusiba, 2002) and is an important element of risk for HIV. See Chapter 40 for more on violence against women.

Rape

Rape is the most common act of violence against women in wartime (Turshen, 2000). It is also a major risk for the contraction of HIV. In war zones such as northern Uganda and Congo, rape is an act of political violence that has exposed victims to trauma and all the risks associated with HIV. Communities often reject women who have been raped, and victims may be unable to access services that could help them address the potential risks of HIV for fear of discrimination. Research has indicated that in Uganda, women are afraid to ask for money or permission from their husbands to visit HIV/AIDS facilities to inquire about prevention or testing (WHO, 2004).

THE EFFECTS OF HIV/AIDS ON CHILDREN, INCLUDING ORPHANS

The status of children in Africa is inextricably linked with the plight of women, who are usually the key child-care providers. Because HIV/AIDS has had devastating results for women, children have similarly been affected. It is a serious threat to children's well-being and safety.

The disease has left many children orphaned. Over five million children have been orphaned or made vulnerable. In some countries like Uganda, war and hunger have exacerbated the problem. Not only has HIV increased the number of orphans in sub-Saharan countries, but many of them are themselves infected and dying. A child's vulnerability begins to increase long before the HIV-infected parent dies. In the face of HIV/AIDS, children are exposed to poverty, pressure to drop out of school, reduced access to health care, deteriorating housing, and worsening material conditions as parents struggle to make ends meet. Psychosocial distress includes anxiety, loss of parental love and nurturing, depression, grief, and the dispersal of siblings among relatives (Martin, 2006). In some cases, children are driven into adult responsibilities for which they are not prepared.

When women are not able to provide for their children, the children may be dispersed among relatives or several households without opportunities for collective grieving. Orphans with HIV have often lost both parents and some of their siblings as well. Even when these children have one living parent, that parent may be too sick to provide guidance and care. Additionally, surviving family members may be too impoverished to provide care. Relatives who emerge as caregivers may themselves be too burdened physically and fiscally.

The plight of orphaned children is immense. Girls are often married off at a young age or seek out older men for economic security. In the absence of such security, they sometimes end up on the street, where social support is reduced and psychosocial distress intensifies. Even for children in less extreme circumstances, psychosocial problems relating to loss and bereavement may affect behavior and development. Stigma associated with AIDS frequently compounds their emotional distress and vulnerability.

Many of these children are deprived of education because there is no one to fund it, and they may also be forced into labor, especially hazardous labor, early in life. In war-ravaged areas, being an unprotected orphan can be especially dangerous; these children often are kidnapped and forced into service as soldiers. Sometimes they are left to fend for themselves. These children are more likely to be heads of households (raising other children) or separated from their siblings and divided among relatives, becoming vulnerable to economic and sexual exploitation.

While most developed nations wrestle with issues of medication and human rights, most poor nations struggle with issues of survival. In many developing countries, HIV/AIDS has resulted in intense financial and psychosocial effects on caregiving. It has disrupted the usual trajectory of family development. Grandparents and other elderly caretakers often assume the responsibilities that would otherwise be fulfilled by their frail and dying children. These aging caretakers often have few resources themselves to manage the stress and demands that HIV puts on the whole family system. All these issues result in serious consequences for children and their caregivers (Cluver & Gardner, 2007; Jacobs & Kane, 2010; Kamya & Poindexter, 2009). African social workers and international aid organizations are working to develop appropriate and feasible programs of substitute care and supportive services for orphans.

OTHER POPULATIONS AT RISK

Other populations affected by HIV/AIDS include drug users, men who have sex with men, sex workers,

and the incarcerated, to name a few. Recent studies show high infection levels among members of these groups in parts of the world. Data are showing new infections among men who have sex with men and users of intravenous drugs in a number of high-income countries. Infections among men who have sex with men are increasing sharply in parts of Asia (UNAIDS, 2008). Men who have sex with men made up more than two-thirds (68%) of all men living with HIV in the United States in 2005, even though only about 5% to 7% of men in the United States reported having sex with other men (CDC, 2009).

Among incarcerated populations, HIV infection appears to be on the rise worldwide. No worldwide figures are available, but some studies have shown that HIV prevalence rates are higher among the incarcerated than the nonincarcerated. In one such study in Jamaica, Andrinopoulos (2008) found that the HIV prevalence rate of 3.3% is higher than the rate in the nonincarcerated population.

Not many studies have examined the sexual behavior of older adults; however, HIV/AIDS seems to be rapidly increasing in this population. Recent studies have focused on populations in developed countries (Lovejoy et al., 2008). These studies have also focused mostly on white populations, ignoring the experiences of persons of color. International efforts that target this population must explore how HIV/AIDS affects the elderly and persons of color.

PROGRAMS AND POLICIES FOR PREVENTION AND TREATMENT

Prevention

The HIV/AIDS epidemic and its impact on all levels of society compels practitioners to devise and enact programs and policies to prevent the spread of the disease. Prevention, behavior change, and access to treatment are crucial, but these efforts are hindered by a number of issues. In sub-Saharan Africa, women often lack power in negotiating sexual relationships with male partners. Any program or intervention needs to take into account the role and position of women in society. Such programs must work to promote condom usage and female protection in the negotiation of sex with male partners.

The experience of women in sub-Saharan African is one measure of the problem of HIV/AIDS in the international arena. In China, too, studies have found that traditional gender norms have played a key role for HIV-infected women in their efforts to tackle this disease and to make sense of their daily lives. Infection has created a conflict between women's intentions to fulfill their conception of womanhood and a decreased ability to do so, which, in turn, has adversely affected their self-perceptions and well-being (Zhou, 2008).

Prevention and intervention are hindered by lack of political will and leadership. Many governments have to decide whether to fund health care, education, and social services or build infrastructure. Some countries are embroiled in complex wars that further strain their meager resources. Social, cultural, and human capital often undergo major challenges that are hard for governments to address in the face of the HIV/AIDS epidemic. In some cases, lack of will and leadership from diverse sectors, as well as poor management of resources, has exacerbated the problems that surround HIV/AIDS. Some religious leaders have condemned the use of condoms and preach vehemently against prevention methods that have been proven to work, further impeding progress against the spread of disease.

Addressing Stigma

Stigma regarding HIV/AIDS has continued to persist since the early days of the disease, constituting one of the largest barriers to coping with the epidemic (UNAIDS, 2008). Education and development of policies to reduce stigma are urgently needed. The HIV/AIDS epidemic poses a major trauma to communities, often resulting in feelings of rejection and isolation. Stigma comes in perceived, internalized, enacted, symbolic, and instrumental forms. *Perceived stigma* refers to people living with HIV/AIDS (PLWHA) and their awareness of negative societal attitudes, reduced opportunity, and negative social identity (Berger, Ferrans, & Lashley, 2001). *Internalized stigma* includes negative beliefs, views, and feelings toward HIV/AIDS and oneself (Lee, Kochman, & Sikkema, 2002). *Enacted stigma* encompasses acts of discrimination toward people with HIV/AIDS, such as violence and exclusion (Herek, Capitanio, & Widaman, 2002; Nyblade, 2006). *Symbolic stigma* refers to othering, blaming, and shaming of groups associated with HIV/AIDS (Deacon, 2006; Herek & Capitanio, 1999). *Instrumental stigma* has been described as measures taken to protect oneself and one's health (Herek et al., 2002).

The complexity of defining HIV-related stigma stems in part from its interaction with cross-cultural differences, structural inequalities, discrimination by health-care professionals, and social processes that are not always focused on the individual (Campbell & Deacon, 2006; Parker & Aggleton, 2003). Stigma may also be compounded by negative societal attitudes toward the route of infection (e.g., sex work, drug use) and demographic characteristics (e.g., gender, ethnicity) (Herek & Capitanio, 1999; Reidpath & Chan, 2005).

Stigma and discrimination are major barriers to HIV prevention. In many cultural groups, the problem of cultural silence is prevalent. Cultural silence is linked to denial and is often a risk factor that increases vulnerability, while the breaching of cultural silence serves as a protective factor that can enhance resilience among people. Indeed, social meanings attached to the epidemic often silence the people and communities that are affected and make them invisible. Efforts to address HIV/AIDS on the international scene must seriously consider the impact of stigma and discrimination in various communities. Social workers can play useful roles in direct outreach and in advocacy campaigns to reduce stigma.

Access to Treatment

Availability and delivery of antiretroviral drugs (ARVs) pose serious concerns. Access to ARVs continues to be a major problem, especially in developing countries. In some parts of the world, such as Africa, the lack of effective delivery systems and infrastructure continues to pose a threat to the administration of ARVs. The prohibitive cost of administering these drugs must also be reckoned with, even with global attempts to provide them at minimal costs. While availability has been an issue in developing countries, optimism about treatment has surfaced a return to risky sexual practices among some groups, especially where ARVs are readily available and affordable. It is therefore important to enact policies and programs that continue to address such behaviors and attitudes. Another important issue to note is the continued integration of traditional health practices with the promise of ARVs.

Programs that work toward the reduction of mother-to-child transmission are a necessity. Preventing vertical transmission is a critical piece in preventing the spread of the virus, especially since there is currently no cure for the disease. A threefold strategy is needed to prevent babies from acquiring HIV from their infected mothers: (1) preventing HIV infection among prospective parents, (2) avoiding unwanted pregnancies among HIV-positive women, and (3) preventing the transmission of the virus from HIV-positive mothers to their infants during pregnancy, labor, delivery, and breast-feeding—now possible through the use of ARVs (Kanabus & Noble, 2005). Women of reproductive age who live with HIV face major challenges in making decisions related to pregnancy. In some countries in Africa, where it is important to have children or a progeny, these decisions create more confusion for women. Social workers can play a major role in helping women make informed decisions and facilitating access to medical and social services.

MOVING FORWARD

Prevention and treatment programs and policies must also attend to the broader societal work on gender equity and violence prevention. The link between violence and HIV risk is well documented (Rountree & Mulraney, 2010). Gender inequality and imbalance are at the root of the problems facing women and society at large. The power imbalance at many levels of society puts women at serious disadvantages not only for warding off HIV/AIDS but also for accessing services to address HIV/AIDS in their lives and providing for their children. Any conclusive strategy must therefore target gender inequality and listen to women's concerns with an ear that not only comforts them in their plight but challenges them to seek healthier ways of relating to the issues that affect their lives.

Because the issues that affect HIV/AIDS are also broader public-health issues, any intervention must take into account entire communities and design intervention programs that promote wellness, prevent disease, and thereby increase the quality and prolongation of life. It is a daunting task, and public-health practice must walk a tight path as it designs culturally competent intervention programs at intrapersonal, interpersonal, and community levels. In practice, these three levels must be seen as intertwined and outcomes of interventions at each stage as having direct, indirect, and reciprocal effects on each other. It is important to increase awareness of both personal and community responsibility for health.

To reverse the HIV/AIDS epidemic, prevention strategies need to be designed through community organization and community building. In this process, community groups are engaged in identifying common problems or goals, mobilizing resources, and designing and implementing strategies for reaching the goals using culturally relevant approaches.

Any effort that targets women must also focus on men, especially in African societies. Men and women need to be educated on domestic violence and its effects on society. Programs that target gender attitudes and norms should be stressed, with a special focus on preparing young males for future relations with women. Such a focus should also attend to issues of shame attached to rape and violence as well as behavior-change communication strategies. Ultimately, everyone must be encouraged to examine the damaging effects of silence on the overall health of the community today and in the future. More research and education programs are needed in order to stop violence, improve health, reduce gender equality, and empower women.

CONCLUSION

For best outcomes, any approach must not only address factors that directly affect societal norms, it must also examine both the infrastructural factors that directly or indirectly facilitate the spread of HIV and the structural factors related to developmental issues over which the individual and the health system have little control. The focus should be a comprehensive model that targets the entire health and social system. Any efforts on the international scene must examine what happens on the local scene, noting how the global and the local are intricately intertwined.

REFERENCES

Andrinopoulos, K. M. (2008). Examining HIV/AIDS within the context of incarceration in Jamaica. *Dissertation Abstracts International, Section B: The Sciences and Engineering, 69*(4-B).

Ankrah, E. M. (1992). AIDS in Uganda: Initial social work responses. *Journal of Social Development in Africa, 7*(2), 53–61.

Berger, B. E., Ferrans, C. E., & Lashley, F. R. (2001). Measuring stigma in people with HIV: Psychometric assessment of the HIV Stigma Scale. *Research in Nursing & Health, 24*(6), 518–529.

Campbell, C., & Deacon, H. (2006). Unravelling the contexts of stigma: From internalization to resistance to change. *Journal of Community & Applied Social Psychology, Special Issue: Understanding and Challenging Stigma, 16*(6), 411–417.

Centers for Disease Control and Prevention (CDC). (2009. Basic statistics [Data file]. Retrieved from http://www.cdc.gov/hiv/topics/surveillance/basic.htm.

Cluver, L., & Gardner, F. (2007). The mental health of children orphaned by AIDS: A review of international and southern African research. *Journal of Child and Adolescent Mental Health, 19*(1), 1–17.

Cohen, B., & Tussell, J. (Eds.). (1996). *Preventing and mitigating AIDS in sub-Saharan Africa.* Washington, DC: National Academy Press.

Craft, S. M., Delaney, R. O., Bautista, D. T., & Serovich, J. M. (2007). Pregnancy decisions among women with HIV. *AIDS and Behavior, 11*(6), 927–935.

Deacon, H. (2006). Towards a sustainable theory of health-related stigma: Lessons from the HIV/AIDS literature. *Journal of Community & Applied Social Psychology, Special Issue: Understanding and Challenging Stigma, 16*(6), 418–425.

Gysels, M., Pool, R., & Nnalusiba, B. (2002). Women who sell sex in Ugandan trading town: Life histories, survival strategies and risk. *Social Sciences & Medicine, 54,* 179–192.

Herek, G. M., & Capitanio, J. P. (1999). AIDS stigma and sexual prejudice. *American Behavioral Scientist, 42*(7), 1130–1147.

Herek, G. M., Capitanio, J. P. & Widaman, K. F. (2002). HIV-related stigma and knowledge in the United States: Prevalence and trends, 1991–1999. *American Journal of Public Health, 92*(3), 371–377.

Jacobs, R. J., & Kane, M. N. (2010). HIV-related stigma in midlife and older women. *Social Work in Health Care, 49*(1), 68–89.

Kamya, H., & Poindexter, C. (2009). Mama Jaja: The stresses and strengths of HIV-affected Ugandan grandmothers. *Social Work in Public Health, 24,* 4–21.

Kanabus, A., & Noble, R. (2005). Preventing mother-to-child transmission of HIV. Retrieved on April 30, 2005, from www.aegis.com/news/ips/2004/IP040730.

Lee, R. S., Kochman, A., & Sikkema, K. J. (2002). Internalized stigma among people living with HIV-AIDS. *AIDS and Behavior, 6*(4), 309–319.

Lovejoy, T. I., Heckman, T. G., Sikkema, K. J., Hansen, N. B., Kochman, A., Suhr, J. A., Garske, J. P., & Johnson, C. J. (2008). Patterns and correlates of sexual activity and condom use behavior in persons 50-plus years of age living with HIV/AIDS. *AIDS and Behavior, 12*(6), 943–956.

Martin, R. (2006) Children's perspectives: Roles, responsibilities and burdens in home-based care. *Journal of Social Development in Africa, 21*(1), 106–129.

Mermin, J., Musinguzi, J., Opio, A., Kirungi, W., Ekwaru, J. P., Hladik, W., Kaharuza, F., Powning, R., & Bunnell, R. (2008). Risk factors for recent HIV infection in Uganda. *Journal of the American Medical Association, 300*(5): 540–549.

Nyblade, L. C. (2006). Measuring HIV stigma: Existing knowledge and gaps. *Psychology, Health & Medicine, Special Issue: Perspectives on Health-Related Stigma, 11*(3), 335–345.

Parker, R., & Aggleton, P. (2003). HIV- and AIDS-related stigma and discrimination: A conceptual framework and implications for action. *Social Sciences & Medicine, 57*(1), 13–24.

Piot, P. (1994). Differences between African and western patterns of heterosexual transmission. In A. Nicolai (Ed.), *HIV epidemiology: Models and methods* (pp. 77–82). New York: Raven Press.

Reidpath, D. D., & Chan, K. Y. (2005). HIV/AIDS discrimination in the Asia Pacific (editorial). *AIDS Care, Special Issue: Structural and Institutional Forms of HIV Discrimination: An Analysis from the Asia Pacific, 17*(2), S115–S116.

Rountree, M. A., & Mulraney, M. (2010). HIV/AIDS risk reduction intervention for women who have experienced intimate partner violence. *Clinical Social Work Journal, 38,* 207–216.

Turshen, M. (2000). The political economy of violence against women during armed conflict in Uganda. *New School for Social Research, 67*(3), 803–815.

UNAIDS: The Joint United Nations Programme on HIV/AIDS [UNAIDS]. (2008). HIV and men who have sex with men in Asia and the Pacific. [Data file]. Retrieved from http://www.unaids.org.

UNAIDS. The Joint United Nations Programme on HIV/AIDS [UNAIDS]. (2009). AIDS epidemic update 2009. Retrieved from http://www.unaids.org.

Vignarajah, K. (2004) Mother-to-child transmission of HIV/AIDS in Uganda. *Journal of Children & Poverty, 10,* 23–35.

Weisberg, J. (2005, January/February). ABCs of AIDS prevention. *Dollars & Sense,* 10–18.

World Health Organization (WHO). (2004). Violence against women and HIV/AIDS: Critical intersections intimate partner violence and HIV/AIDS. *Global Coalition on Women and AIDS, 1,* 1–9.

Zhou, Y. R. (2008). Endangered womanhood: Women's experiences with HIV/AIDS in China. *Qualitative Health Research, 18*(8): 1115–1126.

Human Trafficking

JINI L. ROBY

What is human trafficking? Simply stated, human trafficking, or trafficking in persons (TIP), is the buying, selling, and exploiting of human beings for profit. It is a modern-day form of slavery in which human beings are treated as properties or commodities (Bales, 2005). Human trafficking generally falls into two major categories: labor exploitation and sexual exploitation. Victims can be found in a wide range of work environments, including the commercial sex market, domestic servitude, sweatshops, farms and orchards, construction, factories, bars, restaurants, and many other arenas. In this chapter, we explore the incidence and global flow of people who are caught up in trafficking, contributing factors at various levels, current policy and practice efforts, and implications for social workers around the world.

Trafficking in persons can be viewed from many overlapping theoretical perspectives (Kyle & Koslowski, 2001), including power disparity based on gender and class (Sullivan, 2003), human rights issues (Salt, 2002), economic market forces of supply and demand (Raymond, 2004), and a phenomenon deeply embedded in cultural forces. The ecological model used by social work and its focus on vulnerable populations provides a useful and holistic vehicle for understanding and responding to this social phenomenon (e.g., George, 2002). And because social workers are in direct contact with victims, it is important that they have a basic but substantive understanding of trafficking in order to identify and assist the victims.

The definition of trafficking most universally agreed upon is contained in the Protocol to Prevent, Suppress and Punish Trafficking in Persons, especially Women and Children (hereafter *the Palermo Protocol*), which supplements the United Nations Convention against Transnational Crime (www.unodc.org/pdf/crime/a_res_55/res5525e.pdf):

> "Trafficking in persons" shall mean the recruitment, transportation, transfer, harbouring or receipt of persons, by means of the threat or use of force or other forms of coercion, of abduction, of fraud, of deception, of the abuse of power or of a position of vulnerability or of the giving or receiving of payments or benefits to achieve the consent of a person having control over another person, for the purpose of exploitation. Exploitation shall include, at a minimum, the exploitation of the prostitution of others or other forms of sexual exploitation, forced labour or services, slavery or practices similar to slavery, servitude or the removal of organs.

This definition articulates a list of the activities that constitute trafficking, the methods used, and minimum forms of exploitation to be included. As of August 25, 2010, 147 nations had signed the Palermo Protocol, and 157 countries had become parties to this instrument (United Nations Treaty Collection, 2010).

INCIDENCE AND FLOW OF TRAFFICKING IN PERSONS

Estimates of people involved in human trafficking vary from 4 to 27 million, and of those, 800,000 are believed to be trafficked across national borders (US Department of State, 2008). However, there is no accurate estimate of victims, partly due to the diversity of what is counted as trafficking. For example, the US government estimated that 50,000 victims were brought into its territory in 2000 but cites "thousands of men and women" in the introduction to its 2008 report. In addition, its definition of human trafficking covers only sexual and labor exploitation, excluding the other categories listed in the Palermo Protocol (US Department of State, 2008).

It is also unclear how many victims are involved in forced sexual exploitation compared with those involved in forced labor exploitation. Discussions of human trafficking initially focused on sex trafficking, but recently the focus has been shifting to other forms such as involuntary servitude. According to the International Labour Organization (ILO), there are 12.3 million people in forced labor around the world. Although sex trafficking has received the bulk of public attention lately, the ILO estimates that for every person being sexually exploited, there are nine victims who are exploited for other forms of forced labor (US Department of State, 2010). In contrast, according to the *Global Report on Trafficking in Persons* released by the United Nations Office on Drugs and Crime (UNODC, 2009a), which compiled data from 155 countries, 79% of victims are exploited in the sex market, followed by 18% exploited in other labor. These vastly different estimates may reflect statistical biases, but everyone seems to agree that human trafficking is becoming increasingly feminized, including those victimized by exploitive domestic work under conditions of fraud, coercion, or force. Additionally, this crime is perpetrated by a higher percentage of women compared with crimes in general.

Some people migrate voluntarily and fall prey to trafficking, or they may be moved through legal recruitment. Consider, for example, the victims involved in the following scenario:

> A contract labor agency in [a developing country] recently advertised work at a garment factory in [a developed country]. The ad promised a three-year contract, $125 per month, eight-hour workdays, six days of work a week, paid overtime, free accommodation, free medical care, free food, and no advance fees. Instead, upon arrival, workers (who were obliged to pay exorbitant advance fees) had passports confiscated, were confined in miserable conditions, and prevented from leaving the factory. Months passed without pay, food was inadequate, and sick workers were tortured. Because most workers had borrowed money at inflated interest rates to get the contracts, they were obliged, through debt, to stay.
> —(US Department of State, *2006*, p. 7).

Victims and perpetrators often share the same nationality, and most trafficking occurs within national boundaries (UNODC, 2009a). Victims are recruited either by deception or against their will and placed into exploitation within their own city or across provincial, national, or continental borders. Victims from East Asia, the largest source region, are found in more than twenty countries in all regions of the world. Europe is the destination of the widest range of source countries. However, victims are found in, and originate from, every continent (UNODC, 2009b).

WHAT CONTRIBUTES TO HUMAN TRAFFICKING?

The ecological perspective calls for information on many levels and from multiple dimensions, including how culture, laws and policies, economic conditions, and social mores interact. It is important to recognize that factors *correlated* with human trafficking are not necessarily the *causes* of human trafficking. For example, extreme poverty is often associated with heightened risk of trafficking; however, relatively few poor families succumb to human trafficking, and many participate because they do not understand or suspect trafficking.

Women and girls are mostly involved in sexual exploitation whereas men and boys are mostly involved in labor exploitation, but the two are not mutually exclusive. One of the most invisible groups of trafficked victims is child domestics throughout the world, such as the restavek children of Haiti (Pan American Development Foundation, 2009). Female child domestics suffer a high degree of sexual abuse while their labor is also exploited. Orphaned and unaccompanied children are at increased risk of falling into commercial sex, armed conflict, the drug trade, or other harmful forms of labor (Smart, 2003). Children of families struggling with single parenthood, chronic illness, or substance abuse are also at greater risk. In addition, natural disasters and conflicts exacerbate the risk of trafficking ("Human trafficking expert warns," 2008).

Cultural norms about gender, ethnic minorities, and impoverishment influence attitudes and decisions. For example, in some cultures daughters are expected to support their parents, yet girls and young women lack access to education and employment opportunities to fulfill this cultural mandate. One study found that 60% of all girls from the hill tribes in Thailand were working in brothels to help their families (Brown, 2000). In some societies racial or cultural minorities face the same denial of access to education and other opportunities.

At the national level, the lack of antitrafficking policies or the lack of political will or resources to enforce such policies poses major challenges. For example, the Cambodian government recently passed a comprehensive antitrafficking law (Law on Suppression of Human Trafficking and Sexual Exploitation, 2008); however, corruption and a severe lack of governmental resources hinder services for victims and tertiary prevention efforts. Lack of coordination among countries of origin, transit, and destination also hinders prevention.

INTERVENTIONS: WHAT IS BEING DONE ABOUT HUMAN TRAFFICKING?

Many countries have passed legislation to address human trafficking. By late 2008, 63% of the 155 countries included in the *Global Report on Trafficking in Persons* had passed legislation covering at least the two major aspects of human trafficking (sexual exploitation and forced labor), compared with only 35% in 2003 when the Palermo Protocol went into force (UNODC, 2009a). But laws are only as effective as they are enforced, and many of the countries with the worst trafficking problems have difficulty enforcing laws and protecting victims. When it comes to intercountry trafficking, many sending countries now have extraterritorial laws so that they can convict their citizens who commit an act that would be a crime if committed within their own territory, or they have entered into bilateral extradition treaties. These extraterritorial laws target the activities of sex tourists and recruiting agents abroad. Interpol, the international policing organization, has also become active on the trafficking front.

These efforts are commendable, but policies and enforcement are patchy. For example, the United States passed the landmark Trafficking Victims Protection Act of 2000 (TVPA), which has the stated aim of protecting victims, prosecuting perpetrators, and preventing trafficking. Though this policy is an improvement, critics (Roby, Turley, & Cloward, 2008) have raised concerns that victim protection is compromised by the primary goal of prosecution, which requires the victims to cooperate in the investigation, prosecution, and sentencing of the perpetrators. Another major gap in policy is that most national laws are intended to punish the victims as well as perpetrators. For example, in some countries, all prostitutes are punished regardless of their status as victims of trafficking. In other countries all illegal immigrants are punished without specific inquiry into how they came into the country or their experiences as victims of exploitation.

Recently the global community has acknowledged that the root causes of trafficking must be addressed by providing education and occupational opportunities to economically disadvantaged people in developing countries (Kempadoo, 2005). These efforts include ensuring access to school, educating communities about trafficking, providing employment and microfinancing opportunities for returning victims, advocating for gender parity in higher education, and many others focusing on the empowerment of women and other disadvantaged people.

Implications for Social Work

As previously mentioned, social work provides a holistic framework for understanding human trafficking and facilitates intervention at multiple points of entry. However, a key to effectiveness is working with other disciplines—such as law enforcement, the legislative and judicial systems, education, business, and health and social welfare entities (Van Impe, 2002)—to address human trafficking by serving in direct practice, policy advocacy, and research.

Practice Implications

A threshold challenge in assisting victims is identifying them (Hughes, 2003). Victims do not proactively seek assistance because they may not know there is help, they usually believe they cannot leave, their legal documents have been confiscated by the traffickers or don't exist, they usually do not speak the local language, and they have few, if any, social connections in the area. Even when they know they can receive help, victims who come forward risk getting deported, or worse, being imprisoned or having their families hurt back home. Social workers must be extremely sensitive to the real fears victims face when asking for information from them. Several sources are helpful in recognizing victims. The UNODC (2009a) provides a set of general indicators as well as specific indicators for child victims and victims in domestic servitude, sexual exploitation, begging and petty crime, and labor exploitation (see Table 30.1).

In terms of direct practice, social workers may provide referrals and information, case management, shelter-based work, street outreach, or therapeutic services. They need to have knowledge of a wide range of assistance, such as legal services to protect victims' immigration status and assist them in receiving victim protection services, applying for appropriate visas, and accessing social and financial assistance. In many cases the social worker may have to advocate for the creation of new services or apply existing services and resources in new ways. Direct service with clients who, in addition to the trauma of being victimized, may not speak

TABLE 30.1. GENERAL HUMAN TRAFFICKING INDICATORS

People who have been trafficked may:

- Believe that they must work against their will
- Be unable to leave their work environment
- Show signs that their movements are being controlled
- Feel that they cannot leave
- Show fear or anxiety
- Be subjected to violence or threats of violence against themselves or against their family members and loved ones
- Suffer injuries that appear to be the result of an assault
- Suffer injuries or impairments typical of certain jobs or control measures
- Suffer injuries that appear to be the result of the application of control measures
- Be distrustful of the authorities
- Be threatened with being handed over to the authorities
- Be afraid of revealing their immigration status
- Not be in possession of their passports or other travel or identity documents because those documents are being held by someone else
- Have false identity or travel documents
- Be found in or connected to a type of location likely to be used for exploiting people
- Be unfamiliar with the local language
- Not know their home or work address
- Allow others to speak for them when addressed directly
- Act as if they were instructed by someone else
- Be forced to work under certain conditions
- Be disciplined through punishment
- Be unable to negotiate working conditions
- Receive little or no payment
- Have no access to their earnings
- Work excessively long hours over long periods
- Not have any days off
- Live in poor or substandard accommodations
- Have no access to medical care
- Have limited or no social interaction
- Have limited contact with their families or with people outside of their immediate environment
- Be unable to communicate freely with others
- Be under the perception that they are bonded by debt
- Be in a situation of dependence
- Come from a place known to be a source of human trafficking
- Have had the fees for their transport to the country of destination paid for by facilitators, whom they must pay back by working or providing services in the destination
- Have acted on the basis of false promises

Source: United Nations Office on Drugs and Crime [UNODC] 2011, available at: http://www.unodc.org/pdf/HT_indicators_E_LOWRES.pdf.

the local language or are unfamiliar with the cultural context will provide additional challenges for the practitioner. Social workers also need additional training about the trauma associated with trafficking, the form of exploited labor or activities imposed on victims, the dynamics of victimization, social attitudes tending to blame the victim, and applicable statutes and policies. Further, they must examine and address their own biases and prejudices.

In addition to direct practice with victims, social workers can be involved in training other direct service providers, government officials (such as law enforcement and the judiciary), and nongovernmental organizations and community groups working with trafficked persons or vulnerable families. Social workers may also serve as victim advocates or as expert witnesses.

Policy Implications

Social workers can influence policy by raising public awareness and helping to increase demand for the creation of laws or improvement in the enforcement of existing laws. This is often done as they create or serve on multidisciplinary task forces or in working groups. Social workers can bring special knowledge to the policy table, especially where attitudes of discrimination and insensitivity toward disadvantaged populations prevail. Because social workers understand that trafficking is a manifestation of many layers of societal deficit—such as deeply embedded gender-based policy or discrimination against minority groups—they can help bring attention to those issues. And since social work values client participation, the profession should ensure that laws and policies are formed with the participation of former victims.

Research Implications

Research on human trafficking is in its early stage. Derks, Henke, and Vanna (2006), referring to research done in just one country, point out that "there is no consistency in the way the research on trafficking covers different groups, sectors and places" (p. 2). Salt (2002) believes that the enormous concern for trafficking and human smuggling is running ahead of theoretical understanding and factual evidence. The urgent need for systematic research on human trafficking has been conveyed by Antonio Maria Costa, executive director of UNODC: "I plead with social scientists . . . to generate . . . the information needed for evidence-based, antislavery policy. The crisis we face of fragmented knowledge and disjointed responses intensifies a crime that shames us all" (UNODC, 2009b, p. 3).

Social work is not significantly represented in research on trafficking, but efforts should increase in this arena. With its strong commitment to oppressed and vulnerable populations, social work is a natural fit to conduct research that can be applied in assisting victims and their families as well as in improving policy and programming.

CONCLUSION

Human trafficking is a complex social phenomenon that requires intensive efforts by multiple disciplines. Law enforcement, business, judicial, educational, and social services sectors must work together in sending, receiving, and transit countries. Social work can be involved in this effort as a major player in advocacy, policy development, direct practice, and research.

REFERENCES

Bales, K. (2005). *Understanding global slavery*. Berkeley, CA: University of California Press.

Brown, L. (2000). *Sex slaves: The trafficking of women in Asia*. London: Virago Press.

Derks, A., Henke, R., & Vanna, L. (2006). *Review of a decade of research on trafficking in persons in Cambodia*. San Francisco: The Asia Foundation & USAID.

George, U. (2002). A needs-based model for settlement service delivery for newcomers to Canada. *International Social Work, 45*(4), 465–480.

Hughes, D. (2003). *Hiding in plain sight: A practical guide to identifying victims of trafficking in the U.S.* Retrieved February 25, 2009, from www.uri.edu/artsci/wms/hughes/hiding_in_plain_sight.pdf.

Human trafficking expert warns of risks to children in disaster zones. (2008, May 26). *International Herald Tribune*. Retrieved August 17. 2009 from http://www.human-trafficking.org/updates/852.

Kempadoo, K. (2005). *Trafficking and prostitution reconsidered: New perspectives on migration, sex work, and human rights*. Boulder: Paradigm.

Kyle, D., & Koslowski, R. (2001). *Global human smuggling: Comparative perspectives*. Baltimore: Johns Hopkins University Press.

Pan American Development Foundation (2009). *Lost childhoods in Haiti: Quantifying child trafficking, restaveks & victims of violence*. Washington, DC: Author.

Raymond, J. (2004). Prostitution on demand: Legalizing the consumers as sexual consumers. *Violence Against Women, 10*(10), 1156–1186.

Roby, J., Turley, J., & Cloward, J. (2008). The U.S. response to human trafficking: Is it enough? *Journal of Immigrant and Refugee Services, 6*(4), 508–525.

Salt, J. (2002). Trafficking and human smuggling: A European perspective. *International Migration, 38*(3), 31–56.

Smart, R. (2003). *Policies for orphans and vulnerable children: A framework for moving ahead*. Washington, DC: USAID.

Sullivan, B. (2003). Trafficking in women. *Feminist Journal of Politics, 5*(1), 67–91.

United Nations Office on Drugs and Crime (UNODC). (2009a). *Global report on trafficking in persons: Human trafficking, a crime that shames us all*. United Nations Global Initiative to Fight Human Trafficking (UN.GIFT).

United Nations Office on Drugs and Crime (UNODC). (2009b). *Global report on trafficking in persons: Executive summary*. Author.

United Nations Treaty Collection. (2010). Retrieved August 25, 2010, from http://treaties.un.org/Pages/ViewDetails.aspx?src=TREATY&mtdsg_no=XVIII-12&chapter=18&lang=en.

US Department of State (2010). *Trafficking in persons report* (10th ed.). Washington, DC: Author.

US Department of State (2008). *Trafficking in persons report* (8th ed.). Washington, DC: Author.

US Department of State (2006). *Trafficking in persons report* (6th ed.). Washington, DC: Author.

Van Impe, K. (2002). People for sale: The need for a multidisciplinary approach to human trafficking. *International Migration, 38*(3), 113–191.

Indigenous Peoples and Cultural Survival

JAY T. JOHNSON AND MICHAEL YELLOW BIRD

This chapter provides an overview of the term *Indigenous peoples*,[1] covers the history of the international Indigenous peoples' movement, and discusses the United Nations Declaration on the Rights of Indigenous Peoples, its importance, and its limitations. It concludes with a discussion of social work with Indigenous peoples, past and future.

OVERVIEW

Indigenous peoples is a modern term used by international organizations to describe culturally and geographically diverse groups with diverse histories. Despite considerable cultural divergence, Indigenous peoples share significant symmetries that have evolved from the common experiences of European colonialism. These similarities are founded in an ancestral birthright in the land; a common core of collective interests concerning the protection of their human, territorial, and cultural rights; and the shared experience of dispossession, discrimination, exploitation, and marginalization precipitated through the colonial projects perpetrated against their communities by colonial and neocolonial state administrations.

In addition to the international designation of *Indigenous peoples*, several other terms have been used, including *Aborigines, Indians, Natives, ethnic minorities, First peoples*, and occasionally *the Fourth World* (Corntassel & Primeau, 1995; Manuel & Posluns, 1974). *Indigenous peoples* is the designation used by the United Nations to recognize these and other groups collectively. The cultural survival of Indigenous peoples concerns the protection and restoration of Indigenous peoples' territories, natural resources, sacred sites, languages, beliefs, values, relationships, systems of governance, sovereignty, self-determination, human rights, and intellectual property.

Who Are Indigenous Peoples?

Indigenous peoples reside on all of the inhabited continents of the earth and in all geographical regions: deserts, arctic and subarctic areas, islands, mountains, grasslands, woodlands, rainforests, wetlands, and coastal areas. The global population is estimated to be at least 350 million, which is divided into approximately 5000 cultural groups (IWGIA, 2009). Most identify themselves according to the reciprocal relationships they hold with their physical environments and territories, along with their affiliation in an extended family, clan, band, village, tribe, confederacy, or nation. There is no typical group; each has its own history, worldview, language, dress, food, sacred and secular ceremonies, and social and political organizations. Indigenous peoples may or may not have a stable political, economic, or social relationship with mainstream society.

Defining which groups of peoples can and cannot be considered Indigenous has been a significant challenge for international forums. Elsa Stamatopoulou, former chairperson of the United Nations Permanent Forum on Indigenous Issues, describes these groups as diverse populations who reside on ancestral lands, share a lineage with the original inhabitants of these lands, have distinct cultures and languages, and regard themselves as different from those who have colonized and now control their territories (Stamatopoulou, 1994).

Although the definitions created by a range of organizations and authors have varied over the past fifty years, recently a broad consensus has formed within the international community. Four core principles have been agreed upon in defining Indigenous peoples: First, they generally live within, or maintain attachments to, geographically distinct territories; second, they tend to maintain distinct social, economic, and political institutions within their territories; third, they typically aspire to remain culturally, geographically, and institutionally distinct rather than assimilate fully into national society; and fourth, they self-identify as Indigenous or tribal. Many Indigenous groups believe that defining who is Indigenous is "best answered by indigenous communities themselves" (Corntassel, 2003, p. 75).

Indigenous Peoples' Movement: A Brief History

Beginning in the fifteenth century and continuing for the next 500 years, an assortment of European nations embarked on colonizing what became known as the Americas, Africa, Asia, the Pacific, and the Arctic. As the settler states of the Americas and South Pacific gained their independence beginning with the United States of America in 1776, the subjugation of Indigenous populations shifted from European colonial to settler-controlled, neocolonial administrations. The invasions by European colonizers led to numerous conflicts with Indigenous peoples, who were subjected to introduced diseases in addition to state-sponsored campaigns of murder, enslavement, and cultural destruction, which resulted in staggering losses to their numbers. The diseases, previously unknown to Indigenous peoples, resulted in death rates between 70 and 95 percent, particularly from smallpox, which was spread by European settlers.

Burger (1990, pp. 76–77) writes that the numbers of Indigenous peoples in the Americas "fell from 30 to 5 million" fifty years after first contact with Europeans. The colonization of North America reduced Indigenous populations to 1 million by the 1890s. In Africa, "colonialists shipped at least 10 million slaves to the Americas," and "a quarter of all Bushman had disappeared by 1921 following Dutch settlement and German atrocities in the 1890s." In Australasia, the original population of 500,000 Aboriginal peoples fell to 60,000 by the 1890s, and "Maori numbers fell by 200,000 in just 50 years, leaving 42,000 by 1890." In the Pacific, "the Polynesian population halved and one Micronesian group was left with a fortieth of their number." As the colonizers assumed control of Indigenous peoples and their territories, they maintained this control through the implementation of racialized policies that purloined Indigenous rights, lands, culture, and natural resources. Most Indigenous groups actively resisted these actions (Maybury-Lewis, 2002). More recent resistance to state domination has led to the development of an Indigenous peoples' movement, which has sought international recognition and protections for these groups.

The history of the Indigenous peoples' movement is traced by many to the 1923 appeal by Deskaheh to the League of Nations (the predecessor of the United Nations) on behalf of the Six Nations of the Iroquois Confederacy. Deskaheh, a traditional leader of the Cayuga, sought the support of the League in his claims against the Canadian government, which was imposing a tribal council system of administration on the Six Nations of the Grand River reserve. Despite his failure to address his petition, "The Redman's Appeal for Justice," before the League, Deskaheh did succeed in presenting his case before several ambassadors with the assistance of the mayor of Geneva, convincing them to address his concerns directly with the Canadian government. While he was in Geneva, the Canadian government succeeded in forcing a "democratically elected" government on the Six Nations reserve, and subsequently Deskaheh lost his mandate (Niezen, 2003).

Despite Deskaheh's failure to have his nation recognized by and its case heard before the League of Nations, recognition of the unique political status of Indigenous peoples has nonetheless slowly developed within international forums over the past eighty years. The first significant recognition of the need for protecting Indigenous peoples' rights against the encompassing domination of state governments came in 1957, when the International Labour Organization (ILO) issued its Indigenous and Tribal Populations Convention (No.107), later updated in 1989 by a more strongly worded convention (No.169). Through these conventions, the ILO set in motion an evolving international legal framework that not only recognizes the status of Indigenous peoples as a unique category within international law but also recognizes that Indigenous peoples require protection from the continuing colonial and neocolonial projects of state governments.

Following in the footsteps of the ILO, the United Nations began in 1982 to investigate the demands made by Indigenous peoples for attention to their unique status within the international state system. Although the UN had adamantly affirmed the sovereign rights of peoples colonized by European powers throughout Africa, Asia, and the Pacific to decolonization and self-determination through the Declaration on the Granting of Independence to Colonial Countries and Peoples, the organization had made no move toward addressing the situation of peoples whose lands had been subsumed into settler states, predominately in the Americas and South Pacific, or of those who remained disenfranchised minorities within the newly decolonized states of Africa and Asia. Beginning with the Martínez-Cobo study in 1983, the UN started down a path whose ultimate outcome has been the recognition of Indigenous peoples' rights within an organizational structure that had previously failed to acknowledge any self-determining authority other than through internationally recognized states (UN Sub-Commission on Prevention of Discrimination and Protection of Minorities & Martínez-Cobo, 1987).

Following the recommendation of the Martínez-Cobo study, the UN created the Working Group on Indigenous Populations under the Office of the High Commissioner for Human Rights. The primary aims of this working group were twofold: first, to create a permanent forum for Indigenous peoples within the UN system, and second, to draft a Declaration on the Rights of Indigenous Peoples with the hope that this instrument would provide the next step in further defining the evolving international legal framework for Indigenous peoples' rights (Minde, 2008). With the creation of the UN Permanent Forum on Indigenous Issues in 2000 and the approval by the UN General Assembly of the Declaration on the Rights of Indigenous Peoples in 2007, the international Indigenous peoples' movement has entered a new era. During the vote, 143 nations voted in favor of the declaration, 4 voted against it, and 11 abstained. Not surprisingly, those voting against the declaration were Australia, Canada, New Zealand, and the United States, who have protracted histories of violating the human, cultural, and territorial rights of Indigenous peoples.

THE UNITED NATIONS DECLARATION ON THE RIGHTS OF INDIGENOUS PEOPLES

The importance of the UN Declaration on the Rights of Indigenous Peoples cannot be overstated. First, the UN admits "that indigenous peoples have suffered from historic injustices as a result of, inter alia, their colonization and dispossession of their lands, territories and resources, thus preventing them from exercising, in particular, their right to development in accordance with their own needs and interests (UN General Assembly, 2008, p. 2). Second, the UN recognizes "the urgent need to respect and promote the inherent rights of indigenous peoples which derive from their political, economic and social structures and from their cultures, spiritual traditions, histories and philosophies, especially their rights to their lands, territories and resources," and "the urgent need to respect and promote the rights of indigenous peoples affirmed in treaties, agreements and other constructive arrangements with States" (p. 2). Third, the UN believes that the "Declaration is a further important

step forward for the recognition, promotion and protection of the rights and freedoms of indigenous peoples" (p. 2).

The declaration contains forty-six articles that address "individual and collective rights, cultural rights and identity, rights to education, health, employment, language, and others" (UN Permanent Forum on Indigenous Issues, 2007). Although all of the articles contained in this document are important for social workers to support, the first four provide an overall sense of the rights that are guaranteed by the declaration (UN General Assembly, 2008). Article 1 states that Indigenous peoples have the right to fully enjoy, as a collective or as individuals, all human rights and fundamental freedoms as recognized in the Charter of the United Nations, the Universal Declaration of Human Rights, and international human rights law. Article 2 states that Indigenous peoples are free and equal to all other peoples and have the right to be free from any kind of discrimination in the exercise of their rights, in particular those based on their indigenous origin or identity. Article 3 states that Indigenous peoples have the right to self-determination. By that right they can freely determine their political status and pursue their economic, social, and cultural development. Article 4 says they have the right to maintain and strengthen their distinct political, legal, economic, social, and cultural institutions while retaining the right to participate fully in the political, economic, social, and cultural life of the state, if they so choose.

The Relevance of the UN Declaration on the Rights of Indigenous Peoples

The endorsement of the UN Declaration on the Rights of Indigenous Peoples by a majority of the General Assembly is important for a number of reasons. First, Indigenous peoples throughout the world have been consistently and often brutally marginalized and denied human, political, economic, social, cultural, and territorial rights by occupying settler governments. Second, the Declaration provides a twofold strategy that "aims at empowering indigenous groups by according them control over the issues which are internal to their communities," and "it refers to procedures of participation and consultation in order to ensure that these peoples are involved in the life of the larger society of a State" (Errico, 2007, p. 755). Third, under the continuing colonial policies of many settler governments and agencies, Indigenous peoples face numerous oppressions (Maybury-Lewis, 2002), including *genocide* (deliberate destruction of the people), *ethnocide* (deliberate destruction of the culture rather than the people themselves), *ecocide* (destruction of their natural environments), and *linguicide* (destruction of Indigenous languages).

The recognition of Indigenous peoples' rights by the UN is a step toward dealing with the continuing oppression faced by various Indigenous populations around the globe. Indigenous peoples have consistently been regarded as an impediment to progress and development (Burger, 1990), which has contributed to a settler political discourse that has cast Indigenous populations as backward, "wild," "savage," and "barbarian" (Keal, 2003, p. 67). The neoliberal economic policies fueling globalization have put the poorest populations, frequently Indigenous populations, in greater economic peril as wealth and resources are concentrated in the hands of multinational corporations.

Several national Indigenous rights movements have been born out of the struggle to defend their natural resources and fragile economies against further erosion. The Zapatista movement in the Chiapas state of Mexico was born out of the struggle against the North American Free Trade Agreement, or NAFTA (Yashar, 2005). As another example, the Bolivian movement that brought Evo Morales, an Indigenous farmer, into power was primarily a struggle against the increasing control of multinational corporations over the natural resources of the state (Albó, 2007).

Recently, the Peruvian Congress has acceded to the demands of Indigenous protestors to revoke a free trade agreement with the United States that would have opened Amazonian lands to gas and oil exploration (Cultural Survival, 2009). The development of unwanted mining and hydroelectric dams that contaminate the lands and waters of Indigenous territories poses a major threat to Indigenous peoples. And, since most Indigenous peoples remain under the control of the state and are not free to exercise full autonomy and pursue political, economic, and social development on their own terms consistent with their cultural values and beliefs, protecting their interests remains challenging. The oppressions experienced by Indigenous peoples in these colonial contexts have resulted in a number of grim realities for many groups, including what Burger (1990) refers to as conditions found at the "bottom of the heap" (p. 82): living far below the poverty line; low life expectancy; high rates of illiteracy and unemployment; the least schooling, medical care, and welfare; the worst housing; the lowest salaries; and high rates of disease, violence, and loss of homes and lands.

IMPLICATIONS FOR SOCIAL WORK

There is great hope that the Declaration marks a new era for protecting and acknowledging the sovereignty of Indigenous peoples, but it is only one step in the evolving international legal standards concerning Indigenous peoples. Although the UN General Assembly has passed the Declaration as a resolution, it has yet to be acknowledged as a binding convention under international law. Only Bolivia has so far incorporated the articles of the Declaration into its national legal framework. Social workers have the opportunity to become engaged through their practice and also by encouraging their organizations to support the principles of the Declaration.

Social work has often served at the behest of European colonialism and thus constitutes a threat to the cultural survival of Indigenous peoples throughout the world. Simply put, "colonialism refers to the invasion, subjugation, and occupation of one people by another" (Yellow Bird, 2004, p. 33). Its methods include the colonizers forcing their political, social, intellectual, psychological, and economic ideas and rules over another territory and people (Wilson & Yellow Bird, 2005). It is a brutal, exploitive, and violent experience and institution, and it "has been one of the most destructive processes in human history" (Burger, 1990, p. 76). Most notably, it was social workers in Australia, Canada, New Zealand, and the United States who, under the policy of killing the Native within the child, forcibly removed hundreds of thousands of Indigenous children from their communities and placed them in government and Christian residential schools and settler homes. In this way, social workers were complicit in genocide as defined under the UN Convention on the Prevention and Punishment of the Crime of Genocide. Article 2, part e, states that "forcibly transferring children of the group to another group" with intent to destroy, in whole or in part, a national, ethnical, racial, or religious group constitutes genocide (www.hrweb.org/legal/genocide.html).

Colonialism is motivated by many factors, but greed, self-interest, expansion of the invading colonial empire, and the "white man's burden," which was "the alleged duty of the white peoples to manage the affairs of the less developed nonwhite peoples" ("white man's burden," 2009), appear to be the primary motives. Since colonizers seldom acknowledge colonialism as an ignominious activity despite the death, pain, trauma, loss, and humiliation it has brought to Indigenous peoples throughout the world, its practice can be thought of as "a sickness, an addiction to greed, supremacy, power, and exploitation" (Yellow Bird, 2004, p. 42).

Because "colonialism is embedded in social work" (Yellow Bird & Gray, 2008, p. 65), it has often failed to see its destructive side when "helping" Indigenous peoples address personal and social problems, generally sticking to the mandates of settler-state governments and agencies that advance a narrow Western worldview while ignoring "Indigenous world views, local knowledge, and traditional forms of helping and healing" (Gray, Coates, & Yellow Bird, 2008, p. 1). Indeed, as a helping profession in the Third World, social work has been coined "professional imperialism" (Midgley, 2008, pp. 32–37) and regarded as "essentially a modernist Western invention which has a history of silencing marginal voices and importing, into diverse contexts across the world, Western thinking primarily from the UK and the U.S.A." (Gray, Coates, & Yellow Bird, 2008, p. 1). Undeniably, social work has failed to develop its "knowledge and approaches in tandem with Indigenous Peoples" (Gray, Yellow Bird, & Coates, 2008, p. 49). Social work was an invention of the colonial state and has been largely absent in "advocacy efforts to expose or combat rampant poverty, 'third world conditions,' [and] human rights abuses," and it has not been a "major supporter of efforts to uphold land claims and treaty rights" of Indigenous peoples (Gray, Yellow Bird, & Coates, 2008, p. 49).

Since settler-state governments are often responsible for much of the oppression experienced by Indigenous peoples, it is the colonial enterprise, not the social work discipline, that will likely determine the level of empowerment, justice, and self-determination accorded to Indigenous peoples (Yellow Bird & Gray, 2008). In order for social work to transform its colonizing methodologies, it must fiercely focus on neutralizing the structural mechanisms of colonial society that continue to discriminate against and marginalize Indigenous peoples. Such an approach can be thought of as *Indigenous social work*, which involves decolonizing social work by liberating the profession from executing the oppressive ideas, beliefs, policies, and practices of colonial governments and agencies. Indigenous social work is decolonized social work and represents just cause in social work practice (Briskman, 2008; Weaver, 2008; Yellow Bird & Gray, 2008).

Before social workers can become effective advocates for Indigenous peoples' rights, they must confront the continuing effects of colonialism and the ways in which the profession continues to participate in colonial projects. This will also require more reflection on the complicity of social work in these projects, and in this age of state apologies to Indigenous peoples, perhaps national social work organizations should consider official apologies for their participation in stealing Indigenous children from their families. The decolonization of any profession requires that members first acknowledge their complicity. Second, they must cease their participation. Third, they must openly condemn the past and continuing effects of colonialism. And fourth, they must collaborate with Indigenous Peoples to engage in anticolonial actions against public and private colonial projects.

The decolonization of social work would allow for the acknowledgment and incorporation of Indigenous communities' strengths within social work theory and practice. Too often Indigenous communities are blamed for the compounding effects of several hundred years of colonial projects perpetrated against them. From a strengths perspective, their continued existence in spite of colonialism and their resistance to colonialism demonstrate a strong will to survive. This survival includes the protection and restoration of territories, natural resources, sacred sites, languages, beliefs, values, relationships, systems of governance, intellectual property, and self-determination. Social workers have the opportunity to either support Indigenous peoples' cultural survival or continue with practices that further erode Indigenous rights.

NOTE

1. Following on the precedent set by various organizations, including Indian and Northern Affairs Canada, we are capitalizing words such as Aborigine, Indian, First Nations, and Indigenous.

REFERENCES

Albó, X. (2007). The history of a Bolivia in search of change. *Indigenous Affairs*, 6–21. Retrieved July 7, 2009, from www.iwgia.org/sw20878.asp.

Briskman, L. (2008). Decolonizing social work in Australia: Prospect or illusion. In M. Gray, J. Coates, & M. Yellow Bird (Eds.), *Indigenous social work around the world : Towards culturally relevant education and practice* (pp. 83–96). Aldershot, Hants, England and Burlington, VT: Ashgate.

Burger, J. (1990). *The Gaia atlas of first peoples: A future for the indigenous world*. New York: Doubleday.

Corntassel, J. J. (2003). Who is Indigenous? 'Peoplehood' and ethnonationalist approaches to rearticulating indigenous identity. *Nationalism and Ethnic Politics*, 9(1), 75–100.

Corntassel, J. J., & Primeau, T. H. (1995). Indigenous "sovereignty" and international law: Revised strategies for pursuing "self-determination." *Human Rights Quarterly, 12*(2), 343–365.

Cultural Survival. (2009). A victory for Indigenous Peoples: Controversial free trade laws revoked by Peru's Congress. Retrieved June 30, 2009, from www.cs.org.

Errico, S. (2007). The draft UN Declaration on the Rights of Indigenous Peoples: An overview. *Human Rights Law Review, 7*(4), 741–755.

Gray, M., Coates, J., & Yellow Bird, M. (2008). Introduction. In M. Gray, J. Coates, & M. Yellow Bird (Eds.), *Indigenous social work around the world: Towards culturally relevant education and practice* (pp. 1–12). Aldershot, Hants, England and Burlington, VT: Ashgate.

Gray, M., Yellow Bird, M., & Coates, J. (2008). Towards an understanding of Indigenous social work. In M. Gray, J. Coates, & M. Yellow Bird (Eds.), *Indigenous social work around the world: Towards culturally relevant education and practice* (pp. 49–58). Aldershot, Hants, England and Burlington, VT: Ashgate.

IWGIA. (2009). Indigenous Peoples: Who are they? Retrieved June 24, 2009, from www.iwgia.org/sw641.asp.

Keal, P. (2003). *European conquest and the rights of indigenous peoples: The moral backwardness of international society.* Cambridge, UK, and New York: Cambridge University Press.

Manuel, G., & Posluns, M. (1974). *The Fourth World: An Indian reality.* New York: Free Press.

Maybury-Lewis, D. (2002). Genocide against Indigenous Peoples. In A. L. Hinton (Ed.), *Annihilating difference: The anthropology of genocide* (pp. 43–92). Berkeley, CA: University of California Press.

Midgley, J. (2008). Promoting reciprocal international social work exchanges: Professional imperialism revisited. In M. Gray, J. Coates, & M. Yellow Bird (Eds.), *Indigenous social work around the world: Towards culturally relevant education and practice* (pp. 31–48). Aldershot, Hants, England and Burlington, VT: Ashgate.

Minde, H. (2008). The Destination and the Journey: Indigenous Peoples and the United Nations from the 1960s through 1985. In H. Minde (Ed.), *Indigenous Peoples: Self-determination, Knowledge, Indigeneity* (pp. 49–86). Delft, The Netherlands: Eburon Academic Publishers.

Niezen, R. (2003). *The origins of indigenism: Human rights and the politics of identity.* Berkeley, CA: University of California Press.

Stamatopoulou, E. (1994). Indigenous Peoples and the United Nations: Human rights as a developing dynamic. *Human Rights Quarterly, 16*(1), 58–81.

United Nations General Assembly. (2008). United Nations Declaration on the Rights of Indigenous Peoples. New York: Author.

United Nations Permanent Forum on Indigenous Issues. (2007). *Indigenous peoples, Indigenous voices.* New York: Author.

United Nations Sub-Commission on Prevention of Discrimination and Protection of Minorities, & Martínez-Cobo, J. R. (1987). *Study of the problem of discrimination against indigenous populations.* New York: United Nations.

Weaver, H. N. (2008). Indigenous social work in the United States: Reflections on Indian tacos, Trojan horses and canoes filled with indigenous revolutionaries. In M. Gray, J. Coates, & M. Yellow Bird (Eds.), *Indigenous social work around the world: Towards culturally relevant education and practice* (pp. 71–82). Aldershot, Hants, England and Burlington, VT: Ashgate.

Wilson, A. C., & Yellow Bird, M. (2005). *For indigenous eyes only: A decolonization handbook.* Santa Fe: School of American Research.

Yashar, D. J. (2005). *Contesting citizenship in Latin America: The rise of indigenous movements and the postliberal challenge.* Cambridge, UK, and New York: Cambridge University Press.

Yellow Bird, M. (2004). Cowboys and Indians: Toys of genocide, icons of American colonialism. *Wicazo Sa Review, 19*(2), 33–48.

Yellow Bird, M., & Gray, M. (2008). Indigenous people and the language of social work. In M. Gray, J. Coates, & M. Yellow Bird (Eds.), *Indigenous social work around the world: Towards culturally relevant education and practice* (pp. 59–70). Aldershot, Hants, England and Burlington, VT: Ashgate.

White man's burden. (2009). In *Merriam-Webster Online Dictionary.* Retrieved July 7, 2009, from www.merriam-webster.com/dictionary/white man's burden.

Global Mental Health

JANICE WOOD WETZEL

"There is no health without mental health" (WHO, 2010, p. 1). This World Health Organization declaration stems from the definition of health contained in its constitution: "Health is a state of complete physical, mental and social well-being and not merely the absence of disease or infirmity."

Mental health is viewed from a comprehensive psychosocial strengths perspective whereby we all can realize our potential, cope with the normal stresses of life, work productively, and contribute to the community. Mental illness and emotional distress are often the end result of the absence of positive social and economic circumstances necessary to fulfilling a state of well-being. Even when vulnerability is a function of genetic inheritance or neurological problems, social and economic conditions exacerbate the situation. The same is true for those suffering from AIDS and other physical diseases. There are few issues that are not relevant to mental health and well-being; certainly this is true of the issues discussed in every chapter in this book.

It has become clear to experts in the international arena that mental health problems are becoming increasingly serious. By 2020, WHO projects that the leading cause of both physical and mental disease burden in developing countries, as measured in disability-adjusted life years, will be unipolar (nonpsychotic) major depression in young women. (Burden of disease is a measurement of the incidence and prevalence of a given problem and its impact on society.) By the year 2030, unipolar depressive disorders will become the leading cause of the burden of disease, surpassing physical disease and other mental health problems, for *all* people in high-income countries. It will become the second and third leading cause in middle- and low-income countries, respectively (WHO, 2008).

MENTAL HEALTH, INEQUITABLE SOCIAL CONDITIONS, AND POLICY SOLUTIONS

The World Federation for Mental Health (WFMH) (2008) reports that over 450 million people around the world are living with mental illness. Fewer than half of them are receiving any help at all, resulting in poor work performance, family disruption, and even suicide. The startling statistics and the human toll they represent are often given little attention by not only the general public but also by health-care systems (when they even exist) and policy makers in public and private spheres. Women's vulnerability to mental health problems is directly related to their inferior social and economic position worldwide. Mental health, according to WHO (2001) is unlikely to be achieved in the absence of a supportive familial, social, educational, and work-related economic context. Freedom from violence, discrimination, and unjust treatment across the life span is essential as well.

Social and economic policies help determine whether a child can thrive and develop her full potential or whether her life will be blighted. In rich and poor nations alike, mental health problems are converging. Many developed countries fall short of meeting needs, and developing countries often lack systems of care. In many low-income countries, 75 percent of people do not have access to the treatment they need to function in society.

For these reasons, WHO launched its mental health Gap Action Programme (mhGAP) in Geneva in October of 2008. Although noting that there are needs in developed countries, its aim is to increase services for mental health and substance abuse in low- and middle-income countries (mhGAP, 2008).

At the core of mhGAP is the establishment of productive partnerships based upon reinforcing commitments with existing partners and attracting and energizing new partners. Increasing social, political, and institutional engagement with a range of contributors, interest groups, and organizations is key. In order to be successful, the international community must be involved in partnership with governments, health professionals, civil society, communities, and families. An urgent commitment is needed by all constituencies to respond to this public health need.

Psychosocial interventions include treatment for depression, alcohol, and drug dependence, primarily with cognitive-behavioral and interpersonal therapies and problem solving. Family and community-based psychosocial rehabilitation and care are recommended models of service delivery. Additionally, WHO notes the importance of policies to support these interventions, including restriction of access to common methods of suicide. In all circumstances, attention must be paid to specific contexts, cultural choices, beliefs, and health-seeking behaviors in addition to health-system requirements for implementation. Priorities and methods will vary with the setting and will differ with the country and even areas of the same country. In all cases, basic education and training of professionals and laypeople are essential, as is early intervention, however brief. It is particularly important for rural areas that have few, if any, services.

Addressing Social Determinants of Mental Health

In 2005, the WHO Commission on Social Determinants of Health was set up to address unmet needs. Closing the gap between mental health needs on a global scale and the reality on the ground has become a focal point in its efforts to forge an international movement. The Commission's overarching recommendations include improving the well-being of girls and women and creating social protection policies supportive of all. Key elements needed to repair damaging inequities include addressing inequities between men and women, strengthening governance dedicated to equity, acknowledging that there is a problem, and focusing more on social determinants.

Social determinants of health were brought front and center in July of 2009 at the United Nations in Geneva. The Economic and Social Council and its Annual Ministerial Review held what they call a *high-level segment* to address the overarching theme of implementing the internationally agreed-upon goals and commitments in regard to global public health.

Their focus was on social determinants of health and the impact of the international economic crisis on global public health.

Preceding the event, the Conference of NGOs (CoNGO) held a Civil Society Development Forum to influence the deliberations of the world's governments. Geneva, New York, and Vienna provided the leadership, making a point of including mental health throughout their discourse as a relevant concern otherwise overlooked. From a local and global perspective, workshop themes addressed responding to health inequities, dealing with the shortage of healthcare workers (including social workers and indigenous community workers), slowing the increase in noncommunicable and chronic diseases, financing global access to health (including health technologies), ensuring women's right to health throughout the life cycle, and promoting the prevention and treatment of HIV and AIDS. UN and government representatives, nongovernmental organizations (NGOs), grassroots leaders, and a cadre of young people from around the world expanded on the subject matter in order to bring a comprehensive civil society perspective to the intergovernmental arena. Follow-up conferences in New York and Vienna were designed to build upon the Geneva event. (The Civil Society Development Forum outcome document is available on the CoNGO website: www.ngocongo.org.).

MENTAL HEALTH, STIGMA, AND PSYCHOSOCIAL WELL-BEING

Whether working with marginalized people in wealthier countries or with people from diverse cultures throughout the world, it is well to keep in mind that the words *mental health*, much less *mental illness*, are often off-putting. There is such a stigma, ranging from discomfort to taboos, that people deny symptoms and refuse interventions associated with mental illness. To do otherwise in some cultures can lead to ostracism and the person's family being stigmatized and rejected for years to come. There is a great need for global education on mental health to combat this stigma.

The truth is that most people suffering emotional distress as a result of social or economic conditions are simply behaving normally to stressful situations. To speak of psychosocial well-being and emotional distress rather than mental health and mental illness is more accurate. This is particularly important when assisting disaster and other trauma casualties. Such experiences are representative of natural responses to traumatic events.

The Lancet Global Mental Health Services Movement

An internationally diverse *Lancet* Global Mental Health Group from the United Kingdom issued a series of papers in 2007, launching a global mental health services movement that has captured the attention of international leaders. The series is a call to action and a commitment to track and monitor progress across a range of mental health indicators in the run-up to a global summit on mental health in 2009. The purpose is to change the culture of lost opportunity that has stifled mental health progress.

The series notes that despite attention paid to the mind and human consciousness by Western countries, mental health remains neglected and deeply stigmatized across societies. They acknowledge that the fragile and fragmented services for the disadvantaged in particular are not because efforts weren't made. In 2001, WHO itself devoted its 2001 World Health Report to mental health.

Since that time, WHO has continued to publish reports on mental health, including a briefing alert following the 2004 Asian tsunami that called for psychosocial interventions to normalize the lives of psychologically traumatized survivors rather than by means of Western-oriented psychotherapy (WHO, 2005). Predicting that there would be a massive need for psychosocial support given the estimated one million people involved in the area most affected by the tsunami, the Aceh area of Indonesia, WHO developed a strategic plan that highlighted its particular concerns based on Aceh's sociocultural circumstances. The plan noted that this society holds a deeply religious belief that suffering resulting from disasters and loss of loved ones, houses, and material possessions is the will of God. They are a proud, resilient people. Having recovered from many traumas, both natural and human-made, they are resistant to outside interference, regardless of intentions.

According to WHO (2005), these observations had implications for planned interventions. Among them were *(1)* that trauma-related psychiatric disorders might be substantially less than would be expected; *(2)* attempts by people outside of Aceh to train community leaders in how to respond to widespread psychological distress using Western constructs would likely be misguided and unwelcome; and *(3)* trauma-focused counseling and psychiatric approaches would be ineffective when dealing with psychological and social consequences of disaster that were not consonant with religious and cultural values and beliefs.

The Inter-Agency Standing Committee (IASC) (2007), which includes UN agencies and NGOs, has issued guidelines consistent with WHO's caveats to assist humanitarians in planning, establishing, and coordinating a set of minimum responses to protect and improve people's mental health and psychosocial well-being in the midst of an emergency. They note that there is a significant gap among the world's agencies to identify and effectively coordinate relevant useful practices, to flag potentially harmful practices, and to clarify how different approaches to mental health and psychosocial support are complementary. The IASC guidelines offer essential advice to do just that, all within the context of human rights, as is the case with the *Lancet* series. (See Appendix D for a summary of these guidelines).

The *Lancet* series laments that most organizations have not been able to convert lofty words into tangible actions (2007) despite the fact that many low-income countries are crying out for help. Its core message includes recognition of the fact that mental health is a neglected aspect of well-being that is intimately connected with many other conditions of importance to global health. Resources for mental health are inadequate, insufficient, and inequitably distributed, and they must be scaled up. The *Lancet's* call for action provides a template for a new social movement to strengthen mental health worldwide (*Lancet* Global Mental Health Group, 2007). The social work profession could be an important player in this movement.

Human Rights and Abuses Advocacy

The UN Convention on the Rights of Persons with Disabilities is a landmark agreement passed by consensus (UN, 2006). The inclusion of psychiatric rights was largely due to the significant advocacy efforts of MindFreedom International, an NGO dedicated to consumer rights. Their slogan is, "Nothing about us without us" (www.mindfreedom.org).

Disability Rights International, formerly Mental Disability Rights International (MDRI), is an organization based in Washington, DC, that is committed to advocacy for the human rights and full participation of the seriously mentally ill throughout the world. This organization documents institutional human rights abuses, supports the development of mental disability rights advocacy, and promotes international awareness and oversight of the rights of people with mental disabilities. It also advises governments and NGOs worldwide to plan strategies to bring about effective rights enforcement and service-system reform. Disability Rights International has investigated human rights conditions and assisted mental disability rights advocates in countries all over the world (www.disabilityrightsintl.org).

BEST PRACTICES FOR INTERNATIONAL MENTAL HEALTH AND SOCIAL WORK

The following best practices for the field of international mental health are suggested as considerations for social workers. Most are familiar to the profession, but the provisos may be thought provoking.

Psychosocial Perspective

The strengths perspective, which is concerned with the resourcefulness and resilience of people and has long been embraced by social workers, is an appropriate global orientation, particularly when applied within a psychosocial framework. These dual dimensions are intertwined, requiring assessment of one's psychological state within the context of the family, work, and the larger community, including educational, religious, military, and custodial facilities.

Self-Determination and Cultural Relativism

Human rights in a global context should include respect for alternative cultural practices even when described, as is often the case, as cleansing of evil spirits. Provided that the customs do not abuse, they can be very effective for those who believe in them.

In order to ensure that we are doing no harm—a basic social work principle—the profession's self-determination premise must be reexamined. To its credit, social work has long been concerned with the rights of people to determine their own existence, a value that must be considered seriously. But there are provisos that also must be taken into account. When cultures socialize a person to a given custom, it may not always be in the person's best interest. A case in point is the treatment of women within families and communities all over the world. Theirs is a secondary status at best and a subjugated position all too often. From girlhood, they are taught to believe in their inferiority. As social workers know, people incorporate the opinions of the powerful so as to be loved by their families and society. Hence, we can understand why women who are victims of violence believe they deserve to be punished, and we can understand why millions of women in Africa and the Middle East carry out the practice of genital mutilation even though it is detrimental to their physical and emotional well-being. To assess their cultural compliance

as self-determination when socialization is the real determinant calls into question the benignity of the concept. Although cultural sensitivity and cultural competence are essential social work values to be honored, cultural relativism must not overshadow human rights.

Human Rights–Based Social Work and Gender Mainstreaming

By adopting human rights as the foundational principle upon which all of social work theory and applied knowledge rests, social workers involved with individuals, families, small groups, large communities, or institutions will have a value-based tool with which to apply their knowledge and skills. In so doing, it will become commonplace, whether concerned with direct or policy practice, research, or program development, to assess the theories that inform us. For example, human behavior informs models of practice. Do psychoanalytic theories advance the human rights of girls and women and of boys and men in all cultures around the world, or do they deter their possibility? What of cognitive-behavioral approaches, systems theory, and the spectrum of family therapies? How might we modify what we do to ensure that the human rights of all people from childhood to old age are served? This is called *gender mainstreaming*.

Gender mainstreaming is an analytic UN human rights method designed to ensure the appropriate assessment of policies and programs from the viewpoint of their disparate impact on girls, women, boys, and men across the life span. By extending this approach to direct practice and research in the field of mental health, human rights assessment will include gender analysis regarding everything we do. If our practices are not appropriate for everyone, it is not appropriate that we engage in them (Office of the Special Advisor on Gender Issues and Advancement of Women [OASGI], 2008).

Human Rights and Social Justice

Human rights encompass social justice, an important but insufficient concept in that it is inherently associated with cultural mores that may limit one's rights. Social policy research reveals that "social justice is an evolving hybrid of diverse cultural norms" (Reich, 2008). Human rights, however, transcend civil and political customs in consideration of the basic life-sustaining needs of *all* human beings. Those rights that are inherent in our nature and without which we cannot live as human beings are considered to be human rights (UNESCO, 1994). That includes rights ranging from the right to food and to housing to the right to freedom from racism and racial discrimination and religious intolerance to the rights of women and minorities. *The Right to Health*, published by the UN Office of the High Commissioner for Human Rights (OHCHR) in 2008, includes mental health and its interdependent, indivisible links with other human rights. Without such rights, vulnerability leads to emotional distress and well-being becomes questionable.

Capacity Building and Personal and Social Development

Many definitions of capacity building have emerged since the latter part of the twentieth century when the United Nations Development Programme (UNDP) promoted capacity building to alleviate poverty as an international policy directive. Development was addressed as a primarily rural geographic, societal, and economic phenomenon (Dobie, 2000). As important as that model is for social workers, it is a limited construct because human development must also address emotional well-being and personal growth.

All social development and capacity building, no matter how large the project, begin with individuals, families, small groups, organizations, and communities—the social work neighborhood. No matter the constituency, if its members' development as human beings is ignored, they become vulnerable. Even when working at the country level, *country* is not an abstract concept. It is a "sum of individuals who develop a *consensus* vision" (Dobie, 2000, p. 12). Development, then, is not just a geographic, economic, or societal concept. It is also about human development, emotional well-being, and personal growth.

Capacity 21, instituted by the UNDP in 1992, is more than relevant for social work implementation today. This program was developed because the UNDP concluded that capacity development has largely failed over the years because the capacity of people was not developed in the process (Dobie, 2000).

An organization that has endorsed and implemented this indigenous approach since 1807 is the Brothers of Charity's Caraes, whose home offices are in Rome and Belgium. This organization has worked with marginalized and disadvantaged people on nearly every continent, providing exemplary mental health services and support to people regardless of religious beliefs, gender, sexual orientation, or race. It even has developed schools of psychiatric nursing and social

work in developing countries to ensure that local people are educated to serve their own communities (Stockman, 2008).

It follows, then, that social workers should be concerned with increasing the capacity of people by enhancing their abilities and skills so that they can become fulfilled members of society. Accordingly, when working with organizations and communities, social workers should strive to increase their ability to function by increasing the skills, knowledge, and resources of everyone involved. Whatever the client group, increasing self-awareness in a group context when appropriate to the culture is a universal means of increasing self-esteem, which is essential to personal development.

Train the Trainers Model

Train the Trainers is a model that has evolved from the international women's movement in the developing world over recent decades. It is designed to address the shortage of professionals while empowering women to take charge of their own lives and futures. The model, of course, is just as suitable for men. A participatory, nonhierarchical approach is taken whereby experts train leaders, who in turn train others in an organization or community, who then train others, and so on. The approach has been used in comprehensive health programs, with factory workers, and with microcredit programs, to name just a few venues.

Interventions that use mutual support also strengthen capacity and mental health. Microcredit programs from the renowned Grameen Bank in Bangladesh to Annapurna in India found that they needed to form support groups before they could embark on microcredit training. The women universally had such low self-esteem that they didn't believe they deserved to succeed. In all cases, participants are educated about the importance of the work they do, the need to pay attention to their health given their circumstances, the laws that are in place to protect them but are not implemented, and how to work collectively to implement policies. Even in developed countries, few women are aware of their rights or know how to foster policies to their advantage. It would behoove social workers, both female and male, to become knowledgeable about their own rights as well (Wetzel, 2004).

Participative Social Action Research and Programming

Participatory action research, originated by Kurt Lewin in 1946, grew out of the need to increase knowledge about social systems, according to Marsick (2003). She points out that action research may seem more demanding, but in the long run it promises to be more successful. The reasons make sense. Including the input of stakeholders increases the likelihood that studies will be implemented. In the process, individuals, organizations, and communities develop capacities that enhance success and development at every level. Action research is a cyclical process that begins with diagnosing a problem situation, planning action steps, and implementing and evaluating the outcomes, which in turn leads back to reassessment based on the findings that are followed by effective policy and programs relevant to the real world of the participants themselves. The empowering participatory process of social action research is as effective a mental health intervention as the end result.

CONCLUSION

This chapter has provided an overview of the up-to-date information and concepts relevant to global mental health and its definition, prevalence, policy, and practice issues of concern. The content has been garnered largely from involved international organizations and experts in the field. Terminology that is used by the international community is shared where appropriate for the illumination of social work practice and policy. Content also includes familiar social work nomenclature but suggests that there may be provisos to reconsider in the context of the current reality. The promotion of mental health is essential for social workers in all parts of the world, whether working domestically or globally.

REFERENCES

Dobie, P. (2000). Approaches to sustainability: Models for national strategies: Building capacity for sustainable development. In J. McCullough (Ed.), *Building capacity for a sustainable future*. Geneva: UNDP.

Inter-Agency Standing Committee (IASC). (2007). Guidelines on mental health and psychosocial support in emergency settings. New York: United Nations. Available at www.humanitarianinfo.org/iasc/downloadDoc.aspx?docID=4445&type=pdf.

Lancet Global Mental Health Group. (2007). Movement for global mental health. *Lancet, 370* (9590), 806. doi:10.1016/S0140-6736(07)61243-4.

Lewin, K. (1946). Action research and minority problems. *Journal of Social Issues, 2*(4), 34–36.

Marsick, V. J. (2003). Action research: Building capacity for learning and change. *Human Resource Planning, 26*(2), 14–18.

mental health Gap Action Programme (mhGap). (2008). Mental health gap report. Geneva: Author. Retrieved November 3, 2008, from http://www.who.int/mental_health/mhgap/en/index.html.

Office of the High Commissioner for Human Rights (OHCHR). (2008). *The right to health*. Geneva: UN.

Office of the Special Advisor on Gender Issues and Advancement of Women (OASGI). (2008). Gender mainstreaming. Retrieved November 5, 2008, from www.un.org/womenwatch/osagi/gendermainstreaming.htm.

Reich, M. (2008, October). *Different approaches to social justice*. Presented at the panel on working for change in a rapidly changing society, Council on Social Work Education Annual Program Meeting, Philadelphia.

Stockman, R. (2008, September). *International experiences in the development of mental health care programs.* Presented at the panel on international community mental health education: human rights–based grassroots and professional models, Conference on Reaffirming Human Rights for All: The Universal Declaration at 60. UNESCO, Paris. Retrieved on November 4, 2008, from www.brothersofcharity.org.

UNESCO. (1994). Resolution on United Nations decade for human rights education. Retrieved November 8, 2008, from http://portal.unesco.org/education.

United Nations (UN). (2006). Convention on the protection and promotion of the rights and dignity of persons with disabilities. Retrieved November 3, 2008, from www.disabilityrightsnow.org.au/node/4.

Wetzel, J. W. (2004). Mental health lessons from abroad. In M. C. Hokenstad, Jr., & J. Midgley (Eds.), *Lessons from abroad* (pp. 93–116). Washington, DC: NASW.

World Federation for Mental Health (WFMH). (2008). Making mental health a global priority: World Mental Health Day. Retrieved November 8, 2008, from www.wfmh.org.

World Health Organization (WHO) (2010). Fact Sheet No. 220. Mental Health: strengthening our response (p. 1). Available at: www.who.int/mediacentre/factsheets/fs220/en/.

World Health Organization (WHO). (2008). *Closing the gap in a generation: Health equity through action on the social agenda: Final report of the Commission on Social Determinants of Health*. Geneva: Author. Retrieved November 1, 2008, from www.who.int/social_determinants/.

World Health Organization (WHO). (2005, January). *WHO recommendations for mental health in Aceh* (Prepared by B. Saraceno & H. Minas, with assistance of S. Indradjaya, WHO Indonesia). Available at: www.who.or.id/eng/contents/aceh/WHO_Recommendations_Mental_Health_Aceh.pdf.

World Health Organization (WHO). (2001). The World Health Report 2001: Mental health: new understanding, new hope. Geneva: Author. Available at: www.who.int/whr/2001/en/.

Migration and Refugees

KAREN LYONS AND NATHALIE HUEGLER

Population mobility has been a feature of human existence since time immemorial. For some people migration results from particular crises and is in itself a problematic process with possibly negative effects. It is this concept of *forced migration* that we are primarily concerned with in this chapter. In other contexts migration has been part of the natural order or taken-for-granted history of particular societies or population groups. Quite apart from the need or greed for new land or resources that have motivated explorers and traders over centuries, examples remain of more localized movements as a way of life (which may or may not constitute a problem for those involved or for neighboring communities). These include nomadic people in China, pastoralists living in mountainous terrain (for example, transhumance in Switzerland or Nepal), and Roma people traveling between towns and villages offering casual work or opportunities to sell goods (Lyons, 1999; Lyons, Manion, & Carlsen, 2006).

Modern concerns about migration—within which refugees and asylum seekers constitute a specific, identified category—date from the growth of nation-states (particularly from the nineteenth century) and the twentieth-century development of national immigration policies and international policies and conventions. More recently, migration of people across political boundaries has been identified as a clear symptom of the growing interconnectedness and deepening of globalization (Hoogvelt, 1997). This has provided opportunities for some, with the growth of multinational corporations and modern transport and telecommunications opening up work possibilities that enable skilled workers to commute, so to speak, over ever-larger distances, including crossing national borders, or to relocate across continents for planned periods of time. Even in the case of people in less skilled or secure employment, we have seen the growth of transnational families (for instance, spanning the US–Mexican border; Furman & Negi, 2007).

There can be few societies remaining in the world without links between indigenous populations and extended family members or former acquaintances now settled elsewhere.

From the perspective of social welfare, migration has often been cast as a problem, and indeed, early developments in social work and social services were related to the plight of immigrants in particular societies or the situation of particular populations affected by war. The work of Jane Addams in Chicago from 1889 and that of Save the Children from 1919 in response to the needs of children in the Balkan region are examples of these (Healy, 2001). The extent to which work with immigrants and refugees currently constitutes an area of activity for social workers is related to national policies and legislation; events that have global repercussions, including economic inequalities, natural disasters, and war; and the international mechanisms that have been devised to address some of their particular effects.

This chapter therefore focuses on current characteristics of migration; international, regional, and national policy responses to population mobility; and implications for social work. We conclude with a summary of key points.

VOLUNTARY AND FORCED MIGRATION: SCALE, FLOWS, AND PATTERNS

Before exploring the scale of migration in a global context, we first consider various terms, definitions, and categorizations used to describe the movement of people. A dominant approach among several theoretical frameworks is to consider migration as a process influenced by circumstances that *push* people from one place and factors that *pull* them to another. Following from this, a broad distinction is generally drawn between migrants who move to another country voluntarily to seek a better life (implying a degree of choice and planning) and those who are displaced by forces beyond their control, such as conflicts or disasters (Cox & Pawar, 2006; Lyons & Manion, 2006). The commonly held implication of differentiating between voluntary and forced migration is that they are based on economic and political grounds, respectively, and that this justifies different responses from nation-states in regulating the entry, stay, and access to citizenship for various migrant groups. The discourse, particularly in countries of the Global North or the West, is that economically motivated migration should be managed in line with the overall interests of a state and its citizens, whereas refugees deserve protection based on states' obligations under the 1951 United Nations Convention Relating to the Status of Refugees[1] and its 1967 Protocol.

The International Federation of Social Workers (IFSW) policy statements on migration (2005) and refugees (1998) draw a clear distinction between the two groups, pointing out that in order to preserve the integrity of the international refugee protection framework, it may be necessary to screen and determine the claims of individuals to the right of asylum, applying consistent criteria. On the other hand, some critics of the dualistic approach, which distinguishes between refugees considered deserving of entry and residence and other migrants considered undeserving of such rights in times of economic constraints, argue that many states fail to grant consistent and fair access to protection. At the same time, others point out that in the reality of displacement, political and economic forces are often intertwined (Turton, 2003). There is some acknowledgment that, not least because of increased border control, people migrating for many reasons are forced to use the same routes of clandestine travel and entry, often organized by international networks of human smuggling or trafficking (Crisp, 2007). The extent to which people use the services of smugglers as the only available means to crossing borders, as well as the extent to which they are exploited during and after the actual act of transportation in various forms of bonded labor, prostitution, or other abusive contexts, add further complexity to the situation (Lyons et al., 2006).

According to estimated figures published by the United Nations (2011), 213.9 million people were migrants in 2010, making up 3.1% of the global population. The International Organization for Migration (IOM) (2011a) estimates that around 20 to 30 million people (10% to 15% of all migrants) are unauthorized migrants. This far from homogenous group is often labeled with terms that have varying connotations, such as *undocumented workers*, *illegal immigrants*,

sans papiers, and *failed asylum seekers*, all of which express the precariousness of their presence in destination countries, resulting in a lack of access to even the most basic socioeconomic rights (Lyons & Manion, 2006).

In 2010 the European continent was the region with the highest absolute number of international migrants (69.8 million); however, this accounted for only 9.5% of its total population, compared with 16.8% in Oceania and 14.2% in North America (IOM, 2011b). Among individual nation-states, the United States hosts the largest number of international migrants (42.8 million), followed by Russia (12.3 million), Germany (10.8 million), and Saudi Arabia (7.3 million). Statistics have to be treated with some caution, however; varying national policies are likely to influence reported figures. With an estimated diaspora of 35 million people, China is listed as the top sending country of migrants in 2005, followed by India (20 million) and the Philippines (7 million) (IOM, 2011b).

The United Nations' International Migrant Stock database (2008 Revision) (2011) indicates that 49% of migrants worldwide were women in 2010. Age distribution, particularly the extent to which children are affected by migration, is more difficult to ascertain, mainly because children traveling with adults are often not counted. Little seems to be known about the numbers or motivations of children who migrate independently (Whitehead & Hashim, 2005).

Regarding forced migration, estimates of the United Nations High Commissioner for Refugees (UNHCR) (2010) suggest that at the end of 2009, 43.3 million people had experienced forced displacement through conflicts and persecution. The majority (27.1 million) had been uprooted from their homes and forced to move to other parts of the same country as internally displaced persons (IDPs), but 10.4 million were refugees under UNHCR's responsibility. Definitions are essential when looking at statistics, and it is worth noting that the figures exclude, for example, those displaced through natural disasters as well as 4.7 million refugees supported by the United Nations Relief and Works Agency for Palestine Refugees (UNRWA).

The nationalities of refugees reflect current major conflict zones, with Afghani and Iraqi refugees making up nearly half of the population of concern to UNHCR in 2009. The vast majority of refugees remain within the regions of conflict or disaster, and in 2009, Pakistan, Iran, and Syria were hosting the largest numbers of refugees worldwide (UNHCR, 2010).

Though data on gender and age distribution are only available for a proportion of refugees worldwide, there are indications that children's involvement in forced migration is substantial both in numbers and in terms of the effect on their well-being and development (Ager, 1999; Ahearn, Loughry, & Ager, 1999; UNHCR, 2010; Whitehead & Hashim, 2005).

INTERNATIONAL, REGIONAL AND NATIONAL POLICY RESPONSES TO MIGRATION

Since the mid-twentieth century, a range of international (and regional) conventions and policies have been developed to address the needs of particular migrant groups rather than attempting to regulate migration as a general phenomenon. Various international and regional bodies have sought to advance policies that should be observed in relation to, for instance, refugees or migrant workers. However, while the United Nations Declaration of Human Rights (1948, Article 14) gives people a right to exit their country of birth (to seek asylum), there is no correlating universal right of entry, and the regulation of immigration continues to rest primarily with individual nation-states (Cox & Pawar, 2006; Lyons, 1999). National policies affect not only the circumstances under which some people might be granted right of entry and potentially settlement but also the status accorded to immigrants in relation to citizenship and thus to their political and civic rights, including entitlement to welfare services of various kinds. For instance, over the past decade legislative changes in both the United States and United Kingdom have made it harder for immigrants and asylum seekers to gain citizenship. They have also led to worsening conditions in terms of access to financial benefits and the right to work, resulting in real poverty and demoralization of individuals and families. National policies therefore constitute an important framework for the activities of social workers. However, we will consider first some of the international conventions relevant to this field before identifying immigration policies that have been formulated regionally and nationally.

Refugees have constituted the main focus of international concern. Just as the establishment of the United Nations itself was a response to World War II, UNHCR has been active since shortly after that war, taking responsibility for developing protocols, monitoring implementation, and providing services such as refugee camps and resettlement program. In 2009, the organization had 267 offices in 116 countries with over 6500 staff (UNHCR, 2009). The 1951 Refugee Convention[2] has been crucial in specifying that people seeking asylum should not be returned to countries where they might face threats to their life or liberty. However, the onus is on the asylum seekers to prove that such fears are well founded, and national governments, including for instance the United Kingdom, have sometimes made seemingly arbitrary decisions about which countries are safe for refugees to return to.

Turning to regional alliances, these generally focus on trading relations between member states and other trading blocs, but the European Union (EU) has sought to develop a political role with implications for policy initiatives in relation to migration. These initiatives began as early as 1976, when the Trevi Group was established to counteract "terrorism, radicalism, extremism and violence" (Lyons, 1999, p. 120), drawing an association between international criminality (specifically terrorism) and immigration, which was to resurface globally twenty-five years later.

Further moves were made towards harmonizing national immigration laws over the next decades, leading to a number of shared policies, not least aimed at facilitating the "free mobility of labor" provision of the Maastricht (Single Market) Treaty of 1993. These policies include abolition of shared border controls, common visa and carrier liability policies, detailed checks on non-EU nationals, a list of undesirable aliens, and a stipulation that asylum seekers must apply in their first country of entry and, if refused, are not eligible to seek asylum elsewhere in the EU. The role played by the EU in promoting restrictive immigration policies has earned it the title, Fortress Europe, although with the inclusion of twelve additional states since 2004, it is proving ever harder to police its expanded borders; individual countries, notably those bordering the Mediterranean, Eastern Europe, or the Middle East, tend to operate as corridors for clandestine entry and human trafficking (Lyons et al., 2006).

Turning to national policies, as indicated previously, a significant proportion of immigration is from the Global South to the Global North, and certain countries have earned reputations with regard to public attitudes and policies towards immigration. For much of the twentieth century, the United States, Canada, and Australia were seen as having liberal immigration and settlement policies, notwithstanding either a stated preference for white Europeans (Australia) or legislation that discriminated against Asians (United States). Even the United Kingdom was regarded as a relatively tolerant society, although in terms of granting full nationality rights to immigrants, the UK and also France tended to favor immigrants from former colonies. In contrast, countries such as Belgium, Germany, and Switzerland operated guest-worker systems up to the mid-1970s, failing (in the case of Germany) for a long time to acknowledge that this led to established ethnic minority communities. Consequently, until fairly recently up to three generations of immigrants were debarred from achieving full nationality status (Schierup, Hansen, & Castles, 2006).

However, as discussed, there have been significant shifts towards a tightening of immigration regimes in Europe since the 1990s. These shifts have been in response to a rapid rise in immigrants and asylum seekers as a result of famine and civil wars in a number of African countries, conflict in the Balkan region, and transitions in former Soviet Bloc countries. This more restrictive approach has been mirrored in the United States with introduction of new immigration bills; for instance, the House of Representatives passed the English Language Empowerment Act (1996), apparently in response to the increase in the number of Latinos in the population and fear that Spanish would overtake English as the national language (Van Wormer, 1997). The bill failed to reach a vote in the Senate, however. Harsh and suspicious attitudes towards immigrants and asylum seekers have been even further engendered since 2001 as Western countries have reacted against the perceived threat of terrorist attacks by Muslim fundamentalists following the September 11 (2001) attacks in the United States and, on a smaller scale, the bombing in Bali in 2002, which particularly affected Australian sentiment and policy.

Other countries, such as the Gulf States and Japan, have had more consistent policies about not granting foreign workers permanent resident rights due to a wish to preserve cultural homogeneity (Lyons, 1999), while countries that have traditionally received relatively high numbers of immigrants from diverse countries have had to develop policies aimed at various forms of integration. The degree to which national integration strategies have been based on ideas of cultural pluralism or multiculturalism (traditionally the dominant approach in Canada) versus assimilation (e.g., in France) may themselves pose opportunities or challenges for the activities of social workers.

IMPLICATIONS FOR SOCIAL WORK

As previously noted, from the beginnings of the profession, mobility and migration have featured as major issues in social work in many countries in relation to welfare concerns emanating from both internal (often rural-to-urban) and international migration. Approaches and themes have varied over time, and they continue to be diverse both across and within national contexts. Lyons et al. (2006) suggest that at least three approaches have relevance for social work in the context of migration: specialist therapeutic services, services geared to wider user groups that take account of the particular needs of migrants, and approaches promoting community development and empowerment. The specific needs of the respective migrant populations (e.g., whether services are provided for a group of newly arrived refugees or for an established immigrant community) are likely to shape whether more focus is placed, for example, on emergency practical and material assistance, trauma counseling, and rehabilitation or on interventions that promote community relations and social inclusion (Cox & Pawar, 2006).

Social work practice in this field is influenced by relevant national, regional, and local political and public attitudes towards migration (for example, whether or not a link is drawn on a policy level between immigration control and welfare provision). Another factor is the overall professional location of social work: Services provided through statutory agencies may differ significantly in relation to the boundaries of social workers' roles and the resources available to them compared with services provided by nongovernmental organizations (NGOs) or grassroots initiatives. Similarly, there may be differences regarding the spheres of intervention (i.e., micro, meso, or macro levels) that are considered most appropriate or effective. Particularly in Western countries, more emphasis is often placed on individualized casework or clinical models to provide personal assistance to migrants in adapting to their new lives, while in other societies and cultural contexts, community-based approaches may be favored.

Lyons et al. (2006) consider that loss is a common theme for most migrants, although in what way and how much this is experienced will vary according to their specific circumstances. Cox and Pawar (2006) highlight the importance of access to culturally appropriate trauma counseling for refugees and displaced people, especially if approaches are embedded in existing provisions for assistance and support, in order to avoid any stigmatizing effects. In this context, there are debates about the extent to which refugees are constructed as victims whose needs are pathologized rather than taking into account their voices and resilience (Lyons et al., 2006).

In relation to social work with specific groups, the IFSW policy on refugees (1998) highlights the need for developing services for people who might be particularly vulnerable, such as children, women, and elderly or disabled refugees. In this context, access to the growing body of research on age- and gender-specific experiences of forced migration is likely to constitute an invaluable resource for social workers (see, for example, Ahearn et al., 1999; Kohli, 2007; Pittaway, Bartolomei, & Rees, 2007; Women's Refugee Commission, 2006).

Special Needs of Child Migrants

Turning particularly to children, the rights of migrant and refugee children, whether accompanied by family members or on their own, are reflected in several articles within the United Nations Convention on the Rights of the Child (1989), such as through the prohibition of discrimination on the basis of race, nationality, or status (Article 2) and the emphasis on refugee children's rights to protection and assistance (Article 22) as well as to treatment and recovery following torture, inhumane or degrading treatment, or armed conflict (Article 39). There are a variety of concerns about the effect of migration and exile on the well-being of children. These range from the psychosocial consequences of experiencing war, torture, and disaster to poverty and exclusion, be it through the limitations of life in a refugee camp in developing countries or through denial of access to welfare support for migrant families in countries of the Global North (Ahearn et al., 1999; Briskman & Cemlyn, 2005).

In the context of social work with unaccompanied asylum-seeking children, Kohli (2007) suggests that professionals take on various roles: as *humanitarian helpers* focusing on providing practical assistance and advocacy related to the here and now, as *therapeutic witnesses* to children's emerging stories of persecution, or as *confederates* prepared to embrace the complexities of children's lives in exile and recognize their resiliency. This analysis, although provided in the context of statutory social work with children in the United Kingdom, may be applicable to social work with migrant and refugee populations more generally. On the other hand, given that human rights and social justice are understood as core values for social work (IFSW, 2000), there are debates in some countries about the extent to which professionals have focused too much on "humanizing existing conditions" (Cox & Pawar, 2006, p. 293) or have themselves become, implicitly or directly, involved in immigration control as gatekeepers of access to resources (Humphries, 2004)

rather than taking on roles as advocates or activists for the rights of migrants (Briskman & Cemlyn, 2005). Such debates suggest that social workers need to adopt holistic and ecological approaches (Lyons et al., 2006), based on an awareness of the complex dynamics of migration; relevant local, national, regional, and international frameworks; and the diversity of migrants' and refugees' experiences.

SUMMARY

This chapter has provided an introductory perspective on the scope and diverse nature of international migration as well as on some of the international, regional, and national policies, themes, and debates that influence local social work practice with migrants and refugees. What emerges is that migrants and refugees are by no means a homogenous group but rather people in a wide variety of situations with a wide variety of motivations, needs, and—as a result of states' responses to different forms of migration—rights and entitlements. Despite historic differences in national migration policies, countries of the Global North, while putting considerable effort into restricting access to their territories, have in the past decades placed much emphasis on distinguishing between migrants who have a well-founded fear of persecution and those migrating for economic reasons. Countries of the developing South, on the other hand, have often been faced with the actual fallout from regional crises of displacement. Social workers have developed a multitude of approaches within the field of migration, sometimes based on an existing or statutory mandate. Given a sociopolitical context that is as much in flux as the population they work with, professionals are continually challenged to remain proactive in advocating for the rights of those at risk of being excluded.

NOTES

1. The Convention defines *refugee* as any person who, "owing to well-founded fear of being persecuted for reasons of race, religion, nationality, membership of a particular social group or political opinion, is outside the country of his nationality and is unable or, owing to such fear, is unwilling to avail himself of the protection of that country." It is important to note that in literature relating to refugees, the term is often used in a wider sense, referring more broadly to people who have been displaced outside of their country of origin as a result of war and political oppression (Ager, 1999).

2. By December 2008, 147 states had signed either the 1951 Convention, the 1967 Protocol, or both documents (UNHCR, 2009).

REFERENCES

Ager, A. (1999). Perspectives on the refugee experience. In A. Ager (Ed.), *Refugees: Perspectives on the experience of forced migration* (pp. 1–23). London: Continuum.

Ahearn, F., Loughry, M., & Ager, A. (1999). The experience of refugee children. In A. Ager (Ed.), *Refugees: Perspectives on the experience of forced migration* (pp. 215–236). London: Continuum.

Briskman, L., & Cemlyn, S. (2005) Reclaiming humanity for asylum seekers: A social work response. *International Social Work*, 48(6): 714–724.

Cox, D., & Pawar, M. (2006). *International social work: Issues, strategies and programs*. Thousand Oaks, CA: Sage.

Crisp, J. (2007). Vital distinction: States are having increasing difficulty distinguishing between refugees and migrants. *Refugees*, 148(4): 4–12.

Furman, R., & Negi, N. J. (2007) Social work practice with transnational Latino populations. *International Social Work*, 50(1), 107–112.

Healy, L. (2001) *International social work: Professional action in an interdependent world*. New York: Oxford University Press.

Hoogvelt, A. (1997). *Globalisation and the post-colonial world: The new political economy of development*. London: Macmillan Press.

Humphries, B. (2004). An unacceptable role for social work: Implementing immigration policy. *British Journal of Social Work*, 34(1), 93–107.

International Federation of Social Workers (IFSW). (2005). International policy on migration. www.ifsw.org/en/p38000213.html (accessed October 12, 2008).

International Federation of Social Workers (IFSW). (2000). Definition of social work. www.ifsw.org/en/p38000208.html (accessed October 25, 2008).

International Federation of Social Workers (IFSW). (1998). International policy on refugees. www.ifsw.org/en/p38000216.html (accessed October 12, 2008).

International Organization for Migration (IOM). (2011a). Global estimates and trends. www.iom.int/jahia/page254.html (accessed March 29, 2011).

International Organization for Migration (IOM). (2011b). Regional and country figures. www.iom.int/jahia/ Jahia/about-migration/facts-and-figures/regional-and-country-figures/cache/offonce/ (accessed March 29, 2011).

Kohli, R. (2007) *Social work with unaccompanied asylum-seeking children*. Basingstoke: Palgrave Macmillan.

Lyons, K. (1999). *International social work: Themes and perspectives*. Aldershot: Ashgate.

Lyons, K., & Manion, K. (2006). Migration—an ongoing focus for local and international social workers. In N. Hall (Ed.), *Social work: Making a world of difference* (pp. 195–207). Berne: IFSW.

Lyons, K., Manion, K., & Carlsen, M. (2006). *International perspectives on social work: Global conditions and local practice*. Basingstoke: Palgrave Macmillan.

Pittaway, E., Bartolomei, L., & Rees, S. (2007). Gendered dimensions of the 2004 tsunami and a potential social work response in post-disaster situations. *International Social Work*, 50(3), 307–319.

Schierup, C.-U., Hansen, P., & Castles, S. (2006). *Migration, citizenship and the European welfare state: A European dilemma*. New York: Oxford University Press.

Turton, D. (2003). Conceptualising forced migration. RSC Working Paper No. 12. Oxford: Refugee Studies Centre, University of Oxford.

United Nations High Commissioner for Refugees (UNHCR). (2010). *2009 global trends: Refugees, asylum-seekers, returnees, internally displaced and stateless persons*. www.unhcr.org/4c11f0be9.html.

United Nations High Commissioner for Refugees (UNHCR). (2009). Protecting refugees and the role of UNHCR, 2008–2009. www.unhcr.org/4034b6a34.html.

Van Wormer, K. (1997). *Social welfare: A world view*. Chicago: Nelson Hall.

Whitehead, A., & Hashim, I. (2005). *Children and migration: Background paper for DFID Migration Team, March 2005*. www.livelihoods.org/hot_topics/docs/DfIDChildren.doc (accessed October 12, 2008).

Women's Refugee Commission. (2006). *Displaced women and girls at risk: Risk factors, protection solutions and resource tools*. www.womensrefugeecommission.org/docs/womrisk.pdf (accessed October 25, 2008).

United Nations (2011). *International Migrant Stock: The 2008 Revision*. http://esa.un.org/migration/p2k0data.asp.

Natural and Human-Caused Disasters

MICHAEL J. ZAKOUR

A disaster is the disruption of a society's means for satisfying its needs for material and intangible resources. They are most likely to occur when a hazard affects vulnerable people living in an unsafe environment. Disasters disproportionately affect poor and socially marginalized populations, especially in less developed regions of the world. These communities also suffer greater numbers of disaster deaths and other casualties and lose a higher proportion of total household wealth compared with more affluent communities. Natural and human-caused disasters are increasing in severity and leading to great reduction in the development levels and well-being of affected societies (United Nations International Strategy for Disaster Reduction [UNISDR], 2009). The high levels of disaster vulnerability and low levels of resources in less developed communities and regions represent a lack of social and distributive justice.

OVERVIEW OF DISASTERS AS A SOCIAL ISSUE

Each year disasters kill tens of thousands of people and affect hundreds of millions of people worldwide. In 2008, the International Federation of Red Cross and Red Crescent Societies (IFRC) reported that from January 2004 to April 2008, there were 1108 disasters. Of these disasters, 37% occurred in Asia and the Pacific, 27% occurred in Africa, and 22% occurred in the Americas. Floods or flash floods were the most common type of disaster, accounting for 28% of disasters, while tropical cyclones made up 12%. The United Nations International Strategy for Disaster Reduction (UNISDR) reported that on average, over 200 million people suffered losses from disasters each year between 2000 and 2008 (UNISDR, 2009).

The average annual number of disasters and disaster casualties has increased over the last three decades, rising sharply since 1975 (UNISDR, 2009). From 1975 to 1985, the average annual number of disasters was between 50 and 200. Between 1998 and 2008,

the annual number of disasters rose to between 300 and 450. On average, over 66,800 people were killed annually by natural disasters from 2000 and 2007. However, in 2008, over 235,800 people were confirmed dead from disasters, the largest number for any year on record. The economic damage from natural disasters has also begun to increase, particularly since 1990. Beginning in 1980, eighteen years saw economic losses valued at $50 billion (in 2007 USD) or greater. All but one of these eighteen years occurred in 1990 or later. The five costliest years for disaster losses occurred between 1998 and 2008, with annual losses between $100 billion and $250 billion.

Community vulnerability to disasters is not equally distributed among nations or regions of the world. Africa, with about 14.5% of the world's population, has suffered from a disproportionate percentage of the world's disasters (IFRC, 2008). Though absolute economic losses from natural disasters are highest in developed nations such as the United States and Japan, the number of people affected by disasters per 100,000 inhabitants is highest in less developed and developing nations and regions. Almost 81% of all disaster deaths from 2000 to 2008 were in the less developed or developing regions of Asia, especially Myanmar (Burma), China, Thailand, Indonesia, and the Philippines (UNISDR, 2009).

The increase in disasters, disaster casualties, and annual economic losses is partly explained by the growing scale and globalization of technological, economic, and social systems. Destruction from a localized hazard increasingly leads to regional or transnational disasters (Mileti, 1999). There has also been a trend of rapid population increase in unsafe geographic areas, particularly near coastal and river areas. In developed nations with an aging population, such as the United States, large numbers of older people are relocating to or retiring in coastal areas (Cutter, 2006). In less developed regions, increasing numbers of people reside in unsafe coastal areas with land less than three feet above sea level. These populations tend to be landless and poor. Given the landless and impoverished status of these populations, birth rates are higher than in developed nations because poor families must rely on relatively larger numbers of children to engage in labor and supplement family income. Being landless and poor leads these families to reside in hazard-prone areas such as low-lying delta islands, deforested hillsides, or even large garbage heaps. Because children are more vulnerable to disasters than adults, ever-larger numbers of children live in households residing on hazard-prone land (Wisner, Blaikie, Cannon, & Davis, 2004).

An additional reason for growth in disaster numbers and severity is global climate change (Intergovernmental Panel on Climate Change [IPCC], 2007). Disasters that occur because of human-caused climate change can be thought of as human-caused. Rainfall patterns are already dramatically changing in regions such as Africa and the Middle East. Worldwide, increased mean temperatures lead to droughts and to the rise in mean global sea levels from expansion of water and melting of glaciers and the polar ice caps. Global climate change is leading to less predictable and more destructive weather patterns and more powerful and destructive coastal storms (IPCC, 2007). Hurricanes Katrina and Wilma in 2005 and the 2008 Myanmar cyclone (one of the deadliest on record) provide evidence for this trend toward more powerful storms.

RELEVANCE OF DISASTERS TO INTERNATIONAL SOCIAL WORK

Because of the social work profession's concern for the well-being of communities and societies, international social work practice has increasingly included disaster prevention, response, and recovery as an integral part of social development (Streeter, 1991). Without factoring disaster vulnerability into development projects, development cannot be sustainable. Also, the clients of social work are often the poor and socially marginalized and are disproportionately children, women, the elderly, and ethnic minorities, including people of color. These populations are also the most vulnerable to disasters, as the 2004 Indian Ocean tsunami emphasized.

The profession's concern with social justice is another reason why it is important for social workers to intervene in disasters throughout the world. Linking people to social resources and creating linkages among systems so that they are more accessible are two central aspects of social work's mission (Minahan & Pincus, 1977). Distributive justice is a central priority for social work, and fair and equitable distribution of resources increases the disaster resilience of communities. Consistent with the strengths perspective, international social work helps foster the resilience of less developed communities and populations by increasing their access to resources and by helping people build on and leverage their collective strengths (Lundy, 2004).

THEORETICAL FOUNDATIONS AND DEVELOPMENTS

Conceptual Definitions

Hazards are any conditions that interact with root societal causes of inequality and unsafe living conditions to produce a disaster. *Natural disasters* are triggered when a natural hazard intersects with a population residing in unsafe conditions. *Human-caused disasters* involve hazards that originate in the accidental failure of industrial or technical systems. In this chapter, natural and industrial disasters are distinguished from other types of emergencies, such as mass killings, terrorism, and war. These types of emergencies differ from disasters because conflict emergencies involve the intent by one party to harm or kill others.

Natural hazards include weather and geophysical phenomena as well as fires that originate through accidental or natural sources of combustion in households, neighborhoods, or forested areas. Human-caused disasters result from human or mechanical error leading to toxic emissions, explosions, or potentially life-threatening chemical spills originating from industrial or technological sources. The most destructive industrial disaster in a developing nation was the leakage of cyanide from the Union Carbide plant in Bhopal, India, in 1984. This disaster killed thousands of people and left up to 500,000 people ill and suffering from serious health problems (Rajan, 1999). Though human-caused disasters often lead to assigning blame to other members of society, blame assignment occurs even in natural disasters, though to a lesser degree. For example, just as in Bhopal, where there has been an effort to prosecute the top managers of Union Carbide, the US Army Corps of Engineers is being sued by survivors of Hurricane Katrina for faulty construction of flood walls.

Vulnerability and Resilience

Vulnerability is the level of susceptibility to disasters relative to the level of disaster resilience of social systems, including communities and populations. Vulnerability theory examines the environmental liabilities (risk factors) and capabilities (protective factors) that help explain the susceptibility and resilience of a social system to extremely adverse events such as a disaster. Resiliency theory in social work is used to identify and understand the risk and protective factors that affect the resilience of children and adults in the face of adversity, including exposure to disasters (Zakour, 2008, 2010).

The capabilities of the social, built, and natural environment of a community are a form of social resource or social capital that increases the disaster resiliency of the community. Social resources and social capital are the tangible and intangible resources embedded in social networks and community social structures. Environmental liabilities are risk factors in communities or societies that make members of the society more susceptible to the negative effects of disasters (Zakour, 2010).

Similar to the idea that disasters are designed by societal conditions of inequality (Mileti, 1999), the root causes of disasters are distal social conditions that may not be readily apparent, such as an ideology of inequality or stratification. Dynamic pressures are another type of liability. These pressures include the lack of physical, human, social, and environmental capital as well as rapidly changing conditions related to population growth and crowding, climate change, and environmental degradation. When root causes and dynamic pressures lead to the location of a population in unsafe geographic areas, a hazard can trigger a disaster affecting these communities (Wisner et al., 2004). Population growth and pressure on land use have led to the location of almost 100 million of the world's poor in coastal areas less than three feet above sea level, which are not safe from coastal storms, flooding, and tsunamis.

Resilience is the ability of a social system, community, or society to fully recover after severe adversity such as a disaster. Full recovery of a social system such as a community or society means regaining predisaster or pretrauma levels of functioning. Resilience is largely dependent on access to resources and the ability to mobilize those resources, including physical and social capital, for instrumental uses such as disaster prevention, response, and recovery (Zakour, 2010). Access to resources in many societies is highly inequitable and stratified—the essence of vulnerability and distributive injustice (Oliver-Smith, 2002). An important example of this stratification is the residence of poor populations on hillsides used as garbage dumps or denuded of trees. These populations can only afford to live on such dangerous land, which is highly prone to deadly mudslides; examples are those that occurred in Honduras and Nicaragua in 1998, Venezuela in 1999, and Algeria, Brazil, and the Philippines in 2001 (Wisner et al., 2004).

Current Roles and Contributions of Social Work

With its generalist approach, social work is ideally suited to intervene in disasters because of the multidimensionality of disasters. Disasters affect many dimensions of well-being, and they affect systems at all levels in a society. Effective interventions in disasters at the international level require social work practice from clinical to macro levels. This multidimensionality applies especially to social development. Though international social development and disaster resilience are not one and the same, the level of social development in a society is a primary determinant of both vulnerability and resilience (Zakour, 2010).

Social development increases resilience by increasing the capacity of a community to provide resources for recovery. Effective social development requires micro interventions to decrease psychological disorders and limitations on individual and household functioning due to individual disability. Macro-level interventions in development include increasing the number and capacity of social services organizations, improving cooperation among community organizations and social groups, and improving policy to provide people with increased opportunity for social and economic development. This range of social development strategies was successfully used after Hurricane Mitch in a development and disaster mitigation project in the Lower Lempa River Valley in El Salvador (Lavell, 2004).

International Resources for Disasters

Important resources for information and practice in disasters include the Intergovernmental Panel on Climate Change (IPCC), the International Federation of Red Cross and Red Crescent Societies (IFRC), the UN Office for the Coordination of Humanitarian Affairs (OCHA), the UN International Strategy for Disaster Reduction (UNISDR), faith-based relief organizations such as the United Methodist Committee on Relief (UMCOR), and Social Workers

Across Nations (SWAN), a recent initiative of the National Association of Social Workers in the United States (NASW). The IPCC details the impact of global warming and rising sea levels on physical infrastructure, coastlines, and communities; the increasing severity of disasters; and the resulting psychosocial and mental health issues of disaster victims. The IFRC provides services in disaster management and also social development in the areas of physical and mental health care. The UNISDR and OCHA provide services and information on emergency humanitarian response, especially regarding natural disasters and refugee populations. The work of UMCOR, made possible by charitable contributions and volunteers, focuses on recovery and reconstruction in areas affected by severe disasters. Finally, SWAN helps social workers provide volunteer services on an international level, with a special focus on the needs of the most vulnerable populations and communities.

DISTRIBUTION OF SOCIAL RESOURCES IN DISASTERS

Environmental Capital

The high number of deaths from disasters in less developed nations is often attributable to global resource inequality and stratification of environmental capital. An example of environmental capital in the built environment is infrastructure and the construction or retrofitting of buildings to resist damage from earthquakes. While developed nations (e.g., the United States and Japan) have much of this environmental capital, buildings and infrastructure in developing nations such as Turkey, Haiti, India, and China are less earthquake resistant and are more likely to collapse during an earthquake, potentially killing tens of thousands of people. Access to a built environment resistant to hazards such as earthquakes, tropical storms, and high winds is a critical component of social development. The 2011 earthquake and tsunami in Japan demonstrated the limitations of this approach as even strong building codes could not provide protection against the tsunami.

The large and growing economies of Asia, Europe, and the Americas emit large volumes of greenhouse gases and toxic substances, causing environmental degradation. Pollution and degradation of the environment result in a loss of environmental capital in the natural environment. (See Chapter 27 for more on environment). Global warming and environmental degradation are dynamic forces that increase disaster vulnerability, especially for economically or socially

marginalized communities and populations (Wisner et al., 2004). Partly because of rapid population growth, a lack of drinkable water is becoming an acute problem for billions of people. Glaciers such as those in the Himalayas provide needed fresh water for many of the world's people, yet climate change is rapidly melting these glaciers. Within less than a century, glacial melting will severely limit the supply of fresh water and greatly reduce the environmental capital of billions of people (IPCC, 2007).

Social Networks

To reduce disaster vulnerability, the most effective social work interventions are those that help develop networks of social support and social capital, link the networks together to make them more accessible, and connect vulnerable people directly to the networks. Social networks allow for the redistribution, mobilization, and coordination of services and social resources to effectively mitigate, respond to, and recover from disasters (Gillespie, Colignon, Banerjee, Murty, & Rogge, 1993). In international social work, fostering networks of social support is a key intervention for promoting disaster resilience of households, populations, communities, and societies (Norris, Baker, Murphy, & Kaniasty, 2005). With the profession's focus on relationships, the dignity of the individual, and social justice, social workers are uniquely qualified for fostering community resilience and reducing disaster susceptibility.

Methods of community development that combine locality development, social action, and feminist models can be highly effective for fostering disaster resilience. Development projects that have been able to unify communities and empower women to substantially participate in the development process have been successful in vulnerability reduction (Lundy, 2004). When organizations work together in a cooperative fashion and nonprofit organizations help bridge organizations at the international, national, and local levels, not only can resources be more fairly distributed, but also the voices of local populations are amplified in the political arena (Lavell, 2004).

Through policy interventions, social workers can use voluntary and community organizations to help create synergies in development at regional, national, and international levels (IPCC, 2007). Coordination of the voluntary sector in social development increases resilience and helps create a coordinated network of organizations capable of responding to disasters. Communities need to bolster their existing exchange networks among households and with other communities and villages to leverage available resources for social development and disaster resiliency. This need was illustrated by the inadvertent disruption of mutual support among Turkana pastoralists in East Africa when a Western model of drought relief destroyed the social organization and exchange patterns of historically migratory groups. Western drought aid forced pastoralists, who regularly migrate to obtain water and food, to permanently resettle in refugee camps. This led to the further impoverishment of the affected Turkana and disrupted exchange patterns of mutual aid among groups of pastoralists who relied on this exchange to help them cope with droughts (McCabe, 2002).

Human and Social Capital

Collective social capital is the trust that allows a high level of cooperation in disaster prevention and response among numerous ethnic, cultural, and sociodemographic groups. International social work practice can help increase mutual trust and cooperation among the various sociodemographic and cultural populations in a society. Social workers achieve this through relationship building and the formation of coalitions whose goals are social development and disaster mitigation (Lavell, 2004). Through these community and societal interventions, social workers aid the development of civil society in regions that lack the social participation and voluntary and governmental organizations that help generate collective social capital. These efforts have been underway for some time in the former Soviet Union and neighboring nations in Eastern Europe.

Higher levels of human and social capital at the individual and household levels are also important goals of social development, and these increase resilience in disasters. When individuals or households have access to high levels of human capital, which includes livelihood skills, literacy, and formal education, their disaster susceptibility is reduced and resilience increased. Higher levels of skills and formal education are associated with an increased capacity of individuals, households, and communities to effectively cope with adversity such as disasters (Norris et al., 2005).

Building human capital in a society is the foundation for increased access to social capital embedded in networks of individuals, organizations, and community groups. The existence of adequate social resources and social capital depends largely on high levels of human capital in a community or society. When social development interventions help

to increase and leverage both human and social capital in a community, the community becomes more resilient in the face of adversities such as disasters (Gillespie et al., 1993). Social work community and social development practice in the international sphere can simultaneously foster day-to-day and disaster resiliency. A more disaster-resilient community can help sustain its level of social development, which is important because natural and human-caused hazards can never be entirely eliminated. Fostering social development, the day-to-day well-being of people, and the disaster resilience of communities creates an important development synergy (Zakour, 2008).

SUMMARY AND CONCLUSIONS

Vulnerability is not evenly distributed on a global basis, and factors such as ideologies of social stratification, low levels of development, rising sea levels, and population growth in nations with coastal areas are contributing to increased numbers of severe disasters in many regions (Wisner et al., 2004). Social and development policies from the local to international levels are needed to promote sustainable development, which includes a substantial component of disaster mitigation. In light of global climate change, if these policies are enacted immediately, then important synergies can result between social development and disaster mitigation as well as between development projects in different communities (Zakour, 2008).

Because disasters are not entirely preventable, and it is almost impossible to control natural and sometimes even industrial hazards, the micro and macro practice of international social work must be directed toward fostering the disaster resilience of households, groups, communities, and societies (Zakour, 2010). This focus on disaster resilience represents a decisive shift toward the strengths perspective in disaster social work. Social and distributive justice must occur at all levels of international social work practice, from clinical to community, to help reduce the disaster vulnerability of less developed communities and regions.

Further efforts in vulnerability research are needed for improved identification and understanding of the societal conditions that are among the root causes of disaster as well as to identify and modify the dynamic pressures and unsafe conditions that make communities highly vulnerable to disasters. Efforts should include a major focus on fostering and supporting resiliency, especially in less developed communities around the world. If communities can have more equitable access to human, social, and environmental capital, and the existing strengths of these communities can be leveraged and built on, then their resilience in disaster and nondisaster contexts can be improved. Over the coming decades, fostering community resilience will prove an important challenge for international social work practice in disasters.

REFERENCES

Cutter, S. L., (2006). *Hazards, vulnerability and environmental justice.* London, Earthscan.

Gillespie, D. F., Colignon, R. A., Banerjee, M. M., Murty, S. A., & Rogge, M. (1993). *Partnerships for community preparedness* (Program on Environment and Behavior Monograph No. 54). Boulder, CO: University of Colorado, Institute of Behavioral Science.

Intergovernmental Panel on Climate Change (IPCC). (2007, November). *Summary for policymakers of the synthesis report of the IPCC fourth assessment report.* Retrieved April 12, 2011, from http://www.ipcc.ch/publications_and_data/ar4/syr/en/spm.html

International Federation of Red Cross and Red Crescent Societies (IFRC). (2008). *World disasters report 2008.* Retrieved March 14, 2009, from www.redcross.ie/layout/set/print/content/view/full/1831Red_Cross_Red_Crescent_figures_HIV_disasters.pdf

Lavell, A. (2004). The Lower Lempa River Valley, El Salvador: Risk reduction and development project. In G. Bankoff, G. Frerks, & D. Hilhorst (Eds.), *Mapping vulnerability: Disasters, development & people* (pp. 67–82). London: Earthscan.

Lundy, C. (2004). Community-based social work practice. In C. Lundy (Ed.), *Social work and social justice: A structural approach to practice* (pp. 168–182). Peterborough, ON: Broadview Press.

McCabe, J. T. (2002). Impact of and response to drought among Turkana pastoralists: Implications for anthropological theory and hazards research. In S. M. Hoffman & A. Oliver-Smith (Eds.), *Catastrophe & culture: The anthropology of disaster* (pp. 213–236). Santa Fe, NM: School of American Research.

Mileti, D. S. (1999). *Disasters by design: A reassessment of natural hazards in the United States.* Washington, DC: John Henry Press.

Minahan, A., & Pincus, A. (1977). Conceptual framework for social work practice. *Social Work, 22*(5), 347–352.

Norris, F. H., Baker, C. K., Murphy, A. D., & Kaniasty, K. (2005). Social support mobilization and deterioration after Mexico's 1999 flood: Effects of context, gender, and time. *American Journal of Community Psychology, 36*(1/2), 15–28.

Oliver-Smith, A. (2002). Theorizing disasters: Nature, power, and culture. In S. M. Hoffman & A. Oliver-Smith (Eds.), *Catastrophe & culture: The anthropology of disaster* (pp. 23–47). Santa Fe, NM: School of American Research.

Rajan, S. R. (1999). Bhopal: Vulnerability, routinization, and the chronic disaster. In A. Oliver-Smith & S. M. Hoffman (Eds.), *The angry earth: Disasters in anthropological perspective* (pp. 257–277). New York: Routledge.

Streeter, C. L. (1991). Disasters and development: Disaster preparedness and mitigation as an essential component of development planning. *Social Development Issues, 13*(3), 100–110.

United Nations International Strategy for Disaster Reduction (UNISDR). (2009). 2008 disasters in numbers. Retrieved on March 14, 2009, from www.unisdr.org/eng/media-room/facts-sheets/2008-disasters-in-numbers-ISDR-CRED.pdf

Wisner, B., Blaikie, P., Cannon, T., & Davis, I. (2004). *At risk: Natural hazards, people's vulnerability and disasters* (2nd ed.). New York: Routledge.

Zakour, M. J. (2008). Vulnerability to climate change in the Nile Delta: Social policy and community development interventions. In *Proceedings of the 21st International Conference of Social Work: Social work and human welfare in a changeable community* (pp. 425–451). Cairo: Helwan University.

Zakour, M. J. (2010). Vulnerability and risk assessment: Building community resilience. In D. F. Gillespie & K. Danso (Eds.), *Disaster concepts and issues: A guide for social work education and practice* (pp. 15–33). Alexandria, VA: CSWE Press.

35

Poverty and Human Needs

VIMLA NADKARNI AND GOVIND DHASKE

Poverty remains the most challenging problem of human civilization due to its deep-rooted nature encompassing all walks of life. The academic as well as policy debates pertaining to poverty show several epistemological and ideological variations. Though ongoing globalization has surfaced economic aspects of poverty, it is clear that over centuries and generations, habitats across the world have faced the issues of poverty and its complex manifestations, questioning sustainable human development processes.

Historically, under the influence of social shibboleths, the poor have been blamed for their situation, resulting in poverty reinforcement patterns among policies created by socioreligious polity. Structural theories on poverty have diluted the stringent premises that blame the poor by proving the role of human structures in developing poverty. The wealth and income polarization viewed in the Global South and Global North aggravates a peculiar global poverty dynamic due to the greedy approaches among some economically affluent segments in the developed world and historic classism in the developing world.

Unlike other development issues, poverty probably can be seen as an exclusive problem still undergoing primary debates about its conception. Despite differences, there have been scholarly agreements in the acceptance of determinants of poverty outlining basic human needs essential for a dignified quality of life and well-being. The multidimensional nature of poverty exposes the gaps in the existing development paradigm; hence, the social work profession has a major role to play to ensure that growth processes are fair and just with equitable distribution of resources and benefits to the poor. This chapter looks at poverty and human needs in an integrated framework. Within a perspective-based discussion, it analyzes the role of the social work profession in advancing the practice for policy change.

GLOBAL SCENARIO OF POVERTY

A recent press release by the World Bank (2009) declared that 1.4 billion people (one in four) in the developing world were living below US$1.25 a day in 2005. The same report admitted distressful regional variations wherein East Asia is rapidly overcoming poverty while progress in sub-Saharan Africa is comparatively slow, even stagnant. The Chronic Poverty Research Centre (CPRC) (2008) estimates 442,815,000 chronically poor across the world. They belong to the most complex generational forms of poverty, mainly rooted in systemic and structural barriers.

The geographical variability in poverty distribution can be viewed in the form of polarization in the developed Global North and developing Global South. Africa is the continent with the highest rate of maternal mortality, estimated at 820 maternal deaths per 100,000 live births in 2005. Asia's rate of maternal death is 350 per 100,000 live births (UNICEF, 2008, p. 22). According to a UNAIDS fact sheet (2008), sub-Saharan Africa has two-thirds (67%) of all people living with HIV worldwide. The same report mentions that half of those infected are women. Considering the linkages of women's health with the overall health situation, sub-Saharan Africa is likely to remain trapped under poverty.

In 2007, 37.3 million people were living in poverty in the United States. Child poverty in particular is a growing concern: The poverty rate increased from 17.4% in 2006 to 18.0% in 2007 among children younger than eighteen, according to a recent press release by the US Census Bureau (2008).

DEFINING POVERTY AND HUMAN NEEDS

The definitional conflicts about poverty are significant to interventionists regardless of discipline as they influence policy approaches to the eradication of poverty. Predominantly, the economic, unitary approach of the World Bank indicates extreme poverty as living on less than US$1 per day and moderate poverty as less than $2 per day. The international poverty line has been recalibrated at $1.25 a day using new data on purchasing power parities (PPPs) (World Bank, 2008a, p. 1). The policy obsession with the exclusive economic nature of poverty received a positive stroke with phenomenal research by Nobel Laureate Amartya Sen. He stated that poverty is an income level that does not allow an individual to cover certain basic necessities, taking into account the circumstances and social requirements of the environment (Quesada, 2001).

The UN Millennium Development Goals (MDGs) have given priority to poverty with Goal 1, calling for the world to eradicate extreme poverty and hunger. Targets include reducing by half the proportion of people living on less than a dollar a day, achieving full and productive employment and decent work for all including women and young people, and reducing by half the proportion of people who suffer from hunger. The 2008 Millennium Development Goals report outlines progress on the MDGs; the goal of cutting in half the proportion of people living on less than $1 a day by 2015 remains within reach. However, this achievement will be due largely to extraordinary economic success in most of Asia. In contrast, previous estimates suggest that little progress has been made in reducing extreme poverty in sub-Saharan Africa (UN, 2008, p. 6).

Suggesting that poverty is the consequence of the denial or violation of human rights, Action Aid (2008) states that people living in poverty are often treated as less than human, resulting in a deepening cycle of poverty. The United Nations (2001) has given a comprehensive rights-based definition of poverty as "a human condition characterized by the sustained or chronic deprivation of the resources, capabilities, choices, security and power necessary for the enjoyment of an adequate standard of living and other civil, cultural, economic, political and social rights." Poverty and human needs are mutually correlated in any development context, and their fulfillment signifies the well-being attained by the vulnerable in their political and social locales.

Poverty Measures and Human Needs

Historically, absolute and relative poverty measures have been the primary focal points of poverty interventions through public policies. *Absolute poverty* denotes poverty status based on availability and access to essential commodities. With a top-down absolute poverty measure, the context-specific poverty determinants based on survival needs and cultural practices may get sidelined within policy interventions. *Relative poverty* focuses on income inequality but suffers from methodological problems in assigning poverty status as it ignores quality-of-life indicators.

The Fraser Institute in Canada pioneered the basic-needs approach to poverty measurement with the scientific rationale that poverty is fundamentally a problem of insufficiency and not inequality (Sarlo, 2006). The Panel on Technology for Basic Needs (PTBN) of the United Nations Commission on Science and Technology for Development (CSTD) has defined basic needs as the minimal requirements to sustain life—adequate nutrition, health care, water, and sanitary facilities—as well as access to education and information that enable individuals and communities to be productive and to make rational use of the available basic goods and services (CSTD, 1997, p. 3). Poverty in its visible forms structures a matrix of various human needs. In an analytical review of various major policy documents, Anderson and O'Neil (2006) noted: "*Report on the World Social Situation* (2005), and *Human Development Report* (2005) argue that certain types of inequalities—in access to health care, education, or political rights, for example—have a direct causal impact on poverty by reinforcing the intergenerational transmission of poverty and diminishing individuals' prospects for escaping poverty" (p. 5)(For more on measures, see Chapter 63 on measuring social well-being).

Multifaceted Nature of Poverty

Poverty is not just an issue in itself but acts as a major stressor for various other issues, such as terrorism, violence, lack of access to health care and education, and degradation of environmental and natural resources, resulting in a decline in human development. Poverty has been the cause and consequence of social exclusion, as noted by the Policy Research Initiative (2004) in an important conference on social policy. Further, exclusion occurs when people do not have adequate support to manage key transitions throughout life. "Violence is more common where inequalities are greater, and trends suggest that growing up in poverty often leads to social exclusion, which can contribute to crime. Countries with high rates of poverty and inequality generally have poorer social support and safety nets, more unequal access to education, and fewer opportunities for young people" (The United Nations, Department of Economic and Social Affairs, 2005, p. 6).

The majority of the 1.5 billion people living on $1 a day or less are women (Martin, 2008), and 70% of the world's poor are women. Feminization of poverty in the light of feminization of agriculture needs immediate attention because the sectoral performance of agriculture and agricultural productivity has been rapidly declining across the globe. Estrella (2005) mentioned :

"Women become impoverished because of problems different from those of the men; among them, those related to giving birth (single mothers); affective ruptures (abandonment of families, divorce and widowhood); social problems derived from other types of separations (hospitalization, emigration, imprisonments of husbands or partners); loss of the husband's or partner's work, and definitely, in many instances, problems deriving from affective-economic dependence upon men, which accounts for the greatest intensity in conditions of poverty suffered by the women (in the sense of perceiving less social protection and fewer resources with which to confront poverty)" (p. 1).

The livelihood, nutritional, and health dependency of women and rural folks on agriculture is a prominent feature of rural economies and needs policy incorporation for poverty eradication. The growing unorganized sector, mostly across urban habitats, emerges as a serious concern due to the specific vulnerability of migrants. Pressure on resources and the growing number of congested slums are putting the urban poor at various risks. The Northern market economies need to pay attention to specific poverty features emerging out of market failures whereas the diversifying Southern economies need more balance within dynamics among primary, secondary and tertiary sectors which is resulting in complex forms of poverty.

POVERTY–HEALTH–DEVELOPMENT NEXUS

The instrumental role played by health in quality of life is gaining a substantial place in the policy debates. The majority of the basic human needs can also be seen as important health determinants. The need to provide sanitation both for drinking water and hygiene remains a huge challenge in developing countries. Currently 1.1 billion people lack access to safe water and 2.6 billion lack access to proper sanitation. As a result, more than 4500 children under five years of age die every day from easily preventable diseases such as diarrhea. Many others, including older children and adults but especially women, suffer from

poor health, diminished productivity, and missed opportunities for education (WHO, 2007). *Human Development report (2007/2008)* has mentioned that "Climate shocks are a potent threat to the poor's most valuable assets—their health and their labor and deteriorating nutrition and falling incomes generate a twin threat of increasing vulnerability to illness and fewer resources for medical treatment" (change to UNDP 2007, p. 87, 2007).

One of the major collaborative studies by the World Bank, Department for International Development (DFID), European Commission (EC), and United Nations Development Programme (UNDP) (2002) demonstrates the poverty–environment relationship on three key dimensions of poverty: livelihoods, health, and vulnerability. The impact of this relationship on the rural and urban poor is visible in the destruction of livelihood resources, degradation in health status with exposure to pollution, and decline in environmental health, aggravating the vulnerability of people living in poverty because they have less coping capacity.

Woolf (2007) has mentioned that three trends—increasing poverty, decreasing household income, and widening income inequality—are harbingers of a future wave of poorer health. Growing out-of-pocket expenditures in developing countries and lack of health insurance in the developed world are distressful poverty-related facts that aggravate the drudgery. There is a paucity of context specific research on how poverty and health function in an integrated manner, mutually influencing each other in creating human development.

PUBLIC POLICIES AND POVERTY ALLEVIATION

Human Development report mentions: In our interconnected world, a future built on the foundations of mass poverty in the midst of plenty is economically inefficient, politically unsustainable, and morally indefensible (UNDP, 2005, p. 4). Sachs (2005) stated that the very poor are often disconnected from market forces due to the lack of human capital in terms of good nutrition and health and an adequate education. Sachs emphasized that expenditures towards human capital should reach the poorest of the poor but governments often fail to make such investments (p. 72). Public policy largely derives its theoretical as well as empirical footing in the role of the state in alleviating poverty in the light of defined human needs and the institutional regime that addresses it. Availability and assured access in addition to continual monitoring of basic minimum services characteristically indicate the concern of governments toward vulnerable segments of their populations.

Social security arrangements and safety nets are the primary tools to address the vulnerability of the poor in difficult situations. The World Bank estimated that around 100 million people may have been pushed into poverty because of the high prices of the past two years. African countries and other low-income countries are particularly vulnerable, but even middle-income countries are at risk if they do not get well-developed social safety nets (Spence, 2008).

Creating an enabling environment for the poor to seize emerging opportunities by providing adequate resources is the primary responsibility of governments. Public policies should encompass support to the poor through active institutional systems and efficient service delivery on basic needs fronts and further developmental steps. The policy-making process should incorporate knowledge produced by various development functionaries since mainstream poverty measurement shows some exclusionary features due to a lack of grassroots interface and involvement. Use of inclusive methodologies like qualitative research helps to overcome the epistemological barriers in understanding and intervening for poverty eradication. In addition, the increase in factors that create new vulnerabilities (e.g., global climate change, rapid recession) emphasizes need for advanced poverty monitoring. The extraordinary vulnerability of women, children, the elderly and physically and mentally challenged populations needs well-designed interventions for poverty redress.

POVERTY, HUMAN NEEDS AND SOCIAL WORK

Social work has a concrete role to play in the alleviation of global poverty in terms of advocating against the vulnerability of the poor and poverty patterns. Jordan (2008) mentioned : "Just as physical and ecological sustainability demands that we put a value on the natural resources of the wilderness, forests, seas, and lakes, so well-being requires us to revalue relationships, emotions, respect, and belonging. Social work can be more assertive in insisting on these values for the sake of the poorest in the world, whose value is little considered by present policies" (p. 450). Poverty patterns and their distribution and processes are the core focus of social work interventions. Asunción Lera St. Clair (2006) stated that "the most we can say about the current status of knowledge about global poverty is that it reflects a 'consensus among certain scientists' rather than a 'scientific consensus' (p. 60)." This implies the need for a vigilant approach by social work organizations and social work researchers to the issue of poverty and suffering groups. Cox and Pawar (2006) emphasized community-based strategies for poverty alleviation with a focus on participation, self-reliance, sustainability, and empowerment.

With the failure of the MDGs and World Bank to address the contextual nature of poverty, international social work practice should focus on knowledge production on the dynamic nature of global poverty. Social Work researchers with a value-based research approach should come up with the peculiar issues of poverty which are not captured by the dominant poverty assessment methods. Academia and practitioner organizations have to come forward with advocacy-focused research on poverty for the development of appropriate and effective policies and programs across the globe. International social work organizations must play a significant role in influencing the mind-set of those who govern at the highest levels in order to make poverty the agenda for action in the next decade and thereafter.

CONCLUSION

Perspective building on poverty in international social work education and practice is imperative in the current context of increasing disparities in global development. The dynamic nature of poverty needs a vigilant approach from the social work profession through global alliances with civil society, NGOs, and multidisciplinary professional networks. Social work research should explore the linkages of poverty issues with governance and policy-induced institutional structures, which should inform advocacy and context-specific aspects within poverty eradication policies. Finally, social work interventions should mobilize people to form a constructive movement for policy change on poverty.

REFERENCES

Action Aid. (2008).Human rights–based approaches to poverty eradication and development. Retrieved March 7, 2009, from www.actionaid.org/assets/pdf/RBA%20paper%20FINAL.pdf.

Anderson, E., & O'Neil, T. (2006). A new equity agenda? Reflections on the 2006 *World Development Report*, the 2005 *Human Development Report* and the 2005 *Report on the World Social Situation* (Working paper 265). London: Overseas Development Institute.

Chronic Poverty Research Centre (CPRC). (2008). *The Chronic Poverty Report 2008–09: Escaping poverty traps.* Manchester: Author.

Commission on Science and Technology for Development (CSTD), Panel on Technology for Basic Needs. (1997). *An Assault on Poverty: Basic Human Needs, Science and Technology*. Ottawa, Canada: International Development Research Centre.

Cox, D. & Pawar M. (2006). *International social work: Issues, strategies, and programs*. London: Sage Publication.

Estrella, M. V. (2005). *The feminization of poverty: A global problem*. Accessed on March 06, 2009, at www.globaljusticecenter.org/papers2005/valdes_eng.htm

Jordan, B. (2008). Social work and world poverty. *International Social Work, 51*(4), 440–452.

Martin, J. (2008). Feminization of poverty—women constitute the majority of world's poor. Retrieved on March 7, 2009, from http://poverty.suite101.com/article.cfm/feminization_of_poverty

Policy Research Initiative (PRI). (2004). Exploring new approaches to social policy. Synthesis Report, PRI Conference, Canada.

Quesada, C. (2001). *Amartya Sen and the thousand faces of poverty*. Inter-American Development Bank, Global Policy Forum, US. Retrieved March 7, 2009, from http://www.globalpolicy.org/component/content/article/211/44271.html.

Sachs, J. (2005). *The end of poverty: How we can make it happen in our lifetime*. New York: Penguin.

Sarlo, C. (2006). Poverty in Canada: 2006 update. Vancouver, Montreal, Toronto, and Calgary: Fraser Institute. Retrieved March 7, 2009, from www.fraserinstitute.ca.

Spence, M. (2008). *The Growth Report: Strategies for Sustained Growth and Inclusive Development*. Commission on growth and development. Washington, DC: The World Bank.

St. Clair, A. L. (2006). Global poverty: The co-production of knowledge and politics. *Global Social Policy, 6*(1), 57–77.

UNAIDS. (2008). Fact sheet 08: Key facts by region—2008 report on the global AIDS epidemic. Report on the global AIDS epidemic 2008, August 2008. Geneva: Author.

The United Nations, Department of Economic and Social Affairs (2005). *Report on the World Social Situation 2005: The Inequality Predicament*, A/60/117/Rev.1 ST/ESA/299, New York USA: Author.

United Nations Development Programme (UNDP). (2007). *Human development report 2007/2008: Fighting climate change: Human solidarity in a divided world*. New York: Palgrave Macmillan.

United Nations Development Programme (UNDP). (2005). *Human development report 2005: International cooperation at cross roads: Aid trade and security in an unequal world*. Geneva: Author.

UN (2001) *Poverty and the International Covenant on Economic, Social and Cultural Rights*, UN Committee on Economic, Social and Cultural Rights, E/C.12/2001/10, New York: United Nations.

UNICEF. (2008). *The state of the world's children 2009: Maternal and newborn health*. New York: Author.

United Nations (UN). (2008). *The Millennium Development Goals report 2008*. New York: Author.

US Census Bureau. (2008, August 26). Household income rises, poverty rate unchanged, number of uninsured down. (News release). Washington, DC: Public Information Office, US Dept. of Commerce.

Woolf, S. H. (2007). Future health consequences of the current decline in US household income. *Journal of American Medical Association*, 298(16), 1931–1933.

World Bank. (2009). New data show 1.4 billion live on less than US$1.25 a day, but progress against poverty remains strong. Press Release No:2009/065/DEC. Retrieved March 7, 2009, from http://go.worldbank.org/T0TEVOV4E0.

World Bank. (2008). *World development indicators: Poverty data* (supplement to World Development Indicators 2008). Washington, DC: Author.

World Bank, UK Department for International Development (DFID), Directorate General for Development, European Commission (EC), & United Nations Development Programme (UNDP). (2002). *Linking poverty reduction and environmental management: Policy challenges and opportunities*. Retrieved March 08, 2009, from http://go.worldbank.org/NIMFWINT10.

World Health Organization (WHO). (2007). *The world health report 2007: A safer future global public health security in the 21ˢᵗ century*. Geneva: Author.

36

Racism and Antiracist Strategies

NARDA RAZACK

*Discussions . . . of . . . 'race' and racism shape distinctions, exclusions and privileges
and obstruct the full realization of human rights everywhere.*

UNITED NATIONS, 2001

This chapter focuses on international perspectives on racism. It addresses the saliency of race in an era of globalization and transnationalism. It also emphasizes the importance of including an analysis of racism and oppression in every facet of international social work: pedagogy, research, practice, and policy. The globalization of racism is being discussed as a more current approach to understanding how racism permeates borders, continues to produce the Other, and marginalizes groups of people. Race has played a decisive role in colonial society over the past 500 years and cannot be overestimated (Williams & Chrisman, 1994). In the often-contested postcolonial world, race and racism continue to shape everyday realities, albeit in ways more acutely and often more adversely experienced by nonwhite people. For example, when Northerners go to the South, they work primarily with nonwhite people in the host country and the relationships are raced in different and complex ways. We need to keep in mind, therefore, that *"racism illustrates and symbolizes the colonial relation"* (Memmi, 2000, p. 35).

There is a notable absence of critical race analysis in the international social work discourse. Racism and the process of racialization are evident in postcolonial and international relations and subsequently within international work and collaborations in postcolonial sites. This chapter begins with the current understanding of race and oppression and examples of its pernicious and pervasive nature. Globalization of racism is especially crucial to examine because racial matters are of concern in every corner of the globe. Racism also includes an examination of whiteness for international social work. The consequences of racism continue to be brutal to those on the receiving end. International social workers need to trace the multiple meanings of race in order to understand how race is perceived and practiced differently in Western and non-Western contexts.

LOCATING SOME MEANINGS OF RACE

Racism is a complex term to define and categorize, and striving to provide a broad definition of *race* is problematic since it is a socially constructed term and meanings shift according to political, economic, and global change. Biological and phenotypical concepts of race have been scientifically refuted, yet "race continues to be a powerful *social* construct and signifier" (Morrison, cited in Ladson-Billings, 1998). Racism needs to be understood currently and historically because its intensification and impact change throughout time. Discourses on race have enormous implications for international social work. There is a tendency to react openly to overt and virulent expressions of racism. However, there is still a hesitancy to respond and work through its more systemic and institutionalized manifestations, which are located in personal, professional, and international geographic spaces.

Noting the intersection of race with class and other forms of oppression in our everyday relations makes these arguments even more complex. Goldberg (1993), who explores historical meaning of race and racism, traced the beginnings of racial thinking to the late fifteenth century with the rush to conquer lands and their inhabitants. Others sketch the further development over time of racial classifications and their inseparability from racist evaluations. One stimulus came from the voyages of exploration and so-called discovery that brought Europeans into contact with groups of people different from themselves, especially peoples with different skin colors. The notorious African slave trade contributed importantly to racist thinking; it was already accepted that black was synonymous with evil and sin.

Omi and Winant (1993) describe the historical flexibility of racial meanings and categories as well as conflicts that occur in both the micro and macro levels of analysis, including "the irreducible political aspect of racial dynamics" (p. 4). Kothari's (2006) critiques of racism and ideas of race in discourses of development and practice are needed to understand inconsistencies, inadequacies, and contradictions in policies and practices that occur in this area of work. She also states that ideas and expressed articulations of race are "fluid and multiple, contingent and contextual, ranging from overt to covert and unreflexive" (p. 1). Goldberg (1993) emphasizes that race is a central and enduring element of the modern world. Racism was evident during the Nazi regime when the white race was seen to be the ideal. Colonization of countries has been predicated on the belief in superiority and has been underscored by theft and genocide, including current-day genocide of Aboriginal populations. Economic racism through the exploitation of one country over another has become more apparent through globalization, transnationalism, and capitalism.

Despite all of these charges of ways in which racism manifests itself, the most definitive conclusion is that *racism* is a constructed term and actions against racism have been introduced across the globe, albeit rather haltingly. The United Nations created the Universal Declaration of Human Rights to guard against any kind of distinction and discrimination based on race and color. In 1965, the antiapartheid struggle and the creation of postcolonial states led the UN to adopt the International Convention on the Elimination of All Forms of Racial Discrimination, which consists of twenty-five guiding principles. Its primary goal is to "promote and encourage universal respect for and observance of human rights and fundamental freedoms for all, without distinction as to race, sex, language or religion" (www2.ohchr.org/english/law/cerd.htm). In 1997 the UN General Assembly agreed to hold a World Conference against Racism (WCAR) in the struggle to eliminate all forms of racism and discrimination. The most recent conference was held in Durban in 2009, and its purpose was to recognize the global dimension to race and racism

and to build alliances to combat discrimination. These conferences have become a platform for dissension because of politicized debates on racism.

Cultural Racism

Lentin (2000) argues that a recent de-emphasis on the category of race and an increased focus on ethnicities and ethnic tensions signify a more advanced and sophisticated form of racism. These new and disguised forms of racism accompany the multiculturality of societies where immigration has significantly altered the normative population:

> The increasing 'multiculturality' of western societies is accompanied by a parallel inability to effectively deal with its inevitable consequences—the racist discrimination of ethnically or 'racially' different minorities, who highlight the alterity between the dominant and subordinate groups inherent in today's nation state. (p. 92)

A focus on culture can act as a new form of racism where normative standards are applied to groups of people, marginalizing some and exalting others. Whites are constantly positioned at the top of the hierarchy of relations because they create the ideologies that help to construct these categories. For example, the media, which are controlled by the white majority, often portray blacks as criminals in society, thereby demeaning the entire black population (Benjamin, 2002). Aboriginal people are largely depicted as perpetual drunks. And bell hooks (1995) describes the killing rage that she and many African Americans feel when subjected to racism, adding that addictions, and more dangerously apathy and hardheartedness, are ways to cope with this rage.

Many white people are not attuned to these everyday realities of racism because they believe that overt racist acts are uncommon. They also tend to be unaware of their complicity within institutional and structural forms of racism. We therefore cannot get beyond race and racism since new meanings crop up at every turn. On a cultural and social level, racism is also a social phenomenon and helps to produce the Other, creating distinctions of dominance, power, and privilege versus marginality, subordination, and degeneracy among individuals, groups, countries, and populations. Racism always implies power at the structural as well as the individual level.

International social work needs to transcend the historical comparative analyses of issues, including exchanges and research collaborations. It recognizes the local–global dialectic where peoples move across borders and inhabit spaces of the colonized. It includes the broader forces of colonization and imperialism. The forces of globalization and transnationalism have left particular countries decimated through policies of structural adjustment, and the effects of political wars result in a lack of accountability in perpetrating global abuses.

THE GLOBALIZATION OF RACISM, OR GLOBALIZED RACISMS

Racism is a global phenomenon, and current forms and practices are influenced by the process of globalization. Mary Robinson, former UN High Commissioner for Human Rights, stated that globalization has caused an increase in racism because the income gap between the rich and the poor has widened significantly and poor countries have not made significant gains (UN, 2001). Ten years ago, Castles (1996) wrote that migration was causing rich states to confront racism structurally and directly within their own borders, and he observed that contemporary forms of racisms were intricately linked to other processes of globalization. These observations still ring true in a globalized world. Bonilla-Silva (2000) argues that globalized race relations have become intensified because of diversification through the presence of racial Others in the Western world. Western nations maintain superiority over peripheral nations, and this form of hegemony is referred to as a new form of "informal imperialism" or "dominance without empire" (p. 194).

Jackson and colleagues (2001) state that Europe reluctantly accepts immigrants, especially those who come from countries south of the Mediterranean, and racist practices abound. Flows of people across borders to states that were once homogenous powerfully shift the landscape of these countries. Racist extremists are mobilizing independently across Central and Eastern Europe, which denotes the existence of racism and must be addressed (Mudde, 2005). Zick, Pettigrew, and Wagner (2008) concur that prejudice and discrimination directed at immigrants are widespread across Europe, and Fekete (2005) also states that antiforeigner racism is rampant, especially against asylum seekers in Europe. Additionally, Islam is seen as a threat in Europe and in many other Western countries, and Islamophobia has become a general response (Fekete, 2004). Anti-Muslim racism is on the rise in many countries, and brown and Arab-looking people are subject to various forms of prejudice and discrimination.

Race and caste systems create inequities and human rights violations in India and are key metaphors of sociopolitical struggles in many regions (Blee, 2007; Reddy, 2005). Black students speak of the racism they experience in China (Sautman, 1994), and in parts of Europe the Turks are marginalized as well as the Roma (McLaren, 2003). Essed (1996) has written extensively about the racism immigrants experience in the Netherlands. And Aboriginals continue to suffer genocide in many parts of the world, including Latin America, Australia, the United States, and Canada.

In Canadian society, racialized minority groups have been overtly marginalized and excluded from social, political, and economic structures, both historically as in the forced relocation and the internment of Japanese people during the Second World War (Christensen, 1999) and currently as in the marginalization of people who are Arab-looking. The 2008 election in the United States heralded a significant shift in race relations with the first black president and family occupying the White House. However, racial inequalities are still endemic in American society.

Racism in Professional Exchanges

Race and racism are endemic in international social work and emerge quite potently through exchanges and research collaborations (Razack, 2004). Race is a palpable dynamic in international relations and unfolds quite dramatically during exchanges and research collaborations, especially with partners whose socioeconomic statuses differ markedly. Kothari (2006) states that race is silent in development work, which is inherent in the discourse of international social work since many social workers go abroad and work under the umbrella of international development, especially in Africa. Going abroad principally to gain cross-cultural skills can reproduce Northern superiority regardless of the desire for social justice and equity.

Racism is produced in helping endeavors when we seek to manage diversity by providing information on the cultural traits of a particular ethnic group without analyses of power and privilege. In international social work, especially in the South, more caution needs to be exerted by Westerners in order to avoid fostering imperialism and racism. Smith-Maddox and Solorzano (2002) state that race as a social construction and a force in structuring people's lives is not new, and Roediger (1994) notes that race is evident even when the population is all white. Race continues to have a real impact on society, and race relations continue to be debated and theorized because of shifts in the sociopolitical terrain that create barriers and marginalize certain groups. It is imperative therefore to pay close attention to the dynamics of whiteness in the discourse of race in international social work.

Racializing Whiteness in International Social Work

Whiteness as a category of analysis of racism is largely invisible in the international social work literature. It is a critical area of antiracism studies and is important for international social work. Recent studies on whiteness exhort whites to disrupt their privileged status and act against the perpetuation of white power. Hytten and Warren (2003) analyze how whiteness is inscribed and reified in education. They observe how discourses on whiteness in the classroom can elicit resistance from white students, at times in the form of guilt or by them insisting on being the "good white," thereby protecting and securing dominant positions. Hytten and Warren state that personalizing the realities of whiteness can produce awareness but can also lead to disabling responses when the analysis is centered mainly on the self. These reactions need to be replaced by analyses of subject position and with action-oriented strategies to work against dominance and superiority. The discourse on whiteness needs to be centered within international social work to provide a comprehensive response for action and for change. Thompson (2003) argues that this analysis must include struggles to avoid reinscribing dominance.

It is common for social workers to adopt a neoliberal approach to refute racialized differences. In social work there is the tendency toward feeling white liberal guilt when discussing race, which disables conversation and action (Dominelli, 1998; Razack & Jeffery, 2002; Williams, 1999). Perry (2001) states that white people share a fundamental belief that "white raciality is cultureless" (p. 58) and therefore taken for granted. She argues that there is power in adopting a position that there is no culture, for in doing so, racial superiority is inscribed (p. 59). Weedon (1999) similarly contends that whiteness allows the problem of racism to be the problem of black people and not fundamentally part of the problem of white people. Social workers need to understand how their unearned privilege helps to maintain the status quo (Weedon, 1999). Racism has structural as well as individual advantages for white people,

who tend to be unaware of the privileged position of whiteness. Therefore, racism needs to be problematized by them. A global analysis of whiteness is critical in the terrain of international social work.

Goldberg (2002) illustrates how the state is currently being managed to promote homogeneity, thus certifying white reign and superiority: "White rule rules by going global: colonialism, imperialism . . . anti-communism, globalization. It is the globalizing of white dominance, explicitly or implicitly, by design or structurally, economically, politically, legally, culturally" (p. 196). According to Lipsitz (1998), although whiteness is everywhere in the North, it is difficult especially for white people to see. The subject of whiteness, like race and racism, produces tensions and anxieties when discussed because it forces recognition of privilege and dominance. Whiteness is enacted in subtle and overt ways in institutions and social spaces and is organized to maintain a "world racial order of white dominance" (Goldberg, 2002, p. 199).

The potency of whiteness is evident in foreign postcolonial space. If social workers are able to understand their home context prior to situating themselves in another country, they may be more sensitive to and aware of racism operating abroad. Whites are caught in the web of race relations because of their unearned privilege and their innate tendency to be ignorant (not fully aware) either of the fact of race or of their complicity within repressive societal structures. As Frankenberg (1993) states, whites are taught not to see race and therefore view themselves as colorless. Other (nonwhite) people are therefore raced. Nonwhite students are positioned very differently when they enter the international arena.

Frankenberg (1993) views the social construction of whiteness as being similar to the social construction of racism. She asserts that whiteness "refers to a set of locations that are historically, socially, politically, and culturally produced and, moreover, are intrinsically linked to unfolding relations of domination" (p. 6). Although there is a discourse on whiteness in the literature, it is not a major focus in international social work. Therefore when students and faculty go abroad, for example, they continue to occupy privileged locations because they adopt a position of only viewing difference at an intellectual level; rather than getting politically involved, so many "whitely scripts" are reinscribed (Harding, 1991, pp. 123–127). International social work therefore necessitates knowledge of the social construction of whiteness and its importance for the profession.

SUMMING UP AND IMPLICATIONS

This chapter dealt with how racism and whiteness are critical to the discourse on international social work as it continues to be enacted in a globalized world. Observations of the performance of race and whiteness in global spaces need to be consistently examined for international social work. Analyses of racism and whiteness provide critical perspectives for international social work, and they are also crucial for social work pedagogy, research, and practice. Race has played a decisive role in colonial societies and continues to shape everyday realities for many in a postcolonial world. Analyses of the constructs of race, the structures of racism, and their intersections with other forms of oppression should be mandatory for the profession of social work. Uncovering the presence of racism in the international terrain should become core to the discourse of the field.

REFERENCES

Benjamin, A. (2002). *The Black/Jamaican criminal: The making of ideology.* (Unpublished PhD dissertation). Ontario Institute for Studies in Education, University of Toronto, Canada.

Blee, K. M. (2007). Ethnographies of the far right. *Journal of Contemporary Ethnography, 36*(2), 119–128.

Bonilla-Silva, E. (2000). 'This is a white country': The racial ideology of the Western nations of the world-system. *Sociological Inquiry, 70*(2), 188–214.

Castles, S. (1996). The racisms of globalization. Retrieved March 6, 2009, from www.allenandunwin.com/academic/TEETH2.pdf.

Christensen, C. (1999). Multiculturalism, racism and social work: An exploration of issues in the Canadian context. In G. W. Lie & D. Este (Eds.), *Professional social service delivery in a multicultural world* (pp. 293–310). Toronto: Canadian Scholars Press.

Dominelli, L. (1998). *Anti-racist social work: A challenge for white practitioners and educators.* Philadephia: Temple University Press.

Essed, P. (1996). *Diversity: Gender, color and culture.* Amherst, MA: University of Massachusetts Press.

Fekete, L. (2005). The deportation machine: Europe, asylum and human rights. *Race & Class, 47*(1), 64–91.

Fekete, L. (2004). Anti-Muslim racism and the European security state. *Race & Class, 46*(1), 3–29.

Frankenberg, R. (1993). *White women, race matters: The social construction of whiteness.* Minneapolis, MN: University of Minnesota Press.

Goldberg, D. T. (2002). *The racial state.* Boston: Blackwell.

Goldberg, D. T. (1993). *Racist culture: Philosophy and the politics of meaning.* Oxford: Blackwell.

Harding, S. (1991). *Whose science? Whose knowledge? Thinking from women's lives.* Ithaca, NY: Cornell University Press.

hooks, b. (1995). *Killing rage: Ending racism.* New York: H. Holt.

Hytten K., & Warren, J. (2003). Engaging whiteness: How racial power gets reified in education. *Qualitative Studies in Education, 16*(1), 65–89.

Jackson, J. S., Brown, K. T., Brown, T. N., & Marks, B. (2001). Contemporary immigration policy orientation among dominant-group members in Western Europe. *Journal of Social Issues, 57*(3), 431–456.

Kothari, U. (2006). Critiquing 'race' and racism in development discourse and practice. *Progress in Development Studies, 6*(1), 1–7.

Ladson-Billings, G. (1998). Just what is critical race theory and what's it doing in a *nice* field like education? *Qualitative Studies in Education, 11*(1), 7–24.

Lentin, A. (2000). Race, racism and anti-racism: Challenging contemporary classifications. *Social Identities, 6*(1), 91–106.

Lipsitz, G. (1998). *The possessive investment of whiteness: How white people profit from identity politics.* Philadelphia: Temple University Press.

McLaren, L. M. (2003). Anti-immigrant prejudice in Europe: Contact, threat perception, and preferences for the exclusion of migrants. *Social Forces, 81*(3), 909–936.

Memmi, A. (2000). *Racism.* Minneapolis: University of Minnesota Press.

Mudde, C. (2005). Racist extremis in Central and Eastern Europe. *East European Politics and Societies, 19*(2), 161–184.

Omi, M., & Winant, H. (1993). *Racial formations in the United States from the 1960s to the 1990s* (2nd ed.). New York: Routledge.

Perry, P. (2001). White means never having to say you are ethnic: White youth and the construction of 'culture-less' other. *Journal of Contemporary Ethnography, 30*(1) 56–91.

Razack, N. (2004). *Perils and possibilities: Racism, imperialism and nationalism in international social work.* (Unpublished dissertation). School of Administration and Social Work, Flinders University, Adelaide, Australia.

Razack, N., & Jeffery, D. (2002). Critical race discourse and tenets for social work. *Canadian Social Service Review, 19*(2), 257–271.

Reddy, D. S. (2005). The ethnicity of caste. *Anthropological Quarterly, 78*(3), 543–584.

Roediger, D. (1994). *Towards the abolition of whiteness.* New York: Verso.

Sautman, B. (1994). Anti-Black racism in post-Mao China. *China Quarterly, 138*, 413–437.

Smith-Maddox, R., & Solorzano, D. (2002). Using critical race theory, Paulo Freire's problem-posing method, and case study research to confront race and racism in education. *Qualitative Inquiry, 8*(1), 66–84.

Thompson, A. (2003). Tiffany, friend of people of colour: White investments of antiracism. *Qualitative Studies in Education, 16*(1), 7–29.

United Nations (UN). (2001). *The UN Committee on the Elimination of Racial Discrimination, fact sheet 12.* Geneva: Author.

Weedon, C. (1999). Race, racism and the problem of whiteness. In *Feminism, theory and the politics of difference* (pp. 152–177). Oxford: Blackwell.

Williams, C. (1999). Connecting anti-racist and anti-oppressive theory and practice: Retrenchment or appraisal? *British Journal of Social Work, 29*, 211–230.

Williams, P., & Chrisman, L. (Eds.). (1994). *Colonial discourse and post-colonial theory: A reader.* New York: Columbia University Press.

Zick, A., Pettigrew, T. F., & Wagner, U. (2008). Ethnic prejudice and discrimination in Europe. *Journal of Social Issues, 64*(2), 233–251.

SARS: A Case of a Global Health Threat

NGOH TIONG TAN

Globalization has intensified the threat of rapid spread of disease. In a speech on the global spread of HIV and AIDS, Peter Piot, then head of the Joint United Nations Programme on HIV/AIDS (UNAIDS), noted that although HIV is only transmitted through the most intimate of contact—blood, sexual contact, and mother's milk—it spread to every continent in a few short years (Piot, 2004). This ongoing global pandemic has claimed millions of lives and affected millions more. In 2009, the world was alerted to the threat of a pandemic caused by a quickly emerging form of flu that was initially resistant to any known preventions—the H1N1 flu. Unlike HIV, respiratory viruses can be spread through the air or by touching surfaces recently touched by an infected person; therefore, an even greatest risk of rapid spread exists.

We are reprinting the case study by Ngoh Tiong Tan on the SARS epidemic in this volume. It details how one country addressed the threat of the pandemic and spells out potential roles for social workers. Although some of the interventions are specific to Singapore and may not work in other contexts, Tan's discussion provides a useful example as the world and profession face future global health threats. The following text first appeared as "Crisis theory and SARS: Singapore's management of the epidemic," (2004, June), *Asia Pacific Journal of Social Work and Development*, *14*(1), 7–17, by the same author, reprinted here with permission.

CRISIS THEORY AND SARS: SINGAPORE'S MANAGEMENT OF THE EPIDEMIC

Introduction

The severe acute respiratory syndrome (SARS) crisis had, in the past year, exacted its toll in the world and especially on the countries of Asia—China, Hong Kong, Taiwan, and Singapore. Crisis may be viewed as danger or opportunity or both. We know that crisis, handled appropriately, has great potential for change and growth. Crisis may thus be viewed as a catalyst that disturbs old ways of doing things, evokes new responses, and is a major factor in charting new developments (Young, 1985; Aguilera, 1997; Tan, 2003).

Crisis theory and crisis intervention may be applied to different situations impacting the range of systems, from the individual, family and community, nation, and the world. For the SARS epidemic that stuck in the first half of 2003, the community, national, and international responses followed a model of crisis coping. The management of SARS may thus be viewed as crisis intervention.

This article focuses on crisis theory and its application for the management of the SARS epidemic in the Singapore context.

Crisis and Crisis Theory

Crisis arises when a person or system is unable to deal effectively with a problem or situation (Caplan, 1961; Dixon, 1987; Young, 1983; Hoff, 1995; Aguilera, 1997; Kanel, 2003). Caplan (1961) termed crisis as an acute situational disorder. At the individual level, one is overwhelmed by the feelings or problems such that one is unable to function normally. Crisis is thus an upset of the steady state—the system is in disequilibrium when, for a time, it cannot deal with the problem nor escape or overcome it with the usual problem-solving mechanisms (Caplan, 1961; Hoff, 1995; Mitchell, 1999).

Crisis theory maintains that crisis may result from either a normal inevitable experience or from some unforeseen and traumatic events. It may be linked to earlier unresolved conflicts in the face of anticipated, developmental or unanticipated, accidental or situational crises. Usually a precipitating event marks the final straw in a series of stressful events or the point where coping mechanisms are overloaded (Caplan, 1961; Young, 1983). The initial phase of the states of crisis is marked with severe disorganization, a rise in tension that results from the crisis-provoking event.

Crisis intervention is the process of helping the system to adapt and deal with specific crises. It involves harnessing resources: organizational as well as the various support systems to cope with the problem. Intervention first provides immediate relief of the symptom through alleviation of immediate distress or stopping the maladaptive behavior in crisis (Young, 1983; Coopers, 1990; Roberts, 1995). With reorganization, the system achieves a new re-equilibrium. Crisis intervention is directed at an optimum time for change rather than long-term intervention (Kanel, 2003; Aguilera, 1997; Slaikeu, 1990).

SARS Situation as Crisis

Trocki (2003) attributed Singapore's proactive responses as the reason why the World Health Organization (WHO) was finally able to declare Singapore SARS-free on 31 May 2003. Singapore has been one of the worst SARS-affected countries. The drastic drop in the number of tourists to Singapore and the decrease in trade, right after an economic downturn, pushed the immediately post-SARS unemployment rate to a high of 5.5 percent.

The first SARS case in Singapore was detected on March 1, 2003, and the last case in this outbreak was reported in April 2003. Through secondary and tertiary transmission, in the short one and a half months, SARS quickly affected some 238 people in Singapore, 4 in 10 of whom were health-care workers (ST, Aug 4, 2004; Tan, 2004; Leong et al., 2004).

SARS started during the winter of 2002 in China, Hong Kong, and Vietnam. Besides Asia, SARS has been reported in North America, Europe, and the rest of the world, with the global infection figure estimated at 8398 and the number of deaths totaling 772 from 1 November 2002 to 2 June 2003 (WHO, 2003). The death tally of 33 in Singapore ranked fourth in the world, after China, Hong Kong, and Taiwan.

Little was known about the epidemiology of the coronavirus that caused SARS. It is not easy to combat SARS and, as like most contagious diseases, the social and community response to both treatment and prevention is critical to containing the spread (Tan, 2003). Medically, SARS is a difficult illness to diagnose except that the symptoms are that of fever greater than 38°C, headaches, body aches, dry cough,

and difficulty in breathing (see: Information For Close Contacts Of SARS, http://content.health.com/content/article/63/71890.htm). The key indication is exposure in SARS-affected areas or contact with possible SARS patients.

Applying Crisis Theory in the Management of SARS

The magnitude of the problem and the uncertainty in having to deal with the relatively unknown virus make SARS an overwhelming problem. The usual coping mechanisms no longer work because of the severity or seriousness of the incident and there was no previous experience with this disease. The high rate of infection by the "killer virus," the mounting death toll, and the inability of first the medical institutions and then the general society to cope with the massive problem rendered SARS a national as well as international crisis.

In applying crisis theory to Singapore's management of the epidemic, we need to consider the key concepts and principles of crisis intervention. The key ingredients of crisis management are

1. dealing with feelings and drama associated with crisis;
2. assessing danger and threats within a short time;
3. need for strategic planning and reorganization of the crisis situation;
4. mobilizing of resources to meet the challenge;
5. establishing communication channels and education; and
6. restoring a new level of equilibrium.

This paper will focus on each of the above principles of crisis management.

1. Crisis Response—Dealing With Affect

When the usual ways of dealing with the situation or problem fail, there is increased tension. Symptoms of the SARS crisis, like all crises, thus include heightened feelings and drama. At the peak of crisis, during the disorganization phase, there is often high anxiety, tension, depression, hostility, guilt, shame, and a host of other feelings (Caplan, 1961; Young, 1983; Kanel, 2003). Often, there is also confusion, bewilderment, helplessness, and loss together with an inability to grasp reality, problem solve, or deal effectively with the crisis (Mitchell, 1999; Dixon, 1987).

In applying crisis intervention, one has to deal effectively with feelings and provide support for the system in question. The management of affect includes the need for awareness of and then a release of the emotions, particularly that of distress, anger, guilt, and grief. Verbalization to discharge the tension and permit a sense of mastery is necessary for the energies to be channeled toward constructive crisis resolution. Instead of panic and fear, leaders must give hope and confidence to the community. *Sunday Times* of May 11th, 2003, carried the article "A shoulder to cry on when SARS strikes," where social workers were featured as dealing with the feelings of guilt and grief of family members whose loved ones succumbed to SARS. Other feelings of fear from isolation and anxiety as well as the uncertainties of the disease were also identified.

Establishing contact with people, developing trust, and relationship building are important in crisis management, whether it is with the individual or the community. Social workers help not only the SARS patients but also their family and the community to cope with emotional distress and the regaining of a normal life afterward. Since the stakes for the crisis are high, high-profile management and response are needed as shown by political and religious leaders coming out to allay fears, identifying with the afflicted and comforting those who are grieving.

In the drama of crisis it is important to have symbolic events for public expression of feelings. At the SARS commemoration ceremony, organized by the Ministry of Health, National Healthcare Group, and Singapore Health Services, for example, there was an expression of public grief. The Prime Minister planted a native tree, known to thrive even under adverse condition, as a symbol of the fight against SARS and a sign of national resilience (see: http://straitstimes.asia1.com.sg/mnt/html/webspecial/gallery/sars_com/sars_com06.html). Through all these, the identifying with, and expression of, the feelings allowed a humane approach to the management of the SARS crisis.

2. Assessment of Dangers and Threats

Crisis intervention is a practical approach in dealing with dangers and threats. One of the key tasks in crisis management is to assess lethality and safety needs (Aguilera, 1997; Gililand & James, 1997). A quick and comprehensive assessment of the crisis, person (or system), and situation is necessary in order for constructive intervention to begin.

At the start of the SARS crisis little was known of the disease. On the medical front, the hospital and the university research teams were tasked to deal with the medical emergency. No known vaccine was available, at least not until recently when a new, experimental vaccine against SARS that protects mice from the infectious disease could soon be tested on humans (Reuters, as cited in *ST*, April 1). It was later in the outbreak period that the university's research laboratory was able to identify the genetic code of the coronavirus and developed a tentative diagnostic kit to diagnose SARS.

Meanwhile, to contain the problem it is vital that immediate actions need to be taken to detect infection and prevent its spread. The fight against SARS, at the early stage, would take place at three fronts: immigrations and checkpoints, hospitals, and the home and community (*ST*, Apr 20, 2003, 1). Temperature screening was introduced, early in the SARS outbreak, at places of high human traffic such as offices, schools, and shopping centers. University students, for example, were required to take their temperature before being admitted to examination halls.

As SARS is primarily spread through close person-to-person contact, for prevention of possible transmission, quarantining those infected with the virus and suspected cases as well as those who had come into contact with SARS patients was enforced. Other safety measures include closure of schools, closing down of a wholesale vegetable market, and postponement of public events as well as issuing the travel advisory. The Ministry of Health, for example, urged the public to heed WHO's advice to postpone travel to Beijing, Hebei, Inner Mongolia, Shanxi, Tianjin, and Taiwan until another time (MOH, 2003). The health ministry and other government bodies, including schools and public functions, also required health declarations to be made on a daily or weekly basis.

Vigilance in monitoring of SARS and health practices were heightened and graded in terms of color code, which ranged from red to green alert with the lowest level of alert being green. As a safeguard against the cross-institutional spread of infection, health-care institutions were required to closely monitor health-care workers practicing within ten days of contact with each other and the health-care institution. Electronic contact monitoring and tracing were also introduced. Patients and staff were also divided into clusters and not allowed to cross cluster boundaries. Although some of the procedures (such as twice-daily temperature taking and intrusive health declarations and contact tracing requiring detailed whereabouts of the citizens) were criticized as excessive, nevertheless, the safety needs of the people in the SARS crisis were quickly assessed and attended to.

3. Strategic Planning and Reorganization

Crisis intervention is essentially a problem-solving process with the change agent assuming greater control of the process. The strategy of crisis management is to partialize or redefine the problem, making it more manageable. Prioritizing of the problems and the exploration of possible alternatives is the next step. A workable action plan is then formulated and implemented (Slaikeu, 1990; Kanel, 2003).

One key aspect of problem solving is to keep the client's tasks simple, practical, and achievable. This will restore confidence and autonomy. During the SARS crisis residents, workers, students, and military personnel were taught to take daily body temperatures and asked to see the doctor if they felt unwell. This collaborative approach is important toward maintaining faith in problem-solving abilities of the client system. Involvement of the public in maintaining good health habits reinforced a sense of control in an otherwise difficult and confusing time.

For the effective management of SARS crisis, strategic high-level planning, decision making, and implementation are crucial. An interministerial committee, set up at the onset of the crisis, planned and coordinated the war on SARS in Singapore (*ST*, Apr 20, 2003:1). This approach demonstrated visibly the leadership and the commitment to tackle the problem. It brought together a multidisciplinary and multisectoral team in a coordinated war on SARS.

A high percentage of the SARS victims were health-related personnel. To prevent cross infection and protect both the health workers and the patients, a vital decision was made to designate Tan Tock Seng Hospital as Singapore's SARS hospital and the headquarters for the outbreak (see: http://straitstimes.asia1.com.sg/mnt/html/webspecial/gallery/sars/sars1.html). This decision was a vital one strategically and could only be made at the higher levels of government, specifically by the Minister of Health.

There was a need for legal backups to be developed for effective follow-through of the action plans to fight SARS. In swiftness, a law to control and enforce compliance to prevent the spread of the virus was enacted in just one parliamentary sitting on April 24th, 2003. This legal instrument allowed the government to deal with quarantine breakers. They could be jailed for six months and slapped with a fine even for a first offence. The law also punished those who had contracted a specific disease and put others at risk with their actions.

Collaborative planning is essential for developing a strategy to deal effectively with the crisis. The implementation of a coordinated approach in crisis management enabled the community to reorganize itself.

4. Mobilize Community Support and Resources

The best of plans need resources for effective implementation. Crisis intervention involves the mobilization of resources to enable effective coping and reorganization of the situation (Caplan, 1961; Young, 1983; Gilliland & James, 1997). Given the short time given to mobilize resources, Singapore has done very well in garnering community support and resources to tackle SARS.

A host of community members were enlisted in the fight against SARS. National servicemen were recruited to assist in taking temperatures at hospitals and calling those who were in contact with SARS patients. Contact tracings were also coordinated and performed by Community Development Councils (CDC). Community leaders were incorporated into the team to see to the needs of residents who were quarantined. Through the CDCs and Resident's Committees, food delivery service to those quarantined was organized.

Due to immediacy and urgency of crisis, timing is a critical element in crisis intervention. Resources were expended to provide daily and even hourly updates of the news and information on the situation by the media. Crisis managers were also in touch with ground zero and the situation. Quick decisions and communications necessitate the development of channels and processes that cut across government ministries, businesses, organizations, and civic groups as well as other societal institutions. CISCO guards were enlisted to serve quarantine orders and electronically tag people who broke these orders.

Money, manpower, time, and energy were expended to carry out temperature checks, contact tracing, enforcing quarantine orders, and developing communication with the public. Instead of generating productive work, the government and charitable organizations had utilized existing resources toward combating SARS. To compensate the loss of income by those who were served with quarantine orders, the government provided a Singapore 70 dollars daily allowance, which was administered by the CDC (*ST*, May 11, 2003, 20). The mobilization of resources is essential in positively handling the crisis.

5. Establishing Rapport and Communication

It is important to provide an accurate analysis of the crisis situation with timely and reliable information.

Dialogue sessions and channels of feedback were structured to keep community participation and involvement active. The SARS crisis team had open communication channels with the hospitals as well as the community. The media not only provided information but also incorporated a public education role. Public education is an important strategy for SARS prevention.

In solidarity, and as a community service, a SARS television channel was mounted by three competing media companies. Education programs as well as updates on the latest SARS situation, both the local and overseas, were provided. Public education material, along with a thermometer and mask, were given to all the households in Singapore by the Members of Parliament and grassroots leaders. The illustrated leaflets provided instructions on how to take daily temperatures and what to do when one falls ill and has SARS symptoms.

In establishing rapport with the public and in recognition of those who sacrificed themselves to fight SARS, the Courage Fund was established. The Fund signaled appreciation for the heroes of the war on SARS and boosted the morale of the people. Named in honor of health-care workers, the Fund, in a very short time, collected close to 30 million Singapore dollars (NHG: 2003) and provided relief to the families of SARS victims and awarded bursaries to health-care workers.

6. Restore New Level of Equilibrium

Crisis intervention seeks to restore some kind of equilibrium, preferably higher than or equal to the one before to the crisis (Caplan, 1961; Kanel, 2003). This is also the sign of the end phase of the crisis state.

Finally, long-term solutions and growth through learning of new coping methods such as developing and implementing crisis management protocols and effective intervention for future critical events were made. For both the individual as well as community the exploration of future growth through continued problem solving after the crisis event is important.

There is need to evaluate the crisis experience. Some policies and procedures implemented during the crisis are no longer relevant and need to be taken off. The goal is to identify and implement policies and procedures that can be utilized for future crises. There is also a recognition and appreciation of the contribution of people from all walks of life and different professionals and service providers. The janitor and laundry service providers were hailed along with nurses, ambulance drivers, doctors, and medical social workers.

Immediate effects of precautionary measures introduced during the SARS episode included a cleaner environment, healthier habits, and improved public-health checks. In a society that emphasizes strong work ethics, employees who would go to work even when they were sick during the pre-SARS period are now encouraged to see a doctor and take sick leave. Furthermore, as a side effect, a culture of working and conducting business from home has also taken off.

The result of crisis management of SARS in Singapore has not only reinforced strategies for combating the disease but, more importantly, has strengthened community bonds. Various sectors of the multiethnic, pluralistic society came together as a united front to fight a common enemy. Fears and prejudice were challenged and greater sensitivity, compassion, and transparency in communication have taken its place. The "many helping hands" approach in community organization around the SARS problem has strengthened both formal and informal networks, leading to a more resilient civil society.

Issues in Crisis Intervention

The crisis model is essentially a short-term intervention with individuals, groups, or communities experiencing a major event and its aftermath (Roberts, 1995). The immediate goals of crisis intervention are to understand and make sense of the crisis and to redefine the experience for growth. The worker aims to reduce anxieties, help in the grief process, and manage the crisis. To ensure positive learning, it is vital to reestablish a sense of autonomy by applying personal and community resources to cope with the situation.

What is the prospect of this island state to deal with potentially dangerous and contagious disease breakouts in the future? The Infectious Disease Act of 1976 was invoked during the crisis and its legal teeth made stronger. Other preventive steps include the building of better communicable disease centers, the strengthening of the specialized hospital to deal with SARS and other high-transmission viruses or diseases, and the development of operational structure for interagency coordination. The community's capacity for social defense in dealing with local quarantine matters and the management of resources for social support have been enhanced.

Dealing with SARS in Singapore was not plain sailing. There were some constraints and resistance. In lieu of the crisis situation, where a more directive stance was taken, many lives were affected and the liberty of some people was curtailed. For example, some people ignored quarantine orders and were later physically tagged with electronic monitors to ensure that they remained at home. Confidentiality and privacy of the citizen, wherever possible, should not be sacrificed. Education rather than the use of force or law should be the long-term strategy. Another problem encountered was that there were insufficient facilities to house the massive numbers when a number of the patients of a mental health institution were suspected to have contracted SARS and needed to be quarantined. Government hostels and hotels were mobilized at short notice, but not only were the facilities inadequate, communication problems were also encountered. When SARS struck, there was initial confusion and problems in coordination between the Ministry of Home Affairs and the Ministry of Health. There was also a need to cooperate with the neighboring countries and exercise border checks and safety measures. With great sensitivity, the initial "blame thy neighbor" attitude was turned into a cooperative sharing of useful measures and honest discussion of strategies to contain SARS. As Singapore is an international air hub, the danger of an open-sky policy is in its potential to spread diseases both by importing as well as exporting the viruses. Installation of thermal scanners provided a less intrusive and more effective way of screening both the visitors and people leaving the country.

The meaning aspect of an event, such as the SARS outbreak, depends on the value system and previous experiences as well as the attitude of society toward the events. Dealing with the SARS crisis provided the useful experience to deal with future crises. Preparation for the future includes the identification of likely crisis situations and the establishment of a crisis management plan. Mike Ryan, WHO's coordinator for global alert and response, is of the view that the lessons learned from dealing with SARS would "stand the world in good stead when the new infections or as expected, a flu pandemic breaks out in the future" (WHO: 2003, 4). Perhaps this is why the recent bird flu did not make an outbreak in Singapore.

Singapore's model for combating SARS, despite some shortcomings, has been relatively effective (ST, May 16, 2003:1). This is necessary to win consumer and business confidence, as well as the tourist trade and domestic consumptions affected by SARS. Not only

has the economy rebounded, society has become more prepared for crisis and resilient. Out of a negative situation, something good for the citizenry has resulted. Crisis handled constructively has provided an opportunity for growth not just for individuals but for Singapore society as well.

REFERENCES

Aguilera, D. C. (1997). *Crisis intervention: Theory and methodology*. St. Louis: Mosby.

Caplan, G. (1961). *An approach to community mental health*. New York: Grune and Stratton.

Cooper, L. (1990). *Models of social work practice*. Adelaide: Flinders University.

Dixon, S. L. (1987). *Working with people in crisis: Theory and practice* (2nd ed.). Columbus: Merrill.

Gilliland, B. E., & James, R. K. (1997). *Crisis intervention strategies*. Pacific Grove: Brooks/Cole.

Hoff, L. A. (1995). *People in crisis: Understanding and helping*. San Francisco: Jossey-Bass.

Kanel, K. (2003). *A guide to crisis intervention* (2nd ed.). Pacific Grove, CA: Brooks/Cole.

Leong, I. Y. O., Lee, A., Ng, T. W., Lee, L. B., Koh, N. Y., Yap, E., Guay, S., & Lee, M. N. (2004). The challenge of providing holistic care in a viral epidemic: opportunities for palliative care. *Palliative Medicine, 18*, 12–18.

Mitchell, J. W. (1999). *The dynamics of crisis intervention: Loss as the common denominator*. Springfield, IL: C. C. Thomas.

MOH. (2003). http://app.moh.gov.sg/new/new02.asp?id=1&mid=7520.

Piot, P. (2004). *The global AIDS pandemic*. Keynote presentation at Provoking Hope: A Brown University HIV/AIDS Symposium, Providence, RI.

Roberts, A. R. (1995). *Crisis intervention and time-limited cognitive treatment*. Thousand Oaks, CA: Sage.

Slaikeu, K. A. (1990). *Crisis intervention: A handbook for practice and research* (2nd ed.). Boston: Allyn and Bacon.

Tan, N. T. (2003). Social and community response to the SARS epidemic: The Singapore response. *Journal of Youth Studies, 7*(1), 97–105.

Trocki, C. A. (2003). *SARS threat lifts but leaves its toll*. Canberra: ASEAN Focus Group, Australian National University.

World Health Organization (WHO). (2003). World Health Organization announces new public-private initiative on disease surveillance and response. www.who.int/mediacentre/releases/2003/prwha3/en/.

Young, K. P. H. (1983). *Coping in crisis Hong Kong*. Hong Kong: Hong Kong University Press.

Status of Women

SUSAN MAPP

Those who are oppressed in society always have more difficulty accessing the rights guaranteed to them by the Universal Declaration of Human Rights. This is especially true of women, who have a subordinate status in most societies. Due to this widespread discrimination, women are more likely to live in poverty and are more likely to lack an education compared with men. Although women perform two-thirds of the work in the world, they receive only 10% of the income and own less than 1% of the property (United Nations, 2005). Due to these unique burdens and women's vulnerable position in many societies, a human rights document focusing specifically on the rights of women was adopted by the United Nations in 1979—the Convention on the Elimination of All Forms of Discrimination against Women (CEDAW). This document defines *discrimination* as both intentional discrimination as well as acts that have a discriminatory effect. (More on CEDAW can be found in Chapter 67.)

Despite the adoption of CEDAW, unequal treatment of women continues in every nation in all areas of life, including education, business, and law. The International Federation of Social Workers (IFSW) (2005) notes six critical concerns regarding women in their 2005 International Policy on Women: poverty, the economy, education, health, violence, and girls. In this chapter, the status of women in education, law, health, and employment are discussed; violence is addressed in a separate chapter (Chapter 40).

EDUCATION

Educated women have increased economic capabilities and are more able to play a role in society and have a voice in their life. Education of girls has been found to reduce deaths due to childbirth, lower child mortality and fertility rates, and delay marriage; educated women are also more likely to send their children to school. Despite these advantages, girls face more barriers to achieving an education than do boys.

Globally, there are 117 girls who are not enrolled in primary school for every 100 boys not enrolled, with the gap widening even further in secondary school. As a result, women are more likely to be illiterate than men, impeding their economic success.

These barriers exist for a variety of reasons, including structural barriers, cultural beliefs, and safety concerns. Structural barriers to education can include a lack of female teachers or schools for girls in cultures that do not believe it is appropriate for male teachers to be teaching female students or for female students to be educated with male students. Additionally, many schools in rural Africa do not have private toilet facilities. For example, in Sudan, there is nowhere for girls to relieve themselves, and they will drop out of school rather than embarrass themselves in front of their male classmates by leaving the premises. This only gets worse after girls experience their first menstrual cycle; there is no private place for them to tend to these needs and they will drop out of school rather than be shamed (Abdelmoneium, 2005).

Cultural beliefs can also limit girls' education. Some cultures believe it is not useful to educate girls because they will only grow up to marry and have children. Other girls may start school but not be able to finish due to early marriage or a need to help with the housework and caretaking of younger children at home. This can be influenced by familial poverty—because girls are seen as being valuable at home, where they can assist with household chores, it can be perceived as more expensive to send a girl to school than a boy in terms of lost labor.

Concerns for safety can also act as a barrier to girls' education. Attacks by the Taliban in Afghanistan have made going to school dangerous, and many families are keeping girls home to ensure their safety. In Ethiopia, girls are at risk of being abducted and raped; they are then often married to the rapist because their honor has been ruined. This type of attack (known as *telefa*) is committed primarily while girls are walking back and forth to school, raising fears about this journey (Save the Children Denmark, Ministry of Education, & Ministry of Women's Affairs, 2008).

Teachers also sometimes sexually assault girls, promising them good grades in exchange (Save the Children Denmark et al., 2008). In some areas, due to a lack of qualified teachers, young, low-qualified men are hired, which has led to an increase in sexual harassment of female students (Valerio, Bardasi, Chambal, & Lobo, 2006). For example, in both South Africa and Ecuador, approximately one-third of sexual violence against girls is perpetrated by teachers. In the Netherlands, 27% of students reported being sexually harassed by school staff (Plan International, 2008). Even greater numbers of students experience sexual harassment when peer-to-peer harassment is included. For instance, 83% of female American high school students report experiencing some form of sexual harassment during high school, with 30% experiencing it often (American Association of University Women, 2001).

Strategies to increase enrollment of girls in school include eliminating school fees, working to increase sanitation facilities, and working with male students to help them understand the burdens female students face and encourage them to be supportive of girls. The United Nations has established a special initiative to increase the enrollment of girls—the United Nations Girls' Education Initiative (UNGEI). Additionally, the elimination of gender disparity in all levels of education is a target in the Millennium Development Goals.

UNEQUAL UNDER THE LAW

In 2008, at least twenty-three countries had laws that discriminated against women in such areas as the right to seek divorce, limitations on property ownership, inheritance rights, and credit access, therefore restricting their ability to earn income (Amnesty International, 2008). In some countries, women have differential access to divorce, including reasons why a divorce can be granted and how the divorce can be granted. For example, in Israel, a woman may not initiate a divorce without the consent of her husband because divorce is considered a religious rather than civil matter (Amnesty International, 2004).

Upon divorce, the division of property can also be discriminatory, with men working outside the home being granted greater portions of shared marital property than wives who do not participate in the paid labor force but stay home and care for the children and home. It was not until 2000 that the House of Lords declared that in England and Wales, there should be an even distribution of marital property between an income-earning husband and homemaking wife. Even with this ruling, the first even division did not occur until 2003 (Banda, 2008).

Inheritance laws discriminate against women in some countries, with some cultures passing all property to the husband's natal family due to the desire to retain property within that family as well as the difficulty of dividing property in polygamous societies. However, this leaves widows impoverished and at the mercy of others. In some cases, women are forced to marry the brother of their husband (widow inheritance) or have intercourse with a designated male villager so that her husband's spirit will not remain (widow cleansing). Custody of children can also be an issue. For example, in the Democratic Republic of the Congo, a widow does not have sole guardianship of her children; rather, it is held jointly with members of her husband's family (Banda, 2008).

Some countries place limitations on women's movements, including the right to go out without a male family escort, the right to work (including in mixed-gender environments), the right to a passport without permission of a male relative, and the right to drive. In Saudi Arabia, women are not permitted to appear in public without a male relative, vote, or drive. In Algeria, the 1984 Algerian Family Code treats adult women as minors under the law, stating that women are legally obliged to obey their husbands and that a man may have up to four wives (Salhi, 2003).

The most infamous cases of discriminatory treatment occurred in Afghanistan under the rule of the Taliban from the mid-1990s until the early part of the twenty-first century. During this time, women were not allowed to leave the house without the escort of a close male relative, and when they did leave, they had to be completely covered. They could not seek medical care, even in an emergency, without the escort of a close male relative. They were not permitted to be educated and could not work. This drove many women into desperate poverty and even death because their husbands and other male relatives had been killed during the decades of war. Readers are referred to Benard (2002) for more information on this topic. Women's rights improved after the Taliban was driven from power, but still remain precarious. A number of countries have been working to change their laws, including Bangladesh, Sierra Leone, and Mali. However, acceptance of changed laws is more difficult to achieve, and much work remains to be done.

REPRODUCTIVE AND OTHER HEALTH ISSUES

Due to their reproductive abilities, women are at risk for health issues that do not affect men. Since women are seen as a lower class than men and their reproductive capacity is often seen as different, these medical issues typically do not receive the attention that they should on the micro, mezzo, or macro levels. This is also true in terms of defining human rights; many documents do not include reproductive health, an issue that can be a matter of life and death.

In the United States, which does not have universal health care, the greater need for routine care can incur higher medical costs for women than for men. Insurance plans with high deductibles are a heavier burden to women due to their need for annual care such as mammograms and Pap smears as well as the costs of childbirth. In 2003[1], for those aged eighteen to forty-four, men's average annual medical costs were $463, while women's were $1,266. This spread increased with age: Men aged forty-five to sixty-four had an average annual medical expenditure of $1,849, while for women it was $2,871 (Woolhandler & Himmelstein, 2007).

The ability of women to control their childbearing is medically available, but many women do not have access to contraceptives, which increases the likelihood of an unintended pregnancy. Approximately one in six women in the Global South is estimated to have an unmet need for family planning—she would prefer not to become pregnant but is not using any form of contraception (Population Reference Bureau, 2005). In a number of cultures, it is considered unacceptable for a woman to refuse to have intercourse with her husband for any reason; even if she would prefer not to become pregnant, she cannot refuse him.

When women experience an unintended pregnancy, some opt to have an abortion, whether it is legal or not in their country. For women who are unable to access safe abortion methods, this can lead to high levels of mortality. *Unsafe abortion* is defined by the World Health Organization as "a procedure for terminating an unwanted pregnancy either by persons lacking the necessary skills or in an environment lacking the minimal medical standards, or both" (Population Reference Bureau, 2005, p. 3). More than half a million women and girls die each year from pregnancy-related causes, and about 13% of these deaths result from unsafe abortions. This figure is much higher in some regions of the world; in sub-Saharan Africa it can range up to 50% of maternal deaths (Population Reference Bureau, 2005).

Every day 1400 women and girls die giving birth, with the risk much higher in the Global South, where complications from childbirth are the leading cause of death for women and girls. In fact, 99% of maternal deaths occur in the Global South, typically due to lack of access to medical care, which may be needed for severe bleeding or infection (Population Reference Bureau, 2005). In sub-Saharan Africa, for example, the risk of dying in childbirth is 1 in 13 compared with 1 in 4085 in the Global North. An early pregnancy has a higher risk of maternal death or injury during childbirth. Girls aged ten to fourteen are five times more likely to die as a result of childbirth or pregnancy than those aged twenty to twenty-four, and girls aged fifteen to nineteen are more than twice as likely to die (UNFPA, n.d.a., Child marriage fact sheet). Even more common, though, are long-lasting infections, injuries, and disabilities resulting from childbirth; thirty times more women suffer from these complications than from maternal death (UNICEF, 2003).

One of the primary risks is the development of an obstetric fistula. Typically experienced by young mothers, especially those who are small (as is typically seen in females who are poor and undernourished throughout their lives), a fistula occurs during extended labor. During contractions, the tissue between the uterus and the bowel, as well as between the uterus and bladder rub against each other. When labor is protracted, this friction can result in tissue tearing, creating an opening between the two organs. It is more common in smaller women as the baby will be too large comparatively for the birth to proceed easily. Due to the lack of access to medical facilities, the tear is not repaired, resulting in the woman becoming incontinent. The leakage of urine and/or excrement causes a severe rash as well as a foul odor. As a result, the woman is typically cast off from her husband and her village. If she does not receive surgery to repair the tear, she will often live a shortened life as a result of this societal neglect. Readers are referred to Onolemhemhen (2005) for more information on this topic.

It is estimated that approximately 2 million women are currently living with a fistula, and 50,000 to 100,000 new cases occur every year. These numbers are based on women seeking treatment, and thus the actual numbers are likely much higher (UNFPA, 2006). The problem is concentrated in sub-Saharan Africa due to a combination of reasons—poverty, lack of access to modern health care, the tradition of home birth, and early pregnancy—but it also occurs in other nations where these factors cluster, such as Bangladesh and Afghanistan.

The surgery to repair fistulas is relatively easy. It has about a 90% success rate and costs $300 for the surgery and postoperative care (UNFPA, n.d.b., Obstetric fistula in brief). However, it is typically difficult to obtain because few doctors perform it. To this end, UNFPA has launched the Global Campaign to End Fistula and has been working in a number of countries around the world to work on both prevention and treatment of fistulas (UNFPA, n.d.c., The campaign in brief).

WOMEN AND EMPLOYMENT

In countries around the world, women have less access to gainful employment than do men. They tend to be grouped in sectors deemed as women's labor—the service sector or helping professions in the Global North and agriculture in South Asia and sub-Saharan Africa. They receive less pay for their work than men even once occupation, experience, job level, education, and other factors are taken into account. This gap is 20% in the United States, Brazil, Chile, and Mexico and 15% in the European Union (International Labour Organization, 2009). In Japan, women continue to face barriers to advancing to management in business due not only to cultural gender roles but also the expectation of working late hours, which impedes mothers. In 2005, women held only 10% of managerial positions despite being half of the workforce. The Japanese Equal Employment Opportunity Law is also weak, with its harshest punishment being the publishing of the name of violators (Fackler, 2007).

Some of the most successful examples of empowerment and increased equity in development (both social and economic) have originated within the Global South. In India, many women are employed in such labor as selling vegetables, picking out recyclable materials from trash heaps, and weaving. They were excluded from India's labor laws because these were not recognized professions by the government, which made them vulnerable to exploitation. Ela Bhatt, an experienced labor organizer, helped these women organize and advocate for their rights through the Self Employed Women's Association (SEWA), a labor union she founded in 1972. It is an unusual labor union in that its members consist of poor, self-employed female workers. By organizing and working together, the women are able to advocate for higher wages and less harassment.

Another successful endeavor in helping to alleviate poverty and empower women is microfinance, which involves making small business loans to those living in poverty. The concept originated in Bangladesh by Mohammad Yunus through his Grameen Bank program. He was given the Nobel Peace Prize in 2006 for his work. Although loans were initially made to men and women equally, women are now 96% of the more than six million borrowers. Women are preferred as borrowers as research has found that women are more likely to invest income in their families, resulting in higher increases in child survival rates and child growth. They are also more likely to repay their loans. Evaluations conclude that the Grameen Bank has improved the well-being of female borrowers and their families in terms of income, poverty status, nutrition, and education. However, mild success has been achieved in improving women's social status and empowerment, and there has been little success in altering the social systems that limit women's options, such as the giving of dowry (Bernasek, 2003). More on microfinance can be found in Chapter 64.

PROFESSIONAL ROLE OF SOCIAL WORKERS

Throughout this chapter, issues that affect women solely because of their gender have been discussed, but the impact of poverty and lack of education have also been clear. The research findings of multiple international organizations support the fact that for global social and economic development, the empowerment of women must occur. According to IFSW (2005), since social workers are committed to human rights, we must commit ourselves to helping women and girls because they have not achieved social justice in any society. Due to our ethical grounding in empowerment, social workers are an ideal group to help empower disenfranchised groups. We are able to work both with international nongovernmental organizations (NGOs) and local movements to help women achieve a culturally relevant model of equality.

Due to the varied means through which women experience discrimination, there are a variety of methods that social workers can use to help. Social workers can work on the macro level to help change laws to allow women equal rights under the law, and they can also work on the mezzo and micro levels to increase access to and acceptance of the changes. Increasing access to quality education is a first necessary step, followed by access to productive employment, especially through microfinance operations, to help women be more independent and thus able to fight against harmful practices and unjust laws.

NOTE

1. Data is from 2003, but it is increased to reflect 2006 dollars.

REFERENCES

Abdelmoneium, A. O. (2005). Challenges facing children in education and labour: Case study of displaced children in Khartoum-Sudan. *Ahfad Journal*, 22(2), 64–76.

American Association of University Women (AAUW). (2001). *Hostile hallways: Bullying, teasing and sexual harassment in school*. Retrieved July 6, 2009, from http://www.aauw.org/research/upload/hostilehallways.pdf.

Amnesty International. (2008). *Amnesty International report 2008*. Retrieved May 20, 2009, from http://report2008.amnesty.org/eng/download-report.

Amnesty International. (2004). Making violence against women count. Retrieved August 25, 2006, from http://www.amnesty.org/en/library/info/ACT77/034/2004.

Banda, F. (2008). *Project on a mechanism to address laws that discriminate against women*. Retrieved June 12, 2009, from http://www.ohchr.org/Documents/Publications/laws_that_discriminate_against_women.pdf.

Benard, C. (2002). *Veiled courage: Inside the Afghan women's resistance*. New York: Broadway Books.

Bernasek, A. (2003). Banking on social change: Grameen Bank lending to women. *International Journal of Politics, Culture & Society*, 16(3), 369–385.

Fackler, M. (2007, August 6). Career women in Japan find a blocked path, despite equal opportunity law. *New York Times*. Retrieved August 16, 2007, from http://www.nytimes.com.

International Federation of Social Workers (IFSW). (2005). *International policy on women*. Retrieved from http://www.ifsw.org/p38000218.html.

International Labour Organization. (2009). *Global employment trends for women: March 2009*. Retrieved June 12, 2009, from http://www.ilo.org/wcmsp5/groups/public/—dgreports/—dcomm/documents/publication/wcms_103456.pdf.

Onolemhemhen, D. N. (2005). *A social worker's investigation of childbirth-injured women in northern Nigeria*. New York: University Press of America.

Plan International. (2008). *Learn without fear: The global campaign to end violence in schools*. Retrieved October 13, 2008, from http://plan-international.org/learnwithoutfear/files/learn-without-fear-global-campaign-report-english.

Population Reference Bureau. (2005). *Unsafe abortion: Facts and figures*. Retrieved October 18, 2005, from http://www.prb.org/pdf05/UnsafeAbortion.pdf.

Salhi, Z. S. (2003). Algerian women, citizenship, and the "family code." *Gender and Development*, 11(3), 27–35.

Save the Children Denmark, Ministry of Education, & Ministry of Women's Affairs. (2008). *A study on violence against girls in primary schools and its impacts on girls' education in Ethiopia*. Retrieved October 7, 2008, from www.ungei.org/resources/files/Study_on_Violence_Against_schoolgfils_final.pdf

UNICEF. (2003). *Every day, 1400 girls and women die giving birth*. Retrieved April 20, 2005, from www.unicef.org/media/media_7594.html

United Nations. (2005). *Creating an enabling environment for girls' and women's participation in education*. Retrieved July 24, 2006, from http://www.un.org/womenwatch/daw/egm/enabling-environment2005/docs/EGM-WPD-EE-2005-EP.8%20%20A.pdf

United Nations Population Fund (UNFPA). (2006). *Fast facts: Fistula and reproductive health*. Retrieved August 26, 2006, from http://www.endfistula.org/fast_facts.htm

UNFPA. (n.d.a). *Child marriage fact sheet*. Retrieved March 14, 2009, from http://www.unfpa.org/swp/2005/presskit/factsheets/facts_child_marriage.htm

UNFPA. (n.d.b). *Obstetric fistula in brief*. Retrieved March 14, 2009, from http://www.endfistula.org/fistula_brief.htm

UNFPA. (n.d.c). *The campaign in brief*. Retrieved March 14, 2009, from http://www.endfistula.org/campaign_brief.htm

UNICEF. (2003). *Every day, 1400 girls and women die giving birth*. Retrieved April 20, 2005, from http://www.unicef.org/media/media_7594.html

Valerio, A., Bardasi, E., Chambal, A., & Lobo, M. F. (2006). Mozambique: School fees and primary school enrollment and retention. In A. Coudouel, A. A. Dani, & S. Paternostro (Eds.), *Poverty & social impact analysis of reforms: Lessons and examples from implementation* (pp. 93–148). Washington, DC: World Bank.

Woolhandler, S., & Himmelstein, D. U. (2007). Consumer-directed healthcare: Except for the healthy and wealthy it's unwise. *Journal of General Internal Medicine*, 22(6), 879–881.

FOR MORE INFORMATION

Grameen Bank: www.grameen-info.org.
UN Women: www.unwomen.org.
United Nations Population Fund: www.unfpa.org.
Womenwatch: www.un.org/womenwatch.

39

Veterans, Soldiers, and Military Families

JESSE HARRIS

The military is unique; its members face stresses unlike those of other institutions. It is one of the few occupations where injury and death are constant companions. The armed forces of the world have been called upon to serve many roles, from direct combat to occupational, constabulary (peacekeeping), and even humanitarian. Their fellow citizens have provided social services to fighting forces beginning with the creation of the International Red Cross during the French and Italian war against Austria in 1859 (Friedland, 1977). Some social workers may serve as active members of the military, while others respond to the needs of soldiers, veterans, and military families through civilian roles with governmental and voluntary agencies.

THE SOLDIER

A nation's military may consist of ground forces (army and marines), air fighters (air force), and, if bounded by water, naval forces.[1] The rank structure in most services can be categorized as officer and enlisted, and officers can be further categorized as commissioned and noncommissioned. Most armies use a hierarchical rank structure in which soldiers take pride; therefore, where appropriate, soldiers should be addressed by their rank. Social workers and other health professionals should become familiar with the military rank structure because it is part of the military culture. In some nations the military is predominately conscripts, and in others it is predominately volunteers or a combination of both. Military forces are primarily young men, but some countries include women. In some countries male and female soldiers are allowed to marry one another, which raises the question of child support during deployments. Gays, lesbians, and transsexuals are readily accepted in the militaries of some nations, but their service is a matter of controversy in others (Boene, 2006).

Men and women who serve do so for a variety of reasons, such as from a sense of duty or as a form of temporary employment. Some see military service as a career opportunity and make it their life choice, while others serve to fulfill their obligation as a conscript. A few countries have included children in their ranks (often referred to as *child soldiers*). The use of children is now prohibited by the United Nations Convention on the Rights of the Child (1990), and therefore rebel forces (armies without state sanction) are the most likely to use children. Child soldiers are usually forced into these rebel armies under threat of life, although some may join as a means of economic survival. This subject is elaborated in greater detail in Chapter 22.

Most soldiers come from nonmilitary families and communities, which presents a challenge. Armies must capitalize on the strengths of the new recruits' civilian upbringing while at the same time introducing them to a set of values and skills that may run counter to the culture in which they were raised. It is no secret that the ultimate purpose of this training is to instill new values and to prepare the soldier to engage in warfare. State sponsorship of armies gives legitimacy to the values and standards to which the soldier is expected to adhere. Most men and women in uniform are not hardened soldiers and therefore may require the assistance of mental health personnel as a result of the trauma of war or when values clash (Drescher, Smith, & Foy, 2007). Often overlooked is the fact that most soldiers are young and may have several family-related roles. They may be spouses, fathers or mothers, sons or daughters, and siblings. The role of soldiers coupled with their youth often results in new stresses, including concerns about finance and adequate housing, frequent and unexpected deployments, and separations from loved ones. The unfamiliar and often uncomfortable living conditions may result in both mental and physical problems.

STRESS OF COMBAT ON THE SOLDIER

The rigorous training and discipline of new recruits prepares them for the sights and sounds of battle. It is also given in recognition that soldiers are vulnerable and are potential candidates for emotional and psychiatric breakdowns as a result of combat. Death and injury are the constant companions of the war fighter. Being deployed to a combat zone whether in a direct-combat or combat-support role can result in stress reactions that last long after the conflict is over (Auslander, Soskolne, & Ben-Shahar, 2005). Though not fully understood, trauma resulting from combat is a problem that can be traced to antiquity (Shay, 2002). The macho stance of militaries coupled with poor understanding of the behaviors associated with traumatic experiences often resulted in soldiers being considered weak. They were shunned by their commanders and fellow soldiers or in worst cases, shot. Unfortunately, "breaking in battle" still carries a stigma and is considered unsoldierly. This has resulted in soldiers' reluctance to seek help from mental health professionals. In an effort to reduce psychiatric casualties, some militaries develop instruments designed to screen out recruits prior to entering service. Such efforts, however, have not always proven successful (Wanke, 2002). Other militaries seek to detect current and potential problems with those currently on active duty (Sun et al., 2001).

Various names, causes, and treatments have been applied to the behaviors associated with the trauma of war. The term *soldier's heart* was often used to diagnose US Civil War soldiers who began to present as cardiac patients. Several armies used the term *shell shock* during the First World War (Jones, Fear, & Wessely, 2007). Shell shock described what was thought to be a condition affecting the nervous system as a result of exposure to shells exploding near the trenches. This diagnosis was dropped, however, when it was noted that soldiers who were not near trenches were exhibiting similar behaviors in the aftermath of combat. In later wars such terms as *mental exhaustion*, *combat fatigue*, and *combat neurosis* surfaced. The current diagnosis, post-traumatic stress disorder (PTSD), was introduced into the official psychiatric nomenclature in 1980, after the war in Vietnam (Sussman, 2006).

Just as the names have changed, so have the treatment methods for combat casualties. A common practice was to evacuate soldiers suffering from psychiatric trauma from the combat area and treat them in rear echelons or evacuate them from the area entirely, but eventually evidence began to suggest that it was better to treat the soldiers as close to the combat area as possible. They were given rest and nutrients and then returned to their units, thus saving their dignity and feelings of self-worth (Glass, 1955).

Interesting observations regarding the soldier's stress reaction to combat have been reported. For example, it had been observed that stress reactions seemed to vary with the situation and war. In Korea, it was noted that the soldier's reaction to the stress of combat was to neglect certain health precautions. The result was an increase in cold injuries and in alcohol abuse. Additionally, there was an increase in AWOLs (absent without leave). It was also noted that combat reactions did not occur during the bombing of Pearl Harbor in World War II nor during the retrograde movements in the Korean War after the Chinese pushed back the allied forces. Likewise, few (if any) were reported AWOL. It has been suggested that such behavior would not have served the soldier's purpose (Glass, 1955). The war in Vietnam saw a significant number of soldiers returning with psychiatric injuries but of a different nature, and soldiers frequently engaged in the use of illegal substances and illegal and aggressive behaviors.

The mental health of soldiers and their nation's attitude regarding conflict are related. Soldiers are sensitive to their fellow citizens' approval or disapproval of a war in which they are participating. In the United States, Vietnam became an unpopular war. Returning veterans were not honored with welcome-home parades, nor were they celebrated as heroes. Fox (1972) notes that families welcomed the veterans home but denied them the opportunity to tell their experiences through war stories. The extent to which this may have influenced the mental health of these veterans is a matter of debate, however. In some conflicts the enemy is not necessarily a nation but rather rebellious factions fighting for political or religious ideals, and in these cases the stress of war is as much from the unseen enemy who may not wear a uniform or be conventionally armed as from anything else. Such was the case in Mozambique. In this case too, soldiers were not celebrated as heroes after fighting in that nation's unpopular civil war. At the end of their war, they were required to undergo a cleansing ritual in order to be received back into their community (Granjo, 2007).

In recent conflicts, sophisticated weaponry and scientifically designed armor have been effective in protecting vital organs from penetrating wounds, thus saving lives, but they have not significantly reduced psychological trauma in soldiers (Sussman, 2006). In fact, one could argue the effectiveness of crude homemade devices that have resulted in unexpectedly high numbers of physical and psychological injuries. The high number of psychiatric casualties following deployment in the Middle East in the first decade of the twenty-first century has become a concern (Hoge, Auchterionie, & Milliken, 2006), as has the high suicide rate. Just as potential recruits are screened before entering service, there is a growing recognition of the need to screen soldiers before their reentry into the civilian world. This is especially true for soldiers who have experienced combat or have served in a combat area (Hoge et al., 2006).

THE MILITARY FAMILY

Most families of military men and women stand solidly behind their military family members and are proud of the role they play in support of their country. The family has been a topic of interest in recent years (Booth, Segal, & Bell, 2007). It is now recognized that the family's satisfaction with the military is key to the soldier's decision to remain after the period of obligated service. However, historically neither marriage nor families were recognized as key to the military mission; in fact, families of military personnel were hardly recognized at all. Records from the Civil War and the Revolutionary War in the United States indicate that the soldier was expected to secure his family before going off to war so that they would not be a distraction while he was away in battle (Albano, 1994). The soldier's total commitment was expected to be with his unit and the unit's mission. The old adage, "If the army wanted you to have a family, they would have issued you one," is still heard in many armies of the world.

In most countries where the family is recognized as key to the military mission, such realization came about as a result of grassroots efforts by military spouses. The United States and Netherlands are examples of this (Moelker & van der Kloet, 2006). The degree to which families are accepted in the army (and the degree to which families accept the army) is a direct result of these efforts. Today many countries have some form of family-support policies, programs, and services designed to meet the unique needs of military families and children (Stanley, Segal, & Laughton, 1990). It is also worthy of note that the military has recently recognized that it shares with the civilian sector the issue of domestic violence.

Some armies are vigorously addressing this problem (Harrison & Chantal, 2005).

The family and the military establishment are in a perpetual tugging match. Segal (1986) noted that the army and the family are both "greedy institutions." They both make demands of the soldier and want equal time. The family demands that the soldier attend to the needs of the spouse and children as well as attend to the responsibilities of home. The army, on the other hand, demands the soldier's commitment twenty-four hours a day, seven days a week. Although the family understands the call to duty and tolerates the soldier's long hours and frequent absence, it is under the condition that the soldier resume his or her family role upon returning (provided the absence is not so long as to significantly change the family dynamic).

Just as the military is unique as an institution, so is the military family unique. There are several factors that account for this uniqueness. For example, the soldier and often the family may receive orders to transfer from one location to another several times during the period of service. Each move requires adjustments to new living conditions and new neighbors. However, there may also be reassignments that exclude family members. The reasons for such exclusions vary from lack of family accommodations to the fact that the new assignment may be too dangerous for family members. Separations as a result of deployments, although an acknowledged part of military living, can be stressful for the spouse and children. Moelker and van der Kloet (2006) discuss De Soir's seven stages generally experienced by the spouse with respect to separation: (1) initial shock and protest, (2) disengagement and alienation (beginning in the last days before departure), (3) emotional disorganization, (4) recovery and stabilization, (5) anticipation of homecoming, (6) reunion and reintegration, and (7) stabilization.

It is not unusual for families to experience several separations in a twelve-month period. The degree to which the spouse and children make the adjustments vary depending on several factors, including age and length of time in the service (Wood, Scarville, & Gravino, 1995). Children, especially teenagers, may have special needs. For example, relocations scheduled to occur within a year before high school graduation or other events of significance to the child can be especially stressful. Some militaries find ways to accommodate such problems, such as by delaying the reassignment. Social workers may need to determine if it is in the best interest of the family as well as the child to advocate for a solution.

The long-term absence of parents can be traumatic for children, especially the very young. Social workers should be aware that in countries where single parents are allowed to be service members or where service members are allowed to marry each other, there may be special needs should the parents deploy (Kelly, Bonney, Jarvis, Smith & Gaffney, 2001). The child's ability to adjust under such conditions will vary. If the child is required to relocate, sensitivity must be given to the fact that there may be many difficult adjustments, including adjusting to new caretakers, playmates, schools, and neighborhoods (Lymberg, 2004).

Relocating to foreign countries is another issue of concern. For many families part of the excitement of military living is the opportunity to travel to faraway lands. However, living in a foreign culture has its challenges. Families are required to adjust to new languages and customs. Most families are able to make the adjustment and consider the experience to be positive. Those who are new to the military may find such living stressful and have difficulty connecting with social services designed to make adjustments easier (Durand, Burrell, Knutson, Stretch, & Castro, 2001). In addition, problems of child care, housing, and spouse employment may prove to be challenging for some families.

The Impact of Combat on the Family

The stresses of the soldier are often shared by the family (Durand et al., 2001). Death and injury of deployed soldiers are the family's constant nightmare. The questions most asked by families in anticipation of deployment include the following: Where is she going? When will he return? Is the job dangerous? These concerns are magnified if the soldier is deploying to a combat zone. The degree of stress on families depends on a number of factors, including family dynamics, military experience, and age. Social workers and other mental health workers must be skilled in providing grief and bereavement counseling to families where there is loss of life or life-altering injuries (Bartone, 1996).

However, loss of life and limb are not the only combat tragedies that have lasting impacts on families. Frequent and long-term separations can affect the marriage and family, especially if there were existing problems before the deployments. Soldiers who return suffering from PTSD may prove challenging to families as well. Family members of soldiers diagnosed with PTSD as a result of combat exposure may experience long-term caregiver, financial, and medical burdens. Additionally, PTSD diagnosis in veterans

has been associated with increased somatic and stress symptomatology in families (Solomon, Benbenishty, & Mikulincer, 1991).

A previously overlooked population with regard to stress was women who serve in uniform. With the increase in female soldiers in combat areas, there is now increased interest in their well-being. Research on female soldiers has produced evidence suggesting that during deployment, women are more likely to worry about the care of their children and that their spouse cannot adequately care for the children (Van Breda, 2001). During postdeployment, it is possible that the multiple roles of women (i.e., mother, wife, daughter, soldier) could cause additional stress and have implications for readjustment and reintegration. Functional and structural social support has been identified as a significant protective factor across all stages of the deployment disruption (King, King, Fairbank, Keane, & Adams, 1998). Other protective factors include unit readiness and cohesion, positive homecoming receptions and reunions, positive societal perceptions of the war, and normalization of stress reactions.

While military families brace themselves for the possible injury or death of their loved one, a tragedy of war difficult to comprehend is when a loved one is missing in action (MIA) or has been captured and is a prisoner of war (POW). Army social workers were involved in studies of the families of POWs and MIAs from the Vietnam conflict (McCubbin, Dahl, & Hunter, 1976). They were interested in adaptations to family life based on the knowledge that the husband or father was a POW or MIA. These studies demonstrated the internal conflicts of wives and children of POWs, some of whom had been in captivity up to eight years, and the world of uncertainty for the families. Wives reported experiencing social, psychological, and physical stress. Specifically, they reported feelings of guilt and anxiety, including anxiety regarding possible reunification, loneliness, and assessment of their marriage. They also reported a variety of somatic ailments from general illnesses such as the flu to cardiovascular problems. Children were affected as well. Their behavior ranged from crying easily to encounters with law enforcement.

THE SOCIAL WORKER IN THE MILITARY SETTING

Some countries have social workers who are soldiers in uniform and hold military rank. Among them are the United States, Finland, South Africa, Israel, the Netherlands, Canada, and Great Britain. In many countries the military is supported by a civilian social work force in addition to uniformed social workers (Daley, 2003). The education and training of social workers should prepare them to work with populations of soldiers and families who vary widely in age, ethnicity, race, and experience (Harris & Jones, 2007). Social workers who desire to work with the military should possess skills and training for practicing the traditional social work specializations, including medical social work, psychiatric social work, marital counseling, financial management, and counseling for substance abuse (Martin, Rosen, & Sparacino, 2000; Pryce & Pryce 2006). In some armies social workers are with the soldiers in the combat zone, which means it is crucial that they possess the skills and abilities needed to intervene in situations resulting from combat trauma (Brown, 1984). They should also be prepared to provide consultation to community and unit leaders.

The importance of gaining an appreciation for military culture cannot be overemphasized (e.g., the navy culture is different from that of the army). Social workers must understand that the military of today is significantly different from the military of a generation ago. Further, they must appreciate that although the military is unique, it is at the same time a microcosm of the civilian community from which the soldiers come. For the most part, they are working with a young population and therefore must seek an understanding of the youth culture. Female soldiers are increasing, and therefore social workers need to appreciate the issues of women who serve in this male-oriented culture (Soeters, Winslow, & Weibull, 2006).

In addition, social workers must have an understanding of the stresses experienced by military families as well as the intervention skills required to work with such families. Social workers should understand the impact of the call-up (e.g., conscript or all volunteer) system in their country. Families of soldiers who have been conscripted and families of reservists who have been activated often have different experiences and problems than the families of career soldiers. These families may lack a support system that understands the frustrations of the deployment. The social worker must be aware of the military and civilian resources available to soldiers and their families. To the extent possible, the social worker should establish rapport with the leaders of the soldier's unit. Social workers should also be aware of the issues of family reunification and of the impact on the family if the soldier returns with physical or psychological injuries (Basham, 2008).

Throughout history, militaries have played a significant role in their nations' destinies. Those who serve do so with pride. Likewise, dedicated men and women have supported the warriors by providing social services to them and their families, whether through religious institutions, the Red Cross, or other charitable organizations. Social workers have a definite role to play in the service of their country, helping the men, women, and families who make major sacrifices under difficult conditions.

NOTE

1. The term *soldiers* is used generically to refer to all men and women who serve in the military regardless of their branch of service. The term *army* or *armies* refers to all branches of service.

REFERENCES

Albano, S. (1994). Military recognition of family concerns: Revolutionary War to 1993. *Armed Forces & Society*, 20(2), 283–302.

Auslander, G. K., Soskolne V., & Ben-Shahar, I. (2005). Utilization of health social work services by older immigrants and veterans in Israel. *Health & Social Work*, 30(3), 241–251.

Bartone, P. (1996). Notification and survival: Thinking the unthinkable. In R. J. Ursano & A. E. Norwood (Eds.), *Emotional aftermath of the Persian Gulf War: Veterans, families, communities, and nations* (pp. 315–351). Washington, DC: American Psychiatric Press.

Basham, K. (2008). Homecoming as safe haven or the new front: Attachment and detachment in military couples. *Clinical Social Work Journal*, 36(1), 83–96.

Booth, B., Segal, M. W., & Bell B. D. (2007). *What we know about army families, 2007 update*. Washington: Caliber.

Boëne, B. (2006). The military as a tribe among tribes: Post Modern Armed Forces and Civil-Military Relations? In G. Caforio (Ed.) *Handbook of the Sociology of the Military* (pp. 167–185). New York: Springer.

Brown, P. (1984). Legacies of war: Treatment considerations with Vietnam veterans and their families. *Social Work*, 4, 372–379.

Daley, J. G. (2003). Military social work: A multi-country comparison. *International Social Work*, 46(4), 437–448.

Drescher, K. D., Smith, M. W, & Foy, D. W. (2007). Spirituality and readjustment following war-zone experiences. In C. Figley & W. P. Nash (Eds.), *Combat stress injury: Theory, research, and management*. (pp. 432–458). New York: Routledge/Taylor & Francis Group.

Durand, D. B., Burrell. L., Knutson, K., Stretch, R. K., & Castro, C. (2001, October). *Living OCONUS in a high OPTEMPO environment: How are families adjusting?* Paper presented at the Inter-University on Armed Forces, Baltimore, Maryland, October 19–21.

Fox, R., (1972). Post-combat adaptational problems. *Comprehensive Psychiatry, 13*(5), 436.

Friedland, W. A. (1977). Social work in relief and rehabilitation after wars, at home and abroad. *Journal of Sociology and Social Welfare, 4*(3–4), 530–533.

Glass A. J. (1955). Principles of combat psychiatry. *Military Medicine, 117*(1), 27–33.

Granjo, P. (2007). The homecomer: Postwar cleansing rituals in Mozambique. *Armed Forces & Society, 33*(3), 382–395.

Harris, J. J., & Jones, N. G. (2007). African American military service members and their families: A different environment. In L. A. See (Ed.), *Human behavior in the social environment from an African American perspective* (pp. 133–150). New York: Haworth Press.

Harrison, D., & Chantal, B. (2005). Isolation experienced by female victims of spousal abuse by their military spouses. *Canadian Social Work Review/Revue Canadienne de Dervice Social, 22*(1), 53–70.

Hoge, C. W., Auchterionie, J. L., & Milliken, C. S. (2006). Mental health problems, use of mental health services, and attrition from military service after returning from deployment to Iraq or Afghanistan. *Jounal of the American Medical Association, 295*(9), 1023–1032.

Jones, E., Fear, N. T., & Wessely, S. (2007). Shell shock and mild traumatic brain injury: A historical review. *American Journal of Psychiatry, 164*(11), 1641–1645.

Kelly, M. L., Bonney, J. F., Jarvis, M. S., Smith, K. M., & Gaffney, M. A. (2001). Navy mothers experiencing and not experiencing deployment: Reasons for staying in or leaving the military, *Military Psychology, 13*(1), 55–71.

King L.A., King D. W., Fairbank, J. A., Keane, T. M., & Adams, G. A. (1998). Resilience-recovery factors in post-traumatic stress disorder among women and men Vietnam veterans: Hardiness, postwar social support and additional stressful life events. *Journal of Personality and Social Psychology, 74*, 420–434.

Lymberg, L. (2004). When military parents are sent to war, children left behind need ample support. *Journal of the American Medical Association, 292*(13), 1541–1542.

Martin, J. A., Rosen, L. N., & Sparacino, L. R. (Eds.). (2000). *The military family: A practice guide for human service providers.* Westport, CT: Praeger.

McCubbin, H. I., Dahl, B. B., & Hunter, E. J. (Eds.). (1976). *Families in the military system.* Newbury Park, CA: Sage.

Moelker, R., & van der Kloet, I. (2006). Military families and the armed forces: A two-sided affair? In G. Caforio (Ed.), *Handbook of the sociology of the military* (pp. 201–224). New York: Springer.

Pryce, J., & Pryce, D. (2006). Revisiting social work and the American military family. *Families in Society, 87*(3), 1–12.

Segal M. W. (1986). The military and the family as greedy institutions. *Armed Forces & Society, 13*(1), 9–38.

Shay, J. (2002). *Odysseus in America.* New York: Scribner.

Soeters, J. L., Winslow, D. J., & Weibull, A. (2006). Military culture. In G. Caforio (Ed.), *Handbook of the sociology of the military* (pp. 237–254). New York: Springer.

Solomon, Z., Benbenishty, R., & Mikulincer, M. (1991). The contribution of wartime pre-war and post-war factors to self-efficacy: A longitudinal study of combat stress reaction. *Journal of Personality and Social Psychology, 5*, 279–285.

Stanley J., Segal, M. W., & Laughton, C. J. (1990). Grassroots family action and military policies responses. *Marriage and Family Review, 15*, 207–233.

Sun, J., Wang, H., Wang, W., Yan, M., Xu, J., & Bi, Y. (2001). A study of the symptom checklist-90 on sailors. *Chinese Journal of Clinical Psychology, 9*(1), 40–41.

Sussman, N. (2006). The impact of wartime experiences. *Primary Psychiatry, 13*(3), 12–13.

United Nations Office of the High Commissioner for Human Rights (OHCHR). (1990) Convention on the rights of the child. Retrieved from www2.ohchr.org/english/law/crc.htm.

Van Breda, A. D. (2001). *Resiliency theory: A literature review.* Pretoria, South Africa: South African Military Health Services. Available at www.vanbreda.org/adrian/resilience.htm.

Wanke, P. (2002). Russian/Soviet military psychiatry: 1904–1945. *Humanities and Social Sciences, 63*(5-A), 1961.

Wood, S., Scarville, J., & Gravino, K. S. (1995). Waiting wives: Separation and reunion among army wives. *Armed Forces & Society, 21*(2), 217–237.

Violence Against Women

SUSAN MAPP

Violence against women is widespread around the world, occurring in all countries and to women of all classes. Although men also experience numerous acts of violence, such acts are unlikely to occur specifically due to their gender. Males are also less likely to have the perpetrator be a family member or intimate partner. Violence can take a variety of forms throughout the lives of females, including sex-selective abortion, female genital cutting, honor killings, early marriage, intimate partner violence, and dowry deaths. The prejudice against females runs so deeply in some cultures that it is estimated that there are sixty million "missing" females—girls who were aborted before birth due to their sex, killed at birth, or not given sufficient food or medical care in comparison to their brothers (Amnesty International, 2004).

Violence against women has been declared a violation of human rights as well as a public health emergency by both the United Nations and the World Health Organization (WHO) due to its commonality and consequences. According to WHO (2002), these consequences can include physical injuries, problems with sexual and reproductive health, mental health disorders, physical health problems, an increase in risky behaviors such as substance abuse and sexual risk taking, and even death. This chapter provides an overview of dimensions of violence against women and concludes with a discussion of prevention efforts.

SEX-SELECTIVE ABORTION AND INFANTICIDE

Preference for males over females begins even before birth. Due to cultural norms such as the expense of dowry, a need for physical labor, male children caring for their parents in their old age, or the eldest son lighting the funeral pyre of his father, families can perceive a high need for a son, while daughters are seen as a luxury. This preference can be exacerbated by limits on the number of children, either self-imposed

due to poverty or imposed by the government such as in China. As reproductive technologies have advanced, there is less female infanticide than in previous decades, but there has been a rise in sex-selective abortion. Sex-selective abortion is less likely to result in criminal prosecution of the parents and may be less traumatizing than infanticide.

A recent study in India concluded that ten million girls are missing from expected population over the last twenty years due to sex-selective abortion, even though this procedure has been illegal since 1994 (Jha et al., 2006). Wealthy couples in India will even fly to the United States, one of the few countries where it is legal to test for the sex of embryos prior to implantation, in order to make sure they have a son. In China, there is a high ratio of boys to girls, primarily due to a widely distorted ratio for second births, especially in areas where families are allowed a second child if the first one was a girl (Zhu, Lu, & Hesketh, 2009). This discrepancy among latter-born children has also been found in the United States among families from India, China, and Korea. The gender ratio for first children is equal, but if there is no son in the family, the ratio for second children increases to 1.17 and to 1.5 for the third child. The authors believe this is due to prenatal sex selection and note that the practice continues despite the lack of in-country cultural factors, demonstrating the power of these cultural beliefs (Almond & Edlund, 2008).

To try to alleviate infanticide, governments in both India and Pakistan have been placing cradles outside police stations, hospitals, and charity organizations. Trying to increase the number of women who give birth in hospitals is also seen as an effective method to identify babies at risk and rescue them. In addition, committees have been formed in local villages for this same purpose, and efforts are being made to increase the female literacy rate in order to increase the value of females in society. China has changed laws regarding inheritance by females and is conducting a social marketing campaign for gender equality to reduce the preference for sons.

FEMALE GENITAL CUTTING

The next type of violence that girls may experience is female genital cutting (FGC). This procedure involves partial or total removal of a female's external genitalia for cultural or nonmedical reasons. Approximately 130 million women living today have undergone the procedure (United Nations Secretary-General [UNSG], 2006). The majority of girls undergo FGC between four and fourteen years of age, but it is sometimes performed on infants as well. It is most common in Northeast Africa, where prevalence rates range from 80% to 97% in countries such as Egypt and Eritrea. However, it also occurs in Southwest Asian countries such as Yemen and Iraq.

There are three basic types of FGC, differentiated by the extent of the cutting: clitoridectomy (type I), excision (type II), and infibulation (type III). Type I involves the removal of the clitoral hood and may include the removal of part or all of the clitoris. Type II is the removal of the clitoral hood, the clitoris, and part or all of the labia minora. The most severe form, type III, is the removal of part or all of the external genitalia (clitoris, labia minora, and labia majora) with stitching or narrowing of the vaginal opening. Only a very narrow opening is left (about the diameter of a matchstick) for the passage of urine and menstrual blood.

Extensive damage can result from the procedure, including painful sexual intercourse and menstruation, increased susceptibility to sexually transmitted diseases, infertility, increased risk during childbirth, hemorrhaging, and death. One study found that women who have experienced FGC are more than 50% more likely to die or have their infants die during childbirth than women who have not experienced the procedure. Women who have undergone more severe forms of FGC are more at risk than women who have experienced less severe types (WHO, 2006).

There are several reasons why FGC may be conducted. A primary one is to increase chastity among women and to reduce sexual pleasure for them. It is believed that this will help curb promiscuity as well as protect against sexual assault. Further, the procedure is seen as an important rite of passage in some cultures. The external female genitalia are seen as unhygienic and unsightly in certain societies and thus their removal is seen as beautifying and hygienic. Although often seen in Muslim countries, FGC is not based in that religion and in fact predates it; however, some community leaders will state that it is based in the Koran. Due to the widespread practice of FGC in some cultures, it can be difficult for a girl to marry if she has not undergone the procedure. For this reason, females, including the girl herself and her mother, can be some of the stronger supporters of the procedure. In certain places, a woman who is unmarried is shunned and is barred from employment, making survival nearly impossible. Thus, a girl may have the procedure even if she and her mother are against the idea because if she does not, it could mean social suicide or literal death.

One of the major targets for revising public opinions has been men. Men must be willing to marry a woman who has not undergone the procedure, and fathers must believe it is not necessary in order to maintain family honor. Involving religious leaders to counter the belief that FGC is necessary for religious purposes is also important. In 2007, Egypt started a nationwide campaign against the practice and top religious leaders declared it *haram*, or prohibited by Islam. In Senegal, a grassroots movement that was developed in the native language of the Senegalese at the wishes of the local women and in conjunction with local religious leaders was successful in lowering FGC rates. Culturally sensitive terms were used for FGC, and all villages in the intermarrying community agreed to abandon the practice (Easton, Monkman, & Miles, 2003).

EARLY MARRIAGE

Girls in the Global South are susceptible to being married off at early ages. More than sixty million women aged twenty to twenty-four worldwide were married before the age of eighteen. Rates vary among countries, but South Asia accounts for about half of these girls, with 45% of females married before eighteen (including 65% of Indian girls). Sub-Saharan Africa follows as the region with the next highest rate—40% (United Nations Children's Fund [UNICEF], 2007, 2008).

Although many countries have laws against child marriage, they are often weak or ineffectively enforced. A number of factors increase the likelihood of child marriage, but poverty is a primary one. For women in the lowest quintile of income worldwide, 56% were married as children, compared with 16% in the highest quintile (UNICEF, 2007). If the girl can be married at an early age, her parents no longer have to bear the expense of raising her, and if a bride price is offered, she can be a source of income for the family. Additionally, the family no longer needs to worry about premarital sex. Becoming pregnant outside of wedlock is the worst shame a girl can bring to her family, and early marriage is used to prevent this from occurring.

Girls who are married early face a host of potential negative outcomes. They face a higher risk of domestic violence than those who marry at later ages. They typically have to leave school once they are married or become pregnant, which usually soon follows. Additionally, an early pregnancy has a higher risk of maternal death or injury during childbirth. Girls aged ten to fourteen are five times more likely to die as a result of childbirth or pregnancy than those aged twenty to twenty-four, and girls aged fifteen to nineteen are more than twice as likely to die (United Nations Population Fund [UNFPA], n.d.).

INTIMATE PARTNER VIOLENCE

Approximately one in every three women worldwide (about one billion women) has been beaten, coerced into sex, or otherwise abused by an intimate partner (UNSG, 2006). In Australia, Israel, South Africa, and the United States, between 40% and 70% of female murder victims are killed by their partners. Rates of intimate partner violence (IPV) tend to range between 20% and 30% in most Global North countries, including 22% in the United States, 29% in Canada, 30% in the United Kingdom, and 21% in the Netherlands. These figures include only physical assault and do not include the psychological and sexual violence that often co-occurs (WHO, 2002). The direct and indirect costs of IPV have been estimated at over $5.8 billion in the United States and £23 billion in the United Kingdom—for IPV in that country alone (United Nations, 2009.).

Violence against women is often seen as acceptable due to women's lower societal status. Research has found a high level of victim-blaming attitudes for IPV in the European Union, which can lead to both violence and victims having difficulty accessing assistance (Gracia & Herrero, 2006). Leaving the relationship is not an option for many women for a number of reasons. Women are typically at the highest risk of violence after leaving the relationship. Divorce may not be legal or acceptable, and even if the woman does leave the relationship, she is likely to have difficulty surviving financially due to her lower status and education, making it challenging for her to obtain well-paying work. In many cultures, a woman's status is tied to her role as wife and mother, and if she leaves that role, she loses the little status she did have and faces social stigmatization.

According to WHO (2002), the largest push for change on this issue tends to come from women's organizations, and the first wave of activity in a nation tends to involve efforts toward legal reforms, training for law enforcement, and specialized services for victims, including shelter programs. Despite the widespread nature of IPV, currently less than half of all nations have laws against it. In 2006, 89 states had some legislation addressing domestic violence in some fashion, while 60 of these had a law specifically banning it. In contrast, 102 nations had no law against it (UNSG, 2006). Interventions to reduce IPV have included all-female police stations, treatment for abusive men, and working with health-care providers to identify victims. In the United States, policies have been developed regarding mandatory arrests for IPV, with evaluations finding mixed results for recidivism (WHO, 2002). However, these actions are not sufficient in and of themselves; the laws and services are of little assistance if the attitudes that permit the violence continue unchecked.

Dowry Deaths

One particular form of violence against women within the family is the phenomenon known as dowry deaths. The importance and amount of a bride's dowry has been growing in India despite the fact that the giving and receiving of a dowry has been illegal there since 1961. In order to give an appropriate amount, many families are driven into debt. However, some grooms and their families are not satisfied with the dowry and ask for more. If they do not receive it, they may kill the bride so that the groom is free to marry again and gain another dowry. According to official crime statistics, almost 7000 women were killed in India in 2002 alone due to dowry disputes (UNSG, 2006). In many cases, the murders are disguised as accidental deaths from kitchen fires. A campaign in India has started urging couples to pledge to abstain from giving or receiving a dowry. The Say No to Dowry campaign began in 2002 and has been growing ever since. Kishwar (2005) reminds us, however, that as with all domestic violence cases, the stated reason for the violence can often be simply an excuse for its occurrence. Men may state the fact that dinner was late on the table or poorly cooked as an excuse for violence, but the deaths are not called *lousy-cooking murders*.

Honor Killings

Women are not only at risk of violence from their husbands but also from other family members through so-called honor killings. Approximately 5000 women are murdered each year in honor killings (UNSG, 2006). In some cultures, if a female is perceived to have besmirched the family honor by acting dishonorably, the only way for the family to regain its honor is to kill the female. The offense may be an extramarital affair, being seen in the company of a man who is not her husband, or even being raped. These violations may not even be proven but may be only a suspicion. In some cases of rape, women have not been killed but have been forced to marry their rapist in order to preserve honor. These situations have been documented in Turkey, Pakistan, and Egypt as well as in countries in Europe where people from these countries have immigrated. Although these are all predominately Muslim nations, the crime is not sanctioned by Islam, and it predates the development of Islam as a religion.

Families in which honor killings occur are often poor, and as a father who killed his daughters due to one's adulterous affair stated, "We are poor people and we have nothing else to protect but our honor" (Tanveer, 2005, p. A9). Honor is seen as a valuable possession, and in the case of impoverished families, it may be the only thing of value that they have. Therefore, when it is seen as damaged, it is extremely important to them to reclaim this only possession of value (Sev'er & Yurdakul, 2005).

Although honor killings are outlawed, frequently they are not punished severely. The family will also commonly have the youngest male in the family commit the murder so that the courts will be more lenient with him due to his age. Turkey has begun prosecuting these murders more harshly as part of its bid to join the European Union. As a result, families have moved to pressuring women perceived to have tarnished the family honor to commit suicide or to killing them in a manner to look like suicide (Bilefsky, 2006).

PREVENTION

A number of organizations have begun campaigns to fight violence against women, including the Council of Europe in 2006 and the United Nations in 2008. The study by the secretary-general of the UN on violence against women (2006) noted a number of common interventions that help to lower rates of violence. These include enacting and enforcing laws to criminalize the violence, improving criminal justice systems to effectively respond to such acts, and providing services to victims. Social workers in many countries are involved in providing services to victims of violence, including advice, referrals, and shelter

services; they often also provide training to police and to health-care providers on violence-related issues.

A vital piece in addressing violence is primary prevention—working to change the attitudes and societal structures that allow violence to occur. According to the secretary-general of the United Nations (2006), the root cause of this violence appears to be similar across cultures: the oppression of women stemming from unequal power relations and persistent discrimination. As noted throughout this chapter, a central piece to solving the problem is to involve men and boys in creating change. For instance, FGC cannot be eliminated unless there are men willing to marry women without the procedure, and IPV cannot cease until men are willing to be nonviolent. Programs can be effective in changing attitudes toward gender roles, but many programs tend to be small scale and short term (WHO, 2007). If change is truly to occur, programs must become more widespread and institutionalized.

REFERENCES

Almond, D., & Edlund, L. (2008). Son-biased sex ratios in the 2000 United States Census. *PNAS: Proceedings of the National Academy of Sciences, 105*(15), 5681–5682.

Amnesty International. (2004). *Making violence against women count.* Retrieved April 12, 2011, from http://www.amnesty.org/en/library/info/ACT77/034/2004.

Bilefsky, D. (2006, July 16). How to avoid honor killing in Turkey? Honor suicide. *New York Times.* Retrieved July 18, 2006, from http://www.nytimes.com.

Easton, P., Monkman, K., & Miles, R. (2003). Social policy from the bottom up: Abandoning FGC in sub-Saharan Africa. *Development in Practice, 13*(5), 445–458.

Gracia, E., & Herrero, J. (2006). Acceptability of domestic violence against women in the European Union: A multilevel analysis. *Journal of Epidemiology and Community Health, 60,* 123–129.

Jha., P., Kumar, R., Vasa, P., Dhingra, N., Thiruchelvam, D., & Moineddin, R. (2006). Low male-to-female sex ratio of children born in India: National survey of 1.1 million households. *Lancet, 367,* 211–218.

Kishwar, M. P. (2005). Destined to fail. *Manushi, 148.* Retrieved August 26, 2006, from http://www.manushi.in/docs/74MK%20Article%203-12.pdf.

Sev'er, A., & Yurdakul, G. (2005). Culture of honor, culture of change: A feminist analysis of honor killings in rural Turkey. In P. S. Rothenberg (Ed.), *Beyond borders: Thinking critically about global issues* (pp. 288–306). New York: Worth.

Tanveer, K. (2005, December 29). Pakistani father admits slaying 4 over "honor." *The Patriot-News,* p. A9.

United Nations Children's Fund (UNICEF). (2008). *Child marriage and the law: Legislative reform initiative paper series*. Retrieved February 27, 2009, from http://www.unicef.org/policyanalysis/files/Child_Marriage_and_the_Law(1).pdf.

United Nations Children's Fund (UNICEF). (2007). *Progress for children: A world fit for children statistical review*. Retrieved February 27, 2009, from http://www.unicef.org/publications/files/Progress_for_Children_No_6_revised.pdf.

United Nations. (2009). *Violence against women*. Retrieved from http://www.un.org/en/women/endviolence/pdf/factsheets/unite_the_situation.pdf.

United Nations Population Fund (UNFPA). (n.d.). *Child marriage fact sheet*. Retrieved March 14, 2009, from www.unfpa.org/swp/2005/presskit/factsheets/facts_child_marriage.htm.

United Nations Secretary-General (UNSG). (2006). *In-depth study on all forms of violence against women*. Retrieved May 20, 2009, from http://www.un.org/womenwatch/daw/vaw/v-sg-study.htm.

World Health Organization (WHO). (2007). *Engaging men and boys in changing gender-based inequality in health*. Retrieved June 15, 2009, from http://www.who.int/gender/documents/Engaging_men_boys.pdf.

World Health Organization (WHO). (2006). *Female genital mutilation and obstetric outcome: WHO collaborative prospective study in six African countries. Lancet, 367*, 1835–1841.

World Health Organization (WHO). (2002). *World report on violence and health*. Retrieved from www.who.int/violence_injury_prevention/violence/world_report/en.

Zhu, W. X., Lu., L., & Hesketh, T. (2009). China's excess males, sex selective abortion, and one child policy: Analysis of data form 2005 national intercensus survey. *BMJ, 338*. Retrieved April 16, 2009, from http://www.bmj.com/cgi/reprint/338/apr09_2/b1211.pdf.

FOR MORE INFORMATION

Council of Europe website on violence against women: http://www.coe.int/t/dg2/equality/domesticviolence-campaign/default_en.asp.

United Nations Secretary-General Campaign to End Violence against Women: http://endviolence.un.org.

VAWnet compendium of research on IPV (US focused but has some global information): http://new.vawnet.org/category/index_pages.php?category_id=497.

41

Youth

LINCOLN O. WILLIAMS

Youth work shares a common value base and practice approaches with social work. Both professions are anchored in the democratic paradigm, and in terms of practice and approaches, both professions actively deploy the ecological, empowerment, and advocacy perspectives when dealing with their client groups.

YOUTH PARTICIPATION

The critical problems facing youth in both traditional and modern societies are their lack of power to influence the policies and institutions that shape their lives, their voicelessness in the sense of adult society's refusal to create the structures through which their voices can be heard, and their exclusion from society's main decision-making processes. The lack of participation by youth is a central concern of global agencies such as the United Nations, World Bank, and Commonwealth Youth Programme (Cunningham, McGinnis, Verdú, Tesliuc, & Verner, 2008; Danns et al., 1997; UNICEF and UNFPA, 2002). For example, participation in decision making is a central plank of the UN Convention on the Rights of the Child (1989), which establishes participation as a basic right for all children and young people.

The voice of young people in issues that affect their lives has a transformative effect. For instance, 200 youth in the Inuit community of Kugluktuk held demonstrations in 2007, appealing to their parents to stop drinking, taking drugs, and killing each other and to start looking after their children. The demonstrations were such a shock that a decision was made to control liquor sales, and violence began to decline (www.studentsonice.com/blog/?p=76).

The social upheavals in the Middle East and North Africa offer recent cogent evidence of the transformative effect of youth activism. In a region where 60% of the population is under 30 years old, it is not surprising that young people would be in the forefront of social change. The rallying cry of protesters in Bahrain

was the words of the Tunisian rapper, El General. The basic demand of the young people was to be treated as *citizens* with a voice and not as subjects of a despot.

However, for the vast majority of youth in vulnerable situations, participation requires assistance. It is true that many adults also face these problems as they transition from one life stage to another; hence the need for the assistance of social workers. My contention is that young people are discriminated against in these ways because they are young; it is for this reason that both social work and youth work have a vested interest in adopting a participatory practice approach in dealing with their clients. Clients are encouraged to challenge the oppression that confronts them so that they can take charge of matters that affect them, define their own needs, and participate in the decision-making process. Social workers aim to improve clients' personal capacities to exercise power by, for example, developing their confidence, self-esteem, assertiveness, knowledge, and skills. It is also recognized that these problems are generated not only from the individuals or groups that make up our clientele but also from the social institutions they interact with.

It is incumbent on both social workers and youth workers to ensure that their own institution or agency is open to participation. In this regard, Roger Hart (1997) has developed the concept of a ladder of participation as a tool that organizations can use to assess levels of participation. The ladder starts at the bottom rung with manipulation and moves upward through seven more rungs as follows: decoration, tokenism, youth being assigned and then informed, youth being consulted and informed, adult-initiated programs but shared decisions with youth, youth-initiated and -directed programs, and finally youth-initiated and shared decisions with adults. Applying these practice theories with adults is difficult enough; applying them in working with young people is extremely problematic because it is often not seen as legitimate to extend the democratic process to them, perhaps because, in many countries, a sizable section of the youth population does not have a vote.

DEFINING YOUTH

The United Nations defines *youth* as young people between the ages of fifteen and twenty-four years. There are approximately 1.2 billion young people, constituting 18% of the world's population. Age categorizations of youth vary across the world: In Malaysia it is ages fifteen to forty, in the Caribbean ages ten to twenty-nine, and in Malawi ages fourteen to twenty-five. In Malawi, the National Youth Policy recognizes that "youth is not only a chronological definition, but a term commonly used to describe roles in society ascribed to the young. This policy, therefore, will be flexible to accommodate young people under 14 years and over 25 years depending on their social and economic circumstance" (Williams, 1998, p. 44).

These examples highlight the problem of trying to categorize or define youth. There are several ways of defining it: as a physiological phase, usually denoted by the start of puberty and finishing roughly when the body stops growing; as a psychological phase of transition between childhood and adulthood in which successful negotiation of psychological crises enables individuals to make it to the mature adult stage of the life cycle; as a social category framed by particular social institutions such as school and legislative definitions; or as a phase that is culturally understood by an interplay of musical, visual, and verbal signs that denotes what is young in relation to that which is interpreted as childish or adult.

It is the complex interplay between these various aspects that makes the categorical definition of *youth* inadequate, because it fails to take account of the specific race, gender, class, or cultural context in which young people experience and negotiate their youthfulness. It ignores the problems raised by the assumption that there are clear and absolute differences between childhood, youth, and adulthood. For an excellent refutation of this assumption, see Neil Postman's *The Disappearance of Childhood* (1994), in which he argues that modern communication technology is not only causing childhood to disappear but also is changing the social construction of what it means to be an adult. Finally, the categorical definition encourages the view that youth is a biologically determined process that is neutral, universal, and ahistorical. The implication of this analysis is the recognition that youth is not homogeneous.

The starting point for developing social work practice with youth therefore is to analyze the historical and social forces that have contributed to the context in which young people find themselves. For example, in the United Kingdom, services for youth originated in the Victorian era as an attempt by middle-class interests to save working-class children from the brutalizing effects of industrialization and urbanization (Williams, 1988). Vestiges of these forces are at play today in the social education, intermediate treatment, and life skills remediation programs that are characteristic of UK youth services. This is in contrast, for example, to programs in France, where youth services are directed to stimulate young people's interests in an open and exploratory manner.

In the Caribbean, young people played a significant role in the modernization of their societies in the last century, but today they face a considerable level of exclusion. It is this exclusion and the reasons for it that social workers have to comprehend in order to work effectively with young people in their own context-specific work situations. The Caribbean is a useful example to explore further not only for practice in developing countries but also for practice in urban areas of developed countries that are affected negatively by globalization.

Youth in the Caribbean

In the Caribbean eighty years ago, it was young people who were in the vanguard of constructing postcolonial countries through their participation in labor and fledgling political movements playing an important role in the birth of the politically independent Caribbean (Lewis, 1995). Later, in the 1970s, young people across the region responded to the Black Power movement, to Bob Marley's call to emancipate themselves from mental slavery, and to the aspirations of the Grenadian revolution in 1979. Young people were also active in the attempted coup in Trinidad and Tobago in 1990. Factors such as the unavailability of appropriate opportunities for their development or the denial by adult society of young people's search for personhood were identified as driving their participation in these significant social events that helped shape the modern Caribbean (James-Bryant, 1992).

A lack of opportunities for youth is characteristic of independent Caribbean countries. The inability of postcolonial governments to meet the high expectations—expectations that the politicians themselves helped to build—was due mainly to the adoption of inappropriate models of development, such as capital-intensive industries rather than labor-intensive ones and urban development over rural development. Thus postcolonial youth found themselves in societies in which "the rhetoric of self-reliance, of new visions for youth, of education as a vehicle for democracy, of youth entrepreneurship, all these promises did not materialize in viable amounts" (Deosaran, 1992, p. 66). They also realized that there was not much hope of change because they were not living in societies that had developed a culture of change. They had come to realize that they were living in a political culture where "nepotism crowns geriatric politics" (p. 66). Indeed, young people found that "in large measure, the politics of colonialism have given way to a political independence which provides its own entrenched elites, leaving a blockade against change and youthful succession. The Caribbean is yet to develop a culture of and for change" (p. 67).

Postcolonial Caribbean societies have not only failed to deliver economic security and opportunity but have also failed to imbue the young with an ideology of Caribbeanness that could help them to withstand the materialism and individualism embedded in the culture beamed in from the Global North, principally from the United States. The message for many Caribbean youth is that they will have to migrate—if they can—if they are to achieve their personal and material goals. For those at home who see that they have little opportunity of achieving success through legitimate means, a significant minority will attempt to use illegitimate means to achieve their goals. The growth of the underground economy (euphemistically termed the *informal economy*) assists in the erosion of traditional values and thereby sends the signal to young people that the end justifies the means. The exclusion of youth from the mainstream of Caribbean societies and the powerlessness that youth feel are identified by the major youth organizations in the Caribbean Region, such as the Commonwealth Youth Programme (Danns et al., 1997) and UNICEF and UNFPA (2002). Youth are only recognized seriously in the areas of sport, entertainment, and crime. One of the most significant indicators emerging from a number of studies is a sense of hopelessness, despair, and powerlessness. There clearly exists a crisis of confidence and disillusionment among Caribbean youth.

Youth Culture Globally

On a global level, there are those who argue that youth subcultures are no more than a youthful reflection of the dominant parent culture, which is largely determined by reference to class position. In these youth subcultures, young people often attempt some magical solution to problems confronting the parent culture. In the United Kingdom during the 1980s, for example, the violent confrontation between various soccer firms was interpreted by some radical youth commentators as an attempt by working-class youth to hang onto the territory that their working-class parents had lost due to the closure of factories, mines, and docks.

Some writers (Beck, 1992; Furlong & Cartmel, 2007) argue that in modern societies, a young person's life chances are still largely determined by the unequal distribution of wealth. "Like wealth, risks adhere to the class pattern, only inversely: wealth accumulates at the top, risks at the bottom. To that extent, risks seem to *strengthen*, not abolish, the class society. Poverty attracts an unfortunate abundance of risks. The wealthy (in income, power or education) can *purchase* safety and freedom from risk" (Furlong & Cartmel, 2007, p. 4). Other writers (Adam, Beck, & Van Loon, 2004; Giddens, 1991) argue that modern society is characterized by uncertainty, contingency, complexity, fragmentation, and turbulence and that life is full of risks that are not seen as things that happen to social collectivities such as class, race, or gender but to individuals. People increasingly feel that setbacks and crises are the result of personal shortcomings and not the result of forces that are outside their control. Thus if young people leave school or university and cannot find jobs, they are much more likely to blame themselves for not studying the right courses that the market demands. However, as Beck (2000) reminds us, "No one can say what you must learn in order to be needed in the future" (p. 3).

Such an analysis of a specific historical and sociocultural context enables social workers to appreciate young people's attitudes, behaviors, and values, and it helps them to plan appropriate and effective intervention programs. The starting point for any youth intervention is to recognize that the vast majority (80% to 90%) of young people successfully negotiate the storm and stress of adolescence. After conducting research around the world, Coleman and Hendry (1990) conclude that what youth studies needs to explain is why so many young people make the transition to adulthood so smoothly and without mental crisis—why the majority are so normal, so to speak. They argue that what is needed is a theory of normal youth. Their hypothesis is that young people actively stack their stressors so that they can deal with them one or two at a time. Longitudinal research in the United Kingdom suggests that a young person can usually cope with two risk factors simultaneously, but when three or more are present, the outcome almost always results in some emotional or behavioral problem (Department for Children, Schools and Families [DCSF] & HM Treasury, 2007).

Studies in the Caribbean and in the United Kingdom, for example, show that the vast majority of young people are normal. In the Caribbean, they are generally patriotic, have values similar to those of their parents, feel that their parents are in a position to guide them, feel able to withstand negative peer pressure, have a positive self-image, are not overly materialistic, and highly value their future jobs and careers (Richardson, 1999). In the United Kingdom, the proportion of young people leaving school with good qualifications is trending upward, with 90% of sixteen-year-olds continuing on to some form of further learning, 71% of nineteen-year-olds progressing to a higher qualification, and 50% of sixteen- to nineteen-year-olds providing informal help within their communities. Of those young people who do have crises and need professional intervention, conduct disorder is the most prevalent problem (at 7%)

affecting young people between eleven and fifteen years of age (DCSF & HM Treasury, 2007).

Thus, in working with the vast majority of young people, our objective is one of prevention and seeking to build their resiliency. Program evidence in the United Kingdom, the United States, Latin America, and the Caribbean shows that what young people do in their leisure time—out of school, out of work, or during periods of non-income-generating time—has significant outcomes for their adult lives. Positive outcomes include improved attitudes toward drugs and alcohol use, decreased delinquency and violent behavior, increased knowledge and practice of safe sex, and increased skills for coping with peer pressure. There is also evidence of decreased behavioral problems and improved social communication skills, self-confidence, and self-esteem. It is also interesting to note that the research evidence seems to indicate that structured activities—such as sports, the arts, and volunteer work—are far more effective than unstructured activities. These are further elaborated in Box 41.1.

BOX 41.1
HOW POSITIVE ACTIVITIES CAN IMPROVE OUTCOMES

Although the characteristics of the activity matter more than the activity itself, the evidence shows that different kinds of activities can give rise to different outcomes.

Sport—Offers a way of helping young people to build their confidence and self-esteem, overcome behavioral issues, and acquire life skills in a context more likely to appeal to those who are disenchanted with or disengaged from school. It can also reduce involvement in crime and antisocial behavior and improve attainment, particularly when combined with learning. Evaluation of the Playing for Success initiative demonstrated an increase in both self-confidence and learning.

The Arts—Participating in art, music, drama, and dance can build confidence, self-esteem, and self-discipline and help develop social and teamwork skills. It can also help young people to be more open-minded, better able to make friends and to deal with difficult experiences, and be more creative in their thinking. An evaluation of the Actup youth theater group found that "this positive experience, combined with the support of workshop leaders in which references, advice and practical support . . . was available, had encouraged the young people towards learning to the point where access to and participation in further education became a real possibility."

Volunteering—Making a difference to the community can alter young people's aspirations and the way they see themselves. Evidence from the Young Volunteer Challenge Pilot Program demonstrated the impact of volunteering on different groups of young people. After nine months, those with few or no qualifications experienced an increase in confidence and their ability to handle work situations; better-qualified young people had higher aspirations about future education and employment.

DCSF & HM Treasury. (2007, July). *Aiming high for young people: A ten-year strategy for positive activities.* www.hm-treasury.gov.uk.

There does seem to be growing consensus in the youth literature that there are certain underlying principles characterizing successful youth intervention programs. These are briefly explained in Box 41.2.

At-Risk Youth

For a minority of young people, those deemed to be "at risk," programs and interventions need to be well targeted and sustained (Barker and Fontes, 1996). In a sense, all youth are vulnerable to being at risk simply by being young. It is in these years that the foundational factors that lead to long-term inequality are laid. Particularly risky behaviors include leaving school early without formal qualifications; being jobless; engaging in substance abuse, including tobacco and alcohol; behaving violently; initiating sex at an early age; and engaging in unsafe sexual practices (Cunningham et al., 2008).

It is in these years that young people are most subject to peer pressure, suffer the storm and stress of establishing an individual identity, and try to establish their social and economic independence. Such pressures make it more likely for young people to engage in impulsive and thrill-seeking behavior; even biology is working against them in that the part of the brain that controls impulsive behavior is the last to develop. Socially, young people lack the experience to make the most effective decisions and be able to calculate the possible future impact of their actions. It is surprising, then, that so many young people manage not to succumb to these risks and transit this stage of the life cycle so successfully.

The number of young people at risk varies enormously across the world. There can be no complacency even if numbers are small relative to the population of young people as a whole, because a small percentage can result in social turmoil and the loss of economic

---

BOX 41.2
SOME THINGS DO MAKE A DIFFERENCE FOR YOUTH

Adult support, structure, and expectations: **Successful youth programs connect young people with adults who care about them, who serve as role models for them, who advise, mentor, chide, sympathize, encourage, and praise. The effectiveness of adults is enhanced by program settings that have "coherence and structure, that build on challenging content, that give young people responsibility, and that establish rules and set practical limits for young people." Thus, if a program is to be successful, it needs to be staffed by committed and skilled adults.**

Creative forms of learning: **Teaching methods have to make an attempt to engage the learner and be attuned to the learner's interest. Tutors should strive to find ways of making learning challenging and fun and less of the chalk and talk.**

A combination of guidance and rich connections to the workplace: **The most successful employment projects are those that connect young people to the world of work. Such projects not only have a good job-placement service but also a support service for young people while on job placement.**

Support and follow-up: **Young people whose connections to social institutions may be weak need time and support to build trust in adult and peer relationships. This may take more than the first job. One successful project "highlights the importance of follow-up for two years or past a youth's first job, through the difficulties of the initial employer/supervisor relationship and into the second or third more career-oriented placement."**

Youth as a resource: **Young people respond more positively when they are regarded as resources and contributors to their own development rather than as passive vessels waiting to be filled.**

Implementation quality: **The best plans in the world will come to nothing if there is not an effective implementation strategy, one that is "thoughtful and well managed, incorporating evaluation and continuous improvement into design, fostering communication within the program *and among all partners and levels of governments."***

American Youth Policy Forum. (1988 p. 6). *Some things DO make a difference for youth: A compendium of evaluations of youth programs and practices.* Washington, DC.

BOX 41.3
MEASURING CONNECTEDNESS TO SCHOOLS AND CARING ADULTS

Schools: In addition to school attendance, school connectedness is measured by the degree to which students perceive that school is fair and safe (physically, emotionally, and academically), that teachers are supportive, and that they set high academic standards.

Parent or caring adult: Young people perceive that there is at least one parent or caring adult in their life who is regularly available both physically and emotionally, who expresses love and affection, who monitors behaviors, and who provides feedback in a supportive (nonabusive) manner.

Blum, R. W. (2005). *Protective factors in the lives of youth: The evidence base.* Youth Development Lecture Series. Washington, DC: World Bank, HDNCY. www.worldbank.org/childrenandyouth.

---

production. Although young people at risk are generally poor, no causal relationship has been statistically identified between poverty and risky behaviors. What is more evident from the research is that the odds are stacked against poor young people through lack of adequate education, health, housing, and economic opportunities. The correlations enable us to use poverty status as a means to target programs to those who are most at risk.

EFFECTIVE INTERVENTIONS

The practice implications for social workers working with at-risk youth of course depend on which category of risk the particular young people are in. The literature, however, gives some useful general guidelines that should be helpful for practitioners and policy makers. The data from longitudinal studies in the United States and the Caribbean suggest that two micro-level protective factors are of great significance, namely school attendance and school connectedness together with the sustained presence of a caring adult in the young person's life. The policy implications of these findings point to the importance of investing in keeping young people in school and making schools attractive and productive for them. These investments should be a priority in areas with a high concentration of at-risk youth. The evidence also suggests that special attention should be paid to programs that can increase school attendance, improve the connectedness of students to their school, and foster strong families, parenting, and mentors in the lives of young people. Boxes 41.3 and 41.4 provide additional details on these important factors.

Although it is preferable to set up programs that tackle multiple risks, even those programs that focus on single risk factors can influence multiple risky behaviors. Cunningham et al. (2008) highlight twenty-three elements of a policy portfolio for at-risk youth, of which the following three are of particular importance to social work practice.

BOX 41.4
ENHANCING SCHOOL CONNECTEDNESS

✓ **Introduce policies that increase school attendance** (such as school meals, greater supervision, conditional cash transfers, and other incentives).

✓ **Offer skills building for teachers** in how to positively engage students and eliminate abusive behaviors (through both pre- and in-service professional development).

✓ **Provide greater safety** (both emotionally and physically) in schools (such as ensuring a well-lit building and strictly penalizing abusive behavior).

✓ **Involve parents** in school life (such as regular parent–teacher meetings, parent committees, and oversight).

Blum, R. (2006). Youth development. *Youth Development Notes*, 1(4), Washington, DC: World Bank HDNCY. www.worldbank.org/childrenandyouth.

Secondary School Completion

Completing secondary school is perhaps the most important strategy for reducing all types of risky behavior. These programs not only keep young people off the streets (and thereby reduce the risk of them being arrested) but also buy them more time to mature and thereby to make better decisions. Programs for teenage mothers to complete their secondary education are of critical importance here.

Access to Education Equivalency and Lifelong Learning

For those young people who have dropped out of school, the provision of a second chance of getting a high school equivalency diploma can be critical to reintegrating them into the labor market.

Access to Youth-Friendly Health and Pharmaceutical Services

Many young people know how to avoid pregnancy and sexually transmitted diseases, but they often have difficulty accessing such services, particularly ones that recognize their need for confidentiality. This is especially true in small island states such as those in the Caribbean, but it is also a problem in small towns and villages in developed and developing countries. Outreach programs, mobile services, and health-care staff sympathetic to young people can help to break down geographical and psychological barriers to accessing advice and support.

Social workers should be cautious about deploying strategies that get tough on at-risk youth. There is no evidence that such strategies work. Zero-tolerance programs, shock incarceration programs, and boot camps have not only been shown to be ineffective but can actually lead to an increase in delinquent and criminal behavior (Cunningham et al., 2008; Furlong & Cartmel, 2007). Further, abstinence-only programs have not been shown to reduce the incidence of teen pregnancy or the transmission of sexually transmitted diseases. When a society is in full moral-panic mode and the government has to demonstrate that it is taking tough action to stop the complete breakdown of society, then there is a temptation to introduce such tough measures as increasing custodial sentences for youth convicted of certain crimes, trying young people in adult courts, and placing convicted young offenders in adult institutions. These strategies produce hardened criminals, not young people able to overcome risk.

CONCLUSION

This chapter argues that youth work and social work share a common value base and that the basic problem confronting young people is their lack of participation in the decision-making structures of their societies. The critique of the categorical definition of *youth* implies that social workers need to undertake a thorough sociocultural and historical analysis of the individual or group of young people they intend to work with. The chapter concludes with guidelines for effective intervention strategies for working with the majority of youth as well as the significant minority who could be defined as youth at risk.

These strategies rely on social workers who care for young people and who "serve as role models for them, who advise, mentor, chide, sympathize, encourage and praise" (See Box 41.2 above). They require social workers to establish a positive and strong relationship that is committed to the young peoples' best interests. Whether in a client–social worker relationship or in a youth service program, it is essential for the social worker to negotiate with the young person to build a structured and agreed-upon framework within which a young person can develop. Furthermore, support for the critical transitions from home to school and from school to work requires follow-up and continual support, sometimes over years until the young person is established in adulthood.

REFERENCES

Adam, B., Beck, U., & Van Loon, J. (2004). *The risk society and beyond: Critical issues for social theory*. London: Sage.

American Youth Policy Forum. (1988). *Some things DO make a difference for youth: A compendium of evaluations of youth programs and practices*. Washington, DC.

Barker, G., & Fontes, M. (1996). *Review and analysis of international experience with programmes targeted on at-risk youth*. LASHC Paper Series No. 5. Washington DC: World Bank.

Beck, U. (2000). *The brave new world of work*. Cambridge: Polity.

Beck, U. (1992). *Risk society: Towards a new modernity*. London: Sage.

Blum, R. (2006). Youth development. *Youth Development Notes*, 1(4), Washington, DC: World Bank, HDNCY. www.worldbank.org/childrenandyouth.

Blum, R. W. (2005). *Protective factors in the lives of youth: The evidence base*. Youth Development Lecture Series. Washington, DC: World Bank, HDNCY. www.worldbank.org/childrenandyouth.

Coleman, J. C., & Hendry, L. (1990). *The nature of adolescence*. London: Routledge.

Cunningham, W., McGinnis, L., Verdú, R. G., Tesliuc, C., & Verner, D. (2008). *Youth at risk in Latin America and the Caribbean: Understanding the causes, realizing the potential.* Washington, DC: World Bank.

Danns, G., Henry, B., & LaFleur, P., et al. (1997). *Tomorrow's adults: A situational analysis of youth in the Commonwealth Caribbean.* London: Commonwealth Secretariat.

Department for Children, Schools and Families (DCSF), & HM Treasury. (2007, July). *Aiming high for young people: A ten-year strategy for positive activities.* London: DCSF.

Deosaran, R. (1992). *Social psychology in the Caribbean.* Trinidad and Tobago: Longman.

Furlong, A., & Cartmel, F. (2007). *Young people and social change: New perspectives.* Maidenhead, England: Open University Press.

Giddens, A. (1991). *Modernity and self-identity: Self and society in the late modern age.* Oxford: Polity.

Hart, R. (1997). *Children's participation: The theory and practice of involving young citizens in community development and environmental care.* London: Earthscan.

James-Bryant, M. (1992). *Challenges facing Caribbean youth as the region approaches the 21ˢᵗ century: Survival or destruction.* Submission to the West Indian Commission, *Time for action.* Jamaica: University of the West Indies Press.

Lewis, L. (1995). *The social reproduction of youth in the Caribbean.* Jamaica: University of the West Indies Institute of Social and Economic Research.

Postman, N. (1994). *The disappearance of childhood.* New York: Vintage Books.

Richardson, A. G. (1999) *Caribbean adolescents and youth. Contemporary issues in personality development and behaviour.* Brooklyn, NY: Caribbean Diaspora Press.

UNICEF and UNFPA (2002) *Meeting adolescent development and participation rights. The findings of five research studies in Jamaica.* Kingston, Jamaica.

Williams, L. O. (1998) *Youth and Society-Module 2 of the Diploma in Youth in Development.* London: Commonwealth Youth Programme, 1998.

Williams, L. O. (1988). *Partial surrender: Race and resistance in the youth service.* London: Falmer Press.

USEFUL WEBSITES

Commonwealth Secretariat: www.thecommonwealth.org
United Nations: www.un.org.
World Bank: www.worldbank.org/childrenandyouth.

SECTION V

International Profession and Professional Organizations

International Federation of Social Workers (IFSW)

NIGEL HALL

The International Federation of Social Workers (IFSW) is an international organization representing the interests of social workers around the world, with its secretariat based in Berne, Switzerland. The organization works in cooperation with regional social work bodies, national organizations, and associations of social workers. It organizes international events, publishes policy statements, encourages cooperative initiatives between its members, and links to other international bodies. Celebrating its Golden Jubilee in 2006, the organization is active in human rights and social development and in the promotion of best practices and high professional standards (Hall, 2006a; Healy, 2001). At present, there are national organizations in more than eighty countries, representing over 500,000 social workers across the world. Association members collaborate to develop the common goals of the profession and work on issues of concern to social workers internationally.

STRUCTURE, MEMBERSHIP, AND MAJOR FUNCTIONS

There are five geographical regions of IFSW: Africa, Asia-Pacific, Europe, Latin America and the Caribbean, and North America, each of which is represented by a regional president. Only one national professional organization in each country may become a member of the federation, although this may be a national organization or a coordinating body representing two or more national organizations. Each member association or coordinating body must observe the IFSW Constitution and should require from its members regular professional training based on an organized sequence of social work education that incorporates ethical standards of practice and a body of knowledge compatible with social work principles. There is also a Friends of IFSW program that provides several membership benefits to affiliating social workers,

social work students, and organizations. According to the Friends coordinator, as of March 2010, there were 903 Friends, including 129 life members and 206 student members (A. Trenkwalder-Egger, personal communication, March 29, 2011). This program, which is being reviewed to extend membership further, gives individuals a direct connection to the international organization.

An international, elected executive committee steers the work of IFSW, with a global president and secretary-general heading the body. The General Meeting convenes every two years at the same time as an international conference, while regional seminars and conferences are held regularly in most regions. Conferences were occasionally held jointly with the International Association of Schools of Social Work (IASSW) and the International Council on Social Welfare (ICSW), but at other times they were held separately. The decision has now been made to host these joint conferences regularly, a decision implemented at the 2010 conference in Hong Kong. Before this conference, the three partners agreed to work on a relevant social agenda and position papers on various issues, both to feed into the conference and to help lay the foundation for social work action in the following decade.

Association members collaborate to develop the common goals of the profession and work on issues of concern to social workers internationally, such as human rights (IFSW & IASSW, 1994) and global ethical standards (IFSW & IASSW, 2004). The organization encourages this cooperation by establishing and maintaining relationships with social work associations and representing them to international bodies, sponsoring biennial international symposia and conferences, developing and publishing policy statements to guide social work practice worldwide, advocating for the protection of the human rights of practicing social workers, providing consultation to the United Nations on issues of human development and human rights, and providing means for the discussion and exchange of ideas and experience through meetings, study visits, research projects, and publications. Some of these are elaborated later following a discussion of the history of IFSW.

HISTORY OF IFSW

The history of IFSW stretches back to the First International Conference of Social Work held in Paris in July 1928, where it was agreed that an international association of social workers would be formed. This led to the formation of the International Permanent Secretariat of Social Workers (IPSSW) in 1932. This organization operated from Berlin, Geneva, and Prague until 1956, when IFSW was formed in Munich with twelve national member organizations and a new secretariat was established in New York, sharing an office with the U.S. National Association of Social Workers (NASW). The strengthening of the secretariat also heralded an era of growing membership and achievement of formal representative status with various organizations.

In 1959, IFSW joined its partner organizations, ICSW and IASSW, in sponsoring the journal *International Social Work (ISW)*, which remains one of the most significant refereed journals on international social work available today. In addition, that year IFSW was approved for consultative status with the United Nations Economic and Social Council (ECOSOC), with a special relationship later extended by the United Nations Children's Fund (UNICEF) and the International Labour Organization (ILO). The organization also now has formal partnerships with Amnesty International, CoNGO (Conference of Non-Governmental Organizations in Consultative Relationship with the UN), the Council of Europe, the European Union, the United Nations Human Settlements Programme (UN-HABITAT), IASSW, ICSW, and the Commonwealth Organisation for Social Work (COSW).

In 1972, the IFSW Executive Committee decided to establish a permanent, paid secretariat in Basel, Switzerland, appointing Catherine Chuard (1972–1974) as the secretary-general. Chuard was followed by Andrew (Andy) Mouravieff-Apostol (1975–1992), who was assisted in his work by his wife, Ellen. Both enjoyed extensive networks within the United Nations system, and Ellen remains today as IFSW Main Representative to the UN at Geneva. With the appointment of the next secretary-general,

Tom Johannesen, the secretariat moved to Oslo, Norway, in 1992 and then in 1999 to Berne, Switzerland, where it is located today (Johannesen, 1997).

A major project to achieve an accepted international definition of social work was launched in the late 1970s (Hare, 2004; IFSW, 2002a). This document was endorsed at the Brighton Conference in 1982 and remained unaltered until 1996, when a committee was established to revise and prepare a new definition of social work, ultimately adopted by both practitioners (IFSW) and educators (IASSW) in 2000. The definition reads:

> The social work profession promotes social change, problem solving in human relationships and the empowerment and liberation of people to enhance well-being. Utilizing theories of human behavior and social systems, social work intervenes at the points where people interact with their environments. Principles of human rights and social justice are fundamental to social work.
>
> —(IASSW & IFSW, 2004, p. 2)

Advocacy

The 1980s were particularly active years for IFSW in the areas of human rights and social justice. By this time IFSW had well-established representative teams to the UN in New York, Geneva, and Vienna. This focus of concern led IFSW to a strong engagement in the UN International Year of Peace in 1986, and its contributions were officially recognized by the UN when it was declared a Peace Messenger. Eight years later the UN designated IFSW as Patron of the International Year of the Family for its exemplary support of the UN program.

A highlight in the 1990s was IFSW's strong involvement in the World Summit for Social Development in Copenhagen in 1995. A special issue of the *IFSW Newsletter* was presented to a broader audience, focusing on social work contributions to a new world order for social development in the areas of poverty eradication, unemployment, social integration, and transition in Eastern Europe. The Fourth World Conference on Women in Beijing the same year also had a strong IFSW presence.

The start of the new century brought significant challenges for the social work profession. A worldwide shift in political orientation toward conservative and in some instances ultraconservative governments has meant that working to develop social services has been particularly difficult in more developed countries. This situation may be changing, but the unprecedented recession beginning in 2008 and increased poverty as a result of this and other forces will present new challenges to the profession.

On the international level, issues concerning poverty alleviation, human rights, and HIV/AIDS continue to be major concerns (Ife, 2002). The organization has responded to some of the major international issues experienced in recent years, such as the Asian tsunami, the terrorist attack on New York City, serious human rights violations in the Sudan, and the challenges faced by orphans and vulnerable children in Africa, by publishing statements outlining its concerns and by supporting projects initiated by its regional bodies and in cooperation with partner organizations.

Many outstanding social workers have contributed over the years to IFSW and its development. Among these are Jane Hoey (1892–1968), whose major contribution to social work was in the establishment and enforcement of standards in public welfare administration in the United States. A fund has been established in her name to promote social work in developing regions of the world. Another is Litsa Alexandraki (1918–1986), founder of the Hellenic Association of Social Workers and former IFSW president. Among other achievements, she initiated a program to assist families whose relatives had been killed or separated during the Second World War.

DISCUSSION OF POSITIVE ACTIONS AND INTERVENTIONS: HUMAN RIGHTS AND ETHICS

Social work grew out of humanitarian and democratic ideals, and its values are based on respect for the equality, worth, and dignity of all people. Human rights and social justice serve as the motivation and justification for social work action. As mentioned, IFSW promotes human rights and an awareness of ethical concerns by publishing statements on relevant issues of global magnitude and by raising awareness within the profession about the commitment of social work to human rights. It has also adopted an International Policy on Human Rights and set up a Human Rights Commission with representatives from all IFSW regions. In addition, IFSW encourages the teaching of human rights in all training courses for social workers and promotes the building of awareness and respect for human rights around the world.

There is recognition that in many parts of the world there are competing human rights dilemmas,

so this can be a complex issue. The federation has faced significant challenges at various times in its history, often due to political and ideological differences among its many members. However, the Executive Committee and the General Meeting of the member associations have made every effort to work together as harmoniously as possible and to overcome these issues. One example of this is the conflict in the Middle East and IFSW having both Israeli and Palestinian members; to their credit, these organizations have worked hard to overcome mistrust and antipathy.

The organization has also produced guidance for social workers in implementing human rights treaties and conventions. *Social Work and the Rights of the Child: A Professional Training Manual on the UN Convention* (IFSW, 2002b) is still available in seven languages. In 2009 and 2010, IFSW and IASSW worked together to update the *Human Rights and Social Work* training manual (IFSW & IASSW, 1994); a new version was launched as a web-based resource at the world conference in Hong Kong in 2010. In addition, the IFSW website (www.ifsw.org) is increasing the ability to disseminate information and respond to issues of concern. For example, a regular stream of news is available on http://www.ifsw.org/f38000059.html, public statements are issued on a range of UN days, and IFSW is developing interactive discussion websites for members.

The joint IFSW–IASSW, Ethics in Social Work: Statement of Principles, underpins IFSW's work and is fundamental both to the organization and to the profession generally (IFSW & IASSW, 2004) (see Appendix A). The Permanent Committee on Ethics has been set up, and it is presently reviewing codes of ethics from various associations, developing educational materials on ethical issues, and organizing consultation days on ethics at biennial conferences.

Additionally, other academic publications are published by IFSW and its member associations from time to time. *Social Work and Globalization* (Canadian Association of Social Workers [CASW], 2000) was produced on the occasion of the 2000 IFSW and IASSW joint conference in Montreal. Other publications include a series of edited books on social work in various countries—*Social Work Around the World*—which explores the complexities of globalization and the place of social work in different countries (e.g., Hall, 2006b; Tan & Dodds, 2002; Tan & Envall, 2000; Tan & Rowlands, 2004). Regional newsletters and journals are also published wherever possible.

A series of international policy papers has also been developed and regularly revised. Current policy papers cover displaced persons, globalization and the environment, health, HIV/AIDS, Indigenous peoples, women, migration, aging and older adults, peace and social justice, protection of personal information, refugees and youth, cross-border reproductive services, genocide, and poverty alleviation (view at www.ifsw.org).

VIGNETTES OF IFSW ACTION PROJECTS

Around the world, IFSW and its member associations are actively involved in various projects and activities,

responding to urgent humanitarian concerns following natural or human-made disasters, and trying to ameliorate issues concerning global poverty or social exclusion. Box 42.1 describes examples of three projects in different areas of the world.

LOOKING TO THE FUTURE

The organization has identified that it needs to strengthen its work in the areas of policy, representation, and advocacy and to make this work more topical, coherent, and better coordinated. In particular, IFSW has recognized that it is important to keep its

---

BOX 42.1
ACTION PROJECTS

Response to Asian Tsunami (2004)

The FAST (Families and Survivors of Tsunami) Project was launched by IFSW and its partners as a professional social work response to the humanitarian crisis unleashed by the tsunami in Asia on December 26, 2004. The FAST Project has focused on children, families, and their needs in this postdisaster scenario in several Asian countries. It has seen

- collaboration between local social workers in the affected countries on specific projects,
- facilitation of the social and emotional recovery of communities,
- direct practical action in supporting those affected and in evaluating projects, and
- assistance in developing and supporting personnel who work on specific projects.

Assistance to Young Carers in Africa (2006)

The IFSW Africa Region, working together with COSW and other partners, organized a symposium in Nairobi in May 2006. The symposium consisted of a representative group of stakeholders, including young carers, from Africa and the United Kingdom—eighty people from eleven countries in all. It focused attention on the many challenges facing those in the field of orphaned and vulnerable young children. Outcomes included

- a DVD put together by the young people for use in Africa and the United Kingdom,
- a web-based network for young people who have caring roles,
- press coverage of the needs of young carers in both the African and UK context, and
- continued development of youth projects in Africa.

Work With Poor Urban Residents in Developing Countries (2008)

In recent years, IFSW has contributed to the UN-HABITAT World Urban Forum, including the Fourth World Urban Forum held in Nanjing, China, in November 2008. This cooperation with the UN body responsible for shelter and housing in poorer regions of the world underlines IFSW's commitment to the relief of suffering and poverty. At the Nanjing conference, IFSW's first vice president presented on social work practice in developing cities, which showcased the involvement of social workers in

- microeconomic activities in the cities of Cairo and Nairobi,
- work with slum dwellers in cities around the world to improve living conditions,
- social work in postconflict scenarios (e.g., with internally displaced persons in urban settlements in Kenya), and
- disaster work following earthquakes in Pakistan and Indonesia.

policy statements up to date and relevant through its Policy, Advocacy and Representation Commission. Both IFSW and IASSW have agreed to a four-year process for the review of the international definition of social work and the international statement of ethical principles. Thereafter these core statements will be reviewed every ten years.

Additionally, IFSW is investigating how it can increase its support and capacity building for member organizations and those wanting to join the global body. Income-generating strategies are a priority because further funds are needed to strengthen regions, improve support for members, and further IFSW's visibility. Work is also taking place on projects to improve the image of social work as a profession and build awareness among the general public of the work that social workers do on behalf of society.

In 2007, IFSW launched a World Social Work Day (WSWD), building on the success of the well-established European Social Work Action Day and linked with the annual social work day at the United Nations in New York, which celebrated its twenty-fifth anniversary in 2008. A decision was made at the 2008 Brazil conference that WSWD would be celebrated every year on the third Tuesday in March and that each two-year cycle would be linked with the upcoming world conference.

In general, the experience of IFSW is that there is a renewed political and economic interest in social work and that the profession is increasingly seen as needing to offer solutions to difficult social problems. The functions of social work and the potential contributions of the profession are constantly changing, and in this context there is an ongoing review (with IASSW) of the definition of social work, the statement of ethical principles, and the human rights manual. Major social concerns for IFSW include the challenges of deepening poverty, ways to achieve the Millennium Development Goals, the consequences of HIV/AIDS, and the migration of skilled professionals from the developing part of the world to the developed. The organization is committed to supporting national member organizations in promoting the profession in their respective regions and helping social workers provide a socially meaningful contribution. To accomplish this, review of the structure and character of the organization is needed.

SUMMARY

The success of IFSW depends on the hard work of a small volunteer executive and general committee, who direct and coordinate the work of the secretary-general, global standing committees, regional committees, and project groups. Over the years, these groups have built a significant organization with good reason to celebrate its achievements. Through a number of world and regional conferences, the development of core international documents to guide social work concepts and practices, and ongoing representation at the United Nations and other international bodies, IFSW is a key global voice of international social work practice.

REFERENCES

Canadian Association of Social Workers (CASW). (2000). *Social work and globalization.* Montreal: Author.

Hall, N. (2006a). *Fifty years of international social work: The International Federation of Social Workers celebrates its Golden Jubilee!* Berne, Switzerland: IFSW.

Hall, N. (Ed.). (2006b). *Social work: Making a world of difference.* Berne/Oslo: IFSW/FAFO.

Hare, I. (2004). Defining social work for the 21st century: The International Federation of Social Workers' revised definition of social work. *International Social Work, 47*(3), 146–158.

Healy, L. (2001). *International social work: Professional action in an interdependent world.* New York: Oxford University Press.

Ife, J. (2002). *Human rights and social work: Towards rights-based practice.* New York: University of Cambridge Press.

International Association of Schools of Social Work (IASSW) & International Federation of Social Workers (IFSW). (2004). *Global standards for the education and training of the social work profession.* Retrieved March 31, 2011, from www.ifsw.org/cm_data/GlobalSocial WorkStandards2005.pdf.

International Federation of Social Workers (IFSW). (2002a). Definition of social work. Retrieved March 31, 2011, from www.ifsw.org/en/p38000208.html.

International Federation of Social Workers (IFSW). (2002b). *Social work and the rights of the child: A professional training manual on the UN Convention* (with UNICEF). Berne, Switzerland: Author.

International Federation of Social Workers (IFSW), & International Association of Schools of Social Work (IASSW). (2004). Ethics in social work: Statement of principles. Retrieved *March 31, 2011,* from www.ifsw. org/en/p38000324.html.

International Federation of Social Workers (IFSW), & International Association of Schools of Social Work (IASSW). (1994). *Human rights and social work: A manual for schools of social work and the profession of social work* (with the UN Center for Human Rights). Professional Training Series No.1. Geneva: UNHCR.

Johannesen, T. (1997). Social work as an international profession: Opportunities and Challenges. In M.C. Hokenstad & J. Midgley (Eds.), *Issues in international social work* (pp. 146–158). Washington, DC: NASW Press.

Tan, N. T., & Dodds, E. (Eds.). (2002). *Social work around the world II*. Berne, Switzerland: IFSW Press.

Tan, N. T., & Envall, E. (Eds.). (2000). *Social work around the world I*. Berne, Switzerland: IFSW Press.

Tan, N. T., & Rowlands, A. (Eds.). (2004). *Social work around the world III*. Berne, Switzerland: IFSW Press.

International Association of Schools of Social Work (IASSW)

LYNNE M. HEALY

The International Association of Schools of Social Work (IASSW) is the international professional organization that serves and represents social work education worldwide. It was founded in 1928 and since then has worked to promote the development of social work education and to ensure that the voice of social work education is represented in relevant international deliberations. This chapter gives an overview of the history of IASSW, its structure and membership, major programs, and activities, and it concludes with a discussion of challenges for the future. First, however, the core mission of the organization, which has been remarkably constant since the founding, is presented.

MISSION

The overarching purpose of IASSW is to promote and strengthen social work education around the world. This was as true at the founding as it is today. The most recent formal review of the mission statement took place in 2000 and resulted in the following mission statement:

The International Association of Schools of Social Work is an international association of institutions of social work education, organizations supporting social work education and social work educators. Its mission is:

- To develop and promote excellence in social work education, research and scholarship globally in order to enhance human well-being;
- To create and maintain a dynamic community of social work educators and their programs;
- To support and facilitate participation in mutual exchanges of information and expertise;
- To represent social work education at the international level. (IASSW, 2000).

The 2000 document also states that IASSW aims to promote social justice and social development and adheres to UN human rights declarations and conventions in its work.

A BRIEF HISTORY OF IASSW

The First International Conference of Social Work, held in Paris in 1928, was a landmark event in the history of social work. Almost 2500 delegates participated from forty-two countries, a remarkable achievement for the time (First International Conference of Social Work, 1929). Three enduring international organizations (IASSW, International Federation of Social Workers [IFSW], and International Council on Social Welfare [ICSW]) had their roots in the Paris conference and in the negotiations and relationships formed in preparing for the conference. Dr. René Sand of Belgium was perhaps the lead organizing force behind the conference; he later became the second IASSW president. A significant segment of the conference focused on training for social work under the leadership of Dr. Alice Salomon of Germany.

During the deliberations, the delegates at the training section agreed to form an organization to promote social work education. The first step they agreed upon was "to write to all the training schools of social work asking them whether they would be prepared to become members of an International Association of Schools" (First International Conference of Social Work, 1929, pp. 233–234). Although 1928 is often cited as the founding year, the formal founding of the organization may also be claimed as the first meeting of the International Committee of Schools of Social Work, held in Berlin in June 1929. Representatives from schools in seven European countries (Belgium, Germany, France, Great Britain, Poland, Switzerland, and Czechoslovakia) and a representative of the

International Labour Office (ILO) participated in this organizing meeting (Kniephoff-Knebel & Siebel, 2008). They adopted the following statement of purpose:

> The object of the Committee of Schools of Social Work is to bring about an exchange of opinion and experience between schools of social work and to deal with all problems of international co-operation of these schools, such as the exchange of teachers and students, the organization of a centre of documentation and information, the formation of international social study courses and the participation in the preparation of international congresses for social work. (International Committee of Schools of Social Work, 1929)

The leadership group quickly expanded to include members from the United States. Alice Salomon was selected as the chair and continued as president of the association until the mid-1940s, although her active leadership ceased after her exile to the United States in the late 1930s.

Early Years

In the early years, the organization sponsored seminars to exchange knowledge and strengthen social work education. Most notable were the summer schools—seminars that intensively explored significant topics for social work. There was a strong emphasis on the value of international exchanges of information and ideas. The committee participated in the Second World Conference of Social Work in Frankfurt in 1932 and the Third World Conference in London in 1936. A fourth conference was planned for 1940 but was cancelled due to war.

It is notable that efforts to establish linkages with intergovernmental organizations began almost immediately. The committee established working relationships with the ILO and with the Commission on Social Questions of the League of Nations. A particularly important achievement was the creation of the Centre of Documentation for schools of social work in 1929 in collaboration with the ILO. "For the next ten years the ILO attempted, with moderate success, to collect and index the statutes, programmes of study, annual reports, publications, research and seminar reports, and lists of theses or other student reports from more than 100 schools of social work" (Kendall, 1978, p. 174).

As stated in an earlier article, "In many ways, the timing could not have been worse for the founding

of international organizations for a profession promoting peace and social justice. Immediately after the founding, the world was plunged into a severe economic depression. Unemployment and economic hardships grew. Soon thereafter, nationalism, isolationism and militarism came together with disastrous consequences for the world and for the International Committee" (Healy, 2008, p. 4). World War II decimated the association and interrupted its activities from the late 1930s until 1946, when a small group met and convinced René Sand to take over the presidency.

According to Kendall (1978), 1945 to 1954 were the Restoration Years for the International Committee of Schools of Social Work. As the organization began to regroup, it immediately pursued affiliation with the newly launched United Nations, and in 1947 it was granted class B consultative status with the Economic and Social Council (ECOSOC) as an NGO (nongovernmental organization), underscoring the importance of the mission of representing social work education in global deliberations. The first postwar conference was a modest one held in Atlantic City, New Jersey, in the U.S. in 1948. Ironically, war had almost destroyed the international committee, yet the aftermath of the war created a new demand for social workers, and "by 1948, 359 schools were counted in 41 countries" (Kendall, 1978, p. 177).

Social work and social work education expanded fairly rapidly to the newly independent countries in Asia and Africa. Outreach to schools in Asia and Africa began to convert the European–North American organization into a worldwide one. Of symbolic importance was the locating of world congresses in Japan in 1956, Brazil in 1962, and Kenya in 1974. By 1956, the Board of Directors included members from Australia, Guatemala, Japan, and India in addition to European and North American countries. By the late 1960s, vice presidents were elected from the Philippines, Ethiopia, Panama, and Finland, further solidifying the association's global identity (Kendall, 1989). In 1956, the name of the organization was officially changed to the International Association of Schools of Social Work.

A Major Project Secured

In the early 1970s, IASSW secured grant funding to carry out a major project on education for the social dimensions of family planning. The grant funded a full-time secretary-general and a secretariat. The project involved curriculum development and training seminars for faculty in twenty countries across Africa, Asia, the Caribbean, and Latin America. Pilot schools for project activities were in Turkey, Iran, Korea, the Philippines, Thailand, Indonesia, Jamaica, Sri Lanka, Bangladesh, Vietnam, Pakistan, Ecuador, Hong Kong, Sudan, Zambia, Ghana, Egypt, and Kenya (Kendall, 1977). Numerous publications also resulted from the project. Dr. Katherine Kendall was the first paid secretary-general, a post she had performed earlier as a volunteer and then as part-time staff. Dr. Kendall's involvement in IASSW spanned six decades, beginning in 1950 with her keynote speech to the IASSW Congress.

The family-planning project confirmed IASSW's reputation as a resource for strengthening social work education. In the 1980s and 1990s, IASSW undertook projects to assist the development of social work education in Eastern Europe, Russia, and China. A number of seminars and targeted consultations were held to help former Soviet bloc countries establish or in some cases reestablish social work education. More recently, IASSW has given grants to strengthen the regional association of schools of social work in Africa and to assist in the establishment of subregional organizations in the Caribbean in the 1990s and in Southeast Europe in 2006. Although these efforts have been on a smaller scale than the family-planning project, they underscore that the growth and development of social work education continues to be a priority.

When Kendall retired in 1978, the IASSW Secretariat moved to Vienna and remained there until it closed in 1992, when the board decided to return to a volunteer-run organization due to rising expenses and financial difficulties. Though finances have since permitted the hiring of an administrative assistant based in the office of the president, from 1993 IASSW has functioned without a professional executive officer.

PROGRAMS AND ACTIVITIES

Although IASSW has not been able to launch additional projects of the same scope as the family-planning initiative, it has maintained significant programs to support international exchange and promote social work education. Among these are sponsorship of biennial worldwide conferences, cosponsorship of the *International Social Work* journal (launched in 1958), periodic research on the scope of social work education and publication of databases, assistance in the development of social work education in underserved areas of the world, assistance to regional and subregional organizations for social work education,

and regular representation of social work education at the United Nations. For IASSW, sponsoring conferences and the journal is central to the mission goals of encouraging scholarship, encouraging international exchange, and building a global community of educators. More recently the organization has expanded its efforts to promote scholarship by launching a publication series with Venture Press.

In 1984, IASSW published the *World Guide to Social Work Education*, a volume featuring a detailed description of the educational program in one school in each member country (Kendall & Rao, 1984). In 1998, under the leadership of Ralph Garber, IASSW launched the World Census project, an effort to collect information on all educational programs in social work (Garber, 2000). The results have been disseminated in journal articles and postings on the IASSW website (Barretta-Herman, 2005; Garber, 2000). Plans call for periodic updates of the census to enable IASSW to provide global data on the state of social work education. (See Chapter 54 by Barretta-Herman for more on the World Census.)

In 2004, IASSW began funding multicountry collaborative projects to further international cooperation in areas of interest to social work education. Modest grants are given to successful applicants, whose projects must involve at least three schools from two or more countries. Examples of funded projects are a project that developed a website on field education for Chinese schools of social work; a collaboration of schools in Kenya, the Philippines, and England to develop a curriculum module on disaster management; a project sponsored by eighteen schools in nine countries on indigenous social work education and practice; and a ten-country project on international social work and political conflict resolution to establish a network to enhance social work education and research in conflict and postconflict situations. (For more information, see www.iassw-aiets.org.)

Some IASSW projects are conducted collaboratively with IFSW and ICSW. Periodically, the three organizations have held joint or co-located world conferences, although from 2002 to 2008, the conferences were held separately. An agreement has been reached for a three-way conference collaboration, which was implemented with the world conference in 2010 (Healy & Hall, 2007). A closer relationship exists between IFSW and IASSW, which both identify with the profession of social work. The two organizations have collaborated in the development and adoption of a definition of social work (2000), a revised statement of ethical principles (2004) and the Global Standards for the Education and Training of the Social Work Profession (2004). The two associations have also worked together on human rights, producing a training manual with the United Nations (United Nations, 1994) and more recently working together on an updated version of the human rights manual.

An enduring purpose of IASSW is to represent social work education in international deliberations, especially those of the United Nations. The organization has special consultative status with ECOSOC and is accredited to the Department of Public Information (DPI). This allows a team of members access to UN meetings and participation on the NGO committees linked to the UN. The team in New York represents IASSW on numerous committees, including ageing, mental health, social development, migration, the status of women, and UNICEF (UN Children's Fund). Members also prepare statements to UN bodies, such as the Commission on the Status of Women, and organize workshops held in conjunction with meetings of UN commissions, especially regarding social development and women. At times, IASSW is also represented at the UN in Vienna, Geneva, and Nairobi. (For more details on representing social work at the UN, see Chapter 16.) There is important collaboration with IFSW in UN-related activities, including cosponsorship of the annual Social Work Day at the UN.

MEMBERSHIP AND ORGANIZATIONAL STRUCTURE

Membership in IASSW is open to both social work educational programs and individuals. Programs or schools eligible for what is called *school membership* must offer a tertiary-level educational program preparing students for professional social work. Educators and others with an interest in social work education may become individual members. While individual members are eligible to participate in association activities and committees, their votes in elections and on policy matters only count for one-tenth of a vote. There are member programs in more than seventy countries in all six inhabited continents. Countries with the largest numbers of member schools are the United States and Japan.

The organization is governed by the Board of Directors, made up of both elected and appointed members. The Nominating Committee prepares slates of candidates for the biennial elections of officers and at-large board members. Ballots are sent to all members.

Regional representation is ensured through the inclusion of five regional vice presidents on the Executive Committee and Board of Directors. These officers are selected by their regions and serve IASSW by reason of their regional leadership positions. Currently, three subregional associations are also recognized, and each can elect a member to the Board of Directors: the Association of Caribbean Social Work Educators, the Northern region (previously Nordic), and Southeast Europe. National associations are entitled to a board representative if the country has at least five IASSW member schools. The Board of Directors carries responsibility for the ongoing direction of the association and development and oversight of the budget. Major policy changes and significant changes to the constitution require action by the Delegate Assembly, which meets biennially during the world conference. All IASSW members may participate in the assembly, with programs having one full vote each and individual members having one-tenth of a vote (IASSW, 2009).

Work of the association is furthered through many additional committees and task forces. These include the International Exchange Task Force, teams of UN representatives, the Women's Caucus, and committees on publications, human rights, international projects, language, education, the Katherine Kendall Award, website development and maintenance, and the World Census.

ISSUES FOR THE FUTURE

There are challenges to be faced in the future. Some are new challenges, while others have been recognized for some time but are accentuated by changing conditions in the larger environment. The organization continues to be challenged by language; as membership diversifies, there are pressures to translate more documents and meetings into Chinese, Russian, and Arabic in addition to the existing official languages of French, Spanish, English, and Japanese. It is difficult to resist the dangers of becoming an English-only association.

Development and adoption of the Global Standards for the Education and Training of the Social Work Profession was a great achievement for IASSW. However, the standards are currently only advisory in nature. There is considerable disagreement over the wisdom of moving toward accreditation, but there is also pressure from regional political bodies and concerns that they may preempt the profession and initiate standards for social work education. Thus, IASSW must ensure that the profession retains control over professional standards while remaining sensitive to cultural and historical differences and avoiding premature adoption of rigid standards.

Work on the global standards and on human rights has highlighted the continuing challenges of cultural relativity and indigenization. In addition, the challenges of numerous long-standing and newly emerging global issues—natural disaster, conflict, new health threats, trafficking, and many more—require ongoing revitalization of social work research and curriculum They also intensify the demands for enhanced representation of social work in global bodies and deliberations. Collaboration with IFSW and ICSW will strengthen the capacity to represent social work at the United Nations and other regional and global bodies. Yet, the new collaborations also pose a challenge—the challenge of maintaining a focus on social work education in joint efforts. Meeting each of these challenges is made more difficult by the limited financial and staff resources of IASSW, a global organization that still relies mainly on volunteers for its programs.

In reviewing the IASSW mission and programs, past and present, what stands out is the enduring nature of the organization's goals and functions. As expressed by Feustel (2006), "The history of the IASSW demonstrates lines of continuity that are even more remarkable for the fact that it was caught up in the great historical ruptures of the 20th century" (p. 3). Over the years, IASSW has experienced turmoil caused by the expulsion of its first president by the Nazi regime in Germany, World War II, termination of social work programs in Eastern Europe and China under Communism, internal disputes over the proper course of action in dealing with apartheid South Africa, and financial difficulties that resulted in the loss of a secretary-general and secretariat. Through it all, however, IASSW has remained engaged in its core purposes of promoting and representing social work education and strengthening education through international exchange. This history augurs well for the future of social work education.

REFERENCES

Barretta-Herman, A. (2005). A reanalysis of the World Census 2000. *International Social Work, 48*(6), 794–808.

Feustel, A. (2006). The story of the foundation of the International Association of Schools of Social Work. Accessed at www.iassw-aiets.org.

First International Conference of Social Work. (1929). *Proceedings of the conference.* July 8–13, 1928. Paris: Author.

Garber, R. (2000). World Census of social work and social development education: Interim report. *Social Work and Globalization Special Issue, Canadian Social Work* 2(1) and *Canadian Social Work Review, 17,* 198–215.

Healy, L. M. (2008). A brief journey through the 80-year history of the International Association of Schools of Social Work. In F. W. Seibel (Ed.), *Global leaders for social work education: The IASSW presidents 1928–2008* (pp. 1–25). Ostrava, Czech Republic: ECSPRESS.

Healy, L. M., & Hall, N. (2007). International professional organizations in social work. In L. Wagner & R. Lutz (Eds.), *Internationale Perspektiven Sozialer Arbeit: Ein einfuhrendes Handbuch* [International perspectives in social work]. Frankfurt am Main: IKO. Also available in English at www.ifsw.org.

International Association of Schools of Social Work (IASSW). (2009). Constitution. Accessed February 27, 2009, at www.iassw-aiets.org.

International Association of Schools of Social Work (IASSW). (2000). Mission statement. Accessed February 27, 2009, at www.iassw-aiets.org.

International Association of Schools of Social Work (IASSW), & International Federation of Social Workers (IFSW). (2004). Global Standards for the Education and Training of the Social Work Profession. Accessed at www.iassw-aiets.org.

International Committee of Schools of Social Work. (1929). Protocol adopted 12 June. Accessible at www.alice-salomon-archiv.de/.

Kendall, K. A. (Ed.), & Rao, V. (Compiler). (1984). *World guide to social work education.* Vienna and New York: Council on Social Work Education for IASSW.

Kendall, K. A. (1989). IASSW and social work education in the fifties, sixties, and seventies. In *60 Jahre IASSW.* (pp. 39–46). Berlin: Fachhochschule fur Sozialarbeit und Sozialpadagogik.

Kendall, K. A. (1978). The IASSW 1928–1978: A journey of remembrance. In K. Kendall (Ed.), *Reflections on social work education 1950–1978* (pp. 170–191). New York: IASSW.

Kendall, K.A. (1977). *Final report: International development of qualified manpower for population and family planning activities.* New York: IASSW.

Kniephoff-Knebel, A., & Seibel, F. W. (2008). Foundation and establishment of international co-operation in social work education: The first decade of the International Committee of Schools of Social Work—ICSSW 1928–1937. *International Social Work, 51*(6), 790–812.

Seibel, F. W. (2008). *Global leaders for social work education: The IASSW presidents 1928–2008.* Ostrava, Czech Republic: ECSPRESS.

United Nations. (1994). *Human rights and social work: A manual for schools of social work and the profession of social work.* Geneva: United Nations in collaboration with IFSW and IASSW.

International Council on Social Welfare (ICSW)

DENYS CORRELL

The origins of the International Association of Schools of Social Work (IASSW), the International Council on Social Welfare (ICSW), and the International Federation of Social Workers (IFSW) lie in the same conference held in 1928 in Paris, the First International Conference of Social Work. The name first adopted by the now ICSW was the International Conference of Social Work, since its main purpose was to conduct international conferences of social work. Much of the early history of the international conferences and ICSW can be attributed to the leadership of René Sand, a Belgian medical doctor who made signature contributions to the fields of social work and social welfare. He was a moving force behind the organization of the 1928 Paris conference and went on to serve as ICSW president from 1932 to 1948 (Anciaux, 1988).

There were three international social work conferences before World War II, and after the devastation of World War II, ICSW resumed its activities. Over time, IASSW, ICSW, and IFSW went their separate ways in terms of structure. Early in the twenty-first century, the leadership reestablished the link between the three organizations with the decision to collaborate on at least their biennial conferences and perhaps other policies and activities.

This chapter is not a chronological history but rather an attempt to capture the evolution of ICSW as a global nongovernmental organization (NGO). The history of IASSW, ICSW, and IFSW is covered in other publications (Comité national d'action sociale [CNAS], 2008; Healy & Hall, 2007).

Kate Katzki, long-time secretary-general of the organization, is one of the most renowned figures in the organization's history. In speaking at the sixtieth anniversary of ICSW, Ms. Katzki said, "When one speaks of the history of ICSW one is speaking not only of the history of an organization, but also of the history of people, events and changes; the history of aspirations, fulfilments, and expectations which stretched

beyond the limits of possibilities. All of these contribute to the history of ICSW" (Katzki, 1988). Organizations come and go. Some rise to enormous heights while others disappear. The NGO sector is characterized by a growing proliferation of international organizations. Over the years, ICSW has risen to challenges and adapted its mission and structure to meet the challenges.

There have been ongoing discussions on the purpose of the organization, reflecting the imperative to adapt to constantly changing internal and external factors. In 1983, the ICSW Executive Committee endorsed three major functions:

- "The organization of the International Social Welfare Conferences
- Support for National welfare development
- Relationship with the United Nations" (EC, 1983, p. 16).

Though a global organization, ICSW has recognized that world regions have unique characteristics and needs. Thus, a regional structure within the global environment has evolved.

THE CONFERENCES

Preparations for the early ICSW conferences were thorough and characterized by themes that were relevant to the global situation. While the 1932 conference had the bland title of Social Work and the Family, the speakers focused on the catastrophic economic situations in their own countries. The proceedings of the 1936 conference contain some foreboding of what was to come, with Nazi philosophy expressed in some of the conference papers. In 1947, representatives of twenty countries met in the Netherlands to discuss social problems in the war-stricken areas of Europe. In 1948 after the creation of the United Nations, the conference discussed social work and the United Nations. More recently, the 1994 conference anticipated the landmark World Summit for Social Development with the Tampere Manifesto and Declaration. Many elements of the manifesto and declaration appeared in the subsequent United Nations Copenhagen Declaration and Programme of Action.

The first conference to be held outside Europe and North America was in 1952 in India. In the minutes of the Executive Committee, there is almost a note of surprise at the huge success of the Madras conference (EC, 1953, p. 2). Not withstanding the recognition of success, the Executive Committee registered concern at the "over-emphasis in the program on Indian problems rather than international social welfare" (EC, 1953, p. 2). This issue still arises when a host country or region hijacks the conference program to promote local issues and causes to the neglect of global themes.

SOME DILEMMAS AND DEVELOPMENTS

At times, ICSW has been confronted with dilemmas. After World War II, the Executive Board discussed whether ICSW would invite participation from the Axis countries, particularly Germany and Japan (EB, 1946, p. 4). They adopted the principle that membership and participation should come from countries that are essentially democratic and not fascist. In 1949 the Executive Committee agreed to establish national committees in the formerly fascist countries (EC, 1949, p. 5).

International organizations are often seen as biased toward Europe or North America. As early as 1949, the Executive Committee noted that it needed to have conferences in other parts of the world if it was to "retain its world-wide character" (EC, 1949, p. 6). As noted earlier, this resulted in selecting new conference locations. It has also resulted in ongoing efforts to extend membership to all parts of the world.

Diplomatic issues have arisen. For instance, the membership of Taiwan arose as an issue in relation to the conference in India in 1952. Citizens of Taiwan (then Formosa) could not attend the conference because India did not have diplomatic relations with Formosa. The Executive Committee adopted the principle that "any individual who believes in the purposes of the Conference should be permitted to attend and participate in our conferences" (EC, 1952, p. 5), and this principle has not changed. The Taiwan issue arose again in 1975 and 1976 when several UN agencies, including UNESCO (UN Educational, Scientific and Cultural Organization), put pressure on all organizations that had Taiwan as a member

to terminate that membership. These agencies suggested that if ICSW did not comply, it would jeopardize its UN consultative status. The council decided not to respond directly to the threat but came to an agreement with the Taiwanese member that the member would change its name to the Council of Social Welfare, Taipei, Taiwan (Committee of Representatives [CoRep], 1976, pp. 6–7; EC, 1976, p. 8).

Membership by intergovernmental and governmental bodies has stirred the passions of ICSW from time to time. In 1979 there was a strong debate when some members of the Executive Committee worried that if governments were able to join, "this might affect the non-political character of ICSW" (EC, 1979, p. 9). Others felt that it was acceptable to have governments as members so long as they respected the NGO character of the organization.

The twenty-first century has brought a new stress to the meetings of ICSW. As a result of the issues of terrorism and undocumented migration, individuals from some countries are barred by governments of the hosting countries from attending ICSW conferences.

Regionalism

The council was ahead of its time in recognizing that regionalism was the way forward for influencing social and economic agendas. In 1953 the underlying principles for regional offices were established to facilitate relations and cooperation between members on each continent (Katzki, 1988). Debate occurred in 1961 on whether regional activities strengthened or weakened ICSW as an international organization. The Executive Committee concluded that regional activities would be encouraged, and ICSW regions were given high autonomy in selecting and developing projects (EC, 1961, pp. 6–7).

Until 2000, ICSW had the traditional European and North American bias in its regional design (i.e., North America, Europe, Asia, Africa, and Latin America). In a truly prophetic move, ICSW adopted a ten-region structure (now nine) that largely parallels the membership of regional economic bodies. This structure has enabled ICSW to create dialogue with regional economic entities such as the Association of Southeast Asian Nations (ASEAN) and the Economic Community of West African States (ECOWAS). It is only in the twenty-first century that the regional economic bodies have evolved their missions to encompass social dimensions of development. The regional structure of ICSW has enabled immediate dialogue with these economic entities.

Focus on the Global South

It was not until 1964 that the first African member (Ethiopia) joined ICSW (EC, 1964, p. 4). In 1968 the German National Committee obtained funding from the German government to strengthen social welfare in Africa. Three regional seminars were conducted and ten African national committees joined the membership (Katzki, 1988). This North–South arrangement created considerable interest and support within the Executive Committee.

Following the regional seminars, the Executive Committee decided unanimously to establish a regional office in Addis Ababa, Ethiopia, for East and Central Africa (EC, 1969, p. 9). This was extended in 1970 to two offices, with the second being in Kenya (EC, 1970, p. 7). After a period of strong growth of African membership, the situation deteriorated. The minutes of the Executive Committee in August 1979 state, "ICSW has lost contact with most of its African members, most National Councils have not paid their membership for several years" (EC, 1979, p. 4).

Thus, the history of activity in the Global South has not been consistent. It was not until the World Summit for Social Development in 1995 that a marked change occurred, taking ICSW away from the traditional Northern welfare bias. Some European government development agencies were so impressed with ICSW's contribution to the World Summit that they made considerable financial contributions to ICSW to extend its work in the Global South. The organization has maintained this activity, and there is now a permanent office in Uganda. Regional presidents in the South, usually from poor organizations, are subsidized from donor funds to undertake the responsibilities of their position.

NATIONAL COUNCILS

From the earliest days of ICSW, national councils have been the base of the organization. In 1948 the Executive Committee noted that "several countries had requested information that could be used by them in the organization of National Committees" (EC, 1948, p. 2). A perennial issue is the degree to which "a National Committee was truly representative of social welfare interests within a country" (EC, 1955, p. 7); this issue was further addressed in 1957. And in 1969, the Executive Committee debated questions relating to national councils, including whether there should be government representation on boards and what the function and structure of national councils should be (EC, 1969, p. 4). A major project on strengthening national councils commenced in 1980. The project received support from the Rowntree Trust, Australian Development Assistance Bureau, and Dutch Committee of ICSW. The development of a national council handbook was supported by the Japanese National Committee of ICSW and the Canadian International Development Agency (CIDA).

The UN Copenhagen Declaration and Programme of Action (UN, 1995) established a consensus to place people at the center of concerns for development (UN, 2007). More recently, the 2005 Paris Declaration on Aid Effectiveness (Organization for Economic Cooperation and Development [OECD], 2005) is recognized as a significant juncture in the history of development assistance and cooperation. The concept of general budget support gives the governments of recipient countries more scope to make decisions based on their own priorities. The principle is national ownership. More responsibility is placed on governments to encourage civil society input to policy and budget processes; however, this is in the context of a civil society that is not powerful and organized. For example, "Civil society tends to be weak across Africa" (Hyden, 2008, p. 269).

In the ICSW context, strong National Member Organizations (national councils) are imperative as tools to influence government policy, budgets, and strategies for poverty reduction. They are also powerful agents for strengthening civil society through their capacity to strengthen and support their own local and national member organizations. However, a major obstacle to mobilizing democratic institutions for poverty alleviation is the organizational weakness of people who live in poverty and disadvantage. ICSW works to strengthen the capacity of civil society to participate effectively in programs for poverty reduction and social development. Strengthening the capacity of National Member Organizations is the major component of the ICSW global program.

A curious phenomenon has been the rise in membership of national councils in the Global South and a declining of membership in the Global North. The European and North American membership dominated the council until late in the twentieth century. It is hard to find documentation on the cause of the diminution of membership and activity of national councils in the Global North. One possibility is the rise and entrenchment of the welfare state in many European countries and in North America. Civil society was fundamental to the growth of the welfare state, but as the range of services became increasingly state owned and controlled, the need for intervention by civil society diminished. Some national councils reinvented themselves and found new roles in bringing together service providers and professionals. They have worked on issues such as service quality and protecting services from the ravages of the neoliberal state. Others have not reinvented themselves and have become hollow shells without a mission and membership relevant to this century.

On the other hand, the growth of national councils in Africa is characterized by enthusiasm in the face of inadequate resources and corruption within many states. It is possible to draw a parallel between the growth of national councils in Africa and the growth of the European national councils at the time of the creation of the welfare state. Whereas European countries developed social protection systems a hundred years ago, the African Union only adopted a common understanding of the introduction of social protection in the African states in 2008.

The states of the former Soviet Union provide a rich field for analysis. Democracy is still relatively new, as are NGOs. Old cross-border suspicions are alive. Cross-border trust comes naturally to the African national councils because cross-border conflict is not a major part of the history of that continent; in the former states of the Soviet Union, however, trust is far from automatic. Thus, building a regional spirit is a slow process marked with historic suspicion. A major role was played by ICSW in establishing the first regional grouping of NGOs in the Black Sea region. This has been a challenge since the concept of a national umbrella did not exist in the former states of the Soviet Union. The organization continues to support the International Union of Black Sea NGOs.

WORKING WITH OTHER INTERNATIONAL ORGANIZATIONS

From the early days, ICSW has considered membership from international NGOs (INGOs) to be important and has given such organizations voting rights in meetings of members. At times ICSW has taken a lead in bringing INGOs together. In 1955, ICSW convened a meeting of fifteen INGOs, which resulted in seven submitting a joint statement to the UN Social Commission (EC, 1955, p. 5). This leadership continued until after the World Summit for Social Development, when new and assertive INGOs appeared on the international scene. The late twentieth century was characterized by the rise of INGOs specifically constructed to undertake in-country development activities. They are well resourced compared with

the advocacy NGOs that do not provide direct services.

United Nations and Other International Institutions

The council was one of the first NGOs to be granted consultative status with the United Nations, and it retains the highest level of NGO consultative status. Through its consultative status, ICSW can attend, submit statements to, and speak at meetings conducted under the auspices of the Economic and Social Council (ECOSOC).

In 1946, the Executive Board decided to make immediate contact with the ECOSOC Social Welfare Commission and offer "cordial cooperation" (EB, 1946, p. 7). The Social Welfare Commission was active in the 1940s, and ICSW contributed to the examination of issues such as repression of prostitution, problems of slavery, and care of individuals without citizenship (EC, 1949, p. 12). In the same period, ICSW was granted consultative status with UNESCO and sought consultative status with the World Health Organization (WHO) (EC, 1949, p. 13). Consultative status with the United Nations Children's Fund (UNICEF) was granted in 1952 (EC, 1952, p. 3). The main focus of the organization's UN work is with the UN Commission for Social Development, which has the responsibility of following the commitments of the Copenhagen World Summit for Social Development.

Because the activities of the International Labour Organization (ILO) in the area of social security were within the range of interest of ICSW, the Executive Committee decided in 1959 to apply for inclusion in the ILO's Special List of Nongovernmental Organizations (EC, 1959, p. 8). Sometime between 1959 and 1963, the application was approved (EC, 1963, p. 6).

Although it holds consultative status with UN agencies, ICSW minutes note the difficulty of maintaining adequate representation at UN meetings: "While it is possible to participate through volunteer representation, this method has not proven entirely satisfactory because of the unavailability of qualified individuals who have sufficient time and resources" (EC, 1953, p. 12). The dilemmas of representation were further outlined in the comment that "the International Conference is primarily a forum and therefore cannot take a position on controversial matters" (EC, 1953, p. 12). Representation was raised again in 1957, with doubts expressed about the effectiveness of consultative status if ICSW did not take a position on substantive issues. Further, there was concern that national committees should be involved in the preparation of documents submitted to the UN (EC, 1957, p. 10). To deal with this issue, ICSW has developed considered positions (after consultation with members where possible); it does not tend to make quick statements on immediate issues.

The dilemmas of working with the UN and related agencies continue; the UN has failed to resolve the working relationships with NGOs. A review of relations with civil society was relegated to the UN rubbish bin during Kofi Annan's time as secretary-general. There are opportunities for NGOs to participate in UN activities, but these are restricted and on strict terms.

CONCLUDING THEMES

The Name

Originally, ICSW started as the International Conference on Social Work. The proposal to change the name to the International Council on Social Welfare was formally raised in 1961 (EC, 1961, p. 10). Since then, the issue of the ICSW name has arisen periodically and reveals the evolution of the organization. In 1971, a member of the Executive Committee proposed the name be changed to the International Council on Social Development, "thus showing a wider concept than social welfare" (EC, 1971, p. 7). After debating a name change in 1981, the name *International Council on Social Welfare* was retained with the additional words, "A world organization promoting social development."

Leadership

There can be little doubt that the common characteristic of the successful years of ICSW has been strong leadership. Leaders need to maintain a balance of leadership and consultation with committees and members. Leading an international NGO is a different challenge from leading a national or regional NGO. Timescales to achieve democratic change are longer than at the national level. Achieving democratic involvement is fraught with difficulties. Meetings are only attended by representatives of richer countries unless subsidies are provided to allow members from poorer countries to attend. Electronic communication is generally more democratic but removes the benefit of face-to-face communication and can be notoriously unreliable in poorer countries. In this environment there is the danger of leadership becoming remote from members. The rise of English as the major language of international communication has enhanced participation, although Spanish and French speakers remain the most disadvantaged in meetings despite interpretation.

CONCLUSION

The history of ICSW is characterized by legions of committed social activists who have worked for the improvement of global society. At times the leadership was truly inspired, as was the case at the World Summit for Social Development in 1995. At other times, ICSW has been characterized by dogged resistance to the impending demise of the organization. It is not unusual to see predictions of financial doom in the meeting minutes. Despite moving to the brink of extinction on occasion, ICSW has showed the resilience of its leadership and members. Throughout its history, ICSW has sought to improve the lives of those living in poverty. It has been innovative in its approach to social development. The support of national councils and the prophetic realization that regional development will be a dominating force in the twenty-first century are just two examples of ICSW's global leadership in social development.

REFERENCES

Anciaux, A. (1988). René Sand—Fondateur de L'ICSW. In *ICSW 1928–1988: Celebration of the 60th anniversary* (pp. 25–28). Vienna: International Council on Social Welfare.

Comité national d'action sociale (CNAS). (2008). *International Council on Social Welfare 80 Years of History (1928–2008)*. Rennes Cedex, France: Presses de l'EHESP.

Committee of Representatives (CoRep). (1976). International Council on Social Welfare minutes, Committee of Representatives meeting, July.

Executive Committee (EC). (1983). International Council on Social Welfare minutes, Executive Committee meeting, July.

Executive Committee (EC). (1979). International Council on Social Welfare minutes, Executive Committee meeting, August.

Executive Committee (EC). (1976). International Council on Social Welfare minutes, Executive Committee meeting, July.

Executive Committee (EC). (1971). International Council on Social Welfare minutes, Executive Committee meeting, August.

Executive Committee (EC). (1970). International Council on Social Welfare minutes, Executive Committee meeting, September.

Executive Committee (EC). (1969). International Council on Social Welfare minutes, Executive Committee meeting, August.

Executive Committee (EC). (1964). International Council on Social Welfare minutes, Executive Committee meeting, September.

Executive Committee (EC). (1963). International Council on Social Welfare minutes, Executive Committee meeting, September.

Executive Committee (EC). (1961). International Council on Social Welfare minutes, Executive Committee meeting, August.

Executive Committee (EC). (1959). International Council on Social Welfare minutes, Executive Committee meeting, July.

Executive Committee (EC). (1957). International Council on Social Welfare minutes, Executive Committee meeting, August.

Executive Committee (EC). (1955). International Council on Social Welfare minutes, Executive Committee meeting, September.

Executive Committee (EC). (1953). International Council on Social Welfare minutes, Executive Committee meeting, July.

Executive Committee (EC). (1952). International Council on Social Welfare minutes, Executive Committee meeting, August.

Executive Committee (EC). (1949). International Council on Social Welfare minutes, Executive Committee meeting, September.

Executive Committee (EC). (1948). International Council on Social Welfare minutes, Executive Committee meeting, April.

Executive Board (EB). (1946). International Council on Social Welfare minutes, Executive Board meeting, August.

Healy, L., & Hall, N. (2007). International organizations in social work. In L. Wagner & R. Lutz (Eds.), *Internationale Perspektiven Sozialer Arbeit* [International perspectives in social work] (pp. 223–242). Leverkusen, Germany: Verlag Barbara Budrich.

Hyden, G. (2008). After the Paris Declaration: Taking on the issue of power. *Development Policy Review, 26*(3), 259–274.

Katzki, K. (1988). *Sixty years of ICSW.* ICSW 24th Conference, Berlin, Germany.

Organization for Economic Cooperation and Development (OECD). (2005). *Paris Declaration on Aid Effectiveness.* Available at www.oecd.org/dataoecd/11/41/34428351.pdf.

United Nations (UN). (2007). *Participatory dialogue: Toward a stable, safe and just society for all.* New York: Author.

United Nations (UN). (1995). *The Copenhagen Declaration and Programme of Action: World Summit for Social Development.* New York: Author.

International Consortium for Social Development (ICSD)

FRANK B. RAYMOND AND CHARLES "CHUCK" COWGER

The International Consortium for Social Development (ICSD) is a global organization of individuals and institutions committed to the advancement of social development throughout the world. The organization, started in the 1970s, consists of numerous types of organizations and individuals from many disciplines. Membership now includes educators, practitioners, students, schools of social work, nongovernmental organizations (NGOs), and other organizations concerned with social development. Furthermore, ICSD has expanded to include worldwide representation with regional branches. Although it has increased in size and complexity, the organization remains true to its mission of promoting social development throughout the world.

PHILOSOPHY AND MISSION

For ICSD, the term *social development* refers to building social, economic, and political capacities of individuals, families, communities, nation-states, and international organizations. The organization's work is accomplished by asking key questions, specifying theory, conducting research, using evidence to improve policy and practice, teaching, holding professional meetings, publishing an international journal, and maintaining a website dedicated to promoting ICSD goals. It is organized exclusively for charitable, religious, educational, and scientific purposes under Section 501(c)(3) of the Internal Revenue Code (the tax law in the United States). In all facets of its operations, ICSD seeks to promote gender, racial, ethnic, and cultural diversity.

The organization's philosophy is set forth in the ICSD Constitution (ICSD, 2005). The existence of ICSD is based on the conviction that the goals of human realization, equality, human rights, peace, and social and economic justice can only be achieved through comprehensive, collective, remedial, and developmental efforts. This position assumes that the traditional clinical approaches of the social service professions, which are directed only toward individuals, are insufficient to achieve these goals.

According to this philosophy, the central features that characterize social development and ensure that it is an encompassing approach are identified by the terms *intersystemic, intersectoral, institutional, normative,* and *participatory.* The perspective is *intersystemic* in that attention is paid to the relations among social systems and their impact on each other. It is *intersectoral* by focusing on the political, economic, and cultural dimensions within and between social systems. It is *institutional* by its concern with activities designed to create new institutions or support the renewal of existing ones. This perspective on social development is *normative* in its belief that values of peace, human empowerment, and social, economic, and political justice provide the structure within which social development takes place. Finally, it is *participatory* by its emphasis on the maximum participation of those who will be affected. These features distinguish ICSD efforts and activities from those of other national and international organizations and provide the rationale for its existence. An early study by two ICSD members was particularly important in defining the concept of social development (Meinert & Kohn, 1987).

The ICSD mission is to advance social development by creating conceptual frameworks and effective intervention strategies geared toward influencing local, national, and international systems. It is committed to developing and promoting peaceful solutions to the problems of survival at the local, national, and global levels through use of a social development approach.

HISTORY OF THE
ORGANIZATION

In the early 1970s, faculty members from several schools of social work in the Midwestern United States met informally at the behest of Frank Paiva, then director of the School of Social Work at the University of Missouri. This meeting was held in order to discuss means of achieving the following:

> To discover and refine the knowledge required for social development and to clarify the role of the human service professions in the development process; to explore the development of educational programs and specific curriculum content to reflect the above; to ensure the reflection of the foregoing in the programs of country assistance undertaken by our universities; and to initiate and sustain a continuing process of mutual consultation and cooperative action among schools in the mid-west region towards these ends.
>
> —(Paiva, *1977b*)

Invitations for an initial meeting went to five universities, and all five responded. Paiva, who had earlier worked at the United Nations Division for Social Policy and Development, stated that he called the meeting primarily because he found social work's understanding of social development to be limited. This limited perspective focused on traditional social welfare remedial and preventive programs as opposed to progressive, comprehensive programs that consider all variables relevant to the struggle to attain economic development (Paiva, 1977a).

The initial meeting of this group (i.e., founding members) included John F. Jones, David Hollister, and Rama Pandey (a former colleague of Paiva's at the UN) of the University of Minnesota, Duluth; Tom Waltz and Earl Carter of the University of Iowa; Shanti Khinduka and Richard Parvis of Washington University; Arthur Katz of the University of Kansas; Frank Paiva, John Moore, and Lee Cary of the University of Missouri; and Ezra Kohn of the University of Nebraska. The group met informally in the early 1970s under the name of the Midwest Consortium for International Social Development. In 1975, the group held an organizing meeting in Columbia, Missouri, that included the original six universities plus St. Louis University. Daniel Sanders, of the University of Hawaii, requested and was granted permission to join the group. With the admission of the University of Hawaii, the scope of the group expanded beyond the Midwest. When a memorandum of cooperation was approved

by the membership in 1977, the name was changed to the Inter-University Consortium for International Social Development (IUCISD) in order to accommodate individuals and institutions from other regions who might wish to join (Meinert, 1991).

It became clear that this organization was not going to be able to fulfill its purpose without international activity and participation. In 1980, it held its first international symposium following the International Association of Schools of Social Work (IASSW) Congress in Hong Kong. Daniel Sanders became president of IUCISD in 1981, and with his leadership and that of Richard Parvis, secretary-general, membership expanded considerably over the next seven years. The relationship of peace and social justice to social development became a more central focus, and the biennial symposium became an outlet for significant research and further conceptualization of social development theory. Sustainability, social development technology transfer, women in development, and the integration of peace, social justice, and social development were highlighted at IUCISD symposia.

James Billups served as president from 1990 to 1998. Along with Peter Lee, secretary-general, Billups worked tirelessly to enlarge membership and make the organization more inclusive. By 1998, IUCISD had eighty-three organizational members from thirty-one countries, a European branch had been firmly established, and a new constitution was approved that stipulated board membership from IUCISD regions. Also, individual and institutional membership fees and biennial symposium registration fees were based on a sliding scale using the World Bank – designated levels of development for each country, and the board established a policy that any profits from the biennial symposium would be used for registration scholarships for people from least developed countries for the next symposia.

A professional journal, *Social Development Issues*, was established at the University of Iowa by a founding member of IUCISD, Tom Walz. In the late 1980s, IUCISD became a cosponsor of the journal by paying for subscriptions for each of its members, taking over editorial policy, and appointing editors. In 1998, an agreement was reached with the University of Iowa for IUCISD to assume ownership of the journal.

Succeeding James Billups as president were Chuck Cowger, Shanti Khinduka, Frank Raymond, and Barbara Shank. During this period branches were firmly established in Europe and the Asian-Pacific and Latin America regions, board representation from each region was mandated, and the biennial symposia were moved to the odd years so as not to conflict with the IASSW Congress. Also, the organization began to take advantage of information technology with an impressive website, a listserv for members, and a technical assistance roster.

At the 2005 biennial symposium in Recife, Brazil, the membership approved a change in the name of the organization to the International Consortium for Social Development (ICSD). This change reflected the reality that membership had become global and more diverse and the goals of the organization had expanded since the organization's founding. While universities continued to have the largest numbers of members, other types of organizations such as NGOs and governmental units were playing prominent roles and were important partners in carrying out ICSD goals.

ORGANIZATIONAL STRUCTURE

There are two categories of ICSD membership—individual and institutional. Individual members include educators, students, practitioners, and others committed to the goals of social development. Institutional members include colleges, universities, governmental agencies, and NGOs that have a philosophical orientation compatible with ICSD. Members from regions around the world may petition the board in writing to establish a regional ICSD branch. Members of the established regional branches are full members of the larger organization as well as their respective branches. The regional branches receive a proportional part of the membership dues paid by their members. Each branch carries out its own activities in support of the ICSD mission, including the sponsoring of regional symposia.

The Board of Directors, including both elected and appointed officers and representing all branches, meets at least once a year to establish the organization's policies and central direction. There is also an Executive Council empowered to meet (usually via conference calls) during the interim between board meetings to make decisions on matters requiring immediate attention. In addition, there are several standing committees mandated by the ICSD Constitution that are responsible for carrying out specific tasks. The general membership meets during each biennial symposium (in odd-numbered years) to receive reports from officers and to vote on any proposed changes to the constitution.

MAJOR ACTIVITIES

One of the primary activities by which ICSD seeks to accomplish its goals is its biennial symposium.

This conference provides important means for scholars, professionals, representatives of international agencies, government officials, and others to come together to share professional papers, exchange views, and work toward ICSD goals. Sessions are held in accessible, low-cost locations to encourage attendance. Efforts are made to schedule the symposia at sites where attendance expenses are reasonable, and sites rotate among the several regions. Since the inaugural symposium in Hong Kong in 1980, people from around the world have gathered for ICSD symposia in Great Britain (1982), Canada (1984), Japan (1986), Finland (1988), Costa Rica (1990), the United States (1992), Sri Lanka (1994), Portugal (1996), Egypt (1998), South Africa (1999), Turkey (2001), India (2003), Brazil (2005), Hong Kong (2007), Mexico (2009), and Bangladesh (2011).

Each symposium is cosponsored by a variety of organizations in the host country and in the United States, including other schools and universities, professional organizations such as the Council on Social Work Education (CSWE), human service organizations, foundations, and so on. Additionally, other international organizations such as IASSW, ICSW (International Council on Social Welfare), and IFSW (International Federation of Social Workers) lend their support to the symposium by publicizing the event through their information outlets and having their officers participate in the symposium.

As a further effort to keep the costs of attendance affordable to all, differential registration fees are charged so that participants from countries with low-income economies (as defined by the World Bank) are charged lower fees. Scholarships are made available to students who need financial assistance to attend. Also, a wide range of housing options are offered to conference attendees, often including accommodations in dormitories and private homes. Each symposium also includes several types of tours, such as visits to human service organizations (particularly those engaged in social development) in or near the host city, local learning tours, and pre- or postsymposium study tours. The former appeal primarily to symposium delegates, whereas the latter two appeal equally to symposium delegates and accompanying guests. Local learning tours are either half- or full-day visits to locations in or near the host city. Continuing education credits (CEUs) are awarded to symposium participants who want them. In addition, CEUs are available to participants who take part in the pre- or postconference study tours. Both types of CEUs are usually awarded through the sponsoring school in the United States.

Publications

Another important way ICSD seeks to accomplish its goals is through its publications. It publishes a newsletter semiannually, normally during the months of May/June and October/November. The editor of the *ICSD Newsletter* is appointed by the president for an unspecified term. The newsletter is distributed electronically and helps keep the membership informed of current events related to social development and recent ICSD activities.

As mentioned earlier in the chapter, ICSD also publishes *Social Development Issues*, a refereed journal that serves as a forum for achieving linkages among multiple disciplines, nations, and cultures. The purpose of this journal is to promote the scholarly examination of issues related to social development, social justice, and the development and well-being of individuals and their communities. The journal is committed to the advancement of social, cultural, political, and economic theory, policy, and practice within a global context. It includes manuscripts that address alternative approaches to counteracting obstacles to social development. Diverse topics are addressed, such as life span, gender, and race; the impact of policies, practices, and service-delivery systems on urban and rural communities; comparative studies of health, poverty, and income-maintenance systems; and movements such as global feminism, human rights, and peace. *Social Development Issues* is published by Lyceum Books (lyceum@lyceumbooks.com). The journal is sent to all ICSD members as one of their membership benefits and is also available by subscription.

The ICSD website has become another vehicle for promoting social development (www.icsd.info). Through the website, ICSD serves as a major clearinghouse for information on all aspects of international social development. The website links ICSD members and other interested parties to a multitude of schools, human service organizations, and professional associations concerned with international social development. It is a repository for information on international social problems and issues as well as efforts made to address these. The website also contains information on ICSD activities. This includes a regularly published message from the ICSD president and announcements of upcoming events. Links are provided to the websites for the biennial symposium and the regional conferences of the ICSD branches. Information on the *ICSD Newsletter* and the ICSD journal, *Social Development Issues*, is available on the website. Also, membership information is provided, including links to enable an individual or organization to join.

Technical Assistance Roster

The ICSD technical assistance roster links members to individuals, organizations, and government agencies with special expertise in various aspects of international social development. Areas of expertise include community and economic development, organization and program building, education and training in problem-solving processes, comparative analysis of social development projects, and program evaluation.

FUTURE DIRECTIONS OF ICSD

There are many ways in which ICSD differs from most international organizations dedicated to social work, human services, and education for practice in the social services arena. First, ICSD is unique in its exclusive focus on social development. Although other international associations may concern themselves with some aspects of social development, this area of study and practice is usually one of many areas of attention rather than the main focus. Second, and partly because of its specialized focus, ICSD is smaller than many of these organizations. Professional associations such as IASSW, IFSW, and ICSW have more members and their conferences usually have a greater attendance; the smaller size of the ICSD meetings offers greater opportunities for relationship building and collaboration.

As noted earlier, however, ICSD has grown steadily in membership and global presence over the years, and this expansion is expected to continue. The numbers of individuals and organizations interested in social development are increasing in response to the continuing economic and social deprivation of people throughout the world. No single discipline has all the answers to addressing these needs. Rather, it is important that all disciplines concerned with social development make their unique professional contributions in building a knowledge base, creating social and economic strategies, training practitioners for this field of practice, and developing and implementing programs aimed at improving the lives of those in need.

It is important for these disciplines not to go about these tasks independently; there have been too many instances of social development practitioners duplicating or overlapping each other's work in some locations while other areas of need are ignored. Also, too often those who study or work in the area of social development have no idea of the knowledge, programs, and practices of their colleagues from other disciplines. It is essential that all disciplines concerned with social development work together and share their knowledge and resources, and ICSD provides an ideal means of accomplishing this purpose. Therefore, as those who are committed to social development seek opportunities to study and work with colleagues from other disciplines, it is likely that ICSD will continue to grow.

For several years, ICSD leaders have discussed the organization's growth. Some have expressed concern that the organization will become too big. They enjoy belonging to an association that is not so large that it is impersonal. They enjoy meeting with like-minded colleagues biennially to study together and to share ideas and aspirations, and they like the camaraderie they experience at the ICSD symposia, regional conferences, and committee meetings. Remembering their experiences with other associations that have grown dramatically, they are concerned that some of the small-group atmosphere would be lost if the organization were to become too large.

The ICSD leaders have taken the position that the organization should be as large as it needs to be. There is no interest among the leadership in growth for growth's sake; rather, they believe that ICSD should remain true to its mission and goals in facilitating the advancement of social development throughout the world. To achieve this purpose, ICSD must be inclusive and welcome all who share these aspirations; look for ways of bringing about social development wherever needs exist; seek new, different, and more effective ways of carrying out social development activities; and use every tool available for sharing knowledge, wisdom, and ideas with colleagues who engage in this important area of study and practice. All this means that ICSD will continue to grow in size and scope.

At the same time, the leaders of ICSD want to preserve the qualities that have made the organization so successful and enjoyable for its members. Hence, symposia will be structured to provide ample opportunity for small-group study and social networking among conference attendees. The *ICSD Newsletter*,

and *Social Development Issues* will remain important means of keeping the membership informed of developments in the organization, the field, and the knowledge base for social development practice. The ICSD website will also be critical in keeping members informed about current events, facilitating information exchange among members, and providing information about ICSD to individuals and organizations that may be interested in joining. Finally, ICSD will seek to expand its Branch Chapters throughout all regions of the world. These chapters make it possible for the work of the larger organization to be carried out on a local level. Members who are not able to travel to the biennial symposia may find it possible to attend the regional symposia. Not only do these regional conferences offer the opportunity for members to study and learn together with other colleagues as they would at the biennial symposia, but they can also be tailored more specifically to address the immediate needs and circumstances of the respective world regions and host countries. Together, the global organization and its regional units support continuing progress toward social development, locally and globally.

REFERENCES

International Consortium for Social Development (ICSD). (2005, July). Constitution of the International Consortium for Social Development. Last amended at the general membership meeting of the International Consortium for Social Development in Recife, Brazil.

Meinert, R. (1991). A brief history of IUCISD: From informal interest group to international organization. *Social Development Issues, 13*(3), 1–13.

Meinert, R., & Kohn, E. (1987). Toward operationalization of social development concepts. *Social Development Issues, 10*(3), 4–18.

Paiva, J. F. X. (1977a). A concept of social development. *Social Service Review, 51*(2), 327–336.

Paiva, J. F. X. (1977b). *Memo TO: All Consortium representatives.* July 12.

Global Ethical Principles and Dilemmas

ELAINE CONGRESS

From the beginning, social work has been a value-based profession. Although there has been general consensus about broad principles of social justice, there also has been much debate about what is universal and thus should apply to social workers around the world and what is culturally specific. In a globalized world in which social workers and their clients are increasingly transnational, the quest for global ethical principles is of increasing importance. Yet the tension between the desire for universal ethical principles for all social workers and the recognition of cultural and national differences is not easily resolved.

This chapter presents this issue in four parts—the history and literature on global ethics; a review of the current Ethics in Social Work: Statement of Principles; a discussion of issues and dilemmas that have arisen in the creation and implementation of a statement of ethical principles for all social workers; and a discussion about the future of global ethics.

HISTORY AND LITERATURE ON GLOBAL ETHICS

The desire to identify universal social work values and ethics is not new. Much research on social work values has been national and has looked at the values of members of social work associations. This may be problematic because many social workers do not belong to professional associations, and it might be even more significant to find out the social work values of nonmembers. In an early study in the United States, Abbott (1988) identified social work values in regard to respect for basic rights, sense of social responsibility, commitment to individual freedom (social justice), and support of self-determination, while a recent study in Great Britain (Dominelli, 2004) found that most social workers believe in values such as facilitating self-determination (96%) and creating a just society (72%). It is of concern, however, that 16% of the

social workers sampled in the study reported that social work values do not "underpin their practice" (p. 163).

International research on common social work values has been limited. Abbott (2002) studied professional values of social workers in four areas of the world, including North America, Asia, Europe, and Australia and New Zealand. Using four categories, she found that social workers share certain values, namely respect for basic rights and support of self-determination. Her research, however, did not support a universal sense of social responsibility or commitment to individual freedom. There have been recent attempts to explore similarities and differences between social work values as expressed in the code of ethics in Australia and the United States as well as in Korea and the United States (Congress & Kim, 2007; Congress & McAuliffe, 2006).

Banks (2003, 2006), who studied the codes of ethics in thirty-one countries, found similarities in the stated values and principles of these countries. After her global analysis of codes of ethics, she acknowledged that there were no universally agreed-upon social work values and ethics. However, she did identify three major themes: respect for the dignity and worth of all human beings, promotion of welfare and well-being of service users and society in general, and promotion of social justice, especially among the three Anglo countries—Australia, Great Britain, and the United States. Banks also found that many national codes of ethics seem to be based on the Ethics in Social Work: Statement of Principles document of the International Federation of Social Workers (IFSW) and International Association of Schools of Social Work (IASSW).

In an editorial in *Ethics and Social Welfare*, Hugman (2008) addresses an ongoing concern that social work values are primarily developed and fostered by Western social work educators and represent an attempt to impose Western values on non-Western social workers. In this debate about universalism versus cultural relativism, Yip (2004) argues for a cultural relativist approach, whereas Healy (2007) supports common values that are understood and practiced with cultural sensitivity. Hugman (2008) proposes a new approach, that of capabilities, for helping social workers resolve this dilemma.

ETHICAL STANDARDS OF GLOBAL SOCIAL WORK

History

The Ethics in Social Work: Statement of Principles document was created in 1994 and then revised in 2004 by IASSW, which includes schools of social work in over seventy countries (Healy, 2008), and IFSW, which is composed of professional social work associations from ninety countries. In addition to the 1994 and 2004 Ethics in Social Work documents, the IFSW website (www.ifsw.org) includes codes of ethics from nineteen countries in three official UN languages, namely, English, French, and Spanish. Most codes are from developed Western countries, where English is the dominant language or a strong second language.

In terms of the historical development of an international code of ethics, in 1976 IFSW adopted the first international code of ethics. Ten years later this code was supplemented by a declaration of ethical principles. In 1994 the two documents were merged into one ethical document, the Ethics of Social Work Principles and Standards. At the same time, IFSW established the Permanent Committee on Ethics. Then in 2004, IFSW and IASSW agreed on and adopted a new ethical document—Ethics in Social Work: Statement of Principles.

Content of Ethics in Social Work: Statement of Principles

The first part of Ethics in Social Work: Statement of Principles includes the international definition of social work agreed upon by IFSW and IASSW, which defines social work as a values-based profession. Both organizations see the purpose of their work on ethics as "to promote ethical debate and reflection in the member organizations, among the providers of social work in member countries, as well as in the schools of social work and among social work students. Some ethical challenges and problems facing social workers are specific to particular countries, while others are common" (IFSW, 2004, p. 1). The document affirms the core values of the profession,

explicitly stating that social workers promote human rights and social justice.

In this statement of purpose, both organizations acknowledge that there will be continual ethical debate among social workers. In order to promote universalism and acceptance by all social workers, the statement of principles is very general. The purpose of this is "to encourage social workers across the world to reflect on the challenges and dilemmas that face them and make ethically informed decisions about how to act in each particular case" (IFSW, 2004, p. 1). These ethical challenges are seen as loyalty to ethical prescriptions in the face of conflicting interests such as care versus control and individual versus societal needs within the context of diminishing resources.

The third section of the statement lists the international human rights conventions that should guide global social work practice. The following conventions developed by the UN and approved by most member states are seen as most relevant to social workers:

Universal Declaration of Human Rights

International Covenant on Civil and Political Rights

International Covenant on Economic, Social and Cultural Rights

Convention on the Elimination of All Forms of Racial Discrimination

Convention on the Elimination of All Forms of Discrimination against Women

Convention on the Rights of the Child

Indigenous and Tribal Peoples Convention (International Labour Organization [ILO] convention 169).

It should be noted that the social work document was adopted in 2004, prior to the adoption of the UN Convention on the Rights of Persons with Disabilities.

The fourth section of Ethics in Social Work: Statement of Principles outlines primary social work principles such as human rights and human dignity, including issues such as the right of self-determination, the right to participation, the responsibility to treat each person as a whole, and the responsibility to identify and develop strengths as well as the responsibility to promote social justice by challenging negative discrimination, recognizing diversity, and distributing resources equitably. Challenging unjust policies and practices and working in solidarity are also stressed in this section.

The final section introduces basic guidance on ethical professional practice (IFSW, 2004):

1. Social workers are expected to develop and maintain the required skills and competence to do their job.
2. Social workers should not allow their skills to be used for inhumane purposes, such as torture or terrorism.
3. Social workers should act with integrity. This includes not abusing the relationship of trust with the people using their services, recognizing the boundaries between personal and professional life, and not abusing their position for personal benefit or gain.
4. Social workers should act with compassion, empathy, and care for the people using their services.
5. Social workers should not subordinate the needs or interests of people who use their services to their own needs or interests.
6. Social workers have a duty to take necessary steps to care for themselves professionally and personally in the workplace and in society in order to ensure that they are able to provide appropriate services.
7. Social workers should maintain confidentiality regarding information about people who use their services. Exceptions to this may only be justified on the basis of a greater ethical requirement (such as the preservation of life).
8. Social workers need to acknowledge that they are accountable for their actions to the users of their services, the people they work with, their colleagues, their employers, the professional association, and the law, and that these accountabilities may conflict.
9. Social workers should be willing to collaborate with schools of social work in order to support students getting practical training of good quality and up-to-date practical knowledge.
10. Social workers should foster and engage in ethical debate with their colleagues and employers and take responsibility for making ethically informed decisions.
11. Social workers should be prepared to state the reasons for their decisions based on ethical considerations and be accountable for their choices and actions.
12. Social workers should work to create conditions in employing agencies and in their countries where the principles of this statement and those of their own national code (if applicable) are discussed, evaluated, and upheld.

There is an expectation that some of the principles presented in the Ethics in Social Work document will be further developed in the national codes of IFSW member organizations. Also, it is acknowledged that ethical principles and decisions are not absolute but may be debated. One might question whether the statements in the section that describes professional practice are too culturally specific, such as provision 7, which stresses the importance of confidentiality. Another interesting feature of this section is the statement on self-care—that social workers should take personal and professional care of themselves in order to better serve clients (a concept that does not appear in the US code of ethics).

Challenges With Ethics in Social Work: Statement of Principles

With the diversity of countries and languages, the challenge in developing the statement of principles became apparent. Even within the same language, the same word may have a different meaning and usage in member countries. One example of this is the expression *negative discrimination*. In the United States, the word *discrimination* is most frequently used without a qualifying positive or negative word. To avoid confusion, there is a footnote that clarifies the use of *negative discrimination*: "In some countries the term 'discrimination' would be used instead of 'negative discrimination'. The word negative is used here because in some countries the term 'positive discrimination' is also used. Positive discrimination is also known as 'affirmative action'. Positive discrimination or affirmative action means positive steps taken to redress the effects of historical discrimination against oppressed groups (IFSW, 2004, p. 2).

Dissemination

Distribution of Ethics in Social Work: Statement of Principles continues to be a challenge. The IFSW ethics committee has seen as its goal the dissemination of this document among social workers and students in the member states. Some of this has been accomplished by social work presentations and publications (Banks, 2006; Congress, 2008;

Congress & Healy, 2006; Hugman, 2008) as well as by greater inclusion of the document in social work curricula. It is positive to note that in recent years, many national associations of social workers have used the Ethics in Social Work: Statement of Principles document in developing their codes of ethics (Banks, 2006). Also, the most recent Council on Social Work Education (CSWE) Educational Policy and Accreditation Standards (EPAS) has added the provision that students and social workers in the United States can use the statement of principles in addition to the National Association of Social Workers (NASW) Code of Ethics (CSWE, 2008) in arriving at ethical decisions.

MONITORING ETHICAL COMPLIANCE

All national associations that are members of IFSW must accept and be guided by the Ethics in Social Work: Statement of Principles document. Yet in terms of individual members of professional social work associations, these principles are primarily advisory rather than prescriptive. Very few countries have licensing or registration. In addition to limited national monitoring, there is no global board for monitoring or enforcing the document. Furthermore, the general nature of the document would make enforcement impossible. Even the final section, which focuses on professional practice, would be difficult to assess. For example, it stresses the importance of social workers maintaining skills and competencies to do their jobs. How can this be measured, or is it measureable at all? What type of and how much continuing education do social workers need to perform their job competently? In the United States, licensing requirements for continuing education are diverse, with some states having extensive requirements for post-master's-degree continuing education while other states such as New York do not require continuing education at all. Furthermore, even in countries where social work is an established profession, there often is no licensing of social workers or requirement to maintain skills after acquiring a bachelor or master's degree. Thus, although it would seem important for social workers to maintain their skills, the principle of maintaining social work skills is advisory, not prescriptive or enforceable, similar to other provisions in the document.

CRITIQUE OF THE GLOBAL ETHICAL STATEMENT

An ongoing concern has been that the statement of principles and other global ethics materials are primarily focused on Western values and do not reflect the diversity of social workers and their countries of origin (Congress, 2008; Healy, 2007; Hugman, 2008, Link, 2004; Midgley, 1981; Yip, 2004). In looking at the IFSW website, a review of the posted codes of ethics indicates that they are primarily from developed countries. Some of this might be related to the fact that in many developing countries, social work is a new field and a code of ethics has not yet been created. Often practice begins and then years later is codified. For example, in the United States, social work first began as a profession in the late 1800s, but it did not have a code of ethics until 1920, when Mary Richmond developed the first code of ethics for social workers (Congress, 1999).

In terms of universal approval, Ethics in Social Work: Statement of Principles received approval by all IFSW member states who attended the 2004 meeting in Adelaide and by the International Association of Schools of Social Work. A continual concern is that the membership of the IFSW ethics committee has been primarily Anglo from developed countries. There has been an ongoing effort, however, to seek committee input and participation from social workers all over the world.

How universal are the principles set forth in the Ethics in Social Work: Statement of Principles document? Do they reflect a primarily Western perspective on social work values and ethics? Given the diversity of countries that are members of IFSW and IASSW, are social work values and ethical practice as expressed in this document universal and inclusive of diverse views, or are they unduly influenced by Western national and cultural beliefs? Healy (2007) and Yip (2004) have both expressed concern that the statement of ethical principles may be too grounded in Western values. Healy argues for "a stance in the middle of the universalist relativism continuum," (p. 24) because she is concerned about policies that might compromise human rights, especially for women. Yip, on the other hand, adopts a more ethical relativist, cultural perspective and is concerned that the reliance on human rights as reflected in the document may be at odds with non-Western cultures. Hugman (2008) believes that Yip sees the statement as "unhelpful, even harmful in the development of an authentic Chinese social work" (p. 122).

Hugman (2008) analyzes the Healy (2007) and Yip (2004) articles in terms of their examples on domestic violence. He notes that there is not a strict dichotomy that domestic violence violates the rights of women in Western society but is permissible in non-Western society, pointing out that there are many from Western cultures who believe that it is acceptable to dominate women. Yet this certainly is not the accepted value system of social workers in Western countries, nor probably among most non-Western social workers.

What are the areas in which universalism might conflict with national cultural ethics? As Hugman (2008) indicates, there might be cultural differences regarding the rights of women. Some non-Western countries have very proscribed beliefs about the role of women and the nature of male–female relationships. The statement of ethical principles stresses the elimination of discrimination based on gender differences and this provision may be in conflict with the values of social workers in a country that practices discrimination. Even if countries have oppressive policies toward women, however, many social workers in these countries may not subscribe to these policies. Social workers often find themselves opposing national policies that are discriminatory, such as the anti-immigration and antihomosexuality policies that have been enacted in the United States and other countries.

The confidentiality principle is another example. Ethics in Social Work: Statement of Principles clearly states, "Social workers should maintain confidentiality regarding information about people who use their services. Exceptions to this may only be justified on the basis of a greater ethical requirement (such as the preservation of life)" (IFSW, 2004, p. 2). In the NASW Code of Ethics, privacy and confidentiality are also stressed, with the largest number (eighteen) of code provisions focusing on this theme. There has been concern that the inclusion of this principle on confidentiality in the IFSW–IASSW ethics document may reflect the Western perspective of those who come from countries that are governed by privacy and confidentiality laws, such as the United States. As migration around the world has increased exponentially, social workers often work with clients who may come from cultural backgrounds in which there is more focus on family and community communication rather than individual privacy. For example, a social worker at a US mental health clinic serving primarily Hispanic clients reported that when clients came to her office for the first intake interviews, they arrived with family members Additionally, Healy (2001) reports a dramatic example of a clash between US and African values around confidentiality. A young African man educated in a social work graduate program in the United States sought to maintain confidentiality,

while community members expected that naturally the social worker would reveal information about his adolescent client, who had returned to the village.

If the Ethics in Social Work, Statement of Principles document reflects a primarily Western orientation, one can ask if specific national codes are more reflective of national and cultural differences among member states. Banks (2006) reports that many nations have looked to the Ethics in Social Work document or social work codes that are long established (e.g., United States and Great Britain) in developing their codes, and thus the codes of all countries are similar. If codes are homogenous, they do not reflect the cultural differences of clients, social work, or practice around the world. This may be reflective of a new world of social work in which social workers and clients are increasingly transnational and incorporate diverse national perspectives into their professional practice.

FUTURE OF THE ETHICS IN SOCIAL WORK, STATEMENT OF PRINCIPLES DOCUMENT AND GLOBAL ETHICS

An initial task has been to disseminate the Ethics in Social Work: Statement of Principles document and to educate social workers and social work students worldwide about its existence and content. There have been major efforts in this direction in the United States, Great Britain, and Australia, but it is not clear how much effort has taken place in other countries. A continual challenge has been the need to translate the document into other languages; currently it is only available in English, French, and Spanish on the IFSW website and in English, French, Spanish, Chinese, and Arabic on the IASSW website.

Although professional associations may have looked to the statement of principles in developing their national codes of ethics, the document has not been widely known and used by social workers and students. One step forward in the United States has been the new provision in national curriculum standards (EPAS) that social workers should refer not only to the national (NASW) code of ethics but also to the Ethics in Social Work document in making ethical decisions.

As stated previously, all member states are required to subscribe to the principles of the document, but a monitoring mechanism does not exist. Since much of the document is related to human rights, there has been discussion about collaborating with the human rights committee as one way to begin to monitor code adherence. Also necessary is a process by which complaints of ethical violations can be discussed. Although there is no current mechanism for dealing with or even discussing violations, such activity might be a future project for the IFSW Permanent Committee on Ethics.

A major, more readily attainable goal is to educate social workers about Ethics in Social Work: Statement of Principles and provide examples about how it might be applied. The development of a website and posting of vignettes have been suggested as a possible means to educate social workers around the world about identifying ethical issues and resolving ethical dilemmas.

What is in the future for global ethics? As Banks (2006) notes, the codes of ethics of professional social work associations reflect a growing homogeneity as each association has looked to the other for development and revision of their ethics documents. As the world becomes more globalized and transnational, there will be an increased similarity between social work values in written codes of ethics and in practice around the world. Although much has been written about Western efforts to promote a particular social work worldview, recently there have been major efforts to incorporate multiple voices in leadership positions within international social work organizations (Healy, 2008). With the growth and influence of international social work and its subsequent impact on practitioners around the world, social work ethics will be influenced not only by Western individualist but also non-Western communitarian perspectives. Future ethics documents for global social work will reflect this dual approach and be more inclusive of multiple universal approaches to social work values and ethics.

REFERENCES

Abbott, A. (2002). Measuring social work values: A cross-cultural challenge for global practice. *International Social Work, 42*(4), 455–470.

Abbott, A. (1988). *Professional choices: Values at work.* Silver Springs, MD: National Association of Social Workers.

Banks, S. (2006). *Ethics and values in social work* (3rd ed.). Hampshire: Palgrave McMillan.

Banks, S. (2003). From oaths to rulebooks: A critical examination of codes of ethics for the social professions. *European Journal of Social Work, 6*(2), 133–144.

Congress, E. (2008). Codes of Ethics. In T. Mizhari & L. Davis (Eds.), *Encyclopedia of social work* (20th ed) (pp. 326–331). New York: Oxford University Press.

Congress, E. (1999). *Social work values and ethics: Identifying and resolving professional dilemmas.* Belmont, CA: Wadsworth.

Congress, E., & Healy, L. (2006, Winter). International ethical document adopted. *Social Work Education Reporter, 54*(1), 18–19.

Congress, E., & Kim, W. (2007). A comparative study on social work ethical codes in Korea and the United States: Focused on confidentiality, dual relationships, cultural diversity and impaired colleagues. *Korean Journal of Clinical Social Work, 4*(2), 175–192.

Congress, E., & McAuliffe, D. (2006). Social work ethics: Professional codes in Australia and the United States. *International Social Work, 49*(2), 151–164.

Council on Social Work Education (CSWE). (2008). *Evaluation and Program Accreditation Standards (EPAS).* Alexandria, VA: CSWE.

Dominelli, L. (2004). Practicing social work in a globalizing world. In N. T. Tan & A. Rowlands (Eds.), *Social work around the world III.* (pp. 151–173). Berne, Switzerland: IFSW.

Healy, L. (2008). Introduction: A brief journey through the 80-year history of the International Association of Schools of Social Work. Retrieved March 8, 2009, from www.socwork.net/2008/1/supplement/healy.

Healy, L. (2007). Universalism and cultural relativism in social work ethics. *International Social Work, 50*(1), 11–26.

Healy, L. (2001). *International social work: Professional action in an interdependent world.* New York: Oxford University Press.

Hugman, R. (2008). Ethics in a world of difference. *Ethics and Social Welfare, 2*(2), 118–132.

International Federation of Social Workers (IFSW). (2004). Ethics in social work: Statement of principles. Berne, Switzerland: Author.

International Federation of Social Workers (IFSW). (1994). *The ethics of social work principles and standards.* Berne, Switzerland: Author.

Link, R. (2004). Infusing global perspectives into social work values and ethics. In R. Chathapuram & R. Link (Eds.), *All our futures: Principles and resources for social work practice in a global era* (pp. 69–93). Belmont, CA: Wadsworth.

Midgley, J. (1981). *Professional imperialism: Social work in the Third World.* London: Heinemann.

National Association of Social Work (NASW). (1999). *Code of Ethics.* Washington DC: NASW.

Yip, K. S. (2004). A Chinese cultural critique of the global qualifying standards for social work education. *Social Work Education, 23*(5), 597–612.

SECTION VI

Organizations and Institutions Involved in International Social Work

The United Nations Agencies

STUART WILSON

The United Nations is perhaps best known for its efforts to resolve conflicts around the world, but the majority of its resources are spent meeting the pledge of its charter "to promote higher standards of living, full employment, and conditions of economic and social progress and development" (United Nations Department of Public Information [UNDPI], 2008, p. 149). Organizations such as the United Nations Children's Fund (UNICEF) and the United Nations Development Programme (UNDP) are synonymous with social development. The Office of the High Commissioner of Human Rights (OHCHR) leads the global effort to uphold human rights. This chapter describes how these and other UN organizations interact with the member states of the United Nations to set social and human rights policy. The chapter also emphasizes the direct efforts of UN organizations in improving the lives of human beings.

THE UNITED NATIONS SYSTEM

Before describing the human rights and social development activity of the United Nations, this overview briefly explains the structure of the United Nations and identifies the critical units that are involved in human rights and social development. The organizations often referred to as *UN agencies* (such as UNICEF and UNDP) are more properly known as UN funds and programs and are part of the UN system. There are three key sections of this system: the member states, sometimes referred to as the *United Nations proper* (United Nations System Chief Executives Board for Coordination [CEB], n.d.); the six organs through which the member states work together; and the UN specialized agencies, funds and programs, training and research institutes, and other entities.

At its heart, the United Nations consists of 192 member states. Originally founded in 1945 by 51 nations, it has grown continuously over the last sixty-four years. Montenegro was the 192nd nation-state to join in 2006 (www.un.org/en/members/growth/shtml). Representatives of the member states are involved in some way in almost every organization of the UN system (with the exception of the Secretariat).

The second section of the UN system is the six organs: the General Assembly, the Security Council, the Trusteeship Council (now defunct), the International Court of Justice, the Economic and Social Council (ECOSOC), and the Secretariat. The General Assembly (all member states), the Security Council (five permanent member states and ten rotating elected member states), and ECOSOC (fifty-four rotating elected member states) are forums where member states work together directly to set policy and take action to achieve collective goals. Whereas the General Assembly and ECOSOC are involved with human rights and social development, the priority of the Security Council is peace and security.

The Security Council "function[s] continuously and a representative of each of its members must be present at all times at United Nations headquarters" (UN Security Council, n.d.). The Security Council's main role is to intervene in disputes that have the potential to cause hostilities between nations and to initiate processes to resolve any such disputes. To facilitate this process, Security Council actions may include mediation, cease-fire directives, peacekeeping forces, economic sanctions, and even military action (UN Security Council, n.d.).

The International Court of Justice, located in The Hague, Netherlands, is the only UN organ with headquarters outside New York. It comprises fifteen judges appointed by the General Assembly and the Security Council (International Court of Justice, n.d.).

The Secretariat, with about 40,000 employees worldwide (UN General Assembly, 2008), is one of the UN organs, but this description can be somewhat misleading because the people in the Secretariat are paid employees of the UN with a mandate to serve the UN and not have allegiance to any of the member states. As Kendall (1994) described her experiences during the early days of the UN Secretariat, "We were there as international civil servants and we were international. If we did not think and act as internationalists, we could not have survived" (p. 7). Conversely, the member states are charged with not interfering with the impartiality of any member of the Secretariat. This is different from the General Assembly, the Security Council, and ECOSOC, which are made up of representatives who are responsible for protecting the interests of their member states.

The General Assembly and ECOSOC, which represent member states, and the Secretariat, consisting of UN employees, are the three UN organs that play critical roles in human rights and the setting of social policy. This will be discussed in greater detail in the next section of this chapter.

For the third section of the UN system, the charter provides for the establishment of specialized agencies (under Article 57) and the initiation of programs and funds by the General Assembly (under Article 22). There are fifteen specialized agencies (CEB, n.d.). Examples of well-known ones include the World Health Organization (WHO), the International Labour Organization (ILO), and the United Nations Educational, Scientific and Cultural Organization (UNESCO). These specialized agencies are autonomous organizations with specific negotiated agreements with the United Nations; their role is to "provide support and assistance to countries' development efforts" (UNDPI, 2008, p. 152). Of the fifteen specialized agencies, the ILO has the greatest involvement in social development and is particularly active in social justice and social protection.

There are nine main programs and funds established by the UN General Assembly (CEB, n.d.). These are the United Nations Children's Fund (UNICEF), the United Nations Development Programme (UNDP), the United Nations Population Fund (UNFPA), the United Nations Environment Programme (UNEP), the United Nations High Commissioner for Refugees (UNHCR), the World Food Programme (WFP), the Conference on Trade and Development (UNCTAD), the United Nations Human Settlements Programme (UN-HABITAT), and the United Nations Relief and Works Agency for Palestine Refugees (UNRWA). All these programs and funds have programs involving social development and the protection of human rights. The activities of UNICEF and UNDP will be explained in more detail later in this chapter. The programs and funds,

whose role is to "deal with operational activities for development in program countries," all report to the General Assembly via ECOSOC (UNDPI, 2008, p. 152). In addition to the specialized agencies, programs, and funds, there are two other organizational groupings—research and training institutes and other UN entities. Within the research and training institutes, the organization whose main focus is social development is the United Nations Research Institute for Social Development (UNRISD). Other UN entities include the Office of the High Commissioner of Human Rights (OHCHR) and the Joint UN Programme on HIV/AIDS (UNAIDS), both of which are discussed in greater detail later in the chapter.

HUMAN RIGHTS AND SOCIAL DEVELOPMENT IN THE UN AND ITS ORGANS

The main UN organs involved in human rights and social development are the General Assembly, ECOSOC, and the Secretariat. Although there are substantial similarities in the processes of advancing human rights and enhancing social development, the General Assembly, ECOSOC, and Secretariat interfaces for human rights and for social development are quite different.

Beginning with social development, at the center of the process by which member states debate issues and reach agreement is the General Assembly (in which all member states participate). For discussion and debate, the General Assembly uses six main committees. These are the First Committee (Disarmament and International Security Committee), Second Committee (Economic and Finance Committee), Third Committee (Social, Humanitarian and Cultural Committee), Fourth Committee (Special Political and Decolonization Committee), Fifth Committee (Administrative and Budgetary Committee), and Sixth Committee (Legal Committee) (UN General Assembly, n.d.). The third of these (Social, Humanitarian and Cultural Committee) is the main forum for social development issues. Votes on resolutions proposed by the Third Committee are taken in the full session of the General Assembly.

Economic and Social Council

The organ charged with coordinating economic and social development activities of the UN is ECOSOC. With the input of the many organizations represented by the specialized agencies and the programs and funds, ECOSOC formulates policy that is then forwarded to the General Assembly for discussion and approval. Early in its history, ECOSOC was involved in the spread of social work around the world, adopting a resolution on the necessity of training for social work in 1950 (Billups, 2002).

To develop the various policies on social development, ECOSOC uses a number of commissions as forums for input and debate. These include the Commission for Social Development (CSocD), the Commission on the Status of Women (CSW), and the Commission on Population and Development (CPD). Once policy has been agreed upon and proposed by ECOSOC, the member states, via the Third Committee and the General Assembly, may approve a legally binding resolution such as a convention or a covenant. Nations then have the option to ratify or accede to the convention or covenant, which signals their intent to implement its terms. Once the convention or covenant is effective, a committee is appointed to monitor its implementation. All legally binding conventions and covenants have committees to monitor their implementation by member states. See the chapters 66–69 in Section X for further information on the processes of adoption, ratification, and oversight of UN conventions and covenants.

The social development work of the Third Committee and of ECOSOC is supported by the Department of Economic and Social Affairs (DESA) within the UN Secretariat. In DESA, there are multiple divisions supporting social development, including the Division for the Advancement of Women (see Note 1), the Division for Social Policy and Development, and the Population Division (www.un.org/esa/desa/). The role of DESA is to provide member states with the information and expertise needed to achieve their objectives. Without DESA, the formulation of policy to advance social development objectives would be almost impossible.

Human Rights

The Human Rights Council (HRC) is a subsidiary body of the General Assembly and is responsible for coordinating and mainstreaming all human rights activities within the UN system (Ministry of Foreign Affairs and Trade, 2008). The part of the UN Secretariat that supports the HRC is the Office of the High Commissioner for Human Rights (OHCHR). The commissioner is appointed by the secretary-general and is the UN official responsible for global human rights efforts (Ministry of Foreign Affairs and Trade, 2008).

The OHCHR also provides support to the eight committees that monitor the legal conventions ratified by the General Assembly. These eight committees are the Human Rights Committee; the Committee on Economic, Social and Cultural Rights; the Committee on the Elimination of Racial Discrimination; the Committee on the Elimination of Discrimination against Women; the Committee Against Torture; the Committee on the Rights of the Child; the Committee on the Protection of the Rights of All Migrant Workers and Members of their Families; and the Committee on the Rights of Persons with Disabilities.

Most of the conventions that these committees monitor were initiated and proposed by ECOSOC and its functioning commissions, which illustrates the crossover between social development and human rights. For example, the Committee on the Rights of Persons with Disabilities aims to improve the lives of people with disabilities, but at the same time it necessarily protects their human rights. One other function of ECOSOC that is common to human rights and social development is ECOSOC's role as the portal through which nongovernmental organizations (NGOs) participate in the activities of the UN system; ECOSOC can grant consultative status (general, special, and roster) to NGOs who apply. This status allows the NGOs to be involved in many aspects of UN work. Currently over 3000 NGOs have consultative status (DESA, n.d.). Among them are the International Association of Schools of Social Work (IASSW), International Federation of Social Workers (IFSW), and International Council on Social Welfare (ICSW).

HUMAN RIGHTS AND SOCIAL DEVELOPMENT IN THE UN SPECIALIZED AGENCIES, PROGRAMS AND FUNDS, RESEARCH AND TRAINING INSTITUTES, AND OTHER UN ENTITIES

There are fifteen specialized agencies, nine programs and funds, five research and training institutes, and four other UN entities, not counting some of the subsidiary groups of these thirty-four organizations. Because human rights and social development are at the center of UN work, many of these organizations have programs and projects to advance human rights and enhance social development, but it is beyond the scope of this chapter to describe the relevant work of all these organizations. Examples that may illustrate some of the differences and similarities are the ILO (specialized agency), UNICEF (program and fund), UNDP (program and fund), UNRISD (research and training institute) and UNAIDS (other UN entity).

The ILO differs from all other specialized agencies in that it brings together governments, employers, and employees. It has eighteen main themes, including reducing the use of child labor, promoting economic growth to reduce poverty, creating decent work for all, removing discrimination and promoting equality in the workplace, and providing adequate social protection in all countries (ILO, n.d.). These themes indicate how ILO activities connect with certain programs and funds such as UNICEF and some of the functional commissions of ECOSOC such as the Commission on the Status of Women.

The focus areas of UNICEF are child survival and development; basic education and gender equality; HIV, AIDS, and children; child protection; and policy advocacy and partnerships (UNICEF, n.d.). The fund is active in 190 countries through direct programs led by national committees. In addition to its familiar role of supplying emergency relief at times of disaster, UNICEF also supports programs such as the education and counseling centers run by Vite-n-Hope, which provide children who are at high risk of sexual exploitation with basic literacy and numeric skills (UNICEF, 2008).

The UNDP and its subsidiary program and funds—the United Nations Development Fund for Women (UNIFEM, see Note 1), United Nations Volunteers (UNV), and United Nations Capital Development Fund (UNCDF)—have the primary responsibility for coordinating development work around the world. They have operations in 166 countries, supporting each country's efforts to improve the lives of their people specifically in the areas of poverty reduction, HIV and AIDS, democratic governance, crisis prevention and recovery, and the environment and energy. It also develops the capacity of local people to sustain these development efforts and particularly emphasizes the empowerment of women (UNDP, n.d.).

As mentioned, UNRISD is one of five UN research and training institutions. Based in Geneva and working via a global network of researchers, UNRISD carries out research in six areas: social policy and development; democracy governance and well-being; markets, business, and regulation; civil society and social movements; identities, conflict, and cohesion; and gender and development (UNRISD, n.d.). It provides information and reports to all parts of the UN involved in the various facets of social development.

One of four other UN entities, UNAIDS is a unique organization in that it is cosponsored by ten other UN organizations: six programs and funds (UNICEF, UNDP, UNFPA, UNESCO, WFP, and UNHCR), three specialized agencies (ILO, WHO, and the World Bank), and the UN Office on Drugs and Crime (UNODC). The UNAIDS Secretariat, based in Geneva, operates via regional support teams whose objectives are to halt the epidemic by preventing new infections, to expand access to treatment, to care and provide support for people living with HIV and AIDS, and to expand care, protection, and support for orphans and families affected by the disease (UNAIDS, n.d.). The organization is a formalization of the cooperation of various UN entities that are involved in the same social problem, but similar informal cooperation between UN entities is prevalent for many social issues.

The UN System in Action

The UN system is the source of some of the most important data on global human rights and social development. Typical examples are the Human Development Index (HDI) issued by UNDP, which ranks countries based on their human development achievements (UNDP, 2008); the World Bank's annual World Development Report (WDR), which describes the economic, social, and environmental state of the world (World Bank, n.d.); and the ILO's Global Employment Trends (GET), which reviews the world of work (ILO, 2009).

The UN system also sets global objectives for human development. Spurred by General Assembly resolutions and supported by the Secretariat, the United Nations held eight major international conferences between 1992 and 1996 that discussed human rights and social development (United Nations Information Centre for the Caribbean Area, 2001). These included the World Conference on Human Rights in Vienna in 1993, the World Summit for Social Development in Copenhagen in 1995, and the World Conference on Women in Beijing, also in 1995. These conferences, attended by many heads of state, resulted in declarations and plans of action that set social development goals for all member states. The Copenhagen Declaration and Programme for Action can be found at www.un.org/documents/ga/conf166/aconf166-9.htm. The Beijing Declaration and Platform for Action can be found at www.un.org/womenwatch/daw/beijing/pdf/BDPfA%20E.pdf.

More recently, the General Assembly passed a resolution to hold a world summit in 2000, which resulted in the Millennium Declaration adopted by 189 nations and signed by 147 heads of states and governments (Millennium Development Goals

Indicators, n.d.). Eight Millennium Development Goals (MDGs) were established that set quantifiable targets for social development to be achieved by 2015. The MDGs are a remarkable example of the nations of the world coming together under the auspices of the United Nations to define how and by how much the lives of people could and should be improved. The MDGs can be found in Appendix C of this volume and at www.undp.org/mdg/basics.shtml.

CONCLUSION

The United Nations is not without its critics, but as Winston Peters states, "The United Nations is the world's most vital international institution. Only in the United Nations do all countries come together to devise solutions to and forge collective action on global challenges" (Ministry of Foreign Affairs and Trade, 2008). To respond to these global challenges, which change in nature and priority, and to answer some of the criticisms, the UN is striving for continuous improvement.

For example, in 2007, the One UN pilot was initiated in eight countries (Albania, Cape Verde, Mozambique, Pakistan, Rwanda, Tanzania, Uruguay, and Vietnam). It is not uncommon for multiple UN specialized agencies and UN funds and programs, such as UNDP, UNESCO, WHO, UNFPA, UNHCR, and UNICEF, to have operations in a single country. The intent of One UN was to streamline the work of these multiple agencies by allocating funds from a single budget and nominating the in-country head of UNDP as the in-country UN representative rather than just the head of UNDP. This resulted in saving money; for instance, "in Albania alone, [moving different agencies to single premises] will save $500,000 in the first year" (Itano, 2007, p. 4).

In 2009 at the end of the sixty-third session of the General Assembly, the General Assembly president, Miguel d'Escoto Brockmann, asked the secretary-general to report on the One UN pilot in the next General Assembly session, with a view to extending the concept to additional countries. As Tanzania commented in the same meeting, "the reform process of system-wide coherence at the country level had been 'transformative' in many development areas . . . and had conferred national ownership of the development process in partnership with the United Nations" ("General Assembly president says United Nations must be urgently 'reinvented,'" 2009). This request by the outgoing president to extend the One UN pilot was only one of many far-reaching improvements to the UN system recommended by Brockmann. Like all large organizations, the United Nations can perform more efficiently and effectively, provided that the member states have the collective will to make the necessary changes.This chapter has emphasized that the UN is better represented as the UN system, whose major activity is to improve the lives of people around the world. The member states are at the heart of the system, but there are 40,000 nonaligned individuals in the Secretariat who work tirelessly to support (and sometimes cajole) the member states as they advance human rights and enhance social development. In addition, the UN system has thirty-four more organizations to support the efforts of member states in improving the lives of people in their countries.

NOTE

1. In July 2010, the General Assembly created a new UN entity to address women's issues, the UN Entity for Gender Equity and the Empowerment of Women. The new body, more commonly referred to as UN Women, merged four existing bodies: the Division for the Advancement of Women (DAW); the International Research and Training Institute for the Advancement of Women (INSTRAW); the Office of the Special Advisory on Gender Issues and the Advancement of Women (OSAGI); and the UN Development Fund for Women (UNIFEM). More information about the new entity can be found at www. unwomen.org.

REFERENCES

Billups, J. (2002). *Faithful angels: International social work notables of the late 20ᵗʰ century*. Washington, DC: NASW Press.

General Assembly President says United Nations must be urgently 'reinvented,' as time for reform has passed, in closing statement to 63rd session. (2009, September 16). *US Fed News Service, Including US State News*. Retrieved September 16, 2009, from ProQuest database.

International Court of Justice. (n.d.). The Court. Retrieved September 9, 2009, from www.icj-cij.org/court/index. php?p1=1.

International Labour Organization (ILO). (n.d.). Themes. Retrieved September 11, 2009, from www.ilo.org/global/Themes/lang–en/index.htm.

International Labour Organization (ILO). (2009, January 28). Global employment trends. Retrieved September 18, 2009, from www.ilo.org/global/About_the_ILO/Media_and_public_information/Press_releases/lang–en/WCMS_101462/index.htm#1.

Itano, N. (2007, June 28). Bold gambit for disjointed UN: Oneness. *Christian Science Monitor*, 4.

Kendall, K. A. (1994). The challenges of internationalism in social work: Past, present and future. In L. Healy (Ed.), *The global-local link: International challenges to social work practice* (pp. 3–11). West Hartford, CT: University of Connecticut School of Social Work, Center for International Social Work Studies.

Millennium Development Goals Indicators. (n.d.). The Millennium Declaration. Retrieved September 12, 2009, from http://mdgs.un.org.

Ministry of Foreign Affairs and Trade. (2008). *UN handbook 2008/9.* Wellington, New Zealand: Author.

UNAIDS (Joint UN Programme on HIV/AIDS). (n.d.). UNAIDS regional support teams. Retrieved September 11, 2009, from www.unaids.org/en/AboutUNAIDS/Secretariat/unaids_country_offices.asp.

United Nations Children's Fund (UNICEF). (n.d.). What we do. Retrieved September 11, 2009, from www.unicef.org/whatwedo/index.html.

United Nations Children's Fund (UNICEF). (2008, June 27). Info by country: Pakistan. Retrieved September 11, 2009, from www.unicef.org/infobycountry/pakistan_44654.html.

United Nations Department of Economic and Social Affairs (DESA). (n.d.). NGO branch. Introduction to consultative status. Retrieved September 12, 2009, from www.un.org/ecosoc/ngo/index.html.

United Nations Department of Public Information (UNDPI). (2008). *The UN today.* New York: Author.

United Nations Development Programme (UNDP). (n.d.). About UNDP. Retrieved September 11, 2009, from www.undp.org/about/.

United Nations Development Programme (UNDP). (2008). *Human development reports.* Retrieved September 17, 2009 at http://hdr.undp.org/

United Nations General Assembly. (n.d.). Main committees. Retrieved September 18, 2009, from www.un.org/ga/maincommittees.shtml.

United Nations General Assembly. (2008). *Composition of the Secretariat.* (Document A/63/310). New York: Author.

United Nations Information Centre for the Caribbean Area. (2001). *Major UN conferences since 1992.* Retrieved September 11, 2009, from www.nalis.gov.tt/National-UNDays/UN_INTERNATIONALCONFERENCES.html.

United Nations Research Institute for Social Development. (n.d.). Research. Retrieved September 11, 2009, from www.unrisd.org.

United Nations Security Council. (n.d.). Background. Retrieved September 18, 2009, from www.un.org/Docs/sc/unsc_background.html.

United Nations System Chief Executives Board for Coordination (CEB). (n.d.). Reference material: UN system. Retrieved September 9, 2009, from www.unsceb.org/ceb/home.

World Bank. (n.d.). *World development reports.* Retrieved September 18, 2009, from www.worldbank.org.

Nongovernmental Organizations and Global Social Change

KATHRYN LIBAL AND SCOTT HARDING

A hallmark of the twentieth and early twenty-first centuries has been the emergence of civil society as a force for social change. Healy (2008) defines *international civil society* as "those nongovernmental/ nonprofit organizations that have cross-border linkages" (pp. 366–367). Thus, it entails political processes and relationships that are established outside a given nation-state and its control. Globalization has facilitated the emergence of international civil society through the development of new communication technologies, advances in transportation, and increasing interdependency between nation-states and regions. A variety of nongovernmental organizations (NGOs) have been at the forefront of advocacy for a more just global social order, tackling persistent social inequalities and addressing such macro processes as the global economy and trade, war and armed conflict, international migration, and the realization of human rights, to name a few important domains.

THE RISE OF NGO INFLUENCE ON GLOBAL POLICY AND POLITICS

Since the 1970s, NGOs have been critical actors in local, national, and global processes to promote social development, welfare, and human rights (Roff, 2004). These organizations address humanitarian relief, social development, and human rights concerns at national, regional, and international levels. Some NGOs are primarily service organizations; others do not provide any services but rather focus efforts on advocacy. As NGOs have grown in size and expanded their missions, some relief and development organizations have developed advocacy initiatives as well. Many service-based, operational organizations now work in coalitions on specific short-term campaigns and have networks they can activate for persistent or emerging social problems. In recent years, the division

between humanitarian and development NGOs has become increasingly blurred as protracted crises that have developed because of chronic conflict or environmental disaster fail to be easily solved with short-term direct assistance.

There is a wide range of NGOs in terms of size, purpose, scope, and type of work as well as in terms of their relationships with communities, states, and other organizations (Fisher, 1997). According to the World Bank, NGOs are "private organizations that pursue activities to relieve suffering, promote the interests of the poor, protect the environment, provide basic social services, or undertake community development" (cited in World Association of Non-Governmental Organizations, 2009). Though the term *NGO* can vary in meaning, consensus exists that an NGO must be independent from direct governmental control, it cannot be a political party, it must be nonprofit, and it cannot be a criminal group (Willetts, 2002).

The term *NGO* gained recognition due to the United Nations' efforts to distinguish intergovernmental agency work, such as that of the UN Children's Fund (UNICEF) and the UN Development Programme (UNDP), from the work of other international private organizations. A number of NGOs in the Global North have histories that predate the United Nations, including Save the Children, the International Rescue Committee, and the International Federation of Red Cross and Red Crescent Societies. Such organizations initially focused on humanitarian aid, though over time Save the Children and the International Rescue Committee have initiated development-oriented programming as well as direct political advocacy.

Since the founding of the United Nations in 1945, intergovernmental UN agencies and NGOs have collaborated and sometimes been at odds in humanitarian and development work (UN Department of Economic and Social Affairs, 2009). Following World War II, 41 international NGOs were accorded consultative status with the UN Economic and Social Council (ECOSOC). This gave the NGOs access to intergovernmental advocacy processes and allowed them to work alongside UN agencies in implementing human rights, development, and humanitarian relief programs. In 1992, the number of NGOs with consultative status had risen to more than 700, and by 2009 it had risen to almost 3200. The International Council on Social Welfare (ICSW) and the International Association of Schools of Social Work (IASSW) were among the NGOs granted consultative status in the 1940s.

The expansion of NGO development and relief efforts, as well as rising influence in advocacy and policy making at national and global levels by these groups, is linked to the effects of economic globalization, increased armed conflict, and other humanitarian disasters. The failure of nation-states and the global community to ensure social development and human rights for most people also makes NGOs critical actors (Florini & Simmons, 2000; Lindenberg & Bryant, 2001; Nelson & Dorsey, 2008). UN agencies, as with donor countries to the United Nations, prefer to contract with NGOs, who in turn provide humanitarian and development services to vulnerable populations and those affected by war, famine, and natural disaster.

The proliferation of NGOs has been referred to by some as the "NGOification" of aid and development (Fisher, 1997). This process is linked to neoliberal models of economic growth that stress the need to cut taxes and public spending and to reduce state-run programs that promote social development and social welfare. Thus, a growing reliance on NGOs to deliver aid and administer programming must be seen as part of the devolution of responsibilities once thought to be best administered by states. Over time this led civil society organizations and other nonprofit and for-profit groups to assume many of the key functions related to these activities (Fisher & Karger, 1997).

Although the number of NGOs active in national and international development and humanitarian work has grown enormously in the past forty years, the organizations with the most international influence are concentrated in the Global North (Nelson & Dorsey, 2008). Northern NGOs typically have a longer history, have a bigger infrastructure, receive the majority of international relief and development funds, and have greater access to influencing global policy. Organizations from the Global South have grown in influence since the 1990s, particularly at the national level, but they often rely more heavily upon coalition building and linking with northern NGOs when advocating for policy change at the international level.

As noted earlier, the lines between development and humanitarian organizations have blurred as northern NGOs such as Oxfam International, Save the Children, CARE, World Vision, and Mercy Corps have moved to create programming that addresses both domains. For example, the US-based International Medical Corps (IMC) ostensibly began in the mid-1980s as a relief organization focusing on health provision in humanitarian crisis situations, but it has expanded its programming to include training medical personnel and implementing development programs. It receives millions of dollars in funding from the US government in addition to the funds it raises within the private sector. The group has gained considerable clout in the US Congress and State Department, and thus it is positioned to shape US policies and funding for global humanitarian and development assistance.

Many NGOs from the Global South began at a local, grassroots level and have expanded to become transnational organizations loosely linked through confederations or global networks. Examples of these include the Grameen Bank model of microcredit lending founded in Bangladesh in the 1970s and other economic justice organizations such as the Bangladesh Rural Advancement Committee (BRAC) and the India-based Self Employed Women's Association (SEWA). For example, BRAC asserts that with some 100,000 employees serving 110 million people, it is the largest southern NGO working on development and human rights issues in Asia and Africa (BRAC, n.d.; Smillie, 2009). It now has affiliate organizations in the United States and United Kingdom to mobilize support for development work in the Global South. Through public education and cultivating partnerships, they aim to create "a global network that share[s] values and vision" and "bring[s] together the knowledge, innovation and entrepreneurship to build scalable, sustainable solutions to poverty, disease, illiteracy and environmental degradation around the world" (BRAC, n.d.).

Accountability and Transparency
Many people idealize NGOs as a panacea to the failures of corrupt or weak states and view them as vanguards of democratization, in part because of their stated emphasis on grassroots participation and civic

engagement (Velloso de Santisteban, 2005). Though NGOs are crucial in service delivery and policy advocacy on behalf of vulnerable groups, they also have been subject to criticism for an alleged lack of transparency and accountability, corruption, and inconsistent efforts to integrate the views of local populations into their programming. Scrutiny of NGO work is merited given the enormous resources that are channeled to these organizations and the increasing reliance on them to implement social development and humanitarian programs. NGO Watch, a joint project of the U.S.-based think tanks American Enterprise Institute for Public Policy Research and Federalist Society for Law and Public Policy Studies, monitors international development, relief, and human rights NGOs. In general its work reflects a conservative perspective that challenges the efficacy of international institutions and critiques many NGOs for engaging in biased advocacy on progressive economic and social justice reform.

In response to such criticisms, many international NGOs voluntarily engage in transparency and accountability initiatives. In an effort to address corruption by governments and nongovernmental bodies, Transparency International was formed in the 1990s (Galtung, 2000). This organization successfully initiated a movement for good governance and accountability by NGOs, UN agencies, and national governments. As another example, Humanitarian Accountability Partnership (HAP) International produces an annual report examining corruption and the quality of aid delivery by NGOs and UN agencies. Its 2008 report highlighted a continued need for accountability and quality services in a context where relief and development efforts involve multiple agencies, governments, and NGOs (HAP International, 2009). The NGOs that agree to be monitored by HAP engage in dialogue about developing more effective humanitarian programs and endeavor to overcome deficiencies identified in the monitoring process.

ADVOCACY TO ADDRESS STRUCTURAL ROOTS OF GLOBAL SOCIAL PROBLEMS

Increasingly, an important locus of NGO work is advocacy to promote global social change. Historically the major international development and humanitarian NGOs emphasized service delivery and development projects. Since the 1990s, however, most large organizations now devote resources to advocacy and policy-making efforts in an attempt to tackle the root causes of global social problems.

Advocacy by NGOs has been defined as working for policy change and action to address structural causes of global social problems, "not simply speaking out to alert people of a problem in order to raise funds to support operational work" (Lindenberg & Bryant, 2001, p. 173). As these scholars note, "The scale of modern global social problems as well as the perception that the forces behind them transcend traditional political boundaries and jurisdictions has led many NGOs to explore a more active stance toward advocacy" (p. 175).

Advocacy may be carried out at different levels and with different targets. It may involve mobilizing people through outreach, education, and promotion of constituent lobbying in support of campaigns. An example of this is Amnesty International's Stop Violence Against Women Campaign, which entails public education and mobilization as well as building transnational awareness and linkages to pressure international agencies to address violence against women. Advocacy can be achieved through raising awareness and applying pressure directly on governments or through UN consultation processes. Service-based organizations are often in a unique position to shape global policy, particularly if they have direct insights into human rights, humanitarian, or social development concerns through their programming. Because they are often directly linked to affected individuals and communities, NGOs have the capacity to represent the interests of recipients (Healy, 2008).

Forming Alliances and Coalitions: NGOs and Transnational Advocacy Networks

A number of influential NGO coordination bodies or caucuses have formed over the past twenty years to promote coordination of work and to amplify advocacy efforts. Coordinating bodies are concentrated in the Global North, though some notable southern alliances have formed. The Geneva-based International Council of Voluntary Agencies, established in 1962 as an alliance of NGOs from northern and southern countries, works on development, humanitarian action, and human rights (Walker & Maxwell, 2008). In the United States, InterAction (the American Council for Voluntary International Action) is the largest coalition of US-based international NGOs, including more than 177 member organizations. Established in 1974, InterAction's coalition work is crucial to developing effective responses to global social problems and the formation of policy responses. InterAction has considerable access to US policy-making bodies and plays a key role in coordinating efforts among US-based international NGOs.

An example of a southern NGO coalition is the Southern Caucus of NGOs for Sustainable Development, which was founded in 1994. The Southern Caucus helps disadvantaged communities in developing countries to access information and resources in order to form plans for sustainable development at local and national levels. They also perform advocacy at national and international levels to develop plans of action for eliminating poverty and promoting sustainable economic, social, and environmental development.

Peace Building and Human Rights Advocacy

Many peace-building and human rights NGOs are engaged in advocacy as a primary mission, organizing constituencies and lobbying governments or international bodies such as the World Trade Organization and World Bank in the pursuit of social development initiatives, human rights, and other concerns. Organizations that advocate for human rights play crucial roles in holding governments accountable by applying public pressure via grassroots or constituent mobilization, media and Internet campaigning, and direct dialogue with governments and UN agencies. They also participate in formal monitoring processes of UN human rights treaties by submitting shadow reports that are read by UN human rights committee members along with the official country reports submitted by government parties. Not only do NGOs have an opportunity to submit documentation that may challenge government portrayals of progress or compliance on specific issues, but they are also afforded access to human rights committees conducting country reviews and can engage UN officials directly. Moreover, some NGOs provide input to governments as they develop human rights programs and evaluation, thus creating another channel for advocacy.

Human Rights Watch and Amnesty International are two prominent human rights NGOs engaged in such advocacy since the 1970s. Through investigating and publishing reports on key human rights concerns worldwide, these NGOs seek to influence governments and other international agencies to enforce international human rights standards. The Internet has facilitated this work, allowing journalists, activists, and civil society organizations to access information in their own advocacy efforts. An example of this has been Amnesty International's campaign to challenge the use of torture and harsh interrogation techniques and indefinite detention used by governments like the United States and the United Kingdom in efforts to combat terrorism following the September 11, 2001 attacks in the United States.

Transnational advocacy networking, or NGO-led mobilization across nation-state boundaries, has emerged as a major force in challenging policies and actions of states on human rights issues, the environment, and violence against women. Keck and Sikkink (1998) argue that through linkages among grassroots organizations, local organizations, and larger international NGOs, these groups have the capacity to reach governments that might otherwise ignore the demands of local groups. Successful transnational NGO advocacy has included a global campaign to ban landmines (Mekata, 2000), initiatives to secure debt relief by wealthy countries for the poorest southern countries (Nelson & Dorsey, 2003), and efforts to modify aspects of the economic structural adjustment programs (SAPs) that are required by international lending institutions and that undermine social and economic well-being in developing countries (Abouharb & Cingranelli, 2008).

One of the earliest successful examples of such advocacy networks was developed in Latin America in the 1970s and 1980s. Domestic and international NGOs such as the Mothers of the Plaza de Mayo in Argentina and the Mexican Academy of Human Rights have worked alongside Amnesty International, Americas Watch, and the Washington Office on Latin America to urge the UN and regional human rights bodies to investigate a range of human rights abuses. These groups have successfully pressed the UN Commission on Human Rights (now the Human Rights Council), the UN Human Rights Committee (which oversees the implementation of the International Covenant on Civil and Political Rights), and the Inter-American Commission on Human Rights to investigate egregious violations of civil and political liberties carried out by Chile, Peru, Argentina, and Mexico. As a result of truth commissions and criminal indictments, former dictators, such as Augusto Pinochet of Chile, were successfully prosecuted for human rights abuses. Without global NGO pressure, a climate of impunity would have persisted in many of these countries following the so-called dirty wars from the 1970s to the 1990s.

Willetts (2002) finds that coalition building by NGOs has become a key process for groups that seek to influence national or international social policy. Because of advances in global communications technology and media that are widely available through satellite broadcasts and the web, the scale of such linkages and coalition building has expanded enormously, and with it, the influence of NGOs to shape policy related to human rights, environmental justice, and social development has been strengthened (Keck & Sikkink, 1998). New technologies enable NGOs to better communicate with one another through private intranet systems and allow them to launch sophisticated media and web-based campaigns in support of advocacy goals (Lindenberg & Bryant, 2001). Effective collaboration with the mainstream media can sometimes serve as a lever to address policy concerns, as occurred with a campaign in the mid-2000s to draw attention to ethnic cleansing and the ongoing conflict in Darfur (Haeri, 2008; Hamilton & Hazlett, 2007).

Often such coalitions work together to influence the creation of UN treaties and policies, such as recent efforts to accord violence against women and children the status of human rights violations. Amnesty International, Human Rights Watch, the US-based Center for Women's Global Leadership, and a host of other domestic and international NGOs worked collaboratively over the past fifteen years on advocacy at national, regional, and international levels. Notably, NGO actors successfully pressed the UN secretary-general to appoint a special rapporteur on violence against women and to launch a multicountry investigation of this issue (Keck & Sikkink, 1998). Out of those efforts, the UN General Assembly passed a series of resolutions to direct interagency efforts on eliminating violence against women and has begun to devote more resources to researching and funding initiatives that seek to redress such violence. Similar work at the United Nations, in cooperation with states and NGOs, is now being conducted regarding violence against children. Taken together, NGO advocacy has resulted in the development of UN-based mechanisms to hold states accountable for implementing policies that reduce violence within families and communities worldwide.

Faith-Based NGOs

Many of the most influential NGOs are faith-based organizations, often connected through confederations of churches, synagogues, or mosques that at times transcend national boundaries. Caritas Internationalis, for example, runs projects globally that address humanitarian, development, and social justice initiatives. They are also involved in domestic and international advocacy on behalf of the vulnerable groups they serve. Increasingly, faith-based NGOs are involved in high-level advocacy for the rights of migrant workers in wealthy countries, particularly

when those workers are undocumented and face arbitrary arrest, detention, and deportation.

Episcopal Migration Ministries (EMM) in the United States, for example, lobbies at state and federal levels to overturn punitive national immigration policies. In 2005 they signed the Interfaith Statement in Support of Comprehensive Immigration Reform (EMM, 2005). Along with hundreds of other NGOs, EMM also expressed support for a European Union–based campaign to press European countries to ratify the UN International Convention on the Protection of the Rights of All Migrant Workers and Members of Their Families (UN, 1990). As part of that campaign, Inter Pares (Canada) and Oxfam Novib (Netherlands) provide operational support to December 18, the International Resource Centre on the Human Rights of Migrants. This NGO mobilizes other NGOs to press EU countries to ratify the convention, which has been one of the most challenging campaigns initiated in recent years. By 2010 no northern country had joined the treaty.

Social Work and NGO Advocacy

Social workers increasingly staff local and international NGOs, whether they are providing direct or indirect services, working as community organizers, or serving in advocacy and policy-making roles. These organizations often help generate "community-led, issue-driven efforts towards social change" (Roff, 2004, p. 203) that are consonant with the social work strengths perspective promoting community participation, self-reliance, and advocacy for social justice (Saleeby, 1992). Nonetheless, research on professional social workers' roles and the impact of international social work on NGO advocacy and service provision has been limited. Claiborne (2004) finds that although social workers increasingly serve as project directors and coordinators in service-based and participatory NGOs, they are rarely represented in leadership and administrative positions.

Healy (2008) frames policy advocacy as one of the key dimensions of international social work, noting that developing the capacity of social work to create and implement policy on global social problems is central to the profession's mandate. The participation of representatives of professional associations (e.g., the International Federation of Social Workers [IFSW] and IASSW) in a variety of NGO forums paralleling UN conferences on social development, human rights, and humanitarianism is one important way in which social work influences these policy processes. These organizations use their consultative status to monitor relevant UN issues and to provide input to other NGOs and governments (see Chapter 16). For instance, ICSW has become a significant force in the campaign for the adoption of the Social Protection Floor initiative. Yet social work, particularly in the United States, is often parochial in its focus, minimizing or ignoring the severe global inequalities exacerbated by economic globalization and unequal access to power. Raising consciousness of global social problems among social work professionals, educators, and students, as well as working to increase participation within NGOs, are necessary steps to build leadership capacity to shape social change worldwide.

REFERENCES

Abouharb, M. R., & Cingranelli, D. L. (2008). *Human rights and structural adjustment*. New York: Cambridge University Press.

Bangladesh Rural Advancement Committee (BRAC). (n.d.). BRAC: Alleviation of poverty and empowerment of the poor. Retrieved June 1, 2009, from www.brac.net/index.php?nid=102.

Claiborne, N. (2004). Presence of social workers in nongovernmental organizations. *Social Work, 49*(2), 207–218.

Episcopal Migration Ministries (EMM). (2005). Interfaith statement in support of comprehensive immigration reform. Retrieved June 1, 2009, from www.episcopalchurch.org/documents/InterfaithStatement.doc.

Fisher, W. F. (1997). Doing good? The politics and antipolitics of NGO practices. *Annual Review of Anthropology, 26*, 439–464.

Fisher, R. & Karger, H. (1997). *Social work and community in a private world: Getting out in public*. New York: Longman.

Florini, A. M., & Simmons, P. J. (2000). What the world needs now? In A. M. Florini (Ed.), *The third force: The rise of transnational civil society* (pp. 1–16). Washington, DC: Carnegie Endowment for International Peace.

Galtung, F. (2000). A global network to curb corruption: The experience of Transparency International. In A. M. Florini (Ed.), *The third force: The rise of transnational civil society* (pp. 17–48). Washington, DC: Carnegie Endowment for International Peace.

Haeri, M. (2008). Saving Darfur: Does advocacy help or hinder conflict resolution? *Praxis, 13*, 33–46.

Hamilton, R., & Hazlett, C. (2007). "Not on our watch": The emergence of the American movement for Darfur. In A. de Waal (Ed.), *War in Darfur and the search for peace* (pp. 337–366). Cambridge, MA: Harvard University Global Initiative.

Healy, L. M. (2008). *International social work: Professional action in an interdependent world* (2nd ed.). New York: Oxford University Press.

Humanitarian Accountability Partnership (HAP) International. (2009). *The 2008 humanitarian accountability report*. Retrieved May 15, 2009, from www.hapinternational.org/pool/files/2008-humanitarian-accountability-report.pdf.

Keck, M. E., & Sikkink, K. (1998). *Activists beyond borders: Advocacy networks in international politics*. Ithaca, NY: Cornell University Press.

Lindenberg, M., & Bryant, C. (2001). *Going global: Transforming relief and development NGOs*. Bloomfield, CT: Kumarian Press.

Mekata, M. (2000). Building partnerships toward a common goal: Experiences of the international campaign to ban landmines. In A. M. Florini (Ed.), *The third force: The rise of transnational civil society* (pp. 143–176). Washington, DC: Carnegie Endowment for International Peace.

Nelson, P. J., & Dorsey, E. (2008). *New rights advocacy: Changing strategies of development and human rights NGOs*. Washington, DC: Georgetown University Press.

Nelson, P. J., & Dorsey, E. (2003). At the nexus of human rights and development: New methods and strategies of global NGOs. *World Development, 31*(12), 2013–2026.

Roff, S. (2004). Nongovernmental organizations: The strengths perspective at work. *International Social Work, 47*(2), 202–212.

Saleeby, D. (1992). Introduction: Power in the people. In D. Saleeby (Ed.), *The strengths perspective in social work practice* (pp. 3–20). New York: Longman.

Smillie, I. (2009). *Freedom from want: The remarkable success story of BRAC, the global grassroots organization that's winning the fight against poverty*. Sterling, VA: Kumarian Press.

United Nations (UN). (1990). International convention on the protection of the rights of all migrant workers and members of their families. Retrieved July 10, 2009, from www2.ohchr.org/english/law/cmw.htm.

United Nations Department of Economic and Social Affairs. (2009). *Consultative status with ECOSOC*. Retrieved June 4, 2009, from www.un.org/esa/coordination/ngo/.

Velloso de Santisteban, A. (2005). The poor will always be with us—and so will NGOs. *Development in Practice, 15*(2), 200–209.

Walker, P., & Maxwell, D. (2008). *Shaping the humanitarian world*. New York: Routledge.

Willetts, P. (2002). What is a non-governmental organization? In *UNESCO encyclopedia of life support systems*. Retrieved May 25, 2009, from www.staff.city.ac.uk/p.willetts/CS-NTWKS/NGO-ART.HTM.

World Association of Non-Governmental Organizations. (2009). What are non-governmental organizations (NGOs)? Retrieved June 4, 2009, from www.ngohandbook.org/index.php?title=What_are_Non-Governmental_Organizations_(NGOs)%3F.

WEBSITES FOR NGOs MENTIONED IN THIS CHAPTER

Americas Watch: www.americaswatch.net.

Amnesty International: www.amnesty.org.

Bangladesh Rural Advancement Committee (BRAC): www.brac.net.

CARE: www.care.org.

Center for Women's Global Leadership: www.cwgl.rutgers.edu.

December 18: International Resource Centre on the Human Rights of Migrants: www.december18.net.

Grameen Bank: www.grameen-info.org.

Human Rights Watch: www.hrw.org.

Humanitarian Accountability Partnership: www.hapinternational.org.

InterAction: www.interaction.org/index2.html.

International Committee of the Red Cross: www.icrc.org.

International Council of Voluntary Agencies: www.icva.ch/about.html.

International Rescue Committee: www.theirc.org.

International Medical Corps: www.internationalmedical-corps.org.

Inter Pares (Canada): www.interpares.ca.

Mercy Corps: www.mercycorps.org.

Mexican Academy for Human Rights: www.amdh.org.mx.

Mothers of the Plaza de Mayo: www.madres.org.

Oxfam International: www.oxfam.org.

Save the Children: www.savethechildren.org.

Self Employed Women's Association: www.sewa.org.

Southern Caucus of NGOs for Sustainable Development: http://southsummit.dreamteamtech.com.

Transparency International: www.transparency.org.

World Vision: www.worldvision.org.

Regulators of the Global Economy: The IMF, the World Bank, and the WTO

PETA-ANNE BAKER AND KIMBERLY HINDS

The current global economic crisis and its consequences for the well-being of large sections of the world's population bring renewed attention to the role of global economic institutions such as the International Monetary Fund (IMF), the World Bank, and the World Trade Organization (WTO). These organizations play an active role in establishing the "rules of the game", as in the case of the IMF and the WTO, and in providing economic and technical resources, as in the case of the World Bank. In this chapter we review the origins, roles, and impact of these global financial and trade bodies. Following a description of efforts to make these organizations more responsive to the interests of those who are most disadvantaged, the chapter concludes by identifying ways in which social workers can participate in this process at local and global levels.

The IMF and the World Bank have been well known in the developing world for more than thirty years; for many of these countries, the IMF is the lender of last resort and the World Bank is one of the main sources of development financing. However, serving the needs of emerging and developing states was not part of the original mission of either of these organizations.

ORIGINS AND STRUCTURE OF THE IMF AND THE WORLD BANK

The IMF and World Bank were established in 1944 at the end of World War II. Also known as the Bretton Woods Institutions, after Bretton Woods, New Hampshire, United States, where the conference leading to their establishment was held, the two organizations were created to promote cooperation on trade and other economic matters, including the stabilization of exchange rates (see IMF articles at www.imf.org/ external/pubs/ft/aa/aa01.

htm http://www.imf.org/external/pubs/ft/aa/index. htm). These measures were perceived as necessary to prevent a recurrence of the Great Depression of the 1930s and to assist with the reconstruction of war-torn Europe. As such, their policy time lines were relatively short term, informed by the assumption that the economic and institutional frameworks of the beneficiary countries were sound and the countries only needed limited interventions to stimulate their recovery.

The World Bank comprises the International Bank for Reconstruction and Development (IBRD) and the International Development Association (IDA). The IBRD provides loans to middle-income countries and credit-worthy, low-income countries. The IDA, on the other hand, works exclusively with the world's poorest countries through the provision of interest-free loans and grants (World Bank, 2007). The bank frequently works in conjunction with regional and subregional financial institutions such as the Inter-American Development Bank and the Caribbean Development Bank (CDB).

An expanded group of agencies currently operate within the ambit of the World Bank. They are known as the World Bank Group (World Bank, 2007):

- The International Finance Corporation (IFC) provides financial support and technical assistance for private investment in developing countries.
- The Multilateral Investment Guarantee Agency (MIGA) provides insurance and mediation services to promote investment in politically unstable or other types of high-risk environments.
- The International Centre for Settlement of Investment Disputes (ICSID) handles investment disputes.

Over time and especially in response to the oil crisis of the 1970s and the debt crisis of the 1980s, the IMF and World Bank became increasingly involved in the economic and social affairs of developing countries and the emerging democracies of Eastern Europe. In fact, the IMF created special instruments, the Structural Adjustment Facility and the Enhanced Structural Adjustment Facility, to address the perceived needs of these countries (www.imf.org/external/about/histend.htm).

In 2009, some 185 countries were members of the IMF and the World Bank. (A country must be a member of the IMF in order to become a member of the World Bank.) The structures of both the IMF and World Bank are similar to traditional corporate entities. They are governed by boards of directors elected at the organizations' jointly held annual meetings. The largest shareholders (United States, Japan, Germany, Great Britain, and France) have the greatest power. The directors, who meet only once per year, elect executive directors, who make ongoing decisions about programs and loan applications.

In 2009, the World Bank Executive Director for the United States wielded 16.4% of the total votes, which amounted to 265,219 votes. Although Canada not only votes on its own behalf but also on behalf of eleven English-speaking Caribbean states and Ireland, in 2009 its Executive Director held 3.85% (or 62,217) of the total votes. The votes of forty-four African states (excluding Egypt, Ghana, and Tunisia), totaling 5.36% (or 85,449 votes), were cast by the Executive Directors from two countries: Liberia (3.36%) and Mauritius (1.92%) (see Table 49.1). Two of the most populous countries in the world, China and India, only hold about 6% of the total votes between them.

The major shareholding countries also control key staff appointments in the two agencies, notably the positions of President (World Bank) and Managing Director (IMF). By tradition, the President of the World Bank is a US citizen and the IMF Managing Director has always been a European. At the time of writing, the President of the World Bank Group is Robert B. Zoellick, and the IMF Managing Director is Christine Lagarde.

THE ROLE OF THE IMF AND WORLD BANK

There is a basic division of labor between the IMF and World Bank. The IMF's main contribution is not so much financial (it lends relatively small amounts of money) as political. A country that has an agreement in place with the IMF is seen by potential lenders and investors as taking steps to create an investment-friendly climate. Borrowing countries seek what is described as the IMF's "seal of good housekeeping."

Countries go to the IMF when they encounter problems with their *balance of payments*—that is, they are spending more on imported goods and services than they are earning from their exports. This results in a situation where the country has insufficient funds to secure its basic needs for more than a few months (usually two to three). The IMF can provide funds according to the member country's entitlement, called *Special Drawing Rights (SDRs)*, to help to stabilize the financial situation; this funding is usually referred to as a *stabilization package*. This is the least onerous form of funding because the amount available is within the value of the shares owned by the borrowing country. Additional funding can be provided on increasingly stringent terms. In exchange for this support, countries agree to undertake a range of policy measures that are intended to attract foreign investment and position the country on the road to economic growth.

The classic IMF policy prescription includes the devaluation of the local currency to make exports cheaper on the overseas market and the elimination or significant reduction of public-sector deficits, which is usually achieved by means of staff cuts, reductions in social spending, and the privatization of state-owned enterprises. These loan terms, known as *conditionalities*, are required because the IMF views the cause of the problem to be the excessive involvement of the state in the economic sphere, which distorts the functioning of the free market system (Harrigan & El-Said, 2000; Saner & Guilherme, 2007).

Structural Adjustment Programs

Structural adjustment programs (SAPs) are usually developed and implemented in tandem by the two agencies, and the parenthood of specific aspects is not always clear. However, IMF funds usually provide budgetary support while World Bank loans target designated sectors. Although there were earlier programs of this kind, notably in Chile (under Pinochet) and England (under Thatcher), SAPs became more widely known in the 1980s and 1990s as a host of countries in Africa, Latin America, and the Caribbean adopted the package of reforms involved. The primary purpose of an SAP is to reestablish "the primacy of the marketplace and the opening of the 'adjusting' economy to international trade" (Anderson & Witter, 1994, p. 12). This process increasingly came to include not only loans to reform the role of the state, making it

TABLE 49.1. VOTING POWERS OF SELECTED EXECUTIVE DIRECTORS
OF THE IMF AND WORLD BANK, 2009

Country of executive director	Votes on behalf of	World Bank		IMF	
		Total votes	% of all votes	Total votes	% of all votes
USA	USA	265,219	16.4	371,743	16.77
Japan	Japan	127,250	7.87	133,378	6.02
China	China	45,049	2.79	81,151	3.66
Canada	Antigua and Barbuda	62,217	3.85	80,636	3.64
	Bahamas				
	Barbados				
	Belize				
	Canada				
	Dominica				
	Grenada				
	Guyana				
	Ireland				
	Jamaica				
	St. Kitts and Nevis				
	St. Lucia				
	St. Vincent and the Grenadines				
Liberia (World Bank)	Angola	54,347	3.36	66,763	3.01
Sierra Leone (IMF)	Botswana				
	Burundi				
	Ethiopia				
	Gambia				
	Kenya				
	Lesotho				
	Liberia				
	Malawi				
	Mozambique				
	Namibia				
	Nigeria				
	Seychelles				
	Sierra Leone				
	South Africa				
	Sudan				
	Swaziland				
	Tanzania				
	Uganda				
	Zambia				
	Zimbabwe				
Chile	Argentina	37,499	2.32		
	Bolivia				
	Chile				
	Paraguay				
	Peru				
	Uruguay				

(Continued)

TABLE 49.1. (CONTINUED)

Country of executive director	Votes on behalf of	World Bank		IMF	
		Total votes	% of all votes	Total votes	% of all votes
Mauritius (World Bank) Rwanda (IMF)	Benin Burkina Faso Cameroon Cape Verde Central African Republic Chad Comoros Congo, Democratic Republic of Congo, Republic of Cote D'ivoire Djibouti Equatorial Guinea Gabon Guinea Guinea-Bissau Madagascar Mali Mauritius Niger Rwanda São Tomé and Principe Senegal Togo	31,102	1.92	29,855	1.35
All		1,616,804	100	2,214,607	99.93

Sources: International Bank for Reconstruction and Development—Voting power of executive directors. Retrieved June 22, 2009, from http://siteresources.worldbank.org/ BODINT/Resources/278027-1215524804501/IBRDEDsVotingTable.pdf.
IMF executive directors and voting power. Retrieved June 22, 2009, from www.imf.org/.external/np/sec/memdir/eds.htm.

a facilitator or enabler of economic development, but also loans to support the reform and development of the labor market, including support for education and health.

As the negative impact of SAPs gained increasing attention, the World Bank added social protection—measures to protect the poorest and most vulnerable groups in society—to its menu of programs (Holzmann, 2009; World Bank, 2001). The major instruments in Bank-authored social protection programs are the social fund and the implementation of social safety nets. Social funds are semiautonomous institutions that provide grants for local infrastructure and related projects. Although social funds were intended to be short-term interventions whose functions would be integrated into the actions of the central government authorities, many funds have continued far beyond the five-year timeline originally

envisaged (Glaessner, Lee, Sant'Anna, & de St. Antoine, 1994).

Social-fund projects include small-scale water supply systems, rural roads, and the construction or renovation of schools and health centers. The communities in which these projects are located must provide a percentage of the project cost, usually in the form of sweat equity. From 2002 to 2007, the bank loaned US$621 million and US$386 million for social-fund programs in sub-Saharan Africa and in Eastern Europe and Central Asia, respectively (Holzmann, Sipos, & the Social Protection Team, 2009).

Social safety net programs provide conditional cash transfers and access to basic educational and health services to targeted groups, particularly the very young and the elderly. Between 2002 and 2007, Bank spending on this type of program totaled US$3.401 million, with the Latin America and

Caribbean region receiving the largest portion of these funds at US$1.737 million (Holzmann et al., 2009).

THE FOCUS ON FREE TRADE

A new global organization, the World Trade Organization (WTO), joined the two Bretton Woods institutions in 1995. The WTO was the product of efforts to regulate trading relationships between countries. Its predecessor was the General Agreement on Tariffs and Trade (GATT), which came into force in 1948. Its members were primarily the world's major industrial powers and its focus was on lowering barriers to trade between countries. However, as global trading relationships expanded in both scope and complexity, the search began for a new mechanism of negotiation and cooperation. The WTO emerged after eight years of negotiation from a process known as the Uruguay Round (Ranjan, 2007). (Note that WTO negotiations and agreements traditionally take the name of the location where deliberations first began.)

As of July 2008, there were 153 WTO members, 117 of which were developing countries. Another 30 organizations were at the time of writing negotiating accession to membership. Decisions are made by member countries meeting in the Ministerial Council, which meets at least every two years. A General Council comprising ambassadorial representatives of member countries meets several times a year at the WTO headquarters in Geneva Switzerland. Ongoing decision making and negotiation occur in several specialized councils and committees charged with responsibility for the major portfolios of the organization, including trade in services (GATS) and intellectual property rights (TRIPS) (WTO, 2011).

A distinctive feature of the WTO is that unlike the IMF and the World Bank, WTO decisions are made by consensus among member countries themselves. In this regard, the structure of the WTO is more like the United Nations in that each member is of equal standing. However, fair trade campaigners argue that this similarity is more apparent than real since the process of becoming a member of the WTO called accession requires countries to liberalize their policies not only related to trade but also in sectors such as health and education (WTO, 2011).

Another characteristic of WTO membership is the application of the Most Favored Nation (MFN) rule, under which countries can make no distinction between national and foreign firms. This means, for example, that if a government makes loans available to

indigenous firms at concessionary rates, foreign firms must also receive this concession. In addition, any arrangement negotiated with a firm in one country must be equally available to firms from any other country.

The General Agreement on Trade in Services (GATS) is intended to promote increased investment (including foreign investment) in services in the health, education, and related sectors. Though subscription to this treaty is still voluntary, there are concerns that it could undermine the ability of the state to provide critical health and other services to low-income groups if it can be proven that this has a negative impact on the economic interests of private business. Pollock and Price (2000) describe GATS as "a complex, difficult-to-master set of rules that apply to all 160 service industries including water, telecommunications, health, and education" (p. 1995). There are also fears that the GATS regulations could prevent countries from taking action to prevent developments that could have negative environmental impacts. There are similar concerns that the treaty on Trade-Related Aspects of Intellectual Property Rights (TRIPS) could, among other things, undermine access to low-cost medications such as those used in the fight against HIV and AIDS (Love, 2007).

Advocates for fair trade argue that even if developing countries had the institutional capacity to implement the measures required by WTO regulations, they would be placed at a significant disadvantage relative to more-developed countries (Wallach, 2005). In addition, it has been shown that the United States and the European Union (EU) exercise a disproportionate amount of influence in the WTO (Pollock & Price, 2000).

> To many developing countries who have been subjected to International Monetary Fund (IMF) and World Bank "structural adjustment programs," the demands in the GATS-2000 negotiations to privatize essential public services and to radically deregulate private sector services repeat some of these institutions' most extreme—and in many instance now failed—policy requirements. For developing countries, committing to such demands in the GATS would lock in failed IMF and World Bank policies because under GATS they would be required to offer compensation to all WTO member countries if they sought to reverse the failed policies
> —(Wallach, 2005, p. 11)

ADVOCACY: CHALLENGING THE "THREE HORSEMEN OF THE APOCALYPSE"

The last thirty years have seen the emergence of a global movement aimed at reforming, if not stopping, what many have come to perceive as a significant threat to social well-being and the preservation of the planet. Given the scale of the challenge, it is perhaps not surprising that the language used to describe these efforts has mythical and religious overtones; the heading of this section has been borrowed from the title of a review essay by Benedicte Bull (2004).

Beginning with the formation of the Debt Crisis Network in 1986 and led by groups and organizations in the Global South, initial efforts focused on the debt crisis and the SAPs promoted by the IMF and World Bank. The movement gained momentum in 1990 when the All Africa Conference of Churches issued a call for the year 2000 to be a year of Jubilee, when the countries of Africa would be released from the debts owed to the international financial system. Many famous people, including Archbishop Desmond Tutu, UN Secretary-General Kofi Annan, pop singer Bono, and President Bill Clinton gave their support to Jubilee 2000, a grassroots campaign that ultimately involved hundreds of thousands of people in an international coalition of 110 organizations and national coalitions in sixty-nine countries (Barrett, 2000).

The movement targeted the most influential member countries of the IMF and World Bank to mobilize support within countries, governments, and the IMF and World Bank, asserting that their policies had not only failed but were contributing to people's further impoverishment. These claims were strengthened by developments such as the resignation of Joseph Stiglitz, who, after three years as Chief Economist at the World Bank, crafted what was probably the most public letter of resignation. He accused the IMF and World Bank of being dominated by doctrinaire free market theorists who refused to consider the evidence of the failure of their prescriptions (Stevenson, 1999). Even before Stiglitz's resignation, a multicountry study had found that IMF-imposed conditionalities were the single greatest obstacle to economic growth in the developing world (Bradshaw & Huang, 1991).

The Jubilee 2000 campaign demanded the cancellation of the debts of fifty-two developing countries that the campaigners deemed to be unpayable. These debts were valued at US$300 million. At the end of four years, commitments had been made to cancel approximately one-third of this amount, especially through the Heavily Indebted Poor Countries (HIPC) initiative. However, the realization of even this lower figure was undermined by the insistence of the global financial institutions that governments meet many of the same demands that formed part of their standard adjustment package.

Stiglitz (2003) has noted that both the IMF and World Bank have encouraged developing countries to open their economies to trade with the larger industrialized countries even while the latter maintain their own barriers and prevent the developing nations from taking advantage of their markets. He points out that the industrialized countries have continued to subsidize their agricultural sectors while forcing developing countries to remove subsidies in their own countries. Disagreement between the United States and the EU about the levels of agricultural subsidies was the single most significant contributor to the 2006 breakdown of negotiations on the implementation of the latest set of WTO regulations (the Doha Round).

Campaigns to change the policies of the IMF and the World Bank have gained impetus with the global financial crisis that emerged at the end of the first decade of the twentieth century. They have expanded to include the WTO, which is seen by many as the latest global economic institution to have taken up the cudgels on behalf of the world capitalist system. A significant feature of past and current campaigns has been the effort to make the deliberations of these organizations more transparent and sensitive to the interests of less powerful groups and countries.

Some progress has been made in relation to the World Bank, which has established ongoing working relationships with NGOs and has promoted the use of more participatory approaches in the planning, implementation, and evaluation of its programs. However, even in this case, there is the view that the changes have not gone far enough (Stuart, 2007), and neither the IMF nor the WTO have evidenced a desire for change (Kategekwa, 2009; Third World Network, 2009).[1]

WHAT ROLE FOR SOCIAL WORK?

The role that social workers can play emerges from the core principles of the profession. Notwithstanding official rhetoric, the global economic organizations described in this chapter have come to pose a substantial threat to the sovereignty (self-determination) and well-being of people, especially in developing countries and emerging democracies. Despite claims of less restrictive conditions for assistance to countries affected by the most recent global crisis, the actuality is very different: The countries that have returned to the IMF are facing the same harsh demands of the 1980s and 1990s (Third World Network, 2009).

In identifying the role to be played by social work, there is the real possibility that social workers may feel overwhelmed by size of the issue, which affects not only the lives of people far away but also their own personal and professional lives and the lives of their more immediate client systems (Dominelli, 1999). An important first task is to acquire an adequate understanding of this complex issue that does not lend itself to simple answers. In this regard, it is important to be prepared to be guided by those in the Global South who have had the most extensive experience with the policies of these global institutions and who have accumulated significant expertise in devising strategies to challenge them at local and global levels (Keet, 2000). There is also the opportunity to engage with the growing number of communities in North America and Europe that are losing jobs and benefits as their countries fall in line with WTO regulations.

Social workers can help make information about the impact of these organizations available to affected groups, enabling them to engage with their governments in deliberations about the most appropriate responses to the crisis. A further role, which has long been highlighted as a contribution that can be made even by clinicians, is that of carefully documenting and ultimately disseminating to policy makers the impact of these globally defined policies on users of social services (Schneider & Netting, 1999).

Although there are opportunities for full-time employment with policy advocacy and international development organizations that are seeking to mitigate or change the policies and programs of these institutions, the social work professional has an obligation to find ways to enable those who are most directly affected to speak on their own behalf. Social workers often say clients are the main problem solvers, and they have the right to determine how they want to address an issue. This perspective is as relevant to the roles of global institutions such as the IMF, World Bank, and WTO as it is to more familiar matters such as determining the modality of care for a child or elderly family member.

CONCLUSION

Well over sixty years ago, the dominant political and economic forces in the world established a trio of organizations to regulate financial and trading relationships among their countries. The IMF, the World Bank, and the WTO (previously GATT) have come to exercise a degree of influence that is sometimes characterized as the difference between "life and debt" in over one hundred countries around the world. In fact, the issue is no longer only affecting the countries of the so-called developing world. Workers, families, and entire communities in the Global North are also facing the consequences of a deregulated and privatized world. Though there has been some social work presence in the campaigns that have been launched to challenge these institutions, the profession's commitment to self-determinination and the well-being of the least advantaged calls forth an even greater engagement in actions for change at local and global levels.

NOTE

1. See also the 2003 *Memorandum on Improving Internal Transparency in the WTO* from a coalition of organizations, including the Third World Network, Oxfam International, and the Gender and Trade Network, at www.twnside.org.sg/title2/par/MEMORANDUM_ON_THE_NEED_TO_IMPROVE_IT_Final_version.doc, and *Reforming the Governance of the IMF* from the Group of 24 Developing Nations at www.g24.org/rgover.pdf.

REFERENCES

Anderson, P. & Witter, M., (Eds.) (1994). *Crisis, Adjustment and Social Change- A Case Study of Jamaica in Consequences of Structural Adjustment – A Review of the Jamaican Experience.* Canoe Press. Kingston: Jamaica.

Barrett, M. (Ed.). (2000). *The world will never be the same again.* Jubilee 2000 Coalition & World Vision. Retrieved from www.jubileedebtcampaign.org.uk/download.php?id=284.

Bradshaw, Y. W., & Huang, J. (1991). Intensifying global dependency: Foreign debt, structural adjustment, and third world underdevelopment [Electronic version]. *Sociological Quarterly, 32*(3), 321–342.

Bull, B. (2004). Confronting the "Three Horsemen of the Apocalypse": Critical literature on the World Bank, the International Monetary Fund and the World Trade Organisation [Electronic version]. *European Journal of Development Research, 16*(3), 737–745.

Dominelli, L. (1999). Neo-liberalism, social exclusion and welfare clients in a global economy [Electronic version]. *International Journal of Social Welfare, 8,* 14–22.

Glaessner, P., Lee, K. W., Sant'Anna, A. M., & de St. Antoine, J. J. (1994). *Poverty alleviation and social investment funds—the Latin American experience.* World Bank Discussion Papers No. 261. Washington, DC: World Bank.

Harrigan, J., & El-Said, H. (2000). Stabilisation and structural adjustment in developing countries: The case of Jordan and Malawi [Electornic version]. *Journal of African Business, 1*(3), 63–109.

Holzmann, R. (Ed.). (2009). *Social protection and labor at the World Bank, 2000–08* [Electronic version]. Washington, DC: World Bank.

Holzmann, R., Sipos, S., & The Social Protection Team. (2009). Social protection and labor and the World Bank: An overview [Electronic version]. In R. Holzmann (Ed.), *Social protection and labor at the World Bank, 2000–08* (pp. 1–10). Washington, DC: World Bank.

Kategekwa, J. (2009). *Empty promises: What happened to 'development' in the WTO's Doha Round?* Oxfam Briefing Paper No. 131. Retrieved from www.oxfam.org/en/policy/bp131-empty-promises.

Keet, D. (2000). The international anti-debt campaign: A Southern activist view for activists in 'the North' . . . and 'the South' [Electronic version]. *Development in Practice, 10*(3&4), 461–477.

Love, R. (2007). Corporate wealth or public health? WTO/TRIPS flexibilities and access to HIV/AIDS antiretroviral drugs by developing countries. *Development in Practice, 17*, 2, 208–219.

Pollock, A. M., & Price, D. (2000, December). Rewriting the regulations: How the World Trade Organisation could accelerate privatisation in health-care systems [Electronic version]. *Lancet, 356*, 1995–2000.

Ranjan, P. (2007). *A brief history of the WTO.* InfoChange News & Features. Retrieved from http://infochangeindia.org/index.php?option=com_content&task=view&id=6079&Itemid=61.

Saner, R., & Guilherme, R. (2007). *IMF conditionalities for the least developed countries.* G-24 Policy Brief No. 19. Retrieved from www.g24.org/pbno19.pdf.

Schneider, R., & Netting, F. E. (1999). Influencing social policy in a time of devolution: Social work's great tradition [Electronic version]. *Social Work, 44*(4), 349–357.

Stevenson, R. W. (1999, November 25). Outspoken chief economist leaving World Bank. *New York Times.* Retrieved from www.nytimes.com/1999/11/25/business/outspoken-chief-economist-leaving-world-bank.html.

Stiglitz, J. E. (2003). *Globalization and its discontents.* New York: Norton.

Stuart, E. (2007). *Blind spot: The continued failure of the World Bank and IMF to fully assess the impact of their advice on poor people.* Joint NGO briefing note. Retrieved from www.oxfam.org/en/policy/briefing-notes/bn0709_blind_spot_world_bank_imf.

Third World Network. (2009). *The IMF's financial crisis loans: No change in conditionalities.* Retrieved from www.twnside.org.sg/title2/par/IMF.Crisis.Loans-Overview.TWN.March.2009.doc.

Wallach, L. (2005). *Backgrounder on WTO service sector liberalization and deregulation.* Washington, DC: Public Citizen. Retrieved from www.citizen.org/documents/PC_Gats_Backgrounder_05-05.pdf.

World Bank. (2007). *A guide to the World Bank* (2nd ed.). Washington, DC: Author.

World Bank. (2001). *Social protection sector strategy: From safety net to springboard.* Washington, DC: World Bank. Available at www-wds.worldbank.org/external/default/WDSContentServer/WDSP/IB/2001/01/26/000094946_01011705303891/Rendered/PDF/multi_page.pdf.

World Trade Organization (WTO). (2011). What is the WTO? Retrieved from http://www.wto.org/english/thewtoe/whatis_e/tif_e/agrm7_e.htm

SECTION VII

*International Social Work
Education and Research*

Models of Internationalizing Curriculum

LYNNE M. HEALY AND ROSEMARY J. LINK

The importance of international education for social workers has been recognized for many decades. As early as the 1928 International Conference of Social Work, educators dreamed of founding an international school to train leaders in the field. In 1969, Konopka identified two overarching goals for international education in social work: *(1)* to improve the practice of social work in one's own country and *(2)* "to prepare for intelligent international cooperation in social work practice, theory and research" (p. 3). These remain compelling reasons for internationalizing social work curricula, and they are underscored by the increasing importance of global education in higher education in general.

At the 2009 World Conference on Higher Education, UNESCO (United Nations Educational, Scientific and Cultural Organization) recognized the important role of higher education in preparing students for their work in a global era. "Faced with the complexity of current and future global challenges, higher education has the social responsibility to advance our understanding of multifaceted issues, which involve social, economic, scientific and cultural dimensions and our ability to respond to them. It should lead society in generating global knowledge to address global challenges" (UNESCO, 2009b). There are also regional imperatives fueling the drive to internationalize curriculum. The Bologna Declaration (discussed further in Chapter 59) asks countries in Europe to cooperate with one another to promote collaboration across borders, increased cultural awareness, increased mobility of employment, and greater linguistic ability.

In order to move toward these purposes in ways that are meaningful for social work students and communities, "higher education institutions must be actively engaged in the world around them—through partnerships, providing a global perspective in the education they provide, and connecting the local and the global" (Hill & Green, 2008, p. vii). In social work,

"internationalizing the curriculum will allow social work educators to transcend parochialism, understand similarities and differences among nations, and prepare students for 'emancipatory practice' as they gain new understanding of global inequalities" (Sewpaul, 2001). Focusing on shared problems, the Association of Schools of Social Work in Africa has asked participating schools to seek the strengths and innovations from country to country to help find solutions to cross-border challenges such as AIDS, child soldiers, and poverty (see Chapter 55). Social work education is increasingly responding to these calls for recognition of the international and global responsibilities of higher education, but more work remains.

As chapters in this book demonstrate (for example, chapters 10 through 18 and chapter 71), social workers fulfill multiple roles in the international arena, and the profession has much to contribute to global social policy and programs. Social work educational programs must ensure that professionals are prepared with requisite knowledge, skills, and attitudes for practice in the globalized context of the twenty-first century. This chapter addresses the importance of expanding international content and learning opportunities, discusses learning objectives and models of international curriculum, addresses barriers and facilitating factors in internationalizing curriculum, and concludes with curriculum recommendations.

Current patterns, barriers, and opportunities for optimal curricula will vary in diverse parts of the world. For example, students in many countries where social work is relatively new or where its transplantation is not fully reflected in local scholarship may learn largely from books and journals written in other countries. Thus, they inevitably have a cross-national perspective. These books may not, however, address global problems or be written with a cosmopolitan orientation. Citing a presentation by Abye Tasse in 2003, Dominelli wrote: "Internationalizing the curriculum is a Western preoccupation. People living in the Southern hemisphere have already had their curriculum 'internationalised' either through experiences of colonialism where Western models of knowledge production, acquisition and transfer were imposed upon local ones or globalization had penetrated indigenous knowledges, re-culturalised them and intergrated them into a global system that privileges the West" (2007a, p. 381). While true to some extent, the results of the colonized experience do not ensure useful knowledge or practice skills for addressing current global realities.

In other countries, especially those with strong local scholarship, education may be excessively inward-looking and neglect the global dimension. Thus, while goals and paths will differ, all educational programs in social work would benefit from increased international emphasis. As underscored recently by an educator from Kenya, international social work should "expose learners to different thematics that are affecting the world's peoples." It should "empower learners and practitioners to understand global processes" affecting us all (Wairire, 2008).

The authors recognize that many social work programs in various parts of the world have already added international or global content to their programs. Survey research indicates that coverage varies greatly from country to country and school to school. While some programs have integrated considerable content and have developed courses in international social work, many programs still have limited coverage, and others do not address international or global issues at all (Healy, 1988; Kojima, 1992; Lyons, Manion & Carlsen, 2006; Nagy & Falk, 2000). The suggestions in the remainder of this chapter are intended to assist programs in various stages of development in thinking about best approaches to international social work education.

SETTING GOALS AND LEARNING OUTCOMES FOR INTERNATIONAL EDUCATION

Developing new curricula for social work programs and modifying existing priorities can be daunting tasks. Principles of curriculum design recommend that the process begin by reviewing the mission and educational objectives for the curriculum as a whole and identifying goals and outcomes for the international components. In some instances this first step is supported by references to global reach in the mission of the institution itself. By specifying intended learning outcomes, curriculum content can be carefully selected and teaching methodologies developed to ensure student progress. This is particularly important for a practice-focused profession. The Global Standards for the Education and Training of the Social Work Profession state that each social work educational institution should develop "a specification of its programme objectives and expected higher education outcomes" (IASSW, 2004, 2.1). These program objectives should indicate how "the programme addresses local, national and/or regional/international development needs and priorities" (2.6). Thus, objectives and outcomes should be tailored to the program and based on a combination of universal professional goals and local needs and strengths.

As Hill and Green (2008) noted in their guide to internationalization of curriculum, "although many institutions offer a diverse mix of international learning opportunities, few do so with much intentionality. . . . Without a clear set of goals and a strategy to connect disparate activities and create synergies among them, internationalization may be confined to a set of marginal activities affecting a self-selected group of students and faculty" (pp. ix–x). Healy (1988) discovered a similar pattern in surveys of social work educational programs. Some international social work courses reflected little thought about student outcomes and did not appear to be linked to goals of the overall curriculum.

When designing an international curriculum, it may be helpful to address two questions: How can international content contribute to meeting the overall educational objectives of the institution and program? And what internationally related learning outcomes are important to ensure that graduates are best able to contribute to their context and the wider context of their service users, including their global dimensions? A recent article suggests that internationalizing education achieves academic goals, economic goals (career preparation), social goals (especially social justice and development), and national security goals (producing experts) (Hill & Green, 2008). Adapted to social work, these translate into knowledge goals, practice skills including skills in advocacy, and attitude or values goals. A beginning list of suggested international learning outcomes is presented in Box 50.1 (Healy & Link, 2008).

The outcomes adopted then guide the selection of a curriculum model or models and specific international content.

BOX 50.1
OPTIMAL OUTCOMES FOR INTERNATIONAL LEARNING

Students will demonstrate the following:

- Understanding of globalization as a process or set of processes that affects domestic as well as international social work practice and social issues
- Understanding migration from perspectives of sending and receiving countries (and countries that are both)
- Sensitivity to value dilemmas, especially dilemmas of universal application and cultural relativism, in internationally related work
- Knowledge of the major global human rights laws and their applicability to social work practice
- Ability to analyze a global social policy and beginning skill in international advocacy
- Familiarity with the history, scope, and functions of social work around the world
- Awareness of the impact of the policies of one's own country on conditions and policies in other countries
- Knowledge of major sources of global data on human rights and social development and how to access them
- Knowledge of the ways the profession is organized for international action through its professional organizations
- Knowledge of human diversity, cultural sensitivity, and beginning skill in intercultural communication
- Ability to analyze models of practice and social service innovations from other countries for their adaptability and fit in one's own context.

MODELS OF INTERNATIONAL CURRICULUM

There are numerous models for structuring international curriculum. In selecting a model, social work programs must decide on a number of factors. Will the international curriculum reach all students or a subset of students? Do resources and other considerations permit a comprehensive approach or a focus on carefully selected minimum essentials? Are enough faculty members committed to this initiative so that it can become institutionalized and sustainable rather than the short-term inspiration of one or two people? The selection will be guided by the goals and learning objectives identified by the program in its explication of how international learning will contribute to meeting the program mission and to student preparation.

The most common approaches that reach all students include incorporating international content or modules into required courses in the curriculum and requiring a course on international or global social work. A third model is comprehensive incorporation or infusion of content, usually referred to as the *internationalization approach*. Models that reach only self-selected groups of students offer one or more elective courses, offer a concentration or specialization in international or global social work, or allow independent study with an international focus. Learning can also be enhanced through travel-study courses, international service learning, interactive video classrooms, and cocurricular learning opportunities (non-credit-bearing supplementary lectures, seminars, or films). Field placements or internships are an essential component of social work education and therefore should be included in international learning opportunities. The role of field placements will be mentioned later in this chapter; readers are also referred to Chapter 51.

Given the global nature of current practice, the first priority is to ensure that all students have at least a minimum level of international content and mastery. According to a recent report issued in the United States, "the most effective curricular strategy for internationalization is to infuse intercultural and global issues into the existing curriculum, so that global learning is part of every student's education and is deepened over time, rather than being confined to a single general education course requirement" (Hill & Green, 2008, p. 32).

Educators in social work and the higher education arena in general have encouraged a more comprehensive approach where feasible (Hokenstad, 1984). Healy (1999) defined *internationalization* as "comprehensive infusion of international content into all major required aspects of a social work educational program" (pp. 23–24). Similarly, Cox and Pawar (2006) supported a comprehensive approach: "We strongly suggest that every social work course contain some specific international content" (p. 366). They endorse the idea of comprehensive infusion (which they call *diffusion*) so that every course includes some international content, but they also see dangers in this approach unless it is carefully monitored. They are concerned that "the introduction may be so diffuse in practice that it makes no real impact on students" (p. 366). In this *Handbook*, the authors see a connected approach to infusion and internationalization as optimal. This approach recognizes the global in many local issues, such as housing for migrant workers, and the local in international issues, such as global health threats.

Specialization models prepare practitioners for careers such as international development, work with immigrants and refugees, and global policy (see Chapter 71). Specializations require more substantial content offerings and related field internships and therefore need dedicated resources. Such specializations are not widespread, but they are available in a modest number of schools in some countries, including Denmark, Norway, Canada and the United States. Where feasible, they should be encouraged along with infusion models.

Accreditation and Curriculum Standards

The model chosen for internationalizing a curriculum, whether selective required courses, modules, or infusion, may be strengthened by national curriculum standards. Some countries have incorporated requirements for international curricula into standards and national requirements. In the United Kingdom, for instance, benchmarks are established by the Quality Assurance Agency for Higher Education. An example of a benchmark statement is 3.1.2: "Service delivery context should locate social work within both historical and comparative perspectives, including European and international contexts" (Williams, 2005, p. 23). There are also other requirements for continued professional advancement that address an international perspective. One requirement from the Central

Council for Education and Training in Social Work (CCETSW) states that the professional must "demonstrate knowledge and understanding of the impact of relevant policy, practice and institutions within the European or international context to inform practice or service development" (CCETSW, 1997, as cited in Williams, 2005, p. 23).

Accreditation standards in the United States have waxed and waned on international content over the past half century. Strong requirements were in place in the 1960s, only to be completely absent in curriculum requirements during the 1980s and 1990s. The curriculum policy adopted in 2002 brought renewed attention to global content, requiring that programs prepare students for "the global context of social work practice" and specifically cover global content in curriculum components on oppression and social policy (Council on Social Work Education [CSWE], 2002). The most recent policy, adopted in 2008, acknowledges the importance of a global perspective, mentions the ethical document of the International Federation of Social Workers (IFSW) and International Association of Schools of Social Work (IASSW), and adds human rights as a required topic area. In other ways, however, the statement is weaker and less specific in its references to international or global content (CSWE, 2008). Schools are directed to demonstrate that their students achieve a set of competencies, but global learning is not reflected in the definitions of the competencies. Where official policies require international or global content, programs are more likely to respond by reviewing and strengthening their curricula. The official standards, where they exist, favor content and learning outcomes that reach all students, described previously as an inclusion, incorporation, or infusion approach.

BARRIERS AND FACILITATING FACTORS

Moving into a new content area can be challenging for social work programs. Regardless of the curriculum model selected, there are factors that impede success. The infusion and comprehensive internationalization models suggested in this chapter can be "highly demanding models of curriculum design and instruction" (Healy, 2002, p. 182). However, as experience with internationalization has grown, so have facilitating factors that can assist in the process of curriculum development.

These potential barriers and facilitating factors in curriculum development will be discussed next. The factors differentially affect the various models of change. Obstacles and the ways in which they are experienced also vary from country to country and even program to program. For example, students entering social work programs in the United States often have little background in world history, geography, or economics. In other places, preparation in economics and geography is strong, especially in those countries that are on regional borders, such as Slovenia (four bordering states) and Turkey (gateway from Asia to Europe), and in those countries that are landlocked and depend on access to coastlines and trade routes through others countries, such as Zimbabwe and the *-stan* countries. Thus, the lack of preparation that is a barrier to teaching international social work in the United States may not be experienced elsewhere.

Barriers and Obstacles to Internationalization

As noted in an earlier article (Healy, 2002), barriers to the internationalization of curriculum can be linked to access to resources; attitudes of faculty, administrators, and students; faculty competence; and structural factors in social work education. Lyons et al. (2006) added that "many social work educators either admit to lacking knowledge and confidence to develop curricula appropriately, or, more often, consider that the timetables and syllabuses are already 'too full' to include new units or material" (p. 197).

In the 1980s and 1990s, scholars identified a lack of teaching materials as a significant barrier to international education. The cost of books and journal subscriptions still presents a barrier for programs in many parts of the world. When donations of books and journals flow into new social work programs, whether in Africa or Eastern Europe, they are usually older materials from Western countries. These materials rarely provide international perspectives and can thus impede development of globally relevant curricula (and even relevant curricula in general). Other resource-related barriers include lack of money to support student and faculty travel, lack of money for technology, and lack of money for hiring teachers competent in this area of social work. Language barriers also affect access to resources. More translations of social work books and articles would ensure that professionals and students can benefit from diverse perspectives. Even the premier journal in the field, *International Social Work*, moved from a trilingual to an English-only publication in the early 1980s, although abstracts now appear in six languages.

Significant barriers to internationalization are attitudinal—including the devaluation of international curricula and exchange by faculty and administrators in some countries. Devaluation of international curricula is certainly linked to the absence or minimal inclusion of this content in standards. Social work curricula are already rich in many important topics and courses; educators sometimes express the feeling that the curriculum is crowded and it is hard to find room for new content. Reluctance may also stem from faculty fear of the new and a lack of preparation and confidence to teach in this area. Tye (1999) collected data from fifty-two countries in his study of general global education. Among his findings was the identification of inadequate teacher training in global issues as the most frequent barrier to global education. Limited international content in doctoral programs that prepare social work faculty and neglect of ongoing faculty development in this area suggest that lack of training and preparation are important obstacles to internationalization in social work.

Attitudinal issues may also affect students. As noted, weak preparation in world history, economics, political science, geography, or language may deter students from pursuing international topics or experiences in social work. Students whose focus is on immediate job-related skills may devalue international study, and negative attitudes among administrators of social work schools can have multiplier effects and raise structural barriers. To flourish, international scholarship, partnership activities, and global curriculum development must be taken into account in workloads and standards for faculty evaluation.

Finally, there are curriculum design and pedagogical challenges. The task of selecting learning objectives and content from this vast knowledge area is daunting. Ensuring that the international content addresses the identified learning outcomes and matching these with appropriate teaching methods are additional challenges. Some programs experience tensions between multicultural social work and international social work, and others struggle with balancing indigenization with internationalization. As noted in Chapter 2, the authors propose that multicultural and international social work curriculum models overlap but have distinctive elements. Further, indigenization and internationalization are not in conflict but are both essential approaches for addressing the full context of social work practice.

Facilitating Factors

Fortunately, there are many facilitating factors that encourage internationalization. As noted earlier, some countries have curriculum standards that require international content. In the past decade, there has also been an explosion in availability of materials that can be used to introduce global perspectives. Within professional literature in social work, textbooks on international social work, both comprehensive introductions to the topic and specialized books on particular aspects, have been published by major publishers with global reach. In North America, resource guides to internationalizing social work curricula have been published (Link & Healy, 2005). Journals addressing international and regional themes are a significant source of material for teaching and research. In the English language, these include such periodicals as *International Social Work*, *Social Development Issues*, *Asia Pacific Journal of Social Work and Development*, *Journal of Social Development in Africa*, *Caribbean Journal of Social Work*, *European Journal of Social Work*, and more.

The cost of books and journal subscriptions is high and sometimes prohibitive, disadvantaging some. Although technology is also expensive, computers and Internet access are available in most institutions of higher education. While the digital divide should not be minimized, it is also true that Internet access has given teachers and students in developing countries access to a wide array of materials, including journal articles in the public domain, free electronic journals, papers and course materials posted by individual educators, and a treasure trove of relevant materials from the United Nations and other global and regional organizations. According to UNESCO (2009a), "computers and the internet have allowed previously unimaginable forms of global knowledge transfer." Although all programs do not have equal access, availability of teaching resources is no longer a major barrier to internationalizing social work curricula.

Communication technologies also offer opportunities to directly connect students and teachers in different countries in online discussions, electronically delivered guest lectures, and joint video classrooms. These ideas are discussed at length in Chapter 53 on the use of technology in international social work education. And, opportunities for other types of exchanges offer significant support for international curricula, including formal exchange initiatives, such as those of the Erasmus Programme in Europe, and more individualized faculty-to-faculty exchanges (see Chapter 52 on international exchanges).

However, perhaps the most important facilitating factor is the growing acceptance of the importance of global education in social work. Whereas a decade ago, educators who focused on the global were considered eccentric, "today, if you are not interested in the international you are eccentric" (Tasse, 2005). Students, too, are enthusiastic about global learning, recognizing that "family pathways often begin and end in different communities, regions and countries, so that crossing and re-crossing borders is a norm. Almost all students will practice with people who are of a different culture and national origin to their own" (Link & Healy, 2005, p. v). The increased acceptance and value accorded to global content are reflected in the inclusion of international learning and content elements in national standards for social work education and in many educational programs around the world.

RECOMMENDATIONS

A number of recommendations can be made to strengthen international learning in social work. We suggest that all educational programs *(1)* develop learning outcomes for international curricula that specify how international content will contribute to the preparation of students and to the curriculum and institution as a whole; *(2)* infuse modules into required courses to ensure that all students benefit from a global perspective; *(3)* ensure that internationally related values, knowledge, and skills are linked to students' roles as professionals; and *(4)* emphasize the points of intersection of international and domestic practice and policy concerns. Points 3 and 4 refer us back to Konopka's wise recommendations made more than forty years ago. Faculty development efforts should also be considered, because "faculty development is almost always a prerequisite for student development" (Jones & Kumssa, 1999, p. 212). To implement the ideas included in this chapter, faculty members may benefit from additional training and faculty development opportunities.

International content can and should be integrated into many areas of the social work curriculum and as demonstrated in this book, "The world is here in our schools, in our classrooms, in our field experience" (Link, 1999). Cox and Pawar (2006) recommended a social development approach across the entire curriculum. They also recommended that programs cover international aspects in courses on social policy, cross-cultural social work, history of social work, ethics, law (human rights law), poverty, and community development. Coverage of cross-cultural practice and international practice, global social problems, and material on the international profession were also suggested. These fit well with the learning outcomes suggested earlier in this chapter in Box 50.1.

Field placements should not be neglected. Relatively few students will have the opportunity to complete international field placements. However, most locally offered field placements can offer discussion and practice assignments that address the domestic–global interface; in many instances, international populations are being served and global policies and events are affecting agency practice.

Teaching methods play an important role in student learning. There are many strategies to increase student exposure to the global nature of social work. Modest ones are assigning books and articles written by authors from diverse countries and using teaching materials produced by the international organizations, including the United Nations, World Bank, IFSW, and more. Use of visual materials, such as films and video programs that reflect conditions in other parts of the world, helps students visualize what they are studying. When possible, instructors should attempt to bring—in person or electronically—guest lecturers and discussants from other countries and cultures to their students to further expose them to diverse viewpoints and to underscore the point that knowledge emanates from many places. Mining the rich experiences of students in terms of their diverse experiences and backgrounds can further strengthen cross-cultural understanding.

Ultimately, the rationale for enhancing international curricula in social work programs is to improve the practice of social work and to strengthen its contributions to global justice and human well-being. As Dominelli (2007b) wrote, "Social work educators can ensure that curricula used to train practitioners are infused with the knowledges, values and skills necessary to equip them for the task of revitalizing communities in a globalizing world. In this way, social work education and practice in the international arena can better meet the challenges of globalization to secure social justice for marginalized, socially excluded people and promote equality" (p. 386). UNESCO is convinced that the role of higher education is critical. The 2009 communiqué emphasized the sector's contributions to "the eradication of poverty, to sustainable development and to progress towards reaching the internationally agreed upon development goals, which include the Millennium Development Goals (MDGs) and Education for All" (UNESCO, 2009b). These are surely purposes that social work education worldwide can embrace.

REFERENCES

Council on Social Work Education (CSWE). (2008). *Educational policy and accreditation standards*. Alexandria, VA: Author. Available at www.cswe.org.

Council on Social Work Education (CSWE). (2002). *Educational policy and accreditation standards*. Alexandria, VA: Author.

Cox, D., & Pawar, M. (2006). *International social work: Issues, strategies, and programs*. Thousand Oaks, CA: Sage.

Dominelli, L. (2007a). Challenges in internationalizing social work curricula. In L. Dominelli (Ed.), *Revitalising communities in a globalizing world* (pp. 375–382). Aldershot, Hampshire: Ashgate.

Dominelli, L. (2007b). Conclusions. In L. Dominelli (Ed.), *Revitalising communities in a globalizing world* (pp. 383–386). Aldershot, Hampshire: Ashgate.

Healy, L.M. & Link, R.J. (2008). Infusion of international content into curricula. Presentation at the International Social Work Conference, Boston, Massachusetts, June 6–8, 2008. Sponsored by NADD, CSWE and Boston College.

Healy, L. M. (2002). Internationalizing social work curriculum in the 21st century. In N.-T. Tan & I. Dodds (Eds.), *Social work around the world II* (pp. 179–194). Berne, Switzerland: International Federation of Social Workers.

Healy, L. M. (1999). International social work curriculum in historical perspective. In C. Ramanathan & R. Link (Eds.), *All our futures: Principles and resources for social work practice in a global era* (pp. 14–29). Belmont, CA: Brooks/Cole.

Healy, L. M. (1988). Curriculum building in international social work: Toward preparing professionals for the global age. *Journal of Social Work Education, 24*(3), 221–228.

Hill, B., & Green, M. (2008). *A guide to internationalization for chief academic officers*. Washington, DC: American Council on Education (ACE).

Hokenstad, M. C. (1984). Curriculum directions for the 1980s: Implications of the new curriculum policy statement. *Journal of Education for Social Work, 20*(1), 15–22.

International Association of Schools of Social Work (IASSW). (2004). Global standards for the education and training of the social work profession. Jointly adopted by IASSW and IFSW. Accessed January 14, 2010, at www.iassw-aiets.org.

Jones, J. F., & Kumssa, A. (1999). Professional growth in the global context. In C. Ramanathan & R. Link (Eds.), *All our futures: Principles and resources for social work practice in a global era* (pp. 206–218). Belmont, CA: Brooks/Cole.

Kojima, Y. (1992). Recent trends of international social work education in Japan and Asia. *Yearbook of Social Work Education, 13*, 49–59. Tokyo: Japan Association of Schools of Social Work.

Konopka, G. (1969). Introduction to workshop on teaching of comparative social welfare. In K. Kendall (Ed.), *Teaching of comparative social welfare: A workshop report.* (pp. 1–3). New York: Council on Social Work Education.

Link, R. J., & Healy, L. M. (2005). *Teaching international content: Curriculum resources for social work education.* Alexandria, VA: CSWE.

Link, R. J. (1999). Internationalizing your classroom and field practica: why and how. Update, Association of Baccalaureate Social Work Program Directors, Vol. 21. No .2. p. 13–18.

Lyons, K., Manion, K., & Carlsen, M. (2006). *International perspectives on social work: Global conditions and local practice.* Houndsmills, UK: Palgrave MacMillan.

Nagy, G., & Falk, D. (2000). Dilemmas in international and cross-cultural social work education. *International Social Work, 43*(1), 49–60.

Sewpaul, V. (2001, August 9). Closing plenary speech. 5th Biennial Conference of Caribbean and International Social Work Educators, Nassau, Bahamas.

Tasse, A. (2005, March). *Developments in international social work.* Presentation at the University of Connecticut School of Social Work, West Hartford, Connecticut.

Tye, K. A. (1999). Global education: A worldwide movement. *Issues in global education: Newsletter of the American Forum for Global Education, 150.*

UNESCO (United Nations Educational, Scientific and Cultural Organization). (2009a). *The state of higher education in the world today.* Accessed August 27, 2009, at www.unesco.org.

UNESCO (United Nations Educational, Scientific and Cultural Organization). (2009b). Communiqué from the 2009 World Conference on Higher Education. Accessed August 27, 2009, at www.unesco.org.

Wairire, G. (2008, July). *Defining international social work for the 21st century.* Presentation at the Biennial Conference of the International Association of Schools of Social Work, Durban, South Africa.

Williams, J. (2005). Developing international perspectives in UK curricula: Opportunities and challenges. In K. Lyons (Ed.), *Internationalising social work education: Considerations and developments* (pp. 21–30). Birmingham: Venture Press for the British Association of Social Workers.

International Field Placements

PATRICIA LAGER AND SALLY MATHIESEN

BRIDGING SOCIAL WORK THEORY AND PRACTICE THROUGH INTERNATIONAL FIELD EDUCATION: INTRODUCTION

Through international field experiences, students become immersed in a cross-cultural learning experience where they are challenged to confront different views of human behavior and learn about different systems of social welfare (Healy, 2003). From this vantage point they are able to examine problems similar to those that may exist in their own country that are viewed and remedied in contrasting ways.

For example, the growing interest in international student exchanges is evident by the increasing numbers of American students completing internships in other countries (Mathiesen & Lager, 2007; Rai, 2004). These field placements provide opportunities for substantive student learning and are powerful tools that can prepare students for international practice.

Since social work is viewed differently in many countries, expectations for the learning experiences received in an international location must also vary. Therefore, using a model for placing students abroad can provide a systematic approach to the development and sustainability of an international field program. Such a model should include *(1)* the establishment of a systematic cycle of communication between the parties and *(2)* the incorporation of facilitating factors for maintaining the placement. Each country involved in the development of the program, whether host or guest nation, has expectations that can either facilitate the experience or create barriers to the process. However, a clear understanding of the following global definition of international social work from the International Association of Schools of Social Work (IASSW) and International Federation of Social Workers (IFSW) helps to provide a common area of focus for all parties involved.

The social work profession promotes social change, problem solving in human relationships and the empowerment and liberation of people to enhance well-being. Utilising theories of human behaviour and social systems, social work intervenes at the points where people interact with their environments. Principles of human rights and social justice are fundamental to social work.
—(IASSW & IFSW, *2004*, p. 2)

A number of individual and institutional barriers can arise during the process of establishing international field placements. Many of these barriers can be avoided through a thoughtful planning process that considers certain value-related factors in the establishment of a relationship based on trust, mutuality, and reciprocity between the two institutions. In addition, integrating US standards for field education into an international experience can pose a challenge, requiring significant knowledge of requirements for field education. The goal is to incorporate pertinent experiences that meet required learning objectives while at the same time maintaining flexibility in the expectations of the placement.

This chapter presents the principles and facilitating factors of a model for developing and sustaining international field internships (Mathiesen & Lager, 2007). Key ingredients for institutional support and preparation of students are suggested, followed by a discussion of the articulation and evaluation of outcomes.

BASIC PRINCIPLES AND FACILITATING FACTORS

International social work internships may best be viewed on a continuum. At one end, an internship may consist of an escorted excursion to a neighboring country for a period lasting from one day to several weeks. At the other end of the continuum lies the semester-long field placement where a student is operating more independently while also receiving supervision from the host country. All international internships require clear and consistent understanding between parties to maximize the experience for both the sending and host countries. In addition, the values inherent in a reciprocal view of international student exchanges and internships, based on strong relationships between participants, serve as guiding principles. For field placements specifically, the need is more sharply defined given the extended length of the experience and the need for students to operate more independently in the host country. The following section presents three principles for successful development of field internships and facilitating factors to enhance sustainability.

Principle of Communication

Thorough orientation and preparation of the student and clarification of the expected roles is a cornerstone of effective international efforts. A well-developed orientation program designed to include information that is pertinent to the country and placement is critical to the student's success (Lager, Mathiesen, Rodgers, & Cox, 2010). For example, a predeparture orientation program could include basic expectations of the field program (e.g., suggested work attire, field hours required, daily or weekly work schedule, evaluation expectations and deadlines, evaluation submission guidelines, requirements of the educational contract, corresponding learning objectives and proposed tasks in the placement, region-specific current events). In addition, information relating to the various difficulties the student can expect to experience in adjusting to work in a host setting can be shared (e.g., psychological adjustments, supervision issues and expectations, language barriers, anticipated cultural differences and issues).

In addition to this predeparture orientation, an orientation by the supervisor at the time of arrival can facilitate a student's adjustment to a new system and surroundings. The orientation would focus on important political and governmental issues, the structure of the agency, relevant agency policies and procedures, information regarding the client population the student will be working with and related problem areas, diversity issues and suggested guidelines for responding to encounters in this area, professional behavior and responsibilities, and other job-related tasks and expectations.

Facilitating factor 1: A communication feedback loop with supervisor, field liaison, and student (at a minimum) should include mutual evaluation and debriefing to avoid misunderstandings. When expectations are fully discussed during the development and implementation phases of the placement, and a plan for regular communication is established, there is greater likelihood of a successful outcome for the student, the agency, and the educational program. Therefore, the establishment of a regular schedule of personal contact between the faculty liaison and student is important to this process. This will assist in identifying difficulties immediately and intervening with the supervisor to resolve the issue.

Facilitating factor 2: Contact should be maintained at all levels (micro, mezzo, and macro) with the host country. The importance of a mutuality of purpose in the provision of the international internship is communicated at all levels from the beginning of the planning process. This is helpful to the participants in addressing the inevitable challenges that are associated with most international collaborations that consist of two systems, each with unique organizational and political cultures and educational philosophies.

Facilitating factor 3: Ethics and values for all parties are respected and demonstrated via direct and timely communication of any emerging issues or concerns.

Principle of Mutuality and Reciprocity

As in any sustained relationship where there is ongoing communication of needs and mutual goals, there must also be a feeling that all parties involved are being treated equally and are benefiting from the experience. Mutuality and equality are important factors in these relationships because these qualities lead to both productivity and sustainability (Healy, 2003). As Tice and Long (2009) note, "concerted effort must be paid to ensure that social workers are giving—intellectually, financially, and otherwise—as much as they are taking, in the true spirit of cultural and educational exchange" (p. 242).

Facilitating factor 4: A reciprocal strengths-based approach over time and for all parties is assumed. Each party in the exchange should be able to benefit from the international field placement. The value is undeniable for the visiting student, and the benefits to the host-country participants, including agency and supervisor, should be emphasized. Therefore a plan for reciprocity and mutuality is established in which the host agency can perhaps receive some form of assistance from the student or educational program in return for the experiences and knowledge it has provided throughout the internship This assistance can be in the form of a financial payment for supervision time and provision of learning experiences or the development of a needed project by the student that can be left behind when the placement ends.

Facilitating factor 5: Mutual goals for guest and host nation should be established as part of the relationship-building process. When considering a thoughtful plan for reciprocity, a number of important questions will arise and need to be prioritized. For example, in determining specific roles for student contributions in terms of reciprocity, how can the internship move an agency or program forward? What will the internship leave behind for the host country? How will it be received? How can it be used? What modifications might be needed that can inform future efforts? What barriers may develop for the partnering institution to send students to the sending country? Should an exchange agreement exist? No doubt additional questions will arise throughout the planning and development phases of the internship that will require immediate resolution through honest, open communication between the parties involved.

Facilitating factor 6: Recognition and appreciation of diversity must include cultural differences as well as similarities. The identification of cultural differences and values within a dominant culture and subcultures is an important part of the learning process in which the management of cross-cultural dissonance is a goal of social work practice (Garland & Escobar, 1988) Key learning objectives should include corresponding tasks and discussions surrounding this issue.

Principle of Relationship

To establish clear and comprehensive communication loops with all parties, to develop mutually rewarding goals, and to ensure reciprocity in the exchange, a relationship must be established between the principal partners. This process requires the development of personal relationships that may facilitate resolution of the inevitable challenges that will arise.

Facilitating factor 7: In this developmental model, personal relationships between guest and host countries are placed at the core of the exchange. While the level of relationship will change and deepen over time and the individual participants may change, strong bonds are essential to establish an ongoing opportunity for meaningful student learning rather than the superficiality that can occur with a lack of planning.

Facilitating factor 8: Development of a long-term view of process and outcomes is encouraged and should be reflected in the mutually derived goals for guest and host nations. Recognition of each country's strengths and challenges in pursuing goals will enhance trust and commitment to the process. A consistent

focus on strengths is at the core of a sustainable relationship-building process.

Facilitating factor 9: All participants must assume flexible attitudes as the process of deeper learning about another culture emerges over time. Although political, social, and economic challenges must be considered as relationship factors that affect the feasibility of exchanges, they should not be sole determinants of future efforts.

Facilitating factor 10: Empowerment of individuals and openness for future engagement are emphasized. The dynamic nature of international relationships requires creativity and input from many sources to ensure that opportunities continue to expand. Prospects for the future of the program are discussed between people in both institutions, and organizational support is negotiated with an eye toward sustainability. For example, changes in relationship dynamics often occur with administrative changes in programs, both at the department level and in higher administration. As a result, certain decisions can be made that may affect the sustainability of the partnership and thus adversely affect the quality and sustainability of the internship. Therefore, a commitment to the development of a plan for regular, frequent communication between all parties involved is needed in order for each to establish a high level of trust and clear understanding of pertinent information that needs to be shared.

SUGGESTED GUIDELINES FOR DEVELOPING INTERNATIONAL PLACEMENTS: KEY INGREDIENTS

Institutional Support

When establishing international field placements, one should maintain a focus on the facilitating factors described in the previous section as well as the IASSW–IFSW Global Standards for the Education and Training of the Social Work Profession (2004). More specifically, those standards that relate to program curricula, in particular field education, state that schools should consistently aspire to the following:

- Clear plans for the organization, implementation, and evaluation of the theory and field education components of the program
- A curriculum that helps social work students to develop skills of critical thinking and

scholarly attitudes of reasoning, openness to new experiences and paradigms, and commitment to lifelong learning
- Sufficient duration and complexity of tasks and learning opportunities to ensure that students are prepared for professional practice
- Planned coordination and links between the school and the setting of the field placement
- Provision of orientation to fieldwork supervisors or instructors
- Assignment of field supervisors or instructors who are qualified and experienced, as determined by the development status of the social work profession in any given country, and provision of orientation for fieldwork supervisors or instructors
- Inclusion and participation of field instructors in curriculum development
- A partnership between the educational institution and the agency (where applicable) and service users in decision making regarding field education and the evaluation of students' fieldwork performance
- A field instruction manual for fieldwork instructors or supervisors that details fieldwork standards, procedures, assessment standards, and expectations
- Adequate and appropriate resources to meet the needs of the fieldwork component of the program.

Planned Approach to Development

Developing international field placements can be time consuming and frustrating; therefore, administrative support in the provision of time and sufficient resources is critical to the program's success. As mentioned previously, any plan for a sustainable international field education program must begin with the development of a relationship between the faculty members responsible for the placement of students abroad, the host agency or organization, and the field instructors who will be supervising the students in placement. Many programs choose not to develop international placements due to a lack of relationships with foreign supervisors (Panos, Pettys, Cox, & Jones-Hart, 2004). These relationships, like those between social work practitioners and clients, cannot be established merely by telephone or e-mail but must initially involve face-to-face interaction. The purpose of this process is twofold: *(1)* to gain knowledge of the country, its culture and related systems, and their formal and informal processes and *(2)* to establish

a significant level of trust and mutual respect between the parties that can be sustained over time. Once the relationship is established and there is a mutual agreement to develop and provide placements in which reciprocity and mutuality will occur, careful planning by the home institution suggests inclusion of the following guidelines:

1. Review all expectations of the field program with the supervisor from the host country, in particular the experiences that the students will receive that match learning objectives of the field program. This likely will include the negotiation of an agency agreement, review of evaluation instruments and rating criteria, and so on.

2. Develop a pre-and postdeparture orientation to the culture, government and educational structure, social problems, social service delivery system, client population, potential language barriers, agency policies and procedures, supervision expectations, expectations of field program, etc. The goal of a comprehensive orientation is to move the student beyond an introductory overview of the country to a deeper level of knowledge that will facilitate a positive experience (Mathiesen & Lager, 2007).

3. Develop a procedure for screening students and matching them with the host country, agency, and supervisor. During the matching process, the host agency is identified as the appropriate site based on the student's area of concentration and interests as well as the agency's mission and client population. The screening and matching process is equally important to the success of both international and domestic internships. Also consider the student's travel experience and ability to adapt to the challenges of the country and expectations of the placement. Factors to consider when interviewing a student for placement in a particular country include degree of flexibility and adaptability, previous internship experiences and outcomes, motivation for placement and career goals, academic record, financial barriers, matching of personality style with supervisory expectations and style of supervision, etc. Not all students are appropriate for international work or match well with the experiences offered in certain countries.

4. Establish a plan for the administration of liaison duties through a contract with a faculty member or professional social worker in the area where the student is assigned. Liaison tasks can also be completed through regular telephone contact, videoconferencing, or other means. Consistent communication with the student, either directly or through a liaison, is important and provides the student with a sense of connectedness to the home institution.

5. Negotiate appropriate administrative time and resources to coordinate placements and maintain ongoing personal contact with students and field supervisors. The ability to intervene with the supervisor when problems arise is important to the success of the supervisory relationship and the student's outcomes in the placement.

6. Sufficient resources should be made available to support a well-developed plan for travel to the country in the event of an emergency involving the student. A policy should also be developed and communicated to the student in advance regarding the outcome in the event they are not able to successfully complete the international internship.

There are a number of other factors to consider in establishing international field placements, but overall, a social work program must place value on providing students with cross-cultural learning opportunities abroad and, therefore, commit to establishing these experiences through a thoughtful, well-developed process based on a significant level of knowledge and skill (Lager et al., 2010).

DISCUSSION OF EVALUATION AND INTENDED OUTCOMES

In a discussion of global mental health initiatives, a recent report by the World Health Organization noted that what gets measured gets done, highlighting the importance of monitoring and evaluating both planning and implementation (WHO, 2008). The report notes that "each country will need to decide which indicators to measure and for what purpose" (p. 21). Midgley's (2008) discussion of the need for increased clarity regarding controversial and challenging cultural practices facing social work practitioners around the world suggests the need for leadership from professional social work organizations. He notes

the value of general ethical standards such as those of the National Association of Social Workers (NASW) in the United States and of IFSW as useful tools that need further operationalization.

These same issues—the need for individualized measurement of international efforts and guidance from professional social work organizations—are relevant when the topic is evaluation of international field placements. There is a need for evaluation instruments that have demonstrated reliability and validity in international settings. Wide availability and application of such instruments would be an important advancement for the field because it would permit outcomes to be compared across programs. Though there is a need to reflect on characteristics of international placements that may be unique to one program or country, there are common elements that could be measured. Systematic data collection from all stakeholders would ensure that global ethical guidelines, along with the basic principles of communication, reciprocity and mutuality, and respectful relationships, are infused into international field placements.

Evaluation of the field experience is a standard of social work education in the United States; however, it is not always a requirement of social work programs in other countries, some of which do not offer course credit for field education. The social work program in the home institution is often given the challenge of attempting to comply with the educational objectives of its graduate or undergraduate program through the use of identical evaluation instruments for both domestic and international placements. Frequently these instruments do not fit the learning experiences offered by the host placement, which usually presents complications for the host supervisor in developing an educational plan for meeting required learning objectives on which the student will be evaluated. Therefore, intended outcomes for the student interning abroad will likely be based on the overall expectations of an individual program, which may differ from outcomes of the domestic placements.

The Global Standards for the Education and Training of the Social Work Profession state that social work program curricula, including field education, need to have a clear plan for the "organization, implementation and evaluation of the theory and field education components of the programme" (IASSW & IFSW, 2004, p. 5). The Council on Social Work Education (CSWE) Educational Policy and Accreditation Standards (EPAS) require that field education programs in schools of social work incorporate methods of evaluating students in field placements, which would also include international internships. However, evaluation methods differ greatly among field programs. In order to effectively evaluate outcomes of an international field placement, different measures might need to be used or existing measures modified to fit the experience.

SUMMARY

Though difficult and time consuming, international field placements provide opportunities for student learning that often cannot be duplicated through domestic placements. As noted by Lough (2009), they can be transformative for students in ways that lead to the development of a respect for diversity and a strong commitment to social justice. However, with an eye toward long-term sustainability of an equitable relationship between the parties based on mutuality and reciprocity, a systematic, well-developed plan should be followed in the establishment of international placements by social work programs. Personal contact between the parties is essential to the success of the relationship-building process and future success of the program, so the provision of sufficient resources for this to occur is an integral part of the planning. The purpose of this is twofold: to gain knowledge of the country, its culture and related systems, and their formal and informal processes and to establish a significant level of trust and mutual respect between the parties that can be sustained over time. Other facilitating factors that contribute to the success of the program include institutional support at various levels within an organization and educational system.

Important guidelines for establishing international placements include a process for screening students and matching them to the host country and agency, a comprehensive student orientation prior to departure and at the time of arrival, and a well-designed plan for liaison duties. The IASSW–IFSW Global Standards for the Education and Training of the Social Work Profession and the CSWE policy and accreditation standards should be incorporated into the planning process as well as a country-specific evaluation method that reflects the values and practice standards of the social work profession worldwide.

REFERENCES

Council on Social Work Education (CSWE). (2008). Educational Policy and Accreditation Standards (EPAS). Retrieved March 2, 2009, from www.cswe.org/EPAS/EPAS_start.htm.

Garland, D. R., & Escobar, D. (1988). Education for cross-culture social work practice. *Journal of Social Work Education, 24*(4), 229–241.

Healy, L. M. (2003). A theory of international collaboration: Lessons for social work education. In L. Healy, Y. Asamoah, & M. C. Hokenstad (Eds.), *Models of international collaboration in social work education* (pp. 15–22). Alexandria, VA: Council on Social Work Education.

International Association of Schools of Social Work (IASSW), & International Federation of Schools of Social Work (IFSW). (2004). *Global standards for social work education and training*. Retrieved March 3, 2009, from www.apss.polyu.edu.hk/iassw/index.

Lager, P., Mathiesen, S., Rodgers, M., & Cox, S. (2010). *Guidebook for international field placements and student exchanges: Planning, implementation, and sustainability*. Alexandria, VA: Council on Social Work Education.

Lough, B. J. (2009). Principles of effective practice in international social work field placements. *Journal of Social Work Education, 45*(3), 467–480.

Lyons, K., & Ramanathan, C. S. (1999). Models of field practice in global settings. In C. S. Ramanathan & R. J. Link (Eds.), *All our futures: Resources and principles for social work practice in a global era* (pp. 175–191). Belmont, CA: Brooks/Cole, Wadsworth.

Mathiesen, S. G., & Lager, P. B. (2007). A model for developing international student exchanges. *Social Work Education, 26*(3), 280–291.

Midgley, J. (2008). Perspectives on globalization and culture: Implications for international social work practice. *Journal of Global Social Work Practice, 1*(1). www.globalsocialwork.org/vol1no1_Midgley.html.

Panos, P. T., Pettys, G. L., Cox, S. E., & Jones-Hart, E. (2004). Survey of international field education placements of accredited social work education programs. *Journal of Social Work Education, 40*(3), 467–478.

Rai, G. S. (2004). International fieldwork experience: A survey of US schools. *International Social Work, 47*(2), 213–226.

Tice, C. J., & Long, D. D. (2009). *International social work policy and practice: Practical insights and perspectives*. Hoboken, NJ: Wiley.

World Health Organization (WHO). (2008). *The Mental Health Gap Action Programme: Scaling up care for mental, neurological, and substance use disorders*. Geneva: Author.

Models of International Exchange

ROSEMARY J. LINK AND GABI ČAČINOVIČ VOGRINČIČ

Few social workers in the world can practice in isolation from the global environment. Although the pressure of daily work means that we sometimes get on with the task at hand in the place that is familiar and in the way we know, the impact of globalization and migration means that larger systems perpetually intervene. International exchange in the social work profession has been flourishing for nearly one hundred years—from the days of Toynbee Hall, the settlement house in London visited in 1904 by the US community organizer and peace activist Jane Addams, to the early days of the Tata Institute in Mumbai and its center for international visitors. As explained by Healy in Chapter 8 of this volume, the 1928 International Social Work conference at The Paris called for increased professional opportunities to exchange ideas and practice, with a primary goal being to promote peace in the world. Over the years many goals for international exchange have been added to that of social workers as peacemakers, including expanding cultural awareness, sharing ways to implement human rights and United Nations conventions, exploring a variety of approaches to human service, cooperating in the development of curricula, collaborating in field-work practicums, and generating relationships among students, faculty, and colleagues in ongoing and sustainable ways.

International exchange in social work can mean many things and is well documented (Dominelli & Bernard, 2003; Healy, Asamoah, & Hokenstad, 2003; see also Lager & Mathiesen in Chapter 51 in this volume). Models of interaction range from the traditional study abroad and exchange of students for courses, to faculty-led research dialogue, to tripartite curriculum development such as that encouraged by the Erasmus Programme in Europe (Lyons & Ramanathan, 2004). Recent initiatives include the collaboration of colleagues in Asia who are building master of social work (MSW) programs in Singapore

and China, and parallel to these new ventures are technology transfer and interactive video classrooms, or "lessons without leaving" (Link & Bill, 2005), also discussed in Chapter 53.

The story of exchange is a compelling one. In this chapter, the introduction identifies the current array of international exchange, and the goals and expectations of professional exchange are discussed in relation to curriculum. The varying historical and cultural contexts of the development of international exchange are integrated throughout the narrative. Of a wide array (overuse of variety or varying) of structural approaches, the chapter identifies four key models:

- Traditional study abroad
- Exchange via interactive video classrooms
- Faculty exchange
- Practice and field internship exchange (briefly; this is the topic of Chapter 51)

Finally, the future role of international exchange in the social work curriculum as a whole is reviewed.

INTRODUCTION AND CURRENT ARRAY OF INTERNATIONAL EXCHANGES

We can speak of international exchanges from several perspectives, including structural, social relationship, research, technology, and virtual exchange. In the book *Models of International Collaboration in Social Work Education*, Asamoah (2003) identifies a rich history of exchange in the profession worldwide. A concentration of activity is identified in the early years, with countries of the Global North (i.e., wealthier countries in the West) sending students to countries of the Global South. The exchange was often lopsided, with Western schools devising the goals of short courses most frequently in social policy or international social welfare. As stated by Asamoah (2003):

> Many of the early exchange models are most accurately described as one-way consultations without a true exchange component, and some models lacked cultural relevance and sensitivity . . . there are notable exceptions and some of the ground-breaking firsts for international collaboration in social work were developmentally focused among schools of social work, government agencies, overseas ministries, NGOs and the UN. (p. 3)

There is a new realization that students learn best when they leave their sense of what is normal behind and visit new cultures with respect, curiosity, and the expectation of genuine exchange.

In addition to the early study abroad programs, some of which have been criticized for having more touristic elements than learning through dialogue, there is currently encouragement from professional organizations to add depth to the student experience. The International Association of Schools of Social Work (IASSW), the International Consortium for Social Development (ICSD), and the International Federation of Social Workers (IFSW) encourage programs to build truly reciprocal courses and research projects, such as the University of Connecticut's longstanding program of exchange among students and faculty of the University of the West Indies at Mona. Their work includes faculty research and teaching in their partner schools and a variety of field and course exchanges. Similarly, Durham University in the United Kingdom has extensive collaborative research projects with universities in Europe (Dominelli & Bernard, 2003).

Goals for exchange have been broadening in recent years and include the following:

- Identifying a variety of solutions to common problems, such as child abuse.
- Encouraging social work students to question their own sense of cultural identity and norms so that they become more accepting and welcoming of others.
- Expanding the knowledge of a variety of countries among students so that they understand the original impetus for immigration.
- Developing a sense of the strength of the profession worldwide to foster collaboration,

especially at borders and in questions of human rights such as international adoptions.
- Building a curriculum that is relevant beyond the local situation and that recognizes issues common to social workers worldwide, such as access to health, healthy pregnancy, and safe environments for vulnerable people, including the elderly, people with disabilities, and children.
- Sharing and expanding theory and practice, such as in the work in Ljubljana to cocreate solutions for families. This work builds on the idea of a fourth wave in social work practice—the first being community work, the second being clinical practice and the medical model, the third being psychosocial work with an understanding of the person in the environment, and the fourth being the expectation of working alongside rather than ahead or above service users.

The expectation that international exchanges focus most on student education is also evolving. Faculties in many countries are realizing that there is much to learn from one another in their often completely different approaches to similar issues. For instance, in India, Rachel Singh is a social worker who runs a sewing cooperative in New Delhi. She is inspiring because she combines her knowledge of the person in the environment with empowerment and community organizing. All her workers receive fair trade, and cows in the basement of Singh's center in New Delhi provide milk to families. In India, provision of milk to families and especially to children, is a major drive to increase overall health and prevent childhood diseases as described in Operation Flood (Patel, 2000).

Another innovative example of learning involves the empowerment of service users from the traditional labeling of *victim, welfare recipient*, or *single parent* to *participant* in service provision (Link, 1995; Stones, 1994). Students from the United States visiting a refuge for women recovering from physical and emotional abuse in Exeter, England, were surprised that the women themselves ran the center with the support of the social workers. "But who is in charge?" the students asked, and the reply came, "The service users." "But who is in charge at night?" they asked, with the same response: "The service users."

In a widening network throughout the world, the ideas of Muhammad Yunus (2009), also known as Banker to the Poor, are being played out through social and economic development projects that include microlending and investment. (Microlending is described in more detail by Thomas in Chapter 64 of this volume.) Microlending provides an opportunity for all economic classes, and particularly those experiencing poverty, to participate in credit and wealth building through investment in their labor. Social workers are recognizing that economic circumstances are key to social survival and health and that psychosocial issues are always complicated by economic, environmental, and political ones.

Although the goals of international exchange are ever widening in the social work profession, they cover the essential expectations of cultural values awareness, knowledge expansion, and skill development. In the current phase of this work, there is increased emphasis on preparation for cultural difference. With the increase in migration plus employers crossing borders, there is an understanding that it takes an intentional reorientation when leaving a familiar place to enter a new environment with respect and care.

Expectations were more limited in the early years of exchange; the act of traveling, absorbing the local approach to social work, and returning safely sufficed for many. Now the anticipation includes a more in-depth realization of the vital learning that takes place when the dialogue has been well planned and implemented, including detailed feedback, plans for reentry to familiar domains, and evaluation by all parties.

MODELS OF EXCHANGE

The four models to be discussed are *(1)* study abroad courses; *(2)* interactive video exchange, *(3)* faculty exchange and research, and *(4)* practice and field internship exchange.

Study Abroad Courses

In the 1970s and 1980s, criticism arose of social work courses that simply exported Western views of social work by taking students from the United States to various countries for short courses that used US texts and perspectives. Furthermore, Midgley (1965) was concerned that schools of social work in developing countries were caught up in using methods and theories of Western schools rather than practices that were more appropriate to their context. This social work imperialism extended to courses offered abroad by US faculty that had insufficient respect for and reference to local professionals and educators. At an international conference in Jerusalem, Merlai Desai of the Tata Institute in India expressed frustration at the

notion that codes of ethics are appropriate worldwide. She placed this frustration in the context of American and European social workers assuming that their approach to ethics can be generalized. Desai argued that for countries with a lower gross national product (GNP), there was insufficient infrastructure to oversee licensing and implementation of such codes, and that for many social workers in Asia, a declaration of ethics was enough (Desai, 1998). This dissonance between countries with higher GNPs and those with lower GNPs, or between the Global North and Global South, is further discussed by Barretta-Herman in Chapter 54 of this volume.

Healy (2003) contrasts the period of dominance of Western methods of social work with the current awareness that international exchange is most fruitful when there is respect for local conditions and mutual commitment to goals. She states that "mutuality is the cornerstone of a successful exchange program" and the foundation for the future development of international social work (p. 15). In another discussion of mutuality, Guevara and Ylvisaker (2003) make a helpful distinction between a home model and a host model of exchange (Guevara & Ylvisaker, 2003). In the home model, the faculty at the sending institution generate the syllabus, including goals and service activities that are undertaken by participating students, and the receiving community usually includes nongovernment organizations (NGOs) rather than educational institutions. In the host model, an educational institution receives a group and is responsible for setting up the content, itinerary, and visits to centers of social work.

An ideal for sustainable programs is when an exchange develops over a number of years, such as that of Hokenstad and colleagues at the Department of Social Policy and Social Work at Eötvös Loránd University (ELTE) in Budapest and the Mandel School of Applied Social Sciences at Case Western Reserve University (CWRU) in Cleveland (Healy et al., 2003). This exchange connected Eastern Europe with American partners and included exchange of students and professors across fields of practice, policy, and research.

A similarly longstanding institutional agreement involving exchange of students has been established between the University of Ljubljana, Slovenia, and Augsburg College, Minneapolis (Link & Cacinovic, 2003). In this instance, implicit learning has become equally as important as the explicit curriculum, field visits, and assignments. The Slovenian and US colleagues have discovered multiple levels of implicit learning through living together and participating in different times and rhythms for conversation, rituals, sleeping, and meals; appreciating slow rather than fast food; listening to each other's stories; and walking instead of driving. Another compelling aspect of this experience is the reduction of costs to students following the reciprocal agreement to house, feed, and transport students in the host country, with the countries taking turns to host.

In summary, the study abroad course rarely stands alone. Examples shared here and in the literature indicate that successful initiatives include careful planning with partners, agreements in advance of travel, orientation and cultural preparation for students, mutually accepted goals and plans, and detailed exchange of information prior to physical exchange. Evaluating courses and efforts to build elements of sustainability, learning from past mistakes, and building expectations for the future that are institutionalized (rather than reliant on one or two energetic faculty) are the key to successful work.

Interactive Video Exchange

In 2004 and 2005, a faculty member at a small liberal arts college in the United States responded to a request from the US Department of State for proposals to join ten US schools plus international partners in training to establish video links with universities in a variety of countries (Link & Bill, 2005). Together with a computer consultant, Link traveled to Slovenia and Singapore. Groundwork had been established with colleagues through a previous course exchange where students traveled between Slovenia and the United States in alternating years and with Singapore through earlier research collaboration. Link and colleagues developed a curriculum to exchange ideas through interactive video classrooms between campuses. The emphasis was for social workers to explore world cultures, cross-cultural communication, and peacemaking. Video protocols plus animated learning unfolded as a result of this grant.

The project was a natural extension of the professional concern to connect students with each other across a variety of countries and to appreciate reciprocal learning and interdependence with the world in ways that did not exclude students because of the cost of travel. The project included educating students about cultural awareness, nationalism, social and economic conditions, global citizenship, and the complexity and mirage of borders; exploring global resources such as the United Nations and its agencies; and becoming educational ambassadors with one another. There were four components: orientation to cultural exchange, explicit curriculum, video protocols, and implicit learning.

Orientation to cultural exchange included establishing and building protocols plus increasing awareness of greetings, nonverbal and verbal communication, and cultural awareness. In discussing definitions of culture, participants reviewed high-and low-context approaches to communication as well as individualistic and collective approaches to human development. Carter and Qureshi (1995) state: "Culture is a learned system of meaning and behavior that is passed from one generation to the next," in including values, norms, belief, attitudes, folkways, behavior styles, and traditions that are linked together to form a way of life.

Explicit curriculum development included adding goals to modules within existing courses, including the following:

- Define *culture* (may include the concept of global citizenship).
- Increase students' abilities to explain their own culture and respect others.
- Increase students' understanding of world cultures.
- Identify the variety of cultures and interdependence worldwide.
- Define *global citizenship*.
- Develop cross-cultural communication skills.
- Increase understanding of approaches to human service in a variety of countries.

These modules were implemented within existing courses, enhancing material plus developing new insights for existing objectives. Examples include the concepts of violence and nonviolence, discipline and punishment (students connected this to family experience and widened it to society); social justice, conflict resolution, and restorative justice; social exclusion; and undocumented "disappeared" ones.

Video protocols were an essential aspect of facilitating communication. The protocols included a reminder to students to be aware of their body language (no yawning, no feet on tables, unfolded arms, only head coverings that revealed the face) and to be clear in speech and social demeanor. Greetings included saying who was in the room; everyone had name cards and held them up to indicate when they had a question or contribution to make. The protocols were reviewed from time to time and adjusted according to the location and preferences of the partners. Evaluation included traditional student evaluations, collective focus groups, and faculty e-mail dialogue, which is continuing.

Implicit learning included increasing awareness of global issues in daily life and the environment we work in, such as the way we practice Diwali, Passover, Easter, Ramadan, Kwanza, and holy days across the world. Maps and the globe were displayed and a wide range of opportunities were developed that promoted informal exchange among students. Student e-mail dialogue continued outside the classroom and relationships evolved over longer periods than is the norm with physical exchanges.

Although the emphasis in this section is on one initiative, there were ten parallel projects funded by the US State Department during 2004 and 2005, and reports are available from the schools involved (Link & Bill, 2005). The National University of Singapore also has an advanced approach to interactive video that it uses extensively with international partners, as do the University of Durham and the Massachusetts Institute of Technology (MIT). Interactive video classrooms are a natural corollary to the expansion and availability of accessible technology.

Faculty Exchange

The traditional course exchange and the interactive video exchange among students in the example described previously led to peaceful cooperation on practical and relational levels among the faculty. The relationships that were built reflect aspects of faculty exchange in many parts of the world:

- Writing and researching together
- Developing curricula together
- Having a faculty exchange for teaching

A colleague returned from an overseas visit to a school that may be the recipient of US students from one of the authors of this chapter (Link). The colleague commented that the colleagues in the country visited were unable to understand the US curriculum arrangements, and this sparked lively debate on whether the host needed to understand the curriculum of the senders and whether there should be more of an emphasis on the visitors exploring a new curriculum. International faculty exchange is ideally open-minded, and the sense of normal is released and replaced by storytelling and an invitation to be taught, as in, "Tell me about this community." Faculty visit one another's countries anticipating that they are discovering a community where the patterns of culture, communication, resource sharing, and everyday life are a new ethnography rather than being "less than" or impoverished.

Faculty exchange may include sabbaticals, short-term research, and fully funded collaborative work.

These exchanges offer a parallel process of the learning that is expected of social work students in their multicultural home environments. The key attitude seems to be one of humility, which some faculty can practice, and the key question that faculty may anticipate seems to be this: Do you know enough about this country to visit and teach here?

International Field Placement and Practice

Field placement and practice is perhaps the most recent development in international exchange, and despite a few initiatives toward the end of the last century, it is a particular development of professional social work in the twenty-first century. As explained by Lager and Mathiesen in Chapter 51 of this volume and Mathiesen and Lager, (2007), there are a number of challenges to the establishment of field placements and internships, agreement of expectations, oversight, and evaluation.

The expectations are higher in relation to student skill development for both host- and home-country social work programs than the earliest forays would suggest. Shared language (including student willingness to acquire language skills where they are missing rather than relying on dominant languages such as English) is often a central pathway to a successful experience for both student and supervisor. Also, the dimension of practice teachers (sometimes known as field instructors) who have a variety of styles adds complexity. It is critical to have agreed objectives and plans for implementation even as the initiative is an invitation to negotiate planning and documentation according to the norms of the host country.

SUMMARY

In order to become effective social work practitioners, international exchange has become a necessity (Plummer & Nyang'au, 2009). In the past there was concern that only those with sufficient economic means could travel and participate, but curriculum developments have revealed that there are numerous ways to generate greater awareness of the world. Technology has allowed video classrooms and Internet exchanges. Institutional agreements have established innovative ways to reduce costs for students who visit one another's schools, in some instances paying in country for the visitors and carrying over the arrangement when the visitors become hosts. Also, homestays are an effective and affordable way to engage with a new culture even though they can at first challenge students socially and psychologically (Boyle & Baranti, 1999).

As stated earlier in this chapter, a key goal one hundred years ago was for social workers to be peacemakers. This is still our role. In order to be peacemakers, the profession is building an expectation, even through the difficulty of agreeing on international standards, to hear one another and to respect each other's realities, be it a lack of resources to implement codes of practice or an overemphasis on individual pathology in some parts of the world at the expense of recognizing the structural issues of economic and environmental survival. It is clear that the first steps of international exchange include confronting and acknowledging one's own culture and cultural history, especially if it involves the oppressions of empire. Studying aspects of culture passed from generation to generation so that social workers reach true cultural awareness means confronting and acknowledging one's own skin before meeting and focusing on others (Razack, 2002).

Another critical component of international exchange is the sharing of ways to implement human rights and United Nations conventions. Following the closure of international adoption agencies who ignored the Convention on the Rights of the Child and the arrest of volunteers in Haiti who tried to leave the country with undocumented children, there is ample evidence that there is work to do in fully understanding the value and reach of the international conventions and laws that cross national borders in the interests of vulnerable populations. In essence, exploring a variety of approaches to human service and community organization and development, cooperating in the creation of curricula, collaborating in fieldwork practicum, and generating relationships among students, faculty, and colleagues in ongoing and sustainable ways are all parts of this rich fabric of international exchange.

REFERENCES

Asamoah, Y. (2003). International collaboration in social work education: Overview. In L. Healy, Y. Asamoah, & M. C. Hokenstad (Eds.), *Models of international collaboration in social work education* (Chapter 1, p. 3). Alexandria, VA: CSWE.

Boyle, D., & Baranti, C. (1999). A model for international continuing education: Cross-cultural, experiential professional development. *Professional Development, 2*(2), 57–62.

Carter, R. T., & Qureshi, A. T. (1995). A Typology of Philosophical Assumptions in Multicultural counseling and Training. In J. G. Pontevotta et al, *Handbook of Multicultural Counseling* Thousand Oaks: Sage.

Desai, M. (1998). *Indian declaration of ethics.* Presentation at the International Consortium for Social Development Conference, Jerusalem.

Dominelli, L., & Bernard, W. (Eds.). (2003). *Broadening horizons.* Basingstoke, UK: Ashgate.

Guevara, J., & Ylvisaker, R. (2003). Home and host models of collaboration for service learning: Grand Valley State University programs in El Salvador and South Africa. In L. Healy, Y. Asamoah, & M. C. Hokenstad (Eds.), *Models of international collaboration in social work education* (pp. 81–90). Alexandria, VA: Council on Social Work Education.

Healy, L., Asamoah, Y., & Hokenstad, M. C. (Eds.). (2003). *Models of international collaboration in social work education.* Alexandria, VA: Council on Social Work Education.

Healy, L. (2003). In Healy, L., Asamoah, Y., & Hokenstad, M. C. (2003). *Models of international collaboration in social work education.* Alexandria, VA: Council on Social Work Education.

Link, R. (1995). British Family Centers and Parent Participation: Child Protection Through Empowerment. *Community Alternatives: International Journal of Family Care, 7,* 81–106.

Link, R. & Cacinovic Vogrincic, G. (2003) Learning Together through Faculty and Student Exchange. In Healy, L., Asamoah, Y., & Hokenstad, M. C. (Eds.). (2003). *Models of international collaboration in social work education* (Chapter 3, p. 23). Alexandria, VA: Council on Social Work Education.

Link, R. & Bill, R. (2005). Lessons Without Leaving. Presentation to the Annual Program Meeting, Council on Social Work Education, Nashville.

Lyons, K., & Ramanathan, C. (2004). Models of field practice in global settings. In C. Ramanathan & R. Link (Eds.), *All our futures: Principles and resources for social work practice in a global era* (Chapter 10). Belmont: Brooks/Cole/Thomson.

Mathiesen, S., & Lager, P. (2007). A model for developing international student exchanges. *Social Work in Education, 26*(3), 280–291.

Midgley, J. (1995). *Social development.* London: Sage.

Mirsky, J., & Barasch, M. (1998). Facilitating a reciprocal international exchange in social work. *Professional Development, 1*(3), 20–29.

Patel, A. (1998, February 22). *Operation Flood* [Keynote address]. Second Pan Commonwealth Veterinary Conference, Bangalore.

Plummer, C., & Nyang'au, T. (2009). Reciprocal e-mentoring: Accessible international exchanges. *International Social Work, 52*(6), 811–822.

Razack, N. (2002). A critical examination of international student exchanges. *International Social Work, 45*(2), 251–265.

Stones, C. (1994). *Focus on families: Family centres in action.* Basingstoke, UK: Macmillan.

Yunus, M. (2009). *Banker to the poor.* New York: PublicAffairs.

53

Using Technology for International Education and Research

THOMAS P. FELKE AND GOUTHAM M. MENON

Information and communication technologies have changed the way people connect with one another. The last fifteen years have seen the rise of Internet-based protocols and other technologies that have been beneficial in the way we teach, perform research, and conduct practice. Universities have been quick to adapt to new realities and have led the way in adopting these technologies for education and research. While these changes have been common in economically developed countries, the digital divide with economically less developed nations continues to be of concern. This chapter provides an overview of the current and potential uses of technology in international education and research. Further, it details some of the common tools being used to meet the demand of internationalizing curricula. The chapter also provides case examples of how some programs have used technology to link universities in various continents. Finally, it discusses some of the barriers to using technology as well as some of the new tools available to social work academics and research.

OVERVIEW

The profession of social work has witnessed a growth in the creative use of technology for many decades (Finn & Lavitt, 1994). Patterson (1996) advocated for the development of an online repository of global social work knowledge, while efforts such as telephone support groups (Meier, Galinsky, & Rounds, 1995; Roffman, Beadnell, Ryan, & Downey, 1995), online counseling (Murphy et al., 2009), and online advocacy for international social and economic justice (Quiero-Tajalli, McNutt, & Campbell, 2006) are evidence of the influence of emerging information and communication technologies (ICTs) on professional practice with individuals, families, and groups.

Social work has also been largely affected by ICTs in the area of online education, whether conducted domestically or with an international component. The delivery of course content via the Internet allows students and faculty to interact even though they are in multiple separate locations. A variety of platforms and communication tools have provided faculty and students with news ways for connecting online. For many schools of social work, these tools also provide the means for meeting educational accreditation standards.

The importance of providing social work students with international content has increased over the past decade. The most recent version of the Educational Policy and Accreditation Standards (EPAS) disseminated by the Council on Social Work Education (CSWE) (2010) makes specific reference not only to students learning via a global perspective but also advocates the use of technology in social work programs.

CURRENT USE OF TECHNOLOGY

Technology developments have been used to enhance teaching, supervision, and research in social work. In terms of teaching, ICTs have been used in distance education for both domestic and international purposes. An increasing number of social work programs are using ICTs as either a primary or supplementary method of instruction. Though CSWE does not track the number of programs that offer distance education programs, its website does list twelve US-based programs—ten MSW (master of social work) and two BSW (bachelor of social work) programs—that have such offerings as of July 2010 (CSWE, 2010). The application of ICTs to social work education has also been recognized outside of the United States, as evidenced by the longstanding success of the Open University model in the United Kingdom, Darkwa's (1999) call for the use of such technologies for social work education in Ghana, and other international initiatives such as that conducted by Link and Bill (2007) with academic institutions in Slovenia and Singapore.

This use of ICTs has broadened outside of single-country delivery to cross-national delivery as well (Crowell & McCarragher, 2007). International efforts using distance education include e-mail partnerships (Johnson, 1999), chat rooms (Wong, 2007), and discussion boards (Felke & Healy, 2004). Other uses of ICTs in social work education have included the advising of social work students in international field placements (Maidment, 2006; Panos, 2005).

Much of the technology being used in reaching out internationally revolves around distance education. Given the often prohibitive costs and ancillary issues involved with providing student exchange programs, distance education technologies provide an opportunity for students and faculty to learn and work collaboratively. The following are the major technology tools being used in this endeavor.

Distribution Lists

One of the main forms of distribution lists is the popular Listserv, which allows people to subscribe to various groups that have been set up by list moderators. Messages are sent to a single e-mail address of the list, and the message in turn is distributed to all subscribers. Distribution lists are great ways to generate a community of practice by having members coalesce around a topic of interest. They are easy to manage and require little programming experience.

Chat

This technology is used when there is a need for synchronous communication between groups of people. It is easy to use, but the main drawback is that it is sometimes difficult to get all parties online at the same time when different time zones are in play. A variation of chat is instant messaging, which identifies people who are online and makes it possible to conduct one-on-one or group synchronous communication online. Whereas chat software resides on a server, instant messaging software resides on one's personal computer.

Discussion Boards

For asynchronous communication, the discussion board is the most used technology. It allows people to post questions or remarks on an electronic board and participants can respond to these postings whenever they wish to do so. Its asynchronous nature is ideally suited for international collaborations since people can post at their convenience, hence overcoming the issue of time zones.

Course Management Software

Many universities use course management software (CMS) to conduct online or hybrid classes. Blackboard is one of the most predominantly used commercial CMS products, though other options, such as the open-source Moodle, are gaining in popularity. This type of software brings together various applications in one bundle. Most provide faculty with space to upload syllabi, course reading materials, media presentations, and other documents. Most also include discussion boards, chats, and other communication tools. They can also be used for creating online tests and grading assignments. One drawback of CMS in an international setting is that many universities have strict restrictions on who can access the site. This becomes problematic when faculty members or students from a different university need access to the course materials but are denied the use of the CMS.

Videoconferencing

This is a good tool to use when one wants a visual connection to the person one is communicating with. Typical videoconferencing involves connecting two remote television sets either through satellite or cable technologies. Computers are also now being used to connect people over the Internet using webcams.

Voice Over Internet Protocol (VoIP)

One exciting development in communication technologies is the advent of VoIP. This technology allows people to make long-distance calls free of charge on a computer-to-computer connection. The most used software for VoIP is Skype. This technology has revolutionized the way people connect with each other, especially internationally, and is a useful tool when collaborating with scholars and researchers in multiple locations. The overhead cost is minimal; hence the attraction to this technology.

Web Conferencing

This technology brings together aspects of CMS, videoconferencing, and VoIP. Systems such as Dimdim and WebEX allow people to connect in a myriad of ways, such as through videoconferences, VoIP, or traditional conference calls, using a toll-free telephone line. These systems also provide a platform for participants to share documents and presentations. The cost of these systems tends to depend on the number of participants and level of functionality.

CASE EXAMPLE 1

Over the past ten years, the University of Connecticut (UConn) School of Social Work has undertaken several international social work education initiatives involving ICTs. The collaborations have been developed with students and faculty in various locations, particularly in the Caribbean and Central Asia. Two specific projects highlight the use of ICTs for such ventures.

The first project came about as a result of an existing working relationship between faculty at UConn and the University of the West Indies (UWI). Based on this relationship, an idea was formed to have a UWI faculty member participate in a course being conducted by a professor from UConn (Felke & Healy, 2004). The UWI professor was provided with guest access to the course site on the CMS operated by UConn. The UWI professor posted a case study to the course site, the UConn students reviewed the case study, and then the students and UWI professor had a dialogue via the CMS discussion board. Due to the positive response by students to this initiative, the "lecture" was conducted again the following year and was expanded to include another participant from Cape Verde.

To provide some reciprocity in this initiative, a second project was developed for students at UWI that involved a lecture provided by adjunct UConn faculty focusing on the potential uses of technology for social service administration (Felke & Healy, 2004). The lecture was based on the content of an elective course, Computer Applications in the Human Services, which is offered annually in the administration sequence at UConn. The elective is offered to graduate social work students at UConn in a traditional face-to-face format. Based on conversations with visiting lecturers from UWI-St. Augustine, the idea was generated to provide students at the UWI campus with an overview of the potential uses of technology in social work practice. Two lecturers from UConn developed a narrated PowerPoint slideshow that was loaded as a streaming video into the course site for the elective on the CMS. Students and faculty from UWI were provided with guest accounts to access the CMS and specific course site. The UWI students viewed the presentation and then discussed its content with the two lecturers via the synchronous chat feature available on the course site. The students

were given continued access to the course site throughout the remainder of the semester so as to discuss other topics related to technology and social work administration with the lecturers. The project was well received and laid the groundwork for an additional initiative to be undertaken.

This additional initiative involved an existing relationship between faculty at UConn and Yerevan State University (YSU) in Armenia. The project was first undertaken in 2002 once it was determined that the available technology in Armenia could support such an initiative. This initiative built upon the lessons learned from the projects undertaken with UWI. However, in this case the elective course, Comparative Social Welfare Policy, was designed specifically for this initiative. A professor from UConn with extensive knowledge of social welfare policy designed the course along with a graduate assistant familiar with distance education technology. Students from YSU were provided with guest access to the course site located on the UConn CMS. Photos of all participating students and faculty members were posted to the course site so that participants could put faces with names. The UConn professor posted lectures on a weekly basis. Students at YSU met face-to-face with their instructor each week, while students from UConn did not meet with their instructor at any point during the semester, although the option to do so was offered to them. Students from both universities reviewed the lectures and discussed them via the discussion board within the course site. Students from both universities were organized in cross-national work groups to complete three projects using the discussion board. The results of these collaborations were posted to the course site for all students to review and comment on. This initiative has continued to be offered since 2002 and is now in its eighth offering.

CASE EXAMPLE 2

This case involved the teaching of a multicountry course on human trafficking using interactive television and distribution lists. The University of South Carolina School of Law and College of Social Work initiated a joint course on human trafficking with the University of Indonesia Graduate Law Program, the University of Cologne Faculty of Law, the Diponegoro University Faculty of Law, the Gadjah Mada University Graduate Program in Business and Public Law, and the University of Northern Sumatra Graduate Law Program. The course examined international and domestic laws related to human trafficking from the perspective of the United States, Germany, and Indonesia. Students from law and from social work participated in the semester-long course.

During the first three weeks, US faculty taught classes covering general legal and social science points applicable to human trafficking in the United States. Then the Indonesian faculty taught for four weeks, covering a general national study and criticism of human trafficking in Indonesia, a detailed empirical test study of trafficking between villages in a certain rural area and major urban areas, and child prostitution and trafficking. Finally, the German faculty took over for four weeks to cover European views. The course was taught via interactive television connecting all six universities using the Internet. The classes were scheduled in the early morning in the United States, which enabled the German participants to be in class in the afternoon and the Indonesian participants in the evening. The course used a distribution list (Listserv) to allow all students and faculty to engage in a dialogue after class. Faculty used the Listserv to post questions before the lecture to encourage discussion. All lectures were videotaped and streamed on a university-based website. All reading material for the course was uploaded to the website in English, German, and Bahasa Indonesia. The students had group assignments that provided them with the opportunity to work with students from other countries.

The course was well accepted by the students, and the most frequent comment at evaluation was that having the opportunity to interact with faculty from other countries was instructive. The students also liked the group assignments, though there were some language barriers. The technology that enabled this course was simple to use, and students had the opportunity to see the faculty and students at all the sites using multiple television screens simultaneously.

POTENTIAL BARRIERS

The cases just described are examples of how enriching the student and faculty experience can be when technology is used to reach across international borders. Though the lure to use technology for international collaboration is strong, there are several aspects that must be taken into account to make it a reality.

Differences in time zones can affect the type of technology (i.e., synchronous or asynchronous) that is used in collaborative international efforts. Where significant time differences exist between universities, the use of asynchronous technologies such as e-mail

and discussion boards may be the only option. This may lead to dissatisfaction among students who seek opportunities for real-time communication (Beyth-Marom, Saporta, & Caspi, 2005; Katz, 2002).

One of the primary issues in conducting broad-based international connections using distance education is language. Collaborating partners using web-based discussion tools are generally limited to connections with people who can read and write the same language. Even when language fluency does not present a major issue between collaborators, it may still play a limiting role. One author has found that nonresponse may become a barrier for some people participating in an online collaboration. Although students may hold an acceptable level of language proficiency to participate in discussions, they may not feel comfortable with their proficiency to the point that it limits their participation in discussions.

RECOMMENDATIONS

Collaborations that take place online, whether teaching or research based, require a significant amount of coordination and planning. The most obvious recommendation that can be made is to ensure that thorough planning has been undertaken. It is recommended that collaborations occur between partners with an existing working relationship. The relationships that existed between faculties at the universities discussed in the first case example facilitated the development, implementation, and management of the projects. The author involved with these initiatives had the opportunity to travel to the universities in the Caribbean and Armenia before the implementation of these initiatives, which allowed for an assessment of the technological resources at both locations to see how they matched with those at UConn. Based on this assessment, the author was able to make recommendations about how the collaborations might work using the tools available in the CMS at UConn.

Institutional support for international distance education is critical. In the UConn case example, each endeavor was well supported by both the school and the university administration. Particularly, the support provided by the UConn university information technology support division (UITS) has been instrumental in the ongoing success of these initiatives. The instructional technology adviser collaborated with UITS on each endeavor to investigate systems requirements as well as to develop detailed instructional manuals for international partners. One of the primary supports has been the free access to the UConn CMS that is provided to international students and faculty.

Many of the topics that come up when undertaking an online endeavor may be more easily addressed if an existing working relationship exists. Points to be addressed include the following:

- Division of labor—outlining how the collaborative effort will be conducted and maintained
- Expectations about response—establishing time frames for responding to postings and submitting assignments
- Reciprocity—understanding what is to be provided by each partner in the relationship.

This last point may be the most important because often it is the partner who is more technologically advanced who stands to benefit the most from such an endeavor.

Faculty who will be teaching an international distance-education course should meet with students to discuss certain topics before the start of the course. This is not unlike what generally occurs on the first day of a typical course. However, in addition to discussing topics such as course expectations, assignments, and grading, it is also important to ensure that students have a clear understanding of issues such as netiquette, use of slang and professional jargon, and cultural awareness.

Although the digital divide among less economically developed countries continues to be of concern, many countries have the capacity to participate in cross-national exchanges. While examining the technological capabilities at a university in Armenia, for example, one author found the available technology equaled or surpassed that found at the collaborating US institution. This might have been expected given that Armenia and similar countries entered the technological era at a time when computers with higher processing capabilities were the norm. The more pressing problem in these countries may not be the availability of adequate technology but related issues such as cost and access (Steyaert & Gould, 2009; Wong, Fung, Law, Lam, & Lee, 2009).

USING ONLINE TECHNOLOGY FOR RESEARCH EFFORTS

This chapter has dealt primarily with the use of ICTs for international education; however, any of these technologies could also be used for international research efforts. Though the use of such technologies may seem a logical avenue for international researchers, a review of the social work literature turned up few examples illustrating this level of collaboration.

Listservs can be used to identify possible research partners, funding sources, or key informants on specific topics of interest. In an asynchronous environment, documents and other files, such as data sets or presentations, can be attached to e-mails or posted to discussion boards. Plummer and Nyang'au (2009) provide an example of this usage by discussing a case example on e-mentoring through the use of e-mail. In addition, the use of VoIP or a web-conferencing tool such as WebEx or Dimdim provides international colleagues with opportunities for synchronous sharing, creation, and editing of files.

Another technology that may be used in these types of efforts is online survey software such as SurveyMonkey. These types of programs allow researchers to survey people around the globe while reviewing responses and conducting basic statistical analyses in an online environment.

Many of the issues and recommendations highlighted for using online technologies for international education would also apply to international research collaboration. Additionally, the use of online surveys would require considerations based on research standards and ethics for the use of such tools internationally.

EXAMPLE OF CONDUCTING RESEARCH ONLINE

The NGO Committee for Social Development, in collaboration with the United Nations Non-Governmental Liaison Service (NGLS), conducted a survey on best practices in social integration. The survey was carried out almost entirely online. The survey instrument was posted on the NGLS website in several languages, and a cover letter and a link to the survey were distributed by e-mail to organizations in the networks of members of the NGO Committee for Social Development. Responses using the online instrument were encouraged and most respondents used the online tool. Those with limited access to the Internet were able to print out the survey and fax or mail it in. Responses were received from organizations in sixty-two countries. The responses were analyzed and shared with member governments and civil society organizations participating in the forty-eighth session of the United Nations Commission for Social Development. The report was also posted on the NGO Committee's website and distributed by e-mail to the respondents (NGO Committee for Social Development, 2010).

SUMMARY

As noted by Payne and Askeland (2008), "technology-based distance education has an increasing impact on social work education as well as in lifelong learning" (p. 144). This chapter has sought to highlight the role that ICTs have played in advancing international social work education. Two case examples were presented and others mentioned, but this is by no means a comprehensive record of initiatives that have been undertaken in this regard.

It would seem that the role of ICTs in international social work education is destined to increase as universities search for ways to respond to student demands for international exposure in social work education. Cost will continue to be a barrier to travel for many students, particularly those in less economically developed countries where the profession is growing. Thus, ICTs offer a solid (though far from perfect) alternative for many students and universities around the world.

As technology continues to become more accessible, students and faculty will have even more options for connecting with their colleagues in other countries. Research efforts not only need to continue to be targeted on conventional issues such as time, language, and cultural sensitivity but also need to be expanded to include new issues that will arise along with continuing advances in technology.

REFERENCES

Beyth-Marom, R., Saporta, K., & Caspi, A. (2005). Synchronous vs. asynchronous tutorials: Factors affecting students' preferences and choices. *Journal of Research on Technology in Education, 37*(3), 245–262.

Council on Social Work Education (CSWE). (2010, July 8). *Distance education offerings by accredited programs.* Retrieved August 20, 2010, from www.cswe.org/cms/39516.aspx.

Council on Social Work Education (CSWE). (2010, March 12). *2008 Educational Policy and Accreditation Standards (EPAS).* Retrieved August 20, 2010, from http://www.cswe.org/Accreditation/Handbook.aspx.

Crowell, L. F., & McCarragher, T. (2007). Delivering a social work MSW program through distance education: An innovative collaboration between two universities, USA. *Social Work Education, 26*(4), 376–388.

Darkwa, O. K. (1999). Continuing social work education in an electronic age: The opportunities and challenges facing social work education in Ghana. *Professional Development, 2*(1), 38–43.

Felke, T., & Healy, L. (2004). Creating connections for international learning through distance education technologies: A Caribbean-USA demonstration effort. *Caribbean Journal of Social Work, 3*, 142–158.

Finn, J., & Lavitt, M. (1994). Computer-based self-help groups for sexual abuse survivors. *Social Work with Groups, 17*, 21–45.

Johnson, A. K. (1999). Globalization from below: Using the Internet to internationalize social work education. *Journal of Social Work Education, 35*(3), 377–393.

Katz, Y. J. (2002). Attitudes affecting college students' preferences for distance learning. *Journal of Computer Assisted Learning, 18*(1), 2–9.

Link, R., & Bill, R. (2007). *Lessons without leaving.* Paper presented at the 53rd Annual Program Meeting of the Council on Social Work Education, San Francisco.

Maidment, J. (2006). Using on-line delivery to support students during practicum placements. *Australian Social Work, 59*(1), 47–55.

Meier, A., Galinsky, M. J., & Rounds, K. A. (1995). Telephone support groups for caregivers of persons with AIDS. *Social Work with Groups, 18*(1), 99–108.

Murphy, L., Parnass, P., Mitchell, D., Hallett, R., Cayley, P., & Seagram, S. (2009). Client satisfaction and outcome comparisons of online and face-to-face counselling methods. *British Journal of Social Work, 39*(4), 627–640.

NGO Committee for Social Development. (2010). *Social integration in action: Stories from the grassroots.* New York: Author. Available at http://ngosocdev.wordpress.com.

Patterson, D. A. (1996). An electronic social work knowledge base: A strategy for global information sharing. *International Social Work, 39*(2), 149–161.

Panos, P. T. (2005). A model for using videoconferencing technology to support international social work field practicum students. *International Social Work, 48*(6), 834–841.

Payne, M., & Askeland, G. A. (2008). Globalization and international social work: Postmodern change and challenge. Hampshire, UK: Ashgate.

Plummer, C. A., & Nyang'au, T. O. (2009). Reciprocal e-mentoring: Accessible international exchanges. *International Social Work, 52*(6), 811–822.

Quiero-Tajalli, I., McNutt, J. G., & Campbell, C. (2003). International social and economic justice, social work and on-line advocacy. *International Social Work, 46*(2), 149–161.

Roffman, R. A., Beadnell, B., Ryan, R., & Downey, L. (1995). Telephone group counseling in reducing AIDS risk in gay and bisexual males. *Journal of Gay and Lesbian Social Services, 2*, 145–157.

Steyaert J., & Gould, N. (2009). Social work and the changing face of the digital divide. *British Journal of Social Work, 39*(4), 740–753.

Wong, Y. (2007). Lessons learned in chat room teaching internationally. *Journal of Technology in Human Services, 25*(1/2), 59–83.

Wong, Y., Fung, J., Law, C., Lam, J., & Lee, V. (2009). Tackling the digital divide. *British Journal of Social Work, 39*(4), 754–767.

Comparative Cross-National Research (World Census)[1]

ANGELINE BARRETTA-HERMAN

The development of the Global Standards for the Education and Training of the Social Work Profession by the International Association of Schools of Social Work (IASSW) and the International Federation of Social Workers (IFSW) generated controversy from its inception (IASSW, 2004). The debates center on four issues: globalization or localization; dominance of Western or the Global North's conceptualization of social work over indigenous practice models; multiculturalism or universal values; and global standards or local standards (Gray and Fook, 2004). Gray and Fook argue that the extensive dialogue and debate necessary to reach widespread consensus did not occur on these complex and interrelated issues. To counter the criticisms of insufficient consultation, the footnotes in Sewpaul and Jones (2005) present a description of the process, noting the call for comments, changes in the approach to the standards, debates on terminology, and the decision to describe the statements as standards rather than guidelines. Sewpaul (2005) contends that the criticisms of inflexibility and nonresponsiveness to regional or local realities are acknowledged by referring to the Global Standards as "aspirational" statements. The IASSW and the IFSW, as joint sponsors of the project, view the standards as expressions of their missions to support the profession of social work. However, it can be argued that the consultation was limited because IASSW and IFSW do not represent all practitioners and programs worldwide.

Webb (2003) and Hugman (2005) argue that the case for global social work, hence for global standards, is spurious because social work is bound by, and an expression of, local culture. Noble (2004), referring to many Pacific Rim countries, and Healy (2004), referring to the Caribbean region, contend that geographical isolation, economic realities, the nascent stage of social work education, and language barriers present formidable challenges to achieving those standards. However, Yip (2004) identifies cultural norms (responsibility rather than rights, social norms rather than equality, collectivity rather than individuality) as the greatest barrier to the applicability of the standards in China. For others, the strongest argument against global standards is the threat of stifling the development of indigenous theory and practice "by prematurely prescribing the boundaries of the profession" (Healy, 2004: 593). Lyons (2006) recognizes that practice is rooted in the "local" but argues that "systems of welfare and the practices of social workers are affected by the processes and effects of globalization" (p. 366). She sees the Global Standards as the recognition of the transnational mobility of social workers and as an acknowledgment of the impact of global events on local practice.

The establishment of social work programs worldwide has grown exponentially in the last twenty years, notably in the Pacific Rim, Eastern Europe, and Africa. In 2000 the board of IASSW commissioned a world census of social work programs and established a permanent standing committee charged with tracking program development as part of the IASSW commitment to social work education (Barretta-Herman, 2005; Garber, 2000). The purpose of a membership survey in 2005 was to elicit from member programs mid-decade data on those characteristics of social work programs that had been asked about in the 2000 census. This reanalysis of the 2005 membership survey data was designed partly to explore the assumption that IASSW member schools were meeting the stipulations in the Global Standards.

2005 MEMBERSHIP SURVEY METHOD

The first challenge in the mid-decade survey was to shorten and simplify the 2000 census questionnaire without losing the ability to compare and contrast the membership survey results with the findings from the 2000 census. Three sets of questions were explored in the thirty-five-item, forced-choice survey. The first set of questions was designed to gather the demographic characteristics of the programs, their structure, and the personnel. The second set of questions elicited information on the extent of international exchanges of students and personnel. The last set of questions focused on the content of the curriculum offered in each program. The English version of the survey was translated into French, Spanish, and Japanese.

Electronic distribution of the letter of introduction and the survey began in July 2004. A follow-up request and a second survey were sent within eight weeks of the original e-mailing. The electronic version yielded fewer than fifty surveys despite a very small number of "bouncebacks." Appeals to board members and regional representatives were made requesting assistance in generating responses to the survey by letter and at the 2004 IASSW congress in Australia. Surveys were sent by hard copy in late 2004. By May 2005, it was possible to enter 147 responses into a Statistical Package for the Social Sciences (SPSS) database.

THE RESPONDENTS

The responses from twenty-eight countries represent a 36 percent response rate based on the 410 schools and programs listed as IASSW members in 2002–3. The regional analysis does not include Latin America due to a very low response rate ($N = 1$) (see Table 54.1).

These member schools that responded seemed to be decisively more established than the schools

TABLE 54.1. RESPONSES BY REGION ($N = 147$)

Region	Responses
Eastern and Southern African Association of Schools of Social Work (African region)	12
Asian and Pacific Association for Social Work Education (Asia-Pacific region)	50
European Association for Social Work Education (European region)	32
Asociación Latino Americana de Escuelas de Trabajo Social (Latin American region)	1
North America and Caribbean regions (North America)	52

responding to the 2000 world census (Barretta-Herman, 2005). Over 33 percent of the 127 schools that responded to this question were started before 1970, compared with only 14 percent in the 2000 world census. However, the recent upsurge in programs is also evident, particularly in the Asia-Pacific region, where 22 of the 42 programs in this sample were established after 1980 (see Table 54.2).

As in the 2000 census, the majority of these respondents identified their schools as public institutions (60 percent). Nearly one-third of the member schools indicated they were part of a university campus, demonstrating a level of national or governmental support and recognition of social work's academic and professional standing.

The majority of respondents offered programs at degree and postgraduate levels (see Table 54.3), with less than 15 percent of the institutions responding by region offering nondegree certificates or undergraduate diplomas. The only exception was in the Asia-Pacific region, where 40 percent of respondents

TABLE 54.2. SOCIAL WORK SCHOOLS AND PROGRAM ESTABLISHMENT

Region	Earliest year established	Pre–1926	1926–59	1960s	1970s	1980s	1990s	2000s	Total	Missing	N
Africa	1924	1	5	3		2			11	1	12
Asia-Pacific	1918	2	6	9	3	2	19	1	42	8	50
Europe	1899	2	6	4	7	3	2	2	26	6	32
North America	1908	7	15	9	11	2	3		47	5	52

TABLE 54.3. DEGREE PROGRAMS OFFERED BY REGION

Region	Bachelor	Master	PhD	Doctorate in social work
North America	39	39	19	1
Europe	26	15	10	3
Asia-Pacific	29	27	20	9
Africa	12	12	9	4

said they offered this preprofessional training as part of their regular programming.

Table 54.3 illustrates the number of bachelor- and master-level education programs offered by the respondents across the four regions. Table 54.4 gives an indication of the numbers graduating from these programs. We can note here the limited number of doctoral-level programs reported in each of the four regions and the small number of doctoral graduates. These low numbers constitute a threat to the vitality of the profession and raise concerns for the replacement of professional staff. ("Professional staff" here refers to teaching and field personnel employed by the program.)

While the numbers are an underestimate (partly due to the limited response rate and partly since not all schools are members of IASSW), it seems likely that there is, nevertheless, cause for concern. For instance, data from the USA indicate that only 66 out of the more than 500 programs offer doctoral education; and the Council on Social Work Education reports an average of 250 doctoral graduates annually, a no-growth figure since 1980 (Council on Social Work Education, 2005: 46).

TABLE 54.4. DEGREES CONFERRED IN THE PREVIOUS ACADEMIC YEAR (FEB. 2002–AUG. 2003 OR JAN.–DEC. 2003)

Region	Bachelor	Master	PhD or DSW
North America	1194	2718	80
Europe	1985	363	11
Asia-Pacific	2192	484	25
Africa	398	79	12
Total	5769	3644	128

FINDINGS

The data collected in the membership survey were descriptive and demographic: The focus was on program structure, international activities, and the curriculum. The Global Standards detail nine sets of standards that are further elucidated in 4–15 statements. The membership survey provided relevant data on the expectations contained in the first seven of the nine standards. Below, the abbreviated standard is followed by findings from the survey. (The full text of the standard is available on the IASSW and IFSW websites.)

1. Standards regarding the school's core purpose or mission statement
"All schools should aspire toward the development of a core purpose statement or a mission statement . . ."

Mission statements are seen as providing unifying principles for a program's strategic planning, curriculum development, and resource allocation. The actual statements were not collected for analysis, so it is not known to what extent the mission statements are clearly articulated and reflective of the core values and equity aspirations as stipulated in the standard.

However, nearly 89 percent of respondents in the four regions indicated that they had a school mission statement (approaching 100 percent in the North American region). This stands in sharp contrast to the results of the 2000 world census in which fewer than 35 percent of the respondents stated that they had a mission statement for their program (Barretta-Herman, 2005).

2. Standards regarding program objectives
"2.11 The conferring of a distinctive social work qualification . . ."

Seventy-three percent of the respondents indicated that they offered a bachelor's degree in social work. Although 64 percent offered a master's degree and 40 percent a doctorate, the question did not specify whether the degrees were distinctively labeled as social work degrees.

3. Standards with regard to program curricula including field education
"3.7 Field education should be sufficient in duration . . ."

All regions require field education for their bachelor's degree programs with wide variations in duration (as specified in hours, days, or months). Overall, at the bachelor's level, students were required to complete at least 500 hours either in a "block" (concentrated time period) or over a period of a year. Master's-level students outside the North American region were less likely to be required to complete a field placement. Master's programs in many parts of the world are theoretical or research-oriented and thus are less likely to mandate a structured field experience for their students.

"3.8 Provision of orientation for fieldwork supervisors or instructors"

Programs for field supervisors were offered by nearly all schools in North America (94 percent) and by more than 80 percent of the schools in Europe and Africa. Data were not gathered on the length of such programs or on fieldwork supervisors' qualifications.

4. Standards for core curricula
"4.2.1 Domain of the social work profession
Knowledge of human behavior and development . . . tradition, culture, beliefs, religions and customs . . .

A critical understanding of social work's origins and purposes . . . of national, regional and/or international social work codes of ethics . . ."

Because Standard 4 deals with the content of the core curricula, it is perhaps the most controversial. Respondents were asked to indicate if the courses in the list provided were required of their students in the bachelor's and master's programs. The results are shown in Figure 54.1.

Figure 54.1 confirms that 60 to 73 percent of the member schools require bachelor's-degree students to undertake a course or have course content in human behavior and development; race, ethnicity, and cultural issues; and the ethics and values of social work as recommended in the Global Standards. However, this percentage was lower for master's programs, for which several possible explanations can be offered. For example, a graduate student's study of these areas may be waived if a student holds a bachelor degree in

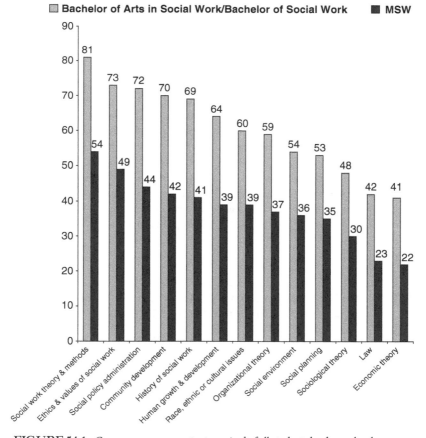

FIGURE 54.1: Courses or course content required of all students by degree level.

TABLE 54.5. RESEARCH COURSE
REQUIREMENTS

Region	Research methods course BSW (%)	Research methods course MSW (%)
North America	61	63
Europe	77	53
Asia-Pacific	70	36
Africa	75	58

social work or if the student has several years of prior work experience.

"4.2.3 Knowledge of social work research and skills in the use of research . . ."

As Table 54.5 illustrates, with the exception of North American respondents, only slightly more than two-thirds of bachelor's-degree students take at least one course in research and substantially fewer master's-degree programs reported requiring course work in research theory and methods. This finding questions the ability of graduates to critically access research findings or to conduct small-scale research fundamental to improving practice.

5. Standards with regard to professional staff
"5.1 The provision of professional staff, adequate in number and range of expertise, who have appropriate qualifications . . ."

In the entire sample, 40 percent of the schools had ten or fewer full-time-equivalent (FTE) professional staff. An additional 40 percent reported eleven to twenty-eight FTEs, indicating that the majority of programs in this sample were small to medium-sized. Whether the ratio of staff to student is adequate cannot be deduced from the data.

In order to access the range of expertise and appropriateness of qualifications, the study considered responses to two questions. The first asked how many of the school's professional staff held degrees in social work or in a related discipline. As Table 54.6 illustrates, both the North American and African regions indicated that at least 75 percent of their staff held a minimum of one social work degree. The results were significantly lower in the European and Asia-Pacific regions, where schools reported staff with degrees in a wide range of disciplines, including sociology, social policy, and education.

Unfortunately, direct evidence for the range of expertise cannot be gathered from the data. However, Table 54.6 shows that between 52 percent of staff in the European region and 84 percent in the African region had practice experience prior to coming to the academy, although only a third of staff are reported to be regularly engaged in practice, consultation, or research outside their institution alongside their teaching.

6. Standards for social work students
"6.1 Clear articulation of its admission criteria and procedures . . ."

Academic qualifications were cited most often as the basis for selection to undergraduate and graduate programs. Interviews were more frequently used as part of the admission process to undergraduate degrees in the European and Asia-Pacific regions (45% and 52% respectively) relative to the North American and African regions (27% and 25% respectively). Interestingly, despite the importance of personal communication and relationship skills in social work practice, the interview was seldom used for admission to a master's degree program in North American (9 percent), compared with 33 percent in European programs.

TABLE 54.6. PROFESSIONAL STAFF WITH SOCIAL WORK DEGREES, PRIOR
AND CURRENT WORK EXPERIENCE

Region	FTEs	With social work degree	With prior work experience	Regularly engaged in practice, consultation or research
North America	1522	1258 (83%)	1110 (73%)	504 (33%)
Europe	697	312 (48%)	363 (52%)	225 (32%)
Asia-Pacific	566	304 (54%)	335 (59%)	161 (28%)
Africa	86	64 (74%)	72 (84%)	31 (36%)

TABLE 54.7. ACADEMIC AND PROFESSIONAL QUALIFICATIONS
OF ADMINISTRATORS

Region	% administrators whose highest academic degree is social work	% administrators who hold a social work academic qualification	% administrators who hold a professional qualification in social work
North America	51	87	87
Europe	47	61	62
Asia-Pacific	50	59	48
Africa	50	92	92

7. Standards for structure, administration, governance, and resources

"7.2 The school has a designated Head or Director who has demonstrated administrative, scholarly and professional competence, preferably in the profession of social work."

The discipline of the administrator's (director's) highest academic credential was listed as social work in just 50 to 51 percent of the cases, with a slightly lower percentage in the European region (47 percent) (see Table 54.7). However, when asked if the academic administrator held a professional qualification in social work, the responses were notably higher, as demonstrated in Table 54.7. In many countries, a clear distinction is made between an academic qualification (a degree awarded by an educational institution) and a professional qualification that requires both practice experience and evidence of competence and may or may not also require a social work degree. However, figures suggest that academic and professional qualifications often operate in parallel, whether or not they are part of an integrated program.

"7.3 The Head or Director has primary responsibility for the co-ordination and professional leadership of the school, with sufficient time and resources to fulfill these responsibilities . . ."

Overall a high level of responsibility (over 75 percent) was reported in ten of the eleven administrative areas listed (including budget/resource allocation, curriculum decisions, staff appointments/hiring and evaluation, and relations with external agencies). Responsibility for building and facility maintenance was 55 percent or less in all four regions, perhaps because so many schools are part of larger institutions and may not have designated buildings. Responsibility for the curriculum, indicated by only 65 percent of the North American region respondents, may be a function of the strong national accreditation bodies in that region that tend to prescribe core curricula.

Although no survey question directly asked about sufficient time and resources, several respondents noted additional responsibilities for the academic administrators, including teaching responsibilities, the supervision of students, a scholarship agenda, university committee work, and resource development (i.e., fund-raising).

"7.10 The school plays a key role with regard to the recruitment, appointment and promotion of staff."

In three of the four regions 75 percent or more of the respondents reported responsibility for professional staff appointment and evaluation. The lower figure in the Asia-Pacific region (58 percent with responsibility for staff evaluation) was accompanied by the explanation that this was a shared responsibility.

LIMITATIONS OF THE STUDY

Cross-national surveys face a number of significant limitations, which demand that their results be considered with a degree of caution. Despite a terminology guide available on each page of the questionnaire, connotation of terms continued to be problematic. There are several classifications of teaching personnel, some of which are described by the same term in different countries. It is impossible to know if the responses to the questions on personnel included those who teach only one course or are full-time. Additionally, considering the challenges of translation, responses to a given question may differ in important ways, thus undermining the validity of the data.

The qualifications issue, although reported above, does not adequately address the reality and complexity of different situations. In many countries with new social work programs, teachers are recruited from other disciplines because specialized education in social work in that country is not available now, never was, or was not available for several decades. This does not begin to address the question of the dramatic variation in qualifying degrees among countries or how the question of previous social work practice was interpreted.

CONCLUSION

Despite the limitations of these data, this reanalysis of the 2005 membership survey provides a level of evidence demonstrating that the majority of the member schools responding to the survey meet several of the expectations in seven of the nine Global Standards. The variations by region reflect the differences in history, cultural norms, and the unique challenges faced by schools in different regions.

Further analysis of the membership data specifically in the areas of international activity and curricular offerings will promote deeper understanding of social work programs. Further research in the areas of the theoretical preparation of students and the requirements of fieldwork experience deserve intensive attention.

Several challenges remain in the continuing efforts to build an international database for social work programs. Despite those challenges, these efforts are fundamental to strengthening the professional identity of social work; providing a basis for comparison between the regions; and demonstrating the growth and development of social work education and training around the world.

ACKNOWLEDGMENTS

The author wishes to express appreciation to the IASSW World Census Committee, to IASSW members for their support, as well as to Michael F. Cogan and Margaret T. Reif of the University of St. Thomas (Minnesota) and Mel Gray of the University of Newcastle University (Australia) for their assistance in the preparation of this article. Special thanks go to work-study students Heidi Paul and Anka Vela for their data entry work.

NOTE

1. Reprinted, with permission from Sage Publications Inc., from Barretta-Herman (2008). Meeting the expectations of the Global Standards: a status report on the IASSW membership. *International Social Work* 51(6): 823–834.

REFERENCES

Barretta-Herman, A. (2005) 'A Reanalysis of the IASSW World Census 2000', *International Social Work* 48(6): 794–808.

Council on Social Work Education (2005) *Statistics on Social Work Education in the United States: 2003.* Alexandria, VA: Council on Social Work Education.

Garber, R. (2000) 'Social Work and Globalization', *Canadian Social Work* 2(1) (Summer) 17 (Special Issue): 198–215.

Gray, M., & J. Fook (2004) 'The Quest for a Universal Social Work: Some Issues and Implications', *Social Work Education* 23(5): 625–44.

Healy, L. M. (2004) 'Standards for Social Work Education in the North American and Caribbean Region: Current Realities, Future Issues', *Social Work Education* 3(5): 581–95.

Hugman, R. (2005) 'Looking Back: The View from Here', *British Journal of Social Work* 35(5): 609–20.

International Association of Schools of Social Work (IASSW) (2004) 'Global Standards for the Education and Training of the Social Work Profession'. Available online at www.iassw-aiets.org (accessed 2007).

Lyons, K. (2006) 'Globalization and Social Work: International and Local Implications', *British Journal of Social Work* 36(3): 365–80.

Noble, C. (2004) 'Social Work Education, Training and Standards in the Asia Pacific Region', *Social Work Education* 23(5): 527–36.

Sewpaul, V. (2005) 'Global Standards: Promise and Pitfalls for Re-inscribing Social Work into Civil Society', *International Journal of Social Welfare* 14(1): 210–17.

Sewpaul, V. and D. Jones (2005) 'Global Standards for the Education and Training of the Social Work Profession', *International Journal of Social Welfare* 14(3): 218–30.

Webb, S. A. (2003) 'Local Orders and Global Chaos in Social Work', *European Journal of Social Work* 6(2): 191–204.

Yip, K. (2004) 'A Chinese Cultural Critique of the Global Qualifying Standards for Social Work Education', *Social Work Education* 23(5): 597–612.

SECTION VIII

Social Work Around the World

Social Work in Africa

LENGWE-KATEMBULA MWANSA

INTRODUCTION

The beginnings of social work in Europe and America were located in the process of social development and growing momentum in the delivery of welfare services. Social work emerged alongside provision of services as a response to growing social problems. It evolved out of the need to help the poor and underprivileged to survive and also to empower them to enter the mainstream of development rather than remaining as vulnerable, oppressed, and marginalized populations (Ambrosino, Heffernan, Shuttleworth, & Ambrosino, 2005; Neukrug, 2008). The church, governments, and individual philanthropists were the drivers in the development of social welfare services.

In particular, history is awash with activities relating to almsgiving or works of mercy based upon Judeo-Christian beliefs and expectations. Christian teachings extolled charity and compassion as a commandment, and this gave impetus to the spirit of caring for the poor. Besides a life of prayer, monks invested time in the care of the deserving poor. With milestone legal instruments such as the Elizabethan Poor Law of 1601, public efforts were strengthened to alleviate the immense suffering of the poor. Almsgiving was also promoted by the philanthropic philosophy of sharing with the less fortunate.

In Europe before the sixteenth century, providing aid to the poor was voluntary and usually supervised by the church. This gave rise to methods of working with individuals, families, groups, organizations, and communities to alleviate human suffering. However, as time went on, paid workers replaced volunteers. Eventually training schools for social work, pioneered by Jane Addams and Mary Richmond, emerged in the United States and United Kingdom to consolidate the methods and skills that had evolved (Neukrug, 2008). These training establishments emphasized the acquisition of methods, skills, and techniques for practice, and a body of knowledge began to develop.

Since these early developments, there have been a variety of conceptualizations of social work as a profession, the dominant orientation being rooted in services to the individual rather than the community. This is not surprising since Western societies are guided by the capitalist ideology, which places a premium on the virtues of individualism, competition, and accumulation. This approach contrasts with the indigenous social welfare service ideology in Africa, which is founded on communalism, kinship systems, and mutual aid (Piccard, 1988). This chapter argues that, although social work in Europe and America evolved out of social service delivery (seemingly a logical consequence), this is not the case in Africa. Western social work and its orientation were transplanted to Africa, and it is believed that this constitutes a major challenge in adopting social work as a method of practice in an African context. Unless Western social work practice is adapted to indigenous systems and environments, its efficacy is dubious. This chapter focuses on the challenges, successes, and prospects of social work in Africa.

BRIEF HISTORY

Social work was brought to Africa as a colonial export from Europe, often under the rubric of commitment to the civilization and improvement of the well-being of native Africans. Essentially, the colonizing powers wanted to bring more territories under their sphere of influence for economic exploitation (Sachs, 2005). In many cases missionaries were instrumental in realizing this objective with their zeal to evangelize (Midgley, 1981), and thus to some extent they were the precursors of colonialism. They were able to enter the hinterland "to carry out not only conversion of the heathens to Christianity but also exploration" (Rea, 1970, 46–53). Their findings were sent back to their countries, providing knowledge of the continent and its wealth. However, alongside their preaching of the gospel, missionaries were the first to introduce modern social welfare services such as schools, training institutions, clinics, and hospitals.

Provision of social services by missionaries has at times been confused with the introduction of social work practice, which came much later in the chain of development. However, it can be argued that social work, in the generic sense, existed in Africa well before colonization in the sense that indigenous knowledge, systems, institutions, and communities were involved in service provision to populations. Western social work practice, mainly curative in nature, was introduced at varying times as the colonization process unfolded in Africa. The practice reflected that of the colonizing countries (Kreitzer et al., 2009).

Colonialism provided the sociopolitical context in which the practice of social work developed. In Ghana, the British began to provide social services in 1939 to deal with the aftermath of an earthquake, and they established the Department of Social Services in 1946 to integrate World War II veterans into society after being away from home for a considerable period of time (UN Survey, 1950). Similar services were instituted for war veterans in Botswana (Hedenquist, 1991). In Zambia, social work emerged with the advent of urbanization and industrialization, especially the copper mining industry. Social welfare services, and indeed social work, were introduced in the mining sector to ensure the well-being of employees.

In Sierra Leone and Togo, the Ministry of Social Welfare and Ministere Du Travail, De Affaires Sociales Et De La Function Publique were introduced in 1974. Similar ministries were established in many other countries, including Ethiopia, Kenya, Cameroon, Ivory Coast, Nigeria, Senegal, Tanzania, and Madagascar (ASWEA Documents, 1973, 1974). In South Africa social work was important as a tool for control of the African population seen as agitators and enemies of the state. At the same time, social work services to the white population enhanced their comfort and livelihood (Sewpaul, 2005). The ulterior motive for the introduction of social work as a tool of exploitation or social control seems to be the story throughout Africa during the preindependence era.

Later on, schools of social work started in various parts of Africa, the first being in South Africa in 1924, Egypt in 1936, Algeria in 1942, Ghana in 1945, Uganda in 1954, Tanzania in 1958, Ethiopia in 1959, Upper Volta (now Burkina Faso) in 1960, Tunisia in 1964, and Zimbabwe in 1964. In the 1960s and 1970s, Mauritania, Nigeria, Rwanda, Sudan, and several other countries established some form of training characterized variously as preservice, certificate,

diploma, and (very few) baccalaureate programs (ASWEA #7, 1974; Healy, 2008). In Zambia, the Oppenheimer College of Social Services started in 1950 to offer a diploma program in social work that was later taken over by the University of Zambia after its inception in 1966. In addition, the bachelor's in social work (BSW) program was introduced by the University in 1974. Other institutions, such as the Mindolo Ecumenical Foundation, Monze Rural Community Development Centre, and Kafue Urban Community Development Centre, trained workers in community development.

Notably, the newly independent countries in sub-Saharan Africa had inadequate social infrastructure to meet the emerging challenges of urbanization and modernization. Training of social work practitioners with designations such as rural animation workers, rural development workers, social workers, community development workers, social promotion workers, and social development workers must be understood in this context.

SOCIAL WORK IN AFRICA

Among the critical local institutions linked to social welfare in African communities have been the chieftaincy, the communal meeting place (known as the Kogtla in Botswana and Insaka in some parts of Zambia), the community, and the extended family system. These have been, and continue to be, used in service delivery and problem-solving processes. However, these institutions have not been fully integrated into social work practice. It is therefore suspected that the lack of relevance, effectiveness, and appropriateness of social work practice in Africa as a whole can be partly attributed to the exclusion of these significant indigenous institutions that play a critical role in the problem-solving process.

Africa in general had a long-standing tradition of social support systems even before the advent of modern social welfare and social work practice. For example, in precolonial Botswana, there were structures in place that dealt with the welfare of families and the community at large. According to Hedenquist (1991), chiefs, villages (communities), and extended families provided for material, cultural, social, and spiritual needs that were important for livelihoods. Communities were organized in such a way that social issues could be dealt with at any level of socialization or when the need arose. For instance, the upbringing of children and the inculcation of societal values and customs were the responsibility of the extended family (Nukunya, 1992). Helping those in need was regarded as a responsibility of communities such that it was customary for those who were well off to assist the poor (Hedenquist, 1991). Institutions such as the extended family system were a form of social security. The social crises that Africa is experiencing today, such as famine and HIV and AIDS, could have been dealt with by engaging these traditional institutions. Interestingly, even though British government officials realized the importance of the extended family system, they did not integrate it into the practice of social work (Botswana Social Welfare Report, 1952).

The replacement of the subsistence economy with a liberal market economy and the process of urbanization resulted in the emergence of towns and cities that consequently brought about a rural-to-urban drift with no guarantee of employment, accommodation, or other social amenities. This situation created social problems such as juvenile delinquency, high rates of unemployment and teenage pregnancy, alcoholism, and violence. As a result of the increasingly negative effects of a market economy and urbanization, social work was introduced in Africa. With this new scenario, different mechanisms or ways of meeting human needs had to replace traditional structures that were no longer effective. It was therefore necessary to introduce social services that would respond to the emerging urban situation.

The practice of social work, it would seem, should have been tailored to the context of the local situation. However, as previously mentioned, the response and the practice knowledge, value base, philosophy, and ideology were transferred from colonizing countries to Africa. Social work training had to be aligned to the nature of the services offered. In other words, the training of social workers had to be directly associated with the employment situations at the time. Consequently, as Lucas (1993) indicates, social work training was largely influenced by Western practices and an ideology that focused more on concepts and principles that were individually oriented and influenced by psychology, psychoanalysis, and group dynamics.

Since then, the practice of social work in Africa has been largely influenced by forms of practice that focus on the individual as the point of departure rather than the community. This situation has been attributed to several factors, including staff who have been educated and trained in the West with a worldview of social work that has been shaped and fashioned by a Western perspective. This has also contributed to the crisis of professional identity among African social workers. Second, those in positions of power with regard to allocation of resources and decision making

are not adequately informed about the role of social work in human development. Hence, the profession has been accorded poor status, working conditions, remuneration, authority, and sovereignty of its practitioners (Chilwane, 2009; Oliphant, 2009). Third, available texts and literature are essentially Western and written for students with Western backgrounds and experience, and fourth, lack of research by local staff that would ideally lead to indigenous literature and curriculum development has led to continued reliance on Western theories, paradigms, and materials. This state of affairs is not limited to social work but is common to many disciplines in Africa (Wight, 2008).

The need to identify indigenous knowledge for curricula and practice cannot be overemphasized (Osei-Hwedie, 2001). Undoubtedly, social work practice will benefit from indigenous knowledge because of the natural fit between knowledge and practice. Critics have argued that lack of an indigenous knowledge base has led to social work practice in Africa being ineffective, assuming the character of maintenance, and failing to resolve inequalities, social injustice, corruption, and poverty.

There are numerous problems common to African countries but unique to respective environments. The twenty-first century has not brought any significant relief to the beleaguered continent. Besides AIDS and corruption, poverty remains the greatest threat to political stability, social cohesion, and the general well-being of millions of Africans. Sub-Saharan Africa is not only the epicenter of HIV and AIDS but of poverty as well. With about 2% of the world population, Africa has two-thirds of the HIV and AIDS cases (32.9 million) and 75% of the global deaths from AIDS. Of every 1000 children in sub-Saharan Africa, 146 die before their fifth birthday. It is estimated that there will be 18 million AIDS-affected orphans in Africa by 2010 (UNAIDS, 2006, 2007). The strain of AIDS on the extended family system has reduced its capacity to fulfill its traditional roles (Dintle, 2003), and the unprecedented numbers of orphans have overwhelmed public, private, and traditional institutions. The challenge for social work practice is to formulate programs for practice that will promote self-reliance and empowerment of orphans, their caregivers, and community-based organizations.

Over 41% of Africans live on less than $1 per day and more than 32% suffer from malnutrition, especially women and children (Hunger Project, 2008). Since the introduction of structural adjustment programs imposed by the International Monetary Fund

(IMF) and World Bank, most sub-Saharan countries have continued to register poor or negative growth with high human poverty indices of above 40% (United Nations Development Programme [UNDP], 2004). This is against the background of declining levels of abject poverty in the rest of the world. Social work can be instrumental in changing the circumstances of the people if curricula are designed to prepare students adequately for professional practice that will respond to the needs and challenges of marginalized and vulnerable groups. Students of social work should be equipped with technologies, information, paradigms, and practice knowledge that will enable them to work with communities for social change.

There are, of course, debilitating circumstances on the African continent that make it virtually impossible for one to successfully operate as a social work practitioner. Most states in sub-Saharan Africa, such as the Democratic Republic of Congo (DRC), Ethiopia, Liberia, Sierra Leone, Somalia, Sudan, and Zimbabwe, suffer from social conditions that make it difficult to build people's capacity to end the vicious cycle of poverty. The current political turmoil in Algeria, Egypt, Libya, Morocco, and Tunisia pose new challenges to the provision of social services to thousands of internally displaced people especially women, children and the elderly running away from conflict areas. The situation remains volatile to tell when peace will finally return to the region.

For instance, Zimbabwe, once a leader in human development, has miserably degenerated into a typical failed state of Africa due to its misrule. With the demise of the economy, massive corruption, hyperinflation and stagflation, and flight of the intelligentsia including social work professionals, social services have crumbled. Zimbabwe today is a country without a national currency. The collapse of social infrastructure such as water and sewage led to the outbreak of cholera and the death of hundreds of people, signaling to the world the desperate situation the country was in. With no resources at hand, social work practitioners, who, like other professionals in the country, go for several months without remuneration, have virtually nothing to offer by way of social services.

However, the multitude of challenges even in a country like Zimbabwe is what makes social work worthwhile, exciting, and challenging in Africa. Without the challenges, the practice would be sterile and uneventful. Challenges must be seen as unlimited opportunities for the practitioner to reach out for innovations and new technologies, techniques, and knowledge. They also provide opportunities for

transformation, empowerment, and the creation of a new era of service. Despite the poor working conditions, social work practitioners are the foot soldiers at the front line of development. They are employed by public, private, parastatal, and donor agencies and nongovernmental organizations offering services such as counseling, group formations, and community mobilization. They work with village development committees to provide, inter alia, HIV and AIDS care, community home-based care facilities, orphan care, reform schools, women's shelters, and hospitals. For example, in Botswana, social work practitioners coordinate disaster management, emergency assessment, relief operations, community rehabilitation, and elderly and destitute provisions.

The major criticism of most of these services, especially destitute services, is that they do not yield any kind of surplus to the recipient or the nation (Weinbach, 1998), nor do they transform the recipients' circumstances of living into self-support. They foster reliance and dependence and create powerlessness on the part of recipients. It is necessary to develop programs that will empower and uplift the recipients to assist them in taking charge of their lives.

CHALLENGES

The terrain for practice in Africa consists of a multitude of challenges. Social work takes place in specific environments that are replete with problems and therefore unfriendly in which to operate. Especially in public agencies, difficulties include poor salary; lack of office accommodation and facilities such as chairs, computers, telephones, office supplies, and transport; and lack of status. This makes working in public agencies extremely stressful, which leads social work professionals to leave for greener pastures in private, parastatal, and nongovernmental organizations where conditions of work are usually better. Furthermore, the low esteem in which social work education and the profession are held has to be acknowledged (Wilson & Mwansa, 2005), along with the low morale and culture of inertia among social work educators and practitioners in sub-Saharan Africa (with, perhaps, the exception of South Africa). The failure by social work to bring about change has opened it to criticism, skepticism, and, at times, outright ridicule. Attempts must be made to develop strategies to boost morale and the image of the profession.

Models of practice require a great deal of innovation and adaptation of Western approaches to suit the unique context of practice. Critics of traditional social work models (Graham, 1999; Schiele, 1994; Turner, 1991) contend that the interventions, practice wisdom, and theoretical foundations of practice models must reflect contextual aspects of life. According to Graham (1999), the African-centered worldview, not Eurocentric ideologies and practice, must inform theory and practice. Western interventions without adaptation may not be appropriate in an African context because they are at odds with the cultural expectations and norms of the people.

The same can be said of social work education and training. In terms of pedagogy, social work in Africa has generally been taught with divergent sets of expectations, values, and methods. The knowledge and value base evolved in Europe and America has been assumed to be transferable to Africa and elsewhere. Some of this can be useful, but only if it is reworked to fit local needs. Although a young profession, social work is growing quickly due to both clinical and developmental needs of the continent, and it offers great potential for employment. However, education and training are constrained by a lack of well-equipped libraries and the slow growth of indigenous literature, which perpetuates dependence on foreign academic literature. Many training institutions continue to rely on staff trained in North America and Europe, with the corresponding views and mind-set. These are transferred to the students in their teaching assignments, maintaining Western imperialism (Midgley, 1986). Community is a primary resource for meeting needs as well as being the client and the location of unmet needs or the point of disparity between needs and resources (Hutton & Mwansa, 1997). It must be brought to the fore alongside the individual, because each is equally important in the quest for homeostasis.

PROSPECTS

The major challenge facing social work in Africa is making a difference in the issues of poverty, HIV and AIDS, civil violence, corruption, the growing food crisis, and the disempowerment of minority groups. To achieve this, social work has to be transformed from its current status of maintenance to one that is able to unleash its potential and create innovative responses to numerous social problems. In this regard, the transformation of social work education and training is of immediate significance. For example, reorientation is necessary to develop curricula, models of instruction, and training methods that facilitate indigenous interventions. At the same time, structures must be established within universities, field agencies,

governments, and partner organizations to accommodate the changes. There is a need to exploit the current atmosphere that includes various formations such as the African Union (AU), the New Partnership for Africa's Development (NEPAD), the Millennium Development Goals, the new wave of democratization, and regional and subregional organizations.

A glimmer of hope is originating in South Africa (Chilwane, 2009; Oliphant, 2009), where Minister Zola Skweyiya has declared social work as a top priority and has launched a "rigorous campaign to make it the career of choice" (Oliphant, 2009, p. 12). Skweyiya expressed the notion that social workers have not been "appreciated and recognised as much as their teacher and nurse counterparts" (p. 12) and declared that the government needs to recognize the profession. In addition, the government of Botswana has initiated discussion on the launching of a Council for Social Work. Perhaps these developments will help to propel the profession forward.

There are a number of nations, tribes, or ethnic groups in Africa. They have developed differently from each other because they have different histories, live in different regions, and have different natural resources with which to work. For example, there are the Masai of Kenya, pygmies and Khoikhoi of the DRC and the Central Republic of Africa, and the Basarwa (Bushmen) of the San ethnic group found in South Africa, Namibia, and Botswana. In Botswana, the vast majority are of the San ethnic group, a sizeable population that makes up 8% to 10% of the total population and is mostly found in the Ghanzi district in the northwest region of the country (Yochum, 2002). Their human rights situation seems to be slowly gaining recognition, providing hope that such minorities will receive equitable treatment. For example, a high profile relocation case they took against the government was ruled in their favour in December 2006 (Botswana High Court, 2006). Social workers need to be creative in recognizing and using diversity and identifying appropriate resources to address divergent needs (Hutton, 1992).

Violence has ripped apart many countries in Africa with telling consequences. The vortex of guns, bullets, and machetes has led to vicious conflicts that have increasingly sucked in large numbers of citizens on the continent. Violence has created untold misery for millions of innocent civilians, especially the elderly, women, and children. The 2008 postelection incidents in Kenya, the xenophobic attacks in some towns and cities of South Africa, and the political violence in Zimbabwe, Darfur (Sudan), Somalia, DRC, and northern Uganda, in which thousands of people have lost their lives, have been internally displaced or become refugees, and have lost personal property and livelihoods, are some examples. The challenge for social work is to prepare a cadre of professionals to work with people to manage anger and conflict and to effect reconciliation in an indigenous context.

CONCLUSION

The prevailing socioeconomic situation in Africa presents a number of challenges for social work education and practice. Social workers are faced with socioeconomic and cultural challenges that require a great deal of innovation. Social work remains a frontline profession and continues to play a critical role in the increasingly complex social problems on the continent. It is necessary, therefore, to establish curricula and practice methods that embrace the local context. Social work educators and practitioners in African countries need to find paradigms that address social issues built on the sociocultural, economic, political, and environmental conditions pertaining to their communities. Social work practitioners should be well versed in the diversified cultural knowledge of people's needs if the profession is to influence their lives in a positive manner and make a meaningful contribution to social development.

REFERENCES

Ambrosino, R., Heffernan, J., Shuttleworth, R, & Ambrosino, R. (2005). *Social work and social welfare: An introduction* (5th ed.). Belmont, CA: Brooks/Cole.

ASWEA, (1973). Relationship between social work education and national social development planning, Document 6. Addis Ababa: ASWEA publication.

ASWEA (1974). Curriculum of schools of social work and community development centres in Africa, doc. 17. Addis Ababa: ASWEA Publication.

Botswana High Court (2006), Roy Sesana vs the Attorney General of Botswana, Misca. No. 52 of 2002, Lobatse High Court.

Botswana Social Welfare Report. (1952). Gaborone: Government printer.

Chilwane, L. (2009, March 18). Social work needs to be recognized and boosted. BusinessDay. http://www.business.co.za.

Dintle, T. (2003). Tswana cultural beliefs and practices: Implications for methods of care for AIDS orphans and other vulnerable children in Botswana. (Unpublished master's thesis). Ohio University, Athens, OH. www.ohiolink.edu.

Graham, J. M. (1999). The African-centered worldview: Towards a paradigm for social work. *Journal of Black Studies, 30*(1), 103–122.

Head, B. (1981). *Serowe: Village of the rain wind.* London: Heinemann.

Healy, L. (2008). *International Social Work: Professional Action in an Interdependent World* (2nd ed.). Oxford University Press, New York.

Hedenquist, J. (1991). *Introduction to social and community development work in Botswana.* Botswana: Ministry of Local Government and Lands.

Hunger Project. (2007). Empowering women and men and their own hunger. http://www.thp.org/?gclid=CJGeqYzWgqgCFQMlfAodrilnqg.

Hutton, M. (1992). *Social work: An extension of community.* Inaugural lecture, University of Botswana, Gaborone.

Hutton, M., & Mwansa, L.-K. (Eds.). (1997). *Social work practice in Africa: Social development in a community context.* Gaborone: Print Consult.

Koontse, M. (1981). *The historical and contemporary factors in the development of communities in Botswana.* (Unpublished dissertation). University of Manchester,

Kreitzer, L., Abukari, Z., Antonio P., Mensha, J. & Kwaku, A. (2009). Social Work in Ghana: A participatory Action Research Project Looking at Culturally Appropriate Training and Practice. *Social work Education, 28*(2), 145–164.

Lucas, T. B. (1993). History of Social Work practice and education in Botswana: A Social Justice and Empowerment Interpretation, Dissertation (MSW) University of Regina, Faculty of Graduate Studies & Research, Canada.

Midgley, J. (1981). *Professional imperialism: Social work in the Third World.* London: Heinemann.

Midgley, J. (1986). Community Participation, Social Development & the state. Vermont: Ashgate Publishing Ltd.

Neukrug, E. (2008). *Theory, practice, and trends in human services: An introduction* (4th ed.). Belmont, CA: Thomson Brooks/Cole.

Nukunya, K. (1992). *Tradition and change in Ghana: An introduction to sociology.* Accra: Ghana University Press.

Oliphant, L. (2009, March 22). Social work top priority: A rigorous campaign has been launched to make social work the career of choice for SA's youth. City Press. www.citypress.co.za.

Osei-Hwedie, K. (2001). *Indigenous practice—some informed guesses: Self-evident and possible.* Paper presented at the Joint University Committee (JUC) Conference on the Theme: Indigenous Social Work. Gaborone, Botswana.

Piccard, B. (1988). *Introduction to social work: A primer* (4th ed.). Chicago: Dorsey Press.

Rea, W. F. (1970). Agony on the Zambezi: The first Christian mission to southern Africa and its failure. *Journal of Social Studies in Southern and Central Africa, 1*(2), 46–53.

Sachs, J. (2005). Sustainable Development. *Time,* 48.

Schiele, J. (1994). Afrocentricity as an alternative world-view for equality. *Journal of Progressive Human Services, 5,* 5–25.

Sewpaul, V. (2005). Social work education in South Africa. *International Association of Schools of Social Work Newsletter, 1,* 8.

Turner, R. (1991). Affirming consciousness: The Afrocentric perspective in child welfare. In J. Chipuungu & B. Leashore (Eds.), *Child welfare: An Africentric perspective.* New Brunswick, NJ: Rutgers University Press.

UNAIDS (2006). Report on the Global AIDS Epidemic. Geneva, UNAIDS.

UNAIDS (2007). Report on the Global AIDS Epidemic. Geneva, UNAIDS.

United Nations Development Programme (UNDP). (2004). *Human development report.* New York: Author.

Weinbach, R. W. (1998). *The social worker as manager: A practical guide to success* (3rd ed.). Boston: Allyn and Bacon.

Wight, D. (2008). Most of our social scientists are not institution based, they are there for hire: Research consultancies and social science capacity for health research in East Africa. *Social Science & Medicine, 66,* 110–116.

Wilson, D., & Mwansa, L-K. (2005). Research proposal for indigenous knowledge-based social work practice with vulnerable children in Southern Africa. (Unpublished proposal). Gaborone, Botswana.

Winslow, R. (n.d.). A comparative criminology tour of the world, Africa: Botswana. www-rohan.sdsu.edu/faculty/rwinslow/africa/botswana.html.

Yochum, P. (2002). *Draft report on indigenous development.* Commonwealth Policy Studies Unit. http://www.europa.eu.int.

Social Work in Asia

NGOH TIONG TAN

This chapter describes the socioeconomic conditions of Asia and the social change and challenges facing this region. It addresses some of the social justice and welfare issues as well as the role of social work and social development in enhancing social well-being.

With tracks toward modernization and globalization, Asia is experiencing rapid economic growth and social change. In the past half century, many of the developing nations in this region have undergone drastic political development and social change. The role of social work is to observe social trends so as to anticipate and meet the changing social needs. It is as important to deal with social issues from a macro and developmental perspective as is to deal with the issues at the micro and interpersonal levels. Social development is thus a vital aspect of social work in Asia.

Asia covers a vast land mass of 17.1 million square miles (44.4 million square kilometers). The forty-nine nations of Asia stretch from the Middle East to the Pacific Ocean. The area of Russia that lies east of the Ural Mountains as well as Central Asia, such as Kazakhstan, Kyrgyzstan, Tajikistan, Turkmenistan, and Uzbekistan, are all part of Asia. The continent is home to about 4.1 billion of the world's 6.7 billion people (Population Reference Bureau [PRB], 2008a).

Six of 10 most populous countries in the world are in Asia: China with 1.32 billion people, India with 1.14 billion, Indonesia with 240 million, Pakistan with 172 million, Bangladesh with 147 million, and Japan with 127.7 million (PRB, 2008a). However, with the one-child policy in place, China's population is expected to decline. Population growth in the Middle East, particularly in Lebanon and Iran, has slowed due to social changes in women's education, later marriages, and attitudes toward childbearing (PRB, 2008b). Several countries with low total fertility rates (TFRs), including Taiwan, with the world's lowest TFR at 1.1 children per woman, and Japan and South Korea, with TFRs of 1.3, are in Asia. With this worldwide trend of declining birth rates, there will be a proportionate increase in the aging population. For example, by the year 2050, 40% of the Japanese population could be over sixty-five years of age. Overall in Asia, the median age is twenty-eight years, which means that the population is still relatively young (PRB, 2008a).

The urban population is growing in Asia, as it is in the rest of the world. Between 2007 and 2050, the urban population is expected to more than double with the projected increase of 1.8 billion people. South and Central Asia is expected to triple its urban population in this time frame (PRB, 2008b). People in cities are expected to consume more food and energy, which will eventually have a negative impact on climate and weather patterns.

ECONOMIC GROWTH, SOCIAL CHANGE, AND INEQUALITY

In the last decades, the fastest growing economies in the world are in Asia. According to United Nations Development Programme (UNDP) (2008), the per capita gross domestic product (GDP) ranged from US$31,267 (Japan) to US$1,027 (Myanmar). The Asian financial centers of Tokyo, Singapore, Hong Kong, and Shanghai have all seen rapid surges in the capital markets. The growth rate of real GDP for Azerbaijan, the highest in Asia, is 25.1 % (in 2007), and the lowest growth rate is found in Brunei Darussalam with .06%. Though the growth rates have decreased during the worldwide economic crisis, it is remarkable that the countries in Asia all registered positive growth for 2007. In addition to the global economic downturn, natural disasters have affected China's GDP growth, which declined from a high of 13.0% in 2007 to 9.0% in 2008 (Asian Development Bank [ADB], 2008).

Social development in Asia is particularly concerned about health care, infant and maternal mortality, and human rights of the vulnerable population. One of the United Nations' development goals is to decrease infant deaths, as exemplified by Hong Kong, which has the lowest infant mortality rate in Asia. As in other parts of the world, the poor in Asia are more susceptible to social stresses and dysfunctions. Poverty is a grave problem, especially in rural regions, and South Asia alone is home to about half of the developing world's poor. The absolute number of poor people in all developing countries is expected to increase slightly (Pandya-Lorch, 2005).

Economic growth in Asia has been uneven. There is a need to bridge the income disparity within countries as well as between countries. The Gini index, an indicator for income inequality, shows that Japan, with a Gini index of 24.9, has the lowest income inequality, while the highest observed inequality is found in Malaysia, with a Gini index of 49.2 (UNDP, 2008).

Inequality is ever present, especially during economic recessions when the economy takes precedence over social welfare. Many Asian countries subscribe to the trickle-down theory that enhancing the economy will result in income redistribution and decrease disparities in wealth. However, Asian policy interventions tackling inequality need to consciously deal with the unequal access to opportunities while simultaneously improving job rewards and incentives, especially for those at the lower end of the job market (ADB, 2007).

The income gap in China is widening, as indicated by a high Gini index of 46.9. This may be accounted for in part by the higher growth in some urban and coastal areas; in addition, the economic reforms of the past twenty-five years have generally benefitted the skilled urban population (UNDP, 2008). To ensure sustainable growth and equitable distribution, it is proposed that incentives be given for improving market efficiency and investing in skills training and education (Luo & Zhu, 2008). To be effective, these measures should target the poor in disadvantaged communities.

SOCIAL JUSTICE AND SOCIAL WELFARE

On the whole, Asian social welfare focuses on providing sound policies and infrastructures, such as adequate health care, education, transportation, and housing, that are essential for social well-being. Adequate protection against unemployment and an enhanced social safety net are both needed to prevent poverty. Policies that are inclusive are generally favored by Asian countries (Tan, 2008).

In the more mature economies of East Asia, social policies are designed to enhance national as well as economic development. Government interventions and policies are aimed at promoting industrialization and growth (Holliday, 2000; Midgley, 1995) and have an overall income redistribution effect. In such countries as South Korea, Malaysia, and Singapore, expenditures in education and health are viewed as investments. The social investment approach has targeted economic returns for public programs. These investments aim to encourage self-reliance and independence as well as meet social needs (Tan, 2008).

Human rights are the basic rights and freedoms. These include civil and political rights, such as the right to life and liberty, freedom of expression, and equality before the law, as well as social, cultural, and economic rights, such as the right to food, to work, and to education (United Nations, 1948). According to Freedom House, many Asian countries are considered "not free," including Kazakhstan, Turkmenistan, Uzbekistan, Tajikistan, Tibet, China, North Korea, Vietnam, Laos, and Cambodia (Freedom House, 2007). In addition, Freedom House (2009a) has stated that "North Korea is a totalitarian dictatorship and one of the most restrictive countries in the world" (p. 1). The regime subjects thousands of political prisoners to brutal conditions and maintains a largely isolationist foreign policy. In Myanmar, exorbitant fuel prices in 2007 led to public protests and subsequent government responses that resulted in thousands of arrests and a number of deaths. In addition, human rights abuses are perpetrated on ethnic minorities, such as the Chin, Karen, and Rohingya tribes. Chin women have reportedly been victims of violence, including being raped and beaten by Burmese soldiers (Freedom House, 2009b).

Both males as well as females in Afghanistan and Timor-Leste, one of the poorest countries in the region, have the lowest life expectancies. Japan has the highest life expectancy at birth at 82.3 years (UNDP, 2008). For the five most populous countries in Asia, life expectancies at birth are the highest for China, which is followed by Indonesia. Life expectancy at birth in India and Pakistan is lower than that of Indonesia. Males in Pakistan registered a slightly higher life expectancy than those in India. Cambodia has the lowest life expectancy at birth in Asia at 58 years (ADB, 2007, 2008; UNDP, 2008).

In general, Asian cultures are gender biased, favoring males. Pakistani and Indian girls between the ages of one and five are 30% more likely to die than boys (Central Asia Health Review [CAHR], 2008).

Maternal death in Afghanistan is highest in Asia and second only to Sierra Leone in the world. Strategies for reducing maternal death include improving access to health care such as obstetric and prenatal care (CAHR, 2008). Social reform and political will are keys to reducing maternal mortality.

The fight against gender inequality must include access for girls to both schools and employment, and restrictions to women's political and social participation and advancement should be removed. Enhancing women's empowerment, voices, and decision making are part of the Millennium Development Goals (MDG) (United Nations Economic and Social Commission for Asia and the Pacific [ESCAP], 2008).

In eleven countries in Asia, more than a tenth of the population lives on less than US$1 a day. In twenty economies, including some of the most populous, more than 10% of the population is malnourished. In around two-thirds of economies, 10% or more of children under five years of age are underweight (ESCAP, 2008). Social development targets in Asia should focus on the poorest and youngest as priorities.

Progress toward the MDGs for Bangladesh, China, India, Indonesia, and Pakistan are of special interest because progress by these countries determines the progress of most of the region (ADB, 2007; ESCAP, 2008). In the 2008 report on MDG progress, countries with slow progress toward the goals for elimination of hunger are Bangladesh, Nepal, Cambodia, Pakistan, China, Papua New Guinea, India, Philippines, Mongolia, and Sri Lanka. Three Asian countries—Kazakhstan, Uzbekistan, and Tajikistan—are regressing in relation to the MDG. The MDG global compact calls for both rich and poor countries to recognize that they share the responsibility to end poverty and that concrete actions will be taken and money, resources, and technology invested to achieve these goals (ESCAP, 2008).

Major diseases encountered in Asia include cholera, typhoid fever, scarlet fever, poliomyelitis, dysentery, and malaria. Cholera and elephantiasis are common in India and China. The spread of AIDS is a concern in Asia, and the World Health Organization (WHO) estimates that 5.8 million people in South and Southeast Asia have AIDS or are infected with HIV. In 2005, 270,000 people in Central Asia (and Eastern Europe) became newly infected with HIV, totaling some 1.6 million people living with HIV or AIDS (World Bank, 2007b). The WHO report targeted vulnerable and marginalized groups in places such as India, Thailand, and Cambodia that have high risk of infection. Sex trafficking alone is reported to victimize some 30 million Asian women, men, and children (World Bank, 2007a).

Mass inoculations and international quarantines are suggested to control many diseases. Smallpox has been wiped out in Asia. However, postwar Laos has just one doctor for every 6400 people (http://www.globaleducation.edna.edu.au/archives/primary/casestud/laos/1/laos.html) and Nepal, Bangladesh, Myanmar, Sri Lanka, Indonesia, and the Philippines have a ratio of 1 doctor to 5000 people. Traditional healers treat a wide range of illnesses, and many Asians still seek traditional medicine and the use of herbal medicines (Encarta, 2009; East-Asian Academy of Cultural Psychiatry [2011], http://www.waculturalpsy.org/01-01/10_EAACP.pdf).

The tropical climate of Southeast, South, and Southwest Asia is conducive for parasites in the soil and water (OECD, 2005). Rivers and streams that supply drinking and bathing water are often used for sewage disposal. Priorities to reduce health problems caused by the environment include safe drinking water and improved garbage and sewage disposal systems (Encarta, 2009; OECD, 2005). Other environmental problems include land and soil degradation, deforestation, and desertification. India and the Philippines have less than one-quarter of their original forest cover, and similar reduction of forest has occurred in Cambodia, Laos, and Indonesia. Slash-and-burn agriculture is still practiced in parts of Southeast Asia as well as in the more remote parts of South Asia and southern China. Thailand instituted a ban on commercial logging in 1988, and to slow production, Indonesia banned the export of unprocessed logs (Encarta, 2009). Sea fishing is important in Asia; for example, Japan is the world's leading fishing country. To ensure sustainable fishing, the farming of fish is a viable alternative to consider (Encarta, 2009).

ROLE OF SOCIAL WORK AND SOCIAL DEVELOPMENT

Asian cultures generally rely on traditional systems of social support provided by the family and community. There is a need for social work to support families as they care for their members. Generally there is an emphasis on employer and employee contributions to the social security systems. Universal social security and welfare programs, like those of the Philippines and Japan, have been introduced in a number of countries. Multidimensional solutions are needed, including social insurance, individual payment and pension funds, taxes, and private sector provisions (Zhang, Gao, & Guo, 2003). It is expected that public welfare expenditures will remain low and social insurance will increasingly be privatized in Asia (Tan, 2008).

Social work has a key role in this vast continent that is making great strides in economic and social development. Social work and social work education have the potential to contribute toward more just and equitable societies and to work with vulnerable populations for a sustainable social welfare (Tan, 2008). For many countries in Asia, developmental strategies must include building human capital through education, skills training, and job creation in addition to the institutional provision of housing, health, and social care.

Social work is being recognized more and more as a valuable profession in Asian societies. Many countries, including Bangladesh, China, Japan, South Korea, Kuwait, Kyrgyz Republic, Malaysia, Palestine, Papua New Guinea, Philippines, Singapore, Sri Lanka, and Thailand, are members of the International Federation of Social Workers (IFSW), with Bahrain, India, Lebanon, and Mongolia being provisional members (IFSW, 2009). The Asian and Pacific Association for Social Work Education (APASWE) (2009) has 99 institutional members in Asia, and 146 schools have registered with the International Association of Schools of Social Work (IASSW, 2009). China and Japan both registered some 200 schools of social work in the past decades. Many of the schools that were founded during colonial times have matured and are taking leadership roles in world social work organizations.

The cutting edge of social work can be observed in Asia as it innovates and localizes for effective practice within challenging cultural contexts. Indigenous social work practices take into account cultural differences in assessment and intervention. The various fields of social work in Asia are expected to take their own courses. Overall, there is a growing civic consciousness in Asian social work practice, but the profession still needs to develop greater citizen participation to respond to community concerns and calamities. There is an emphasis on preventive approaches and citizen participation in dealing with social problems. Preventive and developmental strategies include community self-help, mediation of conflicts using indigenous leaders, and mutual aid associations among clan or ethnic groups (Tan, 2008).

Asian social work tends to be community focused. It is vital to harness community resources to augment professional helping (Tan, 2008; Tan & Rowlands, 2004). Rural community development is especially important in Asia because the rural–urban divide often disadvantages rural society in the provision of social services and resources. Social work needs to forge more effective partnerships with civic society, self-help, and other grassroots movements. Collaboration with businesses, multinational corporations, and governments for resource mobilization is the key strategy for responding to social problems and community issues (Tan, 2007). Cross-disciplinary training and partnerships are essential to enable effective policy development and problem solving.

Many social problems have their roots in the family and community systems; therefore, there is a great need to strengthen Asian families and communities and to help them cope with the rapidly changing social system. In Asia, the focus of social work is on programs that develop families and strengthen the community support network. Although workplace welfare is important, the key strategy is to enhance the already strong kinship networks as the primary source of social support.

Many social problems, such as migrant workers, sex trafficking, international disasters, and health concerns, are borderless and concern everyone. Conflicts due to ethnic tensions are present in Indonesia, Tibet, South Philippines, Sri Lanka, Iraq, and India. In the long run, prevention strategies such as encouraging education and promoting understanding in pluralistic and multicultural societies are vital. In terms of community building, a specialty of social work, there is a need to create a sense of national identity and unity among the diverse groups so as to maintain peace and economic development (Tan, 2008).

Social workers have to deal with a wide range of issues confronting the diverse Asian societies. To be effective, professionals need to be versatile and creative when facing these challenges (Morales & Sheafor, 1998). Social work intervention has to be varied, encompassing research, administration, policy, and institutional approaches to social security, education, housing, and health care. In the new millennium, social work will have to create new indigenous models that are suited to the Asian context of practice.

REFERENCES

Asian Development Bank (ADB). (2008). *Key indicators for Asia Pacific 2008*. Manila: Author.

Asian Development Bank (ADB). (2007). *Interrelationship between growth, inequality and poverty: The Asian experience*. ERD Working Paper No. 96. Manila: Author.

Asian and Pacific Association for Social Work Education (APASWE). (2009). Message from the president.

Retrieved on May 27, 2009, from http://ssteach1. cityu.edu.hk/~apaswe/apaswe_text_version/index. html.

Central Asia Health Review (CAHR). (2008) *Central Asia health review*. Retrieved on May 27, 2009, from http:// en.wikipedia.org/wiki/Central_Asia_Health_Review.

East-Asian Academy of Cultural Psychiatry (2011). WACP Newsletter Vol. 1, No. 1, retrieved April 12, 2011, from: http://www.waculturalpsy.org/01-01/10_EAACP.pdf.

Economic and Social Commission for Asia and the Pacific (ESCAP). (2008). *Future within reach: Regional partnerships for the Millennium Development Goals in Asia and the Pacific*. Bangkok: Author.

Encarta. (2009). Asia. Retrieved on May 27, 2009, from http://encarta.msn.com/encyclopedia_761574726_5/ Asia.html.

Freedom House. (2009a). *Country report: North Korea*. Retrieved on May 27, 2009, from www.freedomhouse. org/template.cfm?page=22&year=2008&country=7424.

Freedom House. (2009b). *Country report: Myanmar*. Retrieved on May 27, 2009, from www.freedomhouse. org/template.cfm?page=22&year=2008&country=7363.

Freedom House. (2007). *A catalyst for freedom and democracy*. Retrieved on May 27, 2009, from http://freedomhouse.org/uploads/special_report/71.pdf.

Holliday, I. (2000). Productivist welfare capitalism: Social policy in East Asia. *Political Studies, 48*(4), 706–723.

International Association of Schools of Social Work (IASSW). (2009). List of member schools. Retrieved on May 29, 2009, from www.iassw-aiets.org.

IFSW. (2009). International Federation of Social Workers. Retrieved on May 29, 2009, from www.ifsw.org.

Luo, X. B., & Zhu, N. (2008). Rising income inequality in China: A race to the top. World Bank Policy Research Working Paper 4700. www-wds.worldbank.org/ external/default/ WDSContentServer/WDSP/IB/20 08/08/25/000158349_20080825160141/Rendered/ PDF/WPS4700.pdf.

Midgley, J. (1995). *Social development: The developmental perspective in social welfare*. Thousand Oaks, CA: Sage.

Morales, A. T., & Sheafor, B. W. (1998). *Social work: A profession of many faces*. Englewood Cliffs, NJ: Prentice Hall.

OECD. (2005). *Full regional assessment survey and workshop on full cost recovery for water utilities in Southeast Asia: sharing international experience and best practices*. Retrieved in 2009 from www.oecd.org/ dataoecd/59/58/34617894.pdf.

Pandya-Lorch, R. (2005). Economic growth and development. Retrieved on May 27, 2009, from www.ifpri. org/2020/briefs/number01.htm.

Population Reference Bureau (PRB). (2008a). *Key findings from Population Reference Bureau's 2008 world population data sheet*. Retrieved on May 27, 2009, from www. prb.org/pdf08/08WPDS_Eng.pdf.

Population Reference Bureau (PRB). (2008b). World population highlights. *Population Bulletin, 63*(3). Retrieved on May 27, 2009, from www.prb.org/ pdf08/63.3highlights.pdf.

Tan, N. T. (2008). International social work and social welfare: Asia. In T. Mizrahi & L. E. Davis (Eds.), *Encyclopedia of social work* (20th ed.). New York: Oxford University Press.

Tan, N. T. (2007, August). *Cross-national collaboration in international social work*. Paper presented at IFSW-Asia Pacific Regional Social Work Symposium, Disaster Management and the Social Work Response. August 27–29, Kuala Lumpur, Malaysia.

Tan, N. T., & Rowlands, A. (2004). *Social work around the world III*. Berne, Switzerland: IFSW Press.

United Nations (UN). (1948). *Universal declaration of human rights*. Geneva: Author.

United Nations Development Programme (UNDP). (2008). Gini index. Retrieved from http://hdrstats. undp.org/en/indicators/147.html.

World Bank. (2007a). AIDS in South Asia: Understanding and responding. http://web.worldbank.org/WBSITE/ EXTERNAL/COUNTRIES/SOUTHASIAEXT/ 0,contentMDK:21019386~pagePK:146736~piPK: 146830~theSitePK:223547,00.html.

World Bank. (2007b). HIV/AIDS in Europe and Central Asia. http://web.worldbank.org/ WBSITE/EXTERNAL/COUNTRIES/ECAEXT/ EXTECAREGTOPHEANUT/EXTECAREGTOPH IVAIDS/0,menuPK:571178~pagePK:34004175~piP K:34004435~theSitePK:571172,00.html.

Zhang, J., Gao, S., & Guo, S. (2003). Financing long-term care: Call to China's social welfare reform. In S. Yao & X. Liu (Eds.), *Sustaining China's economic growth in the 21st century* (pp. 247–263). Routledge: London.

Social Work in Australia and New Zealand

CAROLYN NOBLE AND MARY NASH

Social work in Australia and New Zealand locates its beginnings within the same historical origins as its counterparts in the United Kingdom and United States. The Poor Laws and then the Charity Organization Society (COS) in the United Kingdom and the settlement movement in the United States, which formed the basis for social work in these countries, also influenced the philosophical development of social work in Australia and New Zealand. Although this influence is still seen in the current approaches to social work practice, important distinguishing features fashioned by national, local, and cultural politics are evident. The unique aspects of social work in these two countries will be highlighted in separate sections in this chapter.

Before we move to explore the unique aspects of social work in Australia and New Zealand, a common heritage in the economic and sociopolitical developments after World War II can be identified. Postwar reconstruction in both Australia and New Zealand saw the state heralding a new approach to looking after the well-being of its citizens. Through targeted economic, social, and public-health policies, the state assumed a role that was previously the reserve of individual workers and charity organizations: to look after the community's social, health, and welfare needs and provide a safety net for those who might fall between the gaps in the provision of such services. The state was to ensure the fair and equitable distribution of essential services such as social welfare, health, and education to all, regardless of ability to pay.

For several decades, people in both countries supported the state in this activity; indeed, many regarded access to universal services and programs as their right. During these years of developing a welfare state, social workers played important roles in ensuring the quality of the welfare culture and social service provisions. However, support for a welfare state shifted in the late 1980s when a more conservative philosophy

took hold, arguing that individuals and families should determine which services they should receive and how they might access them. The government gradually assumed a lesser role in the lives of individuals and encouraged the market and consumer choice to determine the type, provision, and distribution of essential services (Mendes, 2008).

This move toward privatization, with its links to neomanagerialism and the new economic rationalism, was implemented with uneven enthusiasm across the two countries. Important changes resulted, such as the privatization of state services, contracting out of existing services, and severe reduction of funding and the provision of services, which significantly affected social workers' practice domains. The role of the social worker changed to offering limited support to individuals within a fiscally restrictive management practice.

Although there are connections between the current state of social work in Australia and New Zealand, there are also noteworthy differences in practice, education, and scholarship in what is now a highly educated practice. These differences have emerged in response to different cultural influences and economic and sociopolitical imperatives. The development of social work in each country is presented next.

AUSTRALIA

The Social Work Workforce: A National Snapshot

There are about 16,000 social workers in Australia. The main employing industries are the health and community services sector (61%) and government administration and defense (27%). Of these 16,000 professionals, 84% hold tertiary qualifications, 87% are women, and 77% are working full time. The average age is forty-one years, and there is no shortage of jobs for people seeking to work in the field. Social work is registered on the government skill shortage list and as a result is attracting increasing interest from international applicants.

The Beginnings of Social Work

The origin of social work in Australia can be traced to paid welfare workers attached to large hospitals in 1929. Known as *almoners*, they were quick to get organized. The Victorian Institute of Hospital Almoners was established around this time, and schools of social work followed in the late 1930s. Now there are twenty- eight schools of social work across the country, monitored in their activities by the Australian Association of Social Workers (AASW), which was established in 1940s.

From its early beginnings, the AASW has evolved into a national organization responsible for ensuring the ethical and practice standards of practitioners, ensuring the educational integrity of university programs, and providing a strong welfare voice in the public arena, focusing on social issues and community concerns. Recently it has provided practical and financial support in times of national and international disasters, especially those that have occurred in the Asia-Pacific region. There are 6400 AASW members. A significant focus is promoting social justice concerns and outcomes in policy and practice and protecting human rights for all members of the community, especially those marginalized by government and private-sector interests, influence, and activities (www.aasw.asn.au).

Professionalism and the Move to Social Work Registration

Social workers choose to become members of the professional association in order to receive the resulting rewards and protections. There is no registration board even though interest was expressed as early as 1968; the complexity of the issues has made it a slow and cumbersome process. The debates are well known. On the one hand is the argument that registration will strengthen professional identity, make social workers accountable to service users and employers, and provide a disciplinary tool when needed. Without registration, the argument continues, social workers are at risk of being sidelined and irrelevant, left without a strong platform from which to speak and make their mission more public and effective.

The other argument wants social work to be self-regulating and encompass a broad church, including other allied social welfare workers. A small but vocal minority sees any move to professionalism as elitist, self-serving, and undermining its mission to fight for social justice, individual and community empowerment, and equality in relation to working with service users. Because the health and welfare industry is changing rapidly, with increasing numbers of workers sharing the same welfare terrain as social workers, including counselors; human service, community, youth, and criminal justice workers; and welfare and disability workers, it seems unrealistic not to include these practitioners in the registration debate (Chenoweth & McAuliffe, 2008; McDonald, 2006).

While the debate continues unresolved, the AASW has developed specific measures to provide practitioners with standards for accountable, ethical, and professional practice. These include a code of ethics, a complaints process, general practice standards, continuing professional education, standards for supervision, accredited social work status, and assessment of overseas qualifications (www.aasw. asn.au). Until the registration issue is decided, these standards exist to monitor and guide professional practice while at the same time making public the principles that inform these practices so that social workers can be held accountable in the public domain.

Practitioner Issues: Areas of Work and Influence

Social work practice includes individual work, family and group work, community work and development, social research and policy, and social activism. The orientation of practitioners spreads across the political spectrum, from focusing on individual, or therapeutic, approaches to focusing on emancipatory approaches that challenge oppressive conditions on social justice and human rights grounds. These approaches to practice are supported by a rich scholarship and research base. Physical and mental health, income support, social welfare, and child protection services have been the traditional areas in which social workers are evident, but there are also many working in community development, policy, and research roles and projects in urban as well as rural and remote communities across the country. These practice domains reflect the multiplicity of theoretical orientations, spreading the spectrum of influence from social control to social care to social change.

An important example of how social work practice spreads across this spectrum is its involvement with Indigenous peoples. On the one hand, welfare workers were the arbitrators and executors of racist policies against Aboriginal and Torres Strait Islander (ATSI) peoples from the early settlement days to the late 1970s. On the other hand, social workers have been on the long and worthy list of activists in challenging institutional discrimination and oppression, leading to good practice outcomes such as the *Bringing Them Home* report on the Stolen Generation (1997). The recently formed National Coalition of Aboriginal and Torres Strait Islander Social Workers Association (NCATSISWA) has played an important role in addressing disadvantage and discrimination in ATSI communities and encouraging full incorporation of alternative cultural knowledge into the social work profession, especially in practice, policy, research, and educational curricula (www.atsisw.org).

Another significant outcome in challenging racism is the recently completed People's Inquiry into Detention. The Australian Council of Heads of Schools of Social Work (ACHSSW) was the reinstate auspicing body for this inquiry, which was conducted in 2006 and 2007, and published its findings in 2008. The book that resulted from this informal, public inquiry tells harrowing stories of untold abuse and neglect by the Australian government from the 1990s to the present day toward the many thousands of asylum seekers who came to Australia by boat as unauthorized persons. Retelling the experiences of survivors, visitors, health personnel, former immigration officials, lawyers, and migration agents, the inquiry drew attention to this disturbing era of social policy. This inquiry resulted in modification of policies pertaining to the detention of refugees to allow for more humane treatment of people seeking asylum in Australia (Briskman, Latham, & Goddard, 2008).

REFERENCES

Briskman, L., Latham, S., & Godard, C. (2008). *Human rights overboard: Seeking asylum in Australia.* Carlton, Australia: Scribe.

Chenoweth, L., & McAuliffe, D. (2008). *The road to social work and human services practice* (2nd ed.). South Melbourne, Australia: Cengage Learning.

Commonwealth of Australia (1997). Bringing them home: The 'Stolen Childrens" Report: National inquiry into the separation of Aboriginal and Torres Strait Islander children from their families. (April). www.hreoc.gov.au/phf/social_justice/bringing_them_home_report.pdf (assessed 2nd March 2011).

McDonald, C. (2006). *Challenging social work: The institutional context of practice.* Basingstoke, UK: Palgrave.

Mendes, P. (2008). *Australia's welfare wars revisited: The players, the politics and the ideologies.* Sydney: UNSW Press.

AUSTRALIAN SOCIAL WORK TEXTS

Allan, J., Pease, B., & Briskman, L. (Eds.). (2003). *Critical social work: An introduction to theories and practices.* Crows Nest, New South Wales: Allen and Unwin.

Briskman, L. (2007). *Social work with Indigenous communities.* Annandale, NSW: Federation Press.

Briskman, L., Latham, S., & Godard, C. (2008). *Human rights overboard: Seeking asylum in Australia.* Carlton, Australia: Scribe.

Chenoweth, L., & McAuliffe, D. (2008). *The road to social work and human services practice* (2nd ed.). South Melbourne, Australia: Cengage Learning.

Fook, J. (2005). *Social work: A critical turn.* Toronto: Thompson.

Gardner, F. (2006). *Working with human service organisations: Creating connections for practice.* Melbourne: Oxford University Press.

Healy, K. (2005). *Social work theories in context: Creating framework for practice.* New York: Palgrave Macmillan.

Ife, J. (2002). *Community development: Community-based alternatives in an age of globalisation* (2nd ed.). Frenchs Forest, Australia: Pearson Education.

Kenny, S. (2006). *Developing communities for the future* (3rd ed.). South Melbourne: Thomson Learning.

McDonald, C. (2006). *Challenging social work: The institutional context of practice.* Basingstoke, UK: Palgrave.

Mendes, P. (2008). *Australia's welfare wars revisited: The players, the politics and the ideologies.* Sydney: UNSW Press.

Napier, L., & Fook, J. (Eds.). (2000). *Breakthroughs in practice: Theorising critical moments in social work.* London: Whiting & Birch.

Pease, B., & Fook, J. (Eds.). (1999). *Transforming social work practice: Postmodern critical perspectives.* St. Leonards, New South Wales: Allen and Unwin.

Weeks, W., Hoatson, L., & Dixon, J. (2003). *Community practices in Australia.* Frenchs Forest, Australia: Pearson Education.

NEW ZEALAND

The Social Work Workforce

New Zealand has over 2,800 registered social workers, but the total number who could be registered (i.e., qualified social workers currently employed) is estimated at 6,000 (Social Workers Registration Board, 2011). The Aotearoa New Zealand Association of Social Workers (ANZASW) has a membership of 3036, with over 500 provisional members (ANZASW 2011–12). The Child, Youth, and Family service of the Ministry of Social Development is the major provider of statutory child protection and safety services.

The Social Workers Registration Board places the nongovernment sector as the major employer of social workers. Included here is the growing number of iwi (tribal) agencies contracted to provide services by Maori for Maori (www.swrb.govt.nz). Social work educators are pleased that the New Zealand Tertiary Education Commission is currently looking at social work education to identify needs, gaps, and priorities in view of the increasing demand for social workers. The demographics of the workforce show that the average age of experienced social workers is in the mid-forties, and many younger social workers are being recruited to work overseas.

Professionalism and the Move to Social Work Registration

Fourteen years after the first social work course began taking students, a national body of social workers was established in 1964 (Nash, 1998). Instead of depending on a professional qualification in social work, ANZASW membership was open to practitioners in listed social work occupations. This was partly a pragmatic measure, because the association could never have sustained itself in the early years with the small number of qualified social workers in the country.

Professionalism has been one of the most contested visions for social work in New Zealand, partly because of a strongly egalitarian and inclusive strand of thinking within the ANZASW. The debates surrounding professionalism in social work have ranged from positive to negative clusters of meaning, focusing on professionalism representing knowledge and sound practice on the one hand and status, elitism, and gatekeeping on the other. Recognition of the place of Te Tiriti o Waitangi (the Treaty of Waitangi) lies at the heart of the social work profession. The ANZASW code of ethics reflects the bicultural partnership and recognition of the importance of Te Tiriti o Waitangi, which inspires members to develop and use Indigenous models of practice (www.anzasw.org.nz).

In 2003, when a sufficient number of qualified social workers—both tangata whenua (people of the land) and tauiwi (all other citizens)—formed a critical mass large enough for professional qualification to become an achievable entry requirement for social work registration, the Social Workers Registration Act was passed. The act established a voluntary system of registration designed to provide service users with safe and competent practitioners. The legislation protects the title of *registered social worker*, which means that unregistered social workers in New Zealand may still call themselves social workers but cannot call themselves registered social workers (http://www.swrb.govt.nz/NA_QnA.html).

Practitioner Issues

Child welfare and the health sector are two particularly prominent fields of social work in New Zealand. An important development in the provision of child protection services is the growing overlap and partnership between statutory agencies and nongovernmental organizations (NGOs), currently referred to as the *differential response model*. Planned changes in the Children, Young Persons, and Their Families Act mean that NGO social workers will carry new responsibilities for assessment work in addition to the excellent preventative and wraparound social work they have always performed. (ANZASW, 2008). Another successful development is the Social Workers in Schools program, which has made professional assistance accessible to children and families in an educational environment.

As many as 1200 ANZASW members, or a third of the membership, work in health or mental health settings, primarily at district health boards. Social work is the largest of the allied health professions (ANZASW, 2008). Many health social workers work with refugees and migrants—a relatively new field for practitioners, reflecting the impact of a steady flow of new settlers who often have pressing needs for assistance to settle and participate in society (Nash, Wong, & Trlin, 2006). Both the state and the community provide certain services to assist the settlement of migrants and refugees, but the type of help available varies geographically and depends to some extent on the migration category (i.e., immigrant or refugee) to which people belong. The interplay between state and community organizations is influenced by the service contracting policies now in place, which inevitably affects the provision of services.

Research

Useful social work research is undertaken in New Zealand, often led by universities that have strong partnerships with service providers. A significant example is the Pathways to Resilience five-year research program run by Robyn Munford and Jackie Sanders. This research project offers a unique opportunity to generate policy and practice-relevant evidence concerning the pathways that children and young people travel leading to involvement with the youth justice, child protection, specialist educational, and community support systems. The findings will inform policy and practice concerning key individual and ecological differences between those who overcome adversity (resilient) and those who do not (nonresilient) and the types of service configurations that most enhance resilience. An illustration of the extensive research platform built over the years by Munford and Sanders can be found in their chapter in *Social Work Theories in Action* (Munford & Sanders, 2005).

Research into migrant and refugee social and community work suggests that although there are new government policy initiatives aimed at assisting new settlers, regular monitoring and evaluation of all resettlement initiatives, including all components of the New Zealand Settlement Strategy, is required to determine and maintain their best fit with assessed needs. In addition, attention should be given to the development and implementation of an ethnic relations policy compatible with New Zealand's official policy of biculturalism. Research findings also indicate that the curriculum and training of community workers, social workers, and NGO volunteers should be developed to more effectively meet the demands and challenges of client needs in a new, specialized field of practice with immigrants and refugees. Here they can build on the work already done in finding effective ways to work respectfully with Indigenous populations.

CONCLUSION

The ANZASW website quotes the Royal Commission on Social Policy (http://anzasw.org.nz/sw-in-nz/), which found the following.

> New Zealanders value three principles in relation to social well-being:
>
> 1. **Voice:** *to be heard and to have one's views taken into account, to be part of decision-making.*
> 2. **Choice:** *active choice based on full information.*
> 3. **Safe prospect:** *the ability to plan with reasonable confidence for the future.*

It seems appropriate to end with this quotation for an international audience, which may then consider to what extent social workers around the world live up to this vision. It is a challenging one that fits the social work goals of social justice, self-determination, and full participation in one's community.

REFERENCES

Aotearoa New Zealand Association of Social Workers (ANZASW). (2008, September 23). Breadth of social work deserves greater recognition [Media release]. www.anzasw.org.nz.

Aotearoa New Zealand Association of Social Workers (February 2011). Noticeboard. ANZASW Christchurch.

Munford, R., & Sanders, J. (2005). Working with families: Strengths-based approaches. In M. Nash, R. Munford, & K. O'Donoghue (Eds.), *Social work theories in action* (pp. 158–173). London and Philadelphia: Jessica Kingsley.

Nash, M., Wong, J., & Trlin, A. (2006). Civic and social integration: A new field of social work practice with immigrants, refugees and asylum seekers in New Zealand. *International Social Work*, 49(3), 345–363.

Nash, M. (1998). *People, policies and practice: Social work education in Aotearoa/New Zealand from 1949–1995.* (Unpublished thesis). School of Social Policy and Social Work, Massey University, NZ. http://muir.massey.ac.nz/bitstream/10179/2014/2/01_front.pdf.

NEW ZEALAND SOCIAL WORK TEXTS

Durie, M. (1994). *Whaiora, Maori Health Development.* Auckland, NZ: Oxford University Press.

Munford, R., & Sanders, J. (Eds.). (2003). *Making a difference in families: Research that creates change.* Crow's Nest, N.S.W., Australia: Allen and Unwin.

Munford, M., & Walsh-Tapiata, W. (1999). *Strategies for change: Community development in Aotearoa New Zealand.* Palmerston North, NZ: School of Sociology, Social Policy and Social Work, Massey University.

Pa'u Tafaogalupe III Mano'o Tilive'a Mulitalo-Lauta. (2000). *Fa'asamoa and social work.* Palmerston North, NZ: Dunmore Press.

Nash, M., & Munford, R. (2001). *Social work in context: Fields of practice in Aotearoa New Zealand.* Palmerston North, NZ: School of Sociology, Social Policy and Social Work, Massey University.

Nash, M., Munford, R., & O'Donoghue K. (Eds.). (2005). *Social work theories in action.* London and Philadelphia: Jessica Kingsley.

Nash, M., & Stewart, B. (Eds.). (2002). *Spirituality and social care: Contributing to personal and community well-being*. London and Philadelphia: Jessica Kingsley.

O'Donoghue, K. (2003). *Restoring social work supervision*. Palmerston North, NZ: Dunmore Press.

Social Workers Registration Board. (2011). Mandatory Social Worker Registration. A discussion paper. (p. 11)

http://www.swrb.govt.nz/files/Mandatory%20registr ation%20Document/Mandatory%20Registration% 20Document.pdf (accessed 22 March 2011).

Truell, R., & Nowland, L. (Eds.). (2002). *Reflections on current practice in social work*. Palmerston North, NZ: Dunmore Press.

Social Work in the Caribbean

PETA-ANNE BAKER AND JOHN MAXWELL

INTRODUCTION

Social work in the Caribbean is as much a product of the region's political and social construction as it is reflective of the modern global reality. As a consequence, traces of early grassroots problem-solving and development strategies can still be located alongside many of the methods and fields of practice found in North American and European settings.

By the broadest definition, the Caribbean is a multiethnic, multilingual archipelago of islands and mainland territories that were formerly Dutch, English, French, and Spanish colonies. (A few countries are still colonies: the islands of the Dutch Antilles; Cayenne, Guadeloupe, and Martinique, which are overseas regions of France; Anguilla, the British Virgin Islands, the Cayman Islands, Montserrat, and the Turks and Caicos Islands, which are British dependencies; and Puerto Rico, which occupies a de facto colonial relationship to the United States.)

The region has a population of nearly forty million people, with Cuba, the Dominican Republic, Haiti, and Puerto Rico contributing over 80% of this number. The English-speaking Caribbean countries, comprising twelve independent island and mainland states and five island colonies, are home to some 16% of the population.

Although the majority of people across the region are of African descent, persons of Asian (especially Indian and to a lesser extent Chinese), European, and Middle Eastern origin are present to varying degrees in the different countries. For example, the people of Cuba are primarily of African and Hispanic origin, while in Guyana persons of Indian origin outnumber those of African ancestry. In a few countries (e.g., Belize, Dominica, Guyana, St. Vincent and the Grenadines, Suriname), groups of indigenous peoples continue to exist. In some countries, a significant number of the inhabitants are mixtures of two or more of racial groups; in others, the groups exist alongside each other with little intermarriage or integration.

CHARACTERISTICS OF SOCIAL WORK PRACTICE IN THE CARIBBEAN

The emergence of social work as a professional occupation in the Caribbean is a twentieth-century phenomenon. Its antecedents lie in the region's dual traditions of self-help and community-based development and of charitable activity by the middle and upper classes in relation to the poor. In the English-speaking Caribbean, the earliest manifestation is found in the period following emancipation in the nineteenth century, when the newly freed Africans and their allies in the non-Conformist churches set about creating a system of free villages and settlements. Schools, Friendly Societies (savings clubs created to provide funds for emergencies), and other institutions of mutual aid characterized the effort at this time. In the early to mid-twentieth century, UNIA (Universal Negro Improvement Association), an international black consciousness movement created by the Jamaican Marcus Garvey, contained several social welfare elements, including a youth corps and a women's service organization, the Black Cross Nurses, which had educational, public health, humanitarian, and leadership development functions.

The official beginning of modern public welfare and of social work in the English-speaking Caribbean is associated with events following a series of labor uprisings in the 1930s, when colonial authorities moved first to coordinate the work of existing voluntary agencies and subsequently to play an increasingly direct role in social service provision (Maxwell, 2002). Although the cause of the uprising was rooted in the poverty and degradation experienced by the working people of the region, the British government chose to focus its resources on the creation of social services rather than on social and economic policies that would result in economic improvement and enhancement of the social status of the black majority (Lewis, 1968).

In most instances social work is practiced within the framework of state-sponsored social services created along the lines of the welfare systems found in the former or current colonial states. It is fair to say that the main field of practice is casework; most practitioners are engaged in delivering services to children in difficult circumstances, vulnerable older adults or persons with disabilities, young and adult offenders, and people who are experiencing short-or long-term difficulties of an economic, social, or medical nature. Most practitioners are generalists, carrying out a range of functions with and on behalf of their various client systems. For example, a worker involved in the delivery of services to children and families would be expected to be able to perform case management functions as well as provide therapeutic interventions on a one-to-one basis or in a group setting. In part, this need arises from the limited number of qualified people available to work in the social services. But there is also the challenge of an inadequate understanding among policy makers and the general public of the scope and complexity of social work (Baker, 2007).

Countries such as Haiti and Curaçao have relied heavily on nonprofit agencies for the delivery of critical services. Consequently, there is a strong emphasis on program management and grant-making skills among practitioners in these countries. Staff in the nonprofit sector across the region also use these skills; however, they are not always professional social workers.

In the field of youth, workers have long been employed by voluntary organizations such as uniformed and church-affiliated groups. They have traditionally engaged in organizing recreational and sporting activities, and initially they were not formally trained. Often it was only at the administrative level of youth development programs that professionally trained workers (social workers or specialist youth workers) were engaged. However, the Commonwealth Youth Program (CYP) Caribbean Centre based in Guyana has promoted training programs for specialist youth workers, and since the 1980s a diploma program has been offered to this group of practitioners. Among other areas, the program builds workers' skills in microenterprise development, which can help to address the problem of widespread youth unemployment (Maxwell, 2002).

The field of community development is one in which the English-speaking Caribbean was an early pioneer. Building on the tradition of cooperation and solidarity that emerged in the postemancipation period, nationalist and community leaders in the mid-twentieth century created programs that galvanized grassroots self-help initiatives. At its height in the 1950s, a network of such groups also wielded considerable political influence in places such as Jamaica, commanding the attention of the executive and public bureaucracy. So distinctive was this program of community mobilization and development that it attracted the attention of the United Nations. One of the foremost architects of the strategy, D.T.M. Girvan, was retained as a consultant to the UN and visited a number of countries in Latin America and Africa to provide advice on the establishment of similar programs in these regions (Girvan, 1993).

Most countries in the Caribbean still have national community development programs. Workers in both government and nonprofit organizations are involved in enhancing the organizational capabilities of community groups to improve the social and economic conditions of their communities. However, official initiatives are often undermined by partisan politics and a culture of clientelism that emerged in the postindependence period. Nongovernmental initiatives are sometimes more successful, although their efforts may be stymied by fluctuating levels of donor support as well as variations in strategy (Francis-Brown, 2000).

In the English-speaking Caribbean, professional social workers have been less in evidence or unequally represented in the delivery of income support programs, in services to the elderly, and in services for persons with disabilities. However, they are an integral part of such programs in other countries in the region and are increasingly becoming engaged in these fields in the Anglo Caribbean.

SOCIAL WORK EDUCATION AND TRAINING

Available information suggests that the earliest university-based social work education program in the Caribbean was developed at the University of Havana in 1943. However, this program closed a few years after the Cuban Revolution in 1959. Many social work functions formerly performed by graduates of this program were assigned to mass organizations such as the Federation of Cuban Women or the Committees for the Defense of the Revolution. Professional training was provided through new technical institutes and social work was closely aligned with the health professions. Professional social work in Cuba was de-emphasized until the 1990s, which saw the dissolution of the Soviet Union and a downturn in the world economy. The reemergence of several social problems contributed to the Cuban government reopening the social work program at the University of Havana and three similar institutions as well as dramatically expanding training for cadres of young paraprofessionals working at the community level to ensure that people in need had access to services (Strug & Teague, 2002).

Professional social work education is currently being developed in the Dutch Antilles, with undergraduate programs being introduced at the University of the Netherlands Antilles in Curaçao and at the University of Aruba. Previously social workers were educated at universities in the Netherlands; however, there has been a growing appreciation of the need to train practitioners in their home countries and to integrate a greater measure of Caribbean content into the curriculum even while meeting the requirements of the Dutch system of education. In like manner, social work education in the French Caribbean is modeled on programs in France, where training is frequently delivered by professional institutes affiliated with the university system.

In the early days of social work education in the English-speaking Caribbean (commencing 1943), short training programs were organized to provide social welfare officers with a foundation of theoretical principles for working with individuals, groups, and communities; skills in applied research; and knowledge of public administration. Concurrently, in the 1940s a limited number of people were being sent to Britain to pursue degrees in social administration, as social work was initially known. In 1961, professional social work education was introduced at the Mona, Jamaica, campus of the relatively newly established University of the West Indies (UWI). This was followed in 1970 by the introduction of a similar program at the University of Guyana (Maxwell, Williams, Ring, & Cambridge, 2003).

The last few years have witnessed a rapid expansion of professional social work education in the English-speaking Caribbean as new universities and colleges have included this discipline in their curricula. The most common qualification is the bachelor degree, with some institutions offering an associate degree in social work. The UWI has continued to lead the way by offering graduate training, including a doctoral program and the opportunity to pursue various areas of concentration such as clinical social work, HIV and AIDS, and administration and management of social services. Graduate social work education is also provided in Martinique through a consortium of French and Québécois institutions.

PROFESSIONAL ORGANIZATIONS, NETWORKING, AND COLLABORATION

National associations of social workers have existed for many years in several countries with varying levels of activity and continuity. The Jamaica Association of Social Workers, for example, was established in 1968. Barbados, Guyana, Martinique, and Trinidad and Tobago are among the other countries with professional social work organizations. These groups have organized introductory and continuing education courses, participated in policy and program development, and above all promoted professional recognition. This has been pursued through work on the development of codes of ethics and seeking formal recognition by legislative means. However, only psychiatric social workers in Trinidad and Tobago have achieved the latter, and work continues on the former.

Even as practitioners struggle locally for recognition, they encounter little difficulty in getting their qualifications recognized outside of the region. In fact, social work graduates are actively recruited to work with the growing Caribbean populations in Britain and North America.

Since 1992, the anglophone Caribbean has been part of and shared in the rotating leadership of the North American and Caribbean Association of Schools of Social Work (NACASSW), one of the five regional bodies of the International Association of Schools of Social Work (IASSW). Caribbean practitioners and educators have attended and made presentations at the joint biennial conferences of the IASSW and the International Federation of Social Workers (IFSW). The region was represented on the boards of the IASSW and IFSW during the 1970s, and it has renewed its presence on the board of the IASSW consistently since 1992.

One of the challenges facing professional social work education in the Caribbean has been the availability of appropriate scholarly material. Whereas there is a wealth of Caribbean research and theorizing in the fields such as politics, economics, and sociology, material for social work application is less available. The expansion and maturation of social work education in the region and the emergence of the Association of Caribbean Social Work Educators (ACSWE) have resulted in some improvements to this situation.

Since 1993, universities in the region have partnered with other organizations to stage the Biennial Conference of Caribbean and International

Social Work Educators. (The ACSWE was an early product of these conferences and has since assumed the role of main sponsor.) The conferences have provided a forum for the dissemination of scholarly work that seeks to apply relevant theoretical concepts to Caribbean social welfare issues, to engage in indigenous theory building, and to offer analytic reviews of best practices from the field. They also have served as a major source of material for the annual peer-reviewed *Caribbean Journal of Social Work*, published since 2002 under the auspices of the ACSWE.

EMERGING FIELDS OF PRACTICE

Rising levels of crime and violence have brought new roles for social workers in the Caribbean. Several mainly nonprofit organizations, especially women's groups, have initiated programs to address the problem of domestic violence, including working with perpetrators. There are also community-based peace-making and mediation initiatives aimed at assisting victims and creating programs to prevent or reduce the formation of gangs (Levy, 2005). These initiatives frequently make use of cultural approaches such as drama and the other creative arts.

In a region prone to hurricanes, earthquakes, and floods, Caribbean social workers are coming to appreciate the impact of environmental factors on the lives of the people with whom they work. Greater attention is now being paid to disaster management and mitigation. This includes not only addressing the mental health aspects of natural hazards but also working to enhance the resilience of communities in the face of such events (Matthews, 2006; Ring & Carmichael, 2006; Rogers, 2006).

The coming into force of several international conventions, such as the Convention on the Rights of the Child (CRC) and the Convention on the Elimination of All Forms of Discrimination against Women (CEDAW), has drawn Caribbean social workers into advocacy with and on behalf of affected groups. There is an increasing investment in public education programs and policy research, and practitioners work closely with international agencies such as UNICEF (UN Children's Fund) and UNIFEM (UN Development Fund for Women). Additionally, with the Caribbean being second only to sub-Saharan African in the incidence of HIV and AIDS, a rapidly emerging area of social work research, advocacy, and intervention is that of working with persons living with or affected by the disease (Barrow, 2006; Jones, Padmore, & Maharaj, 2009).

Global economic and political events and the international policy agenda have exercised considerable influence on the profession's direction in the Caribbean. Even before the onset of the global recession at the end of the first decade of the twenty-first century, most developing countries in the Caribbean underwent drastic economic reforms known as structural adjustment. Early versions of these reforms involved significant reductions in public social spending. Subsequent efforts to mitigate the worst effects of structural adjustment programs include targeted social assistance programs and the creation of specialized social funds providing grant funding to community-based infrastructure works and health and education programs. Though these programs, having been designed by external donor organizations (including the World Bank and International Monetary Fund), tend to make limited use of social work knowledge and skills, there has been a slow but growing social work presence at the policy and operational levels.

School social work is another emerging field of practice in the region as schools increasingly experience the deepening socioeconomic crisis and incidence of violence in their societies. Many school guidance counselors pursue social work training, while a few schools have opted to employ both guidance counselors and social workers. One issue that consistently requires the attention of practitioners in the school setting is the need to attend to children whose parents have migrated, most often to the United States or Canada but also to Britain (Crawford-Brown, 1999; Elliot-Hart, Avery, & Rehner, 2006; Jones, Sogren, & Sharpe, 2004). Another challenge is the need to deal with the problem of violence in schools as well as with the impact of community violence on the school population. Perhaps the greatest challenge for practitioners in this setting, however, is how to respond to students' varying expressions of sexuality, especially homosexuality, in a context of widespread societal disapproval of this orientation (Barrow, de Bruin, & Carr, 2009; Carr, 2003).

Another of the newer fields of practice for Caribbean social workers is work in industrial settings, for example with the oil companies in Trinidad and Tobago, in what is known in the United States as employee assistance programs (EAPs). A small but increasing number of practitioners, usually with graduate-level education, have also ventured into private practice. They are variously engaged in offering clinical and therapeutic interventions, mainly to individuals and families. Experienced professionals also work as consultants, offering educational, research, and project development services to national, regional, and international organizations.

CONCLUSION

Social work in the Caribbean has a rich and varied history, of which there is a growing appreciation. Added to increasing opportunities for networking within the region and exposure to approaches adopted outside the region, this strengthens practitioners' commitment to finding ways of meeting the challenges of their time and acknowledging their membership of the global profession.

REFERENCES

Baker, P. A. (2007). International social work and social welfare: Caribbean In T. Mizrahi & L. Davis (Eds.), *Encyclopedia of social work* (20ᵗʰ ed., pp. 503–506) New York: Oxford University Press.

Barrow, C. (2006, December). Adolescent girls, sexuality and HIV/AIDS in Barbados: The case for reconfiguring research and policy. *Caribbean Journal of Social Work, 5*, 62–80.

Barrow, C., de Bruin, M., & Carr, R. (2009). *Sexuality, social exclusion and human rights: Vulnerability in the Caribbean context of HIV.* Kingston, Jamaica: Ian Randle.

Carr, R. (2003, July). On judgments: Poverty, sexuality-based violence and human rights in 21ˢᵗ century Jamaica. *Caribbean Journal of Social Work, 2*, 71–87.

Crawford-Brown, C. (1999). *Who will save our children? The plight of the Jamaican child in the 1990s.* Kingston, Jamaica: Canoe Press, University of the West Indies.

Elliott-Hart, F., Avery, L., & Rehner, T. (2006, December). Outcome of caregiver interruptions among Jamaican youth. *Caribbean Journal of Social Work, 6*, 91–104.

Francis-Brown, S. (2000). *Spitting in the wind: Lessons in empowerment from the Caribbean.* Kingston, Jamaica: Ian Randle in association with the Commonwealth Foundation.

Girvan, N. (Ed.). (1993). *Working together for development: D.T.M. Girvan on cooperative and community development, 1939–1968.* Kingston, Jamaica: Institute of Jamaica.

Jones, A., Padmore, J., & Maharaj, P. (Eds.). (2009). *HIV-AIDS and social work practice in the Caribbean.* Kingston, Jamaica: Ian Randle.

Jones A., Sogren, M., & Sharpe, J. (2004, October). Children's experiences of separation from parents as a consequence of migration. *Caribbean Journal of Social Work, 3*, 89–109.

Levy, H. (2005, August). Peacemaking on the front line. *Caribbean Journal of Social Work, 4*, 14–27.

Lewis, G. K. (1968). *The growth of the modern West Indies.* New York: Monthly Review Press.

Matthews, L. (2006, December). Caribbean natural disasters: Coping with personal loss and recovery among flood victims in Guyana. *Caribbean Journal of Social Work, 5*, 40–60.

Maxwell, J. (2002, March). The evolution of social welfare services and social work in the English-speaking Caribbean (with major reference to Jamaica). *Caribbean Journal of Social Work, 1*, 11–31.

Maxwell, J., Williams, L., Ring, K., & Cambridge, I. (2003, July). Caribbean social work education: The University of the West Indies. *Caribbean Journal of Social Work 2*, 11–35.

Ring, K., & Carmichael, S. (2006, December). Montserrat: A study of Caribbean resiliency. *Caribbean Journal of Social Work, 5*, 9–28.

Rogers, T. (2006, December). De day we see wind in Grenada! Community level incident debriefing through playback theatre. *Caribbean Journal of Social Work, 5*, 29–39.

Strug, D., & Teague, W. (2002, September). New directions in Cuban social work education: What can we learn? *Social Work Today.* Retrieved May 15, 2007, from www.redandgreen.org/Cuba/Cuban_Social_Work_Education.htm.

FURTHER READING

Allen, L., Baker, P. A., Havens, C., & Healy, L. (Eds.). (2005). Social work with Caribbean people: Perspectives from home and abroad. *Caribbean Journal of Social Work, 4* (Special issue).

Chevannes, B. (2003). Learning to be a man: Culture, socialization and gender identity in five Caribbean communities. Kingston, Jamaica: University of the West Indies Press.

Henry, F., & Plaza, D. (Eds.). (2006). *Returning to the source: The final stage of the Caribbean migration circuit.* Kingston, Jamaica: University of the West Indies Press.

WEBSITES

Oxfam's work in Haiti: www.oxfam.org.uk/resources/countries/haiti.html.

Social Work Development and Practice in Cuba and in the U.S.: www.redandgreen.org/Cuba/Social_Work/sw02-contents.htm.

59

Social Work in Europe

ANNAMARIA CAMPANINI

Social work in Europe began in the twentieth century in many countries. As Lorenz (2006) and Lyons & (and) Lawrence (2006) underline, social work reflects specific cultural and contextual dimensions. Historical backgrounds, social policy trends, pedagogical and disciplinary relationships, and politics all have implications for the way in which social work training has been established in different countries and for the specific manner in which the role of social work has been interpreted. Local factors and European policy developments are also important elements in determining how social work education is evolving in terms of structure, curricula, and pedagogical issues and in determining what kind of role social workers will play (Labonté-Roset, Marynowicz-Helka, & Szmagalski, 2003). This chapter draws a picture of social work in Europe, focusing on three aspects:

the state of the art in social work education,

the role played by social workers, and

the challenges facing social work in postmodern society.

THE STATE OF THE ART IN SOCIAL WORK EDUCATION

Higher education in Europe has been under a profound process of change in the last decade. Since the 1980s, the European Commission has defined a series of measures with the key objectives of developing the European component within the teaching world and further enabling the geographical mobility of students. The Socrates and Erasmus mobility programmes have undoubtedly had a great impact on the creation of a European identity; they have helped to develop a better understanding of social work education and identity in Europe and have encouraged the evolution of a shared knowledge base. One of the needs identified, a need that moved the

European Union to highlight the importance of an intercultural dimension within student learning, is the need to prepare younger generations for life in a society increasingly characterized by cultural and linguistic diversity so that they may identify concrete actions with which to fight racism and xenophobia. The Socrates and Erasmus program measures have enhanced student mobility and the European Credit Transfer System (ECTS); developed joint Programmes (specific title and context) to encourage academic acknowledgment and contribution toward the exchange of experiences and innovative processes, therefore enhancing the quality of teaching; and supported teaching staff exchanges (TS) and intensive programs (IP).

Through the Bologna Declaration (1999), an initiative of twenty-nine European governments, a process was established with the objective of creating a European space of higher education by 2010. The aim was to increase both the employment prospects and geographical mobility of European citizens and to enhance the concept of European higher education in the world (Campanini, 2007).

Many initiatives have been taken during the last decade in social work education, and our intention here is to offer an overview of social work education in Europe. We can refer to some experiences that have involved many countries, such as the thematic networks ECSPRESS (European Consortium of Social Professions in Educational and Social Studies) (Chytil & Siebel,1999) and EUSW TN (European Social Work Thematic Network that lasted from 2002 to 2008, www.eusw.unipr.it). In the book *European Social Work: Commonalities and Differences* (Campanini & Frost, 2004), representatives of twenty-four European nations presented the state-of-the-art social work in their countries. Through this work it was possible to have a clear image of some commonalities and also many differences in social work education at various levels. More recent research has been undertaken, for example by Martínez (2007), specifically on social education across Europe in the wake of the Bologna Process and on fieldwork education in fifteen European countries (Campanini, 2009).

From these studies it is evident that despite the Bologna Process, which aims to harmonize higher education in Europe, meaningful differences among countries persist in a number of ways.

For example, there are differences in the kinds of institutions that provide higher education. Besides countries that have entrusted the formation of social workers in more or less recent times to the university sector, there are countries that have developed learning routes in higher private or public institutes. In some nations (e.g., Poland, Lithuania, Portugal), there is the simultaneous presence of various educational contexts. Also, the church has significant involvement in social work education in Eastern European countries, such as Hungary and Romania, where social work training can be linked with the preparation to become a deacon.

It is interesting to note that the insertion of social work education into the university rather than in other contexts not only produces one different legitimation of the role of the social worker (as evidenced in the Italian experience, where the recognition of the social work profession was consequent to the insertion of social work education into the university) but also leads to a more or less elevated status of the profession. Moreover, access to advanced courses (e.g., research doctorates) can be more difficult if students have not undertaken a university degree but have attended educational institutions such as the Fachhochschulen in Germany or the hogescholen in the Netherlands.

Another difference in social work education among European countries is the duration of the education. At the time of the first research done in the EUSW context, in some places there were curricula of only three years (e.g., Spain, Belgium), while other countries responded to the guidelines issued by the Bologna Declaration by articulating the educational path into a pattern of three years plus two years (e.g., Italy, Norway, Estonia). Some states maintained a curriculum of four years (e.g., Netherlands, Greece, Cyprus, Germany, Iceland), while in other countries the title of social worker was awarded after the attendance of a five-year course (e.g., Portugal). Many changes have occurred due to the need to restructure the educational system in accordance with the Bologna Process, and the situation is still continuously changing as schools attempt to harmonize the differences in the duration of the first and the second cycles (e.g., Sweden decided for a pattern of three and half plus one and half, while Spain defined the curriculum in four plus one).

The disciplinary components of curricula also vary from country to country. It is generally true that the disciplines that form the base of social work education make reference to the human sciences of sociology, psychology, and pedagogy, which are placed side by side with social policy and legal studies. In some Eastern European countries, such as Romania and Hungary, theology is studied.

In professional practice preparation, variously referred to as *placement, fieldwork,* or *practice education,* there are many differences both in relation to the number of hours dedicated to social work theory and supervised practice and regarding the modalities within which the training is carried out.

In a recent analysis of eighteen curricula in fifteen European countries (Campanini, 2009), the number of hours dedicated to field placements ranged from 2050 (in France) to 210 (in Estonia), with different criteria in the definition of the relationship between number of credits and number of hours.

Also different from country to country is the articulation of this experience: Sometimes the field placement is full time in one block (Sweden, Germany), but in many other countries it is spread throughout the whole curricula with a certain number of hours per year. Differences are also evident in the role of other personnel involved with the student in the placement experience: Supervisor, tutor, practice teacher, and field instructor can be some of the different names for the same function, or they can designate the specific roles being played by the same person. Further differences are notable in the evaluation processes, which range from quite general and not greatly affecting the attainment of the degree (e.g., Italy) to being strictly regulated in terms of quality, learning, and student achievement (e.g., United Kingdom).

In relation to teaching methodologies, the role of teachers in social work courses can vary greatly and is strictly related to the idea of the learning process predominant within the individual nation. Active learning has a strong presence in Scandinavian countries, with specific tools and evaluation processes oriented toward helping students to be the principal actors in their own learning process and to develop a critical and self-reflective attitude (Juliusdottir, 2006). Contrary to this, in Italy more conventional methods are based on the traditional notion of an expert lecturer imparting knowledge to educable and eager students.

Within specific systems, even the layout of rooms can reinforce the specific philosophy. In Italy it can be difficult to find flexible shapes and settings away from the formal auditoriums, which restrict teachers in developing more participative methods. In addition, information and communication technologies are slowly entering social work education, for example in the Norwegian-led initiative of a virtual classroom (VIRCLASS), and are useful for organizing pan-European modules with teachers and students from different countries (see the virtual campus experience at www.virclass.net).

Research and theory production are yet another area that differs among countries (Labonté-Roset, 2005). These aspects are important elements for the enhancement of social work education. In some nations, such as Sweden, a long tradition of PhD studies is linked to intensive publication of research in social work. In other countries (e.g., Estonia, Czech Republic, Italy, Spain), this process is a fundamental challenge for the future of social work. There are issues regarding whether social work education should be positioned inside or outside the university, both in relation to the possibility of students achieving research degrees and in relation to the expectation that teachers will actively pursue research (Lyons & Lawrence, 2006).

Finally, the European orientation of social work education varies from country to country. Involvement in European projects and activities is high in nearly all countries, and social work has been pursuing the aim of opening itself to inter-European comparisons in social work education. Many countries are using the opportunities made available by the European community. Several countries have become involved in student mobility and teaching staff exchanges.

These activities have also been developed in some places through European Commission intensive programs on specific topics and through particular initiatives such as international weeks, which are open to contributions from teachers of various nations. The attempt to open education to a wider vision is also demonstrated by the insertion of curricular modules that address various aspects of social work from a comparative perspective. There are initiatives such as summer schools in different countries (e.g., Fachhochschule Alice Salomon in Berlin; University of Lapland in Rovaniemi, Finland; summer schools held in Parma and Dornbirn by EUSW TN), some international master's courses (e.g., MACESS in Maastricht, Goteborg University), and some attempts to create a specific course that awards the title of bachelor of

intercultural and international social work (as in Copenhagen).

In spite of these actions, some difficulties remain. Primarily these are the students' and staff's insufficient knowledge of languages (e.g., France, Great Britain, Italy, Spain) and problems with the temporal structure of the courses and the economic costs of studying abroad, all of which can limit the mobility of students. Some reluctance to operate transnationally might also indicate an inward-facing attitude whereby European engagement and dimensions are still not perceived as opportunities. Students then fail to develop intercultural and international professional competences, which are now seen as core competencies in many parts of Europe.

We can conclude that despite all these differences, there is a strong will to participate in mutually identifying processes to recognize common concerns regarding ethics and principles and a European social work identity. "Examples of social work constituencies in European countries forging links and associations, projects and cooperative activities to engender European social work identities are burgeoning, with the EU itself financing some of this work. In social work education and academia particularly there is perceptible evidence of conscious attempts to develop Europeanisation" (Frost, 2008, p. 350).

THE ROLE PLAYED BY SOCIAL WORKERS

Social work in Europe can be almost universally recognized as a profession, and it may be stated that the requirements mentioned by Flexner (1915) have been fully met. The presence of theoretically sound and transmissible know-how, effective and sufficiently articulated training courses, and a community of professionals who define the criteria to admit new workers and regulate the professional ethics by means of a code of conduct show that social work has become a real profession.

Nevertheless, it is not a unique profession (Chytil, Lorenz, Seibel, & Strieznec, 2000). In Europe the professional role is multifaceted, and under the same term *social work* there can be many methods and also emphasis on diverse aspects in realizing the international definition of social work. Although common features can be identified, such as clear reference to shared principles and values focusing on human beings and their potential, theoretical and methodological approaches undeniably vary with reference to the know-how achieved and the different roles attributed to a number of reference disciplines.

As described, social work education and the way in which curricula stress diverse subjects prepare students to undertake distinct roles and contribute to professional differentiation (Chytil & Siebel 1999). Research and discussions conducted within EUSW TN on the specific roles and activities carried out by social workers in Europe (Campanini & Frost, 2004) have shown the existence of a variety of career paths:

- Counseling and therapeutic route (e.g., Scandinavian countries)
- Educational and pedagogical focus (e.g., Germany, Poland, Luxembourg, and the Netherlands)
- General approach (e.g., Italy and Finland)
- Specialist route with specific attention to child protection, community, and youth work or probation (e.g., Great Britain)
- Charity aid work in countries where there is a major fight against poverty activities (e.g., many Eastern European countries such as Estonia and Lithuania).

As Shardlow & Payne (1998) noted, there is a problem defining common boundaries of social work in Europe, and the range of activities that can fall under the rubric of social work could be quite large. Tasks attributed to social workers in one country may be part of the role of other professionals somewhere else. For example, in Italy, all activities connected with psychotherapy are the exclusive domain of psychologists; also, it is illegal for a trained social worker to work as family therapist. On the other hand, some professions such as social pedagogues (e.g., Germany) do not exist at all in some European states (e.g., Great Britain), which could mean that a pedagogical approach will be taken by social workers. "The shape of social work boundaries is influenced by an enormous number of factors: historical factors as the strength and the influence of other occupational groups; prescription of the state; the legitimate dreams of the population and the self-perception of the social work profession about the scope and range of this activities" (Shardlow & Payne, 1998, p. 155).

At the same time, the European Qualifications Framework (EQF), launched in 2006 by the European Commission, can facilitate a comparison of qualifications and qualification levels in order to promote geographical and labor market mobility as well as lifelong learning through the definition of knowledge, skills, and competences at each qualification level. There is pressure toward a possible harmonization of social

work (Campanini, 2007), both in education and in practice, as well as in the welfare system across Europe. If it is true that we are facing more and more similar problems, we cannot forget the national cultures and traditions that have shaped the role of social work.

Working from this research, Lorenz (2006) suggests finding a decisive element of common identity in the "recognition of such a multidimensional diversity not as a result of mere historical contingencies . . . but as a means of engaging with the individual and collective determinants of identity in the context of which social problems and issues manifest themselves and need to be respected in all form of intervention" (p. 46).

Looking at the employment fields across Europe, the majority of social workers are still within public institutions even though the importance of NGOs (nongovernmental organizations) is increasing everywhere. In some countries there are also a number of independent (freelance, private) social workers, although the number is still small due to the strict connection that the profession has with social services and social policy (Campanini & Frost, 2004).

GLOBAL CHALLENGES

Europe is facing many challenges. These include aging populations at risk of exclusion from participation in mainstream society and facing problems connected with care for illness, disability, and isolation; migration processes (Ricciardelli, Urban, & Nanopoulos, 2009) with their controversial and complex impacts on societies in terms of social inclusion and the embracing of diversity; the effects of globalization on lifestyle and in relationship structures that can cause individual and family problems; the poverty that is still present in many countries; and managerialism and its influence on the organization of welfare systems, which raises the risk that the search for more economically viable forms of service delivery may result in the occasional use of unqualified social workers (Campanini & Frost, 2004, p. 212).

Taking into account these challenges, social work has had to deal with a general shift from state to civil society, from welfare to workfare logic, with an increased presence of third-sector and nonprofit social services and a service delivery market (Fortunato, Friesenhan, & Kantovicz, 2008).

Clients and citizens are increasingly seen as consumers, while the suppliers of social services are turning into producers. Consequently, factors such as effectiveness, efficiency, and service output are becoming more and more important. This neoliberal attitude is affecting the role of social workers by orienting their actions toward bureaucratic, instrumental, and depoliticized responses.

In this scenario there is a great need for committed social work to support personal and social responsibility and to contribute to social cohesion. This requires social workers who are able to invest in the development of the resources of both individuals and communities, involving all the major participants in elaborating and verifying processes and constructive actions; work with individuals within the community and not just groups as a whole; and an appreciation of the viewpoints and mentality of these individuals.

It also necessary that social workers understand the multiple factors (e.g., political, economic) that form the basis of exclusion, oppression, and poverty. They need to be able to tackle social problems while also promoting structural changes.

The impact of globalization at the local level requires "cross-cultural understanding, comparative social policy, concern with global problems, a general worldview, knowledge of a common profession worldwide, international practice, intergovernmental social welfare, and a sense of collegiality with social workers in other countries" (Healy, 2001, p. 7). However, as the global standards and code of ethics underline (www.ifsw.org), we have to stress the importance of awareness of ethnic diversity, cultural, and gender issues in both the training and professional arenas.

The Bologna Process has had a strong impact in creating a common understanding of the challenges that we are facing in society, stressing the need to tune the curricula and defining competences of social work. It has also contributed to the investigation into the European identity of social work (Frost, 2008).

Various associations support this process in Europe, representing both education (European Association of Schools of Social Work—EASSW) and professionals (International Federation of Social Workers—IFSW Europe). These associations organize joint conferences and meetings, voice issues at a European level, and network with other organizations in the social field (e.g., European Network for Social Action—ENSACT) to raise awareness of the role of social work in improving social cohesion in European society.

REFERENCES

Barnes, M. (2002). *Poverty and social exclusion in Europe.* Cheltenam: Edward Elgar.

Campanini, A. (Eds) (2009). *Scenari di Welfare e formazione al Servizio Sociale in un'Europa che cambia.* Rome: Carocci.

Campanini, A. (2007). Introduction. In E. Frost, & M. J. Freitas (Eds.). *Social work education in Europe* (pp. 9–22). Rome: Carocci.

Campanini A., & Frost E. (Eds.) (2004). *European social work: Commonalities and differences.* Rome: Carocci.

Chytil, O., Lorenz, W., Seibel, F. W., & Strieznec, S. (Eds.). (2000). *Preparing the social professions for tomorrow's Europe.* Blansko, Czech Republic: ECSPRESS Edition.

Chytil, O., & Seibel, F. W. (Eds.). (1999). *European dimension in training and practice of social professions.* Blansko, Czech Republic: ECSPRESS Edition.

Flexner, A. (1915). Is social work a profession? *School and Society, XXVI,* 901–911.

Fortunato, V., Friesenhan, G., & Kantovicz, E. (Eds.) (2008). *Social Work in Resctructured Welfare Systems.* Rome: Carocci.

Frost, E. (2008). Is there a European social work identity? *European Journal of Social Work, 11*(4), 341–354.

Healy, L. (2001). *International social work: Professional action in an interdependent world.* Oxford and New York: Oxford Press.

Juliusdottir, S. (2006). The emerging paradigm shift in social work: In the context of the current reform of social work education. *Social Work and Society, 3*(2). www.socwork.net.

Labonté- Roset, C. (2005). The European higher education area and research-orientated social work education. *European Journal of Social Work, 8*(3) 285–296.

Labonté-Roset, C., Marynowicz-Helka, E., & Szmagalski, J. (2003). *Social work education and practice in today's Europe.* Slaskl: Katovice.

Lorenz, W. (2006). *Perspectives on European social work.* Opladen: Barbara Budrich.

Lyons, K., & Lawrence, S. (Eds.). (2006). *Social work in Europe: Educating for change.* Birmingham: Venture Press.

Martínez-Román, M. A. (2007). Social Work Education in Europe: The Bologna Process and the Challenges for the Future of Social Work. In E. Frost, & M. J. Freitas (Eds.). *Social work education in Europe* (pp. 23–37). Rome: Carocci.

Ricciardelli, M., Urban, S., & Nanopoulos, K. (Eds.). (2009). *Globalization and multicultural societies some views from Europe.* Paris: Notre Dame Press.

Shardlow, S., & Payne, M. (1998). *Contemporary issues in social work: Western Europe.* Aldershot: Arena.

WEBSITES

European Association of Schools of Social Work: www.eassw.org.

European Social Work Thematic Network: www.eusw.unipr.it.

European Network for Social Action: www.ensact.eu.

International Federation of Social Workers: www.ifsw.org.

Social Work in Latin America

IRENE QUEIRO-TAJALLI

President Evo Morales said in his inaugural address in 2006, ". . . in the world there are
large and small countries, rich countries and poor countries, but we are equal in one thing,
which is our right to dignity and sovereignty . . ."

DUNKERLEY, 2007

INTRODUCTION

The task of writing about social work in Latin America is daunting given the vast differences and population realities among its countries. There are many ways of defining the area known as Latin America, but for the sake of this chapter, Latin America includes twenty countries: the ten Spanish-and Portuguese-speaking countries of South America; the six Spanish-speaking countries of Central America; Mexico; and Cuba, the Dominican Republic, and Haiti in the Caribbean region (Brea, 2003).

Latin America is a region of tremendous beauty, vast natural resources, and rich cultural traits. Its history, languages, traditions, literature, and the like combine to create a vibrant and culturally diverse region. This Indo-Afro-Latin American continent (Dubini, 2008; Zabala Cubillos, 2002) saw the rise and fall of the Incan, Mayan, and Aztec empires. Its music and dances—tango, calypso, salsa, samba, and a rich range of native folklore—extend throughout the world. Traditional native languages such as Quechua, Kekchi, Mixtec, and Guarani are still spoken to this day. In addition, Latin America has numerous Nobel Prize recipients, including Carlos Saavedra Lamas (Peace, 1936), Gabriela Mistral (Literature, 1945), Miguel Angel Asturias (Literature, 1967), Adolfo Pérez Esquivel (Peace, 1980), Gabriel García Márquez (Literature, 1982), and Mario Vargas Llosa (Literatura, 2010). Elisabeth Shirley Enochs (1955) eloquently described the diversity and unity of the Latin American countries as follows:

Some countries still have large Indian populations living under primitive conditions. Some countries are becoming so rapidly modernized and industrialized that their major cities compare with any big city in Europe and the United States. Some cities are a blend of the old and new, and some, even the capital cities, are virtually museum pieces of Spanish or Portuguese architecture of three or more centuries ago. But all are bound together by a sense of common destiny derived from their love of freedom and dedication to republican forms of government. (pp. 299–300)

On the darker side, Latin America suffered mistreatment and abuse from the conquistadores during the colonization period, the brutality of several military dictatorships in recent history, and the current harsh effects of the "global interconnection of oppression" (Council on Social Work Education [CSWE], 2008, p. 5).

From the 1960s through the 1980s, Latin America suffered through brutal military takeovers and regimes, including those in Brazil (1964), Chile (1973), Uruguay (1973), and Argentina (1976). Some authors talk about the lost decade when referring to the 1980s; however, Latin America has experienced several lost decades in the twentieth century at the hands of military regimes and as a result of the deepening radical economic injustices created by neoliberal policies. In the struggle against such oppression, Latin America has witnessed the courageous struggles of its people from Chiapas in the north to the piqueteros and the landless in the south.

Although Latin America is rich in natural resources, poverty has brought considerable pain to the continent. Alcantara (2005) wrote that in Latin

American countries, the poor accounted for 40.5% and 43.8% of the population in 1980 and in 1999, respectively. Poverty levels vary from country to country; for example, in 2001, 22% of the population in Chile and Costa Rica was living below the poverty level. At the same time, 30% of the population in Argentina, Panama, and the Dominican Republic was living below the poverty line. In the mid-2000s, countries such as Colombia, Ecuador, Nicaragua, and Paraguay experienced poverty levels of 60% and above. Citing a 2005 report from the UN Economic Commission for Latin America and the Caribbean, Saracostti (2007) reports that 40.6% percent of the population still lives in poverty. Globally, and as noted by Laszlo (2001), poverty is not evenly distributed among all; "the poorest 40 percent of the [world] population is left with 3 percent of the global wealth, while the wealth of a few hundred billionaires equals the revenue of half the world's population" (p. 66). This is true in Latin America, where the gap between those who control the resources and those who lack the basic means of existence has increased since the 1990s despite a positive growth of the gross domestic product (GDP) (Barragán, 2001). The economic crisis of mid-2000 has hit hard the economies of Latin American, yet the region is not standing still. Governments are taking measures such as increasing public spending, creating employment, and targeting support to vulnerable groups to help counteract the effects of the crisis.

EVOLUTION OF SOCIAL WORK EDUCATION AND PRACTICE

Social work as a profession crystallized in Latin America in the twentieth century, with the first school of social work created in Chile in 1925 (Healy, 2008). Through the history of the profession, one can see the diversity in its orientation and the scope of its work. This is readily visible in the curricula of social work programs, particularly at the onset of the profession, where the training of social workers, or social assistants, as they were called in some countries, was closely related to medicine, public health, home economics, and law. As mentioned by Alayón (2007), the earlier curricula were so different from current programs that it can be hard to believe that they emerged from the same profession. Also, the length of degree programs varied from a genesis of two and three years to the current four-and five-year programs. Additionally, there are several doctoral programs in the continent. The auspices for social education in Latin America consist of the public and private sectors as well as religious institutions.

Latin American social work education and practice has endured several transitions and has experienced periods of growth, retrenchment, reflection, and defiance based on the historical, sociocultural, political, and economic realities of each country. In each instance these trends have guided the evolution of the profession. Though the profession respects the unique historical characteristics of each country, social workers in Latin America are keenly aware that the profession needs to evolve based on current global realities that are shaping future educational and practice trends. This understanding has provided a broader perspective to better access the needs and social concerns of individuals, groups, and communities.

The social work framework in Latin American stemmed from the intervention of religious and charitable organizations. Early interventions were based on the importance of addressing social problems at the individual level. The intent was to reduce poverty by teaching appropriate work ethics to the poor, which in turn would help them to emerge from their precarious living conditions. Clearly, the positivist and functionalist paradigms were the main underpinnings of social work at that time. This interventive approach was later denounced by various authors (de Paula Faleiros, 2005; Maguiña, 1977) as a means of maintaining control, creating an active labor class to support capitalism, and sustaining the ruling class.

During the 1950s, social work in Latin America was influenced by social work practice in the United States. This practice model included a strong emphasis on theory and skills and was designed to produce social workers who were highly trained, nonjudgmental, and devoid of feelings. Such an approach was later criticized for being mechanical, ritualistic, and unresponsive to the societal dimensions affecting the welfare of the clients. As in previous decades, social workers were perceived as a mechanism of capitalism to enforce social control (Castronovo, 2008; Pereyra, 2008; Roig, 2002).

The well-known reconceptualization process started in the southern countries of the Americas in the 1960s and rapidly spread to the rest of the Latin American world. This process challenged the traditional role of the profession by advancing a critical analysis of the palliative nature of social work and its traditional functions in society (Alayón, 2005; Parra, 2007). The movement emphasized the need to focus less on the deficits of the individual, group, or community and more on the denunciation of oppressive socioeconomic conditions that kept society in the hands of the few and powerful. Theories that guided the thinking of that time included liberation theology, conscientization, and Marxist ideology, among others (Pereyra, 2008). The goal was to create a true Latin American social work profession based on the characteristics and needs of the people. "It was a time of professional divisions between those who considered social work as a support for the political establishment and those who believed that social work should bring social change to oppressive structures" (Queiro-Tajalli, 2008, p. 525).

While the movement was not homogeneous, it began a new dialogue among faculty and practitioners. An important guiding principle was the need to assess poverty by analyzing the forces that created it, namely the passing on of wealth to the industrialized countries. Hence, poverty and the plight of the poor were a direct result of oppressive macrostructures. During the reconceptualization period, social work was recognized as the profession best suited to understand the conditions brought about by unjust socioeconomic situations and to work within the precepts of the popular culture. The movement was guided by the conviction that the focus was to eradicate oppressive societal structures and that the poor had a key role to play in this transformation (Gagneten, 1986, as cited in Pereyra, 2008, p. 6). Such thinking is closely related to Freire's (1970) pedagogy of the oppressed:

> The pedagogy of the oppressed as a humanist and libertarian pedagogy, has two distinct stages. In the first, the oppressed unveil the world of oppression and through the praxis commit themselves to its transformation. In the second stage, in which the reality of oppression has already been transformed, this pedagogy ceases to belong to the oppressed and becomes a pedagogy of all men in the process of permanent liberation. (p. 40)

The emergence of dictatorships in Latin America in the 1970s aborted the process of reconceptualization. The study of social sciences was terminated from universities, causing the removal of educators from institutions of higher education and the elimination of social work jobs, particularly those aiming at popular education in impoverished communities. In the following passage, Moljo (2005) describes the takeover of the Argentine government by the military. This is just one example of the appalling times many Latin America countries went through during that decade.

> March 24, 1976, started the bloodiest period in Argentine history resulting in 30,000 disappeared. All the gains that were generated in both society and social work were buried under a military regime which did not vacillate for a second to crush the hopes of so many countries that Argentina could be a free country. Unfortunately, death was the only outcome of their intervention. (p. 44)

Implicit in this passage is the fact that other Latin American countries under military rule lost one of the beacons fighting against oppressive regimes.

After the resurgence of democracy in several Latin American countries in the 1980s, academicians and practitioners began to deliberate the role of social work. Henceforth the postreconceptualization formation of social work encompassed the various transformations of the profession as it progressed to the present time. Unfortunately, the return to democracy did not mean that the profession became less vulnerable. The crescendo of neoliberal policies in the 1990s dismantled the welfare state of the Latin American countries and left social workers with fewer social policies and fewer resources to address the crushing poverty brought on by privatization, wage suppression, and unemployment (Grassi, 2003; Sherraden, 2009). As Curiel (1991) noted, a culture of structural adjustments was created even though some countries did not qualify for such adjustment given that they were in a position to pay their international debt. The author argues that this culture was created to allow privatization and financial and economic liberalization to take place.

With the collapse of labor in the twentieth century and as governments have increasingly abdicated their social responsibilities, again social work is faced with macro forces of inequality and injustice. But today, these forces include globalization and a new economic order, which in turn calls for a strong advocacy role to ameliorate the drastic effects of such policies. This advocacy is personified in the actions of social work educators and professionals. Regional social work organizations have also made many contributions, such as the Asociación Latinoamericana de Escuelas de Trabajo Social, or Latin American Association of Schools of Social Work (ALAETS); Centro Latinoamericano de Trabajo, or Social Latin American Social Work Center (CELATS); Asociación

Latinoamericana de Enseñanza e Investigación en Trabajo, or Social Latin American Association of Social Work Education and Research; and Red Latinoiberoamericana y Caribeña de Trabajadores Sociales, or Latinoiberoamericana and Caribbean Network of Social Workers (RELATS).

THE SCOPE OF SOCIAL WORK AND LABOR REALITIES FOR SOCIAL WORKERS

Since social work is deeply embedded in the psychosocial, economic, political, and historical perspective of each country, it makes the profession ideal as an agent of change and denouncer of society's human and social inequalities. At the same time, the close relationship of social work practice to national, state, and municipal governments and charitable organizations requires a less radical position when seeking social change. Castronovo (2008) pointed out that the historical role of social work is subordinate to the government as an employer and to other professions in its role of providing supportive services to those professions. Such a close link between government and social work has been seriously compromised given the wave of neoliberal policies that have overshadowed the Latin American countries and curtailed the role of the government as the benefactor of the people (Basta, 2009). Furthermore, some authors (Melano, 2007; Núñez, 2008) have raised an extremely relevant question as to whether social work has sufficient professional autonomy to create new alternatives to the neoliberal project.

Poverty was identified as a main focus of intervention in the early days of the social work profession. From the beginning, poverty was addressed at the individual and family levels. Since the mid-1990s, there have been many areas of concern for Latin American social workers due to the social cost of neoliberal policies, with poverty as the major focus of attention. As expressed by Professor Maria C. Rueda Salazar from the University of La Salle, Bogotá, Colombia, "every year we observe an increase in the poverty rate and as social workers we have to move from the discourse to the reality of the praxis" (personal communication, June 29, 2009). Latin American has a large enclave of urban poor due to internal migration from rural to urban areas, displacement due to gentrification, and immigration from bordering countries, just to name a few. Social workers have a long tradition of working with vulnerable urban populations as part of interdisciplinary teams.

These teams are most often composed of health-care providers, psychologists, architects, educators, and people from other disciplines who provide a holistic response to complex challenges.

Within the discussion of poverty, Saracostti (2007) talks about how social capital can be a valuable model to address poverty. Her perspective is that the solidarity of Latin America countries is a critical approach to reduce poverty within the region. She contends that models of community practice in social work in Latin America, which support the empowerment of poor and disenfranchised communities, must approach poor communities by integrating their viewpoints. In citing examples of programs that incorporated social capital to help eradicate poverty in Latin America, the author makes a strong claim on the potential of developing project evaluation, practice evaluation, and evidence-based practice programs to combat poverty by incorporating social capital.

Given that Latin American has a young population, social work has traditionally had an important role in child and youth welfare as well. Social workers have worked in this field of practice under the auspices of charitable organizations, government programs, and not-for-profit agencies. Latin America has a history of child-labor abuses even to this day, despite protective labor legislation. These jobs include picking bananas, mining coal, working on construction sites, working as street peddlers and shoe shiners, and working as parking lot attendants, to mention but a few.

With the advent of the global economic crisis (Mello, 2007) and massive layoffs, this situation has intensified for many children. In many countries social workers are working with the ministries of education, welfare, and health to prevent school dropouts, protect children on the streets, and find alternatives to family incomes that depend on child labor. However, this is an enormous task considering the extent of the economic crisis. For example, immediately after the collapse of the Argentine economy in 2001, poor families, including children and teens, lacking any type of social protection, resorted to creating their own sources of income by searching through trash on the streets of Buenos Aires, should we delete, and replace with and? collecting paper goods for recycling. This gave birth to the well-known cartoneros movement (Hill, 2006; Koehs, 2005) and the creation of communal cooperatives that sprang up to help people survive the crisis. In some of the projects, social workers have helped the cooperatives with technical and legal advice designed to improve how they function.

However, many countries are still at loss to find resources to provide much-needed educational and training programs to keep children and youth out of the streets and away from abusive labor conditions.

On the other end of the life cycle is the older population. The Latino culture has a strong orientation toward embracing older adults within the family. However, due to difficult economic times, regional conflicts, internal relocation, and immigration, many older adults find themselves separated from their loved ones. At the macro level, older adults have suffered the devaluation of their life savings and retirement funds as well as the curtailment of social and recreational services. The IFSW (International Federation of Social Workers) International Policy on Ageing and Older Adults considers the role of the social worker as a key human services provider in the field of aging by providing social services at the micro level and creating and advocating for policies and services at the macro level to enhance the well-being of older adults (www.ifsw.org/p38000214.html). Many of these functions have been performed by social workers employed by government agencies, nonprofit organizations, and labor unions working in nursing homes, hospitals, clinics, recreational centers, and social welfare ministries.

A dilemma regarding the scope of social work is that of practice within a global context as opposed to practice focusing on territorial ethnic characteristics, needs, and potentials. By using ethnic-sensitive approaches that do not impose ethnocentric modalities dictated by those in positions of power, the social work profession can play a significant role in helping communities cope with globalized poverty, globalized injustice, and social exclusion (Estrada Ospina, 2008) while still helping them to be part of the global economy.

Connected to this thinking is the broader mission of social work, that of bringing societal change. As expressed by Capello and Mamblona (2007), there is a need for social work interventions committed to constructing a new social order free of class exploitation. Some of these discussions have been entertained in earlier periods of the profession, but there seems to be a stronger thrust to do so now by developing new competencies, reinforcing a spirit of inquiry, and building ties with the many social movements existing in the Latin American continent (Capello & Mamblona, 2007; Molina, 2007).

Related to social work functions are the current realities of employment among social workers. As mentioned earlier, social workers have seen their sphere of intervention curtailed, and many times they find themselves in harm's way when operating under military regimes. In the current worldwide economic crisis, employment security among social workers is once more compromised. A research project carried out by a group of professors and students from the University of Buenos Aires (Cademartori, Campos, & Seiffer, 2007) studied the labor conditions of social workers in Argentina. The results of this study show four troubling labor trends:

- A deep fall in salaries due to the devaluation of the national currency dating back to the collapse of the economy in 2001, which has reduced access to amenities and services that social workers had in the past
- Labor instability through new contractual relationships between employers and social workers; jobs are for a limited time and area based on government decisions to keep or eliminate social welfare programs
- A trend of holding multiple jobs given the need to work in several positions to achieve a decent income
- An increase in subemployment or partial employment since most jobs offer fewer hours and low salaries.

Although these results cannot be generalized to other regions, they may provide some insight as to the realities of professional practice in an era of economic uncertainties in Latin America. Furthermore, as social workers participate in grassroots organizing efforts to construct a social order that leads to human, personal, and socioeconomic emancipation and conscientization, the stability of their employment may be further compromised.

SUMMARY

Latin America faces many of the same socioeconomic concerns of other countries of the Global South, including an aging population, an ever-growing population of young people, struggles with economic globalization and the fading hopes of global prosperity, the loss of jobs, the depletion of natural resources, issues of human rights, and of course poverty. Within this landscape, Latin American social workers try to create innovative approaches through grassroots movements to address the sociopolitical and economic realities of the marginalized, the impact of neoliberal policies on vulnerable sectors of society, and the social injustice that they create. The evolving nature of social work as a profession is closely related to the new sources of power, the emerging nature of people's needs, the economic capacity of governments and nonprofit organizations, and the self-organizing of individuals, all within the vast diversity of the Latin American characteristics.

Implicit in the discussion about social work practice in Latin America is the need to prioritize the levels of interventions (micro, mezzo, macro) and the groups that receive these interventions. Also, there seems to be a need to clarify who are the allies of social work (i.e., government, labor unions, social movements emerging in different corners of the continent), and although it may be a difficult task, social workers may need to identify the voices of those who are the casualties of the new economic and social realities of the twenty-first century.

Currently, there is a growing interest in assessing the ethical ramifications of political practices given the sociopolitical transition underway in the Latin American countries. The prolific body of literature voicing the thoughts of the Latin American social workers about constructing a profession that is reflective of the authentic characteristics of the Latin American people is extremely promising. Additionally, social workers have created alternative interventive approaches borne from the realities, needs, and hopes of the people of this great region. Finally, throughout the recent literature there is a strong theme of social work as a profession, independent from other professions and legitimized by its unique interventive practices. The Latin American social work profession has come a long way from the days of the conquistadores, oppressive military regimes, and lost decades.

REFERENCES

Alayón, N. (2007). Acerca del quehacer profesional del trabajo social. In M. R. Pagaza (Ed.), *La profesionalización en trabajo social: Rupturas y continuidades, de la reconceptualización a la construcción de proyectos ético-políticos* (pp. 9–15). Buenos Aires: Espacio Editorial.

Alayón, N. (Ed.). (2005). *Trabajo social Latinoamericano: A 40 años de la reconceptualización*. Buenos Aires: Espacio Editorial.

Alcantara, M. (2005). Politics and society in Latin America at the start of the new millennium. *Social Forces, 83*(4), 1659–1670. Retrieved on July 28, 2009, from www.jstor.org/stable/3598409.

Barragán, M. J. (2001). The coasts of Latin America at the end of the century. *Journal of Coastal Research, 17*(4), 885–899.

Basta, R. (2008). Precariedad laboral y trabajo social: Algunas reflexiones. *Boletín Electrónico Surá, #144,* July, Escuela de Trabajo Social, Universidad de Costa Rica. Retrieved on June 30, 2009, http://www.ts.ucr.ac.cr/binarios/sura/sura-0144.pdf.

Brea, A. (2003). Population dynamics in Latin America. *Population Bulletin, 58*(1), 1–37.

Cademartori, F., Campos, J., & Seiffer, T. (2007). *Condiciones de trabajo de los trabajadores sociales: Hacia un proyecto profesional crítico*. Buenos Aires: Espacio Editorial.

Capello, M., & Mambloma, M. (2007). La travesía de la profesión: los desafíos de construir un proyecto ético-político que se articule con los proyectos de la clase trabajadora. In M. Rozas Pagaza (Ed.) *La Profesionalización en Trabajo Social: Rupturas y continuidades, de la reconceptualización a la construcción de proyectos ético-políticos* (pp. 195–204). Buenos Aires: Espacio Editorial.

Castronovo, R. (2008). La identidad profesional: Esa construcción ilusoria. In R. Castronovo & S. Cavalleri (Eds.), *Compartiendo notas: El trabajo social en la contemporaneidad* (pp. 17–35). Buenos Aires: Universidad Nacional de Lanús.

Council on Social Work Education (CSWE). (2008). Educational policy and accreditation standards (EPAS). Alexandria, VA: Author.

Curiel, A. (1991). Cultura de ajuste. In F. Calderon & M. R. Dos Santos (Eds.), *Hacia un nuevo orden estatal en América Latina: Veinte tesis sociopolíticas y un corolario* (115–116). Chile: Fondo de Cultura Económica, SA.

de Paula Faleiros, V. (2005). Reconceptualizacion del trabajo social en Brasil: Una cuestión en movimiento? In N. Alayón (Ed.), *Trabajo social Latinoamericano: A 40 años de la reconceptualización* (pp. 57–70). Buenos Aires: Espacio Editorial.

Dubini, G. B. (2008). Trabajo social y autonomía cultural comunitaria: La experiencia del método-projecto orígenes e influencias en nuestra América Latina. Buenos Aires: Espacio Editorial.

Dunkerley, J. (2007). Evo Morales, the "two Bolivias" and the third Bolivian revolution: Commentary. *Journal of Latin American Studies, 39,* 133–166.

Enochs, E. S. (1955). The children of Latin America in an age of anxiety. *Journal of Educational Sociology, 28*(7), 299–307. Retrieved on July 7, 2009, from www.jstor.org/stable/2263749.

Estrada Ospina, V. M. (2008). Implicaciones ético-politicas y ético-tecnicas de la formación academica en una sociedad globalizada. *Boletín Electrónico Sura, #147,* October. Retrieved on June 29, 2009, from http://www.ts.ucr.ac.cr/binarios/sura/sura-0147.pdf.

Freire, P. (1970). *Pedagogy of the oppressed*. New York: Seabury Press.

Grassi, E. (2003). *Politicas y problemas sociales en la sociedad neoliberal: La otra década infame (I)*. Buenos Aires: Espacio Editorial.

Healy, L. M. (2008). *International social work: Professional action in an interdependent world* (2nd ed.). New York: Oxford University Press.

Hill, N. (2006, January 26). Hill, N. (2006) Backstory: Lives recycled in Argentina. *Christian Science Monitor.* Retrieved on July 3, 2009, from www.csmonitor.com/2006/0125/p20s01-woam.html.

Koehs, J. (2005). Cuando la ciudadanía apremia: La Ley "Cartonera" y la emergencia del cartonero como actor público. In G. Delamata (Ed.), *Ciudadanía y territorio: Las relaciones políticas de las nuevas identidades sociales* (pp. 157–186). Buenos Aires: Espacio Editorial.

Laszlo, E. (2001). *Macroshift: Navigating the transformation to a sustainable world.* Berrett-San Francisco: Koehler.

Maguiña, A. (1977). Trabajo social: Servicio o actividad productiva? *Acción Crítica, 3,* 17–26.

Martinelli, M. L. (2008). Reflexiones sobre el trabajo social y el proyecto ético-político profesional. *Escenarios. Prácticas Profesionales y Prácticas Sociales Contemporáneas, 13* (Julio).

Melano, M. C. (2007). Desprenderce para devenir: Travesis y destinos del trabajo social Argentino. In M. R. Pagaza (Ed.), *La profesionalización en trabajo social. rupturas y continuidades, de la reconceptualización a la construcción de proyectos ético-políticos* (pp. 33–39). Buenos Aires: Espacio Editorial.

Mello, W. (2007). Education, work and globalization in Brazil. In J. Harris (Ed.), *Alternative gloabalizations, conference documents of the Global Studies Association* (pp. 90–107). Chicago: Changemaker.

Molina, M. L. (2007). Rupturas y continuidades en la formación profesional de la reconceptualización desde una perspectiva crítica, ética y políticamente comprometida con la defensa de los derechos humanos y la construcción de la ciudadanía. In M. R. Pagaza (Ed.), *La profesionalización en trabajo social. rupturas y continuidades, de la reconceptualización a la construcción de*

proyectos ético-políticos (pp. 283–293). Buenos Aires: Espacio Editorial.

Moljo, C. (2005). Trabajadores sociales en la historia: La militancia de los 60 y 70 en Argentina. *Escenarios, 9*(Mayo), 34–44.

Núñez, R. A. (2008). *Redes comunitarias: Afluencias teóricas metodológicas y crónicas de intervención profesional.* Buenos Aires: Espacio Editorial.

Parra, G. (2007). Aproximaciones al desarrollo del movimiento de reconceptualizacion en América Latina: Aportes a la comprensión de la contemporaneidad del trabajo social. *Boletín Electrónico Sura, #127,* February. Downloaded on June 29, 2009, from http://www.ts.ucr.ac.cr/binarios/sura/sura-0127.pdf.

Pereyra, B. (2008). Social work in Latin America: A historical view and the impact of reconceptualization in how the intervention is seen today. Working paper series 2008:4. Retrieved on June 28, 2009, from Social Science Research Network.

Queiro-Tajalli, I. (2008). South America. In T. Mizrahi & L. Davis (Eds.), *Encyclopedia of social work* (20th ed., pp. 522–528). New York: Oxford University Press and the National Association of Social Workers.

Roig, A. A. (2002). *Ética del poder y moralidad de la protesta: Respuestas a la crisis moral de nuestro tiempo.* Mendoza, Argentina: Editorial de la Universidad Nacional de Cuyo.

Saracostti, M. (2007). Social capital as a strategy to overcome poverty in Latin America: An overview. *International Social Work, 50,* 515. http://isw.sagepub.com/cgi/content/abstract/50/4/515.

Sherraden, M. (2009, April). Social work, global poverty, and development. Wrap-up speech at the United Nations Social Work Day, New York.

Zabala Cubillos, M. T. (2002). *Buscando un pensamiento colectivo social en Latinoamérica.* Buenos Aires: Espacio Editorial.

61

Social Work in North America

JULIA WATKINS (UNITED STATES), THERESE JENNISSEN AND
COLLEEN LUNDY (CANADA)

SOCIAL WORK IN NORTH AMERICA: AN INTRODUCTION

In both Canada and the United States, social work emerged at the turn of the twentieth century as a response to the serious health and social problems that accompanied industrial expansion and the rise in immigration. In these early years, there were close connections between the social workers of both countries; they read the same journals, belonged to the same association, attended the same conferences, and crossed the border for education and employment. Although the United States and Canada shared a common heritage of British colonialism, the trajectory of the internal development of the two countries varied significantly. Nonetheless, the larger population base of the United States and its more intense industrial development led to an earlier and more organized role for social workers in the United States, one that strongly influenced their Canadian counterparts.

The heritage of both countries was shaped by the British traditions of the Charity Organization Societies (COS) and the settlement house movement. The COS focused on streamlining charity, providing it to those deemed truly in need and unable to work. The settlement house movement, on the other hand, adopted a philosophy that emphasized the impoverished as neighbors in need and provided services while advancing social reform and social equality. Both of these traditions had a significant impact on the social work profession in Canada and the United States.

The close relationship between Canadian and American social workers has endured through the centuries; however, there were differences in their development that were rooted in indigenous social issues. Canada has a strong French tradition, its relationship with its Aboriginal populations has developed in a particular way, and the existence of large rural and northern populations has presented unique issues for social workers.

The number of social workers and schools of social work is considerably larger in the United States compared with Canada. The National Association of Social Workers (NASW) has a membership of 150,000, while the Canadian Association of Social Workers (CASW) has 17,000 members. Similarly, while the Council on Social Work Education (CSWE) accredits 660 programs, the Canadian Association for Social Work Education (CASWE) accredits approximately 62 university programs. Social work education and practice respond to the unique cultural differences in each country. For example, both the CASW and the CASWE are fully bilingual.

Differences aside, social workers in Canada and the United States are facing similar challenges, namely sustaining a social welfare state and advancing equality in the context of neoliberalism.

SOCIAL WORK IN THE UNITED STATES

Introduction

Social work is recognized as a profession in the United States and is strongly embedded in the larger sociopolitical and demographic characteristics of the nation. Its beginnings focused prominently on achieving social justice for all who sought the opportunities and protections of this new venture on the North American continent, including the immigrant communities and those whose aspirations were clearly defined as integral parts of a society in which opportunity prevailed under conditions of hard work, freedom of expression, faith, and access to the larger benefits accruing to the general society (Austin, 1997; Stuart, 2008). This American dream, however, was not to be realized for many given the historical, political, and economic turbulence of a new nation exploitive of its human capital and driven by the expansionist tendencies of the free market economy. Based in European antecedents, social work emerged in this unique context as a way of fulfilling the dream through social and political action, securing the rights of disenfranchised and economically disadvantaged populations, arguing for racial and gender equality, and seeking social justice as full participation in society, demanded as a constitutional right.

Emergence of the Profession

The social activism that permeated the beginnings of social work in the United States originated in the work of the settlement house and COS movements (Austin, 1997; Edwards, Shera, Nelson Reid, & York, 2006; Stuart, 2008). It was community-based work done from a sense of charity and philanthropy. It was later influenced by the psychodynamic intellectual traditions of Europe in the nineteenth century, and it ushered in an orientation and increased preoccupation with the clinical aspects of professional social work practice. This practice was centered primarily in the private sector and was viewed as an expansion of the scientific philanthropy that was emerging, drawing heavily on the underpinnings of social science disciplines, particularly sociology and psychology. This latter development had a profound influence that can be seen in the fact that the majority of the mental health services in the United States today are provided by social workers (Proctor, 2004).

Historically, there have been inherent tensions between a social work practice defined as social action (macro practice) with more public, community-oriented services and a practice directed with greater enthusiasm at individual, family, and small-group change (micro practice). Those tensions were particularly evident in what would emerge in the twentieth century as the backbone of social work education in the United States. The tensions are exacerbated or weakened depending on the predominant themes in social policy initiatives at any given time in the United States, such as the growing need for public social work services prompted by enactment of the Social Security Act (Kendall, 2002; Stuart, 2008).

Nonetheless, the roles and responsibilities of social workers in the United States have grown over time and include public and private settings; micro and macro practice interventions; culturally, ethnically, and racially diverse populations; and services directed at age- and sector-specific and demographically varied populations. The clearer trend in social work practice has been the continued privatization of services not only for those of more-than-modest financial means but also for those of low-income and poverty financial status (Shera, 2008). The US Department of Labor projects that social work will be one of the fastest growing professions in the United States in the coming decade (Bureau of Labor Statistics, 2007). With the recognition of professional practice at the entry level (baccalaureate) and advanced level (master's), the requirements for employment of social workers in the various sectors of practice have become more closely identified with the education level of the practitioner. Baccalaureate or entry-level practice is generalist by definition and reflects core practice behaviors that also form the base expectations for advanced or specialized practice at the master's-degree level (CSWE, 2008a).

National Association of Social Workers (NASW)

The primary practice organization for social work in the United States is the National Association of Social Workers (NASW). It was created in 1955 from a unification of seven organizations that served various dimensions of social work practice. The mission of NASW is "protecting and advancing the profession of social work and advocating for social justice issues" (Clark, 2008, p. 292). The organization's membership initially numbered approximately 22,000 and is now at 150,000 members, making it the largest association of social workers in the world (Clark, 2008). Chapters are found in each of the fifty states, the District of Columbia, New York City, Guam, Puerto Rico, and the Virgin Islands. The organization has a broad portfolio of initiatives, from certification to public advocacy, publications, continuing education, and promotion of licensure and title protection for social workers (NASW, 2009).

As part of its professional stature and structural recognition in the United States, the profession has a code of ethics that was adopted in 1960 by the NASW Delegate Assembly. This code, which has repeatedly been revised and reaffirmed, sets the ethical practice standards for social work practice in the United States (NASW, 1999).

Social Work Education

Social work education emerged from two major emphases in the early part of the twentieth century (Kendall, 2002). The American Association of Schools of Social Work (AASSW) represented schools that were sponsored primarily "by private social agencies and located in or near urban areas" (p. 4), and the association voted in 1937 to limit its membership to graduate schools only. On the opposite side of the drawing board was the National Association of Schools of Social Administration (NASSA), which represented social work programs in state-supported universities. This organization saw a mandate in the expansion of social programs under the Social Security Act to increase educational access, and therefore it promoted the baccalaureate level of social work education. Professional social work education takes place in colleges and universities across the country that are accredited by one of the six regional accrediting agencies; they represent all of US higher education—public and private, faith based, urban and rural, historically black colleges and universities, Hispanic-serving institutions, and research institutions.

Council on Social Work Education (CSWE)

The arguments about the academic qualification required for professional social work practice culminated in the establishment of the Council on Social Work Education (CSWE) in 1952. This organization grew out of the tensions between the previous two organizations, NASSA and AASSW, particularly from the use of accreditation by NASSA. In her book *Council on Social Work Education: Its Antecedents and First Twenty Years*, Kendall (2002) elaborates on the arguments, politics, and development of the profession. The CSWE mission is to "ensure and enhance the quality of social work education," and it is pursued "through setting and maintaining policy and program standards, accrediting bachelor's and master's degree programs in social work, promoting research and faculty development, and advocating for social work education" (CSWE, 2009a). For this brief report, however, it is more important to provide an understanding of the current educational context in the United States and the quality-assurance function of accreditation.

There are approximately 660 programs accredited by CSWE, the sole accrediting authority of baccalaureate and master's social work programs in the United States, with recognition granted by the Council for Higher Education Accreditation. These programs consist of 198 graduate and 468 undergraduate programs in 523 institutions of higher education. In total, they represent some 50,000 full-time students and 8,000 faculty (CSWE, 2008b).

Accreditation in the United States is carried out under the auspices of a CSWE-based staff and the Commission on Accreditation—twenty-five volunteers who review programs according to published Educational Policy and Accreditation Standards (EPAS) (CSWE, 2008a) promulgated by CSWE. These standards are reviewed and revised every seven years, and within the past fifteen years they moved social work education from a content-based model to an objectives-based model and now to a competency-based model of education for practice and assessment. The conceptualization of an explicit curriculum (the courses that deliver the competency-based education) and an implicit curriculum (the context of the program) embodies a shift not only in how social work education is presented and taught but also in how compliance with accreditation standards is determined for programs at both the baccalaureate and the master's levels (CSWE, 2008a).

Additionally, CSWE (2009b) provides a service for certification and recognition of social work degrees earned in foreign countries. A memorandum of understanding between CSWE and its Canadian counterpart, the Canadian Association for Social Work Education, signed in 2007, recognizes the substantial comparability of degrees granted in these two countries.

As with all accreditation in the United States that is voluntary and accomplished by nongovernmental entities, there has been increasing emphasis on demonstrating outcomes of the educational process based on the mission and goals of the educational institution or the professional program. With the 2008 EPAS, social work education is at the forefront of this movement for accountability and determining practice behaviors that are fundamental to social work practice at the entry and advanced levels.

Social Work Licensure

Social work is regulated by licensure in all fifty states. The requirements and levels of licensure are not uniform from one state to another, and there exists a complicated and sometimes contradictory picture of regulatory practices and an even more complicated interface with social work education. The various state regulatory boards are represented by the Association of Social Work Boards (ASWB), which provides licensing examination and policy guidance to the state boards. All state licensing laws require that, to be eligible to sit for the relevant licensing examination, an applicant must be a graduate of an accredited social work program. Other requirements may be specified, such as the need for postgraduate work experience, supervised practice, and, in some cases, specific coursework (ASWB, 2008). The two associations, ASWB and CSWE, maintain a healthy dialogue regarding the interface of education and regulation.

Challenges

The profession faces challenges that will require attention by the whole of social work to achieve the success required of a robust and intellectually capable workforce. In the current global economic downturn, not only are social work services in greater demand, but they also are often decreased in attempts to reduce expenditures in both the private and public sectors and in education—the pipeline of future leadership of the profession. The larger agenda for social work includes dealing with the encroachment of other professions and quasi professions into the social work domain and requires continually claiming what is social work along with recruiting and retaining social work students and professionals. Simultaneously, social work must increase its cross-disciplinary work to solve the complex, vexing, and interrelated issues of our time—global poverty, ideological extremism, shifting economies, global climate change, and global conflict.

In moving forward to address challenges, the fragmentation of the profession itself poses a major obstacle that, in spite of a recent attempt, has not been successfully addressed in the United States. This failure means continuing the pattern of inefficient use of time and financial resources and, most important, wastefulness of human resources who are prepared to make a difference. Social work in the United States must seek new resources and new ways to maintain its professional status and recognition in order to carry out its mission and engage in healthy sustainability that includes self-critique and continuous assessment of purpose in the globally complex and interrelated world.

REFERENCES

Association of Social Work Boards (ASWB). (2008). *Association of Social Work Boards.* Retrieved October 22, 2009, from www.aswb.org.

Austin, D. M. (1997). The institutional development of social work education: The first 100 years—and beyond. *Journal of Social Work Education, 33,* 599–612.

Bureau of Labor Statistics, U.S. Department of Labor. (2007). Social workers. In *Occupational outlook handbook* (2008–09 ed.). Retrieved October 22, 2009, from www.bls.gov/oco/ocos060.htm.

Clark, E. J. (2008). National Association of Social Workers. In T. Mizrahi & L. E. Davis (Eds.), *Encyclopedia of social work* (20th ed., pp. 292–295). Washington, DC: NASW Press.

Council on Social Work Education (CSWE). (2009a) Mission. Retrieved October 22, 2009, from http://www.cswe.org/About.aspx.

Council on Social Work Education (CSWE). (2008a). Educational policy and accreditation standards. Retrieved October 26, 2009, from http://www.cswe.org/File.aspx?id=13780.

Council on Social Work Education (CSWE). (2008b). *2007 Annual survey of social work programs* [Research brief]. Alexandria, VA: Author.

Edwards, R. L., Shera, W., Nelson Reid, P., & York, R. (2006). Social work practice and education in the U.S. and Canada. *Social Work Education, 25,* 28–38.

Kendall, K. A. (2002). *Council on Social Work Education: Its antecedents and first twenty years.* Alexandria, VA: Council on Social Work Education.

National Association of Social Workers (NASW). (2009). NASW chapters. Retrieved October 22, 2009, from www.socialworkers.org/chapters/default.asp.

National Association of Social Workers (NASW). (1999). *Code of ethics.* Washington, DC: Author.

Proctor, E. K. (2004). Research to inform mental health practice: Social work's contributions. *Social Work Research, 28,* 195–197.

Shera, W. (2008). International social work and social welfare: North America. In T. Mizrahi & L. E. Davis (Eds.), *Encyclopedia of social work* (20th ed., pp. 518–522). Washington, DC: NASW Press.

Stuart, P. (2008). Social work profession: History. In T. Mizrahi & L. E. Davis (Eds.), *Encyclopedia of social work* (20th ed., pp. 156–164). Washington, DC: NASW Press.

SOCIAL WORK IN CANADA

Introduction

Social work as a profession was established in English Canada in the early years of the twentieth century. With roots in the traditions of both the United Kingdom and the United States, the profession evolved from Christian charity work to a secular movement addressing the social dislocations that resulted from the early stages of industrial capitalism in Canada. The history of social work in French Canada, namely the province of Quebec, has its early roots in France, where social work was operated largely by the Roman Catholic Church.

Currently there are almost 40,000 social workers in Canada, with approximately 17,000 who are members of the Canadian Association of Social Workers (CASW). The organization has acquired visibility and recognition as a professional body and has the ongoing challenge of being a bilingual association responding to the needs of a small, diverse membership within a large geographic area.

The major goal of social work in Canada is to equitably facilitate and advocate for the physical, mental, and emotional well-being of all people. Canadian social work strives toward advancing social justice and human rights through an engagement of activities that improve and enhance the well-being of individuals, families, and communities locally, nationally, and internationally. The specific roles of social workers vary among diverse fields of service, but generally their functions can be separated into direct intervention, including community development, and working in social policy and administration. Each of these broad categories of social work can be subdivided into more specific functions depending on the agency or organization within which social workers are employed. For example, social workers can work in family service agencies, children's aid societies, women's shelters, shelters for the homeless, correctional institutions, welfare administration offices, schools, hospitals, government departments (including municipal, provincial, and federal or territorial), unions, nongovernmental organizations, and in private practice.

Brief History

Social work in English Canada is a unique amalgam of the British and American traditions of charity combined with the indigenous experiences of Canada as it entered the phase of industrial capitalism in the mid- to late nineteenth century. Social workers have always been committed to the dual roles of alleviating suffering of the individual, family, and community and promoting broader social, economic, and political change through social action. However, social workers' commitment to social justice has fluctuated over the years, with social activism often playing a secondary role to a more individualist approach.

In the early years of industrial capitalism in Canada, assistance to the so-called deserving poor was provided through churches, benevolent societies, and private charities. As poverty continued to grow, the charities began to coordinate their services, following the lead of the charity organization societies in the United Kingdom and United States. Around the same time (early 1880s), the settlement

house movement took hold in the larger Canadian centers and initially was affiliated with universities. In Quebec, assistance for the poor was provided mainly through religious communities (Catholic, Protestant, and Jewish); the Catholic Church remained dominant in the social life of Quebec until the Quiet Revolution of the 1960s.

At the turn of the twentieth century, a move toward public support of the impoverished began in English Canada, and untrained charity workers were replaced with social workers trained in the United States and United Kingdom. The casework approach, popularized through the work of Mary Richmond, became standard in Canada. In 1914, the first school of social work was instituted at the University of Toronto, followed shortly by a school at McGill University in 1918, and since then schools have developed across the country. In these early years, social work education in Canada emulated that of the United Kingdom and United States.

Following World War I, the demand for social workers in Canada grew dramatically, and after a few years of debating the need for an indigenous organization, the Canadian Association of Social Workers (CASW) was formed in 1926 with 127 charter members from across the country. The role of the CASW involved monitoring employment conditions, establishing standards of practice, and advancing social work as a profession. Initially the CASW was structured as a national organization comprising local branches. Branches continued to be formed across Canada, including both English- and French-speaking branches in Quebec. This decentralized approach worked for several years, but eventually the CASW became a federation of ten provincial and one territorial social work associations. Individual members that join the provincial and territorial associations of social work automatically become members of the CASW. In 1928, the annual Canadian Conference on Social Work was held, and in 1932 the CASW journal, *The Social Worker*, made its first appearance.

During the Great Depression, social workers faced unprecedented levels of poverty for which the profession was poorly prepared. It was during this era that social workers began to take more critical approaches to understanding the nature of unemployment and poverty. Several social workers were influenced by organizations such as the League for Social Reconstruction (LSR) and the Co-operative Commonwealth Federation (CCF), which developed critiques of capitalism. A more radical Marxist tradition was also present in the social work community in Canada, although this tradition is not well documented. Part of the reason for this is that the social democratic traditions of the LSR and CCF were led primarily by men who were not social workers but who worked in social and economic policy, so they left behind written records of their work. The more radical Marxist tradition involved many frontline female social workers (e.g., Mary Jennison, Dora Wilensky, Bessie Touzel, and Margaret Gould) who were effective and well known in their local communities but who were not directly involved in social policy development and therefore left no written legacies. They were members of the US Rank and File Movement and supported the radical social work journal, *Social Work Today*. The archival records are replete with their social activist work.

During and after World War II, social work, and particularly the CASW, became heavily invested in the mechanisms of the welfare state. Several social workers assisted with the development of new social policies and construction of a public social infrastructure for Canada. Several social workers were employed in both federal and provincial government departments. Working within the machinery of the state had a somewhat conservatizing effect on social work, and for several years the professional association was devoted primarily to developing social work into a mainstream profession. This trend, in conjunction with the witch hunts of the Cold War, removed some of the radicalism from the social work of the 1930s.

As schools of social work continued to expand in Canada, the need for establishing common educational standards became clear. Initially Canadian schools of social work were accredited by the US Council on Social Work Education (CSWE), but in 1970 the Canadian Association of Schools of Social Work (now the Canadian Association for Social Work Education) took over this function.

Major Professional Organizations

There are three major social work organizations in Canada. They deal with strengthening and advancing professional practice, improving social work education, and regulating the profession, respectively.

The Canadian Association of Social Workers (CASW)

This organization represents professional social workers in Canada. The primary focus of CASW is to advance and strengthen the profession by providing leadership on national social policy issues and addressing issues of social work practice. Among its many tasks, the CASW maintains an updated code of ethics for its members; develops national policy papers; prepares research papers, reports, and books; provides information to its affiliates across the country; and produces the *Canadian Social Work Journal* and the *CASW Bulletin* in both French and English. The association (here we are referring to the CASW, so we think Association should be in upper case) also participates in national coalitions and international initiatives.

The CASW Board of Directors is composed of one member from each of the provinces and a territorial representative. Presidents of the national association and provinces and territories meet annually, and a biennial conference provides an opportunity for membership input. For several years social workers from Quebec were affiliated with CASW, but in 2005 they withdrew from the association and become independent.

The Canadian Association of Social Work Education (CASWE)

This national bilingual association promotes social work education and develops educational policies and academic standards for baccalaureate and master's programs in Canada. The major functions of CASWE are overseeing accreditation, organizing a yearly conference, and publishing a bilingual journal, the *Canadian Social Work Review*. It is the sole accrediting body for baccalaureate and master's programs in Canada and currently accredits sixty-two social work programs. Additionally, in Quebec, the CASWE funds the Regroupement des Unités de Formation Universitaires en Travail Social du Québec (RUFUTS) to support the francophone population in social work.

The Character of Social Work Education

In most provincial jurisdictions, the bachelor of social work (BSW) is the first level of entry into the profession. It is a four-year degree program that prepares students in generalist practice. Typically, a person with a BSW requires another year of postgraduate work to obtain a master of social work (MSW). Those who have an undergraduate degree in another discipline usually require two years of postgraduate study to obtain an MSW. With the completion of the BSW, students are expected to have the education and skills necessary for assessment;

work with individuals, families, and communities at all levels; research; policy; and advocacy. At the master's and doctoral levels, more emphasis is placed on advanced practice, theory, policy, and research.

Two unique aspects of Canadian social work education is a focus on the history, culture and current realities of both the francophone and Aboriginal communities.

Many social work schools in Canada operate from a structural perspective. This perspective emphasizes the importance of locating individual, family, and community issues within economic, social, and political contexts. Structural social work recognizes that the community in which a person resides, and of which social work is a constituent part, comprises diverse groups of people who have differential access to political and economic power. This perspective of social work is committed to social justice, human rights, and the equality and dignity of all people.

Provincial Regulatory Bodies

Since the early years of the profession, social workers have debated the roles of government registration and licensing of the profession. Regulation is a matter of provincial jurisdiction, and currently in Canada, all of the provinces have governing legislation. The Northwest Territories, Nunavut, and the Yukon Territory are in the process of developing one regulatory body for the North. The stated objective of regulatory bodies is the protection of the public and the promotion of excellence in social work; these bodies ensure that practitioners have the required skills and knowledge and follow the ethical guidelines of the profession.

In Ontario, for example, the Ontario College of Social Workers and Social Service Workers (OCSWSSW), under the authority of the 1998 Social Work and Social Service Work Act, stipulates that any person in Ontario who wishes to use the title *social worker* or *social service worker* must be registered with the OCSWSSW. While this process is still contested in the social work community, the College argues that "regulation brings credibility to the profession. Practitioners of a regulated profession are subject to a code of ethics and standards of practice" However, according to this legislation, an applicant with no social work education can become a registered social worker based on her/his professional experience. (www.ocswssw.org/en/about.htm).

Since professional regulation is a matter of provincial concern, there are a variety of definitions of the social work title and standards of practice across the country, creating a patchwork of regulatory frameworks for social workers.

The roles of all the professional organizations are interdependent. It has been acknowledged in the social work community that greater communication and collaborative efforts among the organizations, both at the provincial and national levels, must occur.

Current Challenges Facing Social Work

Social workers around the world face many serious challenges, including problems stemming from the current global economic crisis, environmental degradation, international conflict, and increased militarism. At a more local level in Canada, these challenges also include a declining welfare state.

The retreat of the welfare state has been taking place since the mid-1970s. It has meant that national standards have been weakened or eliminated; responsibilities for some areas of social welfare have been downloaded from the federal governments back to the provinces and municipalities, which typically have fewer resources. In recent decades there has been an increased reliance on the charitable sector compared with the post-WWII period, when the state began to play a more active role in the welfare of Canadians. These conservative trends not only reduce employment opportunities for social workers, but they also change the nature of social work employment whereby social workers play a more active role in monitoring and regulating their clients' lives and have increasingly fewer opportunities to empower their clients or become involved more directly in social action.

Given these changing economic and social conditions in Canada, the need for a strong and united national social work voice and an international presence is more urgent than ever. Unfortunately the social work profession in Canada is facing an urgent crisis from which it might not easily recover. Recently, the Boards of Directors of the Ontario and Alberta provincial associations decided to withdraw from the Canadian Association of Social Workers (CASW), without consultation of provincial members. Similar to many associations, the CASW's history has been one of struggle and compromise among member organizations. Giving up this struggle reflects a conservative trend that will serve to undermine social work autonomy, professional identity and survival as a profession.

Without a formal structure that provides a national voice and social work visibility, the strength of the profession is seriously compromised. To be manipulated by conservative forces is to abandon a longstanding tradition of struggle, compromise and, in the final analysis, solidarity with each other as social workers and solidarity with the people whose interests we promote both in Canada and internationally. In spite of these challenges, there continues to be a radical trend in social work, but regrettably it is not dominant. The profession has made important strides in advocating for Aboriginal populations; gay, lesbian, bisexual, and transgender communities; and racial minority populations, among several other important issues. However, a sharp critique of class politics has receded and, for the most part, has been replaced with a more subjective and nebulous anti-oppressive focus.

The current chilly climate for social welfare presents serious challenges for the profession, but it also provides tremendous opportunities for the profession to take a strong leadership role in the future direction of social welfare and social work. This is an important time for social work to evaluate its relationship (past, present, and future) with governments, to assess its role in society, and to make concerted efforts to assert itself with a strong social justice agenda that understands the centrality of class dynamics and how they relate to racism, sexism, and other forms of discrimination. It is a time when solidarity among social workers is most urgently needed.

FURTHER READING

Burke, S. (1996). *Seeking the highest good: Social services and gender at the University of Toronto, 1883–1937.* Toronto: University of Toronto Press.

Canadian Association of Schools of Social Work (CASWE). (2001). *In critical demand: Social work in Canada, final report.* Ottawa: CASSW.

Canadian Association of Social Work Education (CASWE). www.caswe-acfts.ca.

Canadian Association of Social Workers (CASSW). www.casw-acts.ca.

Cassidy, H. (1932). *Unemployment and relief in Ontario, 1929–1932.* Toronto: Dent.

Hill, K. (1984). *Oral history of social work in Canada.* Ottawa: CASW.

Irving, A., Parsons, H., & Bellamy, D. (1995). *Neighbours: Three social settlements in downtown Toronto.* Toronto: Canadian Scholars' Press.

Jennissen, T., & Lundy, C. (2011). *One hundred years of social work in English Canada: 1900–2000.* Waterloo: Wilfrid Laurier University Press.

Jennissen, T., & Lundy, C. (2005). Social work profession (Canada). In J. M. Herrick & P. H. Stuart (Eds.), *Encyclopedia of social welfare history in North America* (pp. 381–384). Thousand Oaks, CA: Sage.

Lundy, C. (2004). *Social work and social justice: A structural approach to practice.* Peterborough: Broadview Press.

Shewell, H. (2004). *"Enough to keep them alive": Indian welfare in Canada, 1873–1965.* Toronto: University of Toronto.

Wills, G. (1995). *A marriage of convenience: Business and social work in Toronto, 1918–1957.* Toronto: University of Toronto Press.

SECTION IX

Poverty and Development

International Social Development Projects

LORNE JAQUES AND W. DUFFIE VANBALKOM

Funding agencies commonly employ projects to fund, guide, implement, and monitor development initiatives. Projects are well-defined mechanisms for initiating change and addressing problems through a grant or contract provided to agencies and communities. They typically run for a specific length of time and for a well-defined purpose. This commonly used structure has both advantages and limitations. It can test the efficacy of strategies and avoid long-term commitments. Projects are also easy to monitor and can demonstrate specific outcomes, but there are significant challenges when it comes to ensuring long-term impact. Despite their limitations, projects continue to be a major avenue for both local and international development.

This chapter introduces the ways in which social workers are likely to encounter development projects when they work with communities and partners in least developed countries (LDCs). Well-conceived and well-constructed projects can make a positive contribution to sustainable, dynamic, and transformative development—the implicit goal of all projects.

Building a bridge is a concrete example of a development project. It has a well-defined purpose and can be built over a specific period of time for a specific budget. It facilitates the transportation of people and goods across a natural barrier. It unites families and allows the products of producers on one side to reach consumers on the other while reducing costs or risks of various types. It may be aesthetically attractive, and it represents thousands of person-hours of labor. The bridge has inherent qualities of its own, but it is foremost only a means to an end. All the research, expense, labor, risk, and resources are put together to build something that serves a greater purpose than simply being a symbol of human ingenuity. The bridge has the potential to significantly change the lives of people on either side of the barrier, and its long-term impact may have many indirect benefits for other populations

as well. The truly transformative nature of any project lies in the sustainable impact it has on the lives of people.

Conceptually, international social development projects share many things in common with building a bridge. They involve a variety of inputs, including the skills and talents of the community and frequently external specialists. They address the needs, interests, and problems encountered by local people, and they have specific targeted outcomes in mind from the beginning. Like the bridge, the transformative value lies not simply in the combination of resources invested, but rather in the results that they produce—the new capacities, the solutions, or the end of persistent threats to quality of life. International development projects are means to an end. They can facilitate the movement of people, institutions, and communities across the barriers of inequality, injustice, marginalization, and poverty.

Development should be distinguished from rescue and relief, which are humanitarian responses to short-term events and circumstances that threaten life and well-being. These efforts address the immediate impacts of disasters, be they natural, such as earthquakes or hurricanes, or complex, such as ethnic conflicts or war. Relief efforts secure the immediate safety and basic human needs of the victims. Immediate stabilization is also necessary for long-term change, but humanitarian relief is less about development than immediate survival.

Development in poor countries is also about survival—about extending life expectancies, reducing child and infant mortality, and changing systems that systematically oppress human rights. Social development projects often focus on rediscovering preexisting capacities and building new ones in order to strengthen a community's ability to transform the underlying conditions of oppression. There are as many creative ways to change the world as there are communities, and projects are one of the primary mechanisms by which resources and partners are mobilized.

SOCIAL WORK AND INTERNATIONAL DEVELOPMENT

Humanitarianism is fundamental to the professional values, principles, and concepts of social work, just as it is to the practice of international development. Simply defined, *humanitarianism* refers to an expression of kindness, sympathy, and compassion on behalf of others and specifically for those who suffer. In the world's LDCs, the average per capita annual income is less than $750, an amount that is much less than what people require to meet their minimal needs. In recognition of this global travesty, in 2000 the United Nations established its first Millennium Development Goal, which focused on ending extreme poverty and hunger.

Social workers bring significant value to individuals and communities in the Global South with a framework of practice that is further guided by standards, ethics, and professional discipline. Furthermore, social workers trained in clinical, leadership, and macro practice bring an array of technical skills to international social development projects that align with the needs and interests of the vast majority of the population in many of the world's countries. Social workers accept the moral obligation and have the professional skills to make significant contributions toward all of the Millennium Development Goals (UN, 2008)(see Appendix C), just as they do for the citizens that they serve in developed countries.

Social development projects should build the capacity of local communities to critically examine the root causes of the circumstances that have contributed to their impoverishment and disempowerment. Whether the project is focused on water, agriculture, or any of the other innumerable issues that inhibit development, nearly all development work must eventually address the root causes of poverty through communal engagement. The origins of poverty are always complex and demand deliberate, locally based analysis of their meaning and social construction. Many grassroots organizations, as well as large international nongovernmental organizations (NGOs) and development agencies, undertake a thorough and sophisticated assessment of the circumstances that systematically create barriers to change, limit access to human rights, and oppress freedom.

Implicit in the notion of sustainable, dynamic, or transformative development is the value of participation and legitimate social engagement. Project ineffectiveness and the perpetuation of systemic global injustice are the consequences of the failure to recognize the inherent flaws and contradictions in the relationship between the subjects of development and its objects. A genuine exposure of power imbalances begins and ends with the recognition that projects sponsored by wealthy developed countries and implemented by privileged and well-resourced agencies instantly reveal inequities, especially in places where just staying alive is a priority. Community participation leads to the establishment of functional partnerships that are based on the inherent knowledge and assets that were part of the community before the project was initiated. More importantly, through legitimate engagement, the project comes to be seen as a natural part of the community and not an artificial, time-limited, charity-dependent gift from the outside. These fundamental social work principles are essential to practice at both the individual and macro levels, whether the project is in an inner city in North America or an isolated community in Central Africa.

As a consequence of legitimate social critique, development partners discover that many systemic and persistent social problems can be traced to basic inequities and the related tensions, frustrations, and sense of helplessness. In his seminal work *Development as Freedom*, Amartya Sen (1999) sees the freedom of individuals, and in particular the expansion of people's capabilities, as the fundamental building blocks for societies to escape the "un-freedoms" that inhibit realization of the lives they value (p. 18). Social workers recognize that building capacities and contributing to the creation of new opportunities is the difference between self-fulfillment and stagnation in a state of poverty, economic or otherwise.

Some projects are specifically designed to address issues of injustice and deprivation, while in other projects these are collateral factors. For a project to have an enduring impact, it must seek long-term solutions through solidarity, advocacy, and the search for peaceful solutions that address not only the obvious manifestation of injustice or poverty but also its underlying causes.

Illustration 1

The Latin American Perinatal Health Project focused on reducing the high rates of maternal and infant mortality and morbidity in four of the poorest countries of the region. While the project focused largely on enhancing the skills of the health practitioners and improving health facilities, it became apparent very early that without legitimate engagement of the communities—the women, the men, and the traditional birth attendants in particular—little real change was going to occur. Combining the experience of social development professionals from Canada with local social workers and health promoters led to an extraordinary range of interventions that emphasized participation, tapped the creativity of the local community, and broadened the perspective of health professionals, whose traditional practice was severely challenged in the process. The result was a unique blend of soft technologies such as participatory community games, microprojects, and colorful manuals as well as locally adapted medical techniques and refined procedures. The final outcome was a significant reduction in the number of women and children who died needlessly in the perinatal period.

THE NATURE OF DEVELOPMENT PROJECTS

The achievement of enduring social change through a series of time-limited projects is an incredibly challenging undertaking—indeed, one that has had a disappointing cumulative effect, according to several prominent development writers, including William Easterly (2006), Paul Collier (2007), and Dambisa Moyo (2009). Attempts to redress protracted and structural causes of poverty within the confines of a five-year project, even one that follows participatory principles and addresses underlying causes, is extraordinarily difficult.

Despite the difficulties of sustaining the changes that are possible with a well-designed injection of inputs, projects remain a dominant fixture in development practice. Projects are appealing because the outputs and outcomes are more easily identified, measured, and attributable to the investment of cash, technical assistance, and methodology employed by the proponents. Public pressure has led politicians and senior bureaucrats in wealthy countries to look for measureable results from all investments of public revenues, with international development initiatives often targeted for scrutiny. The expectation is that costs can be controlled, poor outcomes can be reduced or eliminated, and risks can be managed more effectively by limiting investments to specific periods of time and demanding results that can be proven with clearly articulated and measureable indicators.

By virtue of their scale, projects are often sector specific as well. Although many development projects have an explicit focus on agriculture, health,

education, or another field, they also employ social development methodologies. Projects typically also have a relatively narrow geographic reach, and in order to achieve results within time and budget limitations, it is not always feasible to establish a scope that follows local and traditional definitions of *region*. Thus, although project-scale development appeals to the accountants in the ministries of finance in wealthy countries, it faces significant challenges in making an enduring impact on the complex threats to basic human needs.

At the behest of developing countries, alternative approaches have been promoted to overcome the limitations of project-oriented development (OECD, 2005). Government aid agencies such as USAID (US Agency for International Development), DFID (UK Department for International Development), and CIDA (Canadian International Development Agency) and the international financial institutions such as the World Bank have worked with recipient countries to coordinate donations to invest directly in government revenue accounts and implement sector-wide approaches in an effort to achieve greater long-term impact.

At the field level, the Millennium Villages project (Millennium Villages, 2011) which is funded by the government of Japan and private donations, has implemented a comprehensive model of multisectoral development. It is well endowed and espouses the principles of empowerment and local ownership, but it also retains many of the implicit weaknesses of project-oriented development. The long-term efficacy of the model remains to be seen, specifically in relation to the enduring capacity of the Millennium Villages to escape and remain free from extreme poverty beyond 2015.

Critical Skills for Development Work

Project-scale development requires social workers to draw upon both macro practice technical skills and project management abilities. Limited project funding in a highly competitive environment demands that practitioners become active with, and on behalf of, their communities to secure resources for badly needed programs and services. This is especially true in LDCs, where the needs are vast, urgent, and diverse. Social workers must apply their skills at consensus building and inclusive practice to ensure that the needs being addressed are the right ones and the methods employed are just and effective. They need the ability to write a compelling proposal as well as to effectively manage a project with full knowledge of the expectations implicit in a results-based environment. For a community to win a social development project, it must show that it will produce results by

- articulating a problem, need, and context with precision, justified with appropriate preproject study and stakeholder engagement;
- proposing a method that is innovative, true to the principles of local ownership, and reflective of proven and reasonable approaches;
- demonstrating the capacity to manage the resources and risks; and
- integrating the means by which progress toward the outcomes will be monitored and modifications to the programming made to adapt to the ever-evolving circumstances in complex environments.

These four components constitute what is sometimes referred to as the *project cycle*, from project conceptualization to proposal, implementation, monitoring, evaluation, and back to reconceptualization of the issues, problem, and context that led to the project in the first place.

In the context of project-oriented development, the Western social development practitioner ultimately needs the kind of skills that are a product of the same system that created the results orientation. As partners, we can offer our training and skills to produce proposals, management, and reporting that meet the expectations of politicians and bureaucrats in the Global North. At the same time, our values demand redress of systematic oppression as well as a critique of the broader social circumstances that prevent long-term solutions from emerging.

Sustainable and Transformative Development Projects

Notwithstanding the structural limitations of development projects that we have outlined, involvement in well-designed and well-implemented projects is one of the most common mechanisms for social workers to make a positive contribution to alleviating poverty and injustice. Challenges abound because the roots of international development practice can be found in the postcolonial era, when the focus was on changing countries that were considered backward.

The economic growth model favored by northern countries demanded access to inexpensive and readily available resources and inexpensive labor from former colonies. In the latter half of the twentieth century, this exploitation resulted in unbridled growth of the economies of the industrialized north. However, this expansion eventually exposed the massive risks associated with it both in terms of resource depletion and damage to the environment. In 1987, the Brundtland Commission filed its report (Brundtland & World Commission on Environment and Development, 1987) wherein a definition of *sustainable development* became "meeting the needs of the present without compromising the ability of future generations to meet their own needs" (p. 9). Thus, sustainable development continued to be based on an economic growth model, but one that was more conscious of the impact of growth on the environment and the balance between the full cost of development and its benefits.

A more generic use of the term *sustainable* has entered the development vocabulary recently, with reference to the sustainability of the results of international development initiatives. Also based on a neoliberal, market-oriented worldview, it monitors projects for sustainable results to assure donors that the consequences of their investment will endure. Holding onto the results achieved during the life of a project, as well as protecting them once a change process has been initiated and external support concluded, is a related interpretation of sustainability.

Building new capacities and expanding those that existed in the community before the project was initiated is a key strategy for ensuring greater sustainability. This is typically accomplished through training programs or policy reforms in institutions. As Taylor and Soal (2003) point out, "The purpose of development is to apply the resources (the product) through processes that transform relationships in society. The ultimate purpose of development interventions is always to ensure that the excluded, those at the margins, gain greater access to and control over the decisions and resources that directly affect their lives" (p. 1). Capacity building that is reflective and encourages all to be self-critical leads to development that is (constantly) transformative, and it transcends a mere sustainability focus. In planning for comprehensive and integrative development, projects simultaneously consider the macro (societal) level, the mezzo (institutional and organizational) level, and the micro (individual capacity building) level. Even if the scope of a project can only influence one of these directly, broad consideration and donor coordination increase the chances of success.

Key Elements of Successful Projects

Seven key elements (VanBalkom & Goddard, 2007) affect the ability of a project to be sustainable and transformative within the confines of finite time, money, and expertise. These all need to be considered in relation to the three levels where development commonly takes place.

1. *Local ownership:* The legitimate engagement of the community is fundamental practice during the planning, implementation, and evaluation of a social development project. In many contexts, the approach to planning is top–down, with excessive reliance on those in authority and on external experts. This reliance can undermine a participatory approach and legitimate ownership for both process and outcomes.

2. *Effective, transformative, and legitimate leadership:* Effective leaders create organizational cultures that support personal attributes that are transformative, such as lifelong learning, creativity, and innovation. We also need to be cautious not to indiscriminately and inadvertently replace local leadership.

3. *Critical mass of change agents:* Empirical evidence shows that new ideas, enthusiastically embraced in training sessions, are often discarded for the old ways when colleagues, the community, or supervisors show little enthusiasm caused by a lack of understanding or fear of the impact of change on their own lives. Effective implementation of new ideas and the environment in which they can be continually created and tested requires a broad base of support within for the transformation to take hold.

4. *Mature and stable institutions:* Transformational social work projects include creating, strengthening, and supporting the capacities of appropriate institutions that promote continuous progress. Development expresses itself in families, villages, and local organizations—wherever the most disenfranchised struggle to organize their lives. Collectively, they take responsibility for development, and all have a legitimate voice in the process. Whether stable structures are in place or are nurtured into existence with expanded capacity and effectiveness, they provide the legitimate partners for collaboration.

5. *Adequate and dependable resources:* Reasonable financial resources and access to sound technical expertise are necessary for successful transformative initiatives. Anticipating complexities in an environment where there are many competing demands for the attention of impoverished communities and systems stretches the imagination and skills of social development practitioners. Undertaking large and complex objectives with insufficient resources leads to disappointment and undermines relationships.

6. *Enabling political and policy context:* Adequate time is required to analyze the environment and identify key players and institutions. Furthermore, the establishment of a continuous process of stakeholder engagement is a fundamental success strategy, including transparency and accountability to the people one is meant to serve. This is particularly true of the policy makers on whose influence the implementation and continuation of reform processes depends.

7. *Secure and safe environment:* Change at any level is stressful, particularly when the intended outcomes of a development initiative are seen to undermine existing power relations. Social workers play a pivotal role in the anticipation and amelioration of tensions produced by changes to unjust practices. Actions to change the lives of the most vulnerable often impact the lives of the most privileged. Creation of safe spaces for people to connect in a common cause is essential for local ownership of participatory development processes. Without this basic requirement, development can be neither sustainable nor transformative.

Illustration 2

We were engaged in the former Yugoslavia to strengthen educational institutions in a postwar context that continued to suffer from interethnic animosities and conflicting values. The project succeeded in large part because it continuously evaluated and readjusted development approaches to ensure that the seven key factors were addressed. Local leadership and institutions were strengthened to lead the development of 10,000 professionals. Care was taken to address mutually supportive policies and approaches at the macro, mezzo, and micro levels, creating a safe and enabling environment for sustainable change.

CONCLUSIONS

Project-oriented development remains dominant in the funding that social workers encounter when working internationally. Articulating fundamental social work values into the frameworks that are oriented toward demonstrable and measureable results is one of our biggest challenges. This includes, for example, the task of achieving social justice in an individual community when many root causes of injustice originate and persist outside the reach of a relatively narrow project. Recognizing that the failure to achieve food security locally is tied to global forces may be discouraging, but the process of uncovering that reality is also empowering for the community and the social work professional. Targeted strategies that engage the community in legitimate examination of the barriers to long-term change and that address local and short-term needs at the same time must be accommodated in a sustainable social development project.

The original definition of *sustainability* ties projects to a growth-oriented strategy requiring that the environmental impacts are minimized, or at least balanced, such that they do not harm the capacity of nature to sustain both life and livelihoods. Though this environmental context remains fundamental, sustainable development implies something different to social workers concerned with social structures and relationships. Through strategies of legitimate engagement, participation, and social critique, we seek to establish the basics for long-term transformation on behalf of those communities to whom we are committed. Dealing with the immediate and easily perceptible effects of poverty, disenfranchisement, and victimization is still a goal for our projects, but unless the processes that perpetuate them are reformed, such projects cannot be considered sustainable.

REFERENCES

Brundtland, G. H., & World Commission on Environment, Development. (1987). *Our common future.* Oxford: Oxford University Press.

Collier, P. (2007). *The bottom billion.* New York: Oxford.

Easterly, W. (2006). *The white man's burden.* New York: Penguin.

Millennium Villages. (2011). About Millennium Villages. Retrieved from: www.millenniumvillages.org.

Moyo, D. (2009). *Dead aid: Why aid is not working and how there is another way for Africa.* New York: Allen Lane.

Organization for Economic Cooperation and Development (OECD). (2005). The Paris Declaration. Retrieved May 8, 2009, from www.oecd.org/document/18/0,3343,en_2649_3236398_35401554_1_1_1_1,00.html.

Sen, A. (1999). *Development as freedom.* New York: Anchor Books.

Taylor, J., & Soal, S. (2003). *Measurement in development practice: From the mundane to the transformational.* Cape Town: Community Development Resource Association (CDRA). Retrieved from www.cdra.org.za.

United Nations (UN). (2008). *Millennium Development Goals.* Retrieved May 8, 2009, from www.un.org/millenniumgoals/.

VanBalkom, W. D., & Goddard, T. (2007). Sustainable and dynamic development. In G. Anderson & A. Wenderoth (Eds.), *Facilitating change: Reflections on six years of education development programming in challenging environments* (pp. 253–267). Montreal: Universalia.

Measuring Social Well-Being

LYNNE M. HEALY

Development has been a major emphasis of the international intergovernmental organizations and many nongovernmental organizations (NGOs) for five decades. Naturally, there is interest in assessing the degree of progress made. To what extent have the many development approaches and projects been successful in improving human well-being? How can human well-being and a country's state of development most appropriately be measured? This chapter discusses the development of indicators, measures, and indices that have been used to chart development progress or, sometimes, the lack of progress or improvement in the human condition. The chapter concludes with a brief discussion of the challenges in collecting and verifying global data.

Evaluation of development projects has sometimes been neglected. There are many challenges in selecting indicators and accessing usable data. And, there may be reluctance to divert resources from services and programs to fund research and evaluation. Yet, the United Nations, the World Bank, and the Organization for Economic Cooperation and Development (OECD), among others, have explored and developed a succession of models for measurement. In 2000, the United Nations adopted a measures- and targets-based approach to development—the Millennium Development Goals. This approach will be detailed later in the chapter.

GROSS NATIONAL PRODUCT AS A SINGLE MEASURE

As discussed in Chapter 4, development was initially equated with economic development. It is not surprising that the initial measure selected to assess country progress toward development was gross national product (GNP) or gross domestic product (GDP) per capita. The attractiveness of a single measure and lingering belief in the idea that national economic progress leads to social progress and human well-being have kept GNP at the forefront of many

measurement efforts. Its limitations have long been recognized, however. In a new report on global measures, Hoegen (2009) includes a quote from Robert F. Kennedy, who said over forty years ago, "GNP measures everything except that which makes life worthwhile" (p. 9). Kennedy continued:

> The Gross National Product does not allow for the health of our children, the quality of their education, or the joy of their play. It does not include the beauty of our poetry or the strength of our marriages, the intelligence of our public debate or the integrity of our public officials. It measures neither our wit nor our courage, neither our wisdom nor our learning, neither our compassion nor our devotion to our country; it measures everything, in short, except that which makes life worthwhile. (p. 9)

THE MOVE TO MEASURES OF SOCIAL WELL-BEING

Although many recognized that economic growth did not always result in improved human well-being, it took considerable time for this realization to modify measures. Short life expectancies, high rates of infant mortality, poor sanitation, and other conditions often associated with life in less developed countries persisted in some countries with satisfactory improvements in GNP. Furthermore, use of GNP or GDP per capita was imperfect at best since extreme levels of inequality rendered such averages relatively useless as measures of social well-being. If GNP is useful, it is as an expression of resources potentially available to a country for addressing needs, not as a measure of success in doing so.

Estes (1984) reports on early efforts by the OECD to identify components of social well-being. Eight categories of social concerns were agreed upon in the 1970s by a working group: health, individual development through learning, employment and quality of working life, time and leisure, command over goods and services, physical environment, personal safety and administration of justice, and social opportunity and participation. The grouping included forward-thinking ideas about environment and social participation (now labeled *social inclusion*) but lacked the specificity that would make measurement feasible.

In the late 1970s, the Physical Quality of Life Index (PQLI) was put forward as an index by the Overseas Development Council (Estes, 1984). This simple index uses only three social indicators: life expectancy at birth, infant mortality, and adult literacy. Though the index is inadequate in many ways, it was helpful in demonstrating the limitations of using only GNP to measure development progress. As Estes (1984) said, even "a simplified approach to assessing world social progress over time can yield results that are both analytically interesting and politically useful in redirecting global development assistance resources to those nations with the most urgent social needs" (p. 13).

A Social Single Measure: Under-Five Mortality and UNICEF

The United Nations Children's Fund (UNICEF), an agency focused on child well-being, makes considerable use of a single indicator: under-five mortality rate (U5MR), a measure of the number of children who die between birth and exactly five years of age per 1000 live births. More than infant mortality (children who die before their first birthday per 1000 live births), U5MR captures essential elements of social development. The main causes of death among young children in poor countries are poor nutrition, lack of clean water, lack of basic sanitation, lack of access to basic health services (including immunizations), and the conditions arising from interaction of these factors. These are also the conditions of low levels of development. It can also be argued that U5MR cannot be hidden when only small sectors of the population are very well off. Thus, more than GNP or GNP per capita, it corrects for inequality.

The advantages of using U5MR are as follows (UNICEF, 2007): *(1)* "It measures the end result of the development process rather than an input" (p. 149); *(2)* as indicated previously, it results from many types of development efforts (or lack thereof), including malaria prevention, maternal knowledge, income, safe water, sanitation, immunization, and basic health services; and *(3)* it "is less susceptible to the fallacy of the average" (p. 149), thus giving a more accurate picture of the conditions of the majority than income measures do.

As of 2011, U5MR ranged from 209 in Chad to a best rate of 2 in Liechtenstein and San Marino. Iceland, Greece, Finland, Japan, Luxembourg, Norway, Slovenia, Singapore, and Sweden report a U5MR of 3 (UNICEF, 2011). Measured over time, U5MR suggests progress or lack of progress in development. While significant improvements have been made in many countries, others have regressed, sometimes dramatically. The impact of AIDS is sobering. Botswana had reduced its U5MR from 142 in 1970 to 58 in 1990. As of 2007, however, the rate had climbed back to 124 (UNICEF, 2007). The rate is improving again as Botswana works to decrease mother to child transmission of HIV. Rates in other southern and eastern African countries severely affected by AIDS show similar regression and suggest the power of U5MR as an indicator.

The Human Development Index

The Human Development Index (HDI) put forward by the United Nations Development Programme (UNDP) in 1990 in the first Human Development Report is widely used. In addition to their specific score, countries monitor their ranking on the annual list of countries. The HDI is composed of four indicators measuring three aspects of development. The 1990 Human Development Report explained the index and gave country rankings for the first time.

The HDI has three components: life expectancy, educational attainment, and income. Educational attainment is measured with two indicators: adult literacy and school enrollment. Income is measured with GDP per capita expressed in purchasing power parity (PPP) with US dollars. This controls for the variation in prices from country to country. Another aspect of the index is that it uses goalposts for minimum and maximum values of the variables. For example, the minimum level for life expectancy is twenty-five and the maximum is eighty-five. Therefore, a country with an average life expectancy of fifty-five receives a score of .5 (example from www.undp.org). For income, the goalposts are $100 PPP and $40,000 PPP. Theoretically, scores on the index can vary from 0 to 1. As reported in 2009, the 182, countries in the index ranged from a low of .340 for Niger to a high of .971 for Norway (UNDP, 2009). It is noted that two of the four indicators in the HDI—life expectancy and adult literacy rate—are the same as two of the three PQLI indicators (Cingranelli & Richards, 2007).

In addition to the scores and ranks, countries are divided into groupings. In 2009, there were eighty-three very high and high human development countries, with scores ranging from Norway's .971 to Lebanon's .803; there were seventy-five medium human development countries, ranging from Armenia at .798 to Nigeria at .511; and there were twenty-four low human development countries, ranging from Togo at 159th overall with an HDI of .499 to Niger at .340 (UNDP, 2009).

It is interesting that Niger did not have the worst score on any of the three dimensions but was very low in all three (with a life expectancy of 50.8, literacy for only 29% of adults, and a GDP of $627 per capita). Similarly, Norway did not lead in any statistic but is high in all areas. Leaders in 2009 were Japan, with a life expectancy of 82.7; Georgia, with 100% adult literacy; and Liechtenstein, with a per capita GDP of $85, 382. From year to year, some countries are dropped from the HDI when data are unavailable or judged grossly unreliable and others are added.

An important feature of the HDI is that it can be applied not only at a country level but also at sublevels, such as states, provinces, and districts. Recent work applying the HDI concept to the United States has calculated scores for states and congressional districts to highlight inequalities in development in subareas of the country (Lewis, Burd-Sharps & Sachs, 2010).

The Gender-related Development Index (GDI) is also calculated by UNDP. The GDI uses the same statistics as the HDI but with adjustments and penalties for gender inequalities. The GDI for a country is lower where there are gender disparities.

The Human Poverty Index

In a further development in its measurement efforts, in 1997 UNDP introduced two versions of a Human Poverty Index (HPI), one for developing countries and one for high-income countries. The elements of the HPI are similar to the HDI, but the indicators are different to capture levels of deprivation in the population rather than national averages of well-being. Using the three elements of survival, knowledge, and decent standard of living, the HPI for developing countries uses probability at birth of not surviving to age forty, percentage of adults who are illiterate, and two indicators of deprived standard of living: the percentage of people without "sustainable access to an improved water source and the percentage of children below the age of five who are underweight" (UNDP, 2007, Table 3). In the HPI 2 for high-income countries, survival and knowledge are measured by probability at birth of not reaching age

sixty and percentage of adults who are not functionally literate. Two measures of low standard of living are used: the percentage of people living below 50% of the median household disposable income for the country and the rate of long-term unemployment (twelve months or longer) (UNDP, 2007). (See technical note 1 of the 2007–2008 Human Development Report [UNDP, 2007] for more details on the computation of the HPI.)

Social Work Contributions to Measuring Human Well-Being

Simplicity in constructing indices is both an advantage and a disadvantage. The advantages of easy data collection and computation are obvious. But, simple indices can miss many essential elements of human well-being. Social work scholar Richard Estes has developed a comprehensive index of human well-being, the Index of Social Progress (ISP). The ISP was first developed in 1976 and refined over years of work (Estes, 1984). The ISP now "consists of 45 social indicators divided among 10 sectors of development: Education, Health Status, Women Status, Defense Effort, Economic, Demographic, Geographic, Political Chaos, Cultural Diversity, and Welfare Effort" (Estes, 2002, p. 24). Important elements of the ISP are measures of a nation's effort to address problems and various measures of vulnerability, such as susceptibility to natural disasters and existing political chaos. Estes also has used a weighted version of the ISP, WISP, to permit comparisons over time.

Measuring Gender Equality

The OECD launched a new index to measure gender equality in 2009, the Social Institutions and Gender Index (SIGI). It comprises twelve variables grouped into five categories or subindices: family code (early marriage, polygamy, parental authority, inheritance), physical integrity (female genital mutilation, violence against women), son preference (missing women), civil liberties (freedom of movement, freedom of dress), and ownership rights (access to land, access to bank loans, access to property). The SIGI is an unweighted index, with 0 = no inequality and 1 = high inequality.

According to its developers, the advantage of the SIGI is that it measures root causes, such as inheritance practices, son preference, and cultural practices (e.g., requiring son chaperoning), that constrain female equality (Drechsler, 2009). Focusing on measures that suggest causality will assist in developing more effective solutions to gender problems. For example, older measures identify that there are gender gaps in school enrollment. Often, the programmatic response has been to construct schools. The index identifies areas where girls are not allowed to go to school or where girls are married early, forcing them to leave school. In these cases, school construction will not improve enrollment, dictating alternative program efforts (Drechsler, 2009). An important aspect is that the index measures both the existence of certain rights in law (such as the right to access to credit) and de facto access.

To date, the SIGI has been calculated for 102 developing countries. Results on the scoring showed that the top five countries in gender equality were Paraguay, Croatia, Kazakhstan, Argentina, and Costa Rica. The poorest performers were Sudan followed by Afghanistan, Sierra Leone, Mali, and Yemen (OECD, 2009).

There are several critiques of the SIGI. One is that it is applied only to developing countries and not to the members of the OECD, the sponsoring organization. This is due to two factors. First, the mission of the OECD section on development is to focus only on developing countries. More importantly, however, is the nature of the index. As explained by its developers, applying SIGI to rich countries would result in undeserved high rankings. Different measures would be needed to construct a gender equality index for OECD countries, perhaps modeled after UNDP's separate set of poverty measures for rich nations. Some of the SIGI variables have wide agreement; others, such as freedom of dress and female genital mutilation, are criticized as attacks on particular cultures.

Sharon Camp of the Guttmacher Institute (2009) saluted the SIGI effort but critiqued the selection of the indicators and suggested additional ones. An important addition, according to Camp, would be access to safe, legal abortion; illegal and unsafe abortions are a major cause of death and injury among women in some countries. Adding U5MR would provide a health indicator of survival of girls. Another important health indicator might be extent of health insurance coverage for all types of reproductive services. According to Camp, these will be controversial in a "rich man's club."

THE MILLENNIUM DEVELOPMENT GOALS

The Millennium Development Goals (MDGs), adopted by the United Nations in 2000, represent a shift to using measurable targets to plan and assess global progress on development. The change was driven in part by frustration with lack of measurable

progress on core aspects of human well-being, such as education, freedom from disease, and severe poverty. The first seven of the eight goals identify areas for development progress and specific targets and timelines for achievement; most of the goals call for targets to be met by 2015. An example is the first goal, to eradicate extreme poverty and hunger. The targets for 2015 are to cut in half the proportion of people with an income of less than $1 per day and to cut in half the proportion of people suffering from hunger. Other goals, each with one or more specific quantitative targets, are to achieve universal primary education; promote gender equality; reduce child mortality and maternal mortality; make progress in combating AIDS, malaria, and other diseases; and improve environmental conditions and sustainability (UNDP, 2003). Goal 8 calls for the active participation of developed countries to work toward a more equitable global system in arenas such as trade and tariffs, access to technological advances (including pharmaceutical advances), credit and debt, and overseas development assistance. All countries are asked to commit to good governance to ensure that resources are used appropriately. (For a complete list of MDGs and targets, see Appendix C.)

Progress toward meeting the MDG targets has been regularly monitored by the United Nations and other organizations at the national, regional, and global levels. At the outset, UNDP determined that without improvements, it would take sub-Saharan Africa until 2129 to achieve universal primary education and until 2165 to reduce child mortality by two-thirds (UNDP, 2003). Thus the targets set for 2015 are ambitious, although many people will be left vulnerable even if they are achieved. The midpoint monitoring report issued in 2007 showed areas of good progress and areas with bleak outlooks for meeting any of the MDGs. As reported, "The countries of Latin America and the Caribbean have made remarkable progress toward implementing most of the Goals and at least five of the MDG targets appear to have been met," with the region on track to meet others (NGLS, 2007, p. 3). At the same point, "sub-Saharan Africa is not on track to achieve any of the Goals" (NGLS, 2007, p. 2). The MDG 2007 report also cited rich countries for failing to meet their commitments for aid levels and reforms.

As of 2009, poverty rates had fallen in every region and there was still a possibility of reaching the MDG goals by 2015 (UN, 2009). This is in spite of estimates that the number of people living in extreme poverty was fifty-five to ninety million higher than expected due to the global economic crisis (UN, 2009, p. 6). Also reported was some success in reducing the number of people infected with HIV and in increasing access to improved sources of drinking water. Little progress has been made on maternal mortality. Though it appears that the MDGs have not sufficiently mobilized world action to ensure achievement of the targets, the goals can be credited with highlighting areas of progress and failure. As such, they may assist in further channeling aid and reform efforts and spurring continued global action to address gaps in progress.

RECENT AND ONGOING EFFORTS

Several recent efforts have been made to improve upon the HDI and other measures. The OECD is leading the Global Project on Measuring the Progress of Societies. As expressed in its mission statement, the purpose of the project is "to foster the development of sets of key economic, social and environmental indicators to provide a comprehensive picture of how the well-being of a society is evolving . . . and to encourage the use of indicator sets to inform and promote evidence-based decision-making" (OECD, 2007). Many organizations are partnering in the effort, including the World Bank, UNDP, UNICEF, the regional banks, and the European Commission. Extensive research is ongoing and shared through a series of global forums. In 2007, the second global forum resulted in the Istanbul Declaration, laying out the dual goals of international debate and development of a framework; it called for "action to identify what 'progress' means in the 21st century and to stimulate international debate, based on solid statistical data and indicators, on both global issues of societal progress and how societies compare" (Hoegen, 2009). A third global meeting was held in Busan, Korea, in October 2009, and a fourth is planned for India in 2011 or 2012.

The Commission on the Measurement of Economic Performance and Social Progress was established in 2008 at the request of French president Nicolas Sarkozy. The stated intent of the commission is to move beyond traditional economic measures, although it is led by two distinguished economists, Joseph Stiglitz and Amartya Sen, and touts the membership of five Nobel Prize–winning economists. The commission's 2009 report recommends a multidimensional measurement of well-being, including the following eight dimensions: "i. Material living standards (income, consumption, and wealth); ii. Health; iii. Education; iv. Personal activities, including

work; v. Political voice and governance; vi. Social connections and relationships; vii. Environment (present and future conditions); viii. Insecurity, both of an economic and physical nature" (Stiglitz, Sen & Fitoussi, 2009, pp. 14–15). The report has already been criticized as offering little that is new. However, an interesting dimension of the commission's work and report is that it examined both current levels of well-being and ways to measure sustainability.

In July 2010, the Multidimensional Poverty Index (MPI) for developing countries was launched in a paper from the Oxford Poverty and Human Development Initiative (Alkire & Santos, 2010). Ten indicators are used to measure the same three dimensions used in the HDI: health, education, and standard of living. The dimensions are a set of deprivations: a child in the family has died; any household member is malnourished; a child is out of school; no household member has completed five years of school; household lacks electricity and reasonable access to clean water; sanitation does not meet MDG standards; flooring is dirt, sand, or dung; household cooks with wood, charcoal, or dung; and household owns fewer than two of the following—radio, TV, telephone, bike, or motorbike. Using weighted scores, families are defined as multidimensionally poor if they exceed 30% of the deprivations. Results show very different poverty rates from some other measures. Almost 90% of people in Ethiopia are multidimensionally poor, although only about 40% have incomes under $1.25 per day; in Vietnam, more are poor using the income figure (for more information, see the 2010 UNDP Human Development Report).

Other Measures

There are many more measures, indicators, and indices than can be discussed in this brief chapter. One of the more intriguing is the Gross National Happiness (GNH) index, developed by Bhutan. While its very title perhaps illustrates the subjective nature of measuring well-being, the index has attracted global attention (see www.grossnationalhappiness.com). In addition, scholars in human rights have developed various measures of realization of rights (Hertel & Minkler, 2007), indices are being developed to measure fragile and vulnerable states (Hoegen, 2009), and efforts are underway to develop measures of social integration by the UN Commission for Social Development. All underscore the ongoing quest for meaningful measures of human well-being and development progress.

ARE THESE MEASURES USEFUL?

The maturation of measures and ongoing attempts to develop new measures of human well-being have moved the field toward a more sophisticated understanding of development. The MDGs represent an appropriate impatience with progress to date and a demand for more accountability by national governments and the UN system in ensuring documentable improvements in human well-being.

That said, indices can be critiqued on several grounds. First, indices are only as good as the data used to construct them. As stated in the *Millennium Development Goals Report 2009*, "Reliable, timely and internationally comparable data on the MDG indicators are crucial to holding the international community accountable" (UN, 2009, p. 54). Inconsistencies damage the credibility of global efforts. There are many imperfections in data collection and in accuracy. When data elements are severely lacking, countries are left out of some indices. For example, Zimbabwe was recently excluded from the HDI for several years as its data collection systems disintegrated. Countries experiencing conflicts often similarly neglect data collection. Less dramatic errors certainly exist in all data processes, and at times, estimates must suffice. The need to improve data collection in poorer countries is recognized, but expenditures on statistical improvements must be balanced with urgent needs for spending on programs. Good systems can be costly.

Of greatest importance is ensuring that the right things are measured. The efforts reported in this chapter reflect ongoing efforts to guarantee that useful indicators are selected and that the indicators are good proxies for the phenomena being studied. As noted by Jon Hall, director of the OECD Global Project on Measuring the Progress of Societies, use of indicators can result in "achieving the target and missing the point" (Hall, 2009). He cautioned attendees at the 2009 world forum in Busan that while indicators can help policy makers "to clarify and quantify policy objectives and strategies, there is a danger in excessive use of targets." He also noted that indicators will not be useful unless they are accepted by relevant stakeholders in the policy process. The emphasis on measurability can be limiting and damage progress on important development goals. In an article on the MDGs, Hulme (2010) wrote that the "focus on 'measurables' leads to a reduced interest in difficult-to-measure goals, such as human rights, participation and democracy" (p. 16).

Social workers must join the global efforts to determine what measures are needed. Their input is essential to ensure that all relevant elements of human well-being are included in indices. An important example is the effort of International Association of Schools of Social Workers (IASSW) representatives at the United Nations to ensure that mental health is given attention in policy and program discussions of health. Social workers can also be helpful in involving grassroots stakeholders in discussions of what should be measured. Indices will be less robust if critical elements are omitted. As Camp (2009) indicated, the SIGI measures of female physical integrity miss millions of deaths and injuries resulting from unsafe abortion. The SIGI measures, therefore, will be less effective than they might have been in ensuring better policies to protect women.

Social workers can bring their case knowledge into these global policy and measurement discussions. The index developed by Richard Estes almost three decades ago reflected many of the current advances in measuring human well-being; the inclusion of measures of vulnerability to conflict and disaster, measures of effort suggesting national environments conducive to human progress, and use of multiple factors are all aspects under current debate and development, yet are in the Estes index. Perhaps this suggests that social workers are particularly likely to understand the complexity of human well-being.

Measures and indices are optimally a force for progress and a spur to increased effort to address human needs and human rights. They help governments and development organizations to recognize areas of progress and to identify priorities for increased effort. According to Tadeo Chino, former president of the Asian Development Bank, "Sound data represent a key weapon in the battle against poverty" (as cited in Hoegen, 2009, p. 19). As Estes (2002) wrote, "Clearly, it is the poor themselves that provide the best justification for the attention given by comparative researchers to understanding the dynamics leading to concentrations of wealth and poverty in societies" (p. 26). Ultimately, the value of measures is judged by their responsiveness to the human condition.

REFERENCES

Alkire, S., & Santos, M. E. (2010). *Acute multidimensional poverty: A new index for developing countries*. OPHI Working Paper No. 38. Oxford, UK: Oxford Poverty and Human Development Initiative. Accessed October 15, 2010, at www.ophi.org.uk/acute-multidimensional-poverty-a-new-index-for-developing-countries.

Camp, S. (2009, March). *Critique of the SIGI*. Panel presentation at the United Nations Commission on the Status of Women, New York.

Cingranelli, D. L., & Richards, D. L. (2007). Measuring government effort to respect economic and social human rights: A peer benchmark. In S. Hertel & L. Minkler (Eds.), *Economic rights: Conceptual, measurement and policy issues* (pp. 214–232). Cambridge: Cambridge University Press.

Drechsler, D. (2009, March). *The OECD Social Institutions and Gender Index*. Presentation at the United Nations Commission on Status of Women, New York.

Estes, R. (2002). "Poverties" and "wealth": Competing definitions and alternative approaches to measurement. In W. Glatzer (Ed.), *Rich and poor: Disparities, perceptions, concomitants* (pp. 9–32). Dordrecht: Kluwer Academic.

Estes, R. (1984). *The social progress of nations*. New York: Praeger.

Hall, J. (2009, October). *The global project on measuring the progress of societies: A toolkit for practitioners*. Presentation delivered at the World Forum, Busan, Korea. www.oecd.org.

Hertel, S., & Minkler, L. (Eds.). (2007). *Economic rights: Conceptual, measurement and policy issues*. Cambridge: Cambridge University Press.

Hoegen, M. (2009). Statistics and the quality of life: Measuring progress a world beyond GDP. Bonn, Germany: inWEnt Centre for Economic, Environmental and Social Statistics. Accessed January 5, 2010, at www.oecd.org.

Hulme, D. (2010). Lessons from the making of the MDGs: Human development meets results-based management in an unfair world. *IDS Bulletin, 41*(1), 15–25.

Lewis, K., Burd-Sharps, S., & Sachs, J. (2010). *The measure of America 2010–2011: Mapping risks and resiliencies*. New York: NYU Press.

NGLS. (2007, August). 2007: Midpoint for the achievement of the millennium development goals. *NGLS Roundup 129*. New York: United Nations Non-Governmental Liaison Service.

Organization for Economic Cooperation and Development (OECD). (2009). Gender, institutions and development database. Accessed September 25, 2009, at www.oecd.org/document/16/0,3343,en_2649_33935_39323280_1_1_1_1,00.html.

Organization for Economic Cooperation and Development (OECD). (2007). *Mission statement*. Global Project on Measuring the Progress of Societies, 2nd World Conference, Istanbul, Turkey. Accessed January 25, 2010, at www.oecd.org.

Stiglitz, J. E., Sen, A., & Fitoussi, J. P. (2009). *Report by the Commission on the Measurement of Economic and Social Progress*. Accessed January 5, 2010, at www.stiglitz-sen-fitoussi.fr/documents/rapport_anglais.pdf.

United Nations (UN). (2009). *The Millennium Development Goals Report 2009*. New York: UN Department of Economic and Social Affairs.

United Nations Children's Fund (UNICEF). (2011). *The state of the world's children 2011: Adolescence An Age of Opportunity*. New York: Author.

United Nations Children's Fund (UNICEF). (2007). *The state of the world's children 2008: Child survival*. New York: Author.

United Nations Development Program (UNDP). (2010). *Human Development Report 2010: The real wealth of nations*. New York: Palgrave Macmillan for UNDP.

United Nations Development Program, (UNDP). (2009). *Human Development Report 2009: Overcoming barriers: Human mobility and development*. New York: Palgrave Macmillan for UNDP.

United Nations Development Programme (UNDP). (2007). *Human Development Report 2007/2008: Fighting climate change*. New York: Palgrave Macmillan.

United Nations Development Programme (UNDP). (2003). *Human Development Report 2003: Millennium Development Goals*. New York: Oxford University Press.

Microcredit: A Development Strategy for Poverty Reduction

REBECCA L. THOMAS

Microcredit, providing small loans for income-generating activities to people living in poverty, especially in developing countries, has become one of the most popular strategies for development as well as a means for reducing poverty (Anderson, Locker & Nugent, 2002; Mayoux, 1998). Microcredit is often thought of as a grassroots development strategy for self-employment enterprise that generates income (Woller & Woodworth, 2001b). It has therefore become a powerful method of reducing poverty (Latifee, 2003); empowering women, who are the most frequent participants (Anderson et al., 2002; Newaz, 2003); and building community (Mizan, 1994; Thomas & Sinha, 2009).

Inspired by the success of the Grameen Bank model, developed by Professor Muhammad Yunus in Bangladesh, microcredit programs have become a mainstay even of large international organizations, such as the United Nations and the World Bank, along with large and small nongovernmental organizations (NGOs) around the world. There is almost a global consensus that providing microcredit to the poor is a useful standard practice toward the goal of achieving equitable and sustainable gains for economic and social development in the twenty-first century (Microcredit Summit, 1997). In other words, microcredit has established a new way to provide credit services for the poor in a market economy.

This chapter addresses two questions that often arise in the microcredit research and dialogue. First, does microcredit really benefit the poor? Second, is microcredit an effective strategy for poverty reduction? The chapter provides a brief description of microcredit and microfinance and presents an overview of their role, targeted mostly at women, in reducing poverty. The strengths and limitations of the strategy are then discussed. The chapter concludes that despite evidence of positive effects for individuals

and their families from the microcredit movement, poverty reduction must be addressed through multiple strategies.

WHAT ARE MICROCREDIT AND MICROFINANCE?

Microcredit as fashioned by the Grameen model is the practice of providing small loans, primarily to women who have little access to the traditional banking system. These loans are given for the purpose of supporting income-generating activities in the informal economy through self-employment initiatives. Rather than providing collateral, borrowers must adhere to a set of rules, which include accountability to the group of borrowers who are part of a cohort, weekly or biweekly repayments, and savings as a precondition for getting loans (Yunus, 2003). Microcredit operates from the premise that poverty is a result of social processes that prevent the poor from accessing their social resources, including credit, and by extension such life conditions are a violation of human rights. Through microcredit, an alternative avenue of economic opportunity has been created for the poor, thus influencing development (Qudrat-I Elahi & Rahman, 2006). The success of microcredit programs in reaching the poor in rural communities, along with high repayment rates, has led to an expansion of the services now known as *microfinance.*

Microfinance is a development approach that provides financial and social intermediation. The financial components include services such as savings, credit, and insurance, while the social components involve organizing citizens groups to mobilize and create policy change—a bottom–up approach to empower the poor and effect change (Qudrat-I Elahi & Rahman, 2006). In essence, the difference between microcredit and microfinance is the services that they provide. Microcredit mainly provides services in loan distribution and recovery, which is organized by creating small groups and compulsory savings. Microfinance includes microcredit and other services such as insurance and social components that focus on meeting the needs of the borrower or customer and community development (Woller, 2002).

This chapter uses the terms *microcredit* and *microfinance* very specifically. The term *microcredit* here refers to small initial loans, given to program participants either individually or in a group, that are repaid in a specified time. The term *microfinance* includes microcredit along with additional supportive services to assist the recipient of the loan. These terms are not used interchangeably because there are conceptual differences between the two. However, they both operate in a neocapital environment where the goal is income generation based on selling a product or advancing an entrepreneurial endeavor supported in a group environment. If microfinance projects are to be transformative enough to influence sociopolitical and structural change, then development efforts need greater access to similar financial institutions and an understanding of the complex issues related to poverty and empowerment models that include gender equality and human rights.

MICROCREDIT, WOMEN, AND DEVELOPMENT

A literature review reveals a gendered dimension to microcredit loans. Women receive loans for two reasons. First, there is a perception that women are better borrowers because they do not usually default on their loans (Pitt, Khandker, & Cartwright, 2006). They have greater awareness of the needs of their families and tend to devote a higher proportion of their income to children's nutrition and other family basic needs (Goetz & Sen Gupta, 1996). They also are thought not to spend money on unproductive consumption such as alcohol or personal use (Edward & Olsen, 2006; Mallick, 2002). Second, women are twice oppressed because of their poverty and their subordinate status in the household and the general culture (Edward & Olsen, 2006; Mayoux, 1998). In some countries, gender inequalities lead to women not having property rights or rights of inheritance, restrictions in laws related to marriage and divorce, stigma, and limited economic and social developments such as lack of equal opportunities to education, nutrition, and work. In such a context, microcredit and microenterprise have been shown to have positive impact on women and families, thereby promoting development.

Among women, microcredit is found to promote empowerment and expand economic opportunities. In studies of rural women in Bangladesh, Newaz (2003) found that women felt that they had more leverage in making household decisions since they were contributing to the family income as earners. Anderson et al. (2002) also concluded that women felt empowered to influence decisions when they were earning more and contributing to the family economy. Data from Amin's study (1993) indicated that women spend a larger proportion of their earnings on household expenses, such as medicine, food, and education, than men do. Mayoux (2002) confirms the finding that women spend more of their income on household well-being, including their own and their daughters' education and health. Interestingly, Pitt, Khandker, Choudhury, and Millimet (2003) found that microcredit provided to women resulted in improved measures of health and nutrition for boys and girls, while microcredit provided to men made no significant difference to their children's well-being. Schuler and Hashemi (1997) found that as women's income earning potential increased, fertility rates decreased.

These gender-based differentials are of strategic importance to poverty reduction and family welfare and development (Kebeer, 2001). Pitt et al. (2003) concur with other studies that "credit programs lead to women taking a greater role in household decision making, having greater access to financial and economic resources, having greater social networks, having greater bargaining power vis-à-vis their husbands, and having greater freedom of mobility" and "that children seem to be better off when their mothers control relatively more of their family's resources" (p. 817).

However, gender inequalities cannot be easily erased by microcredit and microfinance. Karides (2005) draws our attention to the realities of women who participate in microfinance. As the old adage goes, women's work is never done—they often struggle to balance work, children, and household duties. With few or no formal supports such as state-supported child care or food or income supports, they work long hours, make little income, and would have difficulty securing credit from any other means. Mayoux (1998) found that women who provided low-paid traditional female work though self-employment such as agricultural work or domestic work in people's homes also spent more time in unpaid domestic work and household duties. Thus, their time and economic resources for paid economic activities were more limited and their repayment rates were slower. In such circumstances, women have little time to become involved in other political and social activities to bring change to the local social order.

In addition, women living in extreme poverty often face multiple difficulties such as lack of marketable skills, discrimination, social exclusion, or chronic illness. These circumstances require long-term investment; access to credit alone will neither eradicate poverty nor create opportunities for sustainable development, and further services are necessary to help them solve other pressing issues such as illiteracy, lack of skills, poor health, and lack of savings. Although microcredit can be useful for these women, its ultimate impact will be minimal if it is not provided in conjunction with supporting services that can help them solve noncredit problems simultaneously (Bhatt & Shui-Yan, 2001).

The literature suggests that for microloan programs to be successful—that is, for recipients to repay their loans in small amounts and to earn additional income—multiple layers of support must be provided for the individuals and their families. For example, Khandker (2005) found that in addition to loans, women required the following supports in order to take advantage of the opportunities that microfinance provided: child care, health care, literacy classes, business-related skills training, employment opportunities, and greater control over their fertility and children's education. When such complementary services were provided, the repayment rates of loans increased and the quality of life for families was enhanced. The grassroots microcredit movement must work toward systematic policy change to create nonoppressive and equal opportunities for members of society, especially in an informal economy. The lack of employment opportunities in the formal sector and lack of employability skills have created an environment that calls for the rise of microcredit and microfinance services.

Projects developed by microcredit are varied, from the complex expansion of businesses to capitalizing on meeting the needs of a community. An example of a user of microcredit is Cipriana, a woman from Chiapas, Mexico, who received a loan and used the money to develop a food stand. She sells juices, smoothies, tortillas, sandwiches, soup, and omelets. With her income she can provide for her children and not totally rely on her husband. She stated, "I was a very negative, angry person before. My involvement in AMEXTRA's peace program and micro-lending programs has changed my personality. It wasn't good

for me to be stuck at home. I enjoy interacting with people in the community, so this business has made me much happier" (Melchor, 2009).

Kalpana Rai is another example of how microcredit has been helpful. A few years ago, Kalpana's son took a fairly large loan from a loan shark to invest in a business that failed. She received a microcredit loan and increased the inventory of her already existing business of selling saris door to door. From her profits she has been able to pay down 50% of the principal amount owed to the loan shark. She indicates that her ability to repay her son's loan was made possible by access to added capital and now sees a way out of the clutches of the loan shark (www.pranainternational.org).

In recent years, microcredit has been heavily scrutinized as some for-profit organizations have charged high interest rates. In India, a number of cases have brought criticism and concern regarding the for-profit MF industry. Recent high profile cases of profit-making that appear to be unethical, or exploitative, have triggered national concern in India regarding the rapid growth of the sector, under-repayment and over-indebtedness; rigid repayment schedules; and too little regulation of MF providers (College of Agricultural Banking & Micro Credit Ratings International Limited, 2011). Larger and for-profit MF providers are pressured to sustain growth and profitability and this has resulted in a perception of client exploitation and lack of products and services which are designed for the client. Oversight and transparency of for-profit industries must be provided to ensure that microcredit is true to its original purpose of poverty reduction.

THE IMPACT OF MICROCREDIT PROGRAMS ON POVERTY REDUCTION AND DEVELOPMENT

In many developing countries, because of limited employment opportunities in both rural and urban areas, many of the poor make their living through self-employment in the informal economy. These are the street venders, small-shop owners, artisans, and self-help groups. Credit allows microentrepreneurs to invest in small-scale businesses that are both creative and responsive to the needs of communities, using small start-up capital to earn an income. Woller and Woodworth (2001b) state that "the microcredit movement is based on the explicit recognition of the extent and the importance of the informal economy and the key role played by the financial capital in raising the labor productivity of the poor" (p. 271). To address the extreme poverty in many countries, NGOs, large multilateral institutions, development agencies such as the World Bank and the United States Agency for International Development (USAID), and national governments have focused on microcredit and micro-finance as a viable development strategy. This move-ment is based on a number of studies that provide evidence that microfinance is an effective approach for reducing poverty, especially for the very poor (Daley-Harris, 2007, Khandker, 2005). In addition, the quality of life for women and their families has improved.

Khandker (2005) found that microcredit pro-grams make a difference to poor individuals by raising per capita income and consumption as well as house-hold net worth, thereby increasing the probability that program participants are able to lift themselves out of poverty. The welfare impact of microfinance is also positive for participating and nonparticipating house-holds, indicating that microfinance programs help the poor beyond income redistribution and growth. The programs have spillover effects on the local economy, but the overall impacts are small.

Poor health and poverty are closely linked. One of the strategies developed in Bangladesh to deal with health-related problems and solutions involves microcredit and microfinance programs that include community-based interventions through group participation, exchange of information, and shared knowledge. The findings reported by Strobach and Zaumseil (2002) indicate that even in a short time, there was significant positive development in knowl-edge related to health issues.

Hietalahti and Linden (2006) studied the socio-economic impact of microcredit on women's welfare in northeastern South Africa. Their study focused on how microcredit projects affect rural women's live-lihoods and how they could strengthen women's welfare. They collected data from two projects, the Microcredit Program (MCP) and the Tshomisano Credit Program (TCP). Their results showed that, by mainly targeting women who lived below the poverty line, the TCP was able to reach the poorest of women, while the MCP targeted those who were in a better financial position. Both groups benefited from micro-credit services.

Using existing data, Sanders (2002) compared low-income microentrepreneurs from one of the seven US demonstration programs with low-income self-employed workers not affiliated with the microentrepreneurs and with low-income wage earn-ers who were not self-employed. Sanders found that

despite the initial gains of the new self-employed microentrepreneurs, both groups involved in self-employed endeavors did not show much variability from 1991 to 1995. It would seem that one would see greater gains in those enterprises that had been in business for a longer time. However, several convinc-ing arguments are presented as reasons why low-income entrepreneurs with existing businesses do not maintain their advantage in earnings as their time in business increases.

Sanders (2002) postulates that these businesses begin with relatively small loans, which limit the type of enterprises that they can be involved in. Similar to dead-end wage jobs, low-income entrepreneurs may be caught in a cycle of low earnings with little room for advancement. Furthermore, low-income entrepreneurs encounter structural barriers that limit their access to information, business networks, and markets (Sherraden, Sanders, & Sherraden, 1998, as cited in Sanders, 2002). In addition, racial minori-ties and women may face discrimination from con-sumers and suppliers, which makes it difficult for them to grow their businesses (Borjas & Bronars, 1989). Sanders' findings indicate that these microen-terprise programs result in no significant gains for participants compared with nonparticipants and low-wage workers, but she cautions that these findings cannot be generalized given the limitations of the sample size. On the other hand, she argues that on the basis of equity, disadvantaged people who want to enter self-employment should have an opportunity and access to startup capital.

Similarly, in her research in southeastern Sri Lanka, Shaw (2004) found that the microenter-prise successes of less-poor clients were better than those of the poor. In addition, poor clients in semi-urban areas had more opportunities to earn a higher income than those in rural communities. Shaw found that poorer clients faced geographic, financial, and sociocultural barriers to the most lucrative income-generating enterprises and were forced to enter low-value activities with limited growth opportunities. In addition, poorer households are more likely to have more socially related problems; their mobility and productivity are hampered by poor health and nutri-tion. People from such households might also lack technical and business skills and have lower levels of education, thus making it difficult for them to com-pete in an unstructured, exploitative, and informal economy.

The argument that the poor do not fare as well as the nonpoor is not sufficient reason to abandon the income-generation activities of such families in general. Microcredit has certainly improved the well-being of almost all participants even though there might be differences between the groups. To assist the needs of the extreme poor, microcredit lending must be augmented by the promotion of programs that invest in the overall social and physical infrastructure of a community. Literacy, health promotion, nutrition, and access to social networks along with microfinance services must be provided. In an effort to be successful—that is, to see higher repayment rates by borrowers or rapid growth of businesses by groups who are primed for success—one must not drift from the original mission of microcredit to provide credit access to the poor (Hishigsuren, 2007).

CONCLUSION

Over the past two decades, microcredit and microfinance services have seen rapid growth and have been championed as important strategies for addressing poverty. Targeted especially toward women, microcredit has provided opportunities for self-employment and income generation.

Does microfinance really benefit the poor? The answer is yes. Research demonstrates that microcredit and microfinance programs have brought considerable benefits for many women, especially the marginally poor. Most women and their families experience increased income along with other benefits due to access to credit. Certainly, women with more skills and education benefit more from microfinance than do women with lesser skills and education, but one must not forget that the point of microcredit is to provide access to the poor who do not have any other means.

Critiques of microcredit and microfinance lie on a continuum. At one extreme are those who claim that microcredit and microfinance programs have the capacity to create jobs and business, revitalize low-income communities, and move people out of poverty (Clark & Huston, 1993). On the other end of the spectrum, some researchers have claimed that microenterprise is an antipoverty strategy that is forcing the poor to participate in an economy based on capitalism and the free market without the skills needed to be successful, adding more stress and uncertainty (Banerjee, 1998). Yet others see microcredit and microfinance as a means to bring poor families into the economic mainstream and to help them exit the secondary labor market (Raheim, 1996, 1997).

Poverty, gender inequalities, class, and caste systems all require multipronged efforts to enhance development. Women in developing countries are often bound by gender roles and are therefore faced with many challenges. They juggle multiple responsibilities and are faced with time and money constraints, family responsibilities, and household work along with addition of newly acquired microfinance responsibilities.

Microcredit and microfinance alone will not solve the problem of poverty, and there is a need to further empower economically challenged women. Women's work is never done. Safeguards must be put in place to make certain that their enterprises do not mandate long hours for poor pay in hazardous conditions. The informal sector is very competitive as well as unregulated, beyond the reach of laws and institutions that protect workers and make sure that their rights are maintained. Structural and policy changes must be developed to improve the conditions of informal work. Further, flourishing examples of empowerment approaches, such as the work of the Self Employed Women's Association (SEWA), must be established. Founded in India, SEWA organizes poor self-employed women through work, builds economic organizations such as unions and cooperatives, creates viable links between a country's grassroots and its macro policies, and peacefully reconciles struggle and development.

Does microcredit serves as a strategy for poverty reduction? Although microcredit is indeed an effective strategy to poverty reeducation, it is only one strategy. Microcredit offers a flexible path to empowering women financially, and it will remain a key strategy. However, numerous other services, such as women's support groups, literacy and technical skill building, family or marriage counseling, and especially education and advocacy for and by women locally and regionally and government or employer-supported health benefits and income insurance, are needed if poor women in developing countries are to earn a fair wage for their labor.

REFERENCES

Amin, S. (1993). *Women's productive and reproductive roles.* Paper presented at the SAREC Conference on Dynamics of Complexity, Harare and Stockholm.

Anderson, C., Locker, L., & Nugent, R. (2002). Microcredit, social capital, and common pool resources. *World Development, 30*, 95–105.

Banerjee, M. (1998). Microenterprise development: A response to poverty. In M. Sherraden & W. Ninacs (Eds.), *Community economic development and social work* (pp. 63–83). New York: Haworth Press.

Bhatt, N., & Shui-Yan, T. (2001). Delivering microfinance in developing countries: Controversies and policy perspectives. *Policy Studies Journal, 29*(2), 319–334.

Borjas, G., & Bronars, I. (1989). Consumer discrimination and self employment. *Journal of Political and Economy, 97*(3), 581–605.

Clark, P., & Huston, T. (1993). Assisting the small business: Assessing microenterprise development as a strategy for boosting poor communities. *Self-employment learning project report.* Washington, DC: Aspen Institute.

College of Agricultural Banking & Micro-Credit Ratings International Limited. (2011, January). Seminar on Risk in Indian Microfinance. Presented at the College of Agricultural Banking, Pune India.

Daley-Harris, S. (2007). *State of the Microcredit Summit Campaign report.* Washington, DC: Microcredit Summit Campaign.

Edward, E., & Olsen, W. (2006). Paradigms and reality in microfinance: The Indian case. *Perspectives on Global Development and Technology, 5*(1–2), 31–54.

Goetz, A., & Sen Gupta, R. (1996). Who takes the credit? Gender, power and control over loan use in rural credit programs in Bangladesh. *World Development, 24,* 46–63.

Hietalahti, J., & Linden, M. (2006). Socio-economic impacts of microfinance and repayment performance: A case study of the Small Enterprise Foundation, South Africa. *Progress in Development Studies, 6*(3), 201–210.

Hishigsuren, G. (2007). Evaluating mission drift in microfinance: Lessons for programs with social mission. *Evaluation Review, 31*(3), 205–259.

Karides, M. (2005). Whose solution is it? Development ideology and the work of micro-entrepreneurs in Caribbean context. *International Journal of Sociology and Social Policy, 25*(1/2), 30–62.

Kebeer, N. (2001). Conflicts over credit: Re-evaluating the empowerment potential of loans to women in rural Bangladesh. *World Development, 29,* 63–84.

Khandker, S. (2005). Microfinance and poverty: Evidence using panel data from Bangladesh. *World Bank Economic Review, 19*(2), 263–285.

Latifee, H. (2003). *Microcredit and poverty reduction.* Presented at the International Conference on Poverty Reduction through Microcredit, Taksim-Istanbul.

Mallick, R. (2002). Implementing and evaluating microcredit in Bangladesh. *Development in Practice, 12*(2), 153–163.

Mayoux, L. (2002). *Women's empowerment and participation in micro-finance: Evidence, issues and ways forward.* Retrieved on July 7, 2008, from www.genfinance.info/Case%20Studies/India_genfinance.pdf.

Mayoux, L. (1998). *Women' empowerment and micro-finance programs: Approaches, evidence and ways forward.* DPP working papers No. 41.

Melchor, D. (2009, February). *Financing through solidarity groups: Empowerment beyond savings and borrowing.*

Presented at the United Nations, Commission on the Status of Women, New York.

Microcredit Summit. (1997). Washington, DC: Results Education Fund.

Mizan, N. A. (1994). *In Quest of Empowerment: The Grameen Bank Impact on Women's Power and Status.* Dhaka, Bangladesh: University Press.

Newaz, W. (2003). *Impact of microcredit programs in Bangladesh: An empirical analysis.* Kalevantie, Finland: Tampere University Press.

Pitt, M., Khandker, S., & Cartwright, J. (2006, July). Empowering women with micro finance: Evidence from Bangladesh. *Economic and Cultural Change,* 791–831.

Pitt, M., Khandker, S., Choudhury, O., & Millimet, D. (2003). Microcredit programs for the poor and the health status of children in rural Bangladesh. *International Economic Review, 44,* 87–118.

Qudrat-I Elahi, K., & Rahman, L. M. (2006). Microcredit and microfinance: Functional and conceptual differences. *Development in Practice, 16*(5), 467–483.

Raheim, S. (1997). Problems and prospects of self-employment as an economic independence option for welfare recipients. *Social Work, 42*(1), 44–53.

Raheim, S. (1996). Microenterprise as an approach for promoting economic development in social work: Lessons from the Self-Employment Investment Demonstration. *International Social Work, 39,* 69–82.

Sanders, C. (2002). The impact of microenterprise assistance programs: A comparative study of program participants, nonparticipants and other low-wage workers. *Social Service Review, 76*(2), 331–340.

Schuler, S. R., & Hashemi, S. M. (1997). The influence of women's changing roles and status in Bangladesh's fertility transition. *World Development, 25*(4), 356–357.

Shaw, J. (2004). Microenterprise occupation and poverty reduction in microfinance programs: Evidence from Sri Lanka. *World Development, 32*(7), 1247–1264.

Strobach, T., & Zaumseil, M. (2002). A evaluation of microcredit system to promote health knowledge among poor women in Bangladesh. *Health Promotion International, 22*(2), 129–136.

Thomas, R. & Sinha, J. W. (2009). A critical look at microfinance and NGOs in regard to poverty reductions for women. *Social Development Issues, 31* (2), 30–42.

Woller, G. (2002). The promise and peril of microfinance commercialization. *Small Enterprise Development, 13,* 12–21.

Woller, G., & Woodworth, W. (2001). Microcredit as a grass-roots policy for international development. *Policy Studies Journal, 29,* 202–214.

Yunus, M. (2003). *Banker to the poor: Micro-lending and the battle against world poverty.* New York: Public Affairs.

Variations and Issues of Survival of European Welfare State Models in the Twenty-First Century

SVEN HESSLE

The concept of the welfare state has its roots in Europe (Goul Andersen, Claesen, van Oorschot, & Halvorsen, 2002; Jordan, 2008; Taylor-Gooby, 2004). For that reason one would expect to find in Europe an advanced, ongoing discourse on social policy. But the ambitions of the growing region to become an important economic force in the world might have delayed the social dimension in the European agenda. There are ambitions of a common European social policy, but the convergence efforts seem to meet resistance from national welfare states that may have sociocultural traditions to defend.

In this chapter, it is demonstrated that the social dimension came rather late to the European agenda, and it has so far been subordinated to economic issues. Social policy has showed deviating development in various parts of Europe (Fenger, 2007; Korpi, 2004), especially pronounced when comparing the Nordic region with southern countries and the former Communist countries in transition (Kangas & Palme, 2005; Sjöberg & Ferrini, in press).

EUROPEAN UNION AS A PEACE PROJECT: THE FIGHT FOR EUROPEAN UNITY FROM DIVERSITY

The European Union (EU) is gradually becoming one of the most important and powerful political and economic forces of the world, with about 500 million inhabitants in twenty-seven member states and close to one-third of the world's gross domestic product (GDP) (http://ec.europa.eu.index/). After World War II, decades of nationalism were broken, and unification was pronounced in the 1950s for a future federation of Europe. The main founding members of the community were states that just had been in war, some of them as antagonists: West Germany, Belgium, France, Italy, Luxembourg, and Netherlands.

The European Community (EC) started as a steel and coal community and was broadened to become an economic community. In 1979, the first direct, democratic elections were held for the European Parliament. After the fall of the Iron Curtain, the former East Germany became a member of the community as part of the united Germany.

In 1993, criteria were defined for entering the EU (Copenhagen criteria; http://europa.eu/). They include a stable economy, respect of human rights, the rule of law, a functional market economy capable of competition within the EU, and acceptance of the obligations of membership. The European Council is the institution that evaluates applications from aspiring member states. On the threshold of joining the twenty-seven members are Croatia, the Republic of Macedonia, and Turkey. Other Balkan states (which were recently in war) are standing in line: Albania, Bosnia and Herzegovina, Montenegro, and Serbia. Even Kosovo, recently engaged in internal and regional disputes, has the status of an official candidate.

Establishing the euro as a common currency was accomplished in 2002. About half of the member states have changed their domestic currency to the euro. The EU's single market is based on four laws applicable in all member states: the freedom of movement of people, goods, services, and capital. The Schengen Agreement has opened the borders between member states since 1999, and citizens can pass through without passport controls. This agreement has both advantages and disadvantages, which we will come back to later in the chapter.

The founders of the European common market were initially concerned with establishing a trading partnership that could promote economic development and reduce military conflicts (Taylor-Gooby, 2004). Social policy has not been a priority on the agenda so far. Social issues have been relevant only in connection with labor market policy and trading of goods. This is especially obvious when considering development and human rights issues (Orbie & Babarinde, 2008).

THE SOCIAL DIMENSION IN THE EU

It was not until the middle of the 1990s that social issues became a priority on the European agenda. This discouraging fact is blamed on the basic tension between economic and social goals (Taylor-Gooby, 2004). The tension is a mirror of the clash between open market and welfare state in Europe, especially emphasized by the conflicting theories from the 1940s of Schumpeter and Polanyi. Schumpeter supported a liberal market-oriented model of capitalism and limited state intervention, where market capitalism is a positive-sum game in which both sides of industry benefit, not a zero-sum game between capitalists and working class (Taylor-Gooby, 2004, p. 5). Polanyi, on the other hand, believed that the structures that may be provided by an interventionist welfare state are necessary to enable market capitalism to flourish in the long term. Free markets are unable to operate successfully in the long run because they undermine the conditions of their own success; more generally, economic relationships must be embedded in a fabric of relations through cultural norms, social institutions, and political controls (Taylor-Gooby, 2004, p. 6).

Social policy has mainly been part of the agenda for labor market policies. In an effort to add the social dimension to the economic issues, the European Social Charter was established in 1989 for regulating the fundamental rights of workers. A social fund and a regional fund have been supporting vocational training, labor market integration of people with disabilities, and women's opportunities. But most of the resources have been allocated to meet the needs of the poorer parts of the European community. This is also emphasized in a series of documents from the Council of Europe. Of importance is the documentation concerning the role of social services in sustainable social development, which was collected at a conference held in Berlin in 2001 (Council of Europe, 2003). For instance, the way social service is organized for all social groups as well as for people with special needs is crucial for "a development that meets the needs of the present without compromising the ability of future generations to meet their own needs" (Council of Europe, 2003, p. 108). In this document we find that the basic guideline for social work in sustainable development is professional activity that participates in a process of protection, empowerment, and inclusion of people who are in a position of marginalization or who are in other ways the target of repression or vulnerability (Hessle & Zavirsek, 2005).

The welfare state in Europe has many faces, and the position of social work (and welfare) and consequently the role of social workers in welfare state models varies (Lorenz, 1994, 2001). Besides the wave of neoliberalism, another reason why the convergence of the social dimension has been blocked might be because EU countries have a tendency to defend their distinctive national social policies, embedded as they are in sociocultural and political history. This predicament will be discussed later in the chapter.

MIGRATION AND FORTRESS EUROPE

The EU states have been gradually increasing their cooperation in attempting to establish a common policy and law on matters related to immigration and asylum. Successive agreements, treaties, and action plans have led to obvious advantages but also to the creation of what has been called "Fortress Europe," indirectly causing thousands of deaths of refugees and asylum seekers as well as criminalizing and marginalizing immigrants within the EU (Dominelli, 1998). The statistics on the flow of migrants to and within the EU are difficult to interpret because of the uneven quality of national statistics and the kinds of movements of migrants (http://ec.europa.eu/). For instance, in some parts of the region, where there has been a traditionally generous attitude to immigration, it has been difficult to distinguish between asylum-seeking family reunification and other asylum-seeking or moving categories. There is also a flow of migrants who move from permanent acceptance in one country to family reunion in another country.

The Schengen Agreement eliminated border controls and established a common visa policy between the member countries, with the exception of the United Kingdom and Ireland. The increased freedom of movement within the Schengen area has created problems in connection with the increased control of travelers entering Europe from other parts of the world. An especially sensitive area is the southern Mediterranean, particularly Greece, Italy, France, and Spain, where thousands of mainly African asylum-seeking people enter by boats every day. Common rules regarding visas, asylum rights, and checks at external borders were adopted and coordination of the police, customs, and the judiciary was increased.

The Schengen Information System (SIS) has been set up to deal with immigration. This vast database system, housed in Strasbourg, consists of records on people's identities, as well as on lost or stolen property, which are entered by the Schengen member states and then accessed by other state agencies. Many of the persons listed in the SIS files to date are or have been asylum seekers. Agreements have been made that make it increasingly difficult for refugees and asylum seekers to gain entry to the EU and that increase cooperation on the surveillance, harassment, and deportation of so-called illegal immigrants.

FROM WELFARE STATE TO ENABLING STATE

Neil Gilbert (2002) has explored the ongoing international transformation of the role of the state in relation to market-oriented social policies, referring to it in the title of his book as—, "the silent surrender of public responsibility". Gilbert summarized this ongoing paradigmatic change in Table 65.1. He calls attention to the changing structural conditions that have a normative function for the welfare state programs. These are quite different from the conditions that formed the welfare state a few decades ago. International (and global) competition, the opening of new markets to

the private sector, and the need for a flexible labor force created a new framework for social welfare policies—indeed, a paradigmatic shift.

The observation that social welfare policies converge from the political Left to the Right has been obvious in, for instance, the United States, but is this the case for Europe as well? Would these welfare policy changes be relevant for the European development: (a) *Social inclusion* as the key to entering in the labor force; (b) *empowerment and activation* for finding (and taking) a job instead of relying on state-run welfare benefits, also known as workfare; (c) privatization of the welfare state through *contractual agreements* with private enterprises or NGOs; and (d) the attitude shift from *social rights to obligations*?

One answer to these questions is the UK development under the Labour Government, inspired by Anthony Giddens, as the third way between the conservative dismantling of welfare state and the socialist support for collectivism (Giddens, 1998). The key term here is *social investment state*, where human capital is emphasized as public investment instead of a public welfare safety net. But the true answer to the question about the European social policy movement at the end of the first decade of the twenty-first century is that the European nations have found idiosyncratic ways of handling the welfare state. Some social scientists have labeled this divergent development within a convergent welfare state concept under the broad concept of "welfare mix" (e.g., Powel & Barrientos, 2004). In the next section, models of welfare states are related to diverse paths that individual nations have chosen. The directions some Nordic countries have taken and some Central European nations have entered will be dealt with in sections that follow.

Ideal-Typical Models of Welfare State Policies

So far the focus of this chapter has been on general tendencies concerning social welfare issues on the European continent. The focus now shifts to specific movements in various parts of the European Union. A much-used model for classification is based on Esping-Andersen's well-known welfare state types (Esping-Andersen, 1990). However, this model has proved to be insufficient for describing the development of the welfare state in Europe and other parts of the world, such as Asia (e.g., Fenger, 2007; Korpi, 2004). The Swedish social scientists Walter Korpi and Joakim Palme (1998) developed ideal-type models for welfare state institutions that are useful for labeling

TABLE 65.1. SHIFT IN CENTRAL TENDENCIES FROM WELFARE STATE TO ENABLING STATE

Welfare State	Enabling State
Public provision	Privatization
Delivery by public agencies	Delivery by private agencies
Transfers in the form of service	Transfers in cash or vouchers
Focus on direct expenditures	Increase in indirect expenditures
Protection of labor	Promotion of work
Social support	Social inclusion
Decommodification of labor	Recommodification of labor
Unconditional benefits	Use of incentives and sanctions
Universal entitlement	Selective targeting
Avoidance of stigma	Restoration of social equity
Solidarity of citizenship	Solidarity of membership
Cohesion of shared rights	Cohesion of shared values and civic duties

Source: Gilbert, 2002, p. 44.

the courses that the current social policy in Europe has taken. The point of departure is the social insurance programs, with special emphasis on old-age pensions, sickness benefits, work-accident insurance, and unemployment insurance. The typology is based on the ways in which social citizenship rights in social insurance programs are defined (Korpi, 2004):

- The criteria used for determining the right to benefits
- The principles for determining the levels of benefits
- The form of governance for social insurance programs.

In Figure 65.1, the principal ideal types of welfare state institutions are outlined. It is not the intention here to provide a complete system for labeling the models of welfare states in the European nations. The aim is pedagogical—to show different ways of structuring the social rights of citizens in Europe.

The *targeted model* represents the classical poor laws where the state gives minimum benefits to people whose eligibility to receive assistance is determined by means testing. Australia is often pointed out as representing this model. In Europe, the model existed a few hundred years ago, but the view of social policy changed gradually during the twentieth century. A few former Communist countries under transition seem to follow this means-tested catering for the poor, which not only results in stigmatization of poor citizens but also, paradoxically, creates inequality, which it was originally set up to fight against (Korpi & Palme, 1998).

The *voluntary state-subsidized model* is also classical. The state provides voluntary organizations with tax money to aid members during unemployment or sickness. This institutional model is structured with the least involvement of the state. There is no nation member that can be classified under this model due to the high entrance threshold to the EU. Even if there is so far no common European social insurance model, there is consensus among the member states about the necessity of active state involvement (Korpi & Palme, 1998). But the model might still exist in some Central American countries, such as Guatemala.

The *corporatist model*, with roots in nineteenth-century Germany, emphasizes competition between occupational categories with earnings-related benefits. But it leaves some groups without insurance; for instance, the top income earners are expected to find private insurance solutions. This model seems to have become popular in certain parts of Central and Southern Europe, where family and small enterprises are important. This is not the so-called dual-earner model, which places both men and women in the labor market (Kangas & Palme, 2005); rather, its aim is to enable women to remain at home. Countries with this model include Germany, Austria, Belgium, Italy, and France as well as some of the former Communist countries under transition (Sotiropoulos, Neamtu, & Stoyanova, 2004).

The *basic security model* covers everyone with the same benefits regardless of earlier earnings. The United States, United Kingdom, Ireland, Netherlands, Switzerland, and Denmark are considered to represent this model.

Lastly, there is the *encompassing model*, which was developed in the Nordic countries during the 1950s and 1960s. Universal programs cover all citizens on an earnings-related basis. Norway, Sweden, and Finland (i.e., Scandinavian welfare state model) are current representatives of this model in Europe.

Antonen (2005) described the universalism of the Scandinavian encompassing welfare model as a *Scandinavian social care regime* with the following characteristics:

- There is a *public system* providing social care services.
- Services are available to *all citizens*, irrespective of economic status, gender, or ethnic background.
- The *middle and upper classes* are among the users of public social services.
- The service system at large responds to the *interests of women* (gender equality).
- The system offers *uniform services* all over the country (regional equality).
- Services are produced by *professional care workers*.
- Citizens have *rights* to some social care services.
- Services are delivered *free of charge*, or they are heavily subsidized by local or central governments.
- The *municipalities* are responsible for service provision and the financing of services.

This Scandinavian social care regime is not only a dual-earner model, it also compensates single parents so that they have access to the same economic situation as other families. It is based on a high tax system

Targeted

Minimum state benefits to people in need
based on means test.

Voluntary Subsidized

The state supports voluntary organizations to provide benefits
to sick or unemployed members.

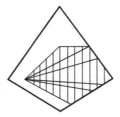

Corporatist

Benefits are related to previous earnings,
but conditions and modes of financing vary
among programs for industrial workers,
farmers, and so on in different conditions.

Basic Security

All are insured in the same program
with flat-rate benefits.

Encompassing

All are insured in the same program with earnings-related benefits.

The diamond-shaped figures represent the socioeconomic structure of the population with the
poor on the bottom and the rich on the top. White surface represents people outside insurance
program; horizontal lines represent flat-rate benefits; vertical lines represent benefits that are
related to previous earnings.

FIGURE 65.1: Ideal-typical models of welfare state institutions (after Korpi, 2004).

that, on a comparison level, results in a high-equality society through income redistribution (Goul Andersen et al., 2002; Korpi & Palme, 1998).

THE EUROPEAN WELFARE STATE DISCOURSE: WINNERS AND LOSERS IN THE FUTURE

Viewed from the European perspective, discourse at the policy level seems to be advocating the establishment of a supranational social policy based on the principles of partnership, pluralism, subsidiarity, and enablement (Council of Europe, 2003), representing a mixture of European welfare state models. These principles are not further elaborated in the Council of Europe documents; rather, they are mentioned as underlying future policy development. The wide diversity of the current twenty-seven European nations necessitates compromise if a supranational social policy is to be implemented, which by no means is a sure thing. The fear of losing social benefits in the process of integration could, for some member nations, be a reason for strong opposition to any departure from national responsibility (Mau, 2005).

What can we expect to be the future direction of social policy in Europe? The principle of *partnership* on the national level entails establishing principles to regulate relationships on both the vertical and the horizontal plane. The vertical plane—modifying the relationship between the state and local authorities with decentralization in mind—could become a major challenge in some nations (e.g., those in the former Soviet Union) and less so or no challenge at all in other nations (e.g., Sweden, which has the most decentralized relationship between state and community government in Europe). On the horizontal plane, the partnership principle refers to the relationships among the various stakeholders (e.g., NGOs) involved in financing and providing a wide range of social services that at times might reflect conflicting social policies.

The principle of *pluralism*, which refers to the state of art in Europe where "there is no one best model for social services financing and provision" (Mau, 2005, p. 175), calls for a model that is adjusted to the contextual conditions. The principle of *subsidiarity* refers to the mainstream of European policy to "enforce minimum social services provision and standards" (Mau, 2005, p. 175), which some governments interpret as the need to increase standards and social responsibility and others as the need to lower the state's social responsibility.

Lastly, the principle of *enablement* refers to current trends in social welfare states, but not necessarily all of them, as was proposed in another section of this chapter. The ongoing privatization and fragmentization of social work has been described as a general phenomenon that is due to neoliberal influences (Dominelli, 2004). These tendencies have created new poverty pockets in the transitional nations, primarily those EU members that were part of former the former Soviet Union (Innocenti Social Monitor, 2006).

These points of departure open up for generalizations across borders and call for a dialogue between international social work stakeholders. One basis for comparison could be the manner and extent to which social work in different countries tackles the task of implementing human rights conventions. Globalization (and especially Europeanization) has consequences for both diversity and standardization in many areas of proactive endeavor, including social work (Lorenz, 2001). Attention must be given to the unique features of each phenomenon for which some kind of action is to be decided on and carried out in line with the previous discussion. Examples are the varying needs of minorities and indigenous people compared with those of other groups in society (essentialism). But it is also necessary to focus on those phenomena that are universal (where we are all alike in basic needs), as expressed in the Universal Declaration of Human Rights and other ratified conventions such as the Convention on the Rights of the Child (Beck, 2007; Hessle, in press).

REFERENCES

Antonen, A. (2005). Empowering social policy: The role of social care services in modern welfare states. In O. Kangas & J. Palme (Eds.), *Social policy and economic development in the Nordic countries* (pp. 88–117). New York: UNRISD and Palgrave Macmillan.

Beck, U. (2007). *Cosmopolitan vision*. Cambridge: Polity Press.

Council of Europe. (2003). *The role of social services in sustainable social development*. Berlin, October 2001.

Dominelli, L. (2004). *Social work: Theory and practice for a changing profession*. Cambridge: Polity Press.

Dominelli, L. (1998). Multiculturalism, anti-racism and social work in Europe. In C. Williams, H. Soydan, & M. R. D. Johnson (Eds.), *Social work and minorities* (pp. 36–57). London: Routledge.

Esping-Andersen, G. (1990). *The three worlds of welfare capitalism*. Cambridge: Polity Press.

Fenger, H. J. M. (2007). Welfare regimes in Central and Eastern Europe: Incorporating post-communist countries in a welfare regime policy. *Contemporary Issues and Ideas in Social Sciences, 3*(2), 36–57.

Giddens, A. (1998). *The third way: The renewal of social democracy*. London: Polity Press.

Gilbert, N. (2002). *Transformation of the welfare state: The silent surrender of public responsibility*. New York: Oxford University Press.

Goul Andersen, J., Clasen, J., van Oorschot, W., & Halvorsen, K. (2002). *Europe's new state of welfare*. Bristol: Policy Press.

Hessle, S. (2008). *Dialog, Kolonisering och Agency Mindset—en utmaning för internationellt socialt utvecklingsarbete* [Dialogue, colonization and agency mindset—a challenge for international development social work]. *Nordisk Socialt Arbeid, 28*, 207–221.

Hessle, S., & Zavirsek, D. (Eds.). (2005). *Sustainable development in social work: The case of a regional network in the Balkans*. Int. proj. No. 5. Stockholm: Department of Social Work, Stockholm University.

Innocenti Social Monitor. (2006). *Understanding child poverty in South-Eastern Europe and the Commonwealth of Independent States*. Retrieved December, 18, 2008, from http://ideas.repec.org/p/ucf/insomo/insomo06-8.html.

Jordan, B. (2008). *Welfare and well-being-Social value in public policy.* Bristol: Policy Press.

Kangas, O., & Palme, J. (Eds.). (2005). *Social policy and economic development in the Nordic countries.* New York: UNRISD and Palgrave Macmillan.

Korpi, W. (2004). The Japanese welfare system in an international perspective. In N. Mauro, A. Björklund, & C. Le Grand (Eds.), *Welfare policy and labour markets* (pp. 47–69). Stockholm: Almqvist och Wiksell International.

Korpi, W., & Palme, J. (1998). The paradox of redistribution and strategies of equality: Welfare state institutions, inequality and poverty in the Western countries. *American Sociological Review, 63,* 661–687.

Lorenz, W. (2001). Social work in Europe: Portrait of a diverse professional group. In S. Hessle (Ed.), *International standard setting of higher social work education* (pp. 9–24). Stockholm Studies on Social Work, No. 17. Stockholm: Stockholm University.

Lorenz, W. (1994). *Social work in a changing Europe.* London: Routledge.

Mau, S. (2005). Democratic demand for a social Europe? Preferences of the European citicenry. *International Journal of Social Welfare, 14,* 76–85.

Orbie, J., & Babarinde, O. (2008). The social dimension of globalisation and EU development policy: Promoting core labour standards and corporate social responsibility. *Journal of European Integration, 30*(3), 459–477.

Powel, M., & Barrientos, A. (2004). Welfare regimes and the welfare mix. *European Journal of Political Research, 43,* 83–105.

Sjöberg, O., & Ferrarini, T. (in press). Welfare state development and health in transition countries. *International Journal of Social Welfare.*

Sotiropoulos, D. A., Neamtu, I., & Stoyanova, M. (2004). The trajectory of post-communist welfare state development: The cases of Bulgaria and Romania. In P. Taylor-Gooby (Ed.), *Making a European welfare state* (pp. 114–130). Oxford: Blackwell.

Taylor-Gooby, P. (Ed.). (2004). *Making a European welfare state.* Oxford: Blackwell.

WEBSITES

Asylum statistics: http://ec.europa.eu/justice_home/doc_centre/asylum/statistics/docs/2003/2003_annual_statistics_report.pdf.

Copenhagen criteria: Copenhagen criteria: http://www.europarl.europa.eu/enlargement/ec/pdf/cop_en.pdf

European Council: www.european-council.europa.eu.

Innocenti Social Monitoring: http://ideas.repec.org/p/ucf/insomo/insomo06-8.html.

SECTION X

Human Rights

Overview of Human Rights: The UN Conventions and Machinery

JOSEPH WRONKA

The International Federation of Social Workers (IFSW) has called social work a "human rights profession, having as its basic tenet the intrinsic value of every human being" (United Nations, 1994, p. 3). The United States National Association of Social Workers (NASW) states that it "endorses the fundamental principles set forth in human rights documents of the United Nations. . . . [And that] human rights be adopted as a foundation[al] principle upon which all of social work theory and applied knowledge rests" (Falk, 1999, p. 17). Countries of the European and African Union, moreover, have developed laws and policies with guidance from human rights documents.

HUMAN RIGHTS FROM THE ASHES OF WORLD WAR II

This powerful social construct, "human rights," now a legal mandate to fulfill human need, emerged from the ashes of World War II. To thwart the Nazi rise to power, there was an international conference at Evian (1938). It ended in failure, because countries did not want to attract attention to their own abuses, such as public lynchings and genocide against Indigenous Peoples in the United States, concentration camps for political dissidents in the Soviet Union, and oppression in Europe's vast colonial empires (Buergenthal, Sheldon, & Stewart, 2002). What occurred as a result was a massacre of ten million, primarily Jews but also Poles, homosexuals, gypsies, and others inimical to the Third Reich, and an estimated seventy-two million killed in that war overall.

For this to never happen again, the United Nations was formed on October 24, 1945. Initially, governments were reluctant to include human rights in its inaugural mandate, the UN Charter, but with the efforts of forty-two nongovernmental organizations (NGOs), they elected Eleanor Roosevelt as chair of a committee that drew up the Universal Declaration of Human Rights, endorsed by the General Assembly with no dissent on December 10, 1948. Now, more than seventy years after Evian, no government would dare say it is against human rights.

INITIAL PROVISOS

People tend to equate violations of human rights with events taking place outside their country of origin. Public discourse may have domestically defined such violations as the misuse of psychiatry in Russia against political dissidents, government crackdowns in Tiananmen Square, female genital mutilation (FGM) in Somalia, and rapes in Darfur. Certainly, these issues are of paramount importance, a gross nature, massive, and revelatory of states' failures to remedy them domestically, major criteria of human rights violations.

Although humanitarian concern should be the basis for advancing human rights, caveats often arise. Government hypocrisy might blind a country to its own psychiatric abuses, as reportedly during the war in Vietnam, US bomber pilots refusing further bombing missions were found mentally ill. Cultural and economic imperialism may have been the basis for media attention to massacres in Tiananmen Square, the final coup the free market needed to make inroads into Communist China; pretext for invasion of Somalia in 1993 may have increased concern for FGM, practiced by 95% of the population; and concern over genocide in Darfur perhaps a masquerade for a desire to control oil reserves there (Wronka, 2008).

Like a sphinx, such provisos challenge us, calling ultimately for courage and the vision of the eagle, as the great spiritual sage of the Sioux, Tashunkewitko, commonly known as Crazy Horse, reminds us ("Crazy Horse/Tashunkewitko," 2006). But, we must always remember that social justice, with human rights as its bedrock, is struggle. The sport is worth the candle.

THE HUMAN RIGHTS TRIPTYCH

To adequately understand the meaning of human rights, it is best to refer to what Rene Cassin, often called the Father of Human Rights, identified as the "human rights triptych" (Szabo, 1982). At the central panel is the Universal Declaration of Human Rights, the authoritative definition of human rights standards, which the late Pope John Paul II referred to as a "milestone in the long and difficult struggle of the human race" (Daughters of St. Paul, 1979). On the right side are documents that have followed the Universal Declaration, which elaborate upon its principles and tend to have more juridical force; on the left side are implementation mechanisms, which commonly monitor a country's compliance with human rights principles.

This triptych can help the global community move toward a human rights culture, which is a "lived awareness" of such principles in one's mind, heart, and body, dragged into our everyday lives. This journey from the mind to heart, ultimately affecting our local and global communities, is undoubtedly a struggle. Moving toward such a culture would entail fundamental changes in the consciousness of humanity. In the end it is about viewing the human person holistically, calling for the empowerment and liberation of all peoples to enhance the well-being and fulfill the human needs of every person, everywhere, yet, within the confines of global commons, calling for an equitable distribution of resources. Such a culture, in which social work can play a major role, is entirely consistent with recent joint statement of principles of the ethics of social work by IFSW and IASSW (International Association of Schools of Social Work), which assert in Article 2, "Principles of human rights and social justice are fundamental to social work."

The Universal Declaration of Human Rights

Written for the educated layperson, not the doctorate in jurisprudence, the Universal Declaration, a philosophical and historical compromise, consists of five crucial notions. The first is *human dignity*, emphasized in Article 1, which comes from numerous religious belief systems, such as Buddhism, Confucianism, Hinduism, and the Judeo-Christian-Islamic tradition. The second is *nondiscrimination*, an expected corollary. Thus, all humans have dignity regardless of "race, color, sex, language, religion, political or other opinion, national or social origin, property, birth or other status," as stated in Article 2.

The third notion is *civil and political rights*, or first generation or negative rights, as stated in Articles 3 through 21, asserting the liberty to pursue the quest for dignity and nondiscrimination, free from the abuse of political authority. Mirroring struggles of the Age of the Enlightenment, examples are freedoms of religion, speech, the press, expression, and peaceful assembly. The fourth notion is *economic, social, and cultural rights*, or second generation or positive rights. Mirroring struggle of the Age of Industrialization, Articles 22 through 27 assert government obligations to provide for basic necessities to ensure an existence worthy of human dignity, such as socially useful work at a reasonable wage, adequate shelter, rest and leisure, food, health care, and security in old age.

The fifth notion is *solidarity rights*, calling for individual duties and intergovernmental cooperation, that is, a "just social and international order." Articles 28 through 30 reflect the failure of domestic sovereignty in the mid-twentieth century and have come to mean rights to a clean environment, development, global distributive justice, peace, humanitarian disaster relief, self-determination, and the common and cultural heritages of humanity, like the oceans, space, and religious places of worship (Wronka, 2008).

Ultimately, these rights are interdependent and indivisible. What good is freedom of speech if a person is homeless or lives in a world at war? Whereas President Obama did mention the generally lesser known economic, social, and cultural rights in his acceptance of the 2009 Nobel Peace Prize in Oslo, his speech lacked mention of peace as a human right. The Universal Declaration is now increasingly referred to as *customary international law*, especially since *Filártiga v. Peña-Irala* (1980), in which a US federal court ruled against a torturer in Paraguay. All countries must abide by its principles. Recently, the Women's International League for Peace and Freedom (WILPF), of which Jane Addams, sometimes called the Mother of Social Work, was the first president, has advocated for a thirty-first article on the right to clean water (2009).

Guiding Principles, Declarations, and Conventions

On the right panel of the triptych are documents tending to expand upon principles of the Universal Declaration, a "good . . . not perfect document," according to Eleanor Roosevelt (United Nations Dept. of Public Information, 1950). They are sometimes called *guiding principles*, which may become *declarations*, then *conventions* or *covenants*. The latter have the most juridical force, with the status of treaty, as is the UN Charter. The US Constitution's Supremacy Clause, Article VI, calls treaties "the Supreme Law of the land . . . [with] judges bound thereby" (Weissbrodt, Fitzpatrick, & Newman, 2001).

Only chosen values endure; nothing substitutes for a global human rights culture. Yet, conventions with monitoring committees, informing governments of human rights violations, are extremely powerful in moving toward such a culture. Becoming signatory is a first step toward ratification. But, even when ratified, governments may include a non-self-executing clause, making the convention nonenforceable in domestic courts, giving it simply symbolic significance (Steiner, Alston, & Goodman, 2007). For example, the International Covenant on Civil and Political Rights asserts in Article 6 that the death penalty shall not be imposed for crimes committed by persons below eighteen years of age. Although ratified by the United States in 1994, the country still executed persons for crimes committed as children, defined as under eighteen in international law, violating the Supremacy Clause. Because ratification stipulated non-self-execution, it was necessary to enact a domestic law to implement the provisions of the convention. The Supreme Court did just that in its *Roper v. Simmons* decision (2005), prohibiting the execution of persons for crimes committed before eighteen, indicating that acts of symbolic significance can have lasting effects.

Eglantyne Jebb, a social worker, drafted documents that later became known as the Declaration of the Rights of the Child (1959), now the Convention on the Rights of the Child (1991) (Healy, 2008). Presently, there are the Guiding Principles on Extreme Poverty and Human Rights, which IFSW and IASSW urged at the sixteenth session of the Human Rights Council (2011) to move toward an international Convention to Abolish Extreme Poverty (CAEP). There is also the Declaration on the Rights of Indigenous Peoples (2007), which social work organizations worldwide hope will become a legally binding convention. In some instances, conventions incorporate the principles of other documents, as occurred when the Convention on the Rights of Persons with Disabilities incorporated the Principles for the Protection of Persons with Mental Illness (1991) and Principles of Medical Ethics relevant to the Role of Health Personnel.

Currently there are eight major human rights conventions: *(1)* the International Convention on the Elimination of All Forms of Racial Discrimination (CERD), 1969; *(2)* the International Covenant on Civil and Political Rights (ICCPR), 1976 *(3)* the International Covenant on Economic, Social and Cultural Rights (ICESCR), 1976; *(4)* the Convention on the Elimination of All Forms of Discrimination Against Women (CEDAW), 1981; *(5)* the Convention against Torture and Other Cruel, Inhuman or Degrading Treatment or Punishment (CAT), 1987; *(6)* the Convention on the Rights of the Child (CRC), 1990; *(7)* the International Convention on the Protection of the Rights of All Migrant Workers and Members of Their Families (CMW), 1993; and *(8)* the Convention on the Rights of Persons with Disabilities (CPD), 2007. (All of these human rights documents can be found in their entirety at www2.ohchr.org/english/law/.)

Like all human rights documents, the conventions have core principles that they elaborate upon. The ICCPR and ICESCR, for instance, assert the principle of self-determination, which they elaborate as "the right of people to freely determine their political status, freely pursue their economic, social, and cultural development and dispose of their natural wealth based on the principle of mutual benefit . . . [and] to enjoy their own culture or to use their own language."

Following are select themes of select conventions (Wronka, 2008). The ICCPR speaks of such rights as *(1) the right to life*, that no person who commits a crime under eighteen and no pregnant woman shall be given the death penalty; *(2) the prohibition against slavery*; and *(3) the obligations of states to realize civil and political rights*, such as nondiscrimination and the equality of men and women.

The ICESCR asserts *(1) the right to work*, meaning full and productive employment and fair wages to ensure a decent living for families; *(2) protections for the family and children*, including paid leave for working mothers before and after childbirth; *(3) the right to the highest attainable standard of physical and mental health*, including the reduction of infant mortality and the improvement of mental hygiene; and *(4) the right to an adequate standard of living*, including improving the methods of production, conservation, and distribution of food and dissemination of the principles of nutrition.

The CRC asserts *(1) nondiscrimination of the child*, that every human under eighteen shall be respected irrespective of the child's, parent's, or legal guardian's race, color, sex, language, and so on; *(2) the best interests of the child are the primary consideration*, that the child has the right to maintain contact with both parents unless contrary to the child's best interests; *(3) economic, social, and cultural rights*, that every child shall have a standard of living adequate for the child's physical, mental, spiritual, moral, and social development; *(4) the right to registration and respect of identity*, which shall be carried out immediately after birth; *(5) the treatment of children in a positive, humane, and expeditious manner*, particularly in regard to family reunification, with no illicit transfer and nonreturn of children; *(6) respect for the views of the child*, giving due weight to the child's maturity; *(7) respect for civil and political rights of children*, with no undue attacks on a child's reputation, with proper acknowledgment of the parents' right to choose a child's religion, with no arbitrary interference with a child's privacy, and with freedom of expression orally in writing or in art, restricted only for the rights of others and protection of public health or morals; and *(8) the importance of the media*, from a diversity of national and international resources, with particular regard to linguistic needs, protected from materials injurious to the child's well-being, with children's books encouraged, produced, and disseminated.

CEDAW asserts *(1) the equality of men and women* in education, employment, policy formation, and before the law; *(2) the modification of cultural and social patterns* to eliminate the idea of superiority or inferiority of either sex; *(3) nondiscrimination on the grounds of maternity and marital status*, with paid maternity leave and prohibition against dismissal on the basis of pregnancy or marital situation; *(4) states' obligations to enable parents to combine family obligations with outside work responsibilities and participation in public life*, including information on nutrition and lactation during pregnancy, the development of facilities for child care, and appropriate services in connection with pregnancy, confinement, and the postnatal period, with free services when necessary; *(5) elimination of discrimination in economic and social life*, including rights to bank loans, mortgages, other forms of financial credit, and participation in recreational activities and all aspects of cultural life; and *(6) particular attention to the situation of rural women*, including the right to self-help groups and cooperatives to obtain equal access to economic opportunities.

Implementation

Implementation is the human rights machinery of the UN. The oil that greases the machine is the political will of the people, which has crystallized into human choices and then rights. Overseeing this entire machinery to formulate and implement human rights principles is the Office of the High Commissioner for Human Rights, established in 1993, who reports to the Secretary-General. Although every organ of the UN concerns itself with human rights in the final analysis, two main implementation mechanisms are monitoring committees for conventions and the Universal Periodic Review (UPR), established in 2007 by the newly formed Human Rights Council in 2006.

Committees cite positive aspects and areas of concern, asking governments that ratified conventions to engage in creative dialogue. Select positive aspects may include citing successes of affirmative action plans (US in response to CERD, 2001); the establishment of a zero-tolerance standard for rape in prisons (US, CAT, 2006); the extension of parental benefits from six months to a year (Canada, ICESCR, 2006); passing the Human Rights Act of 1999 incorporating the covenant into domestic law (Norway, ICESCR, 2007); congratulating the country on its first female president as well as for having 50% women ministers (Chile, CEDAW, 2007); noting with satisfaction the first Arab Israeli citizen appointed to the cabinet and steps to accommodate different cultural and religious traditions of minorities in the workplace (Israel, CERD, 2007); and changes in the penal code criminalizing child pornography, sex tourism, sexual abuse, and trafficking in persons (Morocco, CRC, 2006).

Select examples of areas of concern are that the state does not see the convention applicable in the context of armed conflict (US, CAT, 2006); the persistent discrimination against women with regard to education, equal rights of both spouses within marriage, and management of family assets (Congo, ICCPR, 2006); the persistence of profound structural social and economic inequalities affecting the enjoyment of human rights, particularly economic and social rights, and particularly affecting Afro-descendants and Indigenous Peoples (Venezuela, CERD, 2007); an ineffective birth registration system and lack of parental consent for recruitment of under-eighteens in the military (Bangladesh, CRC, 2006); and deep concern regarding children working in hazardous occupations such as mining, often in precarious conditions that fall short of labor safety standards (China, CESCR, 2006). (UN member states' reports to human rights monitoring committees can be found at www.unhchr.ch/tbs/doc.nsf/newhvdocsbytreaty?OpenView).

Recently initiated by the Human Rights Council, the major nucleus of human rights activity, every four years the UPR monitors all 192 member states' compliance with human rights. Briefly, each state relates before the 47 member states of the Human Rights Council steps taken to advance rights, including a sharing of best human rights practices throughout the world. Recently, Mexico (2009) discussed measures taken to eradicate extreme poverty, the fact that its constitution gives international treaties superiority over federal and local law, and the fact that the federal government has shifted from a welfare approach to a rights-based approach to address needs of vulnerable groups. Delegates recommended that Mexico ensure the full realization of rights of immigrants and address more fully the problems pertaining to high infant mortality and malnutrition among Indigenous peoples. (UPR can be found at www.ohchr.org/EN/HRBodies/UPR/Pages/UPRMain.aspx.)

There are also thematic and country reports by special rapporteurs who present before the Council. Examples of thematic reports include those on extreme poverty and human rights (1996); the right to food (2000); the right to adequate housing (2001); the rights of Indigenous peoples (2001); the human genome (2004); and the sale of children, child prostitution, and child pornography (2008). Examples of country reports include the Palestinian territories (1993), Haiti (1995), Afghanistan (2001), Sudan (2001), Burundi (2003), and Iraq (2003). There is also the 1503 confidential procedure, which, in private forums, has examined situations in roughly ninety countries. This procedure may have played a substantial role in ending *de jure* apartheid in South Africa and the dirty civil wars of Latin America. (Thematic and country reports can be found at www2.ohchr.org/english/bodies/chr/special/index.htm.)

Other UN bodies, such as the General Assembly, Security Council, World Bank, and World Court, also deal with human rights violations. The most notable may be the World Court, which in 2004 asserted that the Palestinian territories were illegally occupied by Israel. But, the General Assembly, which has a one-nation, one-vote policy, may be the most reflective of world opinion.

Ultimately, the mobilization of world opinion to eradicate human rights violations and move toward the creation of a human rights culture is the most important tool of implementation. Information is power. The paradox that thinking is doing is poignant in this struggle for social justice with human rights at its core. Thus, human rights education and world conferences can also play a major role. Human rights education must be broadly construed, including not only formal venues from grammar school to university levels but also informally in families and the media. Norway, for example, flashes a right from the CRC with a brief discussion in between children's cartoons.

This is in contradistinction to the questionable practice of advertising on children's programming, which places the priority on having instead of being, something the French existentialist Gabriel Marcel (1949) presaged as a growing obstruction to human development. Because it is difficult to change values once inculcated, working with youth appears especially vital.

Most recent world conferences, such as in Copenhagen (2009) on climate change, Rome (2009) on food, and Geneva (2009) on racism, and previous ones in Hyogo, Japan, (2005) on disaster reduction; in Johannesburg (2002) on sustainability; and in Beijing (1995) on women attest to our global interconnectedness and the power of the human spirit to overcome adversity. Ultimately, any widespread dissemination of information as it relates to human rights can influence world opinion. The challenge is to make the world aware of human rights in educated layperson's language, as Eleanor Roosevelt urged, rather than elitist terminology, and for the world to live these principles. See Table 66.1 for a summary of these means of implementation.

BEYOND UN CONVENTIONS AND MACHINERY

Regional Developments

Regional developments consist of the African Union (AU), the Organization of American States (OAS), and the Council of Europe (CE), each with its own human rights triptychs. The AU has at its center the African Charter on Human and Peoples' Rights, followed by such documents as the Protocol on the Rights of Women in Africa and the African Charter on the Rights and Welfare of Children. The African Charter also speaks of "the unquestionable and inalienable right to self-determination . . . [and that] colonized and oppressed peoples shall have the right to free themselves from the bonds of domination" (Article 20), calling up states to "undertake to eliminate all forms of foreign economic exploitation particularly that practiced by international monopolies" (Article 21).

The OAS has the American Convention on Human Rights, followed by such conventions as the Inter-American Convention to Prevent and Punish Torture and the Inter-American Convention on the Prevention, Punishment and Eradication of Violence Against Women. The Council of Europe has the most extensively developed human rights machinery. The most poignant document is the European Social

TABLE 66.1. SELECT MEANS OF IMPLEMENTATION FOR
THE HUMAN RIGHTS MACHINERY OF THE UN

Mechanism[1]	Definition
High Commissioner for Human Rights	Office that oversees all of the activities pertaining to human rights activities at the UN
Human rights monitoring committees	Select groups of independent experts whose aim is to engage in creative dialogue with governments, citing positive aspects and areas of concern pertaining to conventions ratified
Universal Periodic Review (UPR)	A process whereby every four years, states must submit before the Human Rights Council steps they have taken to advance human rights
Thematic reports	Assessments of exceptionally serious human rights issues by special rapporteurs that require the cooperation of governments
Country reports	Assessments of a country's human rights record where the situation appears gross, widespread, and unresponsive to domestic remedies
1503 procedure	Confidential process that examines situations in countries similar to those that are subject to country reports
Shadow reports	Reports by NGO's usually in tandem with other concerned groups and individuals that generally supplement reports by governments
Mobilization of world opinion	The penultimate means of implementation, brought about by human rights education, world conferences, and any widespread sharing of human rights materials through technological and other means.

[1]Note that these mechanisms are basically formalized and institutionalized. The forum of the UN and other regional international provide excellent opportunities for creative dialogue and ultimately values transformation consistent with human dignity and rights in the global community. (See, for example, http://www.un.org/webcast/unhrc/archive.asp?go=0146 or links to other links to human rights reports and organizations at www.humanrightsculture.org)

Charter of 1999, which strongly supports second generation rights, delineating roughly forty rights in such areas as social welfare services, dignity at work, and the right to protection against poverty and social exclusion. A major challenge is to create similar regional developments in Asia, the Middle East, and Oceania. The recent 2007 Association of the South East Asian Nations (ASEAN) which expresses adherence to fundamental human rights principles is a step in the right direction.

Implications for Advanced Generalist Social Work Practice

Human rights principles have relevance to every level of social work theory and practice (Ife, 2007; Reichert, 2003, 2006, 2007; Wronka, 2008). Using the advanced generalist social work model, first, there is the meta-macro level, necessitating global interventions. The practitioner can refer to the Universal Declaration that calls for the sharing of scientific advancement in the global community as an argument to give medications to alleviate the effects of AIDS to those unable to afford them in the poorest countries. On the macro (whole-population) level, one can advocate for human

rights education from the elementary to graduate levels, which might eventually create a cultural shift to advance the cause of the lesser known economic, social, cultural, and solidarity rights.

On the meso level, which deals with at-risk populations such as parents before and after childbirth and preschool children, the principles of CEDAW can serve as a basis for governments to provide quality day care and create structural adjustments so families can participate in raising families and working in formalized employment. On the micro level, documents such as the CPD can serve as a guide for effective clinical practice and to inform clients of treatment alternatives, elicit client input, and provide medications to children for their well-being rather than the convenience of adults. On the meta-micro level, which speaks to the realm of the personal and everyday life, human rights can assist in fostering the healing power of support groups and creating communities of compassion. Research action projects can compare the Universal Declaration with constitutions, as in Wronka (1998), revealing significant gaps in the areas of economic and social rights in US federal and state constitutions, urging bills to monitor executive, judicial, and legislative movements toward compliance with human rights standards.

In sum, the human rights profession of social work can legally mandate human need through this powerful social construct arising from the ashes of World War II. caveats, such as governmental hypocrisy, might arise. Yet, human rights principles as elucidated in the human rights triptych, with the Universal Declaration at its core, can serve as effective guides for social work theory and practice, from the meta-macro to meta-micro levels of intervention, with the aim of creating a human rights culture—that is, a lived awareness of these principles in our minds and hearts, carried into our everyday lives.

REFERENCES

Buergenthal, T., Sheldon, D., & Stewart, D. (2002). *Human rights in a nutshell*. St. Paul, MN: West.

Crazy Horse/Tashunkewitko. (2006). Indigenous People's Literature. Retrieved January 15, 2006, from www.indians.org/welker/crazyhor.htm.

Daughters of St. Paul. (1979). USA: The message of justice, peace, and love: Pope John Paul II. Boston: St. Paul Editions.

Falk, D. (1999). International policy on human rights. *NASW News, 44*(3), 17.

Filártiga v. Peña-Irala, 630 F.2d 876 (2d Cir. 1980), 30 June 1980.

Healy, L. (2008). *International social work: Professional action in an interdependent world* (2nd ed.). New York: Oxford University Press.

Ife, J. (2007). *Human rights and social work: Towards rights based practice* (2nd ed.). New York: Cambridge University Press.

Marcel, G. (1949). *Being and having: Etre = avoir*. Westminster: Dacre.

Reichert, E. (Ed.). (2007). *Challenges in human rights: A social work perspective*. New York: Columbia University Press.

Reichert, E. (2006). *Understanding human rights: An exercise book*. Thousand Oaks, CA: Sage.

Reichert, E. (2003). *Social work and human rights: A foundation for policy and practice*. New York: Columbia University Press.

Roper v. Simmons, 543 U.S. 551 (2005).

Steiner, H., Alston, P., & Goodman, R. (2007). *International human rights in context: Law, politics, morals* (3rd ed.). New York: Oxford University Press.

Szabo, I. (1982). Historical foundations of human rights and subsequent developments. In K. Vasak (Ed.), *The international dimensions of human rights* (Vol. 1, pp. 11–41). Westport, CT: Greenwood.

United Nations. (1994). *Human rights and social work: A manual for schools of social work and the social work profession*. New York: Author.

United Nations Dept. of Public Information. (1950). These rights and freedoms. *United Nations Weekly Bulletin*, November 1, 1948–January 15, 1949.

Weissbrodt, D., Fitzpatrick, J., & Newman, F. (2001). *International human rights: Law, policy, and process* (3rd ed.). Cincinnati, OH: Anderson.

Women's International League for Peace and Freedom (WILPF). (2009). Letter to Obama. Retrieved February 14, 2009, from www.wilpf.org/priorities4obama.

Wronka, J. (2008). *Human rights and social justice: Social action and service for the helping and health professions*. Thousand Oaks, CA: Sage.

Wronka, J. (1998). *Human rights and social policy in the 21st century: A history of the idea of human rights and comparison of the Universal Declaration of Human Rights with United States federal and state constitutions* (2nd ed.). Newbury Park, CA: University Press of America.

ADDITIONAL RESOURCES

Websites

Author's website: www.humanrightsculture.org.

Human Rights Education Associates: www.hrea.org/index.php.

International Fourth World Movement, dedicated to the eradication of extreme poverty: www.atd-fourthworld.org.

Resource Center for Human Rights and Social Work at the University of Carbondale: http://socialwork.siuc.edu/resourcecenter/welcome.htm.

University of Minnesota Human Rights Library: www1.umn.edu/humanrts/.

Further Reading

Buitenweg, R. (2007). *Human rights, human plights in the global village*. Atlanta: Clarity.

Farmer, P. (2004). *Pathologies of power: Health, human rights, and the new war on the poor*. Berkeley, CA: University of California Press.

Fellmeth, R. (2006). *Child rights and remedies*. Atlanta: Clarity.

Gil, D. (1998). *Confronting social injustice: Concepts and strategies for social workers*. New York: Columbia University Press.

International Federation of Social Work (IFSW). (2003). *Human rights and the rights of the child*. Berne, Switzerland: Author.

International Fourth World. (2007). *The merging of knowledge: People in poverty and academics thinking together*. Newbury Park, CA: University Press of America.

International Human Rights Internship Program and Asian Forum for Human Rights and Development. (2000). *Circle of rights: Economic, social, and cultural rights activism: A training resource*. Washington, DC: Author.

Lifton, R. (2000). *The Nazi doctors: Medical killing and the psychology of genocide.* New York: Basic Books.

Northeastern University Program on Human Rights and Global Law. (2007). *Human rights for all: A training resource on the local implementation of international human rights to protect human dignity and freedom.* Boston: Author.

Pogge, T. (2002). *World poverty and human rights: Cosmopolitan responsibilities and reforms.* Maldon, MA: Polity.

Symonides, J. (2005). *Human rights: International protection, monitoring, enforcement.* New Delhi: Rawat.

United Nations. (1997). *Human rights and law enforcement: A manual on human rights training for the police.* Geneva: Author.

United Nations High Commissioner for Human Rights. (2005). *Economic, social, and cultural rights: Handbook for national human rights institutions.* Geneva: Author.

United Nations High Commissioner for Refugees. (2006). *Human rights and refugee protection.* Geneva: Author.

Wronka, J. (2003). *The Dr. Ambedkar Lectures on the theme, creating a human rights culture.* Bhubaneswar, India: National Institute of Social Sciences and Social Work Press.

Women and the Human Rights Framework

ELISABETH REICHERT

Around the world, empowering women is now widely considered essential to expanding
economic growth, reducing poverty, improving public health, sustaining the environment, and
consolidating transitions from tyranny to democracy. A near-universal consensus is calling for
fundamental changes in practices that have denied rights to women for centuries.

CHESLER, *2004, pp. A27–A28*

A primary goal of the social work profession is to work with diverse populations. Perhaps the largest of these populations encompasses women and the girl child. Historically, this population has encountered significant discrimination.

Women perform two-thirds of the world's work but earn only one-tenth of all income and own less than one-tenth of the world's property. Two-thirds of the children in the world who are not receiving an education are girls. Women constitute the majority of the world's poor as defined by income level. The number of women living in absolute poverty (i.e., life-threatening poverty) has risen by 50 percent over the last two decades as opposed to 30 percent for men (Human Rights Watch World Report, 2001, p. 456). Because of their greater incidence of poverty, women do not always receive adequate health care. Socioeconomic factors, as well as chance genetic inheritance and geographical availability of nutritional resources, determine a person's health status. Relatively affluent people and those content with their lives enjoy better health status than impoverished and oppressed people who suffer a poor self-image in addition to the disrespect they may encounter in their communities (Deller, 2008; Ife, 2008).

Today, women remain economically disadvantaged in most countries, which makes them both vulnerable to violence and unable to escape it. The correlation between gender and poverty is a problem in all countries, not simply those that are less economically developed (Bissio, 2005; Ishay, 2004; Wetzel, 2007).

Women not only lack power in relation to men, they also encounter diversity of power within their own gender. For instance, a married woman with an upper-class status will likely possess greater privileges in society than an unmarried woman or even a married woman reliant on public assistance. The woman with upper-class status obviously has many more doors open to her in terms of housing, education, esteem within the community, and other opportunities. Such imbalance of power does not occur simply at the individual level; society, government, religious institutions, and other forces maintain this imbalance, which is frequently directed against particular groups, including those based on income (Beneria, 2003; Reichert, 2003).

A woman's access to resources, work, housing, education, and other advantages often determines the level of power she possesses. For that reason, when considering the application of human rights, social workers should always acknowledge how differences in power among groups can result in discrimination and inequality (International Association of Schools of Social Work [IASSW] & International Federation of Social Workers [IFSW], 1994).

HUMAN RIGHTS AND UNIVERSALITY

The notion that human rights are universal and belong to all people is centrally connected to principles of equality. Everyone is born with the same human rights, and everyone should have the same opportunities to enjoy those rights. In a human rights context, equality does not necessarily mean treating everyone in the same manner. When people are in unequal situations, treating them in the same manner invariably perpetuates, rather than eradicates, injustices (Reichert, 2003, 2006a; Staub Bernasconi, 2007; van Wormer 2001). Thus, women often require different treatment than men in order to enjoy the same rights.

For example, to enjoy the human right to work, women may require child care and recognition of the work they typically do in the home. A woman's right to work would then require measures to balance the unequal situations between men and women. Emphasis on the role of a man in raising children and doing work at home could help women achieve this human right. Merely enacting a law stating that women have the same right to a job as men does little in helping women to exercise their human rights to work. Consequently, human rights are not gender neutral. In addressing violations of human rights against women, social workers should recognize the unequal positions of women and men in society and how this situation has become the cultural norm.

WOMEN'S RIGHTS ARE HUMAN RIGHTS

The Universal Declaration of Human Rights does not contain any provisions specific to women. The language of the declaration refers to *man* and uses the pronoun *he* when referring to individuals. Although the declaration introduced innovative and progressive rights for everyone, the articulation of those rights reflects a male-dominated world by incorporating generally male perceptions and priorities. After adoption of the declaration in 1948, central concerns about the male focus persisted. The concept of human rights had not been expanded sufficiently to account for the social, economic, cultural, and political circumstances in which a woman's identity is shaped and experienced. Essentially, the failure of human rights documents and principles to sufficiently highlight the equal status of women to men led to a need to specifically recognize that women's rights are human rights.

In 1975, almost thirty years after the drafting of the Universal Declaration, the United Nations held the First World Conference on Women in Mexico City (United Nations, 1976). At this conference, attendees linked the oppression of women to their inequality. Leaders at the conference also urged governments to eliminate violence against women. To improve the status of women, leaders acknowledged that much needed to be accomplished. Therefore, the UN proclaimed the next ten years as the Decade for Women.

Five years later, at the Second World Conference on Women in Copenhagen, Danish delegates endorsed the Convention on the Elimination of All Forms of Discrimination against Women. This convention aimed to place women on an equal footing with men within any field, including political, economic, social, and cultural arenas. Social workers have called this convention a Magna Carta for the human rights of women (Wetzel, 1993).

CONVENTION ON THE ELIMINATION OF ALL FORMS OF DISCRIMINATION AGAINST WOMEN

The Convention on the Elimination of All Forms of Discrimination against Women, or CEDAW, focuses on elevating the status of women to that of men in the area of human rights. States approving the convention acknowledge that the Universal Declaration of Human Rights and subsequent international covenants all aim to eliminate discrimination on the basis of gender. However, despite these various instruments, extensive discrimination against women continues, and "in situations of poverty women have the least access to food, health, education, training, and opportunities for employment and other needs" (CEDAW, 1979). States party to CEDAW are convinced that the full and complete development of a country, the welfare of the world, and the cause of peace require the maximum participation of women on equal terms with men in all fields. States acknowledge that a change in the traditional role of men as well as the role of women in society and in the family is needed to achieve full equality between men and women. States approving CEDAW agree to adopt measures that would eliminate gender discrimination in all forms and manifestations.

Gender discrimination is defined as follows:

> Any distinction, exclusion, or restriction made on the basis of sex which has the effect or purpose of impairing or nullifying the recognition, enjoyment, or exercise by women irrespective of their marital status, on a basis of equality of men and women, of human rights and fundamental freedoms in the political, economic, social, cultural, civil, or any other field.
>
> —(CEDAW, *1979*, Art. 1)

Any distinction, exclusion, or restriction having the effect as well as purpose of discrimination would include unintentional as well as intentional discrimination.

States approving CEDAW also are required to take appropriate measures in all fields, particularly, the "political, social, economic, and cultural fields, to ensure the full development and advancement of women." States are to take all appropriate measures to "modify the social and cultural patterns of conduct of men and women, with a view to achieving the elimination of prejudices and . . . other practices which are based on the idea of the inferiority or the superiority of either of the sexes or on stereotyped roles for men and women" (Art. 5[a]). States are to suppress all "forms and traffic in women and exploitation of prostitution of women" (Art. 6).

STATUS OF CEDAW

Most countries of the world have approved CEDAW, thereby obligating their governments to enforce provisions within the convention except for any reservations cited by the governments. One notable holdout in approving CEDAW is the United States. Although former president Jimmy Carter signed the treaty in 1980, the US Senate has yet to ratify the document, and ratification does not appear likely. On International Women's Day in 2000, the late Senator Jesse Helms of North Carolina publicly vowed never to allow the Senate to vote on CEDAW. Instead, he promised to leave the treaty in the dustbin for several more decades (Human Rights Watch World Report, 2001). The United States does have legislation that prohibits discrimination against women in the workplace and other areas, but CEDAW would require additional measures to ensure gender equality.

Although most countries have approved CEDAW, many have placed reservations, or conditions, on the acceptance of its provisions (Division for Advancement of Women, 2009). For instance, Algeria has adopted CEDAW but reserves the right to enforce its Family Code over provisions of the convention. One instance where the Algerian Family Code may conflict with CEDAW concerns the code's restrictions on the residence of women. Australia has placed a reservation on enforcement of CEDAW regarding paid maternity leave—it will not always provide paid maternity leave even though CEDAW requires this benefit. Ireland, on the other hand, reserves the right to provide more favorable benefits to women than men where Irish law requires this differential treatment. Malaysia restricts application of CEDAW where it would conflict with the federal constitution and sharia law. Mexico agrees to enforce CEDAW in line with its economic resources. The United Kingdom places a reservation on CEDAW so that it will not apply to its royalty, including determination of succession.

Many of the stated reservations on CEDAW preserve cultural or religious traditions or require consideration of economic resources. Some countries also reserve the right to favor women in terms of social welfare benefits and determination of child custody. The positive aspect of so many countries adopting CEDAW is the clear recognition that discrimination against women should not occur. However, the reservations do allow many exceptions to enter the enforcement of CEDAW, particularly from Islamic countries that wish to preserve their religion (Mayer, 1995). Some of the most intense debates over cultural relativism concern the rights of women (Healy, 2007; Reichert, 2006b, 2007).

SOCIAL WORK SYMPOSIUM ON WOMEN AND HUMAN RIGHTS

At the much publicized Fourth World Conference on Women in Beijing in 1995, delegates to the conference adopted a manifesto for women's rights known as the Beijing Platform for Action (United Nations, 1996). The platform addressed twelve areas of critical concern affecting the well-being of women, including violence, poverty, health, education, and economic participation.

In conjunction with the Platform for Action adopted by the United Nations, Dr. Janice Wetzel organized a social work symposium on human rights to occur during the Beijing conference. This symposium represented the first organized gathering of social workers in conjunction with a UN world conference on women (Reichert, 1998). A primary goal of the symposium was to bring social workers together from all parts of the world to exchange ideas and information.

Two hundred women and men from twenty-seven countries attended the symposium, which highlighted a human rights approach to counter the view that violence against women is a cultural norm. By emphasizing women's rights and human rights, participants hoped to create a common thread among social workers in response to violence. The symposium also encouraged governments to consider cultural background when taking measures against violence. Following the symposium, volunteers drafted a resolution to schools of social work and delegates attending the UN conference. That resolution consisted of a synthesis of programs initiated by women for personal, social, and economic development (Wetzel, 1993, 1996).

1. *Look to the women and listen to the women:* Always begin with the personal experiences of local women, generalizing then to state, national, and international policies so that the connections between all forms of violence become clear.

2. *Require economic self-determination:* Women must lead and define economic and development policies and programs that affect communities. Current policies leave women with a heritage of destruction in health, environment, education, livelihood, culture, and autonomy. Investment priorities must be in the human community.

3. *Free women from fear and domination:* War, dislocation, and state-sponsored violence as well as violence in the street and in the home feed the epidemic. It is a fundamental human right of all women and children to live with respect and without fear.

4. *Value all women's work:* The invisibility and undervaluing of women's work within and outside the home lead to women's status as the poorest, least educated, and most vulnerable to health problems, both physical and mental. Overwork and lack of pay impede human progress.

5. *Place women in decision-making positions:* With women's personal development, relevant social development and action is not only possible but most appropriate and successful.

6. *Promote shared responsibilities in all forms of family and social partnerships:* Human rights include equal sharing of home care and family care. Respect for all forms of families is basic to promoting human rights and building healthy communities.

7. *Invest in health care and education:* The prevention of women's physical and mental illness requires access to appropriate and affordable health services. Literacy, numeracy, and other forms of basic education improve women's economic status, delay pregnancies, and better educate future generations.

8. *Educate all women regarding their legal rights and other laws pertinent to them:* Include in legal education the execution of critical analyses and the development of corrective laws and policies.

9. *Promote positive perceptions of and by women:* Within the context of human rights, provide opportunities for women to share experiences, acknowledge differences, and recognize the value of diversity.

10. *Press for relevant gender-specific data collection and research:* Consider new models, such as participative action research, whereby women themselves select the issues and guide the design, analyses, and implementation of results.

These ten elements provide social workers all over the world with guidance in addressing women's issues and human rights. In conjunction with CEDAW, the Platform for Action, and other human rights documents, the resolution can provide schools of social work with a valuable tool in addressing the human rights of women.

THE IMPORTANCE OF WOMEN'S HUMAN RIGHTS TO THE SOCIAL WORK PROFESSION

In bringing a gender perspective to the understanding of rights, women have struggled to ensure that all human rights—civil, political, economic, social, and cultural—are equally guaranteed to women. The promotion of gender perspective has resulted in increased recognition of interdependence among all human rights. By examining human rights through women's eyes, critical questions emerge: Who in society is a citizen? What are the criteria for consideration as a citizen? Are issues and themes accepted as legitimate political debate truly representative of the concerns of the majority of citizens? These questions all relate to the recognition that women's rights are human rights.

How does the movement to recognize women's rights as human rights have relevance to the social work profession? A primary mission of the social work profession is to advocate for and work on behalf of vulnerable populations. In regard to women, a human rights perspective helps to illuminate the complicated relationship between gender and other aspects of identity such as race, class, religion, age, sexual orientation, disability, culture, and refugee or migrant status.

Viewing women's and girl's lives within a human rights framework provides a new perspective. For example, the movement to draw attention to violence against women and girls emanates from Article 5 of the Universal Declaration of Human Rights. The concept of human rights has helped to define and articulate women's and girls' experiences of violations, such as rape, female genital mutilation, and domestic violence.

Understanding such violence in terms of human rights establishes that states and individuals are responsible for such abuse whether committed in the public or private sphere. A human rights perspective also addresses the issue of how to hold governments and individuals accountable when they are indifferent to such abuses. Human rights provide women all over the world with a common vocabulary by which they can define and articulate their specific experiences, giving each person the entitlement to human dignity (Reichert, 2006a; Wetzel, 2007).

To have relevance to women or any group, human rights need official recognition by governments. Knowing about human rights is only the first step toward recognizing those rights; legal processes must also actively enforce them. Unless women's rights are fundamentally established as human rights, the role of women will always be secondary in overall societal structures. By promoting human rights for women, the social work profession will be working toward its mission of assisting diverse populations that require special attention.

REFERENCES

Beneria, L. (2003). *Gender, development and globalization: Economics as if all people mattered.* New York: Routledge.

Bissio, R. (Ed.) (2005). *Advance social watch report 2005.* Montevideo, Uruguay: Instituto del Tercer Mundo.

Chesler, E. (2004, October). International holdout. *American Prospect: Special Report on Human Rights,* A27–A28.

Convention on the Elimination of All Forms of Discrimination against Women (CEDAW). (1979). G.A. Res. 34/180, U.N. GAOR, 34th Sess., Supp. No. 46 at 193, U.N. Doc. A/34/46, adopted September 3, 1981. New York: United Nations.

Deller Ross, S. (2008). *Women's human rights: The international and comparative law casebook.* Philadelphia. University of Pennsylvania Press.

Division for Advancement of Women. (2009). Convention on the Elimination of All Forms of Discrimination against Women. Department of Economic and Social Affairs, United Nations. Retrieved June 11, 2009, from www.un.org/womenwatch/daw/cedaw/reservations-country.htm.

Healy, L. (2007). Universalism and cultural relativism in social work ethics. *International Social Work,* 5, 11–26.

Human Rights Watch World Report. (2001). *Events of 2000.* New York: Human Rights Watch.

Ife, J. (2008). *Human rights and social work: Towards rights-based practice.* Cambridge: Cambridge University Press.

International Association of Schools of Social Work (IASSW) & International Federation of Social Workers (IFSW). (1994). *Human rights and social work: A manual for schools for social work and the social work profession.* Professional Training Series, no. 1. New York: United Nations.

Ishay, M. (2004). *The history of human rights: From ancient times to the globalization era.* Berkeley, CA: University of California Press.

Mayer, A. E. (1995). Cultural particularism as a bar to women's rights: Reflections on the Middle Eastern experience. In J. Peters & A. Wolper (Eds.), *Women's rights, human rights: International feminist perspectives* (pp. 176–188). New York, Routledge.

Reichert, E. (2007). Human rights in the twenty-first century: Creating a new paradigm for social work. In E. Reichert (Ed.), *Challenges in human rights: A social work perspective* (pp. 1–15). New York: Columbia University Press.

Reichert, E. (2006a). *Understanding human rights: An exercise book.* Thousand Oaks, CA: Sage.

Reichert, E. (2006b). Human rights: An examination of universalism and cultural relativism. *Journal of Comparative Social Welfare,* 22(1), 23–36.

Reichert, E. (2003). *Social work and human rights: A foundation for policy and practice.* New York: Columbia University Press.

Reichert, E. (1998). Women's rights are human rights: A platform for action. *International Social Work,* 15(3), 177–185.

Staub Bernasconi, S. (2007). Economic and social rights: The neglected human rights. In E. Reichert (Ed.), *Challenges in human rights: A social work perspective* (pp. 131–161). New York: Columbia University Press.

United Nations. (1996). The Platform for Action. 4th World Conference on Women, Beijing, September 4–15, 1995. New York: UN Department of Public Information.

United Nations. (1976). *Report of the World Conference of the International Women's Year.* Mexico City, June–July 1975. United Nations Publication no. E.76.IV.I (E/Conf.66/34). New York: United Nations.

Van Wormer, K. 2001. *Counseling female offenders and victims: A strengths-restorative approach.* New York: Springer.

Wetzel, J. (2007). Human rights and women: A work in progress. In E. Reichert (Ed.), *Challenges in human rights: A social work perspective* (pp. 162–187). New York. Columbia University Press.

Wetzel, J. (1996). On the road to Beijing: The evolution of the international women's movement. *Journal of Women and Social Work,* 11(22), 221–236.

Wetzel, J. (1993). *The world of women: In pursuit of human rights.* London: Macmillan.

68

Children's Rights

ROSEMARY J. LINK

Some of the most precious and useful documents to come out of the United Nations in the past fifty years include those conventions that offer a framework to tackle oppression and discrimination, and this especially relates to children. A majority of the world's children have their childhood taken from them by economic and social circumstances. In generating the Convention on the Rights of the Child (CRC) (UNICEF, 1989), countries came together to define *child*, and in so doing, they identified a special status and time of development that is distinct from adulthood and is considered valuable. The convention enshrines the right of a child to be more than a miniature adult. A child is a young human being who, in order to thrive, has the right to be fed, housed, immunized, and educated. Just as important, children should have the right to be heard. Jonathan Kozol (2008) asks us to utilize high-level educational policy and research to guide professional services and intervention but simultaneously to understand the profound need of a child to experience childhood.

The convention was drafted over decades, presented to the United Nations General Assembly by 1989, and voted into international law by 1990, but it is not universally accepted, and some countries have persisted in their resistance to its policy requirements. However, we can be encouraged that 96 percent\of the world's children live in countries that have ratified the convention (www.unicef.org/crc). Exceptions persisting in 2011 include Somalia, torn by war, and the United States, reluctant to approve any law that challenges its sovereignty. Despite the refusal of the United States to ratify, the United Nations Children's Fund (UNICEF) (1997) states that

> the Convention has produced a profound change that is already beginning to have substantive effects on the world's attitude towards its children (Archard, 1993). Once a country ratifies, it is obliged in law to undertake all appropriate measures to assist parents

and other responsible parties in fulfilling their obligations to children (p. 3).

Although full ratification of the law is important, it is not the only reason for understanding and recognizing the CRC. There is also the moral imperative that children's well-being is vital for the future of the world and they have a right to viable life. This notion of accepted international standards has gathered momentum in recent years, especially in relation to issues that cross borders or represent sentiments of common humanity, such as universal concern at the fate of children held on death row or the interdependence of all citizens through global economic and trading systems (e.g., the manufacture of clothing or rugs or the need worldwide for rubber and coffee, commodities that only grow in the tropics).

The CRC is therefore a crucial starting place for international social work and all services concerned with the well-being of children (Link & Ramanathan, 2011). The convention also focuses on children crossing borders and the particular vulnerability of those who migrate or become victims of sexual exploitation and human trafficking. Since 1990, two additional documents have strengthened the intent of the CRC:

i) Optional Protocol to the Convention on the Rights of the Child on the sale of children, child prostitution, and child pornography (UN, May 2000, entry into force January 18, 2002)

ii) Optional Protocol to the Convention on the Rights of the Child on the involvement of children in armed conflict (UN, May 2000, entry into force February 12, 2002).

The Protocol focusing on child prostitution comes following greater public awareness and alarm at the increase in trafficking of children and their sexual exploitation, including internet pornography

(The Guardian, 2009) (www.unicef.org/crc/index_protocols.html). Richard Estes's research for National Geographic on traffic in children between Mexico and the United States was met with shock and in some places disbelief (Estes, 2004). A challenge for social work is that trafficking of children is too well hidden and few people want to believe it is happening in their cities.

The second optional protocol, concerning the involvement of children in armed conflict, follows the terrible reality of children tortured into becoming soldiers, particularly in armed conflicts in Africa, such as in the Darfur region. More detailed attention and research is offered on this issue by Joanne Corbin in Chapter 22 in this volume. Also, Skrebes and Link offer a brief case study of the current situation for children in Sudan (Box 68.1). Building on the introduction to human rights in Chapter 66 (Joseph Wronka), this chapter presents a brief history of children's rights, an overview of the fifty-four articles in the CRC, and case studies to apply this knowledge to social work.

Watching a child spinning a bottle in a market in Cuernavaca, one playing with paper bags blown up to pop under a tree in Philadelphia, or another face painting in the street in Mumbai, this author has seen the resilience of children asserting their right to play. The CRC is a stunning document because it affirms that right. Just as children can die from what they do not know, especially in relation to sexually transmitted diseases, sniffing of chemicals, or chewing tobacco products, they can also thrive in the toughest circumstances when adults respect their needs. This UN instrument serves to inform and to guide social work practice that protects all aspects of a child's life, including play.

HISTORY OF CHILDREN'S RIGHTS

Children are wired to survive, but adults put great challenges in their path, including the historically dominant role of parents to control and discipline through physical punishment. Traditionally children have been treated as the property of their parents, often seen as instruments to improve family economic well-being at the expense of education and healthy development. At the beginning of the twentieth century, children were working in mines, garment factories, and a variety of hazardous occupations in most of the world, including Europe and North America. In countries of the Global South, sometimes referred to as *developing countries* (see Midgley in Chapter 4

of this *Handbook*), children continue to work, chained to looms and bound to employers due to the destitution of their parents.

The CRC did not come about easily. It was debated at the United Nations and internationally throughout the 1970s and was finally passed in 1989. Ratification by the majority of the countries of the world followed during the 1990s, with the notable exceptions mentioned earlier of Somalia and the United States. Somalia lacked representation at the United Nations, and the United States was caught up in political tension and adherence to laws that symbolize its independence of action, including capital punishment for children categorized as adults for serious crimes. It was a dramatic step when Chief Justice Kennedy supported the international outcry and agreed with the convention's definition of child and the need for special protections.

A wealth of practical wisdom and support for children lies in this document and its various articles, which can be clustered as follows: definitions of the child and guiding principles (such as best interests); civil rights; family environment and alternative care; basic health and welfare; education, leisure, and culture; and special protection. The final clauses of the convention address issues of implementation.

In these seven clusters of the fifty-four articles, the convention covers a wide array of issues that are crucial for children's well-being. Some of these have been discussed in earlier chapters, such as the awful oppression of adults coercing children into violence and killing as soldiers, the stress of parents in poverty who are enticed to give up their children for adoption, early betrothal, and the exploitation of child labor. Children need social workers who are well informed, especially when children are vulnerable through disability or being very young (Fraiburg, 1968). All these issues reverberate around the world; no nation is untouched.

Multiple barriers to implementation of the convention and protocols persist, including the perpetuation of physical punishment and all forms of abuse, the complexity of changed identity through adoption or incarceration, indenture, lack of access to education, and few channels for child voices to be heard. Although many of the articles relate to the social and economic well-being of children who are born into acute poverty, there are aspects of children's rights that cross all socioeconomic groups and all cultures. What stands out when first encountering the convention is the optimistic expectation that it will build co-operation. The following paragraphs summarize the articles in ways that illustrate the response of the

BOX 68.1

CHILD PROTECTION INTERNATIONAL IN SOUTHERN SUDAN.

Robyn Skrebes, CPI Steering Committee and Sophie Link, Home Ownership
Preservation Foundation

Sudan has suffered a great deal of strife and violent conflict since colonial rule ended in the mid-1950s. Southern and Northern Sudan have been at war with one another for four of the last five decades, the most recent conflict ending with the signing of the Comprehensive Peace Agreement (CPA) in 2005. Following the signing of the CPA, Southern Sudan began to establish its first central government infrastructure in time immemorial, but four years later it continues to suffer from innumerable issues related to war. Though the government of Southern Sudan has expressed an intent to protect human rights, barriers to implementation are significant. These obstacles can be examined through three main limitations: physical infrastructure, government (capacity and enforcement), and critical social norms.

The conflict and subsequent social implications that have stifled Southern Sudan's development have had a profound effect on human rights, particularly the rights of women and children. In the fall of 2007, Yar and Ajak Mading, ages three and one and a half, were taken under duress from the home of their grandmother in rural Southern Sudan. Upon discovering their abduction, the girls' father walked for three days to make a report to local police, but no efforts were made by the police to find the girls. Scarcity of law enforcement coupled with the lack of fundamental infrastructure in Southern Sudan confounds recovery efforts and makes them rare. Word of the abduction reached the girls' uncle, a graduate student at the University of Minnesota, who mobilized classmates in human rights to work for their return. The students garnered support from US congressional representatives, nongovernmental leaders, and UN agencies working in Southern Sudan. Unfortunately, even under significant international pressure, the Southern Sudanese government was unable to surmount the great difficulties impeding the recovery of Yar and Ajak, and their whereabouts remain unknown. The students created an organization called Child Protection International (CPI), which works to address intercommunal child abduction in Southern Sudan by examining and working to affect its root causes.

A sharp increase in intercommunal violence in Southern Sudan began in 2009. Human Rights Watch reported that in Jonglei, one of the regions most affected by intercommunal clashes, more than 1000 people were killed and 150 women and children were abducted in March and April of 2009 alone.[1] Intercommunal violence is often exemplified by the widespread crime of cattle raiding, an act in which members of one ethnic group forcibly enter the community of another and steal cattle, the most valuable commodity. Such raids frequently result in acts of violence, including murder and abduction, against community members, particularly women and children, and are becoming increasingly dangerous. According to CPI, children are not seen as rights holders, nor as human beings entitled to dignified lives, but rather as commodities to be used and traded. The organization is working to ensure that children are viewed as individuals entitled to legal and social rights by supporting birth registration, which is critical to the protection of identity and would aid in the recovery of abducted children.

Sudan has ratified or assented to several international human rights treaties that are relevant to the protection of women and children, in particular the International Covenant on Civil and Political Rights; the International Covenant on Economic, Social and Cultural Rights; and the Convention on the Rights of the Child. Although the government in word intends to follow through with its commitments to human rights bodies, as evidenced by the passage of legislation such as the Child Act (2009), it has just taken the first steps toward ensuring that basic rights are observed. Obstacles to the implementation of human rights in Southern Sudan are great and will require the ongoing support of the international community. In addition, CPI will continue to be a leader in advocating for child protection in Southern Sudan, including developing innovative approaches to birth registration. For more on CPI, visit www.childprotectioninternational.org.

---

[1] http://www.humansecuritygateway.com/documents/HRW_GapsCivlianProtection_SouthernSudan.pdf

social work profession to what Nelson Mandela describes as a "luminous document." More detailed connection to fields of practice can be found in further readings (Mandela, 2000; Link & Ramanathan, 2011; Reichert, 2007; UNICEF, 2010).

Social work is social policy in action, and the opening statement of the CRC defines *child* as a person under eighteen years of age. When implemented, the absolute rule has the potential to prevent recruitment of child soldiers, discourage early betrothal, expand employment protections, and keep children out of adult prisons. Furthermore, the definition of the child is part of the expectation that "State Parties shall respect and ensure the rights set forth in the present Convention to each child . . . irrespective of the child's parent's race, colour, sex, language, origin, disability, birth or other status" (UNICEF, 1989, Article 2).

The right of all children to have their status defined and to have a name is crucial to their well-being. For social workers in London during the 1980s, "it was normal practice for a child born with a disability and placed for adoption to be called by a capital letter, such as Baby M. Being without a name implies that children do not exist in their own right until named by an adoptive parent, and this reduces their independent status and influences attitudes toward practice" (Link & Ramanathan, 2011, p. 61). In Africa many children are born during war and abducted without registration, which adversely affects their status. The Universal Birth Registration project is using the convention to implement new registration procedures (African Child Forum, 2005). The law affects social work practice in that it demands that social workers support and ensure these protections and the right to a name.

The second group of articles relates to "guiding principles and the best interests of the child, including the right to survival and healthy development" (Wronka, 2002).

Though adults have claimed the rights of parents to know what is best in the healthy growth, development, and discipline of children, the convention commands attention to the safety of children from abusive punishment:

> In all countries of the world, there are children living in exceptionally difficult conditions, and [we recognize] that such children need special consideration . . . and have agreed as follows . . .
> Article 19: State Parties shall take all appropriate legislative, administrative, social and educational

measures to protect the child from all forms of physical or mental violence, injury or abuse, neglect or negligent treatment, maltreatment or exploitation including sexual abuse, while in the care of parent(s), legal guardian(s) or any other person who has the care of the child (www.hrusa.org).

In the United Kingdom in the fall of 2008, there was a great outcry in Parliament and the media at the death of a toddler, Baby P, as a result of violent abuse, including a broken back. Prime Minister Gordon Brown was attacked in debate and assured his constituents that he would "do everything in my power to make sure this does not happen again" (*The Times*, 16 November 2008). Public outrage at the death of this child at the hands of his mother and her boyfriend was expressed in calls for the resignation of the director of social services in the Borough of Haringey. Unrealistic statements were made about preventing such events in the future if only social workers were less trusting and more strict with parents. As stated by the journalist Yasmin Alibhai-Brown (2008), the key issue is the deep ambivalence among adults in their attitude and power over children: "The only people in the country who can still be lawfully hit are children" (p. 37).

The Ombudsman for Children in Norway is perhaps one of the leading examples of children having voice in relation to adult abuse. As a direct result of the CRC, Norwegian family and children policies have given great attention to the ways they meet the expectation of the convention. In Slovenia, the children's shelter, called "Safe House" at Celje uses the CRC as a template for all its work, including keep the child's right to refuse to return home until they feel safe. Similarly, new legislation in Jamaica, the Child Care and Protection Act, is an important government response to the CRC. Attention is now being paid to trafficking, child labor, and child abuse as interest in child protection and parenting have increased (Healy, 2008).

The third cluster of articles refers to civil rights of children as reflected in the setting up of ombudsmen in several countries, first in Norway, then in Sweden and in some US states (including Michigan). These offices uphold the rights and protections that children can seek of their own volition, including the rights of children to be educated, to be freely employed and not exploited, to receive health care and immunization, to be sheltered and to be safe, and to be adjudicated in juvenile courts. Link and Ramanathan (2011) illustrate these rights by pointing to the 1999 case of boys who murdered a toddler in the United Kingdom. The boys were tried before the European Union and now live under new identities with the full protections of the convention. In a similar case, US Supreme Court justice Anthony Kennedy authored a 2005 ruling that referred to the convention and declared that use of the death penalty on juveniles was unconstitutional. This evidence of progress builds on the work of researchers such as Bazemore and Umbreit (1995) who have challenged social workers to increase public understanding of restorative justice for juveniles rather than court decisions based on retribution.

Recently, a distinction has been made between *child labor*, which is defined as "children working in conditions that are excessively abusive and exploitive" (Kent, 2002, as cited in Healy, 2003, p. 92), and *child work*, which is defined as legitimate employment that helps support families and does not interfere with education. Lusk (1992) and Ferguson (Chapter 23 in this *Handbook*) point out that child employment cannot be eliminated entirely. Children themselves want the right to work in fair conditions that do not prevent attendance at school (Leonard, 2004).

Articles 18, 19, 20, and 21 in the fourth cluster of articles include parent responsibility; patterns of care, including alternative care; and international adoption. As vividly explained in Chapter 11 (Rotabi), most social work agencies touch on the lives of families. Agencies offering international adoptions are particularly at risk of malpractice if their staff are not globally aware and educated to use international policy instruments, including the CRC. Link (2007) identifies social work agencies that build their missions on the convention, such as the Southside Family Nurturing Center in Minneapolis and the KLUC center in Ljubljana for youth who are victims of human trafficking.

There is increasing evidence of good practice in adoption agencies, which reflects closer adherence to the tenets of the CRC, including encouraging adoptive parents to ensure that the child remains tied to his or her cultural roots and the family has knowledge of the country of origin. However, this is parallel to serious malpractice, such as the possibility that agency decision making on choice of partner countries is based on political and market availability criteria rather than on social need, a problem described more fully by Rotabi in Chapter 11 of this book.

The fifth cluster of articles relates to health and well-being. Some countries are setting examples for others to follow, including the Italian city of Postoia,

whose government has embraced the convention and declared that children's needs are its first priority. Also, the decision of the Jamaican government to pattern its child welfare services on the convention and the Norwegian decision to make physical punishment illegal under all circumstances, including parental discipline, offer encouragement to policy makers in countries that see international policy as interfering with family and parental rights or attitudes of ownership of their children.

The CRC itself provides an incentive to consider major pieces of domestic social policy legislation that directly affect the quality of life of children, such as welfare reform, through a wider global lens. For example, Bibus, Link and O'Neal (2005) grounded their research on the idea that children and their families and caregivers, regardless of their current plight, have a right to identify the way services affect them and ways such services can be improved. In reference to Article 27, the IFSW manual for social work and the rights of the child states:

> Many people with whom social workers work suffer social exclusion as a result of poverty. They have no realistic hope of securing paid employment and their life chances are blighted by a subsistence existence characterized by malnutrition, poor education and destitution. Breaking into the cycle of poverty requires concerted action at international, national, regional and local level using the resources of people themselves in self-help initiatives such as cooperatives. It requires resource commitment from national governments and a shift from those policies of structural adjustment that pay little regard to human consequences. (IFSW, 2002, p. 36)

It is encouraging that rights to well-being were reinforced in the State of the World's Children 2003 report and that these in turn have been translated into the Millennium Development Goals (UN, 2011). Children everywhere, whether in richer or poorer countries, depend upon access to immunization, education, food, and shelter for their healthy development, but they are often excluded (Figueiredo & de Haan, 1998).

The sixth cluster relates to education, leisure, and culture. Article 31 includes the right to rest: "State Parties recognize the right of the child to rest and leisure, to engage in play and recreational activities appropriate to the age of the child and to participate freely in cultural life and the arts." One of the most striking problems of the twenty-first century is the sharp divide between countries of the Global North, where resources are plentiful, and the Global South, where there is scarcity, famine, and child labor.

Craig Kielburger, the Canadian child labor activist, called upon students to educate themselves about two worlds—one of lavish material goods and waste and the other of the constant struggle to keep food on the table (Kielburger & Kielburger, 2004). Kielburger became interested in child labor when he first read of the assassination of a twelve-year-old boy who was organizing protests against exploitative employers in Pakistan. Kielburger's work has focused on informing people in the Global North of how much they depend on the whole world for such staples as rubber, coffee, and tea as well as the cheap labor that produces goods, such as rugs and clothing.

In addition to disparities between regions in terms of acute poverty, the seventh cluster draws attention to risks for children crossing borders and young people who are exposed to the aftermath of political and social upheaval or war. Continuing the discussion of social exclusion discussed by Lyons and Huegler in Chapter 72, the focus here is the common human conditions and geographic realities surrounding children rather than their individual assets or deficits.

Connected to the awareness of children in terms of geography is the question of national borders and human trafficking, particularly minors, across borders. Article 35 states, "States Parties shall take all appropriate national, bilateral and multilateral measures to prevent the abduction of, the sale of or traffic in children for any purpose or in any form." As discussed by Link (2007, p. 230),

> Trafficking in human beings is included in the European Penal Code and cases of abduction and sexual exploitation have posed complex problems for service providers, particularly in creating agreements with neighboring countries. The European organization EQUAL is well documented by the Society Kljuc (Center for Fight Against Trafficking in Human Beings), and supported by the United Nations Human Rights Commission. Countries may be classified as places of *origin* for trafficking in human beings (THB)—especially children— places of *transit* and places of *destination*.

Some countries that are bordered by several others belong to all these categories, for example Slovenia.

There is increasing awareness of border vulnerability for children who are unaccompanied, and this is addressed earlier in the *Handbook* (Segal, Chapter 10). Also, the United Nations Human Rights Council has coordinated work, together with the Human Rights Commissions of various countries, in implementing the CRC and has supported publications relating to human trafficking in a number of countries, including Afghanistan (Samar, 2005).

It will continue to be a challenge for nations to implement the convention into the next decades. Some countries have taken up the challenge more willingly than others. However, Articles 42 and 43 are clear in the expectations of each state and its administration:

> States Parties undertake to make the principles and provisions of the Convention widely known, by appropriate and active means, to adults and children alike. For the purpose of examining the progress made by States Parties in achieving the realization of the obligations undertaken in the present Convention, there shall be established a Committee on the Rights of the Child, which shall carry out the functions hereinafter provided.

Another form of implementation relates to adult recognition that channels need to be expanded for children's voices to be heard (Martin, 2006). Similarly, it is a built-in assumption that parents will do the best for their children, and overall parents have the law in their favor in terms of control. However, the health of the child is a value that is universally established as paramount by the CRC, and a parent's religious values, for example, may not intervene (Woolfe, 2009).

THE SLOW RECOGNITION OF THE CHILDREN'S RIGHTS MOVEMENT

As social workers become more aware of the way the CRC can inform and guide their work, there is an increasing recognition that children have powerful voices. Kofi Annan recognized this in 2003 when he invited children to the assembly at the UN in Geneva. The following year the Children's World Congress on Child Labor was held in Italy. It "put children at the heart of advocating for the abolition of exploitive labour and national implementation of the CRC" (Leonard, 2004, p. 45). "Children's Views on Children's Right to Work: Reflections From Belfast" (Leonard, 2004) is a powerful expression of their response to being included in adult discourse.

The Convention on the Rights of the Child has become both a source of encouragement for children and a powerful template for human services concerned with families and their children. The articles of implementation (Articles 42–54) and the reporting mechanisms to the United Nations ensure consistency in both planning and implementation. It is an unfolding story to see the various ways the convention has provided frameworks and support for intervention to maintain the human rights of children—a story often overlooked in human services literature and practice.

REFERENCES

African Child Forum. (2005). *Universal birth registration: The challenge in Africa.* www.africanchildforum.org/Documents/Universal%20Birth%20Registration_final.pdf.

Alibhai-Brown, Y. (2008). The only people in the country who can still be lawfully hit are children. The Times, 16 November. p. 37.

Archard, D. (1993). *Children: Rights and childhood.* London: Routledge.

Bazemore, G., & Umbreit, M. (1995). Rethinking the sanctioning function in juvenile court: Retributive or restorative responses to youth crime. *Crime & Delinquency, 41*(3), 296–316.

Bibus, A., Link, R. & O'Neal, M. (2005). The Impact of Welfare Reform on Children's Well-Being. In J. Scott & H. Ward (Eds.), Safeguarding *and Promoting the Well-Being of Children, Families, and Communities.* London: Jessica Kingsley Publishing.

Estes, R. (2004). Child Trafficking. *National Geographic Magazine.*

Figueiredo, J., & de Haan, A. (1998). *Social exclusion: An ILO perspective.* Geneva: International Institute for Labor Studies.

Five hundred children a year abducted from the UK. (2009, August 10). *Guardian,* p. 1.

Fraiberg, S. (1968). Parallel and divergent patterns in blind and sighted infants. *Psychoanalytic Study of the Child, 23,* 264–300.

Garbarino, J. (1999). *Lost boys: Why our sons turn violent and how we can save them.* New York: Free Press.

Gordon Brown Speaks Out. (2008, 16 November). *The Times,* p. 3.

Healy, L. (2008). *International social work: Professional action in an interdependent world.* New York: Oxford University Press.

Jamaica Coalition on the Rights of the Child. (1995). *Children have rights too.* Kingston: Author.

Jeong Trenka, J. (2003). *The language of blood.* St Paul: Borealis Books.

Kielburger, C., & Kielburger, M. (2004). *Me to we: Turning self-help on its head.* Canada: Wiley.

Kozol, J. (2008). Children's Right to be Heard. Keynote to Annual Program Meeting, Council on Social Work Education, Philadelphia. March.

Leonard, M. (2004). Children's views on children's right to work: Reflections from Belfast. *Childhood, 11*(1), 45–61. Quoted in Lyons, K., Marion, K., & Carlsen, D. (2008). International perspectives on social work. Basingstoke: MacMillan Palgrave.

Link, R. (2007). Children's rights as a template for social work practice. In E. Reichert (Ed.), *Challenges in human rights: A social work perspective* (p. 230). New York: Columbia University Press.

Link, R., & Ramanathan, C. (2011). *Human behavior in a just world: Reaching for common ground.* New York: Rowman & Littlefield.

Leonard, M. (2004). Children's views on children's right to work: reflections from Belfast. Childhood, 11(1), 45–61. Quoted in Lyons, K.; Marion, K.; & Carlsen, D. (2008). International Perspectives on Social Work, Basingstoke: MacMillan Palgrave.

Lusk, M. (1992). Street children in Rio de Janeiro. *International Social Work, 35,* 293–305.

Martin, R. (2006). Children's perspectives: Roles, responsibilities and burdens in home-based care. *Journal of Social Development in Africa, 21*(1), 106–129.

Reichert, E. (Ed.). (2007). *Challenges in human rights: A social work perspective.* New York: Columbia University Press.

Samar, S. (2005). The History of the Commission for Human Rights in Afghanistan. New York: UNHRC.

UNICEF. (1989). Convention on the rights of the child. Retrieved in 2005 from www.unicef.org/crc.

UNICEF. (2003). *State of the world's children: Child participation.* New York: Author.

United Nations Millennium Development Goals. www.un.org/millenniumgoals.

Woolfe, W. (2009, June 23). Judge keeps firm hand in Hauser case. *Star Tribune,* A.5.

Wronka, J. (2002). *Human Rights and the Rights of the Child.* Berne, Switzerland: International Federation of Social Work.

Human Rights of People With Disabilities

GUNN STRAND HUTCHINSON

INTRODUCTION

About 650 million people in the world—10% of the total world population—experience various forms of disabilities, according to the World Health Organization (WHO). In addition, 80% of persons with disabilities live in poor countries (WHO, 2008). All over the world, people with disabilities continue to face lower standards of living and barriers to participation in society. People with disabilities are also overrepresented in the population living in poverty. The combination of prejudice, discrimination, and lack of adequate support prevents people with disabilities from achieving an adequate standard of living. The documentation of worldwide discrimination led to the Convention on the Rights of Persons with Disabilities. The aspects of life pinpointed were access to education, employment, transport, housing and buildings in general, and institutionalization. The study also demonstrated that cultural barriers are built on prejudice and discrimination and that legal barriers add to exclusion (Despouy, 2003).

Social work with people with disabilities has not been a focus in professional qualifying courses in social work; professional work with people with disabilities has mainly been seen as a paramedical undertaking. Traditionally the major task in social work has been seen as matching services to assessed need. Little attention has been paid to the barriers facing people with disabilities, the surmounting of those barriers, and the question of the rights of people with disabilities as citizens.

The approach argued for here will build on a human rights perspective, focusing on disabling barriers in society and how social work can enable individuals and groups to participate in society, use their rights, and identify and change disabling barriers. In this approach, matching services to needs will still play a role.

UNDERSTANDING OF DISABILITY

The *disabled people's movement* is a term used to describe the politicization of disability issues, challenging the so-called medical understanding of disability. The movement promotes a model of disability as a form of social oppression rather than personal misfortune or tragedy and sees the propagation of this model and a focus on rights as an instrument for effecting change (Oliver, 2004; Thompson, 2006). Marks (2000) describes the differences between a medical and a social model of understanding disability:

> Disability is a highly contested term. Medicine and its allied professions conceptualize disability as damage to a person's body or medical functioning requiring diagnosis, care or professional treatment. By contrast the social model of disability argues that "the problem" should not be located within an individual person, but rather in a "disabling environment" which excludes and denigrates disabled people. (p. 93)

Although this change in views has been applauded since its emergence in the 1970s, problematic implications of the social model have been commented on. Emphasizing social structures as a cause of disability can make attempts to cure medical problems appear irrelevant. Indeed, real needs may become invisible (Corker & French 1998). Shakespeare (2006) promotes a pluralistic approach to disability, and rather than rejecting research in medical sociology, bioethics, and social care, he advocates that disability studies reengage with the fundamental questions of what disability is and how the lives of people with disabilities can be improved.

This understanding can also be regarded as a sort of synthesis of the individual- and society-based views of disability, where disability occurs at the meeting point between the individual and the environment

(Söder, 1982). This means that people may be disabled in some situations while in others they are not. According to WHO (2001), *disability* is "the outcome or result of a complex relationship between an individual's health condition and personal factors, and of the external factors that represent the circumstances in which the individual lives," and *impairment* is defined as "problems in body function or structure such as significant deviation or loss." Such a relational model of disability emphasizes both societal barriers and the person's impairment. This is an understanding that will be built on in this chapter.

THE RIGHTS OF PEOPLE WITH DISABILITIES

The Universal Declaration of Human Rights of 1948 does not exclude people with disabilities, but over time it became apparent that a positive focus on disability was necessary. The Standard Rules on the Equalization of Opportunities for Persons with Disabilities were adopted by the United Nations in 1993. They are considered to be the most important outcome of the UN Decade of Disabled Persons (1983–1992). The rules are not legally binding but place a moral and political pressure on governments to take action to attain equalization of opportunities for people with disabilities. Despite the adoption of these rules, it became clear that people with disabilities around the world were denied their human rights and marginalized. Thus, it was necessary to adopt a legally binding instrument that placed obligations on states to promote and protect the rights of people with disabilities, and the Convention on the Rights of Persons with Disabilities came into force on May 3, 2008 (UN, 2008).

The convention marks a major shift in the way societies view people with disabilities, with the person being the key decision maker in his or her own life. States that ratify the convention are legally bound to treat people with disabilities as subjects of the law with clearly defined rights to full participation in formulating and implementing plans and policies affecting them. It moves beyond the question of access to the physical environment to broader issues of equality and elimination of legal and social barriers to participation, social opportunities, health, education, employment, and personal development. The guiding principles for the convention are as follows (UN, 2008, p. 5):

a. Respect for inherent dignity, individual autonomy including the freedom to make one's own choices, and independence of persons;
b. Non-discrimination;
c. Full and effective participation and inclusion in society;
d. Respect for difference and acceptance of persons with disabilities as part of human diversity and humanity;
e. Equality of opportunity;
f. Accessibility;
g. Equality between men and women;
h. Respect for the evolving capacities of children with disabilities and respect for the right of children with disabilities to preserve their identities.

The convention is a human rights instrument with a social development dimension that clarifies how all categories of rights apply to persons with disabilities and identifies areas where adaptations have to be made for persons with disabilities to effectively exercise their rights. It reaffirms that *all* persons with *all* types of disabilities must enjoy *all* human rights and fundamental freedoms on an equal basis with others.

IMPLICATIONS FOR SOCIAL WORK

Here I will present an approach to social work based on human rights with a focus on societal barriers and individual needs and dreams. It proposes action in three main categories: supporting individuals in daily living, supporting individuals and groups connecting to services, and changing societal barriers that exclude and discriminate people with disabilities.

Human Rights as a Basis

The convention promotes human rights standards and their application from a disability perspective. The requirement of legally binding provisions that promote full participation as citizens provides a fundamental political mandate for social work.

First, social workers need to be informed about human rights and the convention in order to be able to monitor discrimination and ensure that people with disabilities do not suffer from neglect of their human rights. To have a human rights perspective as a basis for work can also mean asking what implications these rights have for practice, and it means looking at practice and asking what human rights issues are at stake. Ife (2001) calls the first strategy deductive and the second inductive. The deductive approach starts with formal texts and identifying their implications, for example how laws are framed and what rights and duties the laws give people in various situations. The inductive approach starts with private problems that may then be articulated in human rights terms and elevated to a political dimension.

Second, social workers who claim a commitment to human rights should be critically reflective of their own practices. One important human rights principle is the right to self-determination and control over one's own situation. Social workers will have to look at both their agency's policy and their own practice to consider this question.

Societal Barriers and Individuals Needs and Dreams

Most social work starts with meeting individuals and families. In the first meeting, their conceptual framework helps us to see connections and communicate. Our preconceptions influence how we see problems. In assisting people with disabilities, our understanding of disability is most important. Do we conclude that a child does not go to the neighborhood school because he has an intellectual disability, or because the laws exclude him? Do we conclude that a young girl who needs a wheelchair to move around cannot take part in evenings at the youth club because of her impairment, or because the design of the transport system and the club excludes people with wheelchairs?

The way we conceive these problems will also influence the actions we see as necessary. If we look for what hinders participation, our task will be to look for ways to remove or surmount the barriers. This leads to work at a system or societal level.

People with the same impairments are individuals with unique dreams, needs, and interests. Seeing people as individuals must be the basis for social work. It is the quality of life as defined by the individual that is important.

Support for Individuals in Daily Living

To be able to live independently is a civil rights issue concerned with personal autonomy. The institution-based model of personal assistance is connected to a medical understanding of disability: Collect people and engage specialists to serve the person's medical, pedagogical, and psychological needs. The community-based model is more connected to the social or relational model and views the person as part of the society and the local community. Community-based rehabilitation has been promoted by WHO, and during the UN Decade of Disabled Persons (1983–1992), programs were created in more than a quarter of the more developed countries in the world (WHO, 1992). The community-based rehabilitation

model is becoming increasingly adopted throughout the world in both rural and urban areas (Mitchell, 1999). Lightfoot (2004) describes successful programs in Zimbabwe, China, Jamaica, and the Philippines. The independent living movement, initiated by people with disabilities themselves, is now a worldwide movement after having started in North America in 1970 with roots in the civil rights movement (Pelka, 1997). The movement works for self-determination, self-respect, and equal opportunities.

Based on a human rights perspective, living independently as part of a local community and taking part in all aspects of social life are seen as basic rights. To be able to live independently, functionally accessible accommodation is necessary, and many people with impairments will need some sort of support. Support in daily living may include help to manage housework and personal matters, use shops and institutions, travel, attend meetings, visit friends, and generally maintain social networks and interests. The nature and level of support will vary with the person's needs. Personal assistance is a service that has grown from the independent living movement and can be found in many countries. Many consider this service to be the most important tool for securing a good quality of life (Benjamin, Matthias, & Franke, 2000; Morris, 1993).

Thinking in a traditional way, providing support to individuals in daily living might not be considered professional social work. Indeed, many people with disabilities say that they do not want professionals in these jobs because they have experienced professionals as a hindrance in their attitudes and ways of thinking. Professionals themselves are less attracted to such work because the disabled person has so much control over the tasks, which vary a lot and may include menial housework. It is then salutary to recall that empowerment and self-determination are highly valued in social work. Supporting a person in mobilizing strength to take part in an active life as a citizen fulfills these objectives. Working closely with a person and seeing how barriers create private problems makes it possible to work together with the person and to change barriers at a system and societal level. Working with personal support thus provides the possibility of using skills from a wide range of social work knowledge, including group work and community work.

It is nonetheless the case that qualified social workers are seldom engaged in daily personal assistance. People who are engaged in such work are often employed in care services rather than social services. In care services, much of the ethics and organizational arrangements of institutional provision are still in force.

Support for Individual and Groups Regarding Access to Welfare Services

This has traditionally been the main social work job in relation to people with disabilities, and it is still an important task. From a rights perspective, it is not sufficient to connect people to services. Social workers also have to ask if the services are structured, organized, and practiced in a way that is in accordance with the human rights convention. For instance, if a service as important as support in daily living is organized in a way that involves thirty people coming and going, it will be disempowering. The person with a disability will never know who is coming and will have to explain repeatedly how things are to be done. The service is available, but the way it is organized and functions is disempowering and creates barriers for participation as a citizen.

Such situations challenge the social worker to take action. As a first step, the national law and the mandate given to social workers by law and by their employing institution must be clarified. In as far as institutional practice is contrary to the law, the social worker must take steps to effect change. These might include documenting barriers, passing information to decision makers within the institution, challenging the institution, creating alliances, using professional and union organizations, and more. In reviewing alternatives, social workers need to mobilize their mandate. If the law is not in line with international conventions or the mandate is not in line with the law, social workers will need to work with their professional organization to secure change.

Changing Societal Barriers

Through work at the level of support in daily living and in connecting needs to welfare services, social workers will observe how people may be excluded from social participation. With an approach based on human rights, the social worker will identify societal barriers to participation, and it will be apparent that the barriers affect more than one person or one family. The individual life situation is thus connected to societal institutions and social attitudes. When individual problems become common problems, they are amenable to common action. The social worker has a role in promoting and facilitating common action based on common interest where existing organizations are inadequate or where the people concerned are unable to make use of them for a variety of reasons.

We have already discussed the tendency for support in daily living to be disempowering and the action it is possible to take to document and make barriers visible. Another barrier that children face involves mainstream education. In some countries children with disabilities may be excluded by law. In other countries the law does not exclude them but practice hinders inclusion. If countries have ratified the convention, this should not be permissible. In both cases, documentation and exposure of the situation are part of the social worker's job.

The social worker will need to exercise her skills in group and community work. Community work as part of social work has a solid tradition. The defining elements of community work are working together with the people concerned in an empowering way and working for change at a collective level (Ife & Tesoriero, 2006; Twelvetres, 2002).

SUMMARY

The problems connected to disability have not been an important part of social work; rather, they have been considered a matter for paramedical concern. In this chapter, I argue for making problems and challenges connected to disability a more central part of social work. When human rights are defined as a basis for the mandate given to social workers, an approach with a focus on societal barriers and people's needs and dreams is demanded. In turn, this leads to a practice that focuses on providing support to individuals in daily living, connecting individual needs to welfare services in ways that enhance personal autonomy, and cooperating with individuals and groups in acting to remove or surmount societal barriers.

REFERENCES

Benjamin, A. E., Matthias, R., & Franke, T. M. (2000). Comparing consumer-directed and agency models for providing supportive services at home. *Health Services Research*, 35(1), 351–366.

Corker, M., & French, S. (Eds.). (1998). *Disability discourse.* Buckingham: Open University.

Despouy, L. (2003). *Human rights and disabled people.* United Nations, 2003–04, Department of Economic and Social Affairs, Division for Social Policy and Development. Accessed March 8, 2009, from www.un.org/esa/socdev/enable/dispaperdes3.htm.

Ife, J. (2001). *Human rights and social work. Towards rights-based practice.* Buckingham: University Press.

Ife, J., & Tesoriero, F. (2006). *Community development: Community-based alternatives in an age of globalisation* (3rd ed.). Frenchs Forest, Australia: Pearson Education.

Lightfoot, E. (2004). Community-based rehabilitation: A rapidly growing method for supporting people with disabilities. *International Social Work, 47*, 455.

Marks, D. (2000). Disability. In M. Davies (Ed.), *Blackwell encyclopedia of social work.* (pp. 93). Boston: Blackwell.

Mitchell, R. A. (1999). Community-based rehabilitation: The generalized model. *Asia Pacific Journal of Disability and Rehabilitation, 21*(10–11), 522–528.

Morris, J. (1993). *Community care or independent living.* York: Joseph Rowntree Foundation.

Oliver, M. (2004). If I had a hammer: The social model in action. In J. Swain, S. French, C. Barnes, & C. Thomas (Eds.), *Disabling barriers, enabling environments* (pp. 7–12). Thousand Oaks, CA: Sage.

Pelka, F. (1997). *ABC-CLIO companion to the disability rights movement.* Santa Barbara, CA: ABC-CLIO.

Shakespeare, T. (2006). *Disability rights and wrongs.* New York: Routledge.

Söder, M. (1982). *Handikapbegrepet—en analys utifrån WHO terminology och svensk debatt* [The disability concept—an analysis using WHO terminology and Swedish debate]. Utredningsgruppen för handikapåret 1981. Stockholm: Socialdepartementet.

Thompson, N. (2006). *Anti-discriminatory practice* (4th ed.). Basingstoke, UK: Palgrave Macmillan.

Twelvetres, A. (2002). *Community work* (4th ed.). Basingstoke, UK: Palgrave Macmillan.

United Nations (UN). (2008). Convention on the Rights of Persons with Disabilities. Accessed March 8, 2009, from www.un.org/disabilities/default.asp?id=259.

World Health Organization (WHO). (2008). *World report on disability and rehabilitation.* Concept paper. Accessed March 8, 2009, from www.who.int/disabilities/Concept%20NOTE%20General%202008.pdf.

World Health Organization (WHO). (2001). International classification of functioning, disability and health (ICF). Accessed March 8, 2009, from www.who.int/classifications/icf/en/.

World Health Organization (WHO). (1992). *The work of WHO, 1990–1991: Biennal report of the director-general.* Geneva: Author.

Human Rights and Sexual Orientation

GARY BAILEY

Where, after all, do universal human rights begin? In small places, close to home—so close and so small that they cannot be seen on any map of the world. Yet they are the world of the individual person: The neighborhood he lives in; the school or college he attends; the factory, farm or office where he works. Such are the places where every man, woman and child seeks equal justice, equal opportunity, equal dignity without discrimination. Unless these rights have meaning there, they have little meaning anywhere.

ELEANOR ROOSEVELT

HUMAN RIGHTS OVERVIEW

In 1948, the United Nations General Assembly adopted the Universal Declaration of Human Rights (UDHR). The UDHR is also part of the International Bill of Human Rights. The declaration was in response to the experience of the Second World War and represents the first global expression of rights to which all human beings are entitled. It consists of thirty articles that have been elaborated upon in subsequent international treaties, regional human rights instruments, national constitutions, and laws. The International Bill of Human Rights consists of the Universal Declaration of Human Rights; the International Covenant on Economic, Social and Cultural Rights; and the International Covenant on Civil and Political Rights and its two optional protocols. In 1966 the General Assembly adopted the two detailed covenants, which complete the International Bill of Human Rights, and in 1976, after the covenants had been ratified by a sufficient number of individual nations, the bill took on the force of international law. It was adopted by forty-eight countries, including the United States (Williams, 1981).

The thirty articles are expansive. However, the first, and most important in my opinion, states: "All human beings are born free and equal in dignity and rights. They are endowed with reason and conscience and should act towards one another in a spirit of brotherhood." Article 2 best encapsulates what this chapter is about: "Everyone is entitled to all the rights and freedoms set forth in this Declaration, without distinction of any kind, such as race, color, sex, language, religion, political or other opinion, national or social origin, property, birth or other status. Furthermore, no distinction shall be made on the basis of the political, jurisdictional or international status of the country or territory to which a person belongs, whether it be independent, trust, non-self-governing or under any other limitation of sovereignty."

LESBIAN, GAY, BISEXUAL, AND TRANSGENDER HUMAN RIGHTS

According to Amnesty International USA, "We all have a sexual orientation and a gender identity, and this shared fact means that discrimination against members of the Lesbian, Gay, Bisexual and Transgender community, based on sexual orientation and/or gender identity, is an issue that transcends that community and affects all of us" (Amnesty International, n.d).

SEXUAL ORIENTATION DEFINED

Sexual orientation is the emotional, romantic, sexual, or affectional attraction to another person (American Psychological Association [APA], 2005). Although many people believe that sexual attraction is the only determinant of sexual orientation, the desire to share affection or become life partners also plays a role. A gay man, then, is one who is attracted primarily to other men to satisfy sexual and affectional needs. Likewise, a lesbian is attracted primarily to other women to satisfy these needs, and bisexuals are attracted to both men and women.

Although sexual orientation is defined as a preference for sexual and affectional partners of the same sex, it is a relative rather than an absolute concept. Research such as the work of Kinsey and colleagues indicates that sexual orientation falls along a continuum from totally heterosexual to totally lesbian or gay (Kinsey, Pomeroy, & Martin, 1948). In addition, others have shown that sexual orientation may change during the course of one's life from heterosexual to bisexual to lesbian or gay and vice versa (Savin-Williams, 1998).

Sexual orientation is not the same as gender identity or gender role. Gender identity is one's perception of oneself as female or male, and gender role refers to the behaviors generally expected of females and males. Transgender people are people whose gender identity differs from their physical genital characteristics (Maurer, 1999). People who are transgender sometimes undergo gender reassignment surgery or other medical procedures to help create a match between their gender identity and appearance, although such procedures are expensive and many cannot afford or do not choose to undergo this type of intervention (Bailey, 1996).

Intersex is a term referring to "a variety of conditions in which a person is born with a reproductive or sexual anatomy that doesn't seem to fit the typical definitions of female or male" (Intersex Society of North America, 2005, p. 1). Although chromosomal sex is determined at conception, male and female genitalia are identical until about seven weeks of embryonic development. With the influence of hormones, genitalia differentiate into male or female. For some intersex people, the genitalia are not distinguishable as male or female at birth. For others, their chromosomal sex and their genitalia do not match. Intersex anatomy is not always evident at birth and may not become evident until puberty.

Sexual orientation is not synonymous with sexual lifestyle. In other words, people who identify as heterosexual, lesbian, gay, bisexual, transgender, or intersex may be single, with a partner, celibate, monogamous, or polygamous. Although much of the attention around AIDS has focused on gay men, it is not lesbian or gay behavior, or for that matter heterosexual behavior, that spreads AIDS, it is unsafe sexual practices (see Kamya, Chapter 29 of this volume).

Sexual orientation covers sexual desires, feelings, practices, and identification. It can be toward people of the same or different sexes (same-sex, heterosexual, or bisexual orientation). As mentioned, gender identity refers to the complex relationship between sex and gender, a person's experience of self-expression in relation to social categories of masculinity or femininity (gender). One's subjectively felt gender identity may be at variance with one's sex or physiological characteristics.

The Yogyakarta Principles on the Application of International Human Rights Law in Relation to Sexual Orientation and Gender Identity were developed in 2006 by a group of LGBT (lesbian, gay, bisexual, transgender) experts in Yogyarkata, Indonesia, in response to well-known examples of abuse. The principles provide a universal guide to applying international human rights law to violations experienced by lesbians, gay men, bisexuals, and transgender people to ensure the universal reach of human rights protections (www.yogyakartaprinciples.org).

HUMAN RIGHTS ABUSES

Across the globe, there are many places where sexual orientation or gender identity can lead to execution, imprisonment, torture, violence, or discrimination. The range of abuse is limitless and contravenes the fundamental tenets of international human rights law. Human rights abuses based on sexual orientation or gender can include violation of the rights of the child; the infliction of torture and cruel, inhuman, and degrading treatment (UDHR Article 5); arbitrary detention on grounds of identity or beliefs (UDHR Article 9); the restriction of freedom of association (UDHR Article 20); and the denial of the basic rights of due process.

Examples include execution by the state; denial of employment, housing, or health services; loss of custody of children; denial of asylum; rape and otherwise torture in detention; threats for campaigning for LGBT human rights; and regular subjection to verbal abuse. In many countries, the refusal of governments to address violence committed against LGBT people creates a culture of impunity where such abuses can continue unmitigated. Often, such abuses are committed by the state authorities themselves, with or without legal sanction.

Amnesty International has identified two areas of particular importance and focus in relation to LGBT human rights and in their advocacy efforts on behalf of LGBT people worldwide. Those are the decriminilazation of homosexuality and that of marriage equity.

According to Amnesty International decriminalization is when "individuals are detained or imprisoned solely because of their homosexuality—including those individuals prosecuted for having sex in circumstances which would not be criminal for heterosexuals, or for their gender identity— are considered to be prisoners of conscience" and Amnesty International calls for their immediate and unconditional release.

Amnesty International further calls for the decriminalization of homosexuality where such legislation remains, including a review of all legislation which could result in the discrimination, prosecution and punishment of people solely for their sexual orientation or gender identity. All such laws should be repealed or amended.

Amnesty International views marriage equality as "the right of adults to enter into consensual marriage as enshrined in international human rights standards." Article 16, Universal Declaration of Human Rights (UDHR) states that *"Men and women of full age, without any limitation due to race, nationality or religion, have the right to marry and to found a family. They are entitled to equal rights as to marriage, during marriage and at its dissolution."*

Amnesty International further states that "Civil marriage between individuals of the same-sex is therefore an issue in which fundamental human rights are at stake. Amnesty International believes that the denial of equal civil recognition of same-sex relationships prevents many people from accessing a range of other rights, such as rights to housing and social security, and stigmatizes those relationships in ways that can fuel discrimination and other human rights abuses against people based on their sexual orientation or gender identity" (Amnesty International, n.d).

Amnesty International has opposed discrimination in laws which discriminate on the basis of sexual orientation or gender identity and has called upon states to recognize "families of choice, across borders where necessary." They have further stated that "States should not discriminate against minority groups based on identity."

In addition, Amnesty International-USA has actively focused its efforts on ensuring that :

- all allegations and reports of human rights violations based on sexual orientation or gender identity are promptly and impartially investigated and perpetrators held accountable and brought to justice;
- that all necessary legislative, administrative and other measures are taken to prohibit

and eliminate prejudicial treatment on the basis of sexual orientation or gender identity at every stage of the administration of justice;
- Ensure adequate protection of human rights defenders at risk because of their work on human rights and sexual orientation and gender identity.
(Amnesty International, n.d).

In December 2008, the sixtieth anniversary of the Universal Declaration of Human Rights, the UN General Assembly supported a groundbreaking statement confirming that international human rights protections include sexual orientation and gender identity. It was the first time a statement condemning rights abuses against LGBT people was presented in the General Assembly. It was read into the record by Argentine ambassador Jorge Argüello. The declaration, which is nonbinding, was cosponsored by France and the Netherlands. A cross-regional group of states coordinated the drafting of the statement, including Brazil, Croatia, France, Gabon, Japan, the Netherlands, and Norway.

The 192 member states of the UN were divided on the declaration: It passed with support from 66 countries; however, 57 were opposed and 69 abstained. The 27 countries of the European Union, Australia, Canada, Japan, Mexico, New Zealand, and 34 other countries, including most of Latin America, supported the declaration. The 56 predominately Muslim countries belonging to the Organization of the Islamic Conference and other countries either abstained or voted against the declaration.

Sixty states signed an alternative text promoted by the Organization of the Islamic Conference. While affirming the "principles of non-discrimination and equality," they claimed that universal human rights did not include "the attempt to focus on the rights of certain persons" ("UN: General Assembly statement affirms rights for all," 2008).

The opposition to equal rights for homosexuals and transgendered persons is one of the few principles over which *some* predominately Muslim countries belonging to the Islamic Conference of States (ICS) and the Vatican seem to agree agree. The Holy See voiced strong opposition to the General Assembly statement, and its opposition sparked severe criticism by human rights defenders worldwide. Later in a reversal of its previous position, the Holy See indicated to the General Assembly that it called for the repeal of criminal penalties based on homosexual conduct.

The sixty-six countries reaffirmed "the principle of non-discrimination, which requires that human rights apply equally to every human being regardless of sexual orientation or gender identity." They stated they are "deeply concerned by violations of human rights and fundamental freedoms based on sexual orientation or gender identity," and said that "violence, harassment, discrimination, exclusion, stigmatization and prejudice are directed against persons in all countries in the world because of sexual orientation or gender identity." The statement condemned killings, torture, arbitrary arrest, and "deprivation of economic, social and cultural rights, including the right to health." The participating countries urged all nations to "promote and protect human rights of all persons, regardless of sexual orientation and gender identity," and to end all criminal penalties against people because of their sexual orientation or gender identity ("UN: General Assembly statement affirms rights for all," 2008).

Navanetham Pillay, the UN High Commissioner for Human Rights, strongly supported the statement. In a videotaped message, she cited South Africa's 1996 decision to protect sexual orientation in its Constitution. She pointed to the "task and challenge to move beyond a debate on whether all human beings have rights" to "secure the climate for implementation" ("UN: General Assembly statement affirms rights for all," 2008).

According to calculations by ILGA (International Lesbian, Gay, Bisexual, Transgender and Intersex Association) and other organizations, in 2008 more than seventy countries still had laws against consensual sex between adults of the same sex. The majority of these were left behind by colonial rulers. The UN Human Rights Committee, which interprets the International Covenant on Civil and Political Rights, a core UN treaty, held in a historic 1994 decision that such laws are rights violations—and that human rights law forbids discrimination based on sexual orientation. UN treaty bodies have called on states to end discrimination in law and policy ("UN: General Assembly statement affirms rights for all," 2008).

Human rights violations based on sexual orientation and gender identity happen regularly around the world. For example, in the United States, Amnesty International has documented serious patterns of police abuse against lesbian, gay, bisexual, and transgender people, including incidents amounting to torture and ill treatment. In Egypt, Human Rights Watch documented a massive crackdown on men suspected of homosexual conduct between 2001 and 2004, in which hundreds or thousands of men were arrested and tortured. Egypt actively opposed the General Assembly statement. The International Gay and Lesbian Human Rights Commission has documented how, in many African countries, sodomy laws and prejudice deny rights protections to Africans engaged in same-sex practices amid the HIV and AIDS pandemic and can actually criminalize outreach to affected groups. In 2010, an antihomosexuality bill was filed in the Ugandan Parliament.

Other international bodies have also opposed violence and discrimination based upon sexual orientation and gender identity, including the Council of Europe and the European Union. In 2008, all thirty-four member countries of the Organization of American States unanimously approved a declaration affirming that human rights protections extend to sexual orientation and gender identity (Amnesty International, n.d.).

In 2008, the General Assembly adopted a resolution condemning extrajudicial executions, which contained a reference opposing killings based on sexual orientation. Uganda moved to delete that reference, but the General Assembly rejected this by 78–60.

In June 2009, the US House of Representatives adopted the Foreign Relations Authorization Act (HR 2410). Importantly, the bill has groundbreaking provisions that will strengthen the State Department's attention to serious human rights abuses directed against LGBT individuals worldwide. The bill was adopted over Republican objections that "social issues such as gay rights and abortion have no place in a State Department funding bill" (www.state.gov/documents/organization/120655.pdf). The bill does not focus on social issues; it merely creates mechanisms to improve the US government's support for basic human rights, including the rights of women and of LGBT communities abroad.

The bill instructs the US State Department to establish an Office for Global Women's Issues; to create one or more positions within the Human Rights Bureau to monitor international LGBT concerns; to work through US embassies to encourage countries to repeal or reform laws that criminalize homosexuality or consensual homosexual conduct or that otherwise restrict fundamental human rights; to improve human rights reporting on LGBT issues, with a new requirement to include transgender concerns; and to include LGBT issues in human rights training courses for foreign service officers.

Since 1948, when the Universal Declaration of Human Rights was written, much has changed globally and within the social work profession regarding how the lesbian, gay, bisexual, transgender, and intersex (LGBTI) community and the understanding of sexual orientation in general are viewed and responded to.

A decade ago, the international LGBTI community was primarily known as the gay and lesbian community. The inclusion of bisexuals in the gay and lesbian lexicon was being debated, intersex people were commonly referred to as hermaphrodites, and people were dying from, not living with, HIV and AIDS. The representation of gays and lesbians in the media was sketchy at best, and when they did appear, it was as caricatures.

The social work profession has hardly been at the forefront of advocacy for LGBTI people. For example, it was not until the eighteenth edition of the *Encyclopedia of Social Work*, published in 1987, that the first separate articles on lesbians and gay men appear in the encyclopedia.(NASW, 2008). However, in recent years the profession has taken a number of actions to affirm its commitment to lesbian or gay individuals, particularly in the United States. The current National Association of Social Workers (NASW) Code of Ethics (approved 1996, revised 1999 and 2008) contains the following statement: "The social worker should not practice, condone, facilitate or collaborate with any form of discrimination on the basis of race, color, *sexual orientation* [italics added], age, religion, national origin, and marital status, and political belief, mental or physical disability" (p. 22).

At least ten years ago, most LGB (the *I* and not the *T* appeared in the 1990s) organizations had not begun to address issues of race and class. There was a pervasive lack of awareness of how racism, sexism, and internalized oppression were present in the LGBTI community and influenced the ways in which people experienced their sexuality. The phenomenon of men who would not describe themselves as gay or bisexual but who had sex with other men (MSM) was not being discussed in the same way as it is today. Much has changed in the last decade and yet there is still much more to do as both individual social workers and the profession continue to evolve and prepare the next generation of practitioners. Social workers must understand and be prepared to address gay affirmative practice, the intersection of oppressions, and issues across the life span.

THE SOCIAL WORK PROFESSION

In 2010 the International Federation of Social Workers (IFSW) and the International Association of Schools of Social Work (IASSW) joined with the United Nations and other global bodies in denouncing the proposed antihomosexuality legislation that was before the Ugandan Parliament. IASSW (2010) "called upon social work educators in Uganda to engage their students and graduates around what an appreciation of diversity, tolerance, mutual respect, non-violence and a commitment to the promotion of human rights and social justice might mean in their country and beyond. and on social work educators and practitioners around the world to infuse all our discourses and practices with the recognition of our common humanity which binds us together as social work practitioners, service users, educators and students."

In addition, IFSW (2010) stated that "we respect and uphold the international conventions and treaties which explicitly recognize the right of all individuals to give expression to their sexual orientation, among many other basic rights. These global conventions and policies have been developed by common agreement and in the light of experience and research and are reflected in the global ethical principles of social work, endorsed by IFSW and the International Association of Schools of Social Work (IASSW). No further justification of the right to freedom of sexual orientation is needed or appropriate."

DISCRIMINATION AND OPPRESSION

Discrimination and oppression based on sexual orientation and gender identification affect the life experiences of all LGBTI people and social work practice with this population. These negative attitudes and experiences have been blamed on a lack of accurate information about LGBTI people, homophobia, and heterosexism. Homophobia is a fear of lesbians or gay men that is sometimes manifested in expressions of hatred toward them. Heterosexism is "a set of values and structures that assumes heterosexuality to be the only natural form of sexual and emotional expression" (Zimmerman, 1992, p. 342). The inclusion of a chapter on lesbians and gay men in this text does not imply that people by virtue of their sexual orientation require the assistance of social workers. It does, however, imply that some LGBTI people may need the assistance of social workers because they continue to be members of an oppressed group and because they may encounter problems of concern to social workers that people from all walks of life face.

There are many forms of prejudice, discrimination, and oppression faced by LGBTI people. Both individuals and the state have perpetrated violence against them (Herek & Berrill, 1992). This hatred may result in myriad problems, including hate crimes, loss of employment, and heterosexist health and mental health services. Internalizing these negative messages may result in self-hatred and self-destructive behaviors such as alcohol and drug abuse and suicide. In the following section, some problems that LGBTI people face are discussed. Hate crimes and discrimination have specific implications for the gay community. Problems such as AIDS and violent relationships occur in all segments of society but are also addressed here.

Hate Crimes

Hate crimes are perpetrated against others because of hatred of the group to which the victim is presumed to belong. They may be perpetrated because of the victim's sexual orientation, race, ethnicity, or religion. These crimes take many forms including harassment, vandalism, arson, terrorism, assault, sexual assault, and murder. Hate crimes against LGBTI people are increasing (National Coalition of Anti-Violence Programs, 2000). They affect the whole community and are a form of terrorism that creates fear in those who identify as part of the targeted group.

From 1998 to 1999, the number of murders committed against LGBTI people increased thirteen percent in the United States (National Coalition of Anti-Violence Programs, 2000). Hate crimes are generally perpetrated by male adolescents or young adults who are strangers to the victim and who frequently attack in groups (National Coalition of Anti-Violence Programs, 2000). Hate crimes are viewed by many LGBTI activists as socially condoned since no federal laws ban discrimination against lesbian or gays, and historically, certain behaviors between lesbians or gay men have been criminalized (Amnesty International, 2008).

Nondiscrimination and Civil Rights

Since few states have laws that prohibit discrimination based on sexual orientation, LGBTI people may be discriminated against in employment, housing, education, and other activities with the sanction of law. Benefits that most heterosexuals take for granted are generally denied to people in same-sex relationships. Lesbians and gay men are asserting their right to marry through religious or private noncivil ceremonies, and currently same-sex partners in the United States can legally marry in Maine, Massachusetts, New Hampshire, Vermont, Iowa, Connecticut, and in the District of Columbia. New York, Rhode Island, and Maryland recognize same-sex marriages performed in other states. Additionally, California has 18,000 same-sex couples who legally married prior to changes to the state's constitution in 2008.

Internationally, several countries recognize same-sex marriage: Argentina, Belgium, Canada, South Africa, Spain, Sweden, the Netherlands, and Norway. Mexico's Supreme Court ruled in 2010 that all thirty-one Mexican states must recognize same-sex marriages performed in the capital, Mexico City, though its decision does not force those states to begin marrying gay couples. Countries that recognize same-sex marriages performed in other countries include Aruba (Dutch only), Israel, and the Netherlands Antilles (Dutch only). Numerous cities, towns, and municipalities worldwide recognize civil unions and domestic partnerships between people of the same sex (www.glad.org). Without civil unions, power of attorney, or medical directives, same-sex partners may not make medical decisions or even funeral arrangements for each other. Because laws vary by state, it is important to be aware of strategies to protect LGBTI couples and families in regard to inheritance, custody, and other legal decisions.

Since 2009, US gay couples traveling overseas can show passports that feature their married names, letting them take advantage of a little-noticed revision to the US State Department regulations made to comply with an amendment to the Code of Federal Regulations. This amendment allows same-sex couples to obtain passports under the names recognized by their state through their marriages or civil unions (Lavoie, 2009).

Nationally and internationally, LGBTI advocacy groups are challenging and changing laws and policies that negatively affect them. Lesbian or gay sex between consenting adults continued to be illegal in over half of US states until June 2003, when the Supreme Court finally struck down sodomy laws (see *Lawrence v. Texas*). Many companies and some states and municipalities extend health insurance benefits to same-sex couples (also known as domestic partnerships). Under Secretary of State Hillary Rodham Clinton, the US Department of State took steps to grant some of the same benefits to the partners of gay diplomats as those available to spouses in heterosexual marriages. The changes instituted by the State Department include the following rights of domestic partners: diplomatic passports, government-paid travel to and from foreign posts, the use of US medical facilities abroad, eligibility for US government emergency evacuations, and training at the State Department's Foreign Service Institute. Clinton announced the measures after President Obama's decision to grant certain benefits to the same-sex partners of gay federal employees in June 2009 (Phillips, 2009).

Despite progress, there are still many negative stereotypes and attitudes that must be overcome before LGBTI people enjoy the full benefits of society.

Diversity in the Gay Community and Intersection of Oppression

There is much diversity in the gay community, and the rainbow flag is a universal symbol of this diversity. It includes people of any ethnicity, socioeconomic status, age, religion, and political persuasion. Although all LGBTI people share many experiences of oppression and discrimination, it is important to acknowledge the additional issues that women and people of color face.

Lesbians and bisexual women face additional oppression and discrimination due to sexism. Many lesbians felt that gay liberation was insensitive to them as women who rejected the patriarchal ideas embedded in heterosexuality (Bristow & Wilson, 1993). Lesbians and bisexual women worked to expand the objectives of the gay rights movement to include women's issues and to expand the objectives of the women's movement to include lesbian issues. Lesbianism can be considered an important component of feminism's response to sexism because it challenges the idea that women must maintain subservient (hetero)sexual roles with men (gender inequalities globally are also discussed by Dominelli in Chapter 9 of this volume).

People of color also face many challenges that are compounded by their membership in particular ethnic groups: "Growing up in a racist, sexist, and homophobic society, [they] must deal not only with their sexual identity but with their racial or ethnic identity as well" (Hunter & Schaecher, 1995, p. 1057). By coming out as lesbian, gay, or bisexual, people of color may be rejected by members of their own ethnic group and also face racism within the gay community.

Fortunately, many lesbian and gay organizations now include bisexual, transgender, and intersex people in their activities and membership.

There is a shifting context for exploring and teaching about the intersection of sexual orientation with other manifestations of oppressions (Hamilton-Mason, 2007). Racism, sexism, heterosexism, ageism, ableism, anti-Semitism, and classism are abundant in our society and within the LGBTI community. Helms (1999) argues that becoming a practitioner who can effectively address issues of race, ethnicity, and culture begins with recognizing that race and culture are integral psychological aspects of every person and of the social environment in which she functions. Racial and ethnic socialization (how others treat a person because of his perceived race or ethnicity) shapes an individual's feelings, thoughts, or behaviors toward himself and others, and there are those who feel strongly that discrimination against LGBTI individuals is not truly a human and civil rights issue as defined by activities in the 1940s and 1960s. For social workers, these debates are an opportunity to facilitate dialogue about race, class, power, and privilege. Social workers can help identify the similarities that exist between many social movements but also identify their uniqueness.

REFERENCES

American Psychological Association (APA). (2005). *Answers to your questions about sexual orientation and homosexuality*. Retrieved August 1, 2005, from www.apa.org/pubinfo/answers.html.

Amnesty International. (n.d.). *Lesbian, gay, bisexual and transgender human rights*. Retrieved March 15, 2011, from www.amnestyusa.org/lgbt-human-rights/about-lgbt-human-rights/page.do?id=1106573.

Amnesty International. (2008). *Love, hate, and the law: Decriminalizing homosexuality*. Retrieved March 15, 2011, from www.amnestyusa.org/document.php?id=ENGPOL300032008.

Bailey, J. M. (1996). Gender identity. In R. C. Savin-Williams, & K. M. Cohen (Eds.), *The lives of lesbians, gays, and bisexuals: Children to adults* (pp. 71–93). Fort Worth, TX: Harcourt Brace.

Bristow, J., & A. R. Wilson. (1993). *Activating theory: Lesbian, gay, bisexual politics*. London: Lawrence & Wishart.

Hamilton-Mason, J. (2007). The color of fear as racial identity catalyst. In V. Lewis & H. Vasquez (Eds.), *Lessons from The color of fear. Field reports: Using the Color of Fear in the Classroom* (pp. 73–74). Sterling, VA: Stylus.

Helms, J. E. (1995). An update of Helm's white and people of color racial identity models. In J. Ponterotto, J. M. Casas, L. Suzuki, & C. M. Alexander (Eds.), *Handbook of multicultural counseling* (pp. 181–198). Thousand Oaks, CA: Sage.

Herek, G. M., & Berrill, K. (Eds.). (1992). *Hate crimes: Confronting violence against lesbians and gay men.* Thousand Oaks, CA: Sage.

Hunter, J., & Schaecher, R. (1995). Gay and lesbian adolescents. In R. L. Edwards (Ed.), *Encyclopedia of social work* (pp. 1055–1063). Washington, DC: NASW Press.

International Association of Schools of Social Work (IASSW). (2010, May). IASSW statement on Uganda's anti-homosexuality law. Retrieved August 19, 2010, from www.iassw-aiets.org/index.php?option=com_content&task=blogcategory&id=72&Itemid=106.

International Federation of Social Workers (IFSW). (2010). Human rights and social work in Uganda. Retrieved August 19, 2010, from www.ifsw.org/p38002016.html.

Intersex Society of North America. (2005). p. 1. Retrieved June 27, 2011 from www.isna.org/faq

Kinsey, A. C., Pomeroy, W. B., & Martin, C. E. (1948). *Sexual behavior in the human male.* Philadelphia: W.B. Saunders Co.

Lavoie, D. (2009, June 19). Gay couples can use married names on passports. Retrieved from: http://www.seacoastonline.com/articles/20090619-NEWS-90619025.

Maurer, F. (1999). Affirmative practice understanding and working with lesbian, gay, bisexual, and transgender persons. Washington, DC: NASW Press.

National Coalition of Anti-Violence Programs (2000). Retrieved June 27, 2011 from www.ncavp.org/issues/domesticviolence

National Association of Social Workers (NASW). (2008). Code of ethics. Retrieved from: http://www.social-workers.org/pubs/code/default.asp.

Phillips, K. (2009, June 17). Same-sex partner benefits. The Caucus, *New York Times.* Retrieved March 15, 2011, from http://thecaucus.blogs.nytimes.com/2009/06/17/same-sex-partner-benefits/.

Savin-Williams, R.C. (1998). *And Then I Became Gay: Young Men's Stories.* New York: Routledge.

UN: General Assembly statement affirms rights for all. (2008, December 18). Human Rights Watch. Retrieved March 15, 2011, from www.hrw.org/en/news/2008/12/18/un-general-assembly-statement-affirms-rights-all.

Williams, P. (Ed.). (1981). *The International Bill of Human Rights.* Glen Ellen, CA: Entwhistle.

Zimmerman, B. (1992). What has never been: An overview of lesbian feminist literary criticism. In W. R. Dynes & S. Donaldson (Eds.), *Lesbianism* (pp. 341–365). New York: Garland.

SECTION XI

Conclusions: Toward the Future

International Careers in Social Work

AMY BESS AND ROSEMARY J. LINK

This *Handbook of International Social Work* has gathered chapters from across the globe by a variety of authors in thirty-one countries—and more if counting by author country of origin. The collection has presented the concept that social work is a human rights profession that abides by the covenants, policy instruments, and laws of the United Nations and is preparing its labor force to practice across nation-state borders as a norm for the twenty-first century. The chapter on child soldiers, for example, emphasizes the expectation that social workers will implement programs from a child rights perspective, taking into account the full range of political, economic, and social circumstances of situations where children have been conscripted into the military.

The *Handbook* has also demonstrated that problems of social work arising in a particular country often require an examination of cross-border issues. Social workers concerned with child trafficking in Slovenia, for example, work across borders with Italy, Hungary, Austria, and Croatia. There are homeless children who have been separated from their families while crossing frontiers such as between Mexico and the United States and within war-torn regions of Africa, requiring cross-border family tracing.

It is therefore argued that social work is by nature an international profession. However, the recognition that social workers operate in a global context is growing somewhat slowly among practitioners and educators. Potential employers such as international nongovernmental organizations (NGOs) and the United Nations are in the early stages of making this realization as well. As a result, social work remains an underrepresented and often overlooked profession in the international arena, despite the many qualifications that social workers bring to the table and the opportunities that exist (Lopez & Ihrig, 2009). More work needs to be done to bring to light the many types of expertise that social workers bring to this field.

This chapter describes the many opportunities for social workers to practice internationally. The focus here is the specific out-of-country-of-origin experience of social workers who intentionally choose to practice beyond their familiar nation-state borders. Leon Ginsberg's book on careers in social work (2001) included a short piece on international careers, which would no doubt be longer if written in 2010: "Many social workers have long careers in international work because social problems and social welfare programs are a significant part of the agenda of world organizations and social welfare services" (p. 156).

This chapter encourages social workers to include international social work in their career vision, for example by

- taking up direct practice opportunities in another country by working for an international organization, such as an NGO or United Nations agency;
- studying or participating in a field placement in a new country, ideally in a different experience of social and economic development; or
- volunteering or taking advantage of fellowship opportunities in a global nonprofit organization.

To complement the discussion of international opportunities, the chapter includes narrative from a number of practicing international social workers as well as a list of resources for further information. The chapter has four sections:

I. Emergency humanitarian aid and international development careers with NGOs, multilateral organizations, and bilateral organizations
II. International social work careers arising from cross-border practice

III. How to get started in international social work—international volunteer opportunities and personal and professional qualifications to consider

IV. Guide to career resources providing general tips and advice, job-search websites, and resources on fellowships and volunteer opportunities.

EMERGENCY HUMANITARIAN AID AND INTERNATIONAL DEVELOPMENT CAREERS

The fields of international development and humanitarian aid offer a wide array of careers for social workers. Work settings can range from war-torn or disaster-affected areas requiring short-term emergency humanitarian aid to stable environments where long-term development work is undertaken. The roles and skills required of social workers vary widely as well. This section tries to capture the diversity of positions ideal for social workers by examining types of organizations, including NGOs, multilateral organizations, and bilateral organizations, that hire social workers at the various stages of international development.

Nongovernmental Organizations

International nonprofit organizations involved in development or humanitarian aid are often referred to as NGOs. Chapter 48 of this *Handbook* provides an overview of the types of NGOs and the roles they perform in emergency humanitarian aid and international development. Organizations in this field tend to concentrate on either emergency response or long-term development. However, many address the full spectrum of interventions and initiate projects at any point along the development continuum. The range of sectors that NGOs address typically include agriculture, human trafficking, child protection, civil society, climate change, democracy and good governance, disability, displacement, education, emergency relief, food and nutrition, health, HIV and AIDS, hunger, livelihoods and economic development, microfinance, natural resource management, peace building, refugee assistance, reproductive health and family planning, water and sanitation, women's empowerment, and youth.

Given the variety of organizations and issues they address, there is no single standard social work career with an international development or humanitarian aid NGO. A humanitarian aid worker responding to an emergency will have different tasks and draw on a different set of skills than an international development worker in a stable setting. The following discussion highlights social work roles in the various phases of emergency response and humanitarian aid; postconflict stabilization, transition, and recovery; and longer-term sustainable development.

Emergency Response and Humanitarian Aid

In the immediate aftermath of armed conflict or disaster, NGOs address the survival needs of the affected population, alleviate suffering, and protect the most vulnerable. Social workers become involved in interventions at the international, regional, national, community and interpersonal levels, such as by carrying out joint needs assessments, coordinating teams delivering direct services, and establishing family reunification systems. They collaborate with NGO staff and government officials to clarify and implement best practices in social work and case management to support women affected by gender-based violence or vulnerable children who have been separated from their families. They do this by working at the community level, partnering with communities and local agencies, gaining understanding of local definitions of resilience, and building on existing support networks. For example, Amanya Michael Ebye describes his work with the International Rescue Committee in Box 71.1.

Social workers also help to ensure that the delivery of all services promotes the affected community's dignity and psychosocial well-being. Social workers use their knowledge of psychosocial interventions to strengthen emergency response across sectors. They ensure that the delivery of food, shelter, water, and sanitation do not in any way threaten or harm psychosocial well-being. Social workers in this realm must be familiar with the minimum standards for humanitarian aid outlined in the Sphere Project's Handbook titled "Humanitarian Charter and Minimum Standards for Disaster Response" (The Sphere Project, 2004) as well as the Inter-Agency Standing Committee (IASC) Guidelines on Mental Health and Psychosocial Support in Emergency Settings. The IASC is the primary United Nations mechanism for interagency coordination of humanitarian assistance. The guidelines enable humanitarian actors to plan, establish, and coordinate a set of minimum multisectoral responses to protect and improve people's mental health and psychosocial well-being in the midst of an emergency (IASC, 2008).

Social workers are also employed by NGOs to work at the interpersonal level and provide staff care

BOX 71.1

AMANYA MICHAEL EBYE, MA SSPM (International Rescue Committee)[1]

Currently I am the regional director of the International Rescue Committee in the Middle East, where I lead IRC regional programs in providing humanitarian and postconflict assistance to millions of Iraqis and other conflict-affected people in the region.

I have been regional director for three years, during which time I have led teams in negotiating the establishment and registration of our programs in Jordan, Syria, Iraq, the Palestinian territories, and Yemen. My work day to day includes regional programs management, negotiations with governments, strategic planning, representation, and advocacy. As a regional director, I am a member of the IRC Strategic Development Council, a body responsible for developing the IRC global program and operational strategies and supporting their implementation. I have also played an active role in reestablishing the NGO Coordinating Committee for Iraq, initially establishing a funding partnership with NCCI and later chairing its board for six months.

Before transferring to the Middle East, I was the IRC director for the Darfur operation, responsible for the management of one of the biggest IRC humanitarian programs, providing assistance to close to 800,000 displaced people across Darfur. We provided this assistance in partnership with the government and the displaced population. Working with the Darfur program was very challenging.

Between 2001 and 2005, I worked in Tanzania with the IRC, first as field coordinator for a large field site in western Tanzania, providing care and assistance to close to 200,000 Burundian and Congolese refugees. I then led the IRC program in Tanzania as country director responsible for the day-to-day management of the IRC program in three locations in western Tanzania, providing assistance to thousands of Burundian and Congolese refugees.

I had worked in my country, Uganda, between 1997 and 2001 as the humanitarian and peace program coordinator for ActionAid. This was perhaps the most recent turbulent period we have had as a country. We had an insurgency in the north and western parts of Uganda, heightened violence and displacement in eastern Uganda, and an Ebola outbreak in most parts of the country. The need to respond to these issues grew on a nearly monthly basis. My role as humanitarian and peace program coordinator was to work with our teams in the field to improve their emergency response capacity. We were able to expand our response capacity in northern Uganda, setting up an education program in Kitgum and Pader, an emergency response program in Katakwi and Bundibugyo, and a peace-building program in Kapchorwa.

Between 1994 and 1997, I worked with IRC in Rwanda after the genocide, leading a community assistance program responsible for reuniting separated children and creating conditions in the host community to facilitate the return of thousands of separated children from Tanzania and what was then Zaire. Programs included a housing program for rebuilding destroyed houses, a livestock restocking program, a vocational training program for child-headed households, and a transit center for separated children.

Over seventeen years of my career, I have worked in emergency, postconflict, and development programs. I have worked as a field staff, technical staff, middle-level manager, and senior-level manager. I have worked in both insecure and relatively peaceful environments.

I have had the opportunity to work on programs struggling to reunify separated children, programs working hard to provide education to traumatized children in war zones, programs distributing much-needed humanitarian assistance in a disaster, and programs working to prevent violence against women and girls.

(Continued)

BOX 71.1
(CONTINUED)

My social work training and practitioner experience in various countries around the world have provided me with the invaluable tool kit from which I draw references to deal with various problems at hand. But my best teachers have been my staff and the populations we serve. No education or experience is superior to the local knowledge that communities can offer, which has helped me to develop programs in areas where I was not technically competent. Sitting down with the affected population and asking the practical questions keeps my tool kit replenished. Thanks to my social work education and rural upbringing, I am able to draw on the biggest tool kit available: the affected people themselves. I am always humbled by their resilience and resourcefulness.

Over the next few years, I would like to dedicate my work to ensuring that affected populations and national staff have a stronger voice and role in program decisions that are made.

---

and support during humanitarian operations. They work behind the scenes to provide critical care and support to humanitarian aid staff working in extremely challenging environments.

Due to the high-stress environment of emergency programs and the quickly evolving nature of the situation on the ground, positions tend to range from a few months long to one-year renewable contracts. Humanitarian aid workers often move from one emergency to the next; some join emergency response teams where they are quickly deployed to a crisis days after it occurred. They set in place programs for longer-term teams to manage and then move on to the next crisis.

Postconflict or Postdisaster Recovery

When communities are beginning to stabilize and make the transition to postconflict or postdisaster recovery, NGOs shift their focus from life-saving measures to community rebuilding. At this stage, NGOs concentrate on reintegrating communities separated by conflict and operate programs that help communities rebuild social infrastructure, reestablish social norms, and restore trust and social cohesion.

Social work skills of promoting resilience, cross-cultural understanding, and community participation are particularly useful at this stage of intervention. Organizations often hire social workers to work with community members to identify and strengthen existing social networks that support vulnerable children and eliminate abuse, exploitation, and neglect. Their task is to encourage community participation in planning and implementing educational and employment opportunities for youth at risk, for example, or they may identify and build upon a community's resources to respond to the needs of women who have

experienced gender-based violence. Organizations also seek social workers to coordinate community-driven development programs, a strategy to strengthen civil society and its capacity to participate in democratic reform.

Longer-Term Sustainable Development

At this stage, greater opportunities arise for reform of social sectors. Individual NGO projects in earlier stages can be brought to scale and addressed through a more systematic approach due to the increasingly stable environment. Social workers play a key role in bringing together NGOs, government ministries, and other service providers to create a more coordinated professional response to the social welfare needs of communities. They help to identify gaps and needs in social service systems. This may involve working with local social work institutions to strengthen the social work supervisory skills of government ministry staff or to propose new staffing structures and service delivery modalities. There is evidence that governments are increasingly considering strengthening social protection systems and cash transfer programs, and there may be an increasing need for international technical assistance from social workers with backgrounds in areas such as child welfare systems (USAID, 2009). For example, NGOs work alongside UNICEF (UN Children's Fund) and government ministries to develop comprehensive child protection systems and to implement training for managers and child welfare and protection workers.

Sustainable development also requires addressing the long-term needs and strengths of the social work profession. This entails defining the professional status of social workers through credentialing or licensing, building the capacity of national social work associations, ensuring accessibility to professional development, and developing or disseminating common standards of professional practice.

Multilateral Organizations

Multilateral organizations are international organizations that involve a number of countries working in concert. Social workers employed by multilateral organizations such as UN agencies and the World Bank work in many of the same NGO settings just described. For example, UNICEF activates an emergency response at the onset of a crisis and is also present for longer-term development. The World Bank, typically known for its financial assistance to developing countries, is increasingly supporting social development projects in fragile states.

However, the types of roles that social workers play in multilateral organizations differ slightly from those in NGOs. Social workers with the UN or World Bank tend to focus on developing partnerships and policies with government ministries and NGOs. Social workers will call on their knowledge of policy and advocacy, problem assessment, program management, and strengthening of social welfare systems. Multilateral organizations are more likely to hire social workers with long-term international experience. Jobs can be located at headquarters in New York, Washington, or Geneva, but many are located at field offices in countries around the world. Positions can be multiyear or short-term contracts. Short-term consultancies are available to social workers to lead assessments, evaluations, or training programs.

Careers With the United Nations

The United Nations (UN) was founded in 1945 with the mandate to preserve international peace and security. Today, the UN is composed of 192 member states and employs approximately 83,000 people in its extensive system of agencies and programs (UN, 2009). Highlighted next are UN agencies that are most likely to hire social workers.

United Nations Children's Fund (UNICEF)

Created in 1946 after World War II to provide food, clothing, and health care to children, UNICEF has expanded its mission to provide comprehensive services to address the needs and rights of children. The social work presence in UNICEF continues to grow and tends to be concentrated in projects that assess and improve systems of care for children. A social work consultant or staff member of UNICEF may be asked to work with a particular country program, in coordination with government officials and NGOs, to carry out situation analyses of child-related social policies and laws; assess availability and impact of social work services to analyze gaps and needs; develop country-level policies to address family separation in emergencies, alternative care guidelines, or procedures for reintegrating former child soldiers; or develop systems of social support for women and girls who have been, or are at risk of being, vulnerable to sexual abuse, exploitation, and trafficking.

United Nations Development Programme (UNDP)

The main areas of concern of the UNDP are democratic governance, poverty reduction, crisis prevention and recovery, environment and energy, and HIV and AIDs. It has a strong focus on women's empowerment, and social workers might find themselves in careers where they are responsible for integrating a gender, poverty, and human rights perspective into policy, strategy, and program development in a particular country program. Social workers in community development cover a range of issues including gender, poverty, social exclusion, community participation, vulnerability, and human rights.

Joint United Nations Programme on HIV/AIDS (UNAIDS)

This program brings together ten UN system organizations to coordinate a response to help prevent new HIV infections, care for people living with HIV and AIDS, and mitigate the impact of the epidemic. A social worker might develop policy and technical guidelines on HIV-related issues such as gender, reproductive health, counseling and testing, and mental health. They may train service providers to work with marginalized and at-risk populations. Social workers are being called upon to play a greater role in strengthening health systems because there is recognition by regional health administrations that social care is an important part of HIV programs (USAID, 2009).

United Nations High Commissioner for Refugees (UNHCR)

The UNHCR is mandated to resolve refugee problems worldwide and coordinate efforts to provide protection to refugees and displaced persons. It recruits social workers for a multitude of roles, most often in emergency response and postconflict settings. It hires field-level community service officers and protection officers to perform duties, including participating in the needs assessment of refugees, vulnerable groups, and displaced persons; mobilizing communities for identification of unaccompanied and separated children; establishing protection systems to care for children; establishing standard operating procedures to address sexual and gender-based violence; and training staff and partners on community development principles and participatory methods. Typically, a background in community organization and previous work in immigration or humanitarian aid is required.

The agency also seeks social workers in international positions related to refugee resettlement, including psychosocial specialists, child protection workers, and status-determination specialists, to name a few. In these positions, one may work in a country hosting a refugee population prior to resettlement in a third country and be responsible for making best-interest determinations for refugee children, coordinating the provision of psychosocial services and counseling to refugees and survivors of violence and torture, or advocating for women's rights, gender issues, and the protection of refugee women and girls.

Other UN Agencies to Consider

The UN Department of Safety and Security (UNDSS) establishes teams of field stress counselors to provide critical-incident stress counseling to humanitarian aid providers associated with the UN and to build sustainable stress management systems in UN country offices. For example, there are approximately eighty-five professional counselors in the UN system globally that can be accessed by UNICEF staff when needed (Porter & Emmens, 2009).

The United Nations Population Fund (UNFPA) focuses on reproductive health, women's empowerment, and population and development strategies. Examples of roles for a social worker could include managing a portfolio of programs that train children and youth on HIV prevention and conducting analyses of women's exposure to gender-based violence.

Other UN agencies for social workers to consider include the World Health Organization (WHO), which advocates for a strong mental health response as part of its overall health mandate, and the International Labour Organization (ILO), which focuses on gender equality, rights of indigenous groups, child labor, and HIV and AIDS.

World Bank

The World Bank has been steadily increasing its proportion of projects that address social development as a component of its overall approach to promote economic growth, improve services, and strengthen institutions (International Bank for Reconstruction and Development, 2005). Social development activities of the bank are pertinent to social workers, particularly community-driven development, conflict prevention, and reconstruction interventions.

Bilateral Agencies

For the purposes of this chapter, bilateral organizations are national government entities that provide aid to another country. Some of the largest bilateral aid donors are the Australian Government Overseas Aid Program (AusAID), the Canadian International Development Agency (CIDA), the Japan International Cooperation Agency (JICA), Germany's Deutsche Gesellschaft für Technische Zusammenarbeit (GTZ), the United Kingdom's Department for International Development (DFID), and the United States Agency for International Development (USAID).

Whereas countries such as Japan coordinate most of their international aid through a primary agency, the United States spreads its aid across a wide range of entities. These include the State Department's Bureau of Population, Refugees, and Migration (PRM), which provides aid for refugees, victims of conflict, and stateless people globally, and the Office of US Foreign Disaster Assistance (OFDA), which is responsible for providing nonfood humanitarian assistance in response to international crises and disasters and is part of the Bureau for Democracy, Conflict, and Humanitarian Assistance (DCHA) in USAID, along with the Office of Transition Initiatives (DCHA/OTI) and the Office of Food for Peace (DCHA/FFP). International development aid is supported by USAID; the Departments of Defense, Health and Human Services, and Agriculture; and to a smaller extent dozens of other US government entities.

Bilateral aid agencies ultimately fund a significant portion of the NGO work in emergency response previously described in this chapter. These agencies require social work expertise to deploy emergency personnel on disaster assessment teams and to provide ongoing technical expertise to grantees. Several of the agencies, such as DFID, GTZ, and USAID, fund and provide technical support to social development and social protection programs in developing countries and need staff with social work backgrounds. See the Box 71.2 from Maury Mendenhall, who provides technical expertise to USAID on working with orphans and vulnerable children.

Governments also hire foreign service officers to support public diplomacy efforts in other countries,

BOX 71.2
MAURY MENDENHALL, MSW (USAID)

I am a technical adviser for Orphans and Vulnerable Children (OVC) at the United States Agency for International Development (USAID), Bureau of Global Health, Office of HIV/AIDS. I am a Global Health Fellow. My focus is primarily on countries supported through the US President's Emergency Plan for AIDS Relief (PEPFAR). I am responsible for working with USAID missions and other US government, bilateral, and multilateral partners to strengthen the technical capacity of host governments, NGOs, and community-based organizations to address the multidimensional needs of OVC.

Prior to joining USAID, I was a senior technical specialist for the Child and Youth Program at World Learning, the emergency child and youth protection and development coordinator for the International Rescue Committee, a child protection specialist for UNICEF in Southern Sudan, and a Presidential Management Fellow within the US Department of Labor's International Child Labor Program.

It has been helpful to be familiar with clinical social work practice in the United States. However, I tend to consider local social workers to be better positioned to provide direct or clinical social welfare services due to language and cultural issues. I have more frequently applied skills learned in my community development courses (i.e., assessment and survey techniques, community mobilization, advocacy, fund-raising, grant proposal development). As PEPFAR has increased support for systems-strengthening efforts, it has also been helpful to have an understanding of the child welfare system in the United States and various models in other parts of the world.

Advice or tips I have for others interested in starting a career in this field include the following:

- *Travel*—Most of my lucky career breaks have come as a result of being in the right place at the right time. Set up informational interviews with program managers and bring along your CV. Discuss aspects of their program that interest you and ask about current or future job opportunities.
- *Consider working in emergencies*—Organizations working in emergency situations experience significant staff turnaround and are often in urgent need of staff.
- *Learn French*—Programs in French-speaking countries are chronically difficult to staff.
- *Volunteer*—You may be required to take a pay cut in order to transition into a field that is more suited to your interests. However, a little experience goes a long way, particularly from interesting volunteer experiences with well-respected organizations.

and some recruit social workers. The US Department of State, for example, identifies a social work degree as one of several preferred degrees of a foreign service officer.

INTERNATIONAL SOCIAL WORK CAREERS ARISING FROM CROSS-BORDER PRACTICE

Many aspects of cross-border practice are evolving in the social work profession, some of which will be introduced here. They include the work of reconnecting family members who have been separated by traumatic events, the work of protecting children at borders when they are caught up in cross-border activity as undocumented immigrants or trafficked against their will, the legal work of international adoptions, the work of organizations such as the International Federation of Social Workers (IFSW) in supporting initiatives in a variety of countries, and the work of professors exchanging their expertise across borders.

Earlier in this book, the work of International Social Service (ISS) is described, and it represents one of the most readily recognized forms of cross-border practice. Described in Chapter 13, is a network of social service agencies that provide social and legal assistance to families experiencing social problems as a result of migration or displacement. Social workers with ISS may perform intercountry home studies, facilitate assistance to ill citizens repatriated home from foreign countries, or coordinate family tracing.

Often children are abandoned at borders or caught up in trafficking or failed attempts to join family members who have already crossed illegally, and their plight is serious and increasing (Thompson, 2003). The KLUC organization in Eastern Europe has been working out of the Slovenian city of Ljubljana to educate the public and immigration professionals and to provide resource materials at borders directly to young people at risk. One example is their *dictionario*, which contains guidance and resource numbers. It is a small, palm-sized book that looks like an ordinary dictionary so as not to arouse the suspicion of adult traffickers.

Another area of cross-border practice and careers is international adoption. Rotabi explores the various perspectives and professional aspects of international agencies and adoptions in Chapter 11. Although an expanding area of practice for many years, it has also met great controversy, especially where children seem to be imported to wealthier nations from less developed countries where families struggle with poverty. Social workers building careers in this area become familiar with The Hague Convention and the Convention on the Rights of the Child, further described by Link in Chapter 68.

A more recent development in cross-border careers relates to peacemaking. In Box 71.3, the experiences of Michele Braley and Nils Dybvig in

---

BOX 71.3

MICHELE BRALEY AND NILS DYBVIG, FULL-TIME VOLUNTEERS, CHRISTIAN PEACEMAKER TEAMS, BASED IN BARRANCABERMEJA, COLOMBIA

We provide physical and political accompaniment to civilian communities at risk of violence due to the more than forty-year-old armed conflict in Colombia. Physical accompaniment is the work we do to provide an international presence at meetings of human rights and development organizations. Our presence and our witness are deterrents to armed groups that might want to disrupt community-based organizing and peacemaking. Political presence is the work we do to make more visible the conflict in Colombia and to change US foreign policy that is negatively affecting Colombia. We take the stories we have seen and heard in the field and bring them to State Department staff, US legislators, and US-based peace groups to advocate for changes in US foreign policy, including reducing military spending in Colombia and increasing development aid.

Joining Christian Peacemaker Teams (CPT) is the first international work for either of us, although it's not the first time we have lived abroad. Michele is a generalist social worker with experience in community organizing, chemical health, developmental disabilities, and family violence. Nils's career has focused on program planning and development, with an emphasis on programs and policies to end poverty.

The work of CPT reflects our social work values. We work in communities where we are invited, and our presence allows others to make changes in their lives. We don't come in with answers; Colombians are experts on their country and the changes they seek. Our focus is to take responsibility for changing ourselves and our country's foreign policy. As peacemakers, we respect the religious beliefs of the communities where we work and we join with all civilians committed to nonviolence, regardless of religious orientation.

We encourage others interested in international accompaniment work to learn the local language. Though fluency in the local language may not be required, you will feel more useful, be better able to build relationships with local communities, and benefit from gaining firsthand knowledge. We also encourage you to verify that the organization furthers your social work values. Traditional models of international development work have viewed the international worker as bringing resources and expertise that are not available to the local community. This model is based in a strengths perspective that respects self-determination and views individuals and communities as the experts on their own future.

Colombia are presented to illustrate their work to witness and deter violence both within countries and across borders. Former president Jimmy Carter, in his observation of elections in a number of war-torn countries, has also spoken of the power of presence and witness (Carter, 2004). This may be an under-recognized area of intervention for social workers, despite their long-standing commitment to peace and social justice.

In Chapter 42 the International Federation of Social Workers (IFSW) is presented by Nigel Hall, who outlines some of the work of professional visits and exchanges. This organization offers support and resources at many levels of service, such as offering assistance to young carers in Africa whose parents have died.

Another aspect of cross-border practice relates to educational exchanges and the work of professors and students who visit each other's countries and contribute to the education and training of social workers. The chapter in this text on international field placements by Lager (Chapter 51) and the chapter on social work exchanges by Čačinovič Vogrinčič and Link (Chapter 52) describe some of these initiatives.

HOW TO GET STARTED IN AN INTERNATIONAL SOCIAL WORK CAREER

Often when social workers want to enter the field of international social work, they apply for positions and are told that they must have prior international experience. This can be a frustrating, seemingly circular process for those new to the field. Networking and requesting informational interviews are important first steps. An internship, fellowship, or volunteer position can then be the best ways to get a foot in the door. Such positions provide an opportunity to get a better idea of the nature of the work while gaining relevant skills, demonstrating a commitment to the field, and developing a network of contacts for future jobs. Financial constraints can be considerable, and few volunteer positions are paid. Some fellowships are available, but most pertain to midcareer professionals, such as the Global Health Fellows Program at USAID. The Peace Corps, described in more detail in the next section, offers a small stipend, loan deferment programs for some types of loans, and partial loan cancellation for Perkins loans. Eileen Ihrig, currently the Director of International Programs at the Boston College Graduate School of Social Work offers some advice based on her broad experience in Box 71.4.

International Social Work Volunteer Opportunities

A broad array of opportunities exist for overseas volunteer positions. Two groups are highlighted here.

Peace Corps

The Peace Corps was established in 1963 with the goal of promoting world peace and friendship. Peace Corps assignments typically last two years, and volunteers work in the following areas: education, youth outreach, and community development; business development; agriculture and environment; health and HIV and AIDS; and information technology. Volunteers may apply at any point in their career, and the Peace Corps actively recruits midcareer professionals and volunteers over the age of fifty (Peace Corps, 2009).

Social workers with training in working with children, youth, and families may, for example, be assigned to a project to support youth development through youth centers and youth-led NGOs. Social workers with community organizing experience may find themselves in assignments promoting community involvement and carrying out community development projects focused on a range of issue areas, such as formal and nonformal education, youth development, health and HIV and AIDS, and the environment. The Peace Corps has also recruited experienced social workers to be university-level social work teachers in Eastern Europe (Ginsberg, 2001).

United Nations Volunteers (UNV)

The UNV program looks for a wide range of expertise and backgrounds for volunteer positions in development assistance and humanitarian aid. This program is often appropriate for people early in their international careers. The program recruits most volunteers from developing countries. For example, in 2008, out of the 5276 volunteers serving outside their country, only 92 were from the United States (UNV, 2009). A social worker may be recruited to be a gender specialist to work on mainstreaming gender issues into aspects of prevention, conflict management, postconflict reconstruction, or peace building. The program has approximately 55 volunteer gender specialists who work with governments and civil society organizations on gender analysis and research, economic empowerment, and gender-responsive budgeting as well as on addressing the impact of armed conflict and gender-based violence (UNV, 2009).

BOX 71.4
EILEEN IHRIG, MSW (Boston College)

Currently, I am the director of international programs at the Boston College Graduate School of Social Work. Prior to joining Boston College in March 2010, I directed the international and MSW/MPH programs at the Tulane School of Social Work beginning in August 2005. As director of international programs, I am responsible for the development, oversight, and coordination of all aspects of the school's international programs, including international field placements and partnership development. I work closely with students to help them prepare for careers in international social work through advising and matching them with international field placements. I also work closely with faculty to assist with the integration of international content into the foundation coursework and to support international courses, student and faculty exchanges, and cross-national collaborative projects and research.

Before joining the Tulane School of Social Work in 2005, I spent ten years working overseas on humanitarian aid projects in transitioning, postconflict, and postdisaster settings. First, I completed two years of volunteer service with Peace Corps in Romania working on social work education and NGO development projects, and I stayed on for an additional year to start a child welfare reform project that focused on enhancing the government's capacity to offer family-based care alternatives for children living in institutions. Subsequently, I implemented a number of child and youth development, NGO development, and health projects in Russia, Tajikistan, and Pakistan with the United Methodist Committee on Relief and Mercy Corps. Just before joining the Tulane School of Social Work in 2005, I worked with ChildFund International (formerly Christian Children's Fund) in Sri Lanka implementing child protection projects in communities affected by the Indian Ocean Tsunami.

I found that my social work education and experience as a practitioner in the United States provided me with an invaluable theoretical foundation and skill set for working cross-culturally in a variety of settings. The ability to conduct an accurate and contextually relevant assessment of individuals, families, communities, and organizations was essential to developing an understanding of the social, political, and cultural context as well as being able to start where the client is. As senior manager, my most frequently used skills included supervisory and interpersonal skills along with skills in strategic planning, organizational development, program development, program management (including budget management), monitoring and evaluation, and teaching and training. Being open, flexible, and respectful and having a good sense of humor has served me well!

It is a challenge to enter the field of international social work. Many employers are reluctant to hire someone who has little or no work experience in a cross-cultural setting. In mapping out your career path, keep in mind that it is most useful to have a desired skill set, international work or volunteer experience, and language skills. Peace Corps, United Nations Volunteers, and other long-term volunteer opportunities are an excellent way to get the necessary international experience. Conducting internships with UN agencies, NGOs, and other international organizations can help you get your foot in the door. Building a professional network will help you to stay employed over time once you have established yourself as an international social worker.

Personal and Professional Qualifications to Consider

As mentioned earlier in this chapter, many international social work positions require a high degree of knowledge and professional expertise in the technical area of the position, whether it is in child protection, HIV and AIDS, or human trafficking, for example. However, organizations often look for entry-level workers with general social work knowledge and professional skills in key areas. These are skills that social workers can develop throughout their studies, field placements, and domestic positions. They are easily translatable to international positions and include grant writing, program design and development; staff training, development, and management; curriculum development; foreign language ability (e.g., French, Spanish, Arabic); strategic planning; and monitoring and evaluation.

It is important to closely examine one's personal motivations and competencies to identify whether international social work is a good fit. International social work outside of one's country of origin can take place in remote areas where basic comforts are limited. In humanitarian aid work, social workers are exposed to risks inherent in unstable settings following a conflict or disaster, including limited local infrastructure, lack of basic law and order, and fragile systems of health care and food delivery. In most settings, work is intense and entails long hours with unpredictable communications systems to stay in touch with family and friends back home. This can lead to high levels of stress that workers must be careful to monitor and address. In addition to an ability to remain calm in stressful situations, other personal competencies important to international work include: flexibility, self awareness, quick problem analysis in new situations, building trusting relationships across cultures, and making difficult decisions confidently and calmly (Emmens & Swords, 2010).

SUMMARY

As this chapter has highlighted, international social work encompasses a wide array of career possibilities. The range of settings, types of employers, and variety of roles that a social worker can experience in this field is far ranging. When initially launching a career, getting a foot in the door may be a challenge. A new international social worker may struggle while trying to gain enough international experience to be qualified for some of the positions described in this chapter. However, the social work profession is increasingly being recognized as a human rights and global profession. This will certainly lead to more and more career opportunities in humanitarian assistance, international development, and cross-border practice as employers, whether they are NGOs or multilateral or bilateral organizations, recognize the value and importance of a strong social work background.

NOTE

1. In 2011, Mr. Ebye was appointed Senior Regional Advisor, IRC, Democratic Republic of Congo.

CAREER RESOURCES ON THE INTERNET

Please note that this is not an exhaustive list and that Web site addresses routinely change.

General Resources

Aid Workers Network (www.aidworkers.net): Offers advice for first-time aid workers, tips for finding a job, and resources for those currently in the field.

Devex (www.devex.com/career_advice): Offers career advice for humanitarian aid and international development workers. Much of the information is available to nonmembers.

Idealist (www.idealist.org): Provides a list of organizations offering global volunteering opportunities (http://www.idealist.org/info/IntlVolunteer) and a list of international development fellowships (http://www.idealist.org/info/Careers/EntryPoints/Fellowships).

Job-Search Sites

A large number of websites exist to help international social workers search for jobs. This list provides the most popular sites by type of employing agency.

NGOs

Alert Net (www.alertnet.org): Started by the Reuters Foundation, this is a humanitarian news network with listings for humanitarian aid jobs.

Devex (www.devex.com): Hosts a job board for international development positions and provides business information related to foreign assistance.

DEVJOBS (www.devjobsmail.com): Provides international job announcements for various fields in a wide range of locations.

DevNetJobs (www.devnetjobs.org): Lists jobs and consultancies in international development.

Eldis (www.eldis.org/go/jobs): Provides job listings, resources, and news related to international development, policy, practice, and research.

Foreign Policy Association (www.fpa.org/jobs): Lists jobs, internships, and volunteer opportunities in relief and development organizations.

Idealist (www.idealist.org): Lists a large number of jobs and provides a free daily e-mail service.

OneWorld (http://us.oneworld.net/jobs): Provides links to international aid and development jobs with NGOs.

ReliefWeb (www.reliefweb.int): Popular site for jobs in emergency humanitarian relief with NGOs.

United Nations

UN Employment (www.un.org/en/employment/): Provides information on how to apply for jobs at the UN.

UN Jobs (www.unjobs.org): Organization that is not affiliated with the UN but provides links to job openings at the UN.

US Government

Franklin Fellowship Program (http://careers.state.gov/ff): Describes an opportunity to work on foreign policy and global issues of importance to the United States.

GlobalCorps (www.globalcorps.com/jobseek.html): Works under contract to USAID/OFDA and DCHA/OTI to recruit personal services contractors (PSCs). The website provides descriptions of open and past positions, guidance on applying for jobs, and information on each office's mission.

Global Health Fellows Program (www.ghfp.net/index.fsp): Works to improve the effectiveness of USAID population, health, and nutrition programs by developing and increasing the capacity of health professionals in Washington, DC, and overseas. The website lists available fellowships and internships.

US Agency for International Development (www.usaid.gov/careers/): Describes the range of opportunities at USAID, from foreign service and civil service positions to personal service contracts to fellowship programs.

US State Department (http://careers.state.gov/): Provides information about careers in the foreign service and civil service.

REFERENCES

Carter, J. (2004, February). Keynote address. Nobel Peace Prize Forum, St. Olaf College, Northfield, MN.

Emmens, Ben & Swords, S. (2010). *CBHA Humanitarian Capacity Building Program Objective 1 Final Report* Consortium of British Humanitarian Agencies (CBHA). Retrieved from: http://www.ecbproject.org/competencylaunch.

Ginsberg, L. (2001). *Careers in social work* (2nd ed.). Boston: Allyn & Bacon.

Inter-Agency Standing Committee (IASC). (2007). *IASC guidelines on mental health and psychosocial support in emergency settings*. Geneva: Author.

International Bank for Reconstruction and Development. (2005). *Empowering people by transforming institutions: Social development in World Bank operations*. Washington, DC: World Bank.

Lopez, L., & Ihrig, E. (2009). Social workers: Ready for the challenge. *Monday Developments, 27*(11), 22–23.

Thompson, G. (2003, November 3). Crossing with strangers: Children at the border; littlest immigrants, left in hands of smugglers. *New York Times*. www.nytimes.com/2003/11/03/world/crossing-with-strangers-children-border-littlest-immigrants-left-hands-smugglers.html.

Peace Corps. (2009). *Performance and accountability report fiscal year 2009*. Retrieved from http://multimedia.peacecorps.gov/multimedia/pdf/policies/annrept2009.pdf.

Porter, B., & Emmens, B. (2009). *Approaches to staff care in international NGOs*. People In Aid/InterHealth. Retrieved from www.peopleinaid.org/pool/files/publications/approaches-to-staff-care-in-international-ngos.pdf.

The Sphere Project (2004). *Humanitarian Charter and Minimum Standards in Disaster Response*. Oxford: Author. Retrieved from: www.sphereproject.org.

United Nations. (2009). Personnel Statistics. Retrieved from www.unsceb.org/ceb/stats/hr/ps/years/2009.

United Nations Volunteer Program (UNV). (2009). *Annual report 2008: Forging paths for peace*. Retrieved from www.unv.org/news-resources/resources/annual-report-2008.html.

US Agency for International Development (USAID). (2009). *Third annual report to Congress on Public Law 109-95, the Assistance for Orphans and Other Vulnerable Children in Developing Countries Act of 2005*. Retrieved from http://pdf.usaid.gov/pdf_docs/PDACN600.pdf.

International Labor Mobility in Social Work

KAREN LYONS AND NATHALIE HUEGLER

INTRODUCTION

As indicated in Chapter 33, mobility of labor is a major theme in migration. However, relatively little attention has been paid to the topic in the field of social work, and we are not aware of any systematic international research into the scale of this phenomenon. One reason for this is that social work is seen as an essentially local activity, bound by the laws and policies of individual states and expected to be in tune with the culture and needs of local communities.

However, this perception has been shifting over the past decade, with increasing acceptance of the implications of globalization for welfare and social work (Healy, 2001). Additionally, the increasing diversity of populations in many societies calls for an increase in cultural competence, partly addressed through requirements at the qualifying training stage but also sometimes met through recruitment policies (including overseas recruitment). The fact that a proportion of social workers[1] choose to work abroad illustrates one aspect of ways in which social work is becoming a more international activity. The term *international social worker* is therefore used in this chapter in preference to *overseas* or *immigrant workers* to describe those who are working in countries other than where they qualified.

In this chapter we draw on a few reports of small-scale studies in particular locations, data from selected regulatory bodies, and our own experience to

- identify motivations for working abroad,
- look at some of the structural and policy issues affecting labor mobility, and
- consider some of the advantages and challenges posed by this phenomenon.

WHY DO SOCIAL WORKERS WORK ABROAD?

There is very little research into social workers' motivations for seeking work outside their home countries. A recent example in the context of the United Kingdom is Hussein, Stevens, and Manthorpe's study on International Social Care Workers in England (2010) which considers social workers as part of the wider group of 'social care workers'. Also within the wider field of health and social care, clues may be derived from studies about the motivations and experiences of nurses who migrate (e.g. Winkelmann-Gleed, 2006). Additionally, literature in the related field of choosing placements abroad, experiential evidence, and anecdotal evidence suggest some models of motivation:

- Altruism and adventure
- Exploring roots and identity
- Professional development opportunities
- Improving life chances.

These categories are not necessarily discrete or comprehensive, but they offer a framework for discussion. Whatever the dominant motivation, whether such movements turn out to be short- or long-term strategies depends on a range of macro and micro factors, including the directions that migration policies, welfare systems, and associated employment opportunities take in sending and receiving countries and the extent to which migrants establish personal relationships and put down roots in their new countries.

Altruism and Adventure

This is perhaps the longest standing form of international social work and is closely tied to motivation for entering social work in general, but in this case the people to be helped live in foreign locations and work abroad provides an opportunity for professionals to broaden their personal horizons and experience new cultures. Generations of social workers have sought work abroad (usually in international voluntary organizations such as the Red Cross) and have usually spent time-limited periods in a particular country before returning home or moving elsewhere. Though the stereotype of such workers is that they are young and unencumbered, there are indications that an increasing number have already worked for some years in their own countries and see such posts abroad as a kind of sabbatical or as an opportunity to share their experience through consultancy work. The direction of this form of mobility has typically been from the Global North to the South and more recently from West to East.

Exploring Roots and Identity

Given the extent to which large scale transcontinental migrations have occurred since the mid-nineteenth century from some European countries (e.g., Greece, Spain, Sweden, UK), there are substantial populations in countries such as Argentina, Australia, Canada, and the United States with family roots in Europe. It is therefore not surprising that one of the reasons for working abroad by some (usually young) social workers is to spend time in their family's country of origin. Seeking social work employment is a way of using their qualifications and gaining professional experience while funding a period of travel and residence that is often significant in terms of personal identity development. The relocation is typically between advanced industrial (or postindustrial) countries that share a common language.

A variation of this model can be seen in the case of the Caribbean region, where slavery transplanted millions of people from Africa. More recent migration to Canada, the United States, and the United Kingdom to take up employment resulted in many children being raised and educated in such countries in the second half of the twentieth century. However, there has since been some evidence of people at later stages in their careers returning to islands such as Jamaica to take up posts, including in social work, and facing the challenges of being seen as outsiders and having to come to terms with a new perspective on their dual identity (Small, 2007; Williams, 2007).

Professional Development Opportunities

This motivation is likely to be present in association with any of the others but is also likely to be dominant in the case of young professionals for whom there are limited opportunities for employment in social work in their own countries or where opportunities for professional advancement are limited by restrictions in the educational qualifications open to social workers. Thus there are examples in Europe of oversupply of qualified social workers relative to jobs available (e.g., Greece, Spain), and of access to doctoral qualifications limited by the type of institution in which

social workers gained their first award (e.g., Greece, Netherlands). Some of these underemployed or unemployed social workers seek work and advanced qualifications in other countries such as Canada or the United Kingdom (Lyons & Lawrence, 2006). There may be differences in the first language of the international social worker, but there are likely to be assumed similarities about comparable or superior standards of welfare provision and social work qualifications and practices in the destination country.

Improving Life Chances

Along with other occupational groups, there will always be a proportion of people who seek employment in social work agencies (and, even more likely, in the wider social care field) abroad because of precarious and poorly paid employment opportunities or even risk to themselves and their families in their own countries. Examples include staff from the Philippines working in social care settings and social workers from countries such as South Africa and Zimbabwe working in children and family fieldwork teams in England. While long-term studies specifically in the field of social work are lacking, there are some indications of different patterns of migration to improve life chances. This includes, for example, workers (often women) who migrate without their families and send remittances to dependants 'back home'; those who bring families with them and plan to make a new life in their adopted country; as well as those who consider migration to one country as a stepping stone for onward migration to another (Hussein et al., 2010). When improving life chances is the dominant motivation, relocation is more likely to involve a move from the Global South to the Global North.

STRUCTURAL FACTORS AND POLICY ISSUES

The previous section was framed largely from the perspective of individual decisions about migration, but recruitment and employment of foreign nationals is also facilitated or discouraged by a variety of structural factors and regional and national policies (e.g., relating to immigration and equivalency of qualifications). Social workers have sometimes benefited from policies that invariably favor issuing work permits to people who have skills that are in short supply in the receiving country.

We can take the example of the United Kingdom to illustrate the impact of national and regional policies. In the early years of the twenty-first century there was an acknowledged shortage of qualified staff, and one strategy was to recruit qualified staff from abroad. This was facilitated by immigration rules since the UK Home Office included social workers among the occupational groups for which employers could get work permits. Such permits were not age restricted, covered married partners and children, and could be issued for up to five years. Recruitment was sometimes by specialist recruitment agencies and sometimes arranged through contacts and initiatives of existing staff (Lyons & Littlechild, 2006). According to data from the General Social Care Council (GSCC), 6,477 internationally qualified social workers were on the professional register in 2010. They came from seventy-nine countries, with high proportions coming from South Africa, India, Australia, the United States and Germany (GSCC, 2011).

However, various efforts have also been made since 2000 to improve the perceptions and standards of social work and to increase the number of home-grown employees, including government publicity campaigns to increase recruitment to training courses, the upgrading of the basic qualification from a two-year nongraduate diploma to a three-year degree and provision of bursaries, the establishment of a register of accredited social workers, and the introduction or promotion of various policies and practices by individual employing agencies aimed at staff development and retention. Some of these initiatives benefited some of the international members of the workforce as well as established employees, but some militated against continuing recruitment from abroad since, for example in the case of registration, the process of recognizing qualifications was lengthened and made more expensive for applicants.

Over a similar period, events were occurring regionally that have also had an impact on the previous pattern of international recruitment. While the European Union (EU) does not control the immigration laws of individual member states, nevertheless it influences how these are framed, and there were tendencies at both national and European levels to make immigration policies more restrictive (Schierup, Hansen, & Castles, 2006). Additionally, the number of countries included in the EU increased from fifteen to twenty-five in 2004 and to twenty-seven in 2007, significantly expanding the region to the south (the Mediterranean) and east (for instance, up to the borders of Russia and Ukraine). One result was an increase in the pool of labor and in labor mobility between countries within the EU (since free movement of labor is one of the tenets of single market). This has affected social work and social care insofar

as there is now greater encouragement to recruit from EU countries (where the rules governing work permits are different) rather than countries farther afield. In 2008, the United Kingdom's Migration Advisory Committee (2008) recommended the removal of social work and social care from the national list of skills-shortage occupations, but more recent reviews have meant that social workers can still be recruited from countries outside the EU, for work with children and families only (UK Border Agency, 2011).

White (2007) has shown that opportunities for international mobility also vary within the region covered by the North American Free Trade Association (NAFTA); for instance, it is easier for a social worker from Canada to gain employment in the United States than it is for one from Mexico. White also gives figures for the number of people overall from particular countries or regions outside North America who are issued work permits and discusses the provisions under which social workers might seek entry to the United States, including meeting the requirements of individual states to be licensed to practice. All applicants also have to satisfy the regulatory body, the Council on Social Work Education (CSWE), that their educational and professional qualifications are comparable to those awarded in the United States. In 2009 and 2010, CSWE carried out 159 international evaluations (110 at the master's level) for applicants from 29 countries (CSWE, 2010).

The issue of comparability of qualifications is a key factor in facilitating or blocking international labor mobility. For instance, the long-established pattern of a four-year qualifying degree for social workers in Australia has meant that some social workers who were keen to emigrate or work there for a temporary period either needed to retake a qualifying course once there or could only access lower-paid jobs for which a professional qualification was not a requirement.

This issue was a factor in the joint drafting of a document by the International Association of Schools of Social Work (IASSW) and International Federation of Social Workers (IFSW), the Global Standards for the Education and Training of the Social Work Profession, agreed upon in 2004 (Sewpaul & Jones, 2005). It seems unlikely that this will result in short- or long-term convergence in the content and patterns of training, and the notion of global standards is not without its critics. However, it is not unreasonable that international bodies should seek agreements about key issues, roles, and purposes of the profession for which students are being trained, even if these are at the meta level; clearly they must take into account the wide variations in conditions in which social work is undertaken and the traditions framing social work education. In such circumstances, and given that the international associations have no regulatory powers, the global standards have appropriately been describedas aspirational rather than prescriptive (Sewpaul, 2005).

ADVANTAGES AND CHALLENGES OF OCCUPATIONAL MOBILITY

In this section, we examine the possible advantages and challenges of international labor mobility in social work from the point of view of the professional and of the providers and recipients of services.

Personal Advantages and Challenges

Literature discussing field placements or study visits abroad have identified a number of advantages to individual social workers, and we can make an initial assumption that these also apply to some of the people who migrate for work. Thus, there are the advantages of broadening one's horizons and contributing to personal and professional development (Lyons & Ramanathan, 1999). Work abroad may also result in the establishment of a way of life that is more secure in terms of both employment opportunities and living conditions.

However, there are also challenges in the adaptation to new and unfamiliar conditions:

- Wider social and cultural context
- Welfare laws and policies
- Organization and practice of social work
- Dominant language, professional language, and colloquial language (slang).

Employing agencies may take more or less account of any special needs of international social workers. For instance, while recruitment agencies in England targeted qualified workers from countries such as Canada, Australia, and South Africa (assuming that such workers would already speak English and would have been trained within educational programs similar to the British system), employing agencies did not necessarily take into account the different emphases in training and practice that workers were exposed to, underestimating the extent to which new workers required orientation and supervisory support. There have also been suggestions that the experience that many such workers brought with them has been undervalued, even resulting in discrimination in

opportunities for promotion or new appointments. Sometimes international social workers from particular countries have addressed practical and professional challenges through collective efforts, such as the establishment of a network of about sixty Zimbabwean social workers in the West Midlands area of England (Tobaiwa, Machiridza, & Muyambi, 2006).

Additionally, as mentioned, the qualifications of social workers from some countries may not be deemed comparable by registration bodies in countries such as Australia or the United States. This limits the posts for which international social workers may apply, with financial consequences and implications for their long-term career development.

Advantages and Challenges to the Providers and Recipients of Services

Apart from the basic advantage of ensuring that vacant posts are filled, employment of international social workers can have considerable advantages for the providers and recipients of services through adding to the knowledge base and skill mix of particular teams, agencies, and services. However, this assumes that agencies aspire to the ethic of a learning organization and value diversity in their workforce and active contributions from all employees.

From the point of view of individual clients or communities, employment of international social workers might mean that teams include people who are more familiar with the circumstances of new arrivals and the languages and religious and ethnic traditions of particular communities. So, for instance, in the British case mentioned previously, some workers were recruited directly from the Asian subcontinent specifically to meet the linguistic and cultural needs of Asian minority populations concentrated in particular areas of London and other cities (Lyons & Littlechild, 2006).

In the longer term there may also be advantages for service developments and thus users in other countries. For instance, there are indications that increasing numbers of social workers have in recent years come to the UK from former Central and East European states (e.g. Poland and Romania) which are now part of the European Union. However, there is some evidence to suggest that not all may plan to stay long term (Hussein et al. 2010) and some are likely to return to home countries to contribute to new developments in their national public or voluntary social services.

Turning to the challenges of labor mobility, it is possible that international social workers may not be tuned into the culture of a local community or may even have communication difficulties related to accent, vocabulary, or knowledge of local slang when interviewing service users. Staff shortages may also mean that services are disrupted and international social workers may be (unfairly) blamed for agency shortcomings and discontinuities. Additionally, there is the risk that service users will hold overt prejudices related to a worker's race or ethnicity, making provision of services even more contentious for all concerned. Simpson (2009) suggests that labor mobility provides an example of the interrelatedness of the 'local' and the 'global' in social work and points out the need for learning processes not just on the part of international social workers, but also their local colleagues' and employers'.

Ethical Issues

Finally, there are both individual and structural dimensions of the ethical issues raised in relation to international labor mobility. Individually, social workers share with the general population the right to exit their country and to seek the best possible conditions for themselves and their families in terms of access to work, health care, and education. Similarly, they should expect to be treated according to the laws and norms of their new country, including those that relate to antidiscriminatory policies and practices, so that their experience is valued and they are not exploited.

However, one of the main concerns about overseas recruitment from some countries, such as South Africa (Lawrence, 2008; Sewpaul, 2006), is the extent to which this deprives the countries of origin of much-needed human resources following investment in training for a field where qualified staff are in short supply (Welbourne, Harrison, & Ford, 2007). For instance, in 2003, it was reported that Zimbabwe's Department of Social Welfare had a 75% vacancy rate, attributed to aggressive recruitment by British agencies (White, 2007). While the general situation in Zimbabwe now gives reason to suppose that, had they stayed, such workers would be facing extreme hardship, this nevertheless illustrates a result of the brain drain and suggests that countries recruiting from less economically developed states may also have responsibilities to those states.

Is it possible or desirable therefore to establish formal codes of practice to help regulate international labor mobility? For instance, the United Kingdom has established a Social Care Code of Practice for International Recruitment (SCCIR) that lists twelve principles upon which international recruitment should be based. However, the code is voluntary, and at the time of writing (2011) only a fairly small number of voluntary, private, and statutory agencies have signed up (SCCIR, 2011). Though stakeholders in Western countries might need to address problems associated with the training and supply of social workers domestically, perhaps there is also a need for individual governments and international bodies to be more proactive in supporting the development of welfare and social work services in the Global South. This may extend to governments or agencies welcoming back social workers who have gained experience abroad, such as through relocation programs and financial inducements (Lawrence, 2008).

SUMMARY

This chapter has offered only a glimpse of a complex phenomenon that merits further enquiry. Although we lack systematic research data about scale, incidence, and other aspects of this phenomenon, we have advanced suggestions about the possible motivations of international social workers, the structural and policy frameworks that might facilitate or inhibit mobility of labor, and the associated advantages and challenges to individuals and the profession. Not least among the challenges is the ethical dimension, which affects service users and providers in both sending and receiving countries; we consider that this could be a focus for further work by various stakeholders, including national and international professional associations.

NOTE

1. Actual numbers are unknown but assumed to be very small.

REFERENCES

Council on Social Work Education (CSWE). (2010). *2009-2010 Annual Report*. Accessed April 03, 2011, at www.cswe.org/File.aspx?id=46133.

General Social Care Council (2011). *IQ Applications Summary Outcome v1.1 (780)–IQ Registrants by Country of Qualification*. (Data provided on request under the UK Freedom of Information Act 2000).

Healy, L. (2001). *International social work: Professional action in an interdependent world*. New York: Oxford University Press.

Hussein, S., Stevens, M., & Manthorpe, J. (2010). International Social Care Workers in England: Profile, Motivations, Experiences and Future Expectations: Final Report. London: Social Care Workforce Research Unit, King's College London.

Lawrence, S. (2008). *An exploratory study to identify some of the issues associated with international migration and employment of social workers.* (Unpublished report on IASSW-sponsored project). London.

Lyons, K., & Lawrence, S. (Eds.). (2006). *Social work in Europe: Educating for change.* Birmingham: IASSW/BASW, Venture Press.

Lyons, K., & Littlechild, B. (Eds.). (2006). *International labour mobility in social work.* Birmingham: BASW/Venture Press.

Lyons, K., & Ramanathan, C. (1999). Models of field practice in global settings. In C. Ramanathan & R. Link (Eds.), *All our futures: Principles and resources for social work practice in a global era* (pp. 174–192). Belmont, CA: Wadsworth.

Migration Advisory Committee (2008). *Skilled, Shortage, Sensible: The recommended shortage occupation lists for the UK and Scotland.* London: UK Border Agency.

Schierup, C.-U., Hansen, P., & Castles, S. (2006). *Migration, citizenship and the European welfare state: A European dilemma.* New York: Oxford University Press.

Sewpaul, V. (2006). Regional perspectives . . . from Africa. *International Social Work, 49*(1), 129–136.

Sewpaul, V. (2005). Global standards: Promise and pitfalls for re-inscribing social work into civil society. *International Journal of Social Welfare, 14*(3), 210–217.

Sewpaul, V., & Jones, D. (2005). *Global standards for the education and training of the social work profession.* Accessed October 29, 2008, at www.ifsw.org/cm_data/GlobalSocialWorkStandards2005.pdf.

Simpson, G. (2009). Global and local issues in the training of "overseas" social workers. *Social Work Education, 28*(6), 655–667.

Small, J. (2007). Rethinking and unravelling the interlocking dynamics of Caribbean emigration and return. In L. Dominelli (Ed.), *Revitalising communities in a globalising world* (pp. 243–254). Aldershot, UK: Ashgate.

Social Care Code of Practice for International Recruitment (SCCIR). (2011). Accessed April 03, 2011, at www.sccir.org.uk.

Tobaiwa, C., Machiridza, D., & Muyambi, I. (2006). Experiences of overseas trained social workers from Zimbabwe. In K. Lyons & B. Littlechild (Eds.), *International labour mobility in social work* (pp. 17–22). Birmingham: BASW/Venture Press.

Welbourne, P., Harrison, G., & Ford, D. (2007). Social work in the UK and the global labour market: Recruitment, practice and ethical considerations. *International Social Work, 50*(1), 27–40.

White, R. (2007). Opportunities and challenges for social workers in the transnational labour force. In L. Dominelli (Ed.), *Revitalising communities in a globalising world* (pp. 361–374). Aldershot, UK: Ashgate.

Williams, L. (2007). Home alone. In L. Dominelli (Ed.), *Revitalising communities in a globalising world* (pp. 255–269). Aldershot, UK: Ashgate.

Winkelmann-Gleed, A. (2006). *Migrant nurses: Motivation, integration and contribution.* Abingdon: Radcliffe.

UK Border Agency (2011) *Tier 2 Shortage Occupation List Government-approved version: 16 March 2011.* Accessed April 03, 2011, at www.ukba.homeoffice.gov.uk/sitecontent/documents/workingintheuk/shortageoccupationlist.pdf.

73

Conclusion

ROSEMARY J. LINK

In gathering the wide array of chapters for this volume, it has become clear that the social work profession is already a global profession. We have brought Jebb's claim (chapter 2 of this Handbook) published in 1929 (note for readers Jebb died in 1928 but the proceedings were published in 1929) that "international social work is indispensable" into demonstrated reality. In the various sections of this book we can see that the more social workers of an international profession learn from each other's cultures, values, and practice, the more we recognize and espouse interdependence. The ideas emanating from Bangladesh and the Grameen Bank can work in Chicago (Yunus, 2007), for example, and the cooperation of women in poverty, be it the Self Employed Workers' Association (SEWA) in India or the Luz y Libertad women's cooperative in Mexico, can show the way for women enduring poverty anywhere in the world.

Social and economic development is no longer the province of a few countries in the Global South, formerly (but no longer) referred to as Third World. Chapter 10 (Segal) of this Handbook, for example, focuses on the migration and refugee journeys that affect all regions. Also, Chapter 48 (Libal & Harding) on humanitarian aid and advocacy organizations and Chapter 14 (Elliott) on social and community development illuminate ways that social and economic development are relevant to all countries, including postindustrial nations of the West and Oceania.

Thus, although a focus on promoting the well-being of people of all ages, cultures, and abilities in their families and communities remains at the core of a social worker's role, there is now widespread acceptance that international exchange, dialogue, and action are keys to the continuing vitality of the profession.

Such development depends on an assertive identity based in a sense of solidarity. In the early part of the twentieth century there was dismay at the critique of social work in Europe and the United States as not being a real profession. Still in the twenty-first century some countries struggle for recognition of the professional status of their work, as explained in Healy's history chapter 8 in this volume. Increasingly, however, social work is accepted as part of a just and human rights–oriented world.

Chapter 54 by Barretta-Herman presents an analysis of the Global Standards for the Education and Training of the Social Work Profession that were developed over hundreds of hours of dialogue and negotiation. These standards represent the progress made through the leadership of the International Association of Schools of Social Work (IASSW) and the International Federation of Social Work (IFSW). Together they engaged many countries in the thorny issues of content, concept, values, culture, and definition in relation to what is a standard, a goal, and an assumption. It is a great step forward in itself to have this document before us, with all its inherent concerns and collective ideals, as we make strides in building professional solidarity without borders (see Appendix B for full text of the standards).

The sense of progress identified in this volume is not without tension, and in this chapter the opportunities introduced in Chapter 1 are highlighted through examples in the sections that relate to practice, while the historic tensions form a parallel reality. The challenges ahead for international social work are clear throughout the text and will similarly be discussed in this concluding chapter so that we move forward thoughtfully, boldly, realistically, and in the calls to action our Mexican colleagues describe as *solidaridad*.

Tensions were identified in Chapter 2 as relating to four factors, and these are now, in conclusion, modified and expanded to six:

1. The challenge and expectation to be both universal (e.g., establishing and upholding human rights) and respectful of indigenous traditions
2. The concern to retain the focus on local capacities and needs while accepting the social and economic forces of globalization, or conversely, accepting globalization but always attending to local context
3. The question of what we mean by *professional* and the concern that credentials not override local experience, expertise, and abilities, especially where resources are stretched and difficult economic circumstances may disguise capacities
4. The ongoing tendency to identify problems, that is, what a community is without or lacking, rather than to identify strengths and capacity building
5. A tension arising from the debate about global standards that *universal* may refer to more resourced countries or former colonizers dictating to less resourced or less powerful nations
6. Codes of practice versus principles.

The case studies in this volume demonstrate that sharing knowledge and research across borders leads to innovation and recognition of universal needs, for example the crisis response to SARS led by Singaporean colleagues such as Tiong Tan; more assertive lobbying for social justice, as in the work of the UK Child Poverty Action Group preventing sanctions to lone parents struggling to find work; and KLUC in Slovenia, leading to the institution of the Ombudsman for Children in Ljubljana. The infusion of international practice need not collide with local traditions of public health or child discipline to recognize that insights in one country, such as from Singapore's response to SARS, can enhance the response of another.

Similarly, as a result of dialogue across nations, the Convention on the Rights of the Child (CRC) sets down expectations for the treatment of children, including that they be free from physical abuse. Local traditions may include hitting, pinching, smacking, and going without food as physical punishments. Parents may say, "It did me no harm to be whipped,"

but as social workers we can encourage them on the path that says clearly, these are the signposts that lead to healthier and more fulfilled lives. From extensive research we know that physical punishment often leads to adult abuse, especially if the adults are tired or hungry themselves (Scott & Ward, 2007). The work is to replace that punishment with strategies for discipline that are nondemeaning and healthy. The hardest part of reading James Garbarino's book, *Lost Boys*, which reports his research with children in prison for extremely violent crimes including murder, is the relentless history of abuse of the boys in families that did not have alternatives in their traditions.

In relation to the second tension, where we aim to retain the focus on local capacities while accepting social and economic forces of globalization, we see both problems and strengths. Recently several countries have included international communities in their employment opportunities, sometimes known as "offshore labor" or "outsourcing." For instance, people in Bangalore, India, now offer the service lines to British Telecom and American AT&T. With the recent economic crises worldwide, however, questions are being asked by politicians in Europe and the United States about unemployment in their hometowns, and offshore jobs are castigated as contributing to economic distress (Akimoto, Chapter 26 of this book). The alternative perspective is that more mobile labor has always resulted in stronger community building—including in countries of the West, such as the waves of immigration from Ireland and Scandinavia to the United States during the nineteenth century, followed by similar patterns of migration from Mexico and Central America to the United States and from Africa to Europe in the twentieth century.

Migration will not slow down in the twenty-first century, as explained in Chapter 33 (Lyons & Huegler), and we would not want it to. After the Second World War in England, British Rail advertised in the Caribbean for people to staff its communications networks. Construction and flower producers in California could not survive without labor from Mexico. Mines in Peru and Chile are dependent on workers from neighboring countries, and many people from India and Pakistan travel to work in Saudi Arabia and the United Arab Emirates.

A different strain of tension lies in the ways we recognize each other's credentials, of particular concern for professional mobility (see Chapter 72). There is currently no global system for accreditation of social workers or social work educational programs. In the absence of global mechanisms, some have suggested that accrediting bodies in countries with well-developed credentialing systems, such as the United States Council on Social Work Education, might extend their reach across national borders. Opponents express concern over applicability of standards to diverse context and lack of representation in standards of development and implementation.

A welcome shift of concepts and practice in recent decades that has been enhanced by international dialogue is the move away from focusing solely on problems or problematic people, to focusing on capacities and opportunities. Instead of visiting another country and saying that they have no this or that, we go with open eyes and hearts and see what they have and how they conserve resources differently (Link & Ramanathan, 2011; see also Lager & Mathiesen, Chapter 51 in this volume).

As vividly explained in several chapters, including by Mwansa (Chapter 55), social workers from Europe and the United States may underestimate the tensions that remain as a result of actual colonization and covert colonization that follow in the path of war or economic policies. The first visit of one of the authors to India proved enlightening in the ways Indian colleagues wanted their visitor to appreciate their successful independence from Britain, their pride in their long-standing democracy, and also the residue of resentment against the so-called mother country of Queen Victoria's reign and that heritage.

Even in the 1950s and 1960s, British children sang songs such as "Rule Britannia" until a conductor refused to endorse the tradition of playing it at the summer concerts in London known as The Proms. True, Britain did "rule the waves" in the Victorian era for all sorts of reasons, including industrial growth, coal and mineral resources, island living, temperate climate, traditions of exploration, and some would say exploitation. When we are raised, however, to think that our country is the most adventurous, biggest, most influential, or best, it is crucial that we step back and ask why and how we perpetuate these beliefs and at what cost to international cooperation and relationships.

In the various chapters of this *Handbook*, we pay attention to the words of our traditions and songs in order to challenge this subliminal and corrosive tendency that a nation has to stand out boasting at the cost of relationships with others. It is also true that colonizers in some instances introduced schemes of irrigation, transport, law, and local government that benefited those colonized. A visit to Srirangapatna in southern India, however, would disabuse anyone of the benefits of oppression. The mahogany tree–lined gardens of the Tippu Sultan's estate are exquisite, but the Indian guide will explain that the British took the sultan's sons hostage in an argument about land in the eighteenth century and later killed them. In their expressed values, social workers combat the forces of oppression every day, and this is reflected in Hölscher's chapter 7 on social justice.

Linked to this tension of the residual effects of colonization in the twenty-first century is the excitement over the newly approved principles of practice generated by ISFW. The organization has encouraged countries to create their own codes of ethical practice while endorsing the principles. Merli Desai has explained, however, that there is a problem in requiring codes of ethical practice across the globe. For many countries at this time, there are inadequate instruments for establishing codes and a lack of resources for the institutions needed to enforce and oversee such licensing and commitment to practice according to codes of behavior (Desai, 1998).

These tensions throughout the profession have now been identified and can be addressed more openly through friendly disentangling in the coming years as the idea of social work without borders gains momentum (Spears, 1999). Parallel to the existing tensions, we also see many opportunities in the pages of this book. Perhaps in line with the increased attention to treaties and conventions formulated by the United Nations, social workers are reflecting national trends to develop more regional and global partnerships. This global context is further confirmed, for example, in the United States, as we realize that one in five Americans speaks a language other than English at home and one in four children has at least one parent who was born in another country (Armas, 2003). This figure relates to the United States in particular but reflects the same trend in Mexico, England, the United Arab Emirates, and the Netherlands.

In addition to the increased mobility of parents, often for economic reasons, we also see an increase in refugees as regions torn with conflict continue to struggle. Often students of social work need to connect the dots, for example in relation to the geography of countries of the world and their close interdependence. All the six countries surrounding Iraq are deeply affected by the US war on terror, especially Jordan and Turkey in terms of refugees. The Afghanistan–Pakistan border is similarly a continuously revolving pathway of refugees. Even more startling to some students, who are used to flying across continents without physically stepping from one country to another, is the application of Turkey to the European Union, meaning that eventually Iraq and Iran could be on the borders of Europe and its geographic and economic allies.

Thus, while the twentieth century saw the tensions and oppressions of the postcolonial eras, for example in India, Pakistan, and African countries, the twenty-first century is facing mobility of labor and social and economic restructuring on a scale that speaks to greater political freedoms, parallel to camouflaged tension. This is reflected in the criticism of the wealthier G8 (Group of Eight) countries meeting in the 1990s to discuss the problems of the world, now expanded to the G20 countries. It is also reflected in the future realignment of superpowers according to population and economic growth.

Also, as discussed in several chapters, the twentieth century was a period of drafting and ratifying human rights legislation, and now we are moving into a century of implementation. The social policy instruments of the United Nations have become templates for action, as demonstrated in the applications of the CRC and the Convention on the Elimination of All Forms of Discrimination against Women (CEDAW) discussed in Chapters 67 to 70 by Wronka, Reichert, Link, Strand Hutchinson, and Bailey.

In working with the seventy-eight international authors and twelve advisory colleagues contributing to this *Handbook*, it is clear that social work is a human rights profession. Often professionals work in the crucible of matching people's needs with government and nongovernment provision or lack of provision of needed infrastructure and services. The history of social work demonstrates that social workers have been benefiting from collaboration for decades and that dialogue with international partners has helped to shape the profession and expand our thinking at all levels of practice.

Internationalizing social work encourages professionals to work co-operatively, to avoid isolation and to benefit from shared assessment of interventions that are successful. The gathering of papers for this volume in small part represents this new endeavor for the twenty-first century and has been an inspiring journey. In Chapter 2, Healy referred to linking the impact of globalization with a call for professional action on global practice and policy issues, including four professional functions as elements of international social work and a fifth from the work of Cox

and Pawar (2006). These expanded professional functions need greater attention in future education and training and are reviewed here in the light of insights within the volume and the connecting chapters:

1. **Domestically based practice and policy advocacy in situations with international dimensions:** See Section III for common themes in domestic practice, working with refugees, working with street children, and working with illegal immigrants. Practice can benefit from knowledge of UN policy instruments such as the CRC and CEDAW and is especially informed by the framework of articles that expand the questions and tools that can be employed.

2. **International professional exchange of personnel and ideas:** This is an expanding area of work as presented in Sections V, VI, and VII. Organizations such as the International Consortium for Social Development (ICSD) and IASSW hold conferences in all parts of the world to bring social workers together in conversation. Prompted by the leaps in technology, especially through electronic exchanges, student and professional dialogue across continents is at an all-time high (Felke and Menon, Chapter 53). International social work field placements are also a significant source of professional exchange and learning (Lager & Mathiesen, Chapter 51).

3. **Practice in international relief and development organizations:** Section IV and IX vividly depict this fast-expanding area of work. In Chapter 71, Bess and Link identify career paths that build opportunities for this practice, and case studies bring this work to life in several chapters, including from South Africa (Chapter 71) and the Sudan (Link & Skrebe, Chapter 68, box 68.1). Chapter 48 identifies the range of UN agencies and nongovernmental organizations (NGOs) involved in this work (Libal & Harding), and the summary of NGOs illuminates this area of growth in the profession. Similarly, Northcott, Rosicky, Elvin, Ayoub and Lambert explain the expanding role of intercountry casework in Chapter 13: "Broadly conceptualized, the definition of *international social service* is a three-pronged one: social work in a particular country with individuals from outside of that

country (immigrants and refugees, for example), social work that requires working across international borders (international adoption, abduction, document and relative tracings, home studies, child welfare checks), and, finally, social work undertaken by social workers of one country in another country (ISS-USA, 2010)."

4. **Participation in global policy formulation, including human rights and advocacy influencing civil society (Healy, 2008):** Section IV and X address social work involvement in global social movements, including peace, professional committees, and advocacy at the UN, as well as global dialogue on practice issues ranging from adoptions to public health initiatives.

5. **Global and local promotion of social work education and practice:** Cox and Pawar added global and local promotion of social work education and practice to the work of Healy (2008). Social work is widely recognized as a profession instilled with cultural respect to make global exchange go beyond individualistic and therapeutic export toward cooperation, where issues of global context are addressed (see Sections I, II, VII, and VIII). Bosch (Chapter 17) and Lager and Mathiesen (Chapter 51) highlight how social work, perhaps more than most professions, is naturally prepared to seek cross-cultural encounters and expansion of efficacy in cross-cultural communication.

Despite discrete chapters and the expertise of specific authors, many themes in the *Handbook* overlap, such as the impact of gay, lesbian, bisexual, transgender, and intersex (LGBTI) issues as an element of aging; child welfare and the status of women; and the impact of migration on mental health. This overlap reinforces these ideas and perhaps represents the interdependence of the profession's many specialties. It is recognized that some topics are underrepresented in this volume. This conclusion identifies a more holistic approach to the complete volume by applying the five elements identified previously to the major themes of the book. These are the functional themes of what social workers are doing globally, while the values base and theoretical underpinnings of human rights, development, and social justice are discussed as the inspiration and overarching principles flowing through this endeavor.

At a recent human rights conference, Risa Kaufman spoke of interagency cooperation, especially between groups in San Francisco who have implemented CEDAW into their practice and into state and local ordinances (Kaufman, 2009). Her summary of best practices speaks to the growing awareness of ways that we can incorporate the highest or macro levels of policy making, especially through the United Nations, at the local level. Kaufman's summary includes the following:

1. Monitoring and documentation, such as using special rapporteurs to report on the state of local services, including housing, or the impact of war (see, for example, the box on the rapporteur for Southern Sudan in Chapter 68 on children's rights by Skrebes and Link)
2. Assessing local policy in light of international standards
3. Engaging in human rights education
4. Consistently investigating complaints of domestic and interpersonal violence in the context of human rights so that law enforcement officials come to recognize it
5. Incorporating human rights into advocacy training, connecting discrimination with the expectations of the relevant policy instruments
6. Coordinating at local, state, national, and international levels.

Thus, the future of social work depends on international exchange, and one area that continues to develop is exchange with the help of information technology. In Chapter 53, Felke and Menon describe the variety of ways that technology enhances education, especially in bringing the United Nations into the classroom. Also, Link and Bill's experience through a US Department of Education educational ambassador grant gives concrete examples of the benefits to cultural understanding that come through video classrooms and electronic exchanges among students, faculty, and practitioners. Most colleges and universities have regular access to the Internet (though access to electric power fluctuates in some cities), and students who are frequently described as the digital generation automatically expect to be in touch with one another. Often language and location place false boundaries on this communication, and social work education can take the lead in encouraging broader perspectives.

The United Nations has launched the Millennium Development Goals initiative, introducing social work students to the concept of measures of social well-being, such as the human development indicators researched and reported in Chapters 63 and 64 and described in detail by UNICEF and Progress of Nations reports (UNICEF, 2010). Sometimes social well-being has been measured simply in terms of income and wealth, but gradually we have acknowledged that the richest countries in the world cannot enhance social well-being until they improve access to a variety of criteria that enhance well-being through the life cycle, such as prenatal health programs, immunization, and effective and well-resourced schools (*Des Moines Register*, 2010).

Connected to more innovative ways of thinking about well-being and the common human condition is the importance of wealth creation as a strategy for alleviating poverty. As a result of the US National Association of Social Workers (NASW), IFSW, and the In Her Own Image network of case studies, social workers the world over can learn, for example, that a rice mill in northern India is owned and operated by women (In Her Own Image, 1994). Similarly, Operation Flood has brought the fruits of the milk marketing operations to the local level in India (Patel, 1998), and in the American Midwest, the grocery chain known as Hy-Vee is employee owned and operated and focuses on local produce.

There is work still to do among social workers to recognize the value of enterprise and to seek the support of successful corporations and entrepreneurs in community development. A new era of philanthropy is taking us to higher levels of international innovation and unexpected alliances, such as the work of the Gates and Aqualia foundations. Though the global economic crisis of the first decade of the twenty-first century has slowed or caused the deconstruction of welfare state–funded services, there is a parallel growth in corporate responsibility. The exploitation by transnational companies such as Enron, Guinness, Parmalat, Van Heusen, and Exxon is being tackled with new legislation, transparency, and consumer expectations. When we buy carpets and rugs, we want to know that they have not been sewn by children chained to looms (Kielberger & Kielberger, 2006).

CLOSING SUMMARY

Throughout the process of building this reference text, the authors have followed principles set out in our contracts. These include writing without favoring our countries of origin, avoiding putting countries of the Global North first. The book promotes the work of IFSW and IASSW. It also encourages social workers to use global policy instruments, to know the resources of the United Nations, and to embrace human rights as an essential part of social work in the coming decades. Also, the chapters on migration, children crossing borders, and the impact of wars illustrate the reasons why it is imperative for social workers to research the implications of geography and social and economic history and to better know their world. Every chapter speaks to the need of the profession to be truly global in its reach and human relationships.

Sometimes we have failed, or we needed to heavily edit our work, but sometimes we have discovered the new perspectives that come with a lens that looks at the world from a point somewhere in the universe, a point of deep appreciation, even inspiration. This well-resourced, beautiful planet of greens and blues holds such extraordinary social and economic wealth and potential for peaceful coexistence. The *Handbook* speaks to the potential that can be fully realized with the bold and innovative work of social workers in concert with people in their communities and all the professions of teachers, accountants, doctors, engineers, writers, entrepreneurs, lawyers, and advocates, reaching across borders, in the context of our common humanity.

REFERENCES

Armas, G. (2003). Percentage of non-English speaking Americans surges. Associated Press. Retrieved 18 March 2011 from: http://www.boston.com/news/nation/washington/articles/2003/10/09/percentage_of_non_english_speaking_americans_surges/.

Cox, D. & Pawar, M. (Eds.) (2006). *International Social Work: Issues, Strategies, and Programs*. Thousand Oaks, CA: Sage.

Desai, M. (1998). Challenges for social work profession towards people-centred development. *Indian Journal of Social Work, 59*(1), Part 2, 531–558.

Garbarino, J. (1999). *Lost Boys: Why Our Sons Turn Violent and How We Can Save Them*. New York: Free Press.

Hancock, M. (1997). Principles of Social Work Practice: A Generic Practice Approach. London: Routledge.

Healy, L. M. (2008). *International Social Work: Professional Action in an Interdependent World*(2nd ed.). New York: Oxford University Press.

Kaufman, R. (2009, October). Case Study Presentation at Human Rights Conference, Connecticut University, West Hartford, CT.

Kielberger, C. & Kielberger, M. (2006). *Me to We: Finding Meaning in a Material World*. New York: Fireside.

Link, R. & Ramanathan, C. (2011). *Human Behavior in a Just World: Reaching for Common Ground*. New York: Rowman & Littlefield.

Media Network Guide. (1994). *In Her Own Image.* Video. New York: Media Network.

Patel, A. (1998, February). *Operation Flood.* Keynote Address to the Second Pan Commonwealth Veterinary Conference. Bangalore, India.

Scott, J., & Ward, H. (Eds.). (2007). *Safeguarding and Promoting the Well-being of Children, Families and Communities.* London: Jessica Kingsley Publishers.

Spears, L. (1999). *Insights on Leadership.* New York: Wiley.

Yunus, M. (2003). *Banker to the Poor.* Public Affairs.

Ethics in Social Work: Statement of Principles

International Federation of Social Workers and International Association of Schools of Social Work (2004)

1. PREFACE

Ethical awareness is a fundamental part of the professional practice of social workers. Their ability and commitment to act ethically is an essential aspect of the quality of the service offered to those who use social work services. The purpose of the work of IASSW and IFSW on ethics is to promote ethical debate and reflection in the member organizations, among the providers of social work in member countries, as well as in the schools of social work and among social work students. Some ethical challenges and problems facing social workers are specific to particular countries; others are common. By staying at the level of general principles, the joint IASSW and IFSW statement aims to encourage social workers across the world to reflect on the challenges and dilemmas that face them and make ethically informed decisions about how to act in each particular case. Some of these problem areas include:

The fact that the loyalty of social workers is often in the middle of conflicting interests.

The fact that social workers function as both helpers and controllers.

The conflicts between the duty of social workers to protect the interests of the people with whom they work and societal demands for efficiency and utility.

The fact that resources in society are limited.

This document takes as its starting place the definition of social work adopted separately by the IFSW and IASSW at their respective General Meetings in Montreal, Canada, in July 2000 and then agreed jointly in Copenhagen in May 2001 (section 2). This definition stresses principles of human rights and social justice. The next section (3) makes reference to the various declarations and conventions on human rights that are relevant to social work, followed by a statement of general ethical principles under the two broad headings of human rights and dignity and social justice (section 4). The final section introduces some basic guidance on ethical conduct in social work, which it is expected will be elaborated by the ethical guidance and in various codes and guidelines of the member organizations of IFSW and IASSW.

2. DEFINITION OF SOCIAL WORK

The social work profession promotes social change, problem solving in human relationships, and the empowerment and liberation of people to enhance well-being. Utilising theories of human behaviour and social systems, social work intervenes at the points where people interact with their environments. Principles of human rights and social justice are fundamental to social work.

3. INTERNATIONAL CONVENTIONS

International human rights declarations and conventions form common standards of achievement, and recognize rights that are accepted by the global community. Documents particularly relevant to social work practice and action are:

Universal Declaration of Human Rights

The International Covenant on Civil and Political Rights

The International Covenant on Economic Social and Cultural Rights

The Convention on the Elimination of All Forms of Racial Discrimination

The Convention on the Elimination of All Forms of Discrimination against Women

The Convention on the Rights of the Child

Indigenous and Tribal Peoples Convention (ILO Convention 169).

4. PRINCIPLES

4.1 Human Rights and Human Dignity

Social work is based on respect for the inherent worth and dignity of all people, and the rights that follow from this. Social workers should uphold and defend each person's physical, psychological, emotional, and spiritual integrity and well-being. This means:

1. Respecting the right to self-determination— Social workers should respect and promote people's right to make their own choices and decisions, irrespective of their values and life choices, provided this does not threaten the rights and legitimate interests of others.
2. Promoting the right to participation—Social workers should promote the full involvement and participation of people using their services in ways that enable them to be empowered in all aspects of decisions and actions affecting their lives.
3. Treating each person as a whole—Social workers should be concerned with the whole person, within the family, community, societal, and natural environments, and should seek to recognize all aspects of a person's life.
4. Identifying and developing strengths—Social workers should focus on the strengths of all individuals, groups, and communities and thus promote their empowerment

4.2 Social Justice

Social workers have a responsibility to promote social justice, in relation to society generally, and in relation to the people with whom they work. This means:

1. Challenging negative discrimination*—Social workers have a responsibility to challenge negative discrimination on the basis of characteristics such as ability, age, culture, gender or sex, marital status, socioeconomic status, political opinions, skin colour, racial or other physical characteristics, sexual orientation, or spiritual beliefs.

---

* *In some countries the term "discrimination" would be used instead of "negative discrimination." The word negative is used here because in some countries the term "positive discrimination" is also used. Positive discrimination is also known as "affirmative action." Positive discrimination or affirmative action means positive steps taken to redress the effects of historical discrimination against the groups named in clauses 4.2.1 above.*

2. Recognising diversity—Social workers should recognize and respect the ethnic and cultural diversity of the societies in which they practice, taking account of individual, family, group, and community differences.
3. Distributing resources equitably—Social workers should ensure that resources at their disposal are distributed fairly, according to need.
4. Challenging unjust policies and practices— Social workers have a duty to bring to the attention of their employers, policy makers, politicians, and the general public situations where resources are inadequate or where distribution of resources, policies, and practices are oppressive, unfair, or harmful.
5. Working in solidarity—Social workers have an obligation to challenge social conditions that contribute to social exclusion, stigmatization, or subjugation, and to work toward an inclusive society.

5. PROFESSIONAL CONDUCT

It is the responsibility of the national organizations in membership of IFSW and IASSW to develop and regularly update their own codes of ethics or ethical guidelines, to be consistent with the IFSW/IASSW statement. It is also the responsibility of national organizations to inform social workers and schools of social work about these codes or guidelines. Social workers should act in accordance with the ethical code or guidelines current in their country. These will generally include more detailed guidance in ethical practice specific to the national context. The following general guidelines on professional conduct apply.

1. Social workers are expected to develop and maintain the required skills and competence to do their job.
2. Social workers should not allow their skills to be used for inhumane purposes, such as torture or terrorism.
3. Social workers should act with integrity. This includes not abusing the relationship of trust with the people using their services, recognizing the boundaries between personal and professional life, and not abusing their position for personal benefit or gain.
4. Social workers should act in relation to the people using their services with compassion, empathy, and care.

5. Social workers should not subordinate the needs or interests of people who use their services to their own needs or interests.

6. Social workers have a duty to take necessary steps to care for themselves professionally and personally in the workplace and in society, in order to ensure that they are able to provide appropriate services.

7. Social workers should maintain confidentiality regarding information about people who use their services. Exceptions to this may only be justified on the basis of a greater ethical requirement (such as the preservation of life).

8. Social workers need to acknowledge that they are accountable for their actions to the users of their services, the people they work with, their colleagues, their employers, the professional association, and to the law, and that these accountabilities may conflict.

9. Social workers should be willing to collaborate with the schools of social work in order to support social work students to get practical training of good quality and up-to-date practical knowledge.

10. Social workers should foster and engage in ethical debate with their colleagues and employers and take responsibility for making ethically informed decisions.

11. Social workers should be prepared to state the reasons for their decisions based on ethical considerations, and be accountable for their choices and actions.

12. Social workers should work to create conditions in employing agencies and in their countries where the principles of this statement and those of their own national code (if applicable) are discussed, evaluated, and upheld.

Approved by the General Meeting of the International Federation of Social Workers and the General Assembly of the International Association of Schools of Social Work in October 2004 in Adelaide, Australia.

For more information, see www.ifsw.org or www.iassw-aiets.org.

Global Standards for the Education and Training of the Social Work Profession[1]

Adopted at the General Assemblies of IASSW and IFSW, Adelaide, Australia, in 2004.

VISHANTHIE SEWPAUL (IASSW CHAIR) AND DAVID JONES (IFSW CO-CHAIR)

INTRODUCTION

Note: The full version of the global standards includes several appendices that explain the process followed by the professional organizations in developing the standards. Only the text of the actual standards is published here. For the full version, readers are referred to www.iassw-aiets.org or www.ifsw.org.

INTERNATIONAL DEFINITION OF SOCIAL WORK

In July 2001, both the IASSW and the IFSW reached agreement on adopting the following international definition of social work:

> *The social work profession promotes social change, problem solving in human relationships, and the empowerment and liberation of people to enhance well-being. Utilising theories of human behavior and social systems, social work intervenes at the points where people interact with their environments. Principles of human rights and social justice are fundamental to social work.[2]*

Both the definition and the commentaries that follow are set within the parameters of broad ethical principles that cannot be refuted on an ideological level. However, the fact that social work is operationalised differently both within nation-states and regional boundaries, and across the world, with its control and status-quo maintaining functions being dominant in some contexts, cannot be disputed. Lorenz (2001) considered the ambiguities, tensions, and contradictions of the social work profession, which have to be constantly negotiated and renegotiated, rather than resolved, to constitute its success and challenge. It is, perhaps, these very tensions that lend to the richness of the local global dialectic, and provide legitimacy for the development of global standards. According to Lorenz (2001:12): "It is its paradigmatic openness that gives this profession the chance to engage with very specific (and constantly changing) historical and political contexts while at the same time striving for a degree of universality, scientific reliability, professional autonomy and moral accountability."

CORE PURPOSES OF THE SOCIAL WORK PROFESSION

Social work, in various parts of the world, is targeted at interventions for social support and for developmental, protective, preventive, and/or therapeutic purposes. Drawing on available literature, the feedback from colleagues during consultations, and the commentary on the international definition of social work, the following core purposes of social work have been identified:

- Facilitate the inclusion of marginalised, socially excluded, dispossessed, vulnerable, and at-risk groups of people.[3]
- Address and challenge barriers, inequalities, and injustices that exist in society.
- Form short- and longer-term working relationships with and mobilise individuals, families, groups, organisations, and communities to enhance their well-being and their problem-solving capacities.
- Assist and educate people to obtain services and resources in their communities.
- Formulate and implement policies and programmes that enhance people's well-being,

promote development and human rights, and promote collective social harmony and social stability, insofar as such stability does not violate human rights.

- Encourage people to engage in advocacy with regard to pertinent local, national, regional, and/or international concerns.
- Act with and/or for people to advocate the formulation and targeted implementation of policies that are consistent with the ethical principles of the profession.
- Act with and/or for people to advocate changes in those policies and structural conditions that maintain people in marginalised, dispossessed, and vulnerable positions, and those that infringe the collective social harmony and stability of various ethnic groups, insofar as such stability does not violate human rights.
- Work towards the protection of people who are not in a position to do so themselves, for example children and youth in need of care and persons experiencing mental illness or mental retardation, within the parameters of accepted and ethically sound legislation.
- Engage in social and political action to impact social policy and economic development, and to effect change by critiquing and eliminating inequalities.
- Enhance stable, harmonious, and mutually respectful societies that do not violate people's human rights.
- Promote respect for traditions, cultures, ideologies, beliefs, and religions among different ethnic groups and societies, insofar as these do not conflict with the fundamental human rights of people.
- Plan, organise, administer, and manage programs and organizations dedicated to any of the purposes delineated above.

1. STANDARDS REGARDING THE SCHOOL'S CORE PURPOSE OR MISSION STATEMENT

All schools should aspire toward the development of a core purpose statement or a mission statement which:

1.1 Is clearly articulated so those major stake-holders[4] who have an investment in such a core purpose or mission understand it.

1.2 Reflects the values and the ethical principles of social work.

1.3 Reflects aspiration toward equity with regard to the demographic profile of the institution's locality. The core purpose or mission statement should thus incorporate such issues as ethnic and gender representation on the faculty, as well as in recruitment and admission procedures for students.

1.4 Respects the rights and interests of service users and their participation in all aspects of delivery of programmes.

2. STANDARDS REGARDING PROGRAMME OBJECTIVES AND OUTCOMES

In respect of programme objectives and expected outcomes, schools should endeavour to reach the following:

2.1 A specification of its programme objectives and expected higher education outcomes.

2.2 A reflection of the values and ethical principles of the profession in its programme design and implementation.

2.3 Identification of the programme's instructional methods to ensure they support the achievement of the cognitive and affective development of social work students.

2.4 An indication of how the program reflects the core knowledge, processes, values, and skills of the social work profession, as applied in context-specific realities.

2.5 An indication of how an initial level of proficiency with regard to self-reflective[5] use of social work values, knowledge, and skills is to be attained by social work students.

2.6 An indication of how the program meets the requirements of nationally and/or regionally/internationally defined professional goals, and how the program addresses local, national, and/or regional/international developmental needs and priorities.

2.7 As social work does not operate in a vacuum, the program should take account of the impact of interacting cultural, economic, communication, social, political, and psychological global factors.

2.8 Provision of an educational preparation that is relevant to beginning social work professional practice with individuals, families, groups, and/or communities in any given context.

2.9 Self-evaluation to assess the extent to which its program objectives and expected outcomes are being achieved.

2.10 External peer evaluation as far as is reasonable and financially viable. This may be in the form of external peer moderation of assignments and/or written examinations and dissertations, and external peer review and assessment of curricula.

2.11 The conferring of a distinctive social work qualification at the certificate, diploma, first degree, or postgraduate level as approved by national and/or regional qualification authorities, where such authorities exist.

3. STANDARDS WITH REGARD TO PROGRAMME CURRICULA INCLUDING FIELD EDUCATION

With regard to standards regarding programme curricula, schools should consistently aspire toward the following:

3.1 The curricula and methods of instruction being consistent with the school's programme objectives, its expected outcomes, and its mission statement.

3.2 Clear plans for the organisation, implementation, and evaluation of the theory and field education components of the programme.

3.3 Involvement of service users in the planning and delivery of programmes.

3.4 Recognition and development of indigenous or locally specific social work education and practice from the traditions and cultures of different ethnic groups and societies, insofar that such traditions and cultures do not violate human rights.

3.5 Specific attention to the constant review and development of the curricula.

3.6 Ensuring that the curricula help social work students to develop skills of critical thinking and scholarly attitudes of reasoning, openness to new experiences and paradigms, and commitment to lifelong learning.

3.7 Field education should be sufficient in duration and complexity of tasks and learning opportunities to ensure that students are prepared for professional practice.

3.8 Planned coordination and links between the school and the agency/field placement setting.[6]

3.9 Provision of orientation for fieldwork supervisors or instructors.

3.10 Appointment of field supervisors or instructors who are qualified and experienced, as determined by the development status of the social work profession in any given country, and provision of orientation for fieldwork supervisors or instructors.

3.11 Provision for the inclusion and participation of field instructors in curriculum development.

3.12 A partnership between the educational institution and the agency (where applicable) and service users in decision-making regarding field education and the evaluation of student's fieldwork performance.

3.13 Making available, to fieldwork instructors or supervisors, a field instruction manual that details its fieldwork standards, procedures, assessment standards/criteria, and expectations.

3.14 Ensuring that adequate and appropriate resources to meet the needs of the fieldwork component of the programme, are made available.

4. STANDARDS WITH REGARD TO CORE CURRICULA

In respect to core curricula, schools should aspire toward the following:

4.1 An identification of and selection for inclusion in the programme curricula, as determined by local, national, and/or regional/international needs and priorities.

4.2 Notwithstanding the provision of 4.1 there are certain core curricula that may be seen to be universally applicable. Thus the school should ensure that social work students, by the end of their first Social Work professional qualification, have had exposure to the following core curricula, which are organised into four conceptual components:

4.1.1 Domain of the Social Work Profession

- A critical understanding of how socio structural inadequacies, discrimination, oppression, and social, political, and economic injustices impact human functioning and development at all levels, including the global.
- Knowledge of human behaviour and development and of the social environment, with particular emphasis on the person-in-environment transaction, life-span development, and the interaction among biological, psychological, sociostructural, economic, political, cultural, and spiritual factors in shaping human development and behaviour.

- Knowledge of how traditions, culture, beliefs, religions, and customs influence human functioning and development at all levels, including how these might constitute resources and/or obstacles to growth and development.
- A critical understanding of social work's origins and purposes.
- Understanding of country-specific social work origins and development.
- Sufficient knowledge of related occupations and professions to facilitate interprofessional collaboration and teamwork.
- Knowledge of social welfare policies (or lack thereof), services, and laws at local, national, and/or regional/international levels, and the roles of social work in policy planning, implementation, and evaluation and in social change processes.
- A critical understanding of how social stability, harmony, mutual respect, and collective solidarity impact human functioning and development at all levels, including the global, insofar as that stability, harmony, and solidarity are not used to maintain a status quo with regard to infringement of human rights.

4.2.2 Domain of the Social Work Professional

- The development of the critically self-reflective practitioner, who is able to practice within the value perspective of the social work profession, and shares responsibility with the employer for their well-being and professional development, including the avoidance of "burnout."
- The recognition of the relationship between personal life experiences and personal value systems and social work practice.
- The appraisal of national, regional, and/or international social work codes of ethics and their applicability to context specific realities.
- Preparation of social workers within a holistic framework, with skills to enable practice in a range of contexts with diverse ethnic, cultural, "racial"[7] and gender groups, and other forms of diversities.
- The development of the social worker who is able to conceptualise social work wisdom derived from different cultures, traditions, and customs in various ethnic groups, insofar that culture, tradition, custom, and ethnicity are not used to violate human rights.

- The development of the social worker who is able to deal with the complexities, subtleties, multidimensional, ethical, legal, and dialogical aspects of power.[8]

4.2.3 Methods of Social Work Practice

- Sufficient practice skills in, and knowledge of, assessment, relationship building, and helping processes to achieve the identified goals of the programme for the purposes of social support, and developmental, protective, preventive, and/or therapeutic intervention—depending on the particular focus of the programme or professional practice orientation.
- The application of social work values, ethical principles, knowledge, and skills to confront inequality, and social, political, and economic injustices.
- Knowledge of social work research and skills in the use of research methods, including ethical use of relevant research paradigms, and critical appreciation of the use of research and different sources of knowledge[9] about social work practice.
- The application of social work values, ethical principles, knowledge, and skills to promote care, mutual respect, and mutual responsibility among members of a society.
- Supervised fieldwork education, with due consideration to the provisions of Item 3 above.

4.2.4 Paradigm of the Social Work Profession
Of particular current salience to professional social work education, training, and practice are the following epistemological paradigms (which are not mutually exclusive) that should inform the core curricula:

- An acknowledgement and recognition of the dignity, worth, and the uniqueness of all human beings.
- Recognition of the interconnectedness that exists within and across all systems at micro, mezzo, and macro levels.
- An emphasis on the importance of advocacy and changes in sociostructural, political, and economic conditions that disempower, marginalise, and exclude people.
- A focus on capacity-building and empowerment of individuals, families, groups, organisations, and communities through a human-centred developmental approach.

- Knowledge about and respect for the rights of service users.
- Problem-solving and anticipatory socialisation through an understanding of the normative developmental life cycle, and expected life tasks and crises in relation to age-related influences, with due consideration to sociocultural expectations.
- The assumption, identification, and recognition of strengths and potential of all human beings.
- An appreciation and respect for diversity in relation to "race," culture, religion, ethnicity, linguistic origin, gender, sexual orientation, and differential abilities.

5. STANDARDS WITH REGARD TO PROFESSIONAL STAFF

With regard to professional staff, schools should aspire toward:

5.1 The provision of professional staff, adequate in number and range of expertise, who have appropriate qualifications as determined by the development status of the social work profession in any given country. As far as possible a master's-level qualification in social work, or a related discipline (in countries where social work is an emerging discipline), should be required.

5.2 The provision of opportunities for staff participation in the development of its core purpose or mission, in the formulation of the objectives and expected outcomes of the programme, and in any other initiative that the school might be involved in.

5.3 Provision for the continuing professional development of its staff, particularly in areas of emerging knowledge.

5.4 A clear statement, where possible, of its equity-based policies or preferences, with regard to considerations of gender, ethnicity, "race," or any other form of diversity in its recruitment and appointment of staff.

5.5 Sensitivity to languages relevant to the practice of social work in that context.

5.6 In its allocation of teaching, fieldwork instruction, supervision, and administrative workloads, making provision for research and publications.

5.7 Making provision for professional staff, as far as is reasonable and possible, to be involved in the formulation, analysis, and the evaluation of the impact of social policies, and in community outreach initiatives.

6. STANDARDS WITH REGARD TO SOCIAL WORK STUDENTS

In respect of social work students, schools should endeavor to reach the following:

6.1 Clear articulation of its admission criteria and procedures.

6.2 Student recruitment, admission, and retention policies that reflect the demographic profile of the locality that the institution is based in with active involvement of practitioners and service users in relevant processes. Due recognition should be given to minority groups[10] that are underrepresented and/or underserved. Relevant criminal convictions, involving abuse of others or human rights violations, must be taken into account given the primary responsibility of protecting and empowering service users.

6.3 Provision for student advising that is directed toward student orientation, assessment of the student's aptitude and motivation for a career in social work, regular evaluation of the student's performance, and guidance in the selection of courses/modules.

6.4 Ensuring high quality of the educational programme whatever the mode of delivery. In the case of distance, mixed-mode, decentralised, and/or Internet-based teaching, mechanisms for locally based instruction and supervision should be put in place, especially with regard to the fieldwork component of the programme.

6.5 Explicit criteria for the evaluation of student's academic and fieldwork performance.

6.6 Nondiscrimination against any student on the basis of "race," colour, culture, ethnicity, linguistic origin, religion, political orientation, gender, sexual orientation, age, marital status, physical status, and socioeconomic status.

6.7 Grievance and appeals procedures that are accessible, clearly explained to all students, and operated without prejudice to the assessment of students.

7. STANDARDS WITH REGARD TO STRUCTURE, ADMINISTRATION, GOVERNANCE, AND RESOURCES

With regard to structure, administration, governance, and resources, the school and/or the educational institution should aspire toward the following:

7.1 Social work programmes are implemented through a distinct unit known as a Faculty, School,

Department, Centre, or Division, which has a clear identity within the educational institution.

7.2 The school has a designated Head or Director who has demonstrated administrative, scholarly, and professional competence, preferably in the profession of social work.

7.3 The Head or Director has primary responsibility for the coordination and professional leadership of the school, with sufficient time and resources to fulfill these responsibilities.

7.4 The school's budgetary allocation is sufficient to achieve its core purpose or mission and the programme objectives.

7.5 The budgetary allocation is stable enough to ensure programme planning and sustainability.

7.6 There are adequate physical facilities, including classroom space, offices for professional and administrative staff, and space for student, faculty, and field liaison meetings, and the equipment necessary for the achievement of the school's core purpose or mission and the programme objectives.

7.7 Library and, where possible, Internet resources, necessary to achieve the programme objectives, are made available.

7.8 The necessary clerical and administrative staff are made available for the achievement of the program objectives.

7.9 Where the school offers distance, mixed-mode, decentralised, and/or Internet-based education there is provision of adequate infrastructure, including classroom space, computers, texts, audiovisual equipment, community resources for fieldwork education, and on-site instruction and supervision to facilitate the achievement of its core purpose or mission, programme objectives, and expected outcomes.

7.10 The school plays a key role with regard to the recruitment, appointment, and promotion of staff.

7.11 The school strives toward gender equity in its recruitment, appointment, promotion, and tenure policies and practices.

7.12 In its recruitment, appointment, promotion, and tenure principles and procedures, the school reflects the diversities of the population that it interacts with and serves.

7.13 The decision-making processes of the school reflect participatory principles and procedures.

7.14 The school promotes the development of a cooperative, supportive, and productive working environment to facilitate the achievement of programme objectives.

7.15 The school develops and maintains linkages within the institution, with external organisations, and with service users relevant to its core purpose or mission and its objectives.

8. STANDARDS WITH REGARD TO CULTURAL AND ETHNIC DIVERSITY AND GENDER INCLUSIVENESS

With regard to cultural and ethnic diversity schools should aspire toward the following:

8.1 Making concerted and continuous efforts to ensure the enrichment of the educational experience by reflecting cultural and ethnic diversity, and gender analysis in its programme.

8.2 Ensuring that the programme, either through mainstreaming into all courses/modules and/or through a separate course/module, has clearly articulated objectives in respect of cultural and ethnic diversity, and gender analysis.

8.3 Indicating that issues regarding gender analysis and cultural and ethnic diversity are represented in the fieldwork component of the programme.

8.4 Ensuring that social work students are provided with opportunities to develop self-awareness regarding their personal and cultural values, beliefs, traditions, and biases and how these might influence the ability to develop relationships with people, and to work with diverse population groups.

8.5 Promoting sensitivity to, and increasing knowledge about, cultural and ethnic diversity, and gender analysis.

8.6 Minimising group stereotypes and prejudices[11] and ensuring that racist behaviours, policies, and structures are not reproduced through social work practice.

8.7 Ensuring that social work students are able to form relationships with, and treat all persons with respect and dignity irrespective of such persons' cultural and ethnic beliefs and orientations.

8.8 Ensuring that social work students are schooled in a basic human rights approach, as reflected in international instruments such as the Universal Declaration on Human Rights, the United Nations Convention on the Rights of the Child (1989), and the UN Vienna Declaration (1993).[12]

8.9 Ensuring that the programme makes provision for social work students to know themselves both as individuals and as members of collective sociocultural groups in terms of strengths and areas for further development.

9. STANDARDS WITH REGARD TO VALUES AND ETHICAL CODES OF CONDUCT OF THE SOCIAL WORK PROFESSION

In view of the recognition that social work values, ethics, and principles are the core components of the profession, schools should consistently aspire toward:

9.1 Focused and meticulous attention to this aspect of the programme in curricula design and implementation.

9.2 Clearly articulated objectives with regard to social work values, principles, and ethical conduct.

9.3 Registration of professional staff and social work students (insofar as social work students develop working relationships with people via fieldwork placements) with national and/or regional regulatory (whether statutory or nonstatutory) bodies, with defined codes of ethics.[13] Members of such bodies are generally bound to the provisions of those codes.

9.4 Ensuring that every social work student involved in fieldwork education, and every professional staff member, is aware of the boundaries of professional practice and what might constitute unprofessional conduct in terms of the code of ethics. Where students violate the code of ethics, programme staff may take necessary and acceptable remedial and/or initial disciplinary measures, or counsel the student out of the programme.

9.5 Taking appropriate action in relation to those social work students and professional staff who fail to comply with the code of ethics, either through an established regulatory social work body, established procedures of the educational institution, and/or through legal mechanisms.

9.6 Ensuring that regulatory social work bodies are broadly representative of the social work profession, including, where applicable, social workers from both the public and private sector, and of the community that it serves, including the direct participation of service users.

9.7 Upholding, as far as is reasonable and possible, the principles of restorative rather than retributive justice[14] in disciplining either social work students or professional staff who violate the code of ethics.

NOTES

1. All reference to "social work" in this document is to read as the "social work profession," and reference to the "social worker" is to read as the "social work professional."

2. Some colleagues have criticized this definition, expressing the view that it did not adequately cover their contexts. A colleague from the Hong Kong Polytechnic University expressed concern about the lack of emphasis on responsibility and the collective within the Western paradigm. He proposed the following additions to the definition (written in bold italics): "The social work profession promotes social change *as well as social stability*, problem solving *as well as harmony* in human relationships, and the empowerment and liberation of people to enhance well-being. Utilising theories of human behaviour and social systems *and respecting unique traditions and culture in different ethnic groups*, social work intervenes at points where people interact with their environments *and where individuals go well with their significant others*. Principles of human rights and social justice *as well as responsibility and collective harmony* are fundamental to social work *in various countries*."

3. Such concepts lack clear definition. Persons who fall into the categories of being "marginalized," "socially excluded," "dispossessed," "vulnerable," and/or "at risk" may be so defined by individual countries and/or regions.

4. Stakeholders include the educational institution itself; the "profession" however organized or informal including practitioners, managers, and academics; social work agencies as potential employers and providers of fieldwork learning opportunities; users of social work services; students; the government where this funds the institution and/or sets standards; and the wider community.

5. Self-reflexivity at the most basic level means the ability to question: What are we doing? Why are we doing it? Is it in the best interests of the people whom we are working with? Such reflexivity is necessary and desirable irrespective of the context one practices in, whether the emphasis is on, for example, liberal democracy, communitarianism, autocracy or authoritarian sociocultural systems, or democratic socialism.

6. Field placements take place in different settings, within formal organisations or through direct links with communities, which may be geographically defined or defined by specific interests. Some schools have established independent student units in communities, which serve as the context for fieldwork.

7. The concepts "racial" and "race" are in scare quotes to reflect that they are sociostructural and political constructs, wherein biological differences among people are used by some dominant groups to oppress, exclude, and marginalise groups considered to be of minority status.

8. Quoted from Dominelli, L. (2004). *Social work: Theory and practice for a changing profession*. Polity Press: Cambridge.

9. Pawson, R. et al (2003). *Types and quality of knowledge in social care*. Social Care Institute for Excellence. http://scie.org.uk/sciesproducts/knowledgereviews/KRO3summaryonlineversion071103.pdf.

10. "Minority groups" may be defined in terms of numerical representation and/or "minority" in terms of socioeconomic and/or political status. It remains an ambiguous and contested concept and needs to be defined and clarified within specific social contexts.

11. While cultural sensitivity may contribute to culturally competent practice, the school must be mindful of the possibility of reinforcing group stereotypes. The school should, therefore, try to ensure that social work students do not use knowledge of a particular group of people to generalize to every person in that group. The school should pay particular attention to both in-group and intergroup variations and similarities.

12. Such an approach might facilitate constructive confrontation and change where certain cultural beliefs, values, and traditions violate peoples' basic human rights. As culture is socially constructed and dynamic, it is subject to deconstruction and change. Such constructive confrontation, deconstruction, and change may be facilitated through a tuning into, and an understanding of particular cultural values, beliefs, and traditions and via critical and reflective dialogue with members of the cultural group *vis-à-vis* broader human rights issues.

13. In many countries voluntary national professional associations play major roles in enhancing the status of social work, and in the development of Codes of Ethics. In some countries voluntary professional associations assume regulatory functions, for example disciplinary procedures in the event of professional malpractice, while in other countries statutory bodies assume such functions.

14. Restorative justice reflects the following: a belief that crime violates people and relationships; making the wrong right; seeking justice between victims, offenders, and communities; people are seen to be the victims; emphasis on participation, dialogue, and mutual agreement; is oriented to the future and the development of responsibility. This is opposed to retributive justice, which reflects: a belief that crime violates the State and its laws; a focus on punishment and guilt; justice sought between the State and the offender; the State as victim; authoritarian, technical, and impersonal approaches; and orientation to the past and guilt.

REFERENCE

Lorenz, W. (2001). Social work in Europe: Portrait of a diverse professional group. In S. Hessle (Ed.) *International standard setting of higher social work education*. Stockholm: Stockholm University.

The Millennium Development Goals and Targets

Adopted in 2000 by the United Nations

INTRODUCTION

The Millennium Development Goals, or MDGs, emanate from the Millennium Declaration, a resolution adopted by the General Assembly of the United Nations at the close of the Millennium Summit held from September 6–8, 2000. The MDGs express a set of goals and targets (some more measurable than others) to reduce human misery and preserve the environment for a sustainable future. Additional targets were added after 2000. The goals and the Millennium Declaration state the need for partnership among all countries, regardless of their economic status. In general, however, Goals 1 through 7 relate to the situation in developing countries, while Goal 8 identifies the agenda for a fairer world system of trade and resource allocation. The MDGs have been published in many formats; the following was taken from the United Nation's Millennium Development Goals website.

Goal 1: Eradicate extreme poverty and hunger.

Target 1.A: Halve, between 1990 and 2015, the proportion of people whose income is less than $1 per day.

Target 1.B: Achieve full and productive employment and decent work for all, including women and young people.

Target 1.C: Halve, between 1990 and 2015, the proportion of people who suffer from hunger.

Goal 2: Achieve universal primary education.
Target 2.A: Ensure that by 2015, children everywhere, boys and girls alike, will be able to complete a full course of primary schooling.

Goal 3: Promote gender equality and empower women.

Target 3.A: Eliminate gender disparity in primary and secondary education, preferably by 2005 and in all levels of education no later than 2015.

Goal 4: Reduce child mortality.
Target 4.A: Reduce by two-thirds, between 1990 and 2015, the under-five mortality rate.

Goal 5: Improve maternal health.

Target 5.A: Reduce by three-quarters, between 1990 and 2015, the maternal mortality ratio.

Target 5.B: Achieve universal access to reproductive health.

Goal 6: Combat HIV/AIDS, malaria, and other diseases.

Target 6.A: Have halted by 2015 and begin to reserve the spread of HIV/AIDS.

Target 6.B Achieve, by 2010, universal access to treatment for HIV/AIDS for all those who need it.

Target 6.C: Have halted by 2015 and begun to reserve the incidence of malaria and other major diseases.

Goal 7: Ensure environmental sustainability.

Target 7.A: Integrate the principles of sustainable development into country policies and programs and reserve the loss of environmental resources.

Target 7.B: Reduce biodiversity loss, achieving, by 2010, a significant reduction in the rate of loss.

Target 7.C: Halve by 2015 the proportion of people without sustainable access to safe drinking water and basic sanitation.

Target 7.D: Have achieved by 2020 a significant improvement in the lives of at least 100 million slum dwellers.

Goal 8: Develop a global partnership for development.

Target 8.A: Develop further an open, rule-based, predictable, nondiscriminatory trading and financial system (includes a commitment to good governance, development, and poverty reduction—both nationally and internationally).

Target 8.B: Address the special needs of the least developed countries (includes tariff and quota-free access for exports, enhanced program of debt relief for and cancellation of official bilateral debt, and more generous official development assistance for countries committed to poverty reduction).

Target 8.C: Address the special needs of landlocked countries and small island developing states

Target 8.D: Deal comprehensively with the debt problems of developing countries through national and international measures in order to make debt sustainable in the long term.

Target 8.E: In cooperation with pharmaceutical companies, provide access to affordable essential drugs in developing countries.

Target 8.F: In cooperation with the private sector, make available the benefits of new technologies, especially information and communications technologies.

Source: *Millennium Development Goals.* (2010, October 26). Retrieved from www.un.org/ millenniumgoals/.

The IASC Guidelines on Mental Health and Psychosocial Support: A Quick Guide for Social Workers

MARTHA BRAGIN

In recent years, natural disasters and armed conflict have called forth large-scale emergency humanitarian action in both Global North and South. Many specialists in mental health and psychosocial well-being became concerned that in the absence of guidelines as to how community resilience should be supported, both humanitarian actors and even government agencies have been the cause of, and not the solution to, psychosocial distress. There have been all too many reported instances in which outsiders have been permitted to practice in situations of extreme gravity and do harm through importing external methods of coping while marginalizing rather than strengthening indigenous systems. There have also been widely reported instances of failure to provide for the basic rights and dignity of citizens through lack of collaboration with community-based organizations and leaders, such as those noted during and after Hurricanes Katrina and Rita in the United States (Kulkarni et al., 2008). Therefore, a consensus developed that international coordinating bodies should set standards for mental health and psychosocial support in emergency settings. These included guidelines for providing emergency services in ways that support resilience and well-being.

International humanitarian coordination efforts are directed by the Inter-Agency Standing Committee (IASC). The IASC, which issued the guidelines, was established in response to General Assembly resolution 46/182, with the mandate to coordinate humanitarian action around the world and establish and advocate for best practice in humanitarian assistance. It is headed by the director of the UN Office for the Coordination of Humanitarian Affairs (OCHA) and consists of the heads of United Nations agencies,

the International Federation of Red Cross and Red Crescent Societies, the International Committee of the Red Cross, and the consortia of international nongovernmental organizations (Bragin, 2010).

In 2005 the IASC established a task force to develop guidelines on mental health and psychosocial support in emergencies.[1] The purpose of the guidelines was to outline a set of responses to be employed during and immediately after emergencies to support psychosocial well-being, increase resilience, minimize risk, and provide care for mentally ill persons and those who are severely affected by the disaster. The guidelines highlight the importance of mobilizing disaster-affected persons to organize their own supports and participate fully in every aspect of the relief and recovery effort (van Ommeren & Wessells, 2007). The guidelines were launched for implementation in 2007.

The majority of people affected by disaster or mass violence, while changed in many ways, appear to be able to endure their experiences and even to find a measure of meaning and happiness in life following their ordeal, while others, about 5 to 6 percent, suffer from severe stress reactions (Jones, 2008). Therefore, a simultaneous, multilayered approach to the way services are provided is called for, one that targets every aspect of biopsychosocial well-being, and not simply the prevention and response to psychological trauma (Bragin, 2010).

The guidelines outline the layers of care that should be provided, ensure the maintenance of psychosocial well-being, and include all members of the affected population. The following pyramid appears in the guidelines and outlines those layers.

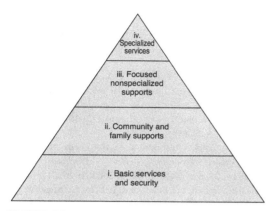

FIGURE D.1: Layers of Care (IASC, 2007).

i.   **Basic services and security.** These are the supports needed by the entire population and must be provided to all survivors immediately.

ii. **Community and family supports.** These supports are group oriented and subclinical. They involve many members of the community. Often they are designed by community members and supports are brought to bear as requested.

iii. **Focused, nonspecialized supports.** The third layer represents the supports necessary for the still smaller number of people who additionally require focused individual, family, or group interventions by trained and supervised workers. This layer also includes psychological first aid.

iv. **Specialized services.** The top layer of the pyramid is for those members of the community who are mentally ill and need access to medication and continued care and those who are having a severe reaction to the events and require professional treatment (Bragin, 2010).

THE FIRST LAYER

This is the most critical layer of the pyramid and applies to all members of the population. The majority of people will cope well over time if they can have their basic needs addressed in security and dignity. People need to be able to do the following:

- Keep their families together and know where to go to report or locate missing family members
- Have access to clear, accurate, and updated information about the nature of the emergency
- Have access to clear and accurate information about safe, centralized locations in which to obtain necessities:

  - ✓ Clean water
  - ✓ Sanitary facilities (safe water for bathing)
  - ✓ Food
  - ✓ Emergency health care
  - ✓ Shelter.

- Have opportunities to participate in creating solutions and be consulted every step of the way
- Be provided with protection from danger and advocacy for their human rights
- Know that the local authorities are able to continue to do their jobs.

THE SECOND LAYER

The second layer of the pyramid addresses the specific needs of large populations such as the following:

- Children and adolescents
- The elderly
- Marginalized groups
- Those who have lost family members.

THE THIRD LAYER

The third layer of support requires the development of ongoing and appropriate supports that address the needs of those who have suffered violence, loss, or atrocity. The supports are provided in collaboration with and according to the standards of their cultures and communities.

THE TOP LAYER

The top layer of the pyramid addresses the needs of those who required mental health services prior to the disaster. They will need these services to continue during the disaster and afterward. Special care will have to be taken to ensure that those in institutional care are not neglected or harmed. In addition, some people will develop symptoms specifically related to the disaster, and they, too, should be treated with culturally competent and clinically sound mental health services.

HOW THE GUIDELINES WORK

The guidelines facilitate best practice by providing a poster listing twenty-five areas to be addressed in an emergency, from the first to the top layer of the intervention pyramid. The poster is accompanied by twenty-five action sheets that operationalize their implementation and by a short Do No Harm slide show that attempts to target harmful practices and offer alternative beneficial ones. There is now a convenient, shorter checklist that can be taken to the field when disaster strikes. The guidelines also provide links to more detailed information should it be needed. They are currently available in English, Spanish, Chinese, Arabic, French, and Russian.

TO LEARN MORE

This link will connect you to all of these products:

www.humanitarianinfo.org/iascweb2/pageloader. aspx?page=content-products-products& productcatid=22.

The following chapter illustrates the use of the guidelines with international case examples: Bragin, M. (2010). Clinical social work in situations of disaster and terrorism. In J. Brandell (Ed.), *Clinical social work practice* (2nd ed., pp. 373–407). Thousand Oaks, CA: Sage.

NOTE

1. The author served on this task force representing CARE International.

REFERENCES

Bragin, M. (2010). Clinical social work in situations of disaster and terrorism. In J. Brandell (Ed.), *Clinical social work practice* (2nd ed., pp. 373–407). Thousand Oaks, CA: Sage.

Jones, L. (2008). Responding to the needs of children in crisis. *International Review of Psychiatry, 20*(3), 291–303. doi: 10.1080/09540260801996081.

Kulkarni, S., Bell, H., Beausoleil, J., Lein, L., Angel, R., & Mason, J. (2008). When the floods of compassion are not enough: A nation's and a city's response to the evacuees of Hurricane Katrina. *Smith College Studies in Social Work, 78*(4), 399–425.

van Ommeren, M., & Wessells, M. (2007). Interagency agreement on mental health and psychosocial support in emergency settings. *Bulletin of the World Health Organization, 85*(11), 822.

INDEX

Printed in the USA/Agawam, MA
August 30, 2017